Approaches to Chan, Sŏn, and Zen Studies

SUNY series in Chinese Philosophy and Culture
―――――――――
Roger T. Ames, editor

Approaches to Chan, Sŏn, and Zen Studies

Chinese Chan Buddhism and Its Spread throughout East Asia

Edited by

ALBERT WELTER, STEVEN HEINE,
and JIN Y. PARK

Foreword by

ROBERT E. BUSWELL JR.

Cover photograph of Jingshan Monastery outside Hangzhou by Albert Welter.

Published by State University of New York Press, Albany

© 2022 State University of New York

All rights reserved

Printed in the United States of America

No part of this book may be used or reproduced in any manner whatsoever without written permission. No part of this book may be stored in a retrieval system or transmitted in any form or by any means including electronic, electrostatic, magnetic tape, mechanical, photocopying, recording, or otherwise without the prior permission in writing of the publisher.

For information, contact State University of New York Press, Albany, NY
www.sunypress.edu

Library of Congress Cataloging-in-Publication Data

Names: Welter, Albert, 1952– editor. | Heine, Steven, 1950– editor. | Park, Jin Y., editor. | Buswell, Robert E., Jr., 1953– other.
Title: Approaches to Chan, Sŏn, and Zen studies : Chinese Chan Buddhism and its spread throughout East Asia / edited by Albert Welter, Steven Heine, and Jin Y. Park.
Description: Albany : State University of New York Press, 2022. | Series: SUNY series in Chinese philosophy and culture | Includes bibliographical references and index.
Identifiers: LCCN 2022009791 | ISBN 9781438490892 (hardcover : alk. paper) | ISBN 9781438490908 (ebook) | ISBN 9781438490885 (pbk. : alk. paper)
Subjects: LCSH: Zen Buddhism—Philosophy. | Zen Buddhism—East Asia—History.
Classification: LCC BQ9268.6 .A67 2022 | DDC 294.3/927—dc23/eng/20220315
LC record available at https://lccn.loc.gov/2022009791

10 9 8 7 6 5 4 3 2 1

Contents

Foreword   ix
    Robert E. Buswell Jr.

Preface   xiii

Introduction   1

Section I
Chinese Chan and the Greater East Asian Region

1. The Spread of Chan Buddhism: Linguistic and Cultural Constraints   11
   John Jorgensen

2. The Hangzhou Region and the Spread of East Asian Buddhism   35
   Albert Welter

3. A Greater Vehicle to the Other Shore: Chinese Chan Buddhism and the Sino-Japanese Trade in the Seventeenth Century   69
   Jiang Wu

Section II
The Japanese Zen Nexus

4. The Transmission of the *Blue Cliff Record* to Medieval Japan: Textuality and Historicity in Relation to Mythology and Demythology   97
   Steven Heine

5 Interpreters, Brush-Dialogue, and Poetry: Translingual
   Communication between Chan and Zen Monks   127
   Jason Protass

6 Doves on My Knees, Golden Dragons in My Sleeves:
   Emigrant Chan Masters and Early Japanese Zen Buddhism   167
   Steffen Döll

7 The Lute, Lyric Poetry, and Literary Arts in Chinese Chan
   and Japanese Zen Buddhism   193
   George A. Keyworth

Section III
The Korean Sŏn Nexus

8 Pure Rules and Public Monasteries in Korea   215
   Juhn Y. Ahn

9 Gender and Dharma Lineage: Nuns in Korean Sŏn Buddhism   239
   Jin Y. Park

10 Mindful Interactions and Recalibrations: From Chinul
   to T'oegye   263
   Kevin N. Cawley

Section IV
Chan, Zen, and Sŏn in the Modern Period

11 Taixu's History of the Chan Tradition   291
   Eric Goodell

12 Zen Internationalism, Zen Revolution: Inoue Shūten and
   Uchiyama Gudō and the Crisis of Buddhist Modernity in
   Late Meiji Japan   319
   James Mark Shields

13 The Struggle of the Jogye Order to Define its Identity as a
    Meditative School in Contemporary Korea   345
        Bernard Senécal

Bibliography   385

Contributors   431

Index   435

Foreword

The study of East Asian Buddhism has long been held back, to my mind, by the tendency of scholars to approach the religion within the confines of discrete national and linguistic boundaries. Once Buddhism had been introduced into and established in a new region, the tradition has from that point on typically been treated by scholars in splendid isolation from its neighbors. The result is that we have ended up with substantial works of scholarship on Chinese Buddhism, or Japanese Buddhism, or Korean Buddhism, but rarely coverage that cuts across traditions. But treating Buddhism in China, Korea, and Japan in terms of independent national traditions obscures, I believe, the many points of synergy that connect one tradition to another. In fact, the Buddhist world writ large, but especially the northeast Asian strands of the religion, have been inextricably interconnected since Buddhism's introduction into new regions. And these connections allowed cultural and religious knowledge to flow in multiple directions, not simply following the better-known "eastward diffusion" from India and Central Asia to China, Korea, and Japan but also in contrary directions. Such flows I have called "countercurrents" of influence. To highlight this tendency of Buddhism to move not just from the center to the periphery but also from the periphery to the center, I long ago referred to the early Korean kingdom of Paekche—the kingdom that introduced Buddhism to the Japanese archipelago—as the "Phoenicia of East Asia" and noted that its well-developed sea lanes, going from the eastern Chinese littoral to the Korean peninsula to the Japanese isles, ensured that Buddhist developments in any one area would find their way across the entire region with surprising speed. I still believe that taking such a regional approach to Buddhism is the most effective way of assessing both the interconnections between, and even the unique developments within, the different regional traditions of East Asia. I would even go so far as to suggest that there are strong grounds for proposing that there is an "East Asian" or "Sinitic" tradition of Buddhism that is something more than the sum of its separate national traditions.

Modern Chan scholarship has been no exception to this tendency to remain trapped within the confines of national traditions. Just one particularly egregious example is the tendency in some Western studies of Japanese Zen to refer to Chinese Chan teachers using the Japanese pronunciations of their names, as if these figures on the Chinese mainland were simply earlier appendages of the mature Japanese tradition. In fact, from virtually the inception of the tradition in China, monastics from these neighboring traditions were active participants themselves in these incipient Chinese schools. This was especially so for the Korean Sŏn tradition, which evolved simultaneously with the Chinese Chan school. In my own work, I have also highlighted the fact that several leading figures in the early Chinese Chan tradition were actually from Korea or of Korean heritage. Indeed, when its proponents are identified as hailing from across the region, or even across the continent, this begs the question: How "Chinese" was "Chinese Buddhism"? On a related note, I think it is also worth lamenting the fact that the study of Chan has proceeded in large measure with little regard for its connections with other influential strands of East Asian Buddhism, such as Tiantai, Huayan, and Tathāgatagarbha—and this even when Chan teachers were clearly in touch throughout most of history with adherents and advocates of these other strands of the religion.

It would of course be going much too far to suggest that there are no distinctive features of the regional traditions of the Chan school. We could readily make a long list: for example, blending gongan introspection with recitation of the Buddha's name in Ming- and Qing-dynasty Chinese Chan; the framing of Sŏn practice on a foundation of Hwaŏm doctrine in the Korean Sŏn tradition; and the elaborate curricula of kōan training in the Japanese Rinzai tradition. But we cannot really know what is distinctive about a particular tradition without a thorough evaluation of developments across the region. In my view, these distinctive features also do not overwhelm the many points of synergy that are just as, if not more, critical to understanding the tradition on its own terms.

In fact, the Chan school has always retained such an expansive view of its own tradition. Since the school's incipiency in East Asia, the school itself claimed to derive from a pedigree that could be traced back to the Buddhist homeland of India and the person of the Buddha himself. All of the different East Asian traditions traced their own iterations of this school back to this same lineage of teachers. And teachers in all of the East Asian traditions consistently studied and cited the writings of their predecessors and sometimes their contemporaries in legitimating their own accounts of their tradition. Chan never perceived itself in terms of national traditions; so why have we scholars of Chan taken the lazy way out?

This volume will take a major step forward in ensuring that scholarship on Chan conforms to this expansive vision of itself that the Chan tradition has always retained. This volume is the first comprehensive attempt to look at Chan Buddhism within a broader regional context that cuts in multiple directions across national boundaries. The chapters in the volume explore both specific developments within the various traditions of Chan as well as the manifold points of synergy and intersection across the national traditions. Thanks to its innovative approach, from this point forward, scholars will no longer have the luxury of hunkering down within the comforting confines of their preferred national and linguistic boundaries but will be compelled to confront those points of contact and symbiosis between traditions. In taking this crucial step, our three coeditors and thirteen contributors have done yeoman's service in outlining a new way forward for the field of Chan studies.

Robert E. Buswell Jr.

Preface

The current volume took shape through generous funding by the American Council of Learned Societies and Ching Ching-Kuo Foundation that resulted in a conference "Creating the World of Chan, Sŏn, and Zen: Chinese Chan Buddhism and Its Spread throughout East Asia," hosted by the Department of East Asian Studies, College of Humanities, and the Center for Buddhist Studies at the University of Arizona in late March 2018. Other contributors included the Khyentse Foundation, Fo Guang University, and Chung Hwa Institute of Buddhist Studies and the Sheng Yen Educational foundation. Most of the chapters included originated as presentations at the conference. The conference coincided with the inaugural ceremony for the University of Arizona Center for Buddhist Studies, with Master Guangquan (光泉), abbot of Lingyin Monastery in Hangzhou and head of the Hangzhou Buddhist Academy, providing the Keynote Khyentse Foundation Lecture, "Telling the Story of Chinese Buddhism: Promoting Exchange and Mutual Learning Among Civilizations" (讲好中国佛教故事: 推动多元文明交流互鉴).

Due to space limitations and other considerations, many of the presentations could not be included in the present volume. Among them were Shūdō Ishii, professor emeritus at Komazawa University, "An Intellectual History of Kōan: An Initial Study"; Guodeng Feng, Zhejiang University, "Buddhist Immigration in Song Dynasty"; Yi-hsun Huang, Fo Guang University, "Chan Isn't Just Meditation: The Role of *Zhizheng zhuan* (智證傳) in Chan Nuddhis"; Gaoxing Qiu, China Jiliang University, "Relationship between Dahui Zonggao and Monks and Laymen from the Perspective of Social Networks"; Chen-kuo Lin, National Chengchi University, ""How a Chan Buddhist Copes with the Method of hetū-vidyā—A Case Study of Miyun Yuanwu (1566–1642) in the Debate on the Thesis on the No-Motion of Things"; Ken Holloway, Florida Atlantic University, "Searching for Zen Roots: from Guodian to Vimalakirti"; Morten Schlütter, University of Iowa, "The transmission of the Platform Sutra to Korea and Japan"; Sungwook Kim, Columbia University, From Center to Peripheries: Encounter Between Sŏn Buddhism and Popular Religions in Late Chŏson Korea"; and Kirill Solonin, Renmin University, "Hongzhou Chan in the Tangut Texts." Robert Buswell, UCLA, presented a second Khyentse Foundation keynote lecture: "Is Zen "Enlightenment" Sudden or Gradual? Insights from the Korean Buddhist Tradition." We are grateful to all the participants and other conference attendees who contributed to the success of the proceedings. We are also grateful to the support team of the School of International Languages, Literatures, and Cultures in the College of Humanities at the University of Arizona, who provided logistical support before, during, and after the conference.

The notion for the conference was originally conceived by the editors at the "Beach Bar" of a Waikiki Hotel during a conference in Honolulu, inspired by sand, waves, and fizzy drinks. We hope that this may inspire others to fulfill aspirations conceived in similarly unexpected ways. We are also indebted to the late John R. McRae, who planted the seed for a conference with a similar theme some time ago.

Introduction

Zen enthralled the scholarly world throughout much of the twentieth century, and Zen studies became a major academic discipline in its wake. Interpreted through the lens of Japanese Zen and its reaction to events in the modern world, Zen studies incorporated a broad range of Zen-related movements in the East Asian Buddhist world. As broad reaching as the scope of Zen studies was, it was clearly rooted in a Japanese context, and aspects of the "Zen experience" that did not fit modern Japanese Zen aspirations tended to be marginalized and ignored. The current edited volume, *Approaches to Chan, Sŏn, and Zen Studies: Chinese Chan Buddhism and Its Spread throughout East Asia*, acknowledges the move beyond "Zen studies," to recognize the changing and growing parameters of the field. The volume focuses on Chan Buddhism and its spread across the greater East Asian region with special attention to impacts on Japanese Zen and Korean Sŏn. The volume also includes aspects of the modern dynamics in each of these traditions.

Toward the end of the twentieth century, some of the biases inherent in Zen studies, barely a half century old, began to be exposed, and the parameters of the field shifted markedly into new directions. These included a growing recognition that the Zen label was a mark of its Japanese context, and as much as Korean Sŏn and Chinese Chan were included, these were incorporated very much in Japanese Zen terms. As a result, Chinese Chan and Korean Sŏn began to be recognized in their own right, independent of Japanese Zen, but still framed in large measure by it. In addition, the Japanese Buddhist sectarian framework, including Zen sectarianism, began to be exposed as products of the Japanese context and not universally valid frames of reference. Furthermore, a consensus formed that the so-called golden age of Zen forged by Tang dynasty masters was largely the product of an early Song dynasty Chan revisionism, and that it was actually in the post-Tang period when classical Chan teaching was framed in the terms it came to be known throughout various East Asian contexts. As important as the Dunhuang manuscripts were in revolutionizing our understanding of early Chan, we now know that this background was far less central to the formation of classical Chan than was once supposed. It was really during the tenth to thirteenth centuries that Chan identity was consolidated and major aspects of classical Chan emerged: *denglu* (燈錄, K. *tŭngnok*, J. *toroku*) transmission histories, *gong'an* (公案, K. *kongan*, J. *kōan*;) case studies, *yulu* (語錄, K. *ŏrok*, J. *goroku*) dialogues and interactions, and *qinggui* (清規, K. *ch'ŏnggyu*, J. *shingi*) rules for Chan monastic conduct as key elements of Chan. Beyond China, the developments during this period were foundational for the Sŏn tradition in Korea including seminal figures like Chinul and Dōgen for the Zen tradition in Japan.

One of the questions raised by this volume is whether the three traditions of Chan, Sŏn, and Zen can or should be held in common. The contents and structure of the volume speak to the shared heritage of the three traditions, even while their modern iterations are largely independent. Obviously, each of the traditions may be studied independently, and efforts to do so are highly encouraged. Yet, historically, the three are intertwined by shared texts, customs, and institutional conventions, not to mention a common distribution of human personnel, especially during formative periods.

Section and Chapter Summaries

The current volume is organized around four sections. Section I: "Chinese Chan and the Greater East Asian Region" explores Chan as an instrument of regional dynamism.

John Jorgensen's "The Spread of Chan Buddhism: Linguistic and Cultural Constraints" provides the broadest scope for considering Chan in the volume, surveying the spread of Chan within and beyond China, including not only Korea and Japan but also Tibet, the Tanguts, Khitan, Jurchen, Bai, and Vietnam. Jorgensen contends that the appetite for Chan was mixed, depending on the region, and that it was an uneven process determined by such things as the Chan use of colloquial versus literary language and the agrarian values of common people. Jorgensen proposes a unique scheme to account for Chan's spread: radical Chan used colloquial language that carried the values of ordinary farmers and people that Literary

Chinese did not; conservative Chan preferred Literary Chinese in order to attract the elites. While the Zen persona prided itself in idiosyncratic, colloquial dialogues interpreted as gateways into the profound, Jorgensen shows how this was not necessarily the case and that Chan colloquialisms were often seen as impediments, rather than conduits, to understanding.

Albert Welter's "The Hangzhou Region and the Spread of East Asian Buddhism" outlines the rationale for a paradigm whereby Chan functions as inspiration for regional identities built on a new religious model. It reviews how an earlier paradigm in Buddhist studies served to ignore, denigrate, or marginalize East Asian developments, except as contributors to an Indo-centered narrative. It explores how Chan actively reimagined itself from around the tenth century, while acknowledging residual passive influences from the Indian Buddhist tradition, transforming Chinese Buddhist customs and practices to create a new intrinsic East Asian tradition. The geographical area integral to this new creation was the greater Hangzhou region, including roughly the boundaries of the Wuyue kingdom during the Five Dynasties and Ten Kingdoms period of Chinese history (contemporary Zhejiang province). The Hangzhou region pioneered new conceptions of Buddhism that became influential not only in the rest of China but also in Korea and Japan, creating a triangular nexus of interrelated Chan, Sŏn, and Zen traditions. It introduces a conception of Chan/Sŏn /Zen studies that firmly distances itself from the Japan-based Zen studies model, a move already current in scholarly circles, and affirms the focus of an intrinsic East Asian regional model, making explicit a turn that has become implicit to the field.

Jiang Wu's "A Greater Vehicle to the Other Shore: Chinese Buddhism and Sino-Japanese Trade in the Seventeenth Century," explores the role of Chinese Buddhism in Sino-Japanese Trade during the seventeenth century. It is noticeable but often neglected that along with the boom in trade volume and the number of ships calling at Nagasaki, a group of Chinese monks, under the leadership of Yinyuan Longqi (1592–1673), settled in Japan successfully during the latter half of the seventeenth century and founded the unique Ōbaku tradition. Despite their religious contribution, these Chinese monks were actively involved in Sino-Japanese interactions and the Chinese monasteries where they resided were patronized by Chinese merchants in Nagasaki. Drawing upon sociological concepts, this study shows that in Nagasaki, Chinese Buddhism had become the source of human, social, and cultural capitals for building Chinese merchants' collective identity.

In short, the three chapters in Section I may be measured in terms of their approaches to the study of Chan: as an assessment of the linguistic appetite across regions for colloquial idioms or literary conventions, as a force of regional dynamism and creativity, and as an influential partner in regional trade networks.

Section II explores "The Japanese Zen Nexus," unraveling ways in which Japan built upon and fostered a tradition rooted in the new paradigm.

Steven Heine's "The Transmission of the *Blue Cliff Record* to Medieval Japan: Textuality and Historicity in Relation to Mythology and Demythology," examines issues of textuality and historicity in relation to mythology and symbology regarding one of the most impactful Chinese Chan masters of the Song dynasty, Yuanwu Keqin, author of the *Blue Cliff Record*. The analysis shows how scholarly engagement is useful in trying to disentangle the complications of invented tradition complicated by various legends and rumors about the origins and fate of the text in order to ascertain a more genuine historiographical account of Yuanwu's influences on early Japanese Zen.

Jason Protass's "Interpreters, Brush-Dialogue, and Poetry: Translingual Communication between Chan and Zen Monks," examines how in the early stages of the transmission of Chinese Chan to Japan, especially during the thirteenth and fourteenth centuries, monks from both countries often struggled to communicate with one another. Based on their shared poetic skills and meditative practice, however, they found creative ways to overcome any gaps through techniques such as matched rhyme poems and brush-dialogue conversations, which allowed for constructive interactions even if one party did not understand the other's language.

Steffen Döll's "Doves on My Knees, Golden Dragons in My Sleeves: Emigrant Chan Masters and Early Japanese Zen Buddhism," moves beyond the figures that have thus far defined our understanding of Zen (Kamakura period founders Eisai and Dōgen, the Ōtōkan-masters, and the Edo-period reformers Takuan, Bankei, and Hakuin) to the period in which Zen established itself in Japan institutionally—the periods of the Five Mountains (J. *gozan*) as well as the so-called proto-*gozan* in the thirteenth and fourteenth centuries. It looks specifically at the Song and Yuan dynasty Chan masters emigrating to Japan from the arrival of Lanxi Daolong in 1246 until Yishan Yining's death in 1317.

George Keyworth's "The Lute, Lyric Poetry, and Literary Arts in Chinese Chan and Japanese Zen Buddhism," outlines reasons why Xinyue

Xingchou (J. Shin'etsu Kōchū, 1639–1696) has been virtually ignored by scholars in East Asia and in the West and provides an overview of him as a poet, artist, lute player and instructor, and scholar-monk in seventeenth-century Japan. It examines how Xinyue wrote poetry to express the taste of Chan and also explores how Xinyue famously rekindled an interest in the Chinese lute and the special relationship between Zen and the literary arts among Buddhist monastics and secular intellectuals.

In terms of their approaches, these chapters employ methods such as textuality and historicality in relation to mythology and symbology, examine the role of techniques such as matched rhyme poems and brush-dialogue conversations, introduce a cadre of monks who have often been ignored and their instrumental role in shaping actual rather than imagined Zen institutional culture, and in looking at Zen and the literary arts through the Zen master as poet, artist, lute player and instructor, and scholar-monk.

Section III: "The Korean Sŏn Nexus" explores ways Korea shaped the Chan tradition inherited from China in its own unique ways.

Juhn Ahn's "Pure Rules and Public Monasteries in Korea," responds to the question of when and how Sŏn Buddhism became an institutional reality in Korea by examining the biographies of so-called Sŏn pioneers and also the rise of the public Chan monastery as an institution in Korea. It shows that the earliest attempt to import this institution from Song China was made in the late eleventh century by the Korean monk Tamjin who visited the grand public monastery (C. *shifangcha*) Jingyinchansi in 1077, as a result of an official Korean embassy to China, how Susŏnsa lineage monks creatively borrowed elements from Song-style public monasteries to establish legitimacy and give themselves a competitive edge, and how Chinul's *Admonitions to Beginning Students* was chosen as a substitute over the Song Chan manual, *Pure Rules for Chan Monasteries*, as a monastic system native to and best suited for the immediate needs of Chosŏn. As such, Ahn shows the dynamism of adoption and adaptation at play in establishing Pure Rules at public monasteries in Korea.

Jin Y. Park's "Gender and Dharma Lineage: Nuns in Korean Sŏn Buddhism," examines the role of nuns in Korean Sŏn Buddhism by examining materials from three different time periods in Korean Sŏn history relating to nuns' practice. In addition to the precedents from the thirteenth and fourteenth centuries that the first two examples provide, Park discusses the characteristics of the nuns' dharma lineage in modern Korea and raises fundamental questions regarding the patriarchal and authoritarian character implicit in mind-to-mind transmission and the way it inhibits and serves to delegitimize nun practitioners and their attempts to form their own authentic Sŏn lineages. For this, she points directly to the claims of T'oeong Sŏngch'ŏl (1912–1993), who questioned the validity of the Sŏn tradition established by Pojo Chinul (1158–1210), the putative founder of the Jogye Order, and his more accommodating style that leaves room for more scope and flexibility in interpretation. This issue is joined further in the contribution of Bernard Senécal in the next section.

Kevin Cawley's "Mindful Interactions and Recalibrations: From Chinul to T'oegye," examines how Chan and Sŏn penetrated and redrew the Confucian understanding of the mind, emphasizing the need for seriousness, restraint, and mindfulness. Specifically, it compares T'oegye's ideas on self-cultivation with Chinul's ideas on continued gradual cultivation. Methodologically, Cawley draws on the broader intellectual "history of effect," taken from Gadamer's term "effectual history" (G. *Wirkungsgeschichte*), to examine the "after-effects" of Chan Buddhism that cross-fertilized the spiritualism of Neo-Confucianism, especially its "study of the mind" (C. *xinxue*, K. *simhak* 心學). Cawley exposes how the influential redrawing of the Confucian tradition, known in the West as Neo-Confucianism, is nearly impossible except as an "after-effect" of the Chan tradition.

In terms of approaches, these chapters address issues relating to the institutionalization of Sŏn Buddhism in Korea, the history of female participation in Sŏn Buddhism and its modern dispensation, and the continuum between Sŏn and Confucian understandings of the mind.

While previous chapters, especially Park's, have drawn us into how these traditions may affect understandings in the modern world, Section IV: "Chan, Zen, and Sŏn in the Modern Period" takes us squarely into it.

Eric Goodell's "Taixu's History of the Chan Tradition" looks at the figure of one of Chinese Buddhism's most important reformers. It contextualizes Taixu's (1890–1947) work in historical, biographical, and religious terms, and discusses Taixu's perspective on Chan's relationship with intellectuals. It identifies his implicit references to Hu Shih's works and concludes with an analysis of Taixu's approach to continuity in the Chan tradition and his decision to include Chan as an explicit component of his program of Humanistic Buddhism, the movement that has been so impactful for modern Chinese Buddhism.

James Mark Shields's "Zen Internationalism, Zen Revolution: Inoue Shūten, Uchiyama Gudō and the Crisis of (Zen) Buddhist Modernity in

Late Meiji Japan" examines the work of two late Meiji Buddhist reformers who affiliated with Zen: Inoue Shūten, a contemporary of Suzuki Daisetsu, was an avowed pacifist and internationalist, and Sōtō sect priest Uchiyama Gudō. It compares and contrasts the "radical" ideas of Inoue and Uchiyama, focusing on their use of Chan and Zen precedents to justify and explain their progressive positions, while setting their arguments in the broader context of Meiji intellectual debates, both within and outside of Japanese Buddhism. It also explores the reasons why Zen was more often than not a "conservative" force in modern Japan.

Bernard Senécal's "The Struggle of the Jogye Order to Define its Identity as a Meditative School in Cotemporary Korea" investigates the sudden/graduate debate in modern Korean Buddhism, ignited by T'oeong Sŏngchŏl (1912–1993) who challenged Pojo Chinul's (1158–1210) position as the founding patriarch of the Jogye Order. Through a critical appraisal of Sŏngchŏl's life, thoughts, and publications, the chapter challenges the authenticity of Sŏngchŏl's claim for sudden/sudden awakening and practice.

Collectively, these three chapters provide windows into important aspects of Chan, Zen, and Sŏn, and suggest how these modern traditions, while built upon common roots and trunks, have each developed in unique ways. While Chan, Zen, and Sŏn continue to be an important aspect of Buddhism in China, Japan, and Korea, respectively, they struggle—as many religions—to maintain relevance in the face of the challenges of modernity and secularizing forces. Whether projected as an element in a tradition of Humanistic Buddhism, as a force in the pull between progressive and conservative Buddhist movements, or in terms of doctrinal debates in the dynamics of factional identity, Chan, Zen, and Sŏn continue to resonate religiously and culturally. Contemporary practitioners continue to struggle over how to interpret their traditions and how to conceptualize authentic models of cultivation based on it. These chapters, each in their own way, demonstrate the importance of Chan, Zen, and Sŏn's pasts to the present. Born of a common heritage, their traditions deviate in the face of the unique challenges they each face.

While the volume hopes to sharpen the refocusing of Chan, Sŏn, and Zen studies that has occurred in recent decades, it is far from the final word and should be seen as contributing to larger conversations. Our attempt here is to be suggestive rather than comprehensive and to inspire future studies that will continue to reinvigorate the field in some of the ways suggested by the chapters in this volume.

Section I
Chinese Chan and the Greater East Asian Region

Chapter 1

The Spread of Chan Buddhism
Linguistic and Cultural Constraints

John Jorgensen

Introduction

Linguistic and cultural restraints meant that Chan was rejected by illiterate societies and could only be accepted by societies that adopted Chan as part of a wholesale Sinification. Chan developed a distinctive language, the Chan koine. To understand many forms of Chan required more than a facility with Literary Chinese or the Buddhist Hybrid Sinitic that was used in translations of Buddhist texts and the composition of doctrinal treatises.

The earliest Chan texts used few colloquialisms. The language was closer to a simplified Literary Chinese than to the spoken language. However, in the mid-eighth century, especially beginning with Shenhui (神會, 684–758), promoters of radical forms of Chan used much colloquial language, which developed into the Chan koine. The more conservative Chan monks, especially those who advocated basing Chan on the doctrinal teachings (C. *jiao* 教), favored Literary Chinese and Buddhist Hybrid Sinitic.

Literary Chinese was the standard written language adopted by societies that sought Sinification in order to centralize government and who adopted an elitist Buddhism. The colloquial used by Chan radicals was considered vulgar by the elites as it often included scatological and abusive language.[1] It carried the values of the common people, with frequent references to farming practices, farming implements, and water buffalos.² Chan radicals used the koine to refer to grain prices, butchers, markets, and everyday activities. References to the values of farmers are summed up in the Chan slogan, "If you do not work for a day, you do not eat for a day."

Therefore, when non-Chinese who could not speak colloquial Chinese (but could use Literary Chinese) tried to read Chan texts full of the koine, they were often nonplussed. Non-Chinese who had adopted Literary Chinese as part of the Sinification process were also likely to share the opinions of the Chinese elites, thinking that only Literary Chinese was civilized (*wen* 文). Thus, colloquial language did not deserve to be written down. Such attitudes toward the different forms of Chinese had implications for the spread of Chan.

The Hinterlands of China

Chan did not gain a foothold in illiterate societies, despite its slogan of nonreliance on written words. Certain regions within the borders of China during the Tang and Song periods had no Chan monasteries. There was no presence of Chan in the highlands of Fujian and the northeast of Guangdong; in a strip from southern Guangdong across to southern Yunnan; most of the Gansu corridor, and all areas to a line north of Dunhuang across to Shanhaiguan; and the eastern part of the Shandong Peninsula.³

In the late Tang, one Chan monk, Sanping Yizhong (三平義忠, 781–872), attempted to convert the She people of the Fujian hinterland. An illiterate people, the She practiced slash-and-burn agriculture, could not understand Chan, and only adopted apotropaic Buddhist practices.⁴ When Yizhong and his associates attempted to convert illiterate peoples like the She and the Gelao (Huineng's mother was supposedly a Gelao and Shitou was said to have come from a Gelao tribe),⁵ they had to use colloquial language. Many of these groups resisted Sinification strenuously.

Beyond China

On the borderlands of China and beyond there were many literate societies. Some were not Sinified and did not share the Chinese lifestyle of sedentary farming. Others adopted the Chinese lifestyle but perhaps not all of their values.

Tibetans

Tibetans developed an empire and a bureaucracy that used a script. They accepted few Chinese values and ultimately rejected Chan, even though it had an afterlife disguised as forms of radical Esoteric Buddhism. The Tibetan and Tang empires were often enemies. A factor that militated against the Tibetan acceptance of Chan was their adoption of an Indian-based script and the activities of Indian Buddhist missionaries.[6]

On a mission to the Tang capital in 756, the Tibetan emissaries encountered the Korean Chan master Musang (無相, 684–762 or 680–756). He gave them three sutras on basic Buddhism but no Chan texts.[7] After a brief period of anti-Buddhist rule, the Tibetan elites were curious about Chan, so when they captured Dunhuang from Tang China in 782, they invited Chan master Moheyan (摩訶衍, n.d.) from Dunhuang to participate in a "debate" with Indian Buddhist monks at Samye Monastery.[8] Chan was ostensibly rejected for being antinomian and ignorant of fundamental Indian Mahāyāna doctrines. There was a political and cultural dimension to the rejection as the Tibetan empire was still hostile toward the Chinese. The Tibetans opted for the nonthreatening Indian Buddhist culture.[9] The Tibetans were probably not exposed to the radical Hongzhou (洪州) Chan,[10] only to the radical ideas of Shenhui, whose rhetoric would have been meaningless when taken out of the Chinese context of an internal dispute over the meaning of Chan. The Tibetans eventually rejected all forms of Chan.

Dunhuang

Dunhuang, an oasis society, is emblematic of societies with mixed populations of Chinese and non-Chinese who engaged in trading and pastoralism. Dunhuang, a trading outpost of Chinese civilization, was a major hub for Buddhism. It received texts of various kinds of Chan; Northern, Niutou (牛頭), Shenhui, and the conservative Chan of Zongmi (宗密, 780–841). However, there are very few traces of the radical Hongzhou Chan. The reason for this was not geographical isolation, as Hongzhou Chan texts reached Korea and Japan. Rather, the reason seems to have been that the Chinese of the northwest, who lived a different lifestyle to the Chinese of central and south China, preferred Esoteric Buddhism. Chan texts from Dunhuang show the influence of the Esoteric Buddhism of metropolitan north China from the eighth century[11] and was probably further incubated by relations with the non-Chinese of the Dunhuang region.

Dunhuang was also a center from where non-Chinese people gained knowledge of Chan. The Uighurs, for example, made several translations from Chan texts[12] of the conservative variety. Despite being great linguists and traders, their script had no Sinitic input, and so I suspect this probably inclined them toward a non-Sinitic doctrinal Buddhism. Eventually they opted for Manichaeism and Islam, religions that used non-logographic scripts and carried no specifically Chinese values.

Tanguts

Tanguts formed a state in the northwest, known in Chinese as Xixia (西夏, 1038–1227). This state displayed tensions between champions of a Tangut self-identity and those favoring Sinification. Literary Chinese was used for some administration and Xixia contained Chinese populations in their towns.[13] The Tangut created their own script, and a number of Chan texts were translated into Tangut.[14] Chan texts in Chinese have been found in Xixia, undoubtedly catering to the ethnic Chinese population.[15] Yet it is evident that the Tanguts favored Esoteric and Huayan Buddhism. However, they translated Chan texts, probably obtained initially from Dunhuang. These were mostly of the Northern Chan type, plus the *Platform Sutra*. Later, the conservative Chan of Zongmi was popular.[16] These Chan texts were either imported from the Chang'an area or from the state of Liao, where a Huayan-Chan mixed with Esoteric Buddhism was popular. The works of Nanyang Huizhong (南陽慧忠, d. 775) were also very popular among the Tangut, but the rather radical content was blunted by editing out elements that conflicted with the ideas of Zongmi.[17] When a text of the radical Hongzhou approach was translated, the Tangut translators apparently failed to fully understand it.[18] They could probably comprehend Literary Chinese but not the Chan koine and the values that radical Chan carried.

Khitan

The Khitan state of Liao (遼, 947–1125) only occupied the sixteen northernmost commanderies of China, yet it had a considerable Chinese population, even in their capital well to the north of the Great Wall.[19] The Khitan devised their own script, yet to be decoded, so it is unknown whether any Chan texts were translated into Khitan. There are texts written in Literary Chinese or Buddhist Hybrid Sinitic (or translated into Tangut) by Huayan scholars such as Daoshen (道辰十殳, 1056?–1147) and Tongli

(通理, 1049–1098), who built on the ideas of Northern Song Huayan masters. This was heavily influenced by the thought of Zongmi, to which were added elements of Esoteric Buddhism.[20] Zongmi's works were published by the Liao on the orders of an empress in 1062.[21] Daoshen wrote about Zongmi's ideas and his work was published in Tangut translation.[22] Daoshen rejected what he and others regarded as the excesses such as vulgar language associated with Song-dynasty Chan and Hongzhou Chan.[23] Rather, he favored the Chan of the Northern Chan master Shenxiu (神秀, 606–706) and the Chan of Zongmi.

The Khitan emperor Daozong (r. 1055–1101), who wrote on Esoteric Buddhism,[24] ordered copies of the *Platform Sutra* and the Hongzhou hagiographical collection, the *Jewel Forest Biographies* (*Baolin zhuan* 寶林傳), be incinerated.[25] He did not approve of radical Chan and the claim that Huineng, a Chinese commoner, preached a sutra. Another Chinese monk influential in Liao, Jiezhu (戒珠, 985–1077) attacked the 'exceptional-ist' Chan notion of "a separate transmission outside of the teachings."[26] Daozong, Jiezhu, and Daoshen championed an "intellectual Chan" that was subordinated to Esoteric Buddhism.[27] Because of this bias against radical Chan, there is no evidence from Liao of the use of the Chan koine.

Jurchen

The Jurchen Jin dynasty (金, 1115–1234) devised scripts for Jurchen, yet to be deciphered, so there is no evidence whether any Chan texts were translated into Jurchen. The Jurchen conquered north China, ruling over a majority Chinese population. A few highly Sinicized individuals such as Yelu Chucai (耶律楚材, 1190–1244) and Chinese Chan masters such as Wansong Xingxiu (萬松行秀, 1166–1246) enabled Linji and Caodong Chan to flourish during the Jin dynasty.[28]

Once the Jurchen had conquered the Khitan, they seem to have translated Literary Chinese into a form of north Chinese colloquial, or at least recorded Chinese colloquial speech.[29] A pidgin Chinese allegedly arose under these conquest dynasties as a lingua franca for Chinese, Khitan, Jurchen, Uighurs, and Mongols. This was used in negotiations with the Southern Song.[30] Snippets of this language have been preserved. It appears that in these multilingual realms that the colloquial language of the Chan masters was generally understandable. Even Emperor Zhangzong of the Jin listened to a sermon by Xingxiu in colloquial Chinese.[31] It is likely that the Jurchen, and then the Mongols, promoted the use and publication of this colloquial material, boosting the circulation of Chan texts, thereby spreading the more radical forms of Chan.

Bai

A greater level of Sinification is found among the Bai (白) people of Yunnan. The Bai used paddy-rice agriculture and were heavily influenced by Chinese civilization from Han dynasty times onward. The Bai elite and some families of Chinese descent in the area used Literary Chinese, mostly as a documentary language.[32] There were many Chinese loan words in the Bai language, and they used Chinese characters to write down Bai words.[33] The elites favored a "classical" Chinese education.[34] In the eighth century the Bai formed the state of Nanzhao (南詔, 649–903). The Buddhism they introduced at the time was primarily the Esoteric Buddhism of China.[35]

Chan was supposedly introduced into Nanzhao by Musang, who lived in Chengdu. Dating errors and the sources suggest this was related not to events in the Nanzhao kingdom but to events in the succeeding Dali (大理) kingdom (937–1253),[36] in which the Gao (高) clan, the second-most important clan after the royal Duan (段) clan,[37] claimed a Chan link with Shenhui, a member of a Chinese Gao clan. The Bai Gao clan produced a number of Chan monks, but there were only four or five generations of Chan monks during the Dali kingdom. The inscription for Zhiyuan (智元, d. 1214),[38] the only one extant for a Dali-period Chan monk, draws on Huayan texts by Chengguan, Zongmi, and Li Tongxuan, as well as a text by Yuanwu Keqin (圓悟克勤, 1063–1135), the teacher of Dahui Zonggao (大慧宗杲, 1089–1163).[39] One Dali master, Jing Miaocheng (淨妙澄), consulted the Linji Chan master Huanglong Huinan (黃龍慧南, 1002–1069).[40] This lineage of Dali Chan masters morphed into Esoteric Buddhism,[41] the dominant Buddhism in the region. Chan in Dali seems to have existed only at Chongsheng Monastery (崇聖寺).[42]

The 1220 stele for Zhiyuan contains only one or two colloquialisms because its focus was on Zongmi's intellectual Huayan-Chan.[43] The influence of the Chinese colloquial was muted because the Song did not encourage interaction with the Bai; their focus was on the northern frontiers.[44] Moreover, the Bai preferred Esoteric Buddhism,[45] while the elites were interested in elegant Literary Chinese that conveyed Confucian values. Thus, the colloquialism of the Chan koine was probably a barrier to the widespread acceptance of Chan.

The Mongols captured Dali in 1253 and Chan reappeared in the region. The conquest enabled Yunnan Buddhists to travel and visit eminent

Chan monks in China proper. Bai monks brought back the Linji Chan of Gaofeng Yuanmiao (高峰原妙, 1238–1295) and Zhongfeng Mingben (中峰明本, 1263–1323) [46] These Yuan-period monks from Yunnan left no texts. They evidently spoke Chinese and may have preached in Bai.[47] After the Ming conquered Yunnan, the Ming court settled many ethnic Chinese in Yunnan.[48] Most of the monks came from Sichuan into Yunnan and Guizhou.[49] From this time on, it is almost impossible to distinguish the Chan of Yunnan from that of China proper. Their texts are full of the Chan koine. Many Bai, in an attempt to maintain their ethnic identity, turned to the religion of the *azhali* 阿吒力, an amalgam of Esoteric Buddhist ritual and folk religion.[50] The Chan of the Bai was completely absorbed into mainstream Chinese Chan.

Vietnam

The Vietnamese (Kinh), a low-land paddy-rice cultivating people, were long influenced by Chinese culture, having been under Chinese control periodically until they created a state in 930. They recognized Buddhism as a state religion only in 971.[51] Despite the proximity of their heartland in the Red River delta to the Chan centers of Guangzhou, the first Chan texts that we know of were brought to the Lý court in 1020 and 1034 as part of a gift of the Tripitaka by the Song court.[52] The earliest source for the history of Chan in Vietnam, the *Collection of Outstanding Figures in Chan Monasteries* (*Thiền Uyển Tập Anh* 禪苑集英 was compiled ca. 1337. Heavily indebted to the *Jingde era Record of the Transmission of the Lamp* (*Jingde chuandeng lu* 景德傳燈錄) of 1104 for some incidents and Chan koine, it also used some no-longer extant Thiền (Chan) sources.[53] Another text, the *Guide to Chan* (*Thiền Tông Chỉ Nam* 禪宗指南), which is on the Bamboo Grove (Trúc Lâm 竹林) lineage, was written ca. 1320–1321 with a preface by King Trần Thái Tông (r. 1225–1257).[54] Works in a mixture of Chinese and *nôm* (喃, a Vietnamese combination of the radicals and phonetic components of Chinese characters to transcribe Vietnamese words) were written by members of the Trúc Lâm lineage such as King Trần Nhân Tông (r. 1258–1308), Huyền Quang (玄光, 1254–1334), Mạc Đĩnh Chi (莫挺之; on a mission to China in 1345), and lay scholar Bạch Liên (白蓮, d.u.). These works are all poems, with Chan allusions, and are clearly elitist.[55]

Thiền in medieval Vietnam was not a recognized school, and the first attempt to establish a Vietnamese Chan school was made when Chinese monks arrived during the Trần dynasty (1225–1400).[56] Most of

18 | John Jorgensen

the Vietnamese Thiền monks had a Confucian education and used Literary Chinese, but they were attracted to Chan literature.⁵⁷ Thus, Chan "in Vietnam is as much a literary function as a religious development."⁵⁸

The Chan element in the *Thiền Uyển Tập Anh* is mostly derivative, and there is little mention of the radical *kanhua* (看話) Chan.⁵⁹ Yet the Chan koine of this text was not simply plagiarized; it was used by the Vietnamese authors to make their own points.⁶⁰ Up until the early fourteenth century it seems that the practice of *gong'an* (公案) and *huatou* (話頭) had only shallow roots, at least until the appearance of the Trúc Lâm school, which may have been modeled on the *kanhua* practices of Zonggao.⁶¹ This type of Chan appeared in Vietnam soon after the Mongols attempted to invade in 1285 and 1287. This was a period of heightened consciousness about Vietnamese identity⁶² and possibly a search for the activist, if not militant, *kanhua* Chan of Zonggao. This may help explain the rise of Linji Chan and Trúc Lâm Thiền in Vietnam.

The Vietnamese, in this patriotic atmosphere, created largely fictitious Thiền lineages as part of a cultural upsurge. However, this Thiền was almost entirely a religion (or fad) of the elite, and very few independent Thiền texts, monasteries, and communities were created.⁶³ Chan in Vietnam had shallow roots, although a little deeper than in the neighboring Bai lands.

KOREA

The Korean Peninsula states adopted paddy-rice agriculture in ancient times and started to use Literary Chinese from 85 CE.⁶⁴ By the seventh century, Silla Korean elites had a sophisticated understanding of Buddhist doctrine the equal of their Chinese counterparts.

Chan was introduced into Silla Korea by Sinhaeng (神行, d. 779) after studying Northern Chan in China. Between 818 and 911, at least eight Silla monks returned from study in Tang China. The earliest three students studied under an heir of Mazu (the founder of Hongzhou Chan), Xitang Zhizang (西堂智藏, 735–814). Later, after the Huichang persecution of Buddhism (842–845) in China, the Koreans studied with members of other lineages.⁶⁵ However, all these masters studied in Jiangxi, south of the Yangzi. They probably went there, rather than to the metropolitan region of Chang'an because the prestige of the Tang court and its associated forms of Buddhism had been diminished by the start of the ninth century,⁶⁶ and the centers of Buddhist activity had moved south. Moreover, the Silla monks followed the trade routes down to the Yangzi basin established by the Korean diaspora.⁶⁷ Most of these monks must have spoken Chinese, for Toŭi (道義, n.d.) the first to study Southern Chan, was in China from 784 to 821.

However, who in their Silla audiences could understand spoken Chinese? When Toŭi returned from China, he found that Koreans regarded his teachings as preposterous, so he retreated into the mountains.⁶⁸ The radical nature of the Hongzhou Chan teachings, plus the problems of translating those practices into Korean, meant the Silla public rejected them. The first signs of the Chan koine appear in a stele inscription for a monk in 940, soon after the Silla fell in 935.⁶⁹ Between 940 and 1085 there are snippets of dialogue using the Chan colloquial in the stele inscriptions, a genre that demanded the use of Literary Chinese. There is a gap in the appearance of such Chan koine in stele inscriptions from 1085 until the 1235 stele for Hyesim (慧諶, 1178–1234).⁷⁰

From 940, during the reign of the Koryŏ founder,⁷¹ some of these Koryŏ-period inscription authors may have been associated with Chinese Song merchants and emigres, some of whom may have supported several Sŏn masters.⁷² Virtually no records exist of Sŏn masters using the Chan koine up until the time of Chinul (知訥, 1158–1210). Two works alleged to have been by the Sŏn monks Muyŏm (無染, 800–888) and Sunji (順之, d. 893) before this time are only found in compilations dating from 1219, 1245, and 1293 and may be post-Chinul texts.⁷³ Neither contain much of the Chan koine.

The first evidence of the Chan koine from this later period is a quote from a Chan *yulu* (recorded sayings) made by Yi Chahyŏn (李資玄, 1061–1125): "All the universe is in the novice's (your) eyes, so where will you squat [to shit]?"⁷⁴ Sŏn in Koryŏ was reduced in influence by the activities of the prince-monk Ŭichŏn (義天, 1051–1101), who returned from Song China in 1086. He promoted a more doctrinal Buddhism,⁷⁵ and he despised writing in anything other than Literary Chinese. However, there was resistance from Yi Chahyŏn and his associate, the monk Hyejo (慧炤, d.u.), who went to Song China before 1086, where he succeeded to the Dharma of the Yunmen-lineage monk Jingyin Daozhen (淨因道臻, 1014–1093).⁷⁶ Yi Chahyŏn and Hyejo seem to have taught the *gong'an* Chan of Xuedu Chongxian (雪竇重顯, 980–1052),⁷⁷ which required knowledge of the Chan koine. Judging from the titles of their no-longer extant writings, Yi Chahyŏn and Hyejo's disciple, Tan'yŏn (坦然, 1069–1158), probably wrote on enlightening master-student dialogues of the radical Chan variety but combined this with scriptural study of the conservative type.⁷⁸ Similarly, Hag'il (學一, 1050–1144) read the works of Huihong (慧洪, 1071–1128),⁷⁹ which are usually labeled "lettered Chan," a mixture of the radical and conservative aspects of Chan.

Thus, by the early twelfth century, there was a revival of Sŏn. The Song dynasty tried to enlist Koryŏ's assistance against the Liao, with relations formally reopened in 1069 and commercial trade permitted from 1085.⁸⁰ This facilitated greater travel between the two countries. Moreover, Ŭichŏn's activities, as a member of the royal house, posed a threat to the independence of Sŏn after his return from Song China in 1086, and so Yi Chahyŏn and Hyejo mounted a counterattack, reviving Chan.

Changes in the international situation also affected developments in Sŏn. The Jurchen rebelled against their Liao overlords in 1114, eliminated the Liao state in 1125, captured the Northern Song capital in 1126 and forced Koryŏ to limit its relations with the remnant Southern Song. Jin pressured Koryŏ between 1127 and 1130.⁸¹ Disaffected by the appeasement policies of the Koryŏ court, the Korean military revolted, and military strongmen took over in 1170. Many aristocratic Buddhists and members of the doctrinal schools attacked the military dictators in 1174 and 1217.⁸² Some members of Hyejo's lineage or school were exiled by the military dictator in 1197.⁸³

Chinul's teacher, Chonghwi (宗暉, n.d.) was probably associated with Hyejo's lineage. Chinul passed the Sŏn examination in 1182, but he regarded Koryŏ Buddhism to be corrupt and so distanced himself from it and its patrons.⁸⁴ Chinul had three "enlightenments," the first on reading the *Platform Sutra*, the second on reading a Huayan text by Li Tongxuan (李通玄, 635–730), and lastly by reading the *Letters of Dahui* (*Dahui shu* 大慧書) by Zonggao. Chinul was therefore knowledgeable of the Chan koine, possibly learning some of this from Chonghwi or the heirs of Hyejo, or from Song merchants. Hyesim (1178–1234), Chinul's chief disciple, who concentrated on propagating the *kanhua* Chan of Zonggao, was an even more prolific writer and the Chan koine appears throughout his writings and in his stele inscription.⁸⁵ Although Chinul tried to avoid connections with the military, Hyesim did not, for the military favored the blunt language and activist Chan of Zonggao with his reputation for promoting a policy of military confrontation with the Jin. Hyesim was aware of external threats to Koryŏ, which probably enticed him to welcome the patronage of the military.⁸⁶

In 1217, Khitan rebels against the Mongols plundered northern Koryŏ. The Mongols pursued the Khitan across the border and forced

Koryŏ to pay tribute. In 1231 the Mongols invaded.[87] Hyesim wrote a gāthā (Buddhist verse) on behalf of the Koryŏ defense forces, stating that sitting in seclusion is selfish and without bodhisattva compassion.[88] This promoted the activist radical Sŏn and attacked conservative quietist Sŏn. Hyesim and the military dictators were in agreement. Zonggao and Hyesim used military metaphors and scatological phrases.[89] The military supported the publication of Sŏn works and Chinul's lineage was not the only Sŏn group to benefit.[90]

From 1270 to 1356, the Koryŏ government was in Mongol hands. Koryŏ kings were clients of the Mongols and married Mongol princesses. Three of the kings had Mongol mothers.[91] This split Koryŏ into a monarchist, pro-Mongol faction and a militarist anti-Mongol faction. Chinul's heirs were on the anti-Mongol side, which limited their development.[92] Some Sŏn monks took advantage of the opportunities[93] being part of the Mongol empire opened up for study in Yuan China. Following the failure of the attempted invasions of Japan by the Mongols via Koryŏ in 1281, the oppression of the Korean people was lessened and the benefits of the Mongol empire started to be experienced, with a flourishing of literature, the proper study of Neo-Confucianism and of foreign languages and scripts, and the greater availability of books.[94] Sŏn monks began to travel in numbers to Yuan China from where they brought new books and ideas, even inviting teachers such as Tieshan Shaoqiong (鐵山紹瓊, n.d., came to Koryŏ in 1304 and stayed three years) and Zhikong (指空, Śūnyadiśya, d. 1363) to Koryŏ,[95] leading to a resurgence of *kanhua* Chan in late Koryŏ.

Through their connections with Koryŏ court ladies married to Mongol emperors and princes, Sŏn monks such as T'aego Pou (太古普愚, 1301–1382) even lectured in Chinese in court-sponsored monasteries in Yandu, the Yuan capital, and a record of excerpts of one of Pou's sermons given there between 1341 and 1348 appears in a textbook written for Koreans to learn the type of Chinese (non-Literary Chinese) used in Yuan China.[96] These Sŏn monks spoke Chinese, which meant Koreans had increased access to the latest developments in Chinese Chan. Sŏn in Korea thereafter was an amalgam of the radical *kanhwa* Chan and the conservative Chan of Zongmi.

JAPAN

Japan, a paddy-rice growing country that began its Sinification in the sixth century, was different from Korea and Vietnam because it developed a script for Japanese well before the Koreans (1443) and the Vietnamese (mid-thirteenth century) developed their own scripts. This allowed the Japanese to gloss and translate Buddhist texts more accurately and to record Zen dialogues in the language they were conducted in, primarily Japanese.

Information on Chan was conveyed to Japan from the 650s and Saichō (最澄, 767–822) brought back many texts, some containing Chan koine, from China in 805.[97] His successors in the Tendai school brought more such texts, but the practices they described were always subsumed within Tendai.[98] There was no establishment of an independent Zen school. An attempt to introduce *gong'an* Chan of Yuanwu Keqin was made in 1175, but this sunk without a trace.[99]

Dainichi Nōnin (大日能忍, d. 1196+) understood Chan via more conservative Chan texts that had little of the Chan koine.[100] This realization came at a time when the military rose to power and became the Kamakura shogunate in 1192, leading to a retreat of the aristocratic Tendai and Shingon Buddhism from the center of power. Chan appeared, once again associated with the rise of the military, foreign threats, and new forms of literature.[101]

The Chan of Nōnin was an outcome of two conflicting forces: a popular, antinomian, "Zen" of street entertainers and hustlers; and an aristocratic "Zen" that was part of the Tendai school. The popular "Zen" figures, called "naturally [enlightened] laymen," spouted Chan slogans like "a separate transmission outside of the teachings." They claimed that even the ignorant could see the nature of the mind without effort or keeping the precepts.[102] Nōnin built his monastic headquarters on an island in the Yodo River because it was on a major transport hub where the "Zen" hustlers gathered. His teaching of "this mind is the Buddha," a slogan typical of Hongzhou Chan, "sentient beings are Buddha," and that the precepts are not required, attracted many people.[103] Nōnin also studied Northern Chan texts and the "conservative" *Record of the Source Mirror* (*Zongjing lu* 宗鏡録) of Yongming Yanshou (永明延壽, 904–975) that championed the agreement of Chan and doctrine.[104]

Nōnin's Bodhidharma school (Daruma-shū 達磨宗) became extremely popular,[105] and the Tendai establishment tried to have it and other claimants to the mantle of Zen suppressed. The other claimants tried to distinguish themselves from the Daruma-shū because of its alleged antinomianism. Yōsai (栄西, 1141–1215, a.k.a. Eisai), a Tendai monk who introduced Chan from China in order to reform Tendai from within,[106] directly attacked the Daruma-shū. Dōgen (道元, 1200–1253), who returned from Song

China in 1227, indirectly attacked the Daruma-shū via criticism of Linji and Zonggao from 1243 because many former Daruma-shū adherents had joined his assembly. Ironically, these adherents eventually took over Dōgen's Sōtō Zen.[107]

While the texts used by the Daruma-shū were largely Northern Chan texts and the *Zongjing lu*, the Daruma-shū teaching of "this mind is Buddha" and the like appear close to Mazu's Hongzhou Chan. While the Daruma-shū text, *Treatise on the Attainment of Bodhisattva Awakening* (*Jōtō shōgaku ron* 成等正覚論) relies heavily on the *Zongjing lu*,[108] the *Treatise on Seeing the Nature and Becoming Buddha* (*Kenshō jōbutsu ron* 見性成佛論) of 1297, possibly a record of Nōnin's replies to doctrinal questioners, written primarily in Japanese, frequently quotes from the *Jingde chuandeng lu* and occasionally from the *Essential Gateways of All-at-once Enlightenment* (*Dunwu yaomen* 頓悟要門) by Dazhu Huihai (大珠慧海, n.d.), a disciple of Mazu, and from Nanyang Huizhong, Yunju 雲居, Shenhui, and Zongmi. It quotes a mixture of early conservative and radical forms of Chan such as "the Buddha does not liberate sentient beings."[109]

After Nōnin was attacked for lacking a certification and a lineage, he sent disciples in 1189 to visit Chan master Zhuoan Deguang (拙庵德光, 1121–1203) seeking acknowledgment of Nōnin's enlightenment, which they received.[110] Deguang was a disciple of Zonggao, but there is no evidence that Nōnin and the Daruma-shū taught *kanhua* Chan. Nōnin founded an independent school, and he probably used the more radical texts that contained Chan koine after 1189.

Yōsai, as a Tendai monk, was a conservative reformer who linked the teaching of Zen with the protection of the state. He claimed that Zen was a counter to the arguments stemming from belief in the End Period of the Dharma (J. *mappō* 末法). Yōsai emphasized the unity of doctrine and Zen and the upholding of the vinaya. He stressed that Nōnin's denial of the precepts was undermining Buddhism and the state. Hence, in 1198, Yōsai wrote *On Promoting Zen to Protect the Country* (*Kōzen gokoku ron* 興禪護国論). Addressing Japan's leaders, who were versed in Literary Chinese, he largely avoided Chan koine and *gong'an*, quoting the Chan koine in one short section on Zen.[111] Yōsai learned Chan in Southern Song in 1168 and again from 1187. He studied Linji Chan for over three years, returning to Japan in 1191.[112]

Yōsai was thus likely familiar with the Chan koine. However, Yōsai did not subscribe to "exceptional-ist" Chan. He advocated study of the Tripitaka, obedience to the regulations in the *Pure Regulations for Chan*

Cloisters (*Chanyuan qinggui* 禪苑清規), and the joint practice of Chan and the teachings as found in the *Zongjing lu*.[113]

Dōgen returned from Song China to Japan in 1227. He had learned some colloquial Chinese during his stay, but he may not have spoken this language, using written conversations (J. *hitsudan* 筆談) instead.[114] Thus, in his early works, Dōgen used minimal Chan koine, even when discussing radical Chan *gong'an*.[115] Some of his earliest works, dating from 1233, have no Chan koine. By 1241 and 1242, Dōgen was more creative with the language, consciously misinterpreting it.[116] Dōgen's language became a hodgepodge of Japanese, Buddhist Hybrid Sinitic, and the Chan koine,[117] meaning Dōgen's works were destined for internal monastic consumption only and consequently remained in obscurity for centuries.[118] Such eccentric language meant that students had to be provided with oral explanations.

Dōgen was also increasingly responding to the influence of former Daruma-shū members.[119] Nōnin and his followers had used a mixture of Japanese in *katakana* script and some Chan terminology, which may have been what truly influenced Dōgen to write in a mixture of Japanese and the Chan koine. He also needed his attacks on Linji and Zonggao to use exact quotes, not just Japanese paraphrases, in order to be convincing. As Dōgen rejected the syncretic tendencies of the Daruma-shū and Yōsai, replacing the exceptionalism of "a separate transmission outside of the teaching" with a "super exceptional-ism,"[120] he needed to quote his authorities exactly in Chinese, adding his comments in Japanese.[121] In 1244, he wrote attacking the idea that the Buddhist learning of the monkhood and laity is equal, saying, "Because this is simply eating and drinking the shit and piss of the laity, one will be in the same category as a dog."[122] This is the language of radical Chan. He had moved away from a more conservative use of language,

Later, Japanese understanding of the Chan koine increased as more students went to study in China. Enni Ben'en (円爾弁円, 1201–1280) returned to Japan in 1241 after seven years of study in Southern Song. He brought back Chan as a job lot: texts, regulations, rituals, meditation techniques, architecture, and even cooking.[123] Ben'en read the Chan koine and used it in teaching his lay patron.[124] This trend continued, and these new Zen monasteries, especially those headed by Chinese abbots, may well have been bilingual societies, miniature Chinese domains within the body of the broader Japanese culture.[125]

However, as time passed, this knowledge of the Chan koine faded. When Yishan Yining (一山一寧, 1247–1317) arrived in Japan in 1299, he had to lecture on Chan texts "character by character."[126] He attracted so many students that he had to limit numbers via a qualifying examination on Chinese. He found that many Japanese Zen monks could not understand the simplest of colloquial words in standard Chan texts.[127]

Meanwhile the numbers of monks traveling between China and Japan increased.[128] After the attempted Mongol invasions of Japan failed, sea trade between Japan and Yuan China prospered, and many monks took advantage of this to travel, study, and trade.[129] Thus, the linguistic situation in Japanese Zen monasteries of this period was complex, as some monasteries had Chinese abbots, others Japanese abbots who had studied in China, and yet others with no monks who had been to China. Dialogues ranged from those in spoken Chinese, those in a mixture of Japanese and Chinese, and those using only Japanese. Some communicated by writing, and sometimes interpreters were used.[130]

Eventually, most Zen monks did not learn to speak Chinese and may have never understood the true meaning of the Chan dialogues and *gong'an*, pretending to understand the Chan koine, which was misinterpreted and ossified into fixed readings such as *zuomosheng* (作摩生) becoming *somosan*, meaningless for those who only knew Literary Chinese.[131] Once Chinese masters stopped coming to Japan from 1358,[132] this misunderstanding was perpetuated until the arrival of monks from Mt. Huangbo (黃檗山) in China in 1654 at the end of the Ming inspired a revival of the study of the Chan koine and colloquial Chinese. In the intervening period, the literary leanings of the Linji Gozan monks inclined them toward an elaborate Literary Chinese and away from the colloquial Chan koine, though some Zen masters did write in literary Japanese.

Conclusion

The existing culture of a society was a major determinant of whether or not it fully embraced Chan. Illiterate societies did not adopt Chan, even when surrounded by ethnic Han Chinese, which tells us that Chan is indeed dependent on letters. Societies that used scripts not derived from Chinese, such as Tibetan, also largely rejected Chan. Societies that had scripts possibly inspired by logographic principles, such as Tangut, adopted the more conservative Chan, especially that of Zongmi. They rejected the radical Hongzhou and *kanhua* styles of Chan that were largely expressed in a koine informed by a colloquial Chinese that carried the values of sedentary farmers. Societies of more mobile, even nomadic, peoples like the Khitan, Jurchen, Tanguts, and Tibetans found this unacceptable. These societies, living in harsher environments, also preferred Esoteric Buddhism with its apotropaic and protective spells over Chan. More Sinified societies, who used Literary Chinese as their language of record, adopted Chan, but only superficially. The Bai, like the Tibetans, Tangut, Khitan, and Jurchen, also preferred their version of Esoteric Buddhism. Societies that were profoundly Sinified, like the Koreans and Japanese, could accept radical Chan but only after considerable exposure to Buddhism and Chan. The partly Sinified and profoundly Sinified societies—the Vietnamese, Bai, Koreans, and Japanese—were also later influenced by the threats of the Jurchen Jin and the Mongols. These threats heightened a sense of ethnic identity and the rise of the military in their societies (excluding the Bai). The radical *kanhua* Chan of Zonggao was sponsored by the military, who found its activism, sense of patriotism, and blunt language appealing. This is evident in Koryŏ Korea, Kamakura Japan, and with the thirteenth-century Vietnamese kings.[133] After the Mongol threat abated, the advantages brought by the Yuan dynasty, such as the widespread printing of books that were far more available than in the Song, the promotion of Neo-Confucian education, the ability to travel widely, the study of foreign languages leading to a greater facility with written forms of "colloquial" Chinese, helped consolidate the adoption of Chan in Korea, Japan, Yunnan, and possibly even in Vietnam.

Notes

1. Jeffrey Lyle Broughton, *Zongmi on Chan* (New York: Columbia University Press, 2009), 218–19, n92.

2. See index in Yanagida Seizan, *Sodōshū sakuin* (Index to *Anthology of the Hall of the Patriarchs*), 3 vols. (Kyoto: Kyoto Daigaku Jinbunka kenkyūsho, 1984).

3. Based on maps from Komazawa Daigaku Zengaku daijiten hensansho, *Zengaku Daijiten* [Great dictionary of Zen studies], vol. 3; maps in Suzuki Tetsuo, *Tō Godai Zenshūshi*—[History of the Chan school in the Tang and Five dynasties] (Tokyo: Sankibō busshorin, 1985), 575–83, and on tables in Wu Zhou, *Zhongwan Tang Chanzong dili kaoshi* [Philological study of the geography of the Chan school in mid-to-late Tang] (Beijing: Zongjiao wenhua chubanshe, 2012), 104–107. For data that includes the Song period, see maps in Lee Kit-wah, "Tang Song Chanzong zhi dili fenbu" [Geographical distribution of the Chan school in the Tang and Song], *Xinya xuebao* 13 (October 1979): 360–62.

4. Nagai Masashi, *Chūgoku Zenshū kyōdan to minshū* [The Chinese Chan school order and the masses] (Tokyo: Uchiyama shoten, 2000), 149–67.

5. John Jorgensen, *Inventing Hui-neng, the Sixth Patriarch* (Leiden: Brill, 2005), 494–97.

6. Paul Demiéville, *Concile de Lhasa: Une controverse sur le quiétisme entre bouddhistes de l'Inde et de la Chine au VIIIe siècle de l'ère chrétienne* (Paris: Institut des hautes études chinoises, 1952), 180–84.

7. Yamaguchi Zuihō, "Chibetto Bukkyō to Shiragi no Kin Oshō" [Tibetan Buddhism and Reverend Kim of Silla], in *Shiragi Bukkyō kenkyū*, ed. Kim Chigyŏn and Chae Inhwan (Tokyo: Sankibō Busshorin, 1973), 5–11.

8. Suganuma Akira, "Chibetto ni okeru Indo Bukkyō to Chūgoku Bukkyō to no tairon" [The debates between Indian Buddhism and Chinese Buddhism in Tibet], *Bukkyō shisōshi* 4 (1981): 188–89.

9. Demieville, *Concile de Lhasa*, 185–92, 224.

10. Sam van Schaik, *Tibetan Zen: Discovering a Lost Tradition* (Boston: Snow Lion, 2015), 9–10, speaking of Dunhuang in the period 750–1000.

11. Tanaka Ryōshō, *Tonkō Zenshū bunken no kenkyū* [Studies on Chan school literature from Dunhuang], (Tokyo: Daitō shuppansha, 1983), 133, 136, 145–146, 501–507.

12. Peter Zieme, "Local Literatures: Uighur," in *Brill Encyclopedia of Buddhism*, vol. 1, ed. Jonathan A. Silk (Leiden: Brill, 2015), 877.

13. Kirill Solonin, "Tangut Identity and the Three Teachings in Tangut State" (unpublished article), 5, 9, 25.

14. Kirill Solonin, "Local Literatures: Tangut/Xixia," in *Brill Encyclopedia of Buddhism*, vol. 1, ed. Jonathan A. Silk (Leiden: Brill, 2015), 853–54.

15. For example, a text of Pure Land-Chan by Cijue (1053/4–1084), see Li Hui and Feng Guodong, "E-zang Heishuicheng wenxian 'Cijue Chanshi quanhua ji' kao" [Study of the *Collection of Encouragements to Practice by Chan Master Cijue*, a document from Heishuicheng (Khara-Khoto) Kept in Russia], *Dunhuang yanjiu* 84-2 (2004): 104–106.

16. Broughton, *Zongmi*, 47.

17. K. Solonin, "The Chan Teaching of Nanyang Huizhong (?–775) in Tangut Translation," in *Medieval Tibeto-Burmese Linguistics, IV*, ed. N. Hill (Leiden: Brill, 2012), 279–83, 296–98.

18. Suoluoning [K. Solonin], "Heishuicheng Xixiawen Hongzhou Chan wenxian chubu fenxi: yi 'Hongzhou zongshi jiaoyi' ji 'Hongzhou zongqu zhujie ji' wei lie" [An initial analysis of Hongzhou Chan Literature in Tangut Script from Heishuicheng: *Hongzhou zongshi jiaoyi* and *Hongzhou zongqu zhujie ji* as examples], *Zhongguo Chanxue* 6: 3–4.

19. Wang Yueting, "Liaochao Huangdi de chongfo jiqi shehui yingxiang" [The veneration of Buddhism by Liao dynasty emperors and its social influence], *Neimenggu Daxue xuebao (Zhexue shehuikexue pan)* 1 (1994): 49.

20. K. Solonin, "The Teaching of Daoshen in Tangut Translation: *The Mirror of Mind*," in Robert Gimello, Frédéric Girard, Imre Hamar, ed. *Avatamsaka Buddhism in East Asia: Origins and Adaptation of a Visual Culture.* (Wiesbaden: Harrasowitz, 2012), 138.

21. Broughton, *Zongmi*, 229, n145; *Chanyuan zhuquanji duxu* [Preface to a collection of Descriptions of the Source of Chan], T48.2015.398a19-21.

22. Solonin, "Daoshen," 142.

23. Solonin, "Daoshen," 150.

24. Kirill Solonin, "The 'Perfect Teaching' and Liao Sources of Tangut Chan Buddhism: A Study of *Jiexing zhaoxin tu*," *Asia Major* 26 no. 1 (2013): 91.

25. Translated in Solonin, "The 'Perfect Teaching' and Liao Sources," 93-94; from *Biezhuan xinfa yi* [Discussion of the mind dharma separately transmitted] by Jiezhu (CBETA ZZ57.953.53; XZJ101.322a-b).

26. *Biezhuan zinfa yi*, XZJ101.321a17-b.

27. Solonin, "The 'Perfect Teaching' and Liao Sources," 97-98.

28. Natasha Heller, *Illusory Abiding: The Cultural Construction of the Chan Monk Zhongfeng Mingben.* (Cambridge, MA: Harvard University Asia Center, 2014), 12-13.

29. Miya Noriko, *Mongoru jidai no shuppan bunka* [The publication culture of the Mongol period] (Nagoya: Nagoya Daigaku shuppankai, 2006), 183.

30. Miya, *Mongoru jidai*, 186-191.

31. Miya, *Mongoru jidai*, 192-193.

32. Megan Bryson, *Goddess on the Frontier and Religion: Ethnicity and Gender in Southwest China* (Stanford, CA: Stanford University Press, 2017), 23, 29.

33. Yeon-Ju Lee and Laurent Sagart, "No Limits to Borrowing: The Case of Bai and Chinese," *Diachronics* 25, no. 3 (2008): 357-385, found at https://hal.archives-ouvertes.fr/hal-00781005. Bai started to borrow from Chinese in the second century CE.

34. Megan Bryson, "Southwestern Chan: Lineage and Texts and Art of the Dali Kingdom (937-1253)," *Pacific World* (3rd series) no. 18 (2016): 72-73.

35. Bryson, *Goddess*, 21-22, 33-34.

36. Alexander C. Soper and Helen B. Chapin, "A Long Roll of Buddhist Images, I," *Artibus Asiae* 32, no. 1 (1970): 14, Chinese text, figure 13; and Bryson, "Southwestern Chan," 81.

37. Bryson, *Goddess*, 38.

38. Bryson, "Southwestern Chan," 84-88, and Duan Jinlu and Zhang Xilu, comp., *Dali lidai mingbei* [Famous stelae of Dali through the ages] (Kunming: Yunnan minzu chubanshe, 2000), 19, 26.

39. Bryson, "Southwestern Chan," 87, 89.

40. Wang Haitao, *Yunnan Fojiao shi* [History of the Buddhism of Yunnan] (Kunming: Yunnan Meishu chubanshe, 2001), 190-192.

41. Wang Haitao, *Yunnan*, 195.

42. Bryson, "Southwestern Chan," 88.
43. Duan Jinlu and Zhang Xilu, comp., *Dali lidai mingbei*, 24.
44. Bryson, *Goddess*, 39, 41, 46.
45. Chen Huan, *Mingji Dian Qian Fojiaoshi* [History of the Buddhism of southwest China in the Ming period], 2 vols. (Shijaizhuang: Hebei jiaoyu chubanshe, 2000), 237 (the chapter with the same name as the main title was first published in 1940).
46. Wang, *Yunnan*, 229–238; Heller, *Illusory Abiding*, 35, 62, 234, 331–32.
47. See Li Xiaoyou, "Nanzhao Dali xiejing shulue" (A Brief Description of Sutra-Copying in the Dali of the Nanzhao Period) in Lan Jifu et al., *Yunnan Dali Fojiao lunwen ji* [Collection of essays on the Buddhism of Dali in Yunnan] (Gaoxiong: Foguang chubanshe, 1991), 294–304.
48. Bryson, *Goddess*, 13.
49. Chen Huan, *Mingji Dian Qian Fojiaoshi*, 266, 362, 366–71.
50. Wang, *Yunnan*, 262.
51. John Jorgensen, "Korea as a Source for the Regeneration of Chinese Buddhism: The Evidence of Ch'an and Sŏn Literature," in *Currents and Countercurrents: Korean Influences on the East Asian Buddhist Traditions*, ed. Robert E. Buswell Jr. (Honolulu: University of Hawai'i Press, 2005), 75.
52. Cuong Tu Nguyen, *Zen in Medieval Vietnam: A Study and Translation of the Thiền Uyển Tập Anh* (Honolulu: University of Hawai'i Press, 1997), 341n41.
53. Nguyen, *Zen in Medieval Vietnam*, 3, 215, but with caveats, 217.
54. Nguyen, *Zen in Medieval Vietnam*, 221–224 and Thich Thien-An, *Buddhism and Zen in Vietnam* (Rutland, VT: Charles E. Tuttle, 1975), 197–199; cf. Kawamoto Kunie, "Vetonamu no Bukkyō" [Vietnamese Buddhism] in *Ajia Bukkyōshi: Chūgoku hen IV: Higashi Ajia sho chi'iki no Bukkyō*, ed. Nakamura Hajime et al. (Tokyo: Kōseisha, 1979), 282.
55. Phạm Thị Huệ, ed. *Mộc Bản Chùa Vĩnh Nghiêm: Thiềm Tông Bân Hạnh* [Woodblocks from Vĩnh Nghiêm monastery: Basic practices of the Chan school] (Hà Nội: Nhàt Xuât Bản Văn Hóa Dân Hộc, 2018). King Trần Nhân Tông abdicated in 1293 to be king-father, and soon after retreated to Yên Tử Pagoda, which was in Vĩnh Nghiêm Monastery(永嚴寺).
56. Nguyen, *Zen in Medieval Vietnam*, 8, 19–21.
57. Nguyen, *Zen in Medieval Vietnam*, 20, 66.
58. Nguyen, *Zen in Medieval Vietnam*, 98.
59. Nguyen, *Zen in Medieval Vietnam*, 35.
60. Nguyen, *Zen in Medieval Vietnam*, 141, 401 note 289.
61. Kawamoto, "Vetonamu," 282, 284; cf. Nguyen, *Zen in Medieval Vietnam*, 48–50; for an uncritical account, see Thich Thien-An, *Buddhism and Zen in Vietnam*, chapter 5.
62. Kawamoto, "Vetonamu," 285–286.
63. Nguyen, *Zen in Medieval Vietnam*, 98.

64. Hŏ Hŭngsik, ed., *Han'guk kŭmsŏk chŏnmun: kodae* [Complete epigraphy of Korea: Ancient period] (Seoul: Asea munhwasa, 1987), 1, 3.

65. See table in Chŏng Sŏngbon, *Silla Sŏnjong ŭi yŏn'gu* [Study of the Sŏn school of Silla] (Seoul: Minjoksa, 1995), 51-52.

66. C. A. Peterson, "Court and Province in Mid- and Late T'ang," in *The Cambridge History of China, volume 3, Sui and T'ang China, 589-906, Part I*, ed. D. Twitchett (Cambridge: Cambridge University Press, 1979), 491, 506-510.

67. Kim Mungyŏng, *Tangdae ŭi sahoe wa chonggyo* [Society and religion in the Tang dynasty] (Seoul: Sŭngsil Taehakkyo ch'ulpanbu, 1984), 64-65; Jorgensen, "Korea as a Source," 89.

68. Yi Chigwan, ed. and trans., *Yŏktae kosŭng pimun: Silla p'yŏn* [The stelae inscriptions for eminent monks through the ages: Silla Collection] (Seoul: Kasan mun'go, 1994 rev. edn), 97, 282.

69. Chōsen Sōtokufu, comp., *Chōsen kinseki sōran* [Complete survey of Korean epigraphy] 2 vols. (Seoul: Asea munhwasa 1976, repr. of 1920 ed., hereafter CKS), 1:146.

70. The 1085 inscription, CKS 1:285; it resumes with CKS 1:452.

71. Yi Chigwan, ed., *Yŏktae kosŭng pimun: Koryŏ p'yŏn 1* (The stelae inscriptions for eminent monks through the ages: Koryŏ Collection 1], rev. ed. (Seoul: Kasan Pulgyo munhwa yŏn'guwon, 2004), 141; colloquial 180, 233.

72. Remco E. Breuker, *Establishing a Pluralist Society in Medieval Korea, 918-1170: History, Ideology and Identity in the Koryŏ Dynasty* (Leiden: Brill, 2010), 235-41; Cho Pŏmhwan, *Silla Sŏnjong yŏn'gu* [Study of the Silla Sŏn school] (Seoul: Ilchogak, 2001), 142-46, although the evidence is circumstantial.

73. For discussion, see Jorgensen, *Inventing Hui-neng*, 735-737; Nishiguchi Yoshio, comp., *Zenmon hōzōroku no kisoteki kenkyū* (Fundamental Studies of the *Sŏnmun pojangnok*) in *Kenkyū hōkoku*, vol. 7 (Kyoto: Kokusai Zengaku kenkyūsho, 2000), 115-116, 127-128; Cho Pŏmhwan, *Silla sŏnjong yŏn'gu*, 7 and Chŏng Sŏngbon, *Silla Sŏnjong ŭi yŏn'gu*, 159, 169.

74. Nishiguchi and Yanagida, translation in Nishiguchi Yoshio, comp., *Zenmon hōzōroku*, 510-16.

75. Jorgensen, "Korea as a Source," 84-85.

76. Ch'oe Pyŏnghŏn, "Koryŏ chunggi Yi Chahyŏn ŭi Sŏn kwa kŏsa-Pulgyo ŭi sŏnggyŏk" [The Sŏn of Yi Chahyŏn and the nature of layperson Buddhism in the mid-Koryŏ], reprinted in Pulgyosa hakhoe, comp., *Koryŏ chunghugi Pulgyo saron* (Seoul: Minjoksa, 1986), 204-205. The biography of Daozhen in the *Chanlin sengbao zhuan* [Biographies of the monk-jewels of the Chan monasteries], XZJ137.543a15-16 says that three Koryŏ monks were sent on a mission and were enlightened by Daozhen during the reign of Emperor Shenzong (r. 1068-86). Hyejo was likely one of them. Cho Myŏngje, *Koryŏ hugi kanhwa Sŏn yŏn'gu* [Studies in the Kanhwa Sŏn of the late Koryŏ period] (Seoul: Hyean, 2004), 91-92 says

Tamjin (Hyejo) went to Song China and stayed in the capital of Bianjing for three years.

77. CKS 1.409-410.

78. Hŏ Hŭngsik, "Koryŏ chunggi Sŏnjong ŭi pukhŭng kwa kanhwa Sŏn ŭi chŏngae" [The revival of the Sŏn school and the development of Kanhwa Sŏn in the mid-Koryŏ period], reprinted in Pulgyosa hakhoe, comp., *Koryŏ chunghugi Pulgyo saron* (Seoul: Minjoksa, 1986), 141-42; Chʻoe, "Yi Chahyŏn," 213-14.

79. Chʻoe, "Yi Chahyŏn," 212, n30.

80. Cho Myŏngje, *Kanhwa Sŏn*, 91.

81. Breuker, *Pluralist Society*, 220-223, 230.

82. Kim Kwangsik, *Koryŏ muin chŏnggwŏn kwa Pulgyogye* (The Koryŏ military regime and the Buddhist world] (Seoul: Minjoksa, 1995), 38, 40, 46.

83. Kim Kwangsik, *Koryŏ muin*, 102, 134.

84. Robert E. Buswell Jr., trans., *Chinul: Selected Works*, Collected Works of Korean Buddhism, vol. 12 (Seoul: Jogye Order of Korean Buddhism, 2012), 11-13.

85. CKS 1: 462.

86. Cho Myŏngje, *Kanhwa Sŏn*, 111-112, 117.

87. Juhn Y. Ahn, trans., *Gongan Collections 1*, Collected Works of Korean Buddhism, vol. 7-1 (Seoul: Jogye Order of Korean Buddhism, 2012), 29-30.

88. Quoted in Cho Myŏngje, *Kanhwa Sŏn*, 113-114.

89. For Zonggao, see *Dahui Pujue Chanshi yulu* [Recorded sayings of Chan Master Dahui Pujue], T47.1998A.871b2, *Jianfu Chenggu Chanshi yulu* [Recorded sayings of Chan Master Jianfu Chenggu], XZJ126.435b5-8; for Hyesim, see Ahn, trans., *Gongan Collections 1*, 439-440, though this is a quote.

90. Cho Myŏngje, *Kanhwa Sŏn*, 110-111, 115.

91. William E. Henderson, *A History of Korea* (New York: Free Press, 1971), 120-21, 123.

92. Cho Myŏngje, *Kanhwa Sŏn*, 118-19.

93. Chʻae Sangsik, *Koryŏ hugi Pulgyosa yŏnʻgu* [Study of the Buddhist history of the late Koryŏ period] (Seoul: Ilchogak, 1991), 114-17, table 2-2, 129-130, 143-147.

94. Henderson, *A History of Korea*, 122, 126, 130. The study of languages by official translators is said to have begun in 1276, but which languages other than Chinese is not clear. Song Ki-joong, *The Study of Foreign Languages in the Chosŏn Dynasty* (Seoul: Jimoondang, 2001), 4-6.

95. Cho Myŏngje, *Kanhwa Sŏn*, 133-135, 163; Hŏ Hŭngsik, *Koryŏ Pulgyosa yŏnʻgu*, 710-716.

96. Liang Wuzhen (Yang Ojin), *Hanhaksŏ yŏnʻgu* [Researches on Chinese studies textbooks for Koreans] (Seoul: Pangmunsa, 2010), 255-58. Song Ki-joong, *The Study of Foreign Languages*, 66; Wang Ha, Yu Chaewŏn and Chʻoe Chaeyŏng, *Yŏkchu Pak Tʻongsa ŏnhae* [Annotated translation of the Korean glosses on *Pak*

the Translator] (Seoul: Hakkobang, 2012), 155–58 for text and the medieval Korean translation.

97. *Dengyō Daishi shōrai Etchū roku* (Record of the texts brought from Yuezhou by Saichō), T55.2160.1059b.

98. Imaeda Aishin, *Chūsei Zenshūshi no kenkyū* (Study of the history of the Zen school in medieval Japan] (Tokyo: Tōkyō Daigaku shuppankai, 1970), 1; Bernard Faure, "The Daruma-shū, Dōgen, and Sōtō Zen," *Monumenta Nipponica* 42.1 (1987), 25n1.

99. Ibuki Atsushi, *Zen no rekishi* [History of Chan/Zen] (Kyoto: Hōzōkan, 2001), 184–85.

100. Faure, "Daruma," 357.

101. Ibuki, *Zen no rekishi*, 187–88.

102. Harada Masatoshi, *Nihon chūsei no Zenshū to shakai* [The Zen school and society in medieval Japan] (Tokyo: Yoshikawa Hirobumi kan, 1998), 18, 21–22.

103. Harada, *Zenshū to shakai*, 64–65; Faure, "Daruma," 27.

104. Harada, *Zenshū to shakai*, 57; Faure, "Daruma," 31.

105. Faure, "Daruma," 27–28.

106. Imaeda, *Chūsei Zenshūshi no kenkyū*, 1, 16–17.

107. Faure, "Daruma," 28–31, 46–47.

108. Analyzed in Faure, "Daruma," 32.

109. Furuse Tamami, "*Kenshō jōbutsu ron* no kihonteki seikaku ni kansuru ichikōsatsu" [An examination of the *Kenshō jōbutsu ron*] *Sengokuyama ronshū* 4 (2008): 155, 159, 161, 164.

110. Faure, "Daruma," 28.

111. Yanagida Seizan, translation of *Kōzen gokokuron* in Ichikawa Hakugen, Iriya Yoshitaka, and Yanagida Seizan, *Chūsei Zenge no shisō* [The thought of medieval Zen masters] (Tokyo: Iwanami shoten, 1972) 113–114, 63–64, supplementary notes 397–398.

112. Imaeda, *Chūsei Zenshūshi no kenkyū*, 3–6.

113. Yanagida, translation of *Kōzen gokokuron* in *Chūsei Zenge no shisō*, 472–75.

114. Ishii Shūdō, *Sōdai Zenshūshi no kenkyū* [A study of the history of the Song dynasty Chan school] (Tokyo: Daitōshuppansha, 1987), 364.

115. Watsuji Tetsurō, ed., *Shōbōgenzō zuimonki* [Record of what was heard of the eye of appreciation of the correct dharma], 1929 (Tokyo: Iwanami shoten reprint, 1976), 14.

116. Hee-Jin Kim, "'The Reason of Words and Letters': Dōgen and Kōan Language," in *Dōgen Studies*, ed. William R. LaFleur (Honolulu: University of Hawai'i Press, 1989), 64.

117. See for example, Nakamura Sōichi, *Zenyaku Shōbōgenzō* [Complete translation of the *Eye of Appreciation of the Correct Dharma*], 4 vols. (Tokyo: Shōshin shobō, 1971), 2:228.

118. Carl Bielefeldt, "Recarving the Dragon: History and Dogma in the Study of Dōgen," in *Dōgen Studies*, ed. William R. LaFleur (Honolulu: University of Hawai'i Press, 1985), 23.

119. Faure, "Daruma," 30.

120. See Imaeda, *Chūsei Zenshūshi no kenkyū*, 19–20, a correct Dharma in a lineage from Buddha, but not called Zenshū.

121. Imaeda, *Chūsei Zenshūshi no kenkyū*, 29.

122. Quoted in Imaeda, *Chūsei Zenshūshi no kenkyū*, 49.

123. Martin Collcutt, *Five Mountains: The Rinzai Monastic Institution in Medieval Japan* (Cambridge, MA.: Harvard University Press, 1981), 41–47.

124. *Tōfukuji kaizan Shōichi Kokushi nenpu* [Chronological biography of the founder of Tōfukuji, national teacher Shōichi] edited in 1417 by Giyō Hōshū (1363–1424) in *Dai Nippon Bukkyō zensho* (Tokyo: Bussho kankōkai, 1912), 13b for letter, 137a for instructions.

125. Murai Shōsuke, "Chūsei no gaikō to Zenji Zensō" [Medieval diplomacy and Zen monasteries and Zen monks], in *Chūsei ji'in no sugata to kurashi—Mikkyō, Zensō, yuya* [The forms and livelihood of medieval monasteries; Esoteric Buddhism, Zen monks, and bathhouses], comp. Kokuritsu rekishi minzoku hakubutsukan (Tokyo: Yamakawa shuppansha, 2004), 123.

126. *Issan Kokushi goroku* [Recorded sayings of national teacher Issan], T80.2553.332b26–c3.

127. Heinrich Dumoulin, *Zen Buddhism: A History, vol. 2: Japan*, trans. James Heisig and Paul Knitter (New York: Macmillan, 1990), 36; Iriya Yoshitaka, "Mujaku Dōchū no Zengaku" [The Zen studies of Mujaku Dōchū] in *Kūgeshū: Iriya Yoshitaka tanpenshū* [Collection of spots before the eyes: Collection of short essays by Iriya Yoshitaka] (Kyoto: Shibunkaku, 1992), 199.

128. Noguchi Yoshitaka, *Gendai Zenshūshi kenkyū* [Study of the history of the Chan school of the Yuan period] (Kyoto: Zenbunka kenkyūsho, 2005), 489–94.

129. Ibuki, *Zen no rekishi*, 196.

130. Kenneth Kraft, *Eloquent Zen: Daitō and Early Japanese Zen* (Honolulu: University of Hawai'i Press, 1992), 8, 51.

131. Yanagida Seizan, *Zen goroku: Sekai no meichō zoku 3* (Chan recorded sayings: Famous works of the world, continued 3] (Tokyo: Chūōkōronsha, 1974), 20.

132. Kraft, *Eloquent Zen*, 3.

133. See also Cho Myŏngje, *Kanhwa Sŏn*, 121–22.

Chapter 2

The Hangzhou Region and the Spread of East Asian Buddhism

ALBERT WELTER

In Search of East Asian Buddhism

The story of East Asian Buddhism has not been told. Or, rather, it has been told in an ineffective and misleading way in the service of other narratives. As I explain below in greater detail, Europeans became enthralled with the Buddhism of India, a land in which Buddhism had played virtually no role for a thousand years. The various Buddhisms that took root and persevered throughout Asia were looked upon with suspicion and contempt, as degraded perversions of the allegedly pure Indian form that Śākyamuni had devised. Beyond Europe, Japan was an early adopter of modern Buddhist studies methodologies. As an Asian country with a long Buddhist history and the first Asian country to modernize according to the European colonial model, Japan made great contributions to the modern study of Buddhism. Yet it, too, was enthralled with the model of Buddhist studies formulated in Europe and fixated on India. Japanese Buddhist sectarian groups with an interest in their own traditions took a different approach, one rooted in Chinese developments but with an eye toward their culmination and fruition in Japan. China, the heartland of East Asian Buddhist developments throughout the East Asian region, fell, so to speak, through the cracks. Given the pull of these two narratives, one European and the other Japanese, Chinese Buddhism became a handmaiden to the inventions of others, as a degraded extension of

Indian Buddhism, on the one hand, and as a prelude to the fulfillment of Buddhist aspirations in Japan, on the other.

The approach I take here is not so much about new research on East Asia as about how previous research has been conceptualized in ways that have not served to highlight accurately the characteristics and features of East Asian Buddhism, their intrinsic meaning and impact. Take, for example, the way the story of East Asian Buddhism is told today in university courses and academic textbooks. The story begins in India, and in many cases, hardly leaves India. Buddhism begins with the life of the Buddha and his environs—geographic, intellectual, and social. It continues through the story of its early developments—the first Buddhist councils, the spawning of different sects and schools. Never mind the fact that this story of Buddhist origins is a decidedly retrospective one, written down centuries after the events allegedly occurred. As a result, it tells us about the Buddha as imagined by his distant descendants, rather than a record of the actual events as they occurred at the time. Subsequently, we are treated to the story of its diffusion beyond the Buddha's initial homeland to include large swaths of the Indian subcontinent. Finally, we are introduced to Mahāyāna reformation movements and the dispersion of Buddhism throughout greater Asia—into Southeast Asia, Central Asia, and finally, to East Asia.[1]

Yet, it would be wrong to fault the authors of these works for a conceptual framework nearly all have succumbed to in one form or another. In addition, Buddhism is such a vast and complex subject, covering its geographic expanse and regional iterations, not to mention its historical contours and social, political, and intellectual dimensions, makes comprehensive treatment all but impossible. Compromise is the order of the day, and a focus on India and Indian-based developments provides a necessary short cut that few avoid. We have all been implicated to some degree in the assumptions that have guided the modern study of Buddhism, projected back on to the story of its origins and dissemination. The task of reimagining East Asian Buddhism, as a result, entails an excursus into the modern field of Buddhist studies, and how and why it was conceived.

Although notions regarding Buddhism had reached the West from antiquity,[2] these had relatively little impact. Previous reports regarding Buddhism from travelers like those form the Flemish Franciscan missionary Willem von Ruysbroeck (c. 1220–c. 1293)[3] and the Venetian explorer Marco Polo (1254–1324),[4] reports from other Catholic missionaries, etc., likewise had relatively little impact. As is well known, European contact with Asia during the so-called Age of Discovery (end of fifteenth to eighteenth century) precipitated an era of globalization and colonialism that our current versions of modernism and world order (political, economic, social, cultural, educational, and so on) are rooted in. Less well known are the religious and intellectual encounters that occurred at this time. The recent work of Urs App has uncovered how knowledge of Buddhism, initiated in Europe during the sixteenth century, led to an interpretation of Buddhist doctrines that produced the notion of a single "Oriental philosophy" seen as a kind of primordial philosophy preeminent throughout the entire "Orient," from Egypt to Japan, an atheism rooted in notions of "nothingness" and "emptiness."[5] This became the first period of serious intellectual engagement between Buddhism and the West. Noteworthy landmarks of this interaction include the work of the German philosopher Arthur Schopenhauer (1788–1860).[6] The impact of the "discovery" of Buddhism in nineteenth-century Europe was momentous. During the height of European colonialism, Buddhism, along with other non-European religions and intellectual traditions, came to the attention of Western intellectuals through the writings of Christian missionaries, scholars, and imperial civil servants who worked and administered in lands where Buddhism was a dominant force.

By the late nineteenth century, the impact of Buddhism on the European West was particularly felt on two fronts. On the popular front, one can point to Sir Edwin Arnold's *The Light of Asia*, published in 1879, which depicts the life, character, and philosophy of Prince Gautama, the founder of Buddhism, and was subsequently translated in numerous languages, including Hindi.[7] On the scholarly front, there was the legendary Max Müller, whose fifty-volume series on the *Sacred Books of the East* beginning in 1879, included many Buddhist classics translated into English for the first time.[8] As with all transitional moments in the history of ideas, the so-called discovery of Buddhism came with a particular worldview that emanated from its European provenance.

The term "Protestant Buddhism" was introduced by Gananath Obeyesekere, who observed that in the late nineteenth century, a Śrī Lankan, Anagarika Dharmapala (1864–1933), became the leader of a Buddhist protest/revival movement. In Obeyesekere's analysis, the term conveyed two meanings: as a new form of Buddhism to protest against Christian missions, and as a movement that mirrored Protestant Christianity in structure and content.[9] Dharmapala was a modernist who promoted a vision of Buddhism as a religion compatible with science and

Western values, such as democracy. Along with Henry Steel Olcott and Helen Blavatsky, the creators of the Theosophical Society, he was a major reformer and revivalist of Ceylonese Buddhism and an important figure in its Western transmission.[10]

The concept was also applied more recently in academic Buddhist studies circles by Gregory Schopen ("Archaeology and Protestant Presuppositions in the Study of Indian Buddhism"), to include the Protestant presuppositions of European "discoverers" of Buddhism.[11] Schopen concluded: "It is possible, then, that this conception has determined the history of the study of Indian Buddhism and that—as a consequence—our picture of Indian Buddhism characterization may reflect more of our own history and values than the history and values of Indian Buddhism."[12] The conception Schopen is referring to includes such things as an overriding textual orientation privileging sacred "canonical" writings as ideal and actual representations (i.e., that carefully contrived ideal paradigms are adequate reflections of historical reality [4–5]); excluding what practicing Buddhists did and believed in the history of their own indigenous traditions (14); the devaluation of material aspects of religion—reliquaries, shrines, and images—as perversions of "true religion" (20–21); and that this conception of where "true religion" is located originates in sixteenth-century Protestant polemics (22).

In line with these presuppositions, the field of Buddhist studies, following Schopen, has been plagued with Protestant overtones from its inception. One way to calculate this influence is to correlate Protestant aspirations with the frames of early Buddhist studies. Early Buddhist interests were preoccupied by the life and teachings of Śākyamuni, as suggested by Arnold's *Light of Asia*, referred to above, and Olcott's description of his faith as a "pure, primitive Buddhism"; in the process, he eschewed the tradition of his Sinhalese mentors in favor of an adapted tradition that "[facilitated] the interaction between Protestantism and Buddhism in the late-nineteenth-century."[13] It goes without saying that the "pure, primitive Buddhism" imagined by Olcott and others was a creative fabrication suitable for Buddhist reformers but hardly a premise for the academic study of Buddhism.

Schopen was not the first to notice the spell to which the scholarly study of Buddhism had succumbed. As early as 1973, David L. Snellgrove made explicit the problems associated with the Protestant inspired quest for the historical Buddha:

Despite the admonitions of responsible scholars, writers of books on Buddhism still tend to assume that a reasonably historical account of the life and personal teachings of Śākyamuni Buddha may be extracted from the earliest available canonical accounts. This quest of the historical Buddha began as a Western nineteenth-century interest, imitating both in its pre-suppositions and its methods of inquiry the parallel quest of the historical Jesus of Nazareth.[14]

Snellgrove elaborated this position further in his assessment of the famous nineteenth-century German Indologist, Hermann Oldenberg's widely read work, *Buddha, sein Leben, seine Lehre, seine Gemeinde* (*Buddha, His Life, His Doctrine, His Order*):

Within the terms of his enunciated principles, Oldenberg's work is responsible and scholarly. He has created a figure of the historical Buddha, which has been now popularly accepted by Westerners, and by Westernized Asians. However, cast as it is in the mold of European nineteenth-century liberal and rational thought, it might seem to bear on examination no relationship to the religious aspirations and conceptions relating to Śākyamuni Buddha, as revealed in the earliest Buddhist literature. Furthermore it can easily be shown that the whole process of deliberately abstracting everything of an apparent unhistorical and mythical character, all too often leads away from any semblance of historical truth. This is because the elements that are deliberately abstracted, usually those relating to religious faith and the cult of the Buddha as a higher being, may be older and thus nearer the origins of the religion, than the supposed historical element. This easily reveals itself at best as an honest but comparatively late attempt at producing out of floating traditions a coherent story, and at the worst as a tangle of tendentious fabrications produced to justify the pretensions of some later sectarian group.[15]

To make explicit the Protestant paradigm suggested in the motivations to focus on the study of early Buddhism, let me suggest the following parallels: (1) Śākyamuni was viewed as the true originator of Buddhism, akin to the position of Jesus in Christianity; (2) the *Dialogues of Buddha*, the alleged record of Śākyamuni's teachings, were likened to the Christian New Testament, the record of Jesus's activities and teachings; (3) subsequent elaborations and explanations of Buddhist teachings were regarded as a deterioration or corruption of Śākyamuni's original message, just as Catholic doctrinal explanations came to be viewed as a perversion of the "pure," original Christianity developed by Jesus and his early followers as revealed in the New Testament; (4) the quest of the Protestant discoverers of Buddhism for the original, true teachings of the historical Buddha came to be associated with "true Buddhism," in a manner not unlike the Protestant quest for the historical Jesus and "true Christianity."

The influence of Protestant orientations over Buddhism has been well noted. Kevin Trainor, in his review of Reginald Ray, *Buddhist Saints in India: A Study of Buddhist Values and Orientations*, comments that Ray's account "bears more than a passing resemblance to influential nineteenth century narratives of an original authentic monastic tradition that was later corrupted by a Buddhist laity incapable of understanding the Buddha's true teaching."[16] In specific reference to Tibet, Donald Lopez writes how "Mahayana had been condemned by an earlier generation of scholars as a deviation of the Buddha's original teachings."[17] A comprehensive overview of the situation is provided by Catherine Newell, who speaks of how discourses about religion were shaped by expectations dating back to the Reformation.

> Protestantism downplayed the importance and efficacy of religious ritual and the soteriological mediation of a professional clerisy, and asserted the centrality of individual access to texts in understanding a religion. It emphasized the personal rather than the social focus of religion. This rational, ritual-free, "true" Christianity, *based in scripture rather than tradition*, was presented in contrast to Catholicism, which was seen to have moved far away from the original teachings of the Early Church, and to have allowed itself to be sullied by clerical hierarchy, devotionalism and excessive ritual. The superiority of Protestantism over the perceived idolatry and ritual of the Catholic Church was well established in the minds of many of the early European scholars of Buddhist Asia, particularly within the Anglo-German strand of scholarship.[18]

As a result, Newell concludes, the study of Buddhism was divided into two disparate poles: (1) an idealized Buddhism of distant antiquity, reconstructed by scholars based on linguistic criteria giving preference to older texts; and (2) the Buddhism of contemporary Asia, whose practices and preferences stood in marked contrast to the idealized reconstruction.[19] This dichotomy perpetrated an ideal "true" Buddhism construed as a transhistorical essence in contrast to its contemporary manifestations.[20] The latter, in contrast to the former, represented an unmitigated distortion and perversion of the ideal.

The spell cast by the myopic European fascination with Indian (especially early Indian) Buddhism was broken in the early twentieth century through the writings of D.T. Suzuki (Suzuki Daisetsu). Suzuki, well known as a proselytizer of Zen Buddhism in the West, carved out a space for Zen (and by extension Chan) as a legitimate expression of Buddhism beyond the Indian cultural sphere. The victory he won, however, was a mixed one, as he did so with an interpretation of Zen that attempted to transcend the Protestant presuppositions that the discipline of Buddhist studies assumed, cast, à la Snellgrove, "in the mold of European nineteenth-century liberal and rational thought."

Through the work of others, the nature of Suzuki's impact and his inspirations are now well known; but let me review some salient aspects.[21] Suzuki was a student of Western philosophy and lay Zen practitioner who accompanied Zen master Shaku Sōen 釋宗演 (1860–1919) to the United States to attend the World Parliament of Religions in Chicago in 1893 to serve as his translator. Suzuki went on to become an indefatigable proponent of Zen, and his efforts almost single-handedly created a new field of Buddhist studies focusing on Zen (and Chan). Suzuki was broadly interested in Theosophy and even founded a branch in Japan of an offshoot organization in 1911, together with his wife Beatrice Lane Suzuki—also an avid Theosophist.[22] Suzuki also formed an interest in another fashionable movement of the time, Swedenborgianism, based on the writings of the eighteenth-century Swedish mystic and theologian Emanuel Swedenborg. Suzuki was instrumental in introducing the movement in Japan, and actively promoted it for several years.[23] Influenced by William James's notion of mysticism as "pure experience,"[24] Suzuki charted an interpretation of Zen as a singular transformative experience, the fundamental and authentic basis for "one single original Faith, deeply embedded in the human soul."[25] In Suzuki's mind, Zen *satori*, or enlightenment, represented the pivotal moment in religious experience, the very foundation of religiosity and spirituality itself, foundational to all religions that were but a species of this transformative insight. Zen thus represented the seminal moment of religious experience, transcending culture and history, which served as the foundation of all religions. Yet, Suzuki was not content to share Zen experience, to deem it as one mystical experience among many, but situated Zen experience as *the* fountain from which all other religious experiences might be compared (even though other species of mysticism might at times, according to Suzuki, come close).[26] Zen, in Suzuki's interpretation, was neither a religion nor a philosophy, and remarkably, not even Buddhism.[27]

While Suzuki broke the spell of Indo-centrism in Buddhist studies, the effect of his mission was to promote a Japan-centric model in its place. Although aware of the Indian, and especially Chinese context that it grew from, Suzuki insisted that true Zen emerged only with the meeting of Buddhism and Japanese culture in the Kamakura period, when Japan truly awakened to religious and spiritual life. The flowering of this period became "the basis for the Japanese Character, thought, religious faith, and esthetic taste," from which in the future, Suzuki believed "there can be constructed something new of world-wide significance," and that this is "the mission of today's Japan."[28] Zen, according to Suzuki, was instrumental for the Japanese in finding their spiritual depth. "Though it came by way of China, its imported character altogether vanished following its introduction, and it became Japanese," to form "an essential rapport between Zen and the Japanese character."[29]

As a result, the breaking of the spell cast by Indian Buddhism did not lead to a true renaissance of Chan and Zen studies. Suzuki's Zen was firmly rooted in the Protestant religious paradigm that privileged the notion of a true religion that allegedly predated the institutional, ritual, and social encumbrances associated with religious deterioration. Somewhat magically, and mysteriously, Zen emerged in Japan as a pristine form of spiritual nonduality (*the* pristine form of spirituality), which Suzuki would claim as more authentic than even Protestant Christianity. As a result, Zen studies shaped our understanding of Chinese Chan Buddhism in two significant ways: (1) it treated Chinese Chan as prelude to a full expression of Japanese Zen spirituality, effectively marginalizing it; and (2) when it did consider Chinese Chan, it privileged those aspects that confirmed and contributed to the new, modern Japanese interpretation of Zen. Additionally, it should be noted that Korean Sŏn plays no role in Suzuki's interpretation of Zen. The result is that even when the story of East Asian Chan, Sŏn, and Zen was told, it was done inaccurately, outside a proper historical model. Historical events relating to the history of Chan, Sŏn, and Zen were not treated as phenomena intrinsic to their own development but in the service of another narrative. Although East Asian Buddhist scholarship has moved beyond the "Zen studies" paradigm, there is still work to be done in framing an adequate narrative structure to tell the story of Chan, Sŏn, and Zen, especially as it relates to crucial post-Tang periods, which have been virtually ignored until recent decades and are still poorly represented. It is from these periods, rather than the early period or the so-called golden age of the Tang, that Chan saw its most significant developments, the ones that were instrumental in the spread of Chan throughout East Asia.

The History of the Spread of Buddhism: Indo-centric Presuppositions

The story of the spread of Buddhism retains the long shadow of Indo-centrism. Traditions beyond India, particularly in East Asia, have long been inadvertently relegated to subsidiary status, valued as adjuncts to the Indian Buddhist story. A corollary of this is the Sui-Tang centrism that long dominated the study of Chinese Buddhism, which saw its culmination in the developments of Indian-inspired models.

Mapping the spread of Buddhism throughout Asia necessarily involves a historical timeline depicting the expansion of Buddhism throughout India, with a southern trajectory to Śrī Lanka and on to Southeast Asia, and a northern trajectory into Central Asia and on to China (although Buddhism came to China via the "southern" sea route trajectory as well), Korea, and Japan. Yet, as accurate as this narrative is, it tells only part of the story of the spread and impact of Buddhism. It tells a story of the spread of Buddhism in Asia as an abbreviated history that is completed by the eighth century. Readily available maps, used ubiquitously in courses introducing Buddhism, depict the currents in the development of Buddhism based on the assumption of an Indian homeland and dispersion across Asia.[30]

The early phases in the adoption and adaptation of Buddhism in China align with this Indo-centric model. The stages in the development of Buddhism in China are usually charted something like this:[31]

1. Translation stage (examples):

   - An Shigao (安世高, 148 C.E.), basic meditation texts (mindfulness and breathing); e.g., *Da anpan shouyi jing* (大安般守意經).

   - Lokasema (支讖, 168 C.E.), *Perfection of Wisdom* (道行般若經) and *Land of Bliss* (無量清淨平等覺經) sutras.

   - Dharmarakṣa (竺法護, 266–308), *Perfection of Wisdom* (光讚般若波羅密經) and *Lotus Sūtra* (法華經).

   - Kumarajiva (鳩什, 344–413), Mādhyamika texts (三論), *Vimalakirti Sūtra* (維摩經), *Lotus Sūtra* (法華經).

2. Indian Buddhist Schools in China stage (examples):

   - Mādhyamika/Sanlun (Three Treatise) school (三論宗).

   - Yogācāra/Vijñānavāda/Faxiang/Weishi (Consciousness Only) school (法相宗/唯識宗).

3. Chinese doctrinal schools based on Indian Buddhist scriptures stage (examples):

   - Tiantai school (天台宗) based on the *Lotus Sūtra* and *Nirvāṇa Sūtra* (涅槃經).

   - Huayan school (華嚴宗) based on the *Huayan jing* (華嚴經, *Avataṃsaka Sūtra*)

During its period of preeminence, India did indeed serve as the cultural center and homeland of Buddhism. The three stages outlined above are directly dependent on Indian Buddhist textual culture, through the translation of Indian Buddhist sūtras and texts, the formation of Indian Buddhist schools in China, and the development of Chinese doctrinal schools based on the primacy of Indian Buddhist scriptures. Chinese Buddhist pilgrims prioritized the Indian homeland in their search for ever-evolving forms of authentic Buddhism. The trajectory of return is evident in the famous journeys, for example, of Faxian (法顯), Xuanzang (玄奘), and Yijing (義淨), who embarked on pilgrimages to India using both land and sea routes and left records of their travels. Their mapping reinforces the story of India as Buddhist center and homeland, the original and "true" source of Buddhism and Buddhist teachings. Yet, as we know,

Buddhism in India was already in decline by the time of Xuanzang, who describes at various points the dilapidated state of Buddhist monuments he visits.[32]

As we also know, the story of Buddhism in Asia did not end with this decline. Indeed, as Buddhism in India subsided, its teachings were just beginning to take hold in places like Tibet.[33]

The decline of Buddhism in India also had a major impact on Buddhism in China and East Asia, but it was not, as had often been told in previous scholarship, the story of decline. As we begin to think about the development of Buddhism beyond an Indo-centric framework, we start with a recognition that as India ceased to be an active agent for Buddhist developments, Chinese developments became the inspiration for a new East Asian Buddhism. The memory of Indian Buddhism remained a potent force in passive memory, but as pilgrimages between India and China waned and the flow of texts that sustained Buddhism based on Indian developments subsided, China initiated its own indigenous forms of Buddhism without precedent in India, and these new forms constituted the forces animating East Asian Buddhism moving forward. China became the new homeland of an East Asian Buddhism largely shorn of its Indian moorings (even while the Indian imaginary remained vivid). The China/Yellow Sea interaction sphere became the new highway of Buddhist dynamism,[34] as Chinese forms of Buddhism were transmitted throughout the region. Given its vibrant economy, dedication to Buddhism, and location, Hangzhou emerged as an important (the most important?) regional center of Buddhism in China, and the hub of an East Asian Buddhism that radiated outward across the China/Yellow Sea.

Beyond Dunhuang: Resituating Chan Studies

No one can deny the impact that Dunhuang has had on our understanding of Buddhism. The study of manuscripts from the lost library cave at Dunhuang has revolutionized our understanding and entrenched "Silk Road Buddhism" as an accepted focus for workshops, symposiums, courses, and conferences. Yet, Dunhuang has been something of a mixed blessing for Chan studies. While it has admittedly transformed our understanding of early and perhaps "middle" period Chan[35] in ways that were once unimaginable, it has also distracted us from the story of Chan that developed from around the ninth century, the story of Chan, Sŏn, and Zen, as it became a truly East Asian phenomenon, the development of which reverberates down to the present day. If we were to look for a "golden age" of Chan, we would need to look beyond the developments of the Tang dynasty and the cache of Chan-related Dunhuang manuscripts, however much these were crucial to revolutionizing our understanding of early Chan.[36]

I am reminded here of a statement by the Chinese Buddhist scholar Lu Cheng 呂澂 that cautions about an overreliance on Dunhuang: that (to paraphrase) although Dunhuang studies has a certain scope of application and usefulness and can supplement some of the shortcomings of research materials, it should not be overestimated. And as Lu notes, even though this is particularly true of Chan and Zen studies, the entirety of Chan and Zen studies cannot be reduced to what has been uncovered at Dunhuang. The reality is that much of what was uncovered, though insightful for unraveling the dynamics of a formative period of early Chan history, was forgotten to history and had little impact on the later tradition that developed.[37]

Let me point to one example of how the Dunhuang materials have revolutionized Chan and Zen studies, on the one hand, but misled generations of scholars on the other. Phillip Yampolsky's *Platform Sutra of the Sixth Patriarch* (六祖壇經), published by Columbia University Press in 1967, along with the writings of Hu Shih on Shenhui, enthralled the English reading world with its revelations of the complexities at work beyond the seminal transition in Chan history and the advent of the so-called Southern school. As important as Dunhuang versions of the *Platform Sutra* were to the story of early Chan, it was not the received version that was read in China. The greatly expanded "mature version of the text" of the Song and Yuan dynasties compiled for later audiences of Chinese readers actually represents the "mainstream" *Platform Sutra* text to Chinese and East Asian readers.[38] In addition, the seminal status of the *Platform Sutra*, long assumed by modern students and scholars of East Asian Buddhism, is questionable given its late entrance into the Buddhist canon and somewhat rare reference to it in later Buddhist sources.[39] The fallacy of our presumption is concretized in a recent work on Neo-Confucianism that, in a spirit of magnanimity, opens with a chapter of sections translated from the Dunhuang version of the *Platform Sutra*, a version completely unknown to Neo-Confucians in the Song dynasty.[40] This is but one example of how the "law of unintended consequences" has prevailed over the impact of Dunhuang on Chan and Zen studies. Dunhuang has skewed our understanding of the Chan tradition, inadvertently shifting attention away from crucial later developments in the tradition that were not only instrumental in shaping Chan in China in the Song and Ming dynasties but also away from the impact of these developments throughout broader East Asian regions.

Where to Begin? The Wuyue Kingdom and the Creation of an East Asian Buddhism

As Tang authority deteriorated, the southern principality of Wuyue was able to carve out a quasi-independent, politically stable, and economically vibrant regime centered in the regional capital of Qiantang (which later became the Southern Song capital of Hangzhou). Like other southern-based regimes of the late Tang and Five Dynasties periods (e.g., Southern Tang, Min, and Southern Han), Wuyue was built on a plan for revising the glories of the Tang dynasty, predicated on a revival of Tang Buddhist culture, based on a Buddhist vision of society and culture.[41]

The founder of an independent Wuyue, Qian Liu (錢鏐, King Wusu 武肅王, r. 893–932), was granted an imperial posthumous title, Taizu (太祖, Great Ancestor), revealing the pretensions of the Wuyue regime. While Qian Liu was early on persuaded to follow Daoism, under the influence of Luo Yin (羅隱),[42] he eventually turned to Buddhism as the hallmark of his regime. Qian Liu supported Buddhism with a campaign to construct monasteries throughout the region, including the Taiping Cloister (太平院, for housing the famous Tiantai prelate Zhiyi's 智顗 remains), the Huiri Monastery (慧日寺), and the Jiuming Monastery (九明寺) on Mt. Tiantai (天台山).[43] Monks from various regions in China sought refuge under the protection of the Buddhist monasteries that Qian Liu supported, including representatives of Northern and Southern factions of Chan.

Mt. Tiantai, the cradle of the Tiantai school founded by Zhiyi (538–597), was a key spiritual center of the Wuyue region. After the death of Zhiyi and his disciple Guanding (灌頂, 561–632), Tiantai was absorbed into the Buddhism of the capital, Chang'an, and lost its independent status and vitality. It was revived for a time in the eighth century by the sixth patriarch of the school, Zhanran (湛然, 711–782) but fell into decline after his death.[44] Through the support of Wuyue rulers, the school was revived. Zanning (贊寧, 919–1001) claimed Haorui (皓端, 889–961), honored by the Wuyue ruler Qian Chu (錢俶, King Zhongyi 忠懿王, r. 948–978) with a purple robe and named "Great Virtuous Exalter of Dharma" (*dade songfa* 大德崇法), was the successor of the tenth Tiantai patriarch Xuanzhu (玄燭).[45]

The campaign to revive Buddhism in Wuyue culminated in the personal connections and political fortunes of Tiantai Deshao (天台德紹, 891–972) and Qian Chu.[46] Nearly forty years his junior, Qian Chu naturally relied on Deshao for advice, practicing Buddhism under him in a manner more akin to a master-disciple relationship than the natural pattern pertaining between a ruler and his spiritual advisor. Deshao's stature in the region was such that he was praised as the reembodiment of Zhiyi.[47] His influence over Qian Chu resulted in favored treatment for Deshao's students in Wuyue, many of whom studied alongside Qian Chu in Deshao's congregation.[48] Most prominent among them were Zanning, who succeeded Deshao in the role of Wuyue's political advisor, and Yongming Yanshou (永明延壽, 904–975), who assumed the role of spiritual leader in Wuyue. Yanshou's career culminated with the role of abbot at the Yongming Monastery (永明寺, contemporary Jingci si 淨慈寺), a newly established institution in the Wuyue capital that symbolized the central role of Buddhism in the region.

Through the promotion of Buddhism, Wuyue rulers envisioned a revival of the old glory of the Tang, where Buddhism served as a central feature in the definition of civilization and culture. Of all the regions in the south during this period, Wuyue was economically and politically the strongest. Among the southern states, Wuyue also provided the strongest support for Buddhism, and Buddhism served as the strongest cornerstone of Wuyue cultural policy. It is noteworthy, however, that in spite of changes in society and culture that demanded new responses from Buddhism, Wuyue support was driven by conservative forces seeking through Buddhism the recovery of a former glory. While Wuyue Buddhism was embodied largely through support for Chan masters and institutions, it sought to weld these to precedents founded in the doctrinal traditions of Buddhist scholasticism. The style of Chan promoted in Wuyue fostered such arrangements. As a result, although the Wuyue Buddhist revival was carried out largely under the Chan banner, Chan in Wuyue had its own distinct character that identified Chan with former Tang Buddhist traditions, and this identification with the larger Buddhist tradition became a defining feature of Wuyue Chan. The major protagonist of Wuyue Chan was Yongming Yanshou, whose Chan syncretism redefined the contributions of the doctrinal schools of Buddhism and their textual traditions in terms of Chan principles. Yanshou's notion of *zong* (宗) is articulated extensively in his major work on Chan scholasticism, the *Zongjing lu* 宗鏡錄 (Records of the source-mirror).[49]

Yanshou's writings reflect prevailing assumptions regarding orthodox Buddhism inherited in Wuyue. Although Yanshou identifies himself in his writings as a Chan master, his brand of Chan should not be confused with Linji faction teachings that assumed dominance after the Song dynasty consolidation.[50] Yanshou was quite critical of the tenets associated with Mazu and Huangbo's Hongzhou faction and Linji Chan teaching, whether it be the rejection of Buddhist scriptures as a meaningful guide, or the dismissal of Buddhist piety, seated meditation, and other conventional Buddhist practices as impediments to direct apprehension and sudden awakening (*wu* 悟). Yanshou's Chan, true to the orientation toward Buddhism prevalent in Wuyue, reflects broad assumptions in Chinese Mahayana teaching and incorporates the full range of practices that this teaching offers. While Yanshou agrees that these teachings are preparatory, in some sense, and do not reflect the complete awakening experience that Chan affords, these teachings are also part and parcel of true bodhisattva practice, and no true Buddhist would reject them. The myriad good deeds (*wanshan* 萬善) that Yanshou advocates in his *Wanshan tonggui ji* (萬善同歸集, Collected writings on the common end of myriad good deeds) are thus a reflection of the pan-Mahayana universalism promoted by Wuyue policy.[51]

The architects of Wuyue policy were the aforementioned ruler, Qian Chu (King Zhongyi), and his spiritual and political advisor, the Buddhist monk Tiantai Deshao. Qian Chu was a self-espoused *cakravartin*. Although the revival of Mt. Tiantai as a spiritual center in Wuyue, at Deshao's urgings, was a strong priority, as a ruler Qian Chu identified with the stūpa reliquary on Mt. Ayuwang (阿育王山, King Aśoka). According to Buddhist traditions in China, when the famed pro-Buddhist Indian monarch dictated that stūpas containing relics of Śākyamuni be erected throughout his kingdom, some—like the one on Mt. Ayuwang in Wuyue—were erected in China.[52] The presumption that Aśoka's stūpas were erected in China symbolically represents the inclusion of China in the larger Asian Buddhist world.

The Aśokan model in Wuyue was more than symbolic. In imitation of Aśoka's pro-Buddhist program, Qian Chu mounted a massive construction campaign aimed at physically imprinting Buddhism on the Wuyue landscape. The number and scale of construction activities carried out by Wuyue monarchs have been well documented.[53] Indicative of this activity was the aforementioned reconstruction of Mt. Tiantai—including its numerous monasteries and shrines—as a spiritual center, affirmation of the Śākyamuni stūpa on Mt. Ayuwang as a leading symbol, and the prominent construction of Aśoka inspired stūpas throughout the realm. In addition, countless Buddhist monasteries and shrines were either constructed or refurbished throughout the Wuyue region during this period. This was particularly true in the capital, Qiantang (錢塘). Yanshou, for example, received his first posting, at the request of Qian Chu, to assume abbotship of the newly refurbished Lingyin Chan monastery (靈隱禪寺) located on the outskirts of the capital. After a brief tenure there, Yanshou was again asked by Qian Chu to assume abbotship of a large, newly constructed Yongming monastery (永明寺) on the southern shores of the famed West Lake. Yongming monastery functioned as a leading Buddhist institution in Wuyue, the beacon from which Wuyue's leading spiritual advisor, Yanshou, disseminated state-authorized Buddhist teachings throughout the region. A number of Aśoka inspired pagodas (ta 塔) erected by Qian Chu survived into the modern period.

Qian Chu's own writing, a preface penned for Yanshou's *Zongjing lu*, leaves no doubt regarding the supreme role accorded to Buddhism in Wuyue. Qian Chu makes clear the relative status granted to each of China's "three teachings" (*san jiao* 三教).[54]

> There are three teachings within the boundaries of our territory. To rectify [behavior between] rulers and ministers, for affection between fathers and sons, and for cordial human relations. Confucianism—it is my teacher.
>
> 域中之教者三。正君臣。親父子。厚人倫。儒。吾之師也。
>
> In moments of quiet and solitude, look and listen for the unobtainable. From the infinitesimally subtle, one soars to vacuous non-existence. How one rides the wind, directing the world as if it were a play. If the ruler obtains this [kind of understanding], what is well established will not end in ruin. If the people obtain it, they will be granted gifts beyond measure. Daoism—the teacher of Confucianism.

寂兮寥兮。視聽無得。自微妙。升虛無。以止乎乘風馭景。君得之則善建不拔。人得之則延覜無窮。道。儒之師也。

The four noble truths, twelve-linked chain of causation, the three miraculous powers, and the eight liberations—practice these regularly without neglect. Cultivate daily in order to obtain them. As soon as you realize nirvāṇa, you will forever understand what is true and eternal. Buddhism—the source (zong) of Daoism.

四諦十二因緣。三明八解脫。時習不忘。日修以得。一登果地。永達真常。釋。道之宗也。

Ultimately, Wuyue left a defining imprint on Song Buddhism. Its legacy of cultural production included major works that left a lasting impact on Buddhism in the Song dynasty. These include major Buddhist print works: the aforementioned *Zongjing lu* (*Records of the Source-Mirror*) by Yongming Yanshou, a defining work that influenced Buddhist doctrine/ teaching (*jiao* 教); the *Jingde Chuandeng lu* (景德傳燈錄, *Jingde era Record of the Transmission of the Lamp*) by Daoyuan (道源), the classical text of the Chan school (*chan* 禪); and two works on monks and vinaya administration (*lü* 律) by Zanning, the *Song Gaoseng zhuan* (宋高僧傳, *Song Biographies of Eminent Monks*) and *Seng shilüe* (僧史略, *Topical Compendium of the Buddhist Clergy*). Wuyue Buddhism thus provided a template for post-Tang Buddhism that extended over the three major areas of Buddhism: teaching/doctrine (*jiao* 教), meditation (*chan* 禪), and vinaya (*lü* 律). Zanning's writings in the latter area marked a major contribution in this regard, and it may not be too much to suggest that these Wuyue developments be viewed as "supplements" to the three pillars–śila, samādhi, and *prajñā*–of the Eightfold Path, with *jiao* paired with *prajñā*, *chan* with *samādhi*, and *lü* with śila.

In the Footsteps of Eisai: The Hangzhou Region as the New Center of East Asian Buddhism

There are, of course, many developments in Chinese Chan in the Northern and Southern Song dynasties, including the development of *denglu*

Lamp Records (燈錄), *yulu* Dialogue Records (語錄), *gong'an* (J. kōan, K. gong-an) literature (公案) and practice techniques, and *qinggui* Rules for Purification (清規), to name but a few prominent examples. These developments significantly shaped Chan and came to further define it. Each of these developments, however, may also be seen as addendums to the three pillars: *qinggui* for śila (moral precepts), *gong'an* for *samādhi* (meditation practice), and *yulu* for *prajñā* (wisdom acquisition). Taken comprehensively, these developments reshaped the Buddhist landscape throughout China, including Jiangnan and the greater Hangzhou region which continued to be the most important Buddhist region in the Song dynasty, especially in the Southern Song when Hangzhou became the capital. The effect of these developments was most evidently demonstrated when Japanese Buddhist pilgrims began visiting monasteries in the Hangzhou region (including Mt. Tiantai and Mingzhou). In retrospect, we can see that Myōan Eisai (or Yōsai, 明菴栄西, 1141–1215), one of the first Japanese pilgrims to visit Song China, initiated a trickle that turned into a stream of monks between China and Japan who transformed Japanese Buddhism by incorporating the culture and practices of the new Song paradigm.

Eisai made two trips to China, both to the Hangzhou region. In 1168, he made a brief six-month trip to Mt. Tiantai, the origin of the Tendai School in Japan to which Eisai belonged, in the hope of finding a means of renewal for Tendai teaching in Japan during an age of Buddhist decline (*mappō* 末法). To his probable dismay, Eisai found that the monasteries of Mt. Tiantai had been transformed into Chan establishments. Chan was unknown in Japan, at least as an independent school. His return to Japan at this time was uneventful as he resumed his activity as a Tendai-esoteric (*taimitsu* 台密) teacher and practitioner.

In 1187, nearly twenty years later, a more mature Eisai returned to China with an intention to proceed on a pilgrimage to sacred Buddhist sites in India. Passage to India by this time was thwarted by political instabilities making the route inaccessible. The north of China had been seized by the Jurchens, who established the Jin dynasty (金朝, 1115–1234). The Xi Xia (西夏, Western Xia or Tangut) governed access to the important Gansu corridor and the overland route to India. Eisai's petition was denied, although he was permitted to remain in China. The Hangzhou region included many palpable reminders of India that were instrumental to the Buddhism that developed there. Among these were Feilaifeng (飛來峰, The Peak Came Flying [from India]), allegedly recognized as the famed Buddhist preaching site Vulture Peak (靈鷲山, Skt. Gṛdhrakūṭa) by an Indian monk Huili (慧理) who first settled in the region in the fourth century. Feilaifeng faces one of Hangzhou's most famous monasteries, Lingyin si (靈隱寺), and the immediate area also contains three Tianzhu (天竺), or "Indian" monasteries, designated as Upper, Middle, and Lower Tianzhu: Faxi si (法喜寺), Fajing si (法淨寺), and Fajing si (法鏡寺), respectively. The Ayuwang si (阿育王寺, King Aśoka Monastery) in the Mingzhou (Ningbo) region allegedly housed the relics of Śākyamuni Buddha as a result of being deposited there in King Aśoka's dispersion of relics in the third century BCE. According to tradition, arhat disciples of the Buddha dwelled beyond the famed Stone Bridge (石橋) overlooking a waterfall on Mt. Tiantai.[55] In addition to these sights, Eisai also visited the Bodhi tree transplanted to the Hangzhou region from India. Most important, however, was his discovery of the tradition of mind-to-mind transmission (以心傳心), the alleged link between master and disciple that connected Song Chan masters to Śākyamuni and his Indian forebears and animated the new tradition of Chan. Prior to his return in 1191, Eisai received official transmission in this tradition from Linji master Xu'an Huaichang (虛庵懷敞, c. 1125–1195) of the Jingde Monastery (景德寺) on Mt. Tiantong (天童山).

Following Eisai's return, he worked to establish Zen in Japan. He wrote *The Promotion of Zen for the Protection of the Country* (*Kōzen gokokuron* 興禪護国論) in 1198, arguing that Zen was a credible school of Buddhism in Japan, against the objections of the Tendai Buddhist status quo.[56] He also established the first Zen institutions in Japan, Shōfuku-ji (聖福寺) in Kyūshū, Kennin ji (建仁寺) in Heian (平安, later Kyoto), and Jūfuku ji (壽福寺) in Kamakura. From these bases, the Zen brand continues to gather momentum in Japan, with numerous proponents following in his wake, journeying to China to study Chan at famous monasteries in Hangzhou and the wider region, and to receive transmission from illustrious Chan masters. Ryōnen Myōzen (了然明全, 1184–1225), Eisai's dharma-successor at Kennin ji, consciously followed Eisai's route, and passed away in China, at Tiantong si. His student and traveling companion, Dōgen (道元, 1200–1253), commenced his study at Jingde si, where Eisai had studied, but embarked on a course that took him to various leading monasteries throughout the region. Eventually, he received transmission from Caodong (曹洞) master Rujing (如淨) at Mt. Tiantong si, returning to Japan in 1227 or 1228 and eventually establishing the Sōtō lineage.

The trickle of monks travelling to Japan soon became a stream. Among the many who are noteworthy in this regard are Enni Ben'en (圓爾

辯圓, 1202–1280), also a student of Eisai, who received transmission from Wuzhun Shifan (無準師範, 1178–1249) of Jingshan si (徑山寺), and returned to Japan to establish Tōfuku ji (東福寺). Nor was the flow only one way. Chinese Chan masters soon plied the waters across the sea to serve as abbots at a growing number of Zen monasteries in Japan. One cannot underestimate the influence of Wuzhun Shifan and Jingshan si in this regard. He sent students like Wuxue Ziyuan (無學祖元, J. Mugaku Sogen; 1226–1286), who was invited to spread Zen in Japan by Hōjō Tokimune (北条時宗, 1251–1284), the eighth regent of the Kamakura Shogunate, and became founding abbot of Engaku ji (円覚寺) in Kamakura, and Wu'an Puning (兀庵普寧, J. Gottan Funei, 1197–1276), who became abbot of Kenchō ji (建長寺), also in Kamakura. In addition, there was Lanxi Daolong (蘭溪道隆, J. Rankei Dōryū, 1213–1278), who also studied under Wuzhun Shifan and took charge of Kenchō ji at the invitation of Hōjō Tokiyori (北条時頼, 1227–1263). In total, there were numerous monks, both known and unknown, who traveled between Southern Song and Yuan dynasty China and Kamakura Japan and contributed to the transmission of Chan institutional practices to Japan.[57]

The institutional basis for the transmission of Chan from China to Japan was structured around the "Five Mountains" (C. Wushan, J. Gozan, 五山) system instituted in Southern Song China and adopted in Japan by the Kamakura *bakufu*. This is a topic beyond the current focus, and I can only allude to it in passing.[58] While changes over time allowed for some relatively minor variation in the institutions represented on the list, a standard depiction can be displayed as follows (see table 2.1):

Table 2.1. Chan School Five Mountains Monasteries in the Southern Song Dynasty 南宋禪宗五山

Rank	Monastery	Location
Supreme	Tianjie si 天界寺	Nanjing 南京
No. 1	Jingshan si 徑山寺	Hangzhou 杭州, Yuhang 餘杭
No. 2	Lingyin si 靈隱寺	Hangzhou 杭州
No. 3	Tiantong si 天童寺	Ningbo 寧波
No. 4	Jingci si 淨慈寺	Hangzhou 杭州
No. 5	Ayuwang si 阿育王寺	Ningbo 寧波

If we expand the system to include the Ten Temples, they are depicted as follows (see table 2.2).

Table 2.2. Chan School Ten Temples in the Southern Song Dynasty 南宋禪宗十剎

Rank	Monastery	Location
No. 1	Zhong Tianzhu si 中天竺寺	Hangzhou 杭州
No. 2	Wanshou si 萬壽寺	Huzhou 湖州
No. 3	Linggu si 靈谷寺	Nanjing 南京
No. 4	Baoen si 報恩寺	Suzhou 蘇州
No. 5	Xuedou si 雪竇寺	Ningbo 寧波
No. 6	Jiangxin si 江心寺	Wenzhou 溫州
No. 7	Xuefeng si 雪峰寺	Fuzhou 福州
No. 8	Shuanglin si 雙林寺	Zhejiang Jinhua 浙江金華
No. 9	Yunyan si 雲岩寺	Suzhou 蘇州
No. 10	Guoqingsi 國清寺	Zhejiang Tiantai 浙江天台

Given the location of the Southern Song capital in Hangzhou, it is hardly a surprise to find the dominance of Buddhist institutions in the greater Hangzhou region, including Ningbo, Nanjing, Suzhou, Wenzhou, Fuzhou, and Tiantai. As an official network of government-supported monasteries and temples, these naturally served as the focal point for the study of Chan in the Southern Song visited by numerous Japanese pilgrims.

The Gozan system instituted in Japan in the Kamakura period comes with two iterations, one for the imperial capital, Kyoto, and one for the Shogunate capital, Kamakura (see Table 2.3).

Table 2.3. Gozan Monasteries in Japan 日本五山寺

	Supreme Rank: Nanzen-ji 南禪寺	
	Kyoto 京都	Kamakura 鎌倉
First Rank	Tenryū-ji 天龍寺	Kenchō-ji 建長寺
Second Rank	Shōkoku-ji 相國寺	Engaku-ji 圓覺寺
Third Rank	Kennin-ji 建仁寺	Jufuku-ji 壽福寺
Fourth Rank	Tōfuku-ji 東福寺	Jōchi-ji 淨智寺
Fifth Rank	Manju-ji 萬壽寺	Jōmyō-ji 常明寺

Due to circumstances in Japan, the Five Mountains system acquired even more prestige there than in China. The Kamakura Shogunate, seeking to distinguish itself from the pattern of the Heian court, threw its support behind the new form of Buddhism from China, and made the Zen network of temples a cornerstone of the regime's religious policy.

As Steffen Döll writes in chapter 6, for example, when Lanxi Daolong came to Japan, he visited Sennyū-ji (泉涌寺) in Heian, and traveled on to Jufuku-ji (壽福寺) in Kamakura, and ultimately was installed as abbot of the newly repurposed Jōraku-ji (常樂寺) by the regent, Hōjō Tokiyori.[59] Tokiyori built a monastery in Kamakura on the Chinese Chan monastic model, especially using Jingshan as a prototype, resulting in Kenchō-ji. Yishan Yining (一山一寧, J. Issan Ichinei, 1247–1317), a Chinese emigré monk who figures prominently in many chapters in this volume, exemplifies the successful transformation from Chinese Chan to Japanese Zen. As Döll notes, Yishan Yining's success had less to do with his talents as a Zen student, strictly speaking, and more to do with his talent as an administrator, and it is this function, often overlooked, which proved key to the dissemination of Chan-style institutions in Japan.

Chan Influence in Korea

Chan influence in Korea began quite early when compared to Japan, in the Silla period (668–935), resulting in the so-called nine mountain schools (*gusan* 九山), eight of which were lineages descended through Mazu Daoyi (馬祖島一), with the other, the Sumi-san (須彌山) lineage founded by Yiŏm (利嚴, 869–936), derived from Caodong.[60] In spite of this legacy, Korean Sŏn developed its own particular character in the Koryŏ period, when the allegedly radical nature of Sŏn was mitigated through accommodation with the Kyo 教 (or doctrinal) schools, culminating in Chinul (知訥, 1158–1210), considered by many the most influential Korean Sŏn master. Chinul advocated an intrinsic unity between Sŏn meditation and Kyo teachings and in this regard bears a clear affinity with Chinese Chan masters like Zongmi (宗密) and Yanshou, who pioneered similar positions. A major preoccupation for Chinul was an issue that had long percolated in Chinese Chan, the relationship between "gradual" and "sudden" approaches to Buddhist practice and enlightenment. In an attempt to resolve the quagmire, Chinul drew upon the teaching of Zongmi and Dahui Zonggao (大慧宗杲, 1089–1163) to promote his position of "sudden enlightenment" followed by "gradual cultivation" (頓悟漸修). To be efficacious according to Dahui, practitioners must have a deep transformative insight into the nature of emptiness of things and see their intrinsically enlightened nature. Progress in practice is predicated on such insight.

As a result, Chinul's approach to Sŏn, discussed by Cawley in chapter 10 and Senécal in chapter 13, was a distinctive blend of *gong'an* mediational practice combined with scriptural study. Along with Dahui's *gwanhwa* (觀話) "observing the critical phrase (or *hwadu* 話頭) of the *gong'an*" technique, Chinul incorporated a scriptural study approach based largely on Hwaŏm (華嚴) teaching. Far from seeing scriptural study as a passive accompaniment, Chinul's own enlightenment experiences did not come via the personal "mind-to-mind transmission between teacher and disciple, but through contemplation of passages from Buddhist texts. Chinul's approach had a lasting impact on Korean Sŏn that resonated through subsequent Sŏn masters. Chinul's successor, Chin'gak Hyesim (真覺慧諶, 1178–1234), further emphasized the hwadu (C. huatou, "critical phrase") practice. Important Sŏn teachers such as Hyegŭn (慧勤, 1320–1376), T'aego Po'u (太古普愚, 1301–1382), Kihwa (己和, 1376–1433) and Hujŏng (休靜, 1520–1604) continued to develop the model of Korean Sŏn established by Chinul, which became the dominant religious force on government and society and the state religion during the Koryŏ period. These developments were nurtured through periodic contacts between Korean monks and their Chinese mentors. Some of them traveled to China to study with Chinese masters. T'aego Pou traveled to study with Chan master Shiwu Qinhong (石屋清洪, 1272–1352) and received a seal of transmission in the Linji lineage. T'aego was credited as initiating the orthodox Linji Sŏn tradition of "sudden awakening" in Korean Buddhism.

The Korean Sŏn connection to Hangzhou was directly established by Tamjin (曇真, n.d.), as Juhn Ahn dsescribes in chapter 8. While King Munjong's son, Ŭichŏn (義天, 1055–1101), is well known, Tamjin reached Hangzhou a decade earlier, when he accompanied a Koryŏ embassy to China led by the vice-director of public works (*kongbu sirang* 工夫侍郎) Ch'oe Sa-ryang (崔思諒, d. 1092) in 1076, and lived with two other Koryŏ monks at Upper Tianzhu monastery. Key to Tamjin's success was his first-hand knowledge of the new developments taking place in Song China, particularly the spread of imperially recognized public monasteries and the dominance of Chan Buddhism in these institutions. It was here that Tamjin presumably learned, among other things, how to reproduce the Chan mythology of mind-to-mind transmission, how to perform important Chan rituals such as "ascending the hall," and how to carry himself in a way that was consistent with the pure rules of a Chan monastery. Upon his return to Korea, Tamjin was appointed abbot of Kwangmyŏng-sa (廣明寺) and Poje-sa (普濟寺), two important Sŏn monasteries in the capital associated with the royal cult, and was named both royal preceptor and state preceptor.[61] Later on, Tamjin's lineage was appropriated, but the trend he helped usher in whereby Sŏn monks "creatively borrowed elements from Song-style public monasteries to establish legitimacy and give themselves a competitive edge," prevailed.[62]

Repositioning Chan, Sŏn, and Zen Buddhist Studies: The Hangzhou Region and the Spread of East Asian Buddhism

Robert Buswell writes, "One of the enduring topoi used to describe the dissemination of Buddhism is that of an inexorable eastward diffusion of the tradition, starting from the religion's homeland in India, leading through Inner Asia, until finally spreading throughout the entire East Asian region," noting that the account of a monolithic movement eastward is but one part of the story.[63] Complementing Buswell's observation regarding countercurrents in this narrative where influences rebound back toward the center, I hope what I have discussed above serves as a prelude to a reorientation of Chan, Sŏn, and Zen Buddhist studies with a focus on China and particularly on the Hangzhou region. The study of Buddhism has incorporated East Asia in meaningful ways. but the operative narrative has tended toward Indo-centrism. While this makes sense if one considers India the birthplace and homeland of Buddhism, the history of Buddhism covers twenty-five hundred years, and for the last thousand years or so, India has ceased to be a significant ongoing source of Buddhist inspiration, figuring primarily in the passive memory rather than as active agent. This is especially true in the case of China, which actively reimagined Buddhism in unique and indigenous ways to form an intrinsically authentic form of East Asian Buddhism. Hangzhou, a former capital of China during the Song dynasty, was a focal point for these developments.

The Hangzhou region has long been one of the most important cultural hubs in China and has had a wide-ranging impact on Chinese culture and Buddhism, yet it is hardly known outside of China and the East Asian context. Knowledge of its impact in Buddhist studies pales in comparison with Dunhuang, whose manuscripts and artistic artifacts have always been a source of fascination. The region came to prominence in the tenth century, when Hangzhou was known as Qiantang and served as the capital of the state (or kingdom) of Wuyue. It became the capital of the Southern Song dynasty (1127–1279) under the name Lin'an. From the Hangzhou region, new forms of Buddhism spread throughout East Asia, especially to Japan and Korea. As a result, when we speak about East Asian Buddhism today, we are speaking about many forms of Buddhism that were initiated in the Hangzhou region and adopted and adapted in other regions and periods. The most prominent among these is Chan Buddhism, known in Japan as Zen and Korea as Sŏn, the practice of which from the tenth century on is mostly indebted to Buddhist developments in the Hangzhou region.

Notes

1. Typical of this tendency to focus on the story of Buddhism as an India-dominated trajectory is Ruthert Gethin's *The Foundations of Buddhism*, which as the title indicates makes no pretense at broader coverage. The table of contents is as follows:

Introduction
1. The Buddha: The Story of the Awakened One
2. The Word of the Buddha: Buddhist Scriptures and Schools
3. Four Truths: The Disease, the Cause, the Cure, the Medicine
4. The Buddhist Community: Monks, Nuns, and Lay Followers
5. The Buddhist Cosmos: The Thrice Thousandfold World
6. No self: Personal Continuity and Dependent Arising
7. The Buddhist Path: The Way of Calm and Insight
8. The Abhidharma: The Higher Teaching
9. The Mahayana: The Great Vehicle
10. Evolving Traditions of Buddhism

Yet, even those works devoted to broader coverage, such as Andrew Skilton's *A Concise History of Buddhism*, do not fare much better, with roughly three quarters of its pages devoted to "Buddhism in India," and one quarter to "Buddhism Beyond India." The tendency to focus on developments in India, especially the life of Śākyamuni, his teachings, the development of the early Buddhist community, etc., are typical of this genre, as is the coverage of Buddhism beyond India, which treats its subject according to national boundaries. For East Asia, a chapter is dedicated to each of China (ten pages), Korea (two pages), and Japan (six pages), roughly the same coverage that is given to individual schools of Buddhism in India (like Abhidharma, Madhyamaka, and Yogācāra).

2. Instances of Western interactions with Buddhism include the Greco-Buddhism of the Seleucid empire (312–63 BCE) which formed in the wake of Alexander the Great's expansion into Central Asia, and the spread of the Mauryan empire (273–232 BCE) into the Greco-Bactrian kingdom covering Bactria and Sogdiana in Central Asia under Emperor Aśoka. Buddhist ideas filtered into Europe through stories of the Christian saints Barlaam and Josaphat, renditions of the life of Siddhartha Gautama, via translations from Indian sources to Persian, Arabic, and Greek versions.

3. Morris Rossabi, *From Yuan to Modern China and Mongolia: The Writings of Morris Rossabi* (Leiden: Brill, 2014), 670. An account of von Ruesbroeck's travels is provided in William Woodville Rockhill's translation, *The Journey of William of Rubruck to the Eastern Parts of the World, 1253–55* (London: Hayklut Society, 1900), available at http://depts.washington.edu/silkroad/texts/rubruck.html. There is also a translation by Peter Jackson in Peter Jackson and David Morgan, eds., *The Mission of Friar William of Rubruck: His Journey to the Court of the Great Khan Möngke, 1253–1255* (London: Hakluyt Society, 1990).

4. *The Travels of Marco Polo* by Marco Polo and Rustichello of Pisa, the complete Yule-Cordier Edition, including the unabridged third edition (1903) of Henry Yule's annotated translation, as revised by Henri Cordier; together with Cordier's later volume of notes and addenda (1920); http://www.gutenberg.org/cache/epub/10636/pg10636-images.html.

5. *The Cult of Emptiness: The Western Discovery of Buddhist thought and the Invention of Oriental Philosophy* (Rorshach and Kyoto: University Media, 2012).

6. Principally, *The World as Will and Idea*, translated by K. B. Haldane and J. Kemp (London: Kegan Paul, Trench, Trubner & Co.), https://archive.org/stream/theworldaswillan01schouoft/theworldaswillan01schouoft_djvu.txt; also Urs App, "Arthur Schopenhauer and China" (Sino-Platonic Papers Nr. 200, April 2010)," contains appendixes with transcriptions and English translations of Schopenhauer's early notes about Buddhism and Indian philosophy.

7. Full title, *The Light of Asia: Being the Life and Teaching of Gautama, Prince of India and Founder of Buddhism*. On the impact in England, see J. Jeffrey Franklin, "The Life of the Buddha in Victorian England," *ELH (English Literary History)* 72 (Winter 2005): 941–974. On its impact in India, where it was retranslated into several vernacular languages, and if anything, proved even more popular than in England, see Phyllis Granoff, "A Modern Border Crossing: Fakir Mohan Senapati's Life of the Buddha," in Victor H. Mair, ed., *Buddhist Transformations and Interactions: Essays in Honor of Antonino Forte* (Amherst, NY: Cambria, 2017), 121–140.

8. The Sacred Books of the East (SBE) series, comprising fifty volumes, was issued by Oxford University Press between 1879 and 1910, with translations of key sacred texts of Hinduism, Buddhism, Taoism, Confucianism, Zoroastrianism, Jainism, and Islam. Buddhist texts included: *Buddhist Suttas* translated by T. W.

Rhys Davids, *Vinaya Texts* translated by Rhys Davids and Hermann Oldenberg, *The Fo-sho-hing-tsan-king* [Chinese version of the Life of the Buddha translated from the Sanskrit of Asvaghosa] translated by Samuel Beal, *The Saddharma Pundarika or Lotus of the True Law* translated by H. Kern, *The Questions of King Milinda* by Rhys Davids, and *Buddhist Mahayana Texts* translated by E. B. Cowell, F. Max Müller, and J. Takakusu. Also worthy of note is Hermann Oldenberg's widely read work on Buddhism, *Buddha, sein Leben, seine Lehre, seine Gemeinde* [Buddha, his life, his doctrine, his order] (Berlin, 1881) (London: Williams, 1882)], discussed in the text that follows.

9. "Religious Symbolism and Political Change in Ceylon," *Modern Ceylon Studies* 1, no. 43 (1970), 43–63, following Stephen Prothero, "Henry Steel Olcott and "Protestant Buddhism," *Journal of the American Academy of Religion* 63, no. 2 (1995): 281–302.

10. In reference specifically to Olcott, Stephen Prothero refines the term "Protestant Buddhism" to "Protestant Modernism" in light of the fact that reformers like Olcott came out of a late nineteenth-century Anglo-American Protestantism rather than the Weberian Protestantism that Obeyesekere assumed. Prothero comments: "By conflating Protestantism with Weber's representation of it, Obeyesekere and his followers tend to obscure the historical sources of the tradition they describe" (282) and "to view Protestant Buddhism solely as a product of the collision of traditional Theravada Buddhism with Weber's generic Protestantism is, in short, to miss out on ways in which a particular historical form of Protestants namely, nineteenth-century Anglo-American Protestant modernism, contributed mightily to that syncretic tradition." (283).

11. *History of Religions* 31, no. 1 (1991): 1–23.

12. Schopen, "Archaeology and Protestant Presuppositions in the Study of Indian Buddhism," 22–23.

13. Stephen Prothero, "Henry Steel Olcott and "Protestant Buddhism," 285.

14. "Śākyamuni's Final 'Nirvāṇa,'" *Bulletin of the School of Oriental and African Studies* 36, no. 2 (In Honour of Walter Simon) (1973): 399.

15. "Śākyamuni's Final 'Nirvāṇa.'"

16. Keven Trainor, *History of Religions* 37, no. 1 (1997): 96–98.

17. *Prisoners of Shangri-La* (Chicago: University of Chicago Press), 4.

18. "Approaches to the Study of Buddhism," in Bryan S. Turner, ed., *The New Blackwell Companion to the Sociology of Religion*, 390 (emphasis mine).

19. "Approaches to the Study of Buddhism," 391.

20. Donald Lopez, *Curators of the Buddha: The Study of Buddhism under Colonialism* (Chicago: University of Chicago Press, 1995), 7.

21. For a succinct review of Suzuki's life and influence, see Robert Sharf, "Suzuki, D.T.," in Lindsay Jones, ed., *Encyclopedia of Religion*, 2nd ed. (New York: Macmillan, 2005), vol. 13, 1884–87. For a full exposition of Sharf's work on Suzuki, see "The Zen of Japanese Nationalism," in *Curators of the Buddha:*

The Study of Buddhism under Colonialism, ed. Donald S. Lopez Jr. (Chicago: University of Chicago Press, 1995), 107–160. On Suzuki's impact following the World Parliament of Religions, see Judith Snodgrass, *Presenting Buddhism to the West: Orientalism, Occidentalism and the Columbian Exposition* (Chapel Hill and London: University of North Carolina Press, 2003), 245–77.

22. See Thomas A. Tweed, "American Occultism and Japanese Buddhism: Albert J. Edmunds, D. T. Suzuki, and Translocative History," *Japanese Journal of Religious Studies* 32 (2) (2005): 249–281; on Beatrice Lane Suzuki, see Algeo, Adele S., "Beatrice Lane Suzuki: An American Theosophist in Japan," *Quest* 95, no. 1 (2007): 13–17.

23. On Swedenborg, see Erland J. Brock, ed., *Swedenborg and His Influence* (Bryn Athyn, PA: Academy of the New Church, 1988). Suzuki's work, *Swedenborg: Buddha of the North* is available through the Swedenborg Foundation (West Chester, PA: Swedenborg Foundation, 1996).

24. James, *Varieties of Religious Experience*, first published 1902.

25. D. T. Suzuki, Editorial, *Eastern Buddhist* 1, no. 2 (1921), 156 (cited from Sharf, "The Zen of Japanese Nationalism," 18).

26. See, for example, Suzuki's *Mysticism: Christian and Buddhist* (London: George Allen & Unwin, 1957), and his work on the medieval Christian mystic, the Dominican, Meister Eckhart.

27. Suzuki, *An Introduction to Zen Buddhism* (Kyoto, 1934), 14.

28. Suzuki, *Japanese Spirituality*, trans. Norman Waddell (Tokyo: Japan Society for the Promotion of Science, Ministry of Education, Japan, 1972), 46; originally published as *Nihonteki reisei* (Tokyo: Iwanami bunko, 1972; originally written in 1944).

29. Suzuki, *Japanese Spirituality*.

30. See, for example, Gunawan Kartapranata, https://en.wikipedia.org/wiki/History_of_Buddhism#/media/File:Buddhist_Expansion.svg.

31. The stages listed here, and the information associated with them, are meant to be suggestive rather than exhaustive. While there is a progressive historical dimension in the depiction of these stages, it is also true that they are non-exclusive—activities of any stage may and do occur outside the evolutionary scheme presented (e.g., translation may and did occur beyond the "translation stage").

32. As Tansen Sen notes ("The Travel Records of Chinese Pilgrims Faxian, Xuanzang, and Yijing," *Education About Asia* 11, no. 3 (2006): 33n18:

> One of the important developments related to South Asian history described in the work of Xuanzang was the decay of urban centers in the Ganges basin, which included the famous Buddhist pilgrimage sites Kuśinagara (the site where the Buddha attained nirvana) and Vaiśāli (the site where the Buddha gave his last sermon). The decline of urban centers that began in the fourth century and its impact on

monastic institutions are depicted in the travel records of Faxian and Yijing as well. These records have been used to examine the economic conditions in early medieval India and the decline of Buddhism in southern Asia. (http://www.columbia.edu/itc/eacp/japanworks/special/travel_records.pdf).

33. Although Sanskrit Buddhist scriptures from India were first translated into Tibetan during the reign of King Songtsän Gampo (618–649), his successors did little to further the dissemination of Buddhism. By the eighth century, however, King Trisong Detsen (755–797) established Buddhism as the official state religion, inviting Indian Buddhist scholars to his court. According to Tibetan tradition, the famous tantric mystic Padmasambhāva arrived in Tibet during his rule and composed a number of important scriptures, establishing the Nyingma school of Tibetan Buddhism as well as the *Yogācāra-Mādhyamika* school of the Indian Buddhist Brahmin Śāntarakṣita (James Blumenthal, entry on "Śāntarakṣita"in *Stanford Encyclopedia of Philosophy*, https://plato.stanford.edu/entries/saantarak-sita/)

34. Following conceptions promoted by Joan Piggot, *The Emergence of Japanese Kingship*, and Gina Barnes, *China, Japan, Korea: the Rise of East Asian Civilization*.

35. A period suggested by Jan Yün-hua, "Tsung-mi: His Analysis of Ch'an Buddhism," *T'oung Pao* 58 (1972): 1–54.

36. Peter Gregory, "The Vitality of Buddhism in the Sung," suggests that if Buddhism in China were granted the sobriquet of a "golden age," it might be more appropriate to apply it to the Song rather than the Tang dynasty; see Gregory and Getz, eds., *Buddhism in the Sung* (Honolulu: University of Hawai'i Press, 1999), 1–20.

37. *A Brief Account of the Origins and Development of Chinese Buddhist Studies* 中國佛學源流略講 (Beijing: Zhonghua shuju, 1979), 10. The full statement reads: 研究中国佛学，当然要用到敦煌的资料。但是必须说明一下，敦煌文物的发现，确实是震动学术界的大事，但一些西方资产阶级的学者，曾想独占它为猎取名利的资本，因子把他说的高于一切，认为不懂敦煌学，就不能进行佛学研究，而且唯有他们这批人，才能懂得敦煌学，这是应该驳斥的。敦煌学，虽有其一定的适用范围和使用价值，它可以扑充研究资料的某些不足等。但也不能予以过高的估价。从学说源流上讲，固然有史实而无记载的，需要加以扑充，这对于佛学研究自然有好处，例如，我们上面讲的禅宗历史的情况；但决不能说，整个禅宗史全部要靠敦煌资料来决定。另外，有些资料本来就没有发生过什么影响，从而被历史淘汰了，现在被发现，作用也不大。总之，我们对敦煌的资料，应该有一个实事求是的恰如其分的估价。I am grateful to Kirill Solonin for bringing Lu's statement to my attention.

38. A translation of the Yuan text of the *Platform Sutra* (Taishō no. 2008) was completed by John McRae as part of the Bukkyō Dendō Kyōkai (BDK) English Translation Project in 2000; https://www.bdkamerica.org/system/files/pdf/dBET_T2008_PlatformSutra_2000_0.pdf?file=1&type=node&id=467

39. According to Darui Long, the first instance of the *Platform Sutra* in the Chinese Buddhist canon is the Yongle Northern Canon (*Yongle beizang* 永樂北藏) printed in the Ming dynasty reign of Emperor Yongle (r. 1403–1424); private conversation (May 2019). For his recent article on the Yongle Canon, see "The *Yongle Northern Canon* and its Donors," *Studies in Chinese Religions* 2, no. 2 (2016): 173–85.

40. Philip J. Ivanhoe, *Readings from the Lu-Wang School of Neo-Confucianism* Indianapolis: Hackett, 2009).

41. The Five Dynasties are:

Later Liang (後梁, 907–923)
Later Tang (後唐, 923–936)
Later Jin (後晉 (936–946)
Later Han (後漢, 947–950)
Later Zhou (後周, 951–959)

The Ten Kingdoms:
Wu (吳, 892–937)
Nan [Southern] Tang (南唐, 937–975)
Former Shu (前蜀, 907–925)
Later Shu (後蜀, 934–965)
Nan [Southern] Han (南漢, 917–971)
Chu (楚, 896–951)
Wuyue (吳越, 893–978)
Min (閩, 909–945)
Jingnan (荊南, 907–963)
Bei [Northern] Han (北漢, 951–979).

For historical developments in southern kingdoms in the Five Dynasties period, see Ben Brose, *Patrons and Patriarchs: Regional Rulers and Chan Monks during the Five Dynasties and Ten Kingdoms* (Honolulu: University of Hawai'i Press, 2015).

42. On Luo Yin, see Jan de Meyer, "Confucianism and Daoism in the Political Thought of Luo Yin," *T'ang Studies* 10–11 (1992–93): 67–80.

43. Hatanaka Jōen, "Goetsu no bukkyō—toku ni Tendai Tokushō to sono shi Eimei Enju ni tsuite" [Buddhism in Wuyue: With special reference to Tiantai Deshao and his heir, Yongming Yanshou]. *Ōtani daigaku kenkyu nenpō* 7 (1954): 309. On Buddhism during Qian Liu's reign, see Abe Chōichi, *Chūgoku zenshūshi no kenkyū* [A history of Chinese Zen], rev. ed., Tokyo: Seishin shobō, 1987), 129–74.

44. Hatanaka, "Goetsu no bukkyō," 309.

45. *Song Gaoseng zhuan* 7: T 2061.750c27–751.a2.

46. On the relation between Qian Chu (King Zhongyi) and Tiantai Desaho, see Hatanaka, "Goetsu no bukkyō"; Abe, *Chūgoku zenshūshi no kenkyū*, 186–210;

and Welter, *Monks, Rulers and Literati: The Political Ascendancy of Chan Buddhism* (Oxford and New York: Oxford University Press, 2006), 118–19.

47. *Shiguo qunchiu* (Wu Renchen) (Beijing: Zhonghua shuju, 1983), 89, 4b.

48. For a discussion and list of the monks supported by Qian Chu (King Zhongyi), see Abe, *Chūgoku zenshūshi no kenkyū*, 186–210; a list of the important monks who studied with Qian Chu under Deshao and whose biographies appear in fascicle 26 of the *Jingde Chuandeng lu* is given by Ishii Shūdō, *Sōdai zenshūshi no kenkyū* [A history of Zen in the Song Dynasty] (Tokyo: Daito Shuppansha, 1987), 82–83.

49. On Yanshou's scholastic style Chan in the *Zongjing lu*, see Welter, *Yongming Yanshou's Conception of Chan in the Zongjing lu: A Special Transmission within the Scriptures* (New York and Oxford: Oxford University Press, 2011).

50. Welter, "The Problem with Orthodoxy in Zen Buddhism: Yongming Yanshou's Notion of *zong* in the *Zongjing lu* (Records of the Source Mirror)," *Studies in Religion/ Sciences Religieuses* 31, no. 1 (2002): 3–18.

51. On Yanshou and the *Wanshan tonggui ji*, see Welter, *The Meaning of Myriad Good Deeds: A Study of Yung-ming Yen-shou and the Wan-shan t'ung-kuei chi* (New York: Peter Lang, 1993).

52. According to legend, the dispersion of the Buddha's relics to China was facilitated by an episode in which King Aśoka miraculously erected eighty-four thousand stūpas at the same time, each containing a relic of the Buddha—with the elder abbot Yaśas covering the sun with his hand to signal the completion of the work (see Lokesh Chandra, *Life of Lord Buddha from Chinese Sutras Illustrated in Ming Woodcuts* (New Delhi: International Academy of Indian Culture and Aditya Prakashan, Sata-Pitaka Series, Indo-Asian Literatures Volume 627, 2010), 426–427 (Episode 193), with accompanying text referencing the *Ayuwang zhuan* (T55.2042).

53. Abe, *Chūgoku zenshūshi no kenkyū*, 125–216.

54. T48.2016.415b10–15; Welter, *Yongming Yanshou's Conception of Chan in the Zongjing lu*, 226.

55. For a description of this tradition, see Ben Brose, "A Record of the Tiantai Mountains" (MA thesis, University of California Berkeley, 2002), 10–14. Even though no strong connection remains, according to Chang Qing, "Feilaifeng and the Flowering of Chinese Buddhist Sculpture From the Tenth to the Fourteenth Centuries" (PhD diss., University of Kansas, 2005), arhat sculptures were a common motif at Feilaifeng during the Five Dynasties and Song periods.

56. See Welter, "Zen as the Ideology of the Japanese State: Eisai and the *Kōzen gokokuron*," in *Zen Classics: Formative Texts in the History of Zen Buddhism*, ed. Steven Heine and Dale S. Wright (New York: Oxford University Press, 2006): 65–112.

57. For an introduction to these developments, see Heinrich Dumoulin, *Zen Buddhism, A History: Volume 2, Japan* (New York: Macmillan, 1990). On

the role of Lanxia Daolong, see Martin Collcutt, "Lanxia Daolong (1213–1278) at Kenchōji: Chinese Contributions to the Making of Medieval Japanese Rinzai Zen," in *Tools of Culture: Japan's Cultural, Intellectual, Medical, and Technological Contacts in East Asia, 1000s–1500s* (Ann Arbor, MI: Association for Asian Studies, 2009), 135–62. For a look at Japanese pilgrims to China, see Huang Chi-chiang, "Canfang mingshi: nansong qiufa riseng yu jiangzhe fojiao conglin" [Searching for inspiring masters: Japanese pilgrims and Buddhist monasteries in the Jiang-Zhe region during the Southern Song Dynasty], 185–233.

58. For full treatment, see Martin Collcutt, *Five Mountains: The Rinzai Zen Monastic Institution in Medieval Japan* (Cambridge, MA: Harvard East Asian Monographs, 1981).

59. As Döll notes, Jōrakuji was rededicated as Zen monastery on this occasion. Initially, the compound had been a family temple of the Hōjō (北条) clan known as Awafune midō (粟船御堂) that Yasutoki (泰時, 1183–1242) had built for his stepmother.

60. The names are derived from the nine mountains they are associated with (from DDB entry http://www.buddhism-dict.net/cgi-bin/xpr-ddb.pl?q=九山):

> Kaji-san school (迦智山), established at Porimsa (寶林寺) under the influence of Toŭi (道義; d. 825) and his grand student Ch'ejing (體澄; 804–890). Toŭi studied in China under Zhizang (智藏; 735–814) and Baizhang (百丈; 749–814).

> Sŏngju san (聖住山) school, established by Muyŏm (無染; 800–888) who received his inga 印可 from Magu Baoche (麻谷寶徹; b. 720?).

> Silsang san (實相山) school, founded by Hongch'ŏk (洪陟; fl. 830), who also studied under Zhizang.

> Hŭiyang san (曦陽山) school, founded by Pŏmnang and Chisŏn Tohŏn (智詵道憲; 824–882), who was taught by a Korean teacher of the Mazu transmission.

> Pongnim san (鳳林山) school, established by Wŏngnam Hyŏn'uk (圓鑑玄昱; 787–869) and his student Simhŭi (審希, fl. 9c). Hyŏn'uk was a student of Zhangjing Huaihui (章敬懷暉; 748–835).

> Tongni san (桐裡山) school, established by Hyech'ŏl (慧徹; 785–861) who was a student of Jizang.

> Sagul san (闍崛山) school, established by Pŏm'il (梵日; 810–889), who studied in China with Yanguan Qian (鹽官齊安; 750?–842) and Yueshan Weiyan (樂山惟嚴).

> Saja san (獅子山) school, established by Toyun (道允; 797–868), who studied under Nanchuan Puyuan (南泉普願; 748–835).

Sumi-san school (須彌山) founded by Yiŏm (利嚴; 869–936), which had developed from the Caodong (曹洞) lineage.

61. See Ahn, chapter 8.
62. Ahn, chapter 8.
63. "Patterns of Influence in East Asian Buddhism: The Korean Case," in Buswell, ed., *Currents and Countercurrents: Korean Influences on the East Asian Buddhist Traditions* (Honolulu: University of Hawai'i Press, 2005), 1.

Chapter 3

A Greater Vehicle to the Other Shore
Chinese Chan Buddhism and the Sino-Japanese Trade in the Seventeenth Century

JIANG WU

Introduction

The year 1654 was special for Nagasaki (長崎) residents.[1] People in the city were talking about three extraordinary things during the year: there were more ships, more snow, and more monks. Indeed, since the Portuguese and the British were expelled, more Chinese ships filled the vacancy, calling at the port more often. In the winter, kids enjoyed playing in the new abundance of snow.[2] More unusual was the coming of a group of Chinese monks, about six in total, in the summer. A welcoming ceremony was held at the port by all important Chinese interpreter-officers (Tōtsūji 唐通事) and merchants in residence, who wore a mixture of Ming and Qing attires. The two Nagasaki administrators (bugyō 奉行), Kurokawa Masanao (黑川正直, 1602–1680) and Kainoshō Masanobu (甲斐庄正述, 1626?–1660), immediately offered a banquet during the night to entertain the leading monk.

Such a solemn ceremony was prepared for the arrival of what then was the most senior Chinese monk arriving at Nagasaki. His name was Yinyuan Longqi (隱元隆琦, 1592–1673) at age sixty-three. He was an established Chan (J. Zen) master in Wanfu (萬福) monastery in Fuqing (福清), Fujian province, and the leading disciple of Feiyin Tongrong (費

隱通容, 1593–1661), a prominent Linji (臨濟, J. Rinzai) teacher. Yinyuan spent the rest of his life in Japan and distinguished himself by creating a new tradition in Edo Japan, commonly known as Ōbaku (C. Huangbo 黃檗), named after the mountain where he resided in China.³

After he arrived, his influence soon reached outside Nagasaki. In 1655, he was invited to Fumonji (普門寺, Fig. 3.1), a monastery which is located in today's Osaka. In 1658, he was allowed to travel to Edo and had two audiences with the fourth Shogun Tokugawa Ietsuna (德川家綱, 1641–1680) and met with his senior councilors. In 1660, he was granted land to build a new monastery in Uji, Kyoto, known as Manpukuji (萬福寺). Japanese monks, local daimyos, and literary men flocked to this new center of Chinese Buddhism, or more symbolically, of Chinese culture.

Yinyuan was not only a Chan master but also a celebrated poet. He used his poems to document what he saw in Nagasaki and beyond. After he settled in Nagasaki, he had a tour of the city and noticed an interesting phenomenon. He was greatly intrigued by a group of people who made their living by salvaging the silver ingots lost in the river, probably the Isahaya (諫早) River, during their transportation to Nagasaki for foreign

Figure 3.1. Fumonji today. Photo by Jiang Wu, 2013.

trade. The Japanese government collected these savaged ingots and rewarded these divers. As a Buddhist monk, Yinyuan was amused by the scene and wrote a poem to express his view about the nature of money.

看江中撈銀	Watching People Dredging up Silver in the River
百年幻化總非真，	Illusion is always false, Even if lasting for a hundred years.
何必坐馳一夢身。	Why riding on such a phantom body? Even knowing it is a dream.
撈得金銀千萬貫，	You have dredged out gold and silver, Even tens of thousands of them.
不知醒後付何人。	Do you know to whom you are going to give, When awakened from this dream?[4]

Yinyuan's poem shows a typical Buddhist attitude toward money: life is impermanent, and so is money. Silver and gold are precious, but they become useless after death. Yinyuan's attitude toward money seems to suggest that there is no relation between money and Buddhism. Yet, as I will demonstrate in this chapter, the very fact of Yinyuan's arrival in Nagasaki reveals the close relationship between Chinese Buddhism and Sino-Japanese trade. For instance, his invitation was supported by the Nagasaki Chinese merchant community who lavishly donated to Nagasaki Chinese temples. Chinese Buddhism relied on Chinese merchants to sustain its institutions and moreover, in return, under special circumstances provided the much-needed human, social, and cultural capital for the growth of the Nagasaki merchant community. In this context, the economic principle of giving and exchange functioned well: the tangible money needs to be spent in exchange for intangible capital, which can be reinvested to achieve greater Buddhist gain.

CHINESE MONKS AS TRAVELERS IN EAST ASIA

Yinyuan's arrival has to be situated in the revival of Chinese Buddhism, particularly Chan Buddhism in seventeenth-century China. During this period, Chan Buddhism rose quickly, following the initial Buddhist revival led by three eminent Ming monks, Zibo Zhenke (紫柏真可, 1543–1603), Yunqi Zhuhong (雲棲袾宏, 1535–1615), and Hanshan Deqing (憨山德清, 1546–1623). As I have shown in my book on the revival of Chan in seventeenth-century China, after the three eminent masters died, the Buddhist revival entered a new phase in which Chan masters, such as Miyun Yuanwu (密雲圓悟, 1566–1642), Hanyue Fazang (漢月法藏, 1573–1635), Feiyin Tongrong (1593–1662), and Muchen Daomin (木陳道忞, 1596–1674) rose to prominence and dominated the Buddhist world. Chan not only spread in the mainland; this wave of revival also expanded overseas along with the internal migration of the population in China and Chinese emigration to Vietnam and Japan, which had been forced by the Manchu conquest.[5]

Miyun Yuanwu's Linji lineage was the most active and was brought to Vietnam by Shouzun Yuanzhao (壽尊元昭 or Yuanshao 元韶, 1648–1728), who belonged to Miyun Yuanwu's dharma transmission line. He came to Vietnam in 1665 and founded the Nguyên-Thiêu tradition within the Lâm-Tê (C. Linji) school in Vietnam.[6] In addition to Miyun Yuanwu's Linji (Rinzai) tradition, the Caodong (曹洞, J. Sōtō) Chan masters were active in the Guangdong area. In 1695, the Caodong master Shilian Dashan (石濂大汕, 1633–1704) was invited to central Vietnam at the request of the Vietnamese ruler, Nguyên Phúc Chu (阮福週, 1674–1725), who had based his government at Hué (順化).[7]

In Fujian, Miyun Yuanwu's lineage had a strong presence because two of his disciples, Feiyin Tongrong and Yinyuan Longqi, who were natives of Fuqing, where Mount Huangbo was located. In 1630, Miyun was invited to be the abbot at Mount Huangbo. After he left eight months later, Feiyin succeeded him, and after Feiyin his dharma heir Yinyuan Longqi took the position. With Mount Huangbo as a base, Feiyin's and Yinyuan's dharma heirs took control of many local temples in Fujian.[8]

Because of the frequent trade connection between Nagasaki and southern China, monks arrived in Japan in the early seventeenth century. After 1644, more and more established Chan masters with dharma transmissions came to Japan and spread their lineage. Among them, Feiyin's second-generation dharma heir Daozhe Chaoyuan (道者超元, 1599–1662) stayed in Japan briefly from 1651 to 1658. Feiyin Tongrong's first dharma heir, Yinyuan Longqi, was perhaps the most famous because he arrived in Nagasaki in1654 and founded the Japanese Ōbaku school, which will be the focus of this chapter.

In the seventeenth century, the Chinese Caodong lineage had no presence in Japan until one of Juelang Daosheng's (覺浪道盛, 1592–1659)

disciples, Xinyue Xingchou (心越興儔, 1639–1695), also known as Donggao Xinyue (東皋心越), landed in Nagasaki in 1677. Because he belonged to the Caodong lineage, he was not welcomed by Yinyuan Longqi's disciples, who had firmly established themselves since 1654. He was later invited to Mito (水戶) and started the Jushō (壽昌) tradition within the Japanese Sōtō school.

The spread of Chinese Chan Buddhism in Vietnam and Japan shows that Chinese monks became significant travelers and missionaries in the seventeenth century. More importantly, frequent commercial exchange in East Asia paved the way for their presence outside China. To further examine the role of Buddhist monks in the maritime trade in East Asian during the seventeenth century, I will focus on the Chan master Yinyuan and his relationship with the Chinese merchant community at Nagasaki.

Chinese Buddhist Monasteries in Nagasaki

During the sixteenth century, Nagasaki became one of the major centers for expatriate Chinese to live. Its growth was largely attributed to the rise of private trade between China and Japan as the official trade with Japan ended in 1549. The devastating "Wakō" (倭寇) invasion along China's southeast coast, which lasted about twenty-five years, also gave rise to the early Chinese communities in Japan. Some Chinese and the Japanese invaders collaborated and launched attacks from their bases in Japan.[9] In particular, the small Chinese community in Nagasaki, which was the stronghold of Jesuit missionaries in East Asia at that time, grew into a center of Sino-Japanese trade in the seventeenth and eighteenth centuries.

Nagasaki developed out of the need to trade with Europeans and Chinese. Since 1570, the port of Nagasaki was granted special privileges to trade and even became a Jesuit province administered by the Jesuits before these concessions were rescinded during the rising anti-Christian movement systematically under Toyotomi Hideyoshi (豐臣秀吉, 1536–1598) and later the Tokugawa shoguns. As a result of the "Sakoku" (鎖國) policy, only Nagasaki remained open to the Dutch and the Chinese, the only two foreign merchant groups that were permitted to trade in Japan. However, more strict regulations were in place to confine these foreigners in certain areas of Nagasaki. Chinese Buddhism was introduced at this juncture and played a significant role in building solidarity within the Chinese community at Nagasaki.

Japan's radical anti-Christian policy was one of the motives for Chinese residents in Nagasaki to organize themselves more closely around Buddhism. Because the bakufu stipulated that all Japanese residents be registered with a local Buddhist temple, Chinese residents in Nagasaki had to do the same as well. They showed special enthusiasm for Chinese Buddhism. Before Yinyuan Longqi, Chinese Buddhist monks already had a presence in Nagasaki. In 1615, an obscure monk, Zhiguang (智廣), resided in Nagasaki. In 1620, the monk Zhenyuan (真圓) from Jiangxi (江西) province started Kōfukuji (興福寺, Fig. 3.2), also called Nankinji (南京寺), which was sponsored by merchants from the lower Yangzi River area, primarily from Zhejiang and Jiangxi. The monk Mozi Ruding (默子如定, 1597–1657)[10] replaced him in 1632 and in turn Yiran Xingrong (逸然性融, 1601–1668) became the abbot in 1645.[11]

In 1628, Fukusaiji (福濟寺, fig. 3.3a&b) was founded by the Chinese monk Juehai (覺海, ?–1637) and lay patrons from Zhangzhou (漳州) in Fujian. Thus, it was also known as Shōshūji (漳州寺, C. Zhangzhou si). The monastery was developed further under Yunqian Jiewan (蘊謙戒琬, 1610–1673), a monk from Fujian. One year later, Sōfukuji monastery (崇

Figure 3.2. Kōfukuji today. Photo by Jiang Wu, 2013.

Figure 3.3a. Tombs of Fukusaiji Chinese Abbots Juehui, Yunqian, and Ciyue in Nagasaki. Photo by Jiang Wu, 2013.

Figure 3.3b. Signpost in Japanese, English, Korean, and Chinese about the burial site. Photo by Jiang Wu, 2013.

福寺), also called Fukushūji (福州寺), was founded by the monk Chaoran (超然). After the second abbot Baizhuo (百拙) died in 1649, Yinyuan's dharma heir Yelan Xinggui (也嬾性圭, 1630?–1651) was invited to succeed him. Unfortunately, Yelan died in a shipwreck in 1651. In addition, at the same time, Daozhe Chaoyuan was invited from Fujian in 1650. However, he was forced to return to China eight years later as he did not belong to Yinyuan's dharma transmission line.[12]

Chinese Merchants in Nagasaki

Yinyuan's arrival was based on the success of his predecessors. All these émigré monks were closely connected to the merchant groups who distinguished themselves according to their geographical origins in China. The three Chinese monasteries in Nagasaki, for example, are often described as expressions of local connections among people from the lower Yangzi region, Zhangzhou, and Fuzhou respectively. Without exception, Yinyuan and his disciples were connected to the diaspora from a particular locality in Fuzhou, Fuqing County. Not only was Yinyuan born in Fuqing, he also became the abbot of Mount Huangbo, which was located in Fuqing. Although merchants who hailed from Fuqing were generally referred to as being from Fuzhou, they emerged as a powerful faction in the Chinese community at Nagasaki because they differed from other Fujianese due to their unique dialect and seafaring tradition. Being recognized as "Hokchia," Fuqing people formed one of the world's most unique émigré communities.[13]

It is no doubt that the strong presence of Fuqing merchants helped Yinyuan and his disciples, most of them Fuqing natives, to emigrate to Japan in 1654. Among these Fuqing merchants in Nagasaki, five played the most significant role: Lin Taiqing (林太卿, zi Chuyu 楚玉, 1561–1645), He Gaocai (何高材, zi Yuchu 毓楚, 1598–1671), Wang Yin (王引, zi Xinqu 心渠, 1594–1678), Wei Zhiyan (魏之琰, zi Shuanghou 雙侯, 1617–1689), and Lin Gongyan (林公琰, 1598–1683). They were not only influential members in the Fuzhou community but also, due to their wealth and influence, leaders of the entire Chinese community in Nagasaki.[14]

Lin Taiqing hailed from a well-to-do family in Fuqing. It was said that his family was related to the family of the famous Ming general Yu Dayou (俞大猷, 1503–1580), who was a leader in the war against the Wakō invasion. Arriving in Kagoshima (鹿兒島) in 1609, he married a daughter of the Shinohara (篠原) family. Soon after, in 1619, he and his family moved to Nagasaki, where he became well established in the local Chinese community and led the building of Sōfukuji (Fig. 3.4) in 1635. Because of this project, Chaoran was invited to be abbot in 1629. After he died in 1645, his son Lin Shoudian (林守壂, zi Datang 大堂, 1610–1694), whose Japanese name was Hayashi Jinbē (林仁兵衛), succeeded in inheriting his prominent status, serving as chief interpreter (*daitsūji* 大通事) from 1641 to 1662. Lin Shoudian was ordained as a monk under Yinyuan in 1669 and was given the dharma name Duzhen Xingying (獨振性英). He received dharma transmission from Yinyuan's dharma heir Duhou Xingshi (獨吼性獅, 1624–1688) in 1676 and later resided in Tokuenji (德苑寺) in Nagasaki from 1678. His son Lin Fenggao (林豐高, 1634–1709), also known as Futaki Jinbē (二木仁兵衛) or Hayashi Jinyōshi (林甚吉) in Japanese, served as chief interpreter from 1693 to 1700. He was also Yinyuan's lay disciple. The Hayashi family was the primary patron of Sōfukuji and supported Yinyuan and later his disciples Mu'an Xingtao (木庵性瑫, 1611–1684) and Jifei Ruyi (即非如一, 1616–1671).[15]

Figure 3.4. Entrance Gate of Sōfukuji nowadays. Photo by Jiang Wu. 2013.

He Gaocai moved to Nagasaki in 1628 and married a daughter of the Takagawa (高河) family. Together with Lin Taiqing, he was an active patron of Sōfukuji. He also helped to rebuild Kiyomizu Temple (清水寺). He signed the petition to invite Yinyuan and became Yinyuan's lay disciple, receiving the dharma name Xingchong (性崇) from him. After Yinyuan left Nagasaki, he visited him at the new Manpukuji in 1664 and was greatly appreciated by Yinyuan, Jifei, and Mu'an. In particular, he supported Jifei at Sōfukuji. He provided funds to publish Jifei's collection of recorded sayings in 1662 and took care of Jifei when he was about to die. During the same year, 1671, He Gaocai died as well. His son He Zhaojin (何兆晉), also known as Kani Uhyōe (何仁右兵衛), was junior interpreter from 1658 to 1668. He had a particular interest in the seven-string zither and thus befriended the Chinese monk Donggao Xinyue (東皋心越, 1639–1695), who was an excellent zither player and helped to spread this musical tradition in Japan.

Wang Yin, probably a Fuqing native, hailed from the Fuzhou area. He may have engaged in the Sino-Japan trade and arrived in Nagasaki during the 1620s as a merchant. As a prominent figure in the Chinese community, he joined Lin Taiqing and his son to build Sōfukuji. After Lin Taiqing died in 1645, he became the leading patron who invited Yinyuan to reside in Sōfukuji in 1655. (Yinyuan first stayed at Kōfukuji.) After Yinyuan left for Fumonji in Osaka, he continued to support Yinyuan's disciple Jifei. In 1678, he was promoted to the position of administrator of the Chinese community (*tōnengyōji* 唐年行司). After Wang Yin's death in 1678, his son Ōkichirō Uhyōe (王吉郎右兵衛) took over the same administrator job.

Wei Zhiyan was also a Fuqing native. His complex and mysterious journey started from Tonkin (東京) in Vietnam with his brother Wei Zhiyuan (魏之瑗, 1654) who was more famously portrayed as a one-eyed merchant ("Itchien") by the Dutch who traded with him. Wei and his brother controlled the silk trade between Vietnam and Japan. Although he traveled frequently between Tonkin and Nagasaki, his residency in Japan was not approved until 1672. However, even without citizenship, he was active in community works. He was one of the major patrons of Sōfukuji and attended the welcoming ceremony for Yinyuan who moved to Sōfukuji in 1655 and later for Jifei in 1658 (Fig. 3.5). He also co-sponsored the construction of several arch bridges in Nagasaki.[16]

Lin Gongyan was also a prominent Fuqing native active in Nagasaki. He supported the move to invite Yinyuan. His history in Nagasaki can be traced back to 1623 when Lin sailed to Japan. Later, in 1628, he was

Figure 3.5. Plaque donated by Wei Zhiyan and He Gaocai in Sōfukuji. Photo by Jiang Wu, 2013.

appointed administrator of the Chinese community at Nagasaki. His son Lin Daorong (林道榮, J. Hayashi Dōei, 1640–1708) was later promoted to the position of chief interpreter in 1674 and continued to support the Ōbaku monks.[17]

These merchants became powerful in Nagasaki through trade. Their prestige and influence were perpetuated through their descendants who were often appointed as interpreters by the Nagasaki bugyō (administrators). In addition to their commercial and administrative activities, they realized the importance of investing in community works such as building bridges and public facilities. In particular, they patronized Chinese Buddhist monks by financially supporting Chinese temples. Yinyuan's arrival provided a new opportunity for them to lavish their patronage even after he moved out of Nagasaki and founded Manpukuji in Kyoto. As I will show in the next section, the common origin of these merchants and Yinyuan was not the only reason for their patronage. Rather, Chinese Buddhism in Nagasaki became a vehicle that carried important social and cultural assets.

Buddhism as Sources of Human, Social, and Cultural Capital

It is evident that aside from his extraordinary personal capabilities, Yinyuan's success was in part due to the tremendous help he received. However, the question remains why Chinese merchants wanted to support Chinese Buddhism and Buddhist monks like him. As I have pointed out, a stringent anti-Christian policy created the need for the existence of Chinese monasteries in Nagasaki. But what the Nagasaki Chinese merchants did was not to simply fulfill the bakufu's new requirements. Rather, they kept upgrading the monastic buildings and inviting more prestigious monks like Yinyuan. Their efforts suggest that there must have been other deep-rooted reasons for their patronage of Buddhist monasteries. Drawing upon sociological concepts, I would like to point out that Chinese merchants had made smart financial investments by acquiring significant symbolic and intangible capital for greater gains. As I will analyze below, Buddhism first of all provided valuable human resources as many monks were highly trained artisans, doctors, and language instructors who were directly involved in merchants' philanthropic projects. Second, by donating and patronizing Chinese monasteries and through their connections with Yinyuan, merchants acquired significant social capital by establishing a unique network with Japanese aristocrats and officials, thus gaining their trust. Finally, an overwhelming fervor over Chinese culture in the early and mid-Edo periods highlights the cultural aspect of Chinese monasteries as representatives of elite Chinese culture: by patronizing these monasteries Chinese merchants accumulated cultural capital that helped construct their collective identity.

BUDDHISM AS A SOURCE OF HUMAN CAPITAL

The plethora of historical sources on Chinese monks in Japan allows us to look at the composition of these émigré monks. Although these monks were primarily religious specialists who met the spiritual needs of their followers, because of the social and political turmoil during the Ming-Qing transition we have seen a diverse monastic population as people fled to monasteries to escape from their troubled lives. Among them were quite a few talented artisans such as bridge builders, painters, doctors, and Confucian literati. In a sociological sense, their skills, knowledge, experiences, and literary talents were essential elements of human capital. In Nagasaki, because they were allowed to stay permanently in the city and to travel within Japan with permission, these monks appeared to be necessary human resources for Chinese merchant communities to flourish.

A notable example was the building of the double-arched bridge Meganebashi (眼鏡橋, Fig. 3.6) in Nagasaki in 1634 by Mozi Ruding (默子如定, 1597–1657), who hailed from Jianchang (建昌) in Jiangxi (江西). Arriving at Nagasaki in 1632, he visited Zhenyuan and became the second abbot of Kōfukuji. Apparently, he was a talented bridge designer. He was allowed to build bridges in Nagasaki which were supported by Nagasaki merchants such as Wei Zhiyan.[18]

In Japan there was a great need for trained medical personnel, and more than a few Chinese monks became famous for their medical knowledge. The most famous monk-doctor was Duli Xingyi (獨立性易, 1596–1672), who was converted by Yinyuan in 1654 upon his arrival. Before coming to Japan, Duli studied with the famed doctor Gong Tingxian (龔廷賢, 1522–1619) in China and specialized in treating smallpox. In 1653, he came to Guangzhou 廣州 and boarded a ship to Nagasaki in the third month. He was soon acquainted with Zhu Shunshui (朱舜水,

Figure 3.6. Meganebashi in Nagasaki. Photo by Jiang Wu, 2013.

1600–1682) and the Confucian scholar Andō Seian (安東省庵, 1622–1701). After Yinyuan came in 1654, he decided to be ordained as Yinyuan's disciple on the eighth day of the twelfth month of that year. Duli thrived in Nagasaki as a skilled doctor, bridge engineer, and calligrapher. Because of his medical skills, he was invited several times to the Iwakuni (岩国) domain by the lord Kikkawa Hiroyoshi (吉川広嘉, 1621–1679), who asked Duli to build the arched bridge Kintaikyō (錦袋橋).[19]

Monks who acquired medical knowledge also put their skills to use in business. The most successfully run Ōbaku business was the famous medicine shop Kintaien (錦袋円) founded by Yinyuan's Japanese disciple Ryōō Dōkaku (了翁道覺, 1630–1707, dharma heir of Gaoquan Xingdun 高泉性潡). Apparently, he had acquired some medical knowledge during this stay in Nagasaki for curing his own disease. (He castrated himself in order to eliminate his sexual desire and had to attend to his wound constantly.) One day, he claimed that in a dream he received the prescription of a cure-all medicine, later named Kintaishi (錦袋子), from the Chinese monk Mozi Ruding, the bridge builder mentioned earlier. He thus built a shop in Kyoto where he would sell the medicine and was hugely successful. He used the money he earned to fund projects such as distributing the Buddhist canon and books, building a public library, among others. Because of his success, he was able to will a contribution of three hundred taels annually from the profit of selling the medicine to fund the repair projects at Manpukuji.[20]

One of the important skills the monks had was their ability in teaching colloquial Chinese. The constant supply of native Chinese speakers was essential for maintaining a vibrant emigrant community in Nagasaki and promoted the learning of spoken Chinese among the Japanese. In Nagasaki, the demand for learning colloquial Chinese was high, as many second-generation Chinese immigrants were born in Japan and needed to be fluent in spoken Chinese to undertake the role of interpreters and to complete business transactions. Japanese monks also needed to learn Chinese to be able to study with their Chinese masters. Educated monks as regular residents naturally became the best teacher candidates. For Japanese intellectuals, learning colloquial Chinese became fashionable in the early eighteenth century, and Ōbaku monks such as Yuefeng Daozhang (悦峰道章, 1655–1734) were frequently invited to Edo to teach Chinese to top officials such as Yanagisawa Yoshiyasu (柳沢吉保, 1658–1714) and influential intellectuals such as Ogyū Sorai (荻生徂徠, 1666–1728) and Yanagisawa Kien (柳沢淇園, 1704–1758).[21]

Some Japanese monks also became fluent in colloquial Chinese. For example, the Japanese Ōbaku monk Kōkoku Dōren (香國道蓮, 1652–1723), a dharma heir of Huilin Xingji (慧林性機, 1609–1681), was ordained by Yinyuan as a novice in 1657 at nine years old. During his long career among Chinese monks, he became fluent in colloquial Chinese and often served as an interpreter for Chinese monks. In 1713, he was invited by Yanagisawa Yoshiyasu (柳沢吉保, 1658–1714) to his residence and was also befriended by Ogyū Sorai.[22]

Buddhism as a Source of Social Capital

Social capital is a sociological concept that reveals an aspect of human relationships that can be used for achieving greater profits. According to sociologists, social capital is generated through extensive networking in which personal interactions created certain reciprocal obligations among people where eventually trust is developed. As the American sociologist James Coleman defines it, a high level of trust and the extent of obligations held are two essential elements in generating effective social capital.[23] Therefore, the more trust a person or institution is able to build, the more likely support, both moral and financial, will accrue. As a result, this type of relationship is conducive to forming a group identity or civic association. In the case of the role of Chinese Buddhism in the Nagasaki Chinese community, the social capital generated through connections with Chinese monks and monasteries bonded Nagasaki Chinese merchants and residents into a more cohesive community and bridged the gap among Chinese residents who were divided by their origins, and more importantly, between them and the Japanese.

Although all Chinese merchants arrived from the mainland, it is notable that they distinguished themselves by their geographical origins and dialects. The building of the three Chinese temples was clearly an identity marker for different groups of Chinese residents. However, Yinyuan's arrival and later the successful establishment of Manpukuji united all three temples under Yinyuan. They merged into the new Buddhist denomination Yinyuan founded and only monks in Yinyuan's dharma transmission line were allowed to be abbots of these Chinese monasteries. Thus, the new identity of Ōbaku monasteries largely transcended their regional origins. It is true that Yinyuan was close to merchants hailing from Fuqing because of their regional bond, but he quickly became the spiritual leader of all Chinese residents.

It was of great importance for the merchants to forge a positive relationship with Japanese officials as the success of their trade often hinged upon official policies and decisions. Yinyuan's arrival immediately provided a bridge for Chinese merchants. Yinyuan formed a good relationship with two political groups: the shogunal bureaucrats including senior councilors and local daimyō, and the imperial house and court aristocrats.

During his twenty-year stay in Japan, Yinyuan developed an extensive network among local daimyō and all levels of bakufu officials. This network expanded from the regional to the national level. The first two bakufu officers Yinyuan met were the two Nagasaki bugyo, Kurokawa Masanao and Kainoshō Masanobu in 1654, who immediately became Yinyuan's disciples.[24] Lords of neighboring domains such as the Hizen (肥前) lord Nabeshima Katsushige (鍋島勝茂, 1580–1657) were also converted by him. He was soon introduced to the Kyoto deputy Itakura Shigemune (板倉重宗, 1586–1656), who had just retired in 1654. Shigemune sponsored an initiative to invite Yinyuna to Fumonji in today's Takatsuki (高槻), a significant move out of Nagasaki. He soon became Yinyuan's disciple and his strong supporter,[25] as was his successor Makino Chikanari (牧野親成, 1607–1677). Because of the importance of the Kyoto deputy in the bakufu government, Yinyuan was immediately connected to the central government controlled by a group of senior councilors.

The fourth shogun Ietsuna's reign saw the rise of Fudai (譜代) daimyō in the bakufu administration. The ancestors of these daimyō joined Tokugawa Ieyasu before the decisive war in Sekigahara and thus enjoyed special privileges at the shogun's court. The central government was controlled by influential chief councilors such as Sakai Tadakatsu (酒井忠勝, 1587–1662) and Sakai Tadakiyo (酒井忠清, 1624–1681). Tadakatsu showed great interest in Yinyuan and helped Yinyuan acquire a piece of land in Kyoto to build his own temple.[26] Because of the support of bakufu senior officials, Yinyuan was allowed an audience with Ietsuna in the winter of 1658. During his visit to Edo, he met Tadakatsu and other senior councilors. After the founding of Manpukuji in 1660, more local lords and bakufu officials befriended Yinyuan.[27]

Yinyuan also developed a network among members of the imperial family and court nobles. The retired emperor Gomizunoo (後水尾, 1596–1680) was attracted to Yinyuan and received dharma transmission in Yinyuan's lineage.[28] Influenced by their father, some of his sons and daughters, such as Prince Shinkei (真敬, 1649–1706) and Princess Genyō (元瑤, 1634–1727), became converted to Ōbaku as well.[29] Kyoto aristocrats were also attracted to Yinyuan and formed a strong connection with him. Among them, Konoe Motohiro (近衛基熙, 1648–1722) and his son Konoe Iehiro (近衛家熙, 1667–1736) became patrons of Yinyuan and his disciples.[30]

Some of the social connections that Yinyuan had were beyond the reach of Chinese merchants. But keeping a close relationship with Chinese monks did help merchants advance themselves and gain profits. One of the examples might be the case of Wei Zhiyan, a merchant from Fuqing mentioned earlier, who successfully maneuvered among Japanese officials through his various social ties, including his connections with Chinese monks. In theory, the Sakoku policy dictates that no residents in Japan, Chinese or Japanese, should go outside its territory to conduct business. In 1635, Chinese merchants, if not already Nagasaki residents, were not allowed to stay permanently and had to leave after the trading season. But Wei Zhiyan was among the few who had the privilege of traveling between Nagasaki and Tonkin for trading silk even after Wei was granted permanent residence.[31]

Wei Zhiyan took over his brother's business after his brother's death in 1654, the year when Yinyuan arrived. Yinyuan's records showed that Wei Zhiyan was in Nagasaki in 1655, though other sources suggested he was there only from 1658. Because the Wei brothers started their business around the 1640s, in the years after the Sakoku policy was implemented, they were not considered residents of Nagasaki. Wei Zhiyan had to travel back and forth from Tonkin to Nagasaki and left his family to stay in Tonkin due to these restrictions. To perpetuate their family business and to acquire legal residence status in Nagasaki, the Wei brothers needed a prominent presence to confirm their status in the Chinese community. It appears that patronizing Buddhist temples was an accessible way to display their wealth and intention to be good citizens. In 1647, Wei Zhiyan's brother donated 150 taels to cast a bell for Sōfukuji, a significant portion of the total amount of 554 taels. In 1650, he donated a stone platform to Zenrinji (禪林寺) in Nagasaki.

His brother's purpose was widely known among Nagasaki foreigners and even noticed by Adriaen van der Burgh, the chief of the Dutch factory in Nagasaki from 1652 to 1653.[32] However, his brother died in the early morning of the seventeenth day of the eleventh month in 1654, This was when Yinyuan arrived. Wei Zhiyan signed his name on the invitation letter and supported Yinyuan's move from Kōfukuji to Sōfukuji, which the Fuqing merchants controlled. Because of his origins in Fuqing, he and his fellow townsmen formed a special relationship with Yinyuan.[33]

During the years that followed, Wei continued to do business between Tonkin and Nagasaki while supporting Nagasaki temples. In 1669, he donated five hundred taels to Sōfukuji and in 1681, he donated again to repair the main hall of Sōfukuji. On the fifteenth day of the tenth month of 1672, a petition for the Wei family to be naturalized reached the senior councilors in Edo. Eventually, he was granted legal status in 1672. In 1679, he and his two sons Wei Gao (魏高, 1650–1719) and Wei Gui (魏貴, 1661–1738) were given Japanese citizenship. He was allowed to keep his Chinese names, while his sons were given the Japanese surname Ōga (鉅鹿).[34]

Buddhism as a Source of Cultural Capital

As Pierre Bourdieu defines it, cultural capital is a special form of social relations that includes the accumulated cultural skills, knowledge, and educational background that bring power and advantageous social status.[35] Because the type of Chinese Buddhism Yinyuan represented had seamlessly integrated Chinese culture as one central component, it can be said that Buddhism greatly increased the cultural capital of those Chinese merchants who associated themselves with Chinese Buddhist temples in Nagasaki.

The continuous influx of Chinese cultural products from China created an atmosphere of Sinophilism in Japan. In the Edo period, Sinophilism reached such a level that collecting Chinese cultural objects became a fashion among the Japanese upper class. In addition, mastery in Chinese cultural crafts such as poetry writing and calligraphy were greatly valued in Edo society. The worship of an imported tradition, as Marius Jansen argues, was rather metaphorical because it manifested the romantic imagination of China, which only existed in an idyllic world created by Chinese poetry, painting, and moralist discourses.[36] Chinese monks must have realized the huge demand for the products of Chinese elite culture, such as literati paintings, books, antiques, and other objets d'art.

Yinyuan and his disciples were masters of Chinese cultural skills and knowledge. Calligraphy was one of the cultural legacies of the Ōbaku school. Nowadays, three Ōbaku masters, Yinyuan Longqi, Jifei Ruyi, and Mu'an Xingtao, have the honorific title of "The Three Brushes of Ōbaku (Ōbaku sanpitsu 黃檗三筆)," and are commemorated as excellent calligraphers and seal makers (Fig. 3.7).[37]

Ōbaku portrait painting is also widely admired, having influenced Japanese portrait painting significantly.[38] Yang Daozhen (楊道貞, active

Figure 3.7. Feiyin Tongrong's calligraphy in Manpukuji. Photo by Jiang Wu. 2013.

in Japan from ca. 1657 to 1663) was a celebrated portrait painter in the Ōbaku school and taught two renowned Japanese portrait painters, Kita Chōbei (喜多宗雲, Dōku, or Sōun, active ca. 1657–1663) and Kita Genki (喜多元規, fl. 1664–1709). Dapeng Zhengkun (大鵬正鯤, 1691–1774), one of the last few Chinese abbots in Manpukuji, was renowned for his painting of bamboo. His depiction of thick bamboo leaves influenced Japanese literati painting in the eighteenth century.[39]

The new cultural flavor that Ōbaku represented has also been embodied in the architecture of Manpukuji, the Ōbaku headquarters in Uji. Manpukuji's architecture and the modeling of Buddha statues inside the monastery were marveled at as a skillful demonstration of seventeenth-century Chinese architectonics and craftsmanship, which distinguished the Ōbaku style from all other Japanese temple structures modeled on earlier Chinese examples.[40]

All these aspects, more cultural rather than religious, are often regarded as the major characteristics of the so-called Ōbaku bunka (黄檗文化 Ōbaku culture). The distinctive cultural features of Chinese temples in Nagasaki and Uji were an ostensible display of the cultural capital possessed by these Chinese monks. Through patronizing Chinese monks,

Chinese merchants shared this type of "institutionalized" cultural capital, which needed to be objectified and displayed in the process of building Chinese temples.

Conclusion

In economic terms, wealth is represented principally in monetary terms. But this is only one form of wealth. Human, social, and cultural capital are also forms of wealth, often being a source of potential wealth inherited in a social group. However, when such potential is fully developed under certain circumstances, it will also generate more monetary wealth.

This study shows that in Nagasaki the existence of Chinese monasteries became a source for building human, social, and cultural capital for Chinese merchants. The presence of Chinese Buddhist monasteries was the result of collective endeavors of Chinese merchants to enhance group coherence and to bridge gaps with the Japanese elite. It was also noted that the rise of Ōbaku Buddhism in Japan was concomitant with the heyday of Sino-Japanese trade, but this imported tradition declined after the mid-eighteenth century when more restrictions on trade were enforced. Around the 1730s, Manpukuji failed several times to invite Chinese monks from China to head the temple, and the bakufu finally gave up such attempts.[41] In the 1780s, when the last Chinese abbot passed away, the abbotship was thus transferred to the hands of Japanese monks. By that time, trade had also declined significantly: in 1791, the number of Chinese ships was further reduced to ten; and in 1858, there were only three Chinese ships trading at Nagasaki.[42]

Notes

1. I appreciate the constructive comments provided by Elisabeth Kaske, George Souza, and Hans Vogel at the Fourth International Workshop of the Research Group "Monies, Markets, and Finance in China and East Asia, 1600–1900" at the University of Tübingen, April 14–16, 2010, when this chapter was first presented. All mistakes remain my own. I am indebted to Paul Groner and Iioka Naoko who sent their newly completed papers and dissertation to me. Research on Chinese monks in Vietnam has been supported by a Faculty Research Development Grant offered by the Office of International Affairs at the University of Arizona.

2. The weather condition and the unusual events in 1654 were hinted in Yinyuan's chronological biography. See Hirakubo Akira 平久保章, ed., *Shinsan kōtei Ingen zenshū* 新纂校訂隱元全集. 12 vols. (Kyoto: Kaimei shoin, 1979), 10: 5208–09. Abbreviated as IGZS in this chapter. This abnormal weather condition might be a result of the so-called Little Ice Age in the seventeenth century which caused a "general crisis" globally. See Geoffrey Parker, *Global Crisis: War, Climate Change and Catastrophe in the Seventeenth Century* (New Haven, CT, and London: Yale University Press, 2003), especially 3–54.

3. For recent studies on the Ōbaku school in Japan, see Helen Baroni, *Obaku Zen: The Emergence of the Third Sect of Zen in Tokugawa Japan* (Honolulu: University of Hawai'i Press, 2000), James Baskind, "Ming Buddhism in Edo Japan: the Chinese Founding Masters of the Japanese Obaku School" (PhD diss., Yale University, 2006); Jiang Wu, *Leaving for the Rising Sun: Chinese Zen Master Yinyuan and the Authenticity Crisis in Early Modern East Asia* (New York: Oxford University Press, 2015). For a brief discussion of Yinyuan and Sino-Japanese cultural exchange, see Ōba Osamu 大庭修, *Edo jidai no Nit-Chū biwa* 江戶時代の日中秘話 (Tokyo: Tōhō shoten, 1980), 44. See also Joshua Fogel's English translation in "Sino-Japanese Relations in the Edo Period," part 2, *Journal of Sino-Japanese Studies* 8, no. 2 (May 1996): 60, http://chinajapan.org/articles/08.2/08.2oba50-61.pdf. Later incorporated in Ōba Osamu, *Books and Boats: Sino-Japanese Relations and Cultural Transmission in the Eighteenth and Nineteenth Centuries*, trans. Joshua A. Fogel (Portland: Merwin Asia, 2012).

4. IGZS 6: 2820.

5. See Jiang Wu, *Enlightenment in Dispute: The Reinvention of Chan Buddhism in Seventeenth-century China* (New York: Oxford University Press, 2008), especially chap. 3.

6. Shouzun Yuanzhao was considered the founder of the Nguyên-Thiêu (元韶) school of the Lâm-Tê Thiên (臨濟禪) tradition in Vietnam. In 1665, he traveled to Vietnam and arrived in Bình-Đinh province where he founded the Thâp-Tháp Di-Đà (拾塔彌陀) monastery. Later, he settled in Hué, the capital of the Nguyên regime, and built Hà-Trung (河中) monastery and Quôc-Ân (國安) monastery. See Thich Thien-An, *Buddhism and Zen in Vietnam: In Relation to the Development of Buddhism in Asia*, ed. Carol Smith (Rutland and Tokyo: Tuttle, 1975), 148–61. For a study of Yuanzhao, see also Tan Zhici 譚志詞, "Qingchu Guangdongji qiaoseng Yuanshao chanshi zhi yiju Yuenan ji xiangguan wenti yanjiu" 清初廣東籍僑僧元韶禪師之移居越南及相關問題研究, *Huaqiao Huaren lishi yanjiu* 華僑華人歷史研究 2 (2007): 53–58.

7. See Charles Wheeler, "Buddhism in the Re-ordering of an Early Modern World: Chinese Missions to Cochinchina in the Seventeenth Century," *Journal of Global History* 2 (2007): 303–24. See also Jiang Boqin 姜伯勤, *Shilian Dashan yu Ao'men Chanshi: Qingchu Lingnan Chanxue yanjiu chubian* 石濂大汕與澳門禪史: 清初嶺南禪學研究初編 (Shanghai: Xuelin chubanshe, 1999). There were other

lesser known Chinese monks who were active in Vietnam such as Chuyết Công (C. Zhuogong 拙公, 1590–1644) and his disciple Minh Hành (C. Mingxing 明行, 1596–1659). See Tan Zhici 譚志詞, "Shiqi shiba shiji Lingnan yu Yuenan de Fojiao jiaoliu" 十七十八世紀嶺南與越南的佛教交流, *Shijie zongjiao yanjiu* 世界宗教研究 3 (2007): 42–52.

    8. For a study of Huangbo, see Jiang Wu, "Building a Dharma Transmission Monastery: The Case of Mount Huangbo," *Journal of East Asian History* 31 (June 2006): 29–52. Later incorporated in Wu, *Leaving for the Rising Sun*, chap. 2.

    9. John E. Wills Jr., "Maritime China from Wang Chih to Shih Lang: Themes in Peripheral History," in *From Ming to Ch'ing: Conquest, Region, and Continuities in 17th Century China*, ed. Jonathan Spence and John E. Wills (New Haven, CT: Yale University Press, 1979), 201–238.

    10. For his biography, see Hayashi Yukimitsu 林雪光 et al., *Ōbaku bunka jinmei jiten* 黃檗文化人名辞典 (Kyoto: Shibunkaku, 1988), 357. Abbreviated as OBJ in this chapter. See later discussions about his bridge-building activities in Nagasaki.

    11. We know more about Yiran Xingrong as he was the strong advocate for inviting Yinyuan to Japan. He arrived in Japan in 1634 as a merchant trading vegetable seeds. He became a monk in 1644, probably due to his business failures. He was also revered as a painter who brought the Chinese literati painting style to Japan. See Nishigori Ryōsuke 錦織亮介, "Itsunen Shōyū Nempō" 逸然性融年譜, *Kitakyūshū Daigaku Bungakubu kiyō* 北九州大學文學部紀要 59 (1997): 45–64.

    12. For information about the current condition of some of these sites, see Wu, "Huangbo canxue ji" 黄檗參學記). *Ōbaku bunka* 黄檗文華 134 (2014): 267–78. Reprinted in *Hanyu Fojiao Pinglun* 漢語佛教評論6 (2018): 250–74. For the Japanese translation, see "Ōbaku sangaku ki: Ingen zenji yukari no jiin wo megutte" 黄檗參學記: 隱元禅師ゆかりの寺院を巡って. Translated by Yang Kuei-hsiang 楊桂香, Hayashi Masako 林正子, and Tanaka Shōzō 田中昭三. *Ōbaku bunka* 黄檗文華 135 (2015): 204–23.

    13. For recent studies of the Fuqing network in Japan, See Jiang Wu, "Leaving for the Rising Sun: The Historical Background of Yinyuan Longqi's Migration to Japan in 1654," *Asia Major* (3rd series) 17, no. 2 (2004): 89–120; Iioka Naoko 飯岡直子, "Literati Entrepreneur: Wei Zhiyan in the Tonkin-Nagasaki Silk Trade." (PhD diss., National University of Singapore, 2009), especially chapter 4, "The Fuqing Network: Chan Buddhism and Late-Ming Culture," 145–89. Other useful works in English include Louis Jacques Willem Berger, "The Overseas Chinese in Seventeenth Century Nagasaki," (PhD diss., Harvard University, 2003); Aloysius Chang, "The Nagasaki Office of the Chinese Interpreters in the Seventeenth Century," *Chinese Culture* 8, no. 3 (1972): 3–19; Patrizia Carioti, "The International Role of the Overseas Chinese in Hirado (Nagasaki) during the First Decades of the 17(th) Century," in *New Studies on Chinese Overseas and China* ed. Cen Huang, Zhuang Guotu, and Tanaka Kyōko (Leiden: International Institute for Asian Studies, 2000, 31–45); "The Origin of the Chinese Community of Nagasaki, 1571–1635," *Ming Qing Yanjiu* (Napoli) 2006: 1–34; "Focusing on the Overseas Chinese in Seventeenth Century

Nagasaki: The Role of *Tōtsūji* in Light of the Early Tokugawa Foreign Policy," in Nagazuni Yōko, *Large and Broad: The Dutch Impact on Early Modern Asia—Essays in honor of Leonard Blussé* (Tokyo: Tōyō Bunko, 2010), 62–75.

14. For details about these Fuqing people and their descendants, see Miyata Yasushi 宮田安, *Tōtsūji kakei ronkō* 唐通事家係論攷 (Nagasaki: Nagasaki bunkensha, 1979), 388–411; 451–76; 798–819; 961–96. The following accounts are based on Miyata's work.

15. For a recent study of Mu'an and Jifei in English, see Shyling Glaze, "Muan Xingtao: An Obaku Zen Master of the Seventeenth Century in China and Japan" (MA thesis, University of Arizona, 2011); Aihua Zheng, "A Portrait of an Ōbaku Monk: the Life and Religion of Jifei Ruyi (1616–1671)," (MA thesis, University of Arizona, 2009).

16. For details, see Iioka Naoko, "Wei Zhiyan and the Subversion of the '*Sakoku*,'" in *Offshore Asia*, ed. Anthony Reid and Momoki Shiro (Singapore: National Singapore University Press, 2013), 236–58. I want to thank Iioka for sending me her manuscript. See also her "Rise and Fall of the Tonkin-Nagasaki Silk Trade during the 17th Century," *Large and Broad: The Dutch Impact on Early Modern Asia—Essays in honor of Leonard Blussé* (Tokyo: Toyo Bunko, 2010), 46–61.

17. Lin met Yinyuan in 1655 when he was a boy. See IGZS 6: 2972. For the relation between Huangbo and the Hayashi family, see Hayashi Rokurō 林陸朗, *Nagasaki Tōtsūji: daitsūji Hayashi Dōei to sono shūhen* 長崎唐通事: 大通事林道榮とその周邊 (Tokyo: Yoshikawa kōbunkan, 2000), especially 22–26, 42–47, and 66–68. According to Hayashi, Yinyuan's disciple Jifei Ruyi might be a relative of the Lin family.

18. In addition to bridge building, he also specialized in processing jade. OBJ, 375. Wei Zhiyan sponsored the building of an arch bridge in 1679. For details of his activities, see later discussions.

19. Also known as Dai Li (戴笠) or Dai Mangong (戴曼公), Duli hailed from a bureaucratic family in Renhe county (仁和) in Hangzhou. His father was Dai Jingqiao (戴敬橋), who descended from Dai Andao (戴安道) who was a famous literatus in the Jin (晉) dynasty. His family declined after his father's death in 1620. He then chose medicine as his career. See Takai Kyōko 高井恭子, "Minmatsu Kika Chūgokusō no gakushiki nitsuite" 明末帰化中国僧の学識について, *Indogaku Bukkyōgaku kenkyū* 印度学仏教学研究 49, no. 1 (December 2000): 251–53; Xu Xingqing 徐興慶, ed., *Tianxianlaoren Dulixingyi quanji* 天閒老人獨立性易全集. (Taibei: Taida chuban zhongxin, 2015). For a recent study of the reception of Chinese medical knowledge in Japan, see Benjamin A. Elman, "Sinophiles and Sinophobes in Tokugawa Japan: Politics, Classicism, and Medicine During the Eighteenth Century," *East Asian Science, Technology and Society* 2, no. 1 (December 2009): 93–121.

20. For a thorough study in English, see Paul Groner, "Ryōō Dōkaku 了翁道覚 (1630–1707), Ascetic, Philanthropist, Bibliophile, and Entrepreneur: the Creation of Japan's First Public Library," Part I published in *Sange gakkai kiyō* 山

家学会紀要 9 (2007): 1–35; Part II published in *Bukkyō to bunka* 仏教と文化, ed. *Tada Kōshō hakushi koki kinen ronbunshū kankōkai* 多田孝正博士古稀記念論集刊行会, 1–33 (Tokyo: Sankibō Busshōrin, 2009). A revised version was published in *Images, Relics, and Legends: The Formation and Transformation of Buddhist Sacred Sites*, ed. James Benn, James Robson, and Jinhua Chen. (Oakville, ON: Mosaic, 2013), 248–72. I want to thank Paul for providing references and sending me both papers.

21. See Nakata Yoshikatsu 中田喜勝, "Sorai to Chūgokugo: Eppō oshō to sono hitsugo" 徂徠と中国語—悦峯和尚とその筆語, *Kyūshū Chūgoku gakkai hō* 九州中国学会報 15 (June 1969): 52–68. For learning Chinese in Edo Japan, see Rokkaku Tsunehiro 六角恒広, *Chūgokugo kyōikushi no kenkyū* 中国語教育史の研究 (Tokyo: Tōhō Shoten, 1988). Early textbooks on learning Chinese are reprinted in his *Edo jidai Tōwahen* 江戸時代唐話篇, 5 vols, published as supplementary volumes to his *Chūgokugo kyōhonrui shūsei* 中国語教本類集成 (Tokyo: Fuji shuppan, 1998).

22. See OBJ 114–115. Other Japanese monks who were fluent in Chinese include Saiun Dōtō (齊雲道棟, 1637–1713), Daichō Genkō (大潮元皓, 1678–1768), Musen Jozen (無染淨善, 1693–1764), and Tensan Reibyō (天產靈苗, 1676–1743).

23. See James Coleman, "Social Capital in the Creation of Human Capital," *American Journal of Sociology* 94 (1988): S95–S120. See also *Religion as Social Capital: Producing the Common Good*, ed. Corwin Smidt (Waco, TX: Baylor University Press, 2003).

24. For their biographies, see OBJ 55–56, 89–90, 289.

25. For his biography, see OBJ 13–14.

26. For his relationship with Yinyuan, see Hirakubo Akira 平久保章, *Ingen* 隱元 (Tokyo: Yoshikawa Kōbunkan, 1962), 124–125, and Narita Kōtarō 成田鋼太郎, ed., *Sakai Tadakatsu kō nenpu narabini genkōshō* 酒井忠勝公年譜並言行抄 (Tokyo: Tōkyōkyūgikai, 1911), 48–49.

27. Other daimyō and officials who became close to Yinyuan include Suetsugu Heizō III (末次平藏, 1654?–1669), Aoki Shigekane (青木重兼, 1606–1682), Kondō Sadamochi (近藤貞用, 1606–1696), Abe Nobumori (安部信盛, 1584–1673), Ogasawara Tadazane (小笠原忠真, 1596–1667), Seki Nagamasa (関長政, 1612–1689), Tachibana Akitora (立花鑑虎, 1645–1702), Tachibana Tadashige (立花忠茂, 1612–1675), Nagai Naomasa (永井尚政, 1587–1668), Nagai Naoyuki (永井尚徴, 1614–1673), Nabeshima Naozumi (鍋島直澄, 1615–1669), Nabeshima Naoyoshi (鍋島直能, 1622–1689), Nabeshima Katsushige (鍋島勝茂, 1580–1657), Niwa Mitsushige (丹羽光重, 1615–1689), Honda Tadaharu (本多忠晴, 1641–1715), Honda Tadahira (本多忠平, 1632–1695), Matsudaira Katsuyoshi (松平勝義, 1602–1670), Mōri Tsunahiro (毛利綱広, 1639–1689), Makino Naritsune (牧野成常, 1597–1669), etc.

28. In 1663 the emperor summoned Yinyuan's leading Japanese disciple Ryōkei Shōsen (龍溪性潛, 1602–1670), a former Myōshinji (妙心寺) abbot, to his residence and inquired about Yinyuan. In the fourth month of 1664, he summoned Ryōkei again, and through Ryōkei he received the bodhisattva ordination. In 1667, he received Ryōkei's dharma transmission, and formally became Yinyuan's sec-

ond-generation dharma heir and belonged to the thirty-fourth generation in the Linji (Rinzai) line. He frequently bestowed gifts on Yinyuan; upon Yinyuan's death, he granted him the honorific title *Daikōfushō kokushi* (大光普照國師). For details, see Lin Guanchao 林觀潮, "Ingen Ryūki to Nihon Kōshi: Tōzuihen o megutte" 隱元隆琦と日本皇室: 桃蕊編を巡つて. *Ōbaku bunka* 黃檗文華 123 (2002–3): 31–55.

29. Prince Shinkei was the twelfth son of Gomizunoo, and his full title was Ichijōin no miya Shinkeihō shinnō (一乘院宮真敬法親王). He was ordained in 1659. In the spring of 1672, he went to Manpukuji together with Prince Shōrenin no miya Sonchō hōshinnō (青蓮院宮尊澄法親王) to inquire about Yinyuan's teaching. He later received Gaoquan Xingdun's (the fifth Manpukuji abbot) dharma transmission in 1675. See OBJ 14–15. Princess Genyō's full title is Fumyōin no miya Shōzan Genyō hōnaishinnō (普明院宮照山元瑤法內親王). In 1664, she received Ryōkei's bodhisattva precepts and dharma name together with her father. In 1673 when Yinyuan was about to die, she managed to obtain the honorific title for Yinyuan from her father. She became formally ordained after her father died and was greatly respected in the Ōbaku community. See OBJ 576–577. Emperor Gomizunoo had several daughters who were devoted to Buddhism. See also Gina Cogan, *The Princess Nun: Bunchi, Buddhist Reform, and Gender in Early Edo Japan* (Cambridge, MA: Harvard University Asia Center, 2014).

30. Konoe Motohiro was the twentieth generation of the Konoe family, the secondary prime minister (Dainagon 大納言). He visited Yinyuan when Yinyuan stayed at Fumonji between 1655–1660. In 1660, the new temple site was chosen in Uji, a location belonging to his fief. The bakufu took back his land in Uji and exchanged it for another piece of land in Settsu to compensate him. Motohiro happily gave up his land to Yinyuan. Thus the Konoe family and Yinyuan's Manpukuji formed an even more special relationship. His son Konoe Iehiro continued to patronize Manpukuji. He was ordained as a monk in 1725 and took Gaoquan, the fifth abbot of Manpukuji, as his teacher. See OBJ 125–127.

31. The following account is based on Iioka, "Wei Zhiyan and the Subversion of the '*Sakoku*'" and "Literati Entrepreneur: Wei Zhiyan in the Tonkin-Nagasaki Silk Trade."

32. See relevant records in Cynthia Viallé and Leonard Blussé, *The Deshima Dagregisters, Volume XII (1650–1660)* (Leiden: Institute for the History of European Expansion, 2005), 61. Quoted by Iioka in her "Wei Zhiyan and the Subversion of the '*Sakoku*,'" 7.

33. Upon his arrival in Sōfukuji, Yinyuan had a late-night conversation with them, and Wei must have been among them. Yinyuan might have written a poem for him when he heard Wei, referred to as a Tonkin ship owner, arriving safely in 1672. See Yinyuan's poem for welcoming Wei's return to Nagasaki from Vietnam, IGZS 10: 4948

34. Certainly, patronizing monasteries was not the only strategy for Wei Zhiyan to achieve his goal. His other strategies included entertaining Japanese officials at his splendid residence. It should be noted that Wei was a musician

and kept a family band. The music scores used by the Wei family, titled *Wei shi yue pu* (魏氏樂譜), were compiled by Wei Hao (魏皓), known as Gi Shimei (魏子明, 1728–1774) and published in Kyoto in 1768. It is reprinted in *Xu xiu siku quan shu* (續修四庫全書), vol. 1096 (Shanghai: Shanghai guji chubanshe, 1995). For a translation of its preface, see Britten Dean, "Mr Gi's Music Book, an Annotated Translation of Gi Shimei's *Gi-shi gakufu*," *Monumenta Nipponca* 37, no. 3 (Autumn 1982): 317–32. See also William P. Malm, "Chinese Music in the Edo and Meiji Periods in Japan," *Asian Music* 6, no. 1/2 (1975): 147–72. An epitaph for Wei Zhiyan's elder son and his wife, discovered in Quanzhou in 2015, sheds new light on Wei Zhiyan's life and his family history in China, Vietnam, and Japan. For details, see Xue Yanqiao 薛彥喬 and Chen Yingyan 陳穎艷, "Wei Zhiyan shengping ji xiangguan shishi kao" 魏之琰生平及相關史事考. *Wenbo xuekan* 文博學刊 4 (2019): 80–87.

35. Pierre Bourdieu, "The Forms of Capital," in *Handbook for Theory and Research for the Sociology of Education*, ed. J. G. Richardson (New York: Greenwood, 1986), 241–58.

36. Marius B. Jansen, *China in the Tokugawa World* (Cambridge, MA: Harvard University Press, 1992), esp. 80–81.

37. For details about their calligraphic style, see Stephen Addiss, *Obaku: Zen Painting and Calligraphy* (Lawrence, Kansas: Helen Foresman Spencer Museum of Art, 1978).

38. For a study of the Obaku portrait painting, see Elizabeth Horton Sharf, "Obaku Zen Portrait Painting: A Revisionist Analysis" (PhD diss., University of Michigan, 1994).

39. Stephen Addiss, *The Art of Zen: Paintings and Calligraphy of Japanese Monks, 1600–1925* (New York: H. N. Abrams, 1989), 101 and his *Obaku: Zen Painting and Calligraphy*, 36–37.

40. For a brief discussion of Manpukuji architecture, see Sasaki Kōzō 佐佐木剛三, *Manpukuji* 萬福寺 (Tokyo: Chuo koron Bijutsu, 1964), 20–22.

41. For these failed attempts, see Wu, *Leaving for the Rising Sun*, chap. 7.

42. Yamawaki Teijirō 山脇悌二郎, *Nagasaki no Tōjin bōeki* 長崎の唐人貿易 (Tokyo: Yoshikawa Kōbunkan, 1964), 320. For a recent study of the Sino-Japanese junk trade, see Hao Peng, *Trade Relations between Qing China and Tokugawa Japan 1685–1859*, Studies in Economic History (New York: Springer, 2019).

Section II
The Japanese Zen Nexus

Chapter 4

The Transmission of the *Blue Cliff Record* to Medieval Japan

Textuality and Historicity in Relation to Mythology and Demythology

STEVEN HEINE

Overview of the Text and Its Myths

This chapter examines several interconnected text-historical issues involved in understanding the complicated process whereby the *Blue Cliff Record* (C. *Biyanlu*, J. *Hekinganroku*, 碧巖錄), the seminal Chan/Zen Buddhist collection of one hundred kōan (C. *gongan*, 公案) cases, was transmitted from Song-dynasty China to Kamakura-era Japan, where it quickly became a foundational work with an ongoing and profound impact on many elements of Zen theory and practice.[1] The text was first published in 1128 at Mount Jiashan temple (夾山寺, Jiashan si) in Hunan province by followers of its primary author, Yuanwu Keqin (圓悟克勤, 1063–1135, J. Engo Kokugon) of the Linji (臨濟, J. Rinzai) school. In lectures given during the summer retreats of 1111 and 1112, Yuanwu used prose and capping phrase expressions to comment creatively on the *One Hundred Odes* (頌古百則, C. *Baize songgu*, J. *Hyakusoku juko*), a compilation of cases originally selected and given verse remarks in 1036 by Xuedou Chongxian (圓悟克勤, 980–1052; J. Setchō Jūken) of the Yunmen (J. Unmon, 雲門) school. The intertwining of multiple layers of commentary with the source cases is considered extraordinarily creative and thought-provoking yet highly cryptic and confusing.

Long celebrated for an intricate use of articulate yet perplexing explanatory devices as the main masterpiece or "premier work of the Chan/Zen school" (禪門第一書, also 宗門第一書), the two-authored, multileveled discursive structure of the *Blue Cliff Record* represents a peak of Song Chan literary developments. Moreover, since this text arrived in Japan probably sometime in the early fourteenth century, the collection was continually studied and investigated through voluminous interpretations, annotations, and adaptations by numerous luminaries in both the Rinzai and Sōtō (C. Caodong, 曹洞) sects during all phases of medieval, early modern, and modern religious history. Yuanwu's lineage, especially the Songyuan (松源, 1139–1209, J. Sōgen) and Boan (破庵, 1136–1211, J. Hoan) subfactions, has dominated the Rinzai branches that contributed to the tradition of commentarial writings, but representatives of other Zen factions have also participated.

However, what happened to the text in the immediate aftermath of its initial appearance in China leading up to its favorable Japanese reception nearly two hundred years later is problematic and greatly contested. Despite the widely recognized importance of the work supported by vigorous hermeneutic discussions regarding its innovative rhetorical style used to express profound though enigmatic spiritual insights, the *Blue Cliff Record* has had a rather strange and difficult history so that our knowledge of exactly how, when, or by whom it was transferred and first appeared in Japan is shrouded in mystery and misunderstanding. For all the appreciation and acclaim the *Blue Cliff Record* has received because of its open-ended and flexible literary expression of ideas about Zen realization, the compilation has been perhaps the single most controversial and least comprehended work in the vast canon of Chan's classical era.

Confusion about the transmission of the text is mainly caused by the persistence of several prevalent legends or myths that are difficult to fully confirm or deny regarding the work's apparent destruction soon after publication and its reconstitution around 1300, in addition to the status of several different extant versions and their rather obscure appropriations in both countries. My aim is to offer some new materials and observations that help clarify and unravel, without losing a sense of the fundamental areas of uncertainty, two powerful legends that tend to mystify yet disclose the text's legacy: one concerns the apparent incineration in 1140 of the xylographs by Yuanwu's foremost disciple Dahui Zonggao (大慧宗杲, 1089–1163, J. Daie Sōkō); and the second involves the story of Dōgen (道元, 1200–1253) transporting in 1227 the *Blue Cliff Record* on his return to Japan from a four-year journey to China. Both legends have been called into question though by no means rejected by modern researchers; yet the need to try to reconcile a basic contradiction—how could Dōgen have carried the text home during an era when it was supposedly kept out of circulation?—has been impeded by various attempts at demythologization of the respective accounts that tend to accept their underlying ramifications while remaining indifferent to clarifying basic issues of historicity.

Wilhelm Gundert, the first scholar to translate the *Blue Cliff Record* into a Western language (German) beginning in the early 1960s, asserts in the introduction to the first of three (never completed) volumes that the collection arrived in Japan in 1326.[2] This suggestion is plausible enough to be used as a starting point for discussion since it stems from miscellaneous evidence in that, shortly after this date, inventive responses were being developed by leading Japanese masters such as Musō Soseki (夢窓疎石, 1275–1351), who designed temple gardens at Saihōji and Tenryūji based on several kōan cases, and Daitō (大燈, 1282–1337), who penned his own sets of capping phrases (C. *zhuoyu*, J. *jakugo*, 着語) on many cases. However, Gundert does not offer an explanation for his claim and, furthermore, does not seem to consider diverse aspects of the complexity of the overall historical situation or try to assess the meaning (or lack) of the two major myths.

The first legend indicates that the *Blue Cliff Record* was ostensibly torched about a decade after its publication by Dahui, who probably objected to its rhetorical flourishes considered emblematic of the literary or lettered Chan style (C. *wenzi Chan*, J. *moji Zen*, 文字禪) in favor of the shortcut or keyword approach he promoted known as kōan-investigation (C. *kanhua-chan*, J. *kanna-zen*, 看話禪), which represented the nonliterary standpoint (C. *wuzi Chan*, J. *muji Zen*, 無字禪). The tale of Dahui's destructive act, described in several para-texts (four prefaces and five postscripts) attached to the version included in the modern Taishō (大正) canon edition of the *Blue Cliff Record*, is usually supplemented by another account suggesting that, after lying dormant for over a century and a half, the text was rediscovered and reprinted around 1300 by layman Zhang Mingyuan (張明遠, n.d.). This act was probably carried out because of intense interest expressed by Japanese Zen monks who were part of a wave of Rinzai sect travelers to the mainland following the encouragement of the émigré monk, Yishan Yining (一山一寧, 1237–1317, J. Issan Ichinei), who came to Kamakura in 1299 and required that his disciples learn classical Chinese. Yishan's instructions helped stimulate attention to recovering the magnum opus of the pilgrims' lineal forebear, Yuanwu, whose other works were already being disseminated among Zen monks in Japan.

The matter of transmission is problematized by another prominent legend maintaining that the *Blue Cliff Record* was brought to Japan a century before by Dōgen, who supposedly copied the entire text in a single night with the aid of a mysterious folk deity before he left China in a version known as the "One Night *Blue Cliff*" (J. "Ichiya *Hekigan*," 一夜碧巌). Compounding questions about the authenticity of this version, which was held for centuries at Daijōji temple (大乗寺)[3] in the town of Kanazawa but not made available until D. T. Suzuki, a.k.a. Suzuki Daisetsu (鈴木大拙, 1870–1966) published an edition in 1937 with the approval of the temple, is the existence of yet another enigmatic document that is stored at Daitokuji temple in Kyoto known as "Floating Yuanwu" (J. "Nagare Engo," 流れ圜悟). The first half of a succession certificate given to Yuanwu's main Chinese disciple, Huqiu Shaolong (虎丘紹隆, 1077–1136, J. Kukyū Jōryū), the scroll was supposedly placed in a paulownia canister that enabled it to drift ashore on the coast of Satsuma (current Kagoshima prefecture). A national treasure highly valued by connoisseurs of Zen arts, this is the oldest extant document handwritten by a Chan master that is sometimes conflated with Dōgen's "One Night" script because, because it was a work authored by Yuanwu and was similarly transferred in an inexplicable way to Japan and long remained of uncertain origins before modern research confirmed its actual status.

A lesser-known tradition proposes that in late 1267 the *Blue Cliff Record* was brought back to Japan by the Japanese pilgrim Daiō (大應, 1235–1308), who studied at Jingshan temple in China under Xutang Zhiyu (虛堂智愚, 1185–1269, J. Kidō Chigu) from Yuanwu's Songyuan lineage and later became the teacher of Daitō. It is possible that Daiō, perhaps like Dōgen, returned with just Xuedou's *One Hundred Odes* collection, the core text. This is plausible since that text was included in the 1289 Five Mountains (J. Gozan, 五山) temples' edition of Chinese works along with several texts by Yuanwu other than the *Blue Cliff Record*, including the *Essentials of Mind* (C. *Xinyao*, J. *Shinyō*, 心要). Moreover, while the *Blue Cliff Record* apparently remained unavailable in China during the intervening years, we do find that the text is cited occasionally in the similarly structured gongan collection, the *Record of Serenity* (C. *Congronglu*, J. *Shōyōroku*, 從容録), produced in 1224 by Wansong Xingxiu (萬松行秀, 1166–1246, J. Banshō Gyōshū). Wansong propagated Chan while residing in Beijing, where he was supported by Yelu Chücai (耶律楚材, 1190–1244), the famous Khitan diplomat and advisor to Genghis Khan who viewed Zen as the true base of all forms of Buddhism in addition to Confucianism and Daoism.

These issues of textual history are discussed here in light of John McRae's "First Rule of Zen": "It's not true, and therefore it's more important," which refers in this instance to the relative productivity or counter-productivity of accepting some key elements of long-standing legends.[4] I do not seek simply to debunk the myths, yet I also do not wish to curtail investigations by endorsing a demythological approach proposing, for example, that even if Dahui did not burn the *Blue Cliff Record* he was vigorously opposed to its rhetoric or that Dōgen did not copy the text in one night but was nevertheless responsible for transporting it to Japan. These are examples of, to rewrite the typical expression, unjustifiably baptizing a baby once the bathwater is thrown out and thus, by accepting the so-called essential meaning of a discredited myth, unwittingly promoting an unresponsiveness to questions of historicity that need to be probed further—even if there is no satisfactory solution. Instead, my goal is to interpret the legends in a productive way based on recent evidential research to clarify what we do and do not know from different accounts and theories regarding the provenance and dissemination of the *Blue Cliff Record*. This approach allows for a novel way of appreciating (without deprecating) the text through drawing out implications at once revealed and obscured by the main legends.

Textual Structure and History

The *Blue Cliff Record* consists of an extraordinarily complex seven-part discursive structure featuring (2) cases selected and given (3) poetic comments by Xuedou, to which (4 and 6) capping phrases and (5 and 7) prose remarks were added by Yuanwu in addition to an (1) introduction (lost for twenty-one cases). The overall effect of this textual arrangement is to provide an evaluative approach (C. *pingchang*, J. *hyōshō*, 評唱), which literally means a "critical response (*ping/hyō*) by calling out or singing (*chang/shō*, 唱)" and thus evokes schools of music criticism that greatly influenced many aspects of Song Chan discourse. In this way, the gongan to be pondered are raised, praised, rephrased, and appraised from various literary and philosophical perspectives that are not fixed or static but seek to accommodate shifting perspectives.

The hermeneutic outlook of the *Blue Cliff Record*, in which contesting views are "continuously circling one another" (交馳) as part of an ongoing "reversal of conventional judgments" (翻案法), stands in contrast to the homiletic approach of many traditional Chan/Zen sermons (C. *tichang*, J. *teishō*, 提唱) that generally advocate a particular standpoint. The textual structure also differs from the more streamlined style of the equally influential collection from 1229, *Wumen's Barrier* (C. *Wumenguan*, J. *Mumonkan*, 無門關; also called the *Gateless Gate* or *Gateless Barrier*), which includes forty-eight cases, each with a four-line verse and a short prose comment. In numerous examples throughout the *Blue Cliff Record*, highly stylized remarks upend dramatically or otherwise challenge radically staid and stereotypical opinions via a Chan adept's symbolic ability to "overturn a trainee's meditation seat and chase the great assembly" (掀倒禪床. 喝散大眾),[5] or, more expansively, to "push backwards the flow of the great seas, topple Mount Sumeru, and scatter the white clouds" (掀翻大海.踢倒須彌. 喝散白雲).[6]

After entering Japan, the *Blue Cliff Record* collection became a major object of interest and study. Following the early appropriations by Dōgen, Daitō, and Musō, during the Muromachi era the text formed a crucial part of the kōan curriculum of various Zen lineages through an esoteric or secretive sequential process of study (*missan*, 密參) that included the sections, "Before *Blue Cliff*" (J. Hekizen, 碧前) and "After *Blue Cliff*" (J. Hekigo, 碧後), or two separate and variable lists of cases to be investigated prior to and following working through the main body of the *Hekiganroku*. In the Tokugawa era, the monumental figures Tenkei Denson (天桂傳尊, 1648–1735) of the Sōtō sect and Hakuin Ekaku (白隠慧鶴, 1686–1769) of the Rinzai sect both wrote major commentaries,[7] along with those of numerous other monk-scholars, and in post-Meiji Japan advanced modern scholarly discussions have been supplemented by the publication of various translations (J. *gendaigoyaku*, 現代語訳) and introductory works (*nyūmon*, 入門). In addition to much fanfare received by the *Blue Cliff Record*, there have been some prominent examples of critique or neglect, particularly by Bankei (盤珪, 1622–1693), who in advocating the philosophical notion of the "unborn" (J. *mushō*, 無生) argued that the rhetorical flourishes of the *Blue Cliff Record* were unnecessary, much like Dahui purportedly remarked.

There are many moving pieces involved in reconstructing the history of the *Blue Cliff Record*, the story of which stretches from Tang sources at Mount Jiashan temple that influenced Yuanwu, who atypically for a Song leader never resided at any of the main Chan temples in Zhejiang province, to quasi-historical accounts currently told by leaders at this monastery compound, which was revived recently after the devastation of the Cultural Revolution. The story of the text also encompasses medieval Japanese pilgrims, who usually traveled only as far as Ningbo and Hangzhou (not as far as Hunan), where they may have come across remnants of the manuscript, and contemporary critical editions produced in Chinese and Japanese. Table 4.1 provides a comprehensive timeline of

Table 4.1. Timeline for Textual Formation Related to the Question of Transmission to Japan of the Biyanlu(ji)/Hekganroku(shū)

1026/38	Xuedou's *One Hundred Odes* (*Baize songgu*) recorded
1102	Yuanwu's reflections and sermons on Xuedou at Zhaojue temple in Chengdu
1108	Comments on Xuedou by Muan in *Lexicon of the Ancestral Garden* (*Zuting shiyuan*)
1111–12	Yuanwu's main sermons delivered at Jiashan (1st manuscript)
1113–17	Additional delivery of sermons at Daolin temple (2nd manuscript)
1122	Notion of "Literary Chan" (*Wenzi Chan*) promoted by Juefan Huihong
1125	First preface composed at Jiashan
1127	Yuanwu exiled to southern China, along with Dahui
1128	Initial publication of the text at Jiashan
1130	Yuanwu retires to Zhaojue and delivers sermons again (3rd manuscript)
1135	Yuanwu dies after spending his last five years in Chengdu
1140	*Blue Cliff Record* woodblocks destroyed (apparently by Dahui)
1189	*Precious Lessons of the Chan Forest* (*Chanlin baoxuan*) attributes destruction to Dahui
1224	Wansong cites the *Blue Cliff Record* in *Record of Serenity* (*Congronlu*)
1227	Dōgen's "One Night *Blue Cliff*" ("Ichiya *Hekigan*") copied on his departure from China
1267	Daiō's return to Japan from studies under Xutang at Jingshan
1289	Japanese Five Mountains edition (Gozan-ban) publication of the *One Hundred Odes*, in addition to Yuanwu texts
1300–1317	Reconstitution of *Blue Cliff Record* with additional prefaces and postfaces
1326	Introduction of the text to Japan (according to Gundert, vol. I: 25)
1331	Daitō's capping phrase commentaries
1340s	Musō designs temple gardens at Saihōji and Tenryūji
1345	"One Night" version apparently moved from Eiheiji to Daijōji
1472	First Mention of "One Night" Version in *Kenzeiki*
1752	Copying of "One Night" attributed to Hakusan Gongen in Menzan's *Teiho Kenzeiki*
1803	Illustrated edition of *Teiho Kenzeiki zue* enhances Menzan's "One Night" legend
1937	D. T. Suzuki views and soon publishes the "One Night" version
1963	Itō Yuten publishes a comparison of the "One Night" and Taishō editions

some of the major developments that took place over the centuries and affect our knowledge of the text's background and legacy.

The early textual history of the *Blue Cliff Record* is difficult to determine because of abrupt reversals of fortune that leave in their wake a series of unanswered questions about its construction and destruction in addition to how and when it was transmitted to Japan. To what extent was Yuanwu himself involved in the editing and publication of the collection since this was apparently based at Mount Jiashan over fifteen years after his tenure there? Did Dahui commit the act of defiling his teacher's magnum opus, and if so, was it a radical deed or simply part of a long-standing discursive pattern in which Chan masters were sometimes said to burn sūtras, destroy their own notes, and refuse to allow disciples to record their sayings?

Also, to what do we attribute the recovery of the text around 1300, and how was that effort related to influences from Chinese Chan teachers traveling to Japan, often at the behest of political leaders including the Hōjō (北条) shogunate, in addition to Japanese priests making the reverse journey during the thirteenth century? Many of these topics tend to get distorted by sectarian enunciations reflecting rival standpoints concerning the value (or lack) of the *Blue Cliff Record*'s style of discourse, and whether Yuanwu's rhetoric is seen either as a kind of marker leading to or an obstruction delaying the supposedly inevitable development of Dahui's minimalist approach to Chan discourse.

Therefore, the question of how and when the *Blue Cliff Record* made its transition to Japan revolves around the issue of whether this took place either as early as the 1220s with Dōgen's enigmatic "One Night *Blue Cliff*," as argued by proponents of the validity of this version; in the 1260s through Daiō's return, as maintained by some members of his Ōtōkan (応灯関) lineage; or as late as the 1320s when the recovered Chinese text somehow found its way across the waters, as Gundert maintains. Perhaps all theories have some validity in representing different routes to the same end. As shown in Table 4.1, Xuedou's *One Hundred Odes* was circulating independently and was published in Japan as early as 1289. Could Japanese pilgrims such as Dōgen or Daiō have had knowledge (even if partial) of the larger gongan collection prior to the time of its reconstitution?

To consider the complications involved in understanding the *Blue Cliff Record*'s arrival in Japan, it must first be recognized that there were probably three somewhat different versions of the text since Yuanwu redelivered the original lectures at two other monasteries he administered after leaving Jiashan, including Daolin temple (道森寺) in southeastern Sichuan province beginning in 1113 and Zhaojue temple (昭覺寺) in his native town of Chengdu during the 1130s, after he had returned to take care of his ailing mother. Only the first two of three versions are extant—that is, (1) the original version included in the Taishō canon, and (2) the Daolin version that is considered by some modern scholars to correspond to Dōgen's "One Night" version—although neither one is exactly true to the source text that was lost for such a long time. As shown in Table 4.2, which speculates about the structure of the third or Zhaojue version that is listed first, there are numerous discrepancies between the available versions in terms of the sequencing of cases and the wording of some of Yuanwu's prose comments.

Rethinking the Dahui Incineration Legend

How much do we know about the Dahui legend and its significance? The myth is usually cast in terms of a stark contrast between literary and nonliterary approaches to Chan discourse, but is this justified by available sources? The earliest and apparently only extant Song-dynasty work that deals directly with the legend of the destruction of the collection is a passage contained in *Precious Lessons of the Chan Forest* (*Chanlin baoxuan*, J. *Zenrin hōkun*, 禪林寶訓) that was probably produced in the middle of the twelfth century, even though the full text was not published a couple of decades later in 1189. This work, which consists of a series of short excerpts from various teachers regarding the causes of disruption and need for reform in then-current Chan training, was initially compiled by Dahui and was amplified and edited by followers after his death. Although it contains expressions by and about numerous masters, including Wuzu Fayan (五祖法演, 1024–1104, J. Goso Hōen), the teacher of Yuanwu as his prime student—with both masters generally depicted in a favorable light—overall this is a work that reflects the agenda of Dahui's lineage.

The crucial passage forms part of the reflections of Xinwen Tanben (心聞曇賁, n.d.), a lesser-known Linji-Huanglong (臨濟-橫龍, J. Ōryū) lineage monk, about the supposedly regrettable condition of the Chan school at the time. Xinwen argues that an overreliance on literary studies made it evident the *Blue Cliff Record* warranted elimination. He begins by pointing out that while eleventh-century commentators like Fenyang Shanzhao (汾陽善昭, 947–1024, J. Funyō Zenshō) and Xuedou offered stirring verse

Table 4.2. Comparing the Structure of Three Versions of the *Blue Cliff Record*

BLUE CLIFF RECORD VERSIONS

Versions	Places and Dates of Sermons	Ordering of Contents*
Chengdu 成都** *Biyanji* 碧巖集 changed to *Biyanlu* 碧巖錄 =Taisho 48.2003, 10 vols.	Zhaojue Temple 昭覺寺 handwritten manuscript held in Chengdu, Sichuan, from 1130–1135	1. Introduction 垂示 2–3. Main Case with Capping Phrase 本則+着語 4. Case Prose Commentary 本則評唱 5–6. Verse with Capping Phrase 頌+着語 7. Prose Commentary on Verse 頌評唱
Fuben*** 福本	Linguan Temple 靈泉禪院 original version at Mt. Jiashan 夾山 in Hunan 1111–1113	Presumably the same as the common (Taishō) version
One-Night 一夜碧巖 aka *Bukko Hekigan Hakan Gekisetsu* 佛果碧巖破關擊節 2 vols.****	Daolin Temple 道林寺 Sichuan 1114–1118	A. Case Name 題名 1. Instruction 示眾 2–3. Main Case with Capping Phrase 本則+着語 5–6. Verse with Capping Phrase 頌+着語 4. Case Prose Commentary 本則評唱 7. Prose Commentary on Verse 頌評唱

*Each kōan is Raised (舉 Main Case), Praised (頌 Verse), and Appraised (評唱 Prose Evaluative Comments), but the sequence for this varies between the two main versions.
**Also known as the Gozan-ban edition that was the basis for Japanese Five Mountains temples commentary.
***From fifteenth-century commentary, supposedly of the original set of sermons and apparently used in Edo period *shōmono*-style commentaries in Japan that is not divergent from the Taishō edition
****Correspondence between Daolin version and One-Night version asserted by Itō Yūten 1963, 26–27 based on a manuscript long held at Daijōji Temple repository in Ishikawa Prefecture; generally, this is the same as the Taishō edition, but there is no preface, the cases each have a title, there is some minor variation in wording throughout, and the order of twenty-eight cases varies (see also https://www.pref.ishikawa.lg.jp/kyoiku/bunkazai/syoseki/2.html).

comments on *gongan* cases, it was their emphasis on writing skill as an end in itself that eventually led to a severe decline in genuine religiosity:

> During the Tianxi era [1017–1021], by using his talents of eloquence and erudition with splendid intent, Xuedou made innovations while seeking to create new expressions using skillful speech following the example of Fenyang, who [first created the genre of] odes to cases by the ancients. This gained the attention of students at the time, so the style of the Chan lineage from this point on was fundamentally altered to deleterious effect.

> 天禧間雪竇以辯博之才. 美意變弄求新琢巧. 繼汾陽為頌古. 籠絡當世學者. 宗風由此一變矣.[8]

Xinwen further claims that by Yuanwu's time there was no turning back on the part of the leading Chan teachers to try to restore the path of a wordless transmission that was persuasively conveyed in the initially unencumbered encounter dialogues involving Tang masters—that is, without the need for such elaborate explanations or interpretations:

> In the Xuan[he] era [1119–1125] Yuanwu discussed the meaning of [Xuedou's] passages in composing the *Blue Cliff Record*. At that time the greatest masters of the age like Ningdao [n.d.], Sixin [Wuxin, 1043–1114], Lingyuan [Weiqing, d. 1117], and Fojian [Huiqin, 1059–1117] did not try to challenge this approach. Students of our latter days still treasure [Yuanwu's] words. From dawn until dusk, they utter these sayings as if the highest form of learning, but without realizing how wrongful this is or recognizing the unfortunate situation in that it has caused their capacity for thinking clearly to greatly diminish.

> 逮宣政間. 圓悟又出己意離之為碧巖集. 彼時邁古淳全之士. 如寧道者死心靈源佛鑒諸老. 皆莫能迴其說. 於是新進後生珍重其語. 朝誦暮習謂之至學. 莫有悟其非者. 痛哉. 學者之心術壞矣.[9]

The passage concludes on a triumphal note concerning Dahui's supposedly heroic efforts, undertaken during the era of pervasive dharmic decline (*mofa*, J. *mappō*, 末法) when true teachings are understood poorly by people incapable of attaining higher spiritual aspirations, although Xinwen does not accompany or specifically link the destruction of the *Blue Cliff Record* to advocacy for the keyword method:

> At the beginning of the Shaoxing era [1131–1162], Fori (Dahui Zonggao) went to Fujian province and saw that Chan students were being misled. Day and night, he pondered the situation of these learners until finally he felt sure about taking the correct course of action. Fori then smashed the woodblocks and tore up the words [of the *Blue Cliff Record*] to eradicate delusion and rescue those who were floundering by getting rid of excessive rhetoric and exaggeration while destroying false teachings to reveal the truth. Once he did this, patch-robed monks gradually began to realize the error of their ways and no longer reverted to conceptual attachments. If not for Fori's farsightedness and compassionate drive to liberate all beings in the Age of Dharmic Decline, Chan communities today would surely find themselves in great peril.
>
> 紹興初. 佛日入閩見學者牽之不返. 日馳月騖浸漬成弊. 即碎其板闢其說. 以至袪迷援溺剔繁撥劇摧邪顯正. 特然而振之. 衲子稍知其非而不復慕. 然非佛日高明遠見乘悲願力救末法之弊. 則叢林大有可畏者矣.¹⁰

While the Xinwen passage attributes the loss of the *Blue Cliff Record* directly to Dahui from the standpoint of lavishly praising this deed as salvific for the Chan school, other selections from *Precious Lessons* further support indirectly the notion that gongan training had become excessively obtuse. One record indicates that Yuanwu had received a cryptic warning about this from his dharma brother Lingyuan (靈源, d. 1117), which was given an equally terse rebuttal emphasizing that holding to faith and uprightness inevitably overcomes inauthenticity:

> Lingyuan said to Yuanwu, "Even though a patch-robed monk has qualifications to see the Way, if he does not develop a depth of self-cultivation when he puts his ability to use it is certain to become crude and abrasive. Not only is it of no avail in instructing people to enter the gate of Buddha's teaching, but I am also afraid it will only lead to spiritual decline and

humiliation." Yuanwu replied, "The way of learning is kept in trustworthiness, and establishing trustworthiness depends on integrity. . . . The ancients said, 'One may lose clothing and food, but integrity and trustworthiness can never be lost.'"

靈源謂圓悟曰. 衲子雖有見道之資. 若不深蓄厚養. 發用必峻暴. 非特無補教門. 將恐有招禍辱. 圓悟禪師曰. 學道存乎信. 立信在乎誠. 存誠於中. 然後俾眾無惑. . . . 古人云. 衣食可去誠信不可失.[11]

Another example is a highly charged passage cited in the *Precious Lessons* by Wan'an Daoyan (卍庵道顏, 1094–1164, J. Ban'an Dōgan), one of Dahui's main disciples who generally cites Yuanwu in a positive fashion and in this instance does not name him. As part of a wide-ranging repudiation of pervasive false teachings and bad habits Wan'an remarks that masters from the period were no longer using dialogues for constructive discussion among peers. Instead, case interpretations had become a rationale for abbots to arbitrarily contest any rival or adversary who visited their temple. This was done without due cause since the main purpose was to trumpet one's own teaching technique, the basis of which was left hidden to avoid scrutiny since the rules of this game were invariably weighted in favor of the teacher. Therefore, legitimate doubts were not mitigated by this kind of gongan practice, as challengers to any adept were intimidated and forced into psychological submission during the exchange rather than empowered to gain insight and illumination.[12]

The other main early source that highlights some of the reasons for the incineration of the *Blue Cliff Record* by giving credit (or blame) to Dahui comes well over a century later in some of the para-texts. It is impossible to determine whether these passages merely echoed reports from the *Precious Lessons* or if, by then, there was additional information available but left unidentified to support the assertion that Dahui was responsible for the destruction.[13]

The Dahui legend may be looked at from the standpoint of demythologization in that, regardless of the question of uncertain historiography, it symbolizes an ideological conflict between two visions of Chan awakening. But does this reductionism really clarify things, or does it further conceal the relationship between master and disciple because it fails to recognize a likely middle ground? Such an attitude of compromise was expressed in a preface contributed in 1304 by Sanjiao Laoren (三教老人, n.d.), or Elder of the Three Teachings:

Yuanwu was mainly concerned for students of later generations, so he recited Xuedou's verses and commented on them. Dahui was eager to save people from burning or drowning, so he destroyed the *Blue Cliff Record*. Śākyamuni Buddha spoke the entire collection of sūtras but, in the end, he said that he had never spoken a single word. Was he trying to deceive us? Yuanwu's goal was like Śākyamuni preaching the scriptures and Dahui's goal was like Śākyamuni denying that he had ever spoken. . . . Whether you push or pull, the primary concern is that the cart moves ahead. . . . If you see a stream and identify it with the ocean or if you take a pointing finger to be the moon itself, not only will Dahui try to rescue you but Yuanwu will remove sticking points and loosen bonds. A poem written on a portrait by a man from ancient times says, "Mr. Zhang appearing on paper looks distinctly clear, yet if you call him as loud as you can he won't answer." Let those who wish to read [the *Blue Cliff Record*] first contemplate that saying.

圜悟顧子念孫之心多. 故重拈雪竇頌. 大慧救焚拯溺之心多.故立毀碧巖集. 釋氏說一大藏經. 末後乃謂. 不曾說一字. 豈欺我哉圜悟之心. 釋氏說經之心也. 大慧之心. 釋氏諱說之心也 . . . 推之輓之. 主於車行而已. . . . 若見水即海. 認指作月. 不特大慧憂之. 而圜悟又將為之去粘解縛矣. 昔人寫照之詩曰. 分明紙上張公子. 盡力高聲喚不膺. 欲觀此書. 先參此語.¹⁴

According to Sanjiao's short essay, which like the other para-texts embraces the implication that Dahui's putative act of destruction should not be disputed or dismissed even when the remarkable rhetorical quality of the collection is acknowledged, Yuanwu and Dahui were equally praiseworthy because they both functioned in accord with Buddhist traditions. Sanjiao concludes, however, by suggesting that whatever is read in this (or any other) Chan work, is not the same as the reality that it tries to depict. This analogy may be construed as a subtle putdown of the discourse used in the *Blue Cliff Record* while nevertheless supporting the inventiveness of Chan dialogues that deliberately problematize notions of truth.

Examples from the *Precious Lessons* and the para-texts are clear about their respective attitudes toward incineration, with Xinwen approving of this action by saying the text got what it deserved and with Sanjiao and others giving an impartial account supporting the merits of a crucial work that deserved to be reconstructed even if acknowledging that Dahui successfully addressed its demerits. As time went by, the hermeneutic situation became increasingly complicated and variable with commentators trying to carve out more nuanced positions. The reason for the disparity of later outlooks often involves contradictory factors of lineage and patronage that are somewhat external to the text yet invariably exert an influence on almost all subsequent appropriations of Yuanwu's work as well as controversies surrounding its impact.

One factor concerns the complex legacy of Yuanwu's pedagogical efforts when seen in terms of the sociohistorical background of the ongoing development of Chinese Chan discourse. Despite Dahui's notoriety as the most prominent follower of Yuanwu who undermined his erstwhile mentor, as the lineage of Yuanwu stemming from Wuzu unfolded during the late Southern Song and Yuan dynasties and greatly influenced the early period of Zen in Kamakura-period Japan, this school was dominated by adherents of Huqiu, the apparent recipient of "Floating Yuanwu." Huqiu's following, which three generations later divided into the Songyuan and Boan streams, eventually included the prominent gongan commentator Gaofeng Yuanmiao (高峰原妙, 1238–1295, J. Kōhō Gemmyō), the teacher of Zhongfeng Mingben (中峰明本, 1263–1333, J. Chūhō Myōhon) who had mixed views about the use of the keyword in relation to other styles of training. The ascendancy of this movement left Dahui's fellowship as a collateral line, rather than the main branch of the Linji school, and mitigated some of his influence in China and Japan although the keyword approach remained very important.

Members of the lineage via Huqiu, some of whom were reclusive and engaged in mountain austerities while others led large monasteries and interacted with the literati elite in an urban setting, generally were noncombative and sought to overcome instead of exacerbating intra- and intersectarian divergences in ideology and method. They tried to reconcile Buddhist Vinaya or precepts and regulations for monastic discipline with Chan irreverence and iconoclasm, as well as the Chan school's poetic discourse with the Pure Land school's *nianfo* (J. *nenbutsu*, 念佛) recitation.[15] In this context Linji stream followers of various stripes were eager to find ways of explaining that the approaches of Yuanwu and Dahui were complementary or, contrariwise, that both exhibited a comparable amount of rhetorical or practical deficiency. This attitude often led to linking the two thinkers in creative but sometimes artificial or superficial ways.

Related to that development was the enhanced role the Huqiu-based lineage played during the period of émigré monks, that is, Chinese teachers who traveled to Japan to help transmit and establish the Rinzai sect beginning with Lanqi Daolong (蘭溪道隆, 1213–1278, J. Rankei Dōryū) in 1246 as well as a series of Japanese monastics who traveled to China in the late thirteenth century to study at the major temples in Zhejiang province.[16] The émigré monks had a keen interest in establishing and maintaining in Japan a strong sense of sectarian identity and the integrity of their school.

In a trend that was at once consistent with and contrary to a focus on the compatibility of Yuanwu and Dahui as favored by the Huqiu-based heritage, the rise to dominance of the keyword method among practitioners in China and Japan in addition to Korea contributed to a retrospective reading of the *Blue Cliff Record* from the standpoint of asserting the priority of a minimalist interpretation of gongan cases. According to that approach, the collection was seen as important mainly in that it formed a part, whether intentionally or not, of a lengthy but essentially linear or teleological progression leading inevitably to the sparse style of discourse epitomized by examples of the keyword that claimed to fulfill Chan's special transmission not bound by words and letters.

Current scholarship greatly influenced by advocacy of the keyword method generally offers two main views of the relationship between Yuanwu and Dahui. One is what I call the "stepping-stone" thesis, which maintains that Yuanwu's approach was intentionally different yet underneath was unintentionally leaning in Dahui's direction. A complementary view is the "precursor status" thesis, which argues that Yuanwu did intend, whether consciously or not, to move toward a contraction or reduction of rhetoric and probably realized on some level the extent to which he remained trapped by his era's disposition toward lettered Chan. Therefore, from either standpoint, Dahui's method brought out the genuine significance of the work of Yuanwu, who would have been willing to acknowledge or even applaud his disciple's new approach.

Rethinking the Dōgen "One Night" Legend

The historicity of the account of what Dahui may or may not have done will likely remain undetermined but one way or another the text of the *Blue Cliff Record* was lost for a long time before being retrieved and partially reconstructed from available fragments by the combined efforts of lay and clerical supporters in the early fourteenth century. Would Dōgen have had access in the mid-1220s to a text that was otherwise unavailable in China for another seventy-five years? In fact, modern scholars have shown that Dōgen cites Yuanwu frequently but probably never directly from the *Blue Cliff Record*, and that the "One Night" legend very likely was not formed until a couple of hundred years after his death.¹⁷ Demythologization suggests that the significance of this folklore is to highlight that Dōgen's impressive use of commentarial techniques altering the wording and content of cases was greatly influenced by the interpretative style of the *Blue Cliff Record*. However, a failure to investigate fully the origins and implications of the "One Night" myth may be detrimental to understanding the rhetoric of both Xuedou and Yuanwu in relation to either Dahui or Dōgen.

Even if it is assumed that the notion of Dōgen copying the *Blue Cliff Record* in a single evening with the help of a deity usually associated with the sacred peak of Mount Hakusan (白山) located near Eiheiji temple (永平寺) is recast to symbolize his general knowledge of kōan compilations he gained in China, a couple of basic questions must be probed: How could Dōgen have acquired the source text during the 150-year period when, according to nearly all other indicators, it was lost or kept out of circulation? Also, why is it that Dōgen rarely if ever cites the *Blue Cliff Record* when he refers to dozens of other Song Chinese writings?

Dōgen's role in the process of transmission is crucial because he was the first Japanese Zen monk to collect and comment extensively on kōan literature based on a wide variety of sources he mastered. While it is certainly possible or even likely that he adopted the evaluative (*pingchang*) standpoint of the *Blue Cliff Record* without having seen or copied this text, Dōgen's direct link to the collection is supported by the modern discovery of an alternative version that he supposedly brought with him upon his return to Japan. Dōgen's putative rendition was supposedly kept at Eiheiji temple until a late thirteenth-century fire caused it to be moved to Daijōji, where it was mentioned in records dating to 1345 and held in secrecy for centuries thereafter.

This version was viewed and published by D. T. Suzuki, with the permission and encouragement of Daijōji's managers and further analyzed by several scholars including during the early years following Suzuki, Itō Yūten (伊藤猷典, n.d.) and Takeuchi Michiō (竹内道雄, 1922–2014), among others. This caused a sense of excitement yet uncertainty about the status of the work that led to new theories about whether it might represent an alternative version or was a fabrication. According to the Sōtō sect's account, after a period of a few decades during which the manuscript may have fallen into the hands of Rinzai monks, eventually it ended up at a Sōtō monastery associated with fourth patriarch Keizan Jōkin (瑩山紹瑾,

1268–1325) and his disciples located in Ishikawa prefecture north of Eiheji. Although for centuries this version was kept as a sectarian secret stored in the temple repository and not disclosed despite persistent rumors and queries, the text was finally examined in 1937 and published in 1942 by Suzuki under the title *Yuanwu's Keeping the Beat to Smash the Barriers at the Blue Cliff* (仏果碧厳破関撃節 *Bukka* [C. *Foguo*] *Hekigan hakan gekisetsu*). It is now a national treasure held at the Ishikawa prefectural museum in Kanazawa with a photo-facsimile also available at Komazawa University in Tokyo and additional later versions held elsewhere.[18]

In 1963 Itō produced an authoritative edition of the "One Night" version featuring a passage-by-passage comparison with the Taishō version.[19] He argues that the "One Night" version was a variation based on the Daolin temple edition that was essentially the same as the mainstream text but with some minor yet crucial structural as well as wording differences. Table 4.3 highlights differences in the structure of the two versions,

Table 4.3. Comparison of Structural Differences between the Taishō and One-Night Versions

Taishō Version	One-Night Version
Introduction	Introduction
	Yuanwu
Main Case	Main Case
	Xuedou
Case Capping Phrase*	Verse
Case Evaluative Remark**	
Xuedou	
Verse	
	Case Capping Phrase*
	Case Evaluative Remark**
Verse Capping Phrase*	Verse Capping Phrase*
Verse Evaluative Remark**	Verse Capping Remark**

*Notes embedded in text
**Reference materials and interpretation

with the "One Night" edition linking case to verse rather than separating them through the appearance of capping phrases and prose commentary placed in between these subsections. In addition, Table 4.4 shows that the "One Night" version's sequence of cases differs in twenty-eight instances

Table 4.4. The "One Night" Version Follows the Sequence of *One Hundred Odes*

Taishō and One Night *Blue Cliff Record* Case Differences

Case Name	Taishō Version	One Night Version
Getting Huangchao's Sword	66	68
Great Adept Fu Expounds a Scripture	67	69
What's Your Name?	68	70
Nanquan's Circle	69	71
Guishan Attends Baizhang	70	72
You Shut Up Too	71	73
Baizhang Questions Yunyan	72	74
The Permutations of Assertion and Denial	73	75
Jinniu's Rice Pail	74	76
Wujiu's Unjust Beating	75	80
Have You Eaten?	76	81
Yunmen's Cake	77	82
Sixteen Bodhisattvas Bathe	78	83
All Sounds	79	84
A Newborn Baby	80	85
Shooting the Elk of Elks	81	86
The Stable Body of Reality	82	66
The Ancient Buddhas and the Pillars	83	67
Vimalakirti's Door of Nonduality	84	87
A Tiger's Roar	85	88
The Kitchen Pantry and the Main Gate	86	89
Medicine and Disease Subdue Each Other	87	90
Three Invalids	88	91
The Hands and Eyes of Great Compassion	89	92
The Body of Wisdom	90	93
Yanguan's Rhinoceros	91	78
The Buddha Ascends the Seat	92	79
Daguang Does a Dance	**93**	77

as it follows the pattern of the original version of the *One Hundred Odes*, which varies from that of the *Blue Cliff Record*, thus giving a sense of authenticity to the alternative edition.

However, this documentation does not firmly establish a direct connection of the "One Night" version to Dōgen, whose own works may allude to the *Blue Cliff Record* in a small handful of occasions although he never mentions the title, even though his writings feature numerous citations with sometimes critical comments of other works by Xuedou and Yuanwu. On the other hand, a small piece of evidence that does appear to link Dōgen is that in a few instances he uses wording that is almost identical to the "One Night" version. One key example occurs in the "Sustained Practice" ("Gyōji") fascicle of the *Treasury of the True Dharma Eye* (正法眼藏, *Shōbōgenzō*). Here a lengthy passage of prose commentary discusses how Xuanzong (宣宗, 810–859) who succeeded his ruthless brother Wuzong (武宗, 814–846) as emperor, was persecuted for his spiritual prowess and interest in Buddhism when the jealous sibling was still in power. According to case 11 in the Taishō version, "Xuanzong was beaten almost to death, thrown out into the back gardens and drenched with filthy water to revive him." In a more fanciful "One Night" version that is consistent with the wording in "Sustained Practice," "Wuzong summoned Xuanzong and ordered that he immediately be put to death for having climbed up onto the throne of Wuzong's father in the past. His corpse was placed in a flower garden behind the palace and waste matter was poured over it, whereupon he came back to life."[20]

There are two main reasons to argue against linking Dōgen to the "One Night" version. The first reason is based on textual evidence or, rather, the lack of it. Dōgen produced two kōan collections during the mid-1230s, a period when he was still seeking to find his own distinctive rhetorical voice before the main comments on cases were composed for the *Treasury of the True Dharma Eye* and the *Extensive Record* (*Eihei kōroku*, 永平広録). The first text was the *Treasury of 300 Cases* (*Shōbōgenzō sanbyakusoku*, 正法眼蔵三百則) collection from 1235, a preparatory listing of kōan without any remarks; and the other was Dōgen's verse comments (C. *songgu*, J. *juko*, 頌古) in volume 9 of the *Eihei kōroku* from 1236, which includes one or two four-line poems for each of ninety kōan cases (for a total of 102 poems) in a style Dōgen abandoned after this initial project. Both texts seem to show a deep familiarity with many of the cases cited in the *Blue Cliff Record*, as do Dōgen's later writings, but he does not actually cite the Chinese collection.

According to Table 4.5, which is based on the research of Ishii Shūdō (石井修道, 1944–), Dōgen did not use the *Blue Cliff Record* as the source for a single one of the kōan cases cited in the *300 Cases*, and also probably did not reference the Chinese collection in the *Verse Comments* collection, even though he cites other works by Yuanwu and Xuedou over forty times in the *300 Cases*. There are thirty cases that are the same in the two collections.[21] In addition Dōgen refers to the writings of Yuanwu a couple of dozen times in *Treasury of the True Dharma-Eye* and *Extensive Record*, but in these instances he invariably mentions passages from the Yuanwu *Record* or *Essentials of Mind* rather than the *Blue Cliff Record*. The single main source for Dōgen's citations of cases, according to Ishii, is the *Essentials of Chan Collection* (C. *Zongmen tongyaoji*, J. *Shūmon tōyōshū*, 宗門統要集), an important compendium of sayings from 1093. Could it

Table 4.5. Dōgen's Lack of Direct Citations to the *Biyanlu* in the *300 Case* Collection Compared to Other Prominent Song Chan Sources

Sources in vols of 300 Cases	ONE	TWO	THREE	TOTAL
Biyanlu	0	0	0	0
Jingde Chuandeng lu	13	19	10	42
Dahui Yulu	9	0	2	11
Hongzhi Yulu	7	19	17	43
Huangbo Yulu	2	0	0	2
Tiansheng Guangdeng lu	1	1	1	3
Xuedou Songgu	1	1	1	3
Yuanwu Yulu	10	7	21	38
Zhengfayan zang	1	5	1	7
Zongmen Liandeng huiyao	4	3	0	7
Zongmen Tongyao ji	45	43	41	129
Uncertain	7	3	6	16
Totals	**100**	**101**	**100**	**301**

Adapted from Ishii Shūdō, *Chugoku Zenshū wa* (Kyoto: Zen bunka kenkyūsho, 1988), 572; additional texts he considered include the *Linji lu* and *Zhaozhou lu*. Note: (1) although the text is often called the *300 Case Collection* (*Shōbōgenzō sanbyakusoku*), the actual total number of cases varies depending on the manuscript; and (2) the *Zongmen tongyaoji ji* is usually dated sometime between 1093 and 1193 and was apparently well distributed at the time of Dōgen's visit to China, although it eventually got lost, according to Ishii, or was incorporated into the contents *Zongmen Liandeng huiyao* of 1183.

be that any apparent textual connections represent a coincidence since Dōgen drew from the same voluminous body of materials contained in transmission of the lamp collections, recorded sayings, and other miscellaneous Chan texts from the Song dynasty that also are reflected in the *Blue Cliff Record*?

The second argument against linkage is historical and involves a deconstruction of the fundamentally nonfactual basis for traditional sectarian claims that center around what is generally referred to as a "legend" (*densetsu*, 伝説) concocted from hagiographical materials crafted centuries after Dōgen's death.[22] It is said in sectarian biographies, mainly the *Record of Kenzei* (建撕記, *Kenzeiki*) from 1472 (with important manuscript variations and revisions until 1803), that Dōgen copied the collection in a single night. As shown in Table 4.6 the original version of the *Kenzeiki* does not mention divine assistance, but in later editions several mythical elements of the account began to be included. Dōgen received the help of a deity in copying, which took place just after he received medicine

Table 4.6. Evolution of *Kenzeiki* Expressions Regarding the "One Night" Version

Kenzeiki Version	"One Night" Deity
1472 *Kenzeiki*	No deity mentioned
1530 manuscript	Daigenshūri Bosatsu
1589 manuscript	Dojishin
1680 manuscript	Hakusan Myōri Gongen
1694 manuscript	Daigenshūri Bosatsu
1738 manuscript	Daigenshūri Bosatsu / Dojishin
1752 *Teiho Kenzeiki* by Menzan	Hakusan Gongen
1803 *Teiho Kenzeiki Zue*	Hakusan Gongen

Notes: (1) The 1680 manuscript gives a longer version of how the Hakusan deity was dispatched from Daijōji temple in Japan to aid Dōgen; (2) In all the early *Kenzeiki* manuscripts the anecdote about the *One Night Blue Cliff* appears a few sequences prior to Dōgen's departure from China (see Kawamura's 1975 edition, 26–27). But in the *Teiho Kenzeiki* (31–32) as well as the illustrated *Teiho Kenzeiki Zue* this is depicted as the last event in China that takes place just after the Inari deity visits Dōgen in China to provide some medicine and before the trip back to Japan during which One Leaf Kannon miraculously helps Dōgen through a storm at sea; neither episode is mentioned in previous versions of the text; (3) the 1589 manuscript known as the Zuichō-bon, considered by Kawamura to be the most reliable source, is the only one that does not identify the god with a famous deity.

from the Japanese folk deity Inari, who came to China to provide tonic for an ailment, and just before he embarked by boat on an arduous journey, during which he was assisted through a storm by the grace of bodhisattva Guanyin (J. Kannon, 觀音), the main deity of the island of Putuoshan (普陀山) located near the coast and past which almost all ships coming to and going from the port of Ningbo must have sailed.

The earliest mention of a deity assisting Dōgen in making a copy refers to Daigenshūri Bosatsu (C. Daquanxiuli Pusa, 大權修理菩薩), who was associated with waterways and travelers, especially at Ayuwang temple near the port of Ningbo, where seafaring monks and other travelers were transported between China and Japan. By the time of this reference the deity that originated in China had become established as a protector god at many Japanese Sōtō and Rinzai temples. One version of *Kenzeiki* refers simply to a local god or *dojishin* (C. tutishen, 土地神), which is a generic term for an autochthonous deity who inhabits and guards most Buddhist temples in East Asia, while another version links this divinity with Daigenshūri.

In the 1680 manuscript, a lengthier narrative changes the reference to the avatar Hakusan Myōri Gongen (白山妙理權現), the tutelary god of the sacred mountain in Echizen province near where Eiheiji was built that has long been used for retreats by monks from the temple. The 1752 version of the main sectarian biography, the *Annotated Record of Kenzei* (*Teiho Kenzeiki*, 訂補建撕記) by Menzan Zuihō (面山瑞方, 1683–1769), the leading Edo period Sōtō scholiast who added many hagiographical ingredients in his extensively annotated version of the text, refers to the divinity as Hakusan Gongen and specifies that he helped complete the last twenty cases. The *Illustrated Annotated Record of Kenzei* (*Teiho Kenzeiki zue* 訂補建撕記圖會) from 1803, featuring floating world-type drawings of scenes in Dōgen's life that gained wide popularity, reinforced Menzan's account with an image of the divinity assisting Dōgen. Some hagiographical materials go further by introducing into the legend the idea that Dōgen's mentor Rujing (如淨, 1163–1227, J. Nyojō) secretly disclosed the *Blue Cliff Record* after Dōgen's awakening experience in 1225 at an early stage of their interaction, while studying gongan literature together and maintaining that a miniature manifestation of Daigenshūri joined Dōgen in his boat to help protect the manuscript from watery threats.

In considering arguments for and against the notion that the "One Night *Blue Cliff*" is a legitimate version we must recognize that even if the text is a valid albeit unorthodox edition of the original Yuanwu publication (which no doubt has been altered over the centuries) this circumstance alone would not prove that it is attributable to Dōgen. A different theory supported in part by Itō's examination of textual history is that this version may have entered Japan in the early 1300s around the same time as the edition that is now included in the Taishō canon, and it became associated with the Sōtō sect at temples mainly to the north of Kyoto while Rinzai-based Five Mountains temples in the capital held the mainstream edition that was also used by Rinka (林下) temples located near the central area of the country.

Conclusion: Outlines of a Theory

Based on textual and field research that cannot help but rely to some extent on various legendary accounts, I offer the thesis that Yuanwu was probably not directly involved in the publication process as the literary production and distribution was handled locally by monks at Jiashan temple well over a decade after he taught there.[23] Moreover Yuanwu, who was never invited to become a leader of one of the prestigious Zhejiang-area temples, may have been considered controversial by imperial authorities and the *Blue Cliff Record* was thought of as subversive for opening with a case in which the emperor is snubbed by Bodhidharma and for including as case 3 Xuedou's comments that were banned by an eleventh-century ruler for seeming to give priority to the authority of Buddhas as spiritual rulers of society over and above regal leadership. Regardless of what Dahui may or may not have done to the *Blue Cliff Record*, circulation likely was quite limited from the beginning and then got cut off almost entirely by the mid-twelfth century due largely to suspicions about the political implications of its religious message, rather than concerns for its elaborate rhetoric.

Whatever may have happened next, the text did not disappear altogether after its destruction or elimination from circulation by the middle of the 1100s. Might Dōgen have been exposed to a surreptitiously kept copy of the collection that he brought home as a kind of contraband? We must take into account that all of the major temples he visited in Zhejiang province were by then under the sway of Yuanwu's lineage, which had been spread by his disciple Huqiu and followers. It is plausible to think that abbots located at these sites would have clandestinely kept copies of the *Blue Cliff Record* and had a strong urge to pass on this and related materials to Japanese pilgrims, so that Yuanwu's teachings could gain traction in a new land unfettered by native political restrictions. It is also interesting to note the Chinese émigré monks coming to Kamakura, especially Lanqi, founding abbot of Kenchōji (建長寺) in 1253, and Wuxue Zuyuan (無學祖元, 1226–1286, J. Mugaku Sogen), founder of Engakuji (円覚寺) thirty years later, had fled China to find solace in Japan. This was in contrast to Wansong and his disciple in Beijing who also composed gongan collections, Linquan Conglun (林泉從倫, n.d., J. Rinkan Shōlin), who succumbed at least in part because of their trepidation in the face of Mongols. Then, the *Blue Cliff Record* was recovered during the early decades of the Yuan dynasty when controversies surrounding the meaning of Xuedou's and Yuanwu's words would have been eclipsed by the impetus of followers of the latter's lineage to transmit their prestigious predecessor's work to Japan.

Demythologization maintains that the legend of the "One Night" version, stripped of references to divinities and other miracles, underlines the crucial role Dōgen played in introducing the burgeoning field of gongan/kōan commentary to his native country whether or not he saw, let alone copied and brought over, the *Blue Cliff Record*. As William Bodiford points out in *Sōtō Zen in Medieval Japan*, Dōgen used more than 580 kōan cases in his teachings.[24] In the *Treasury of the True Dharma-Eye* Dōgen elaborates on at least fifty-five cases that are quoted in their entirety, and in various passages he cites more than 280 dialogues. In the sermons included in the first eight volumes of the *Extensive Record*, ninety-nine kōans are quoted and over one hundred more are mentioned at least briefly in addition to the ninety cases cited in Dōgen's verse comments collection also included in the *Extensive Record*.

Dōgen was immersed in Song-dynasty Chan works, and his own writing cannot be understood without referencing this; yet he also realized that he needed to adapt these materials rapidly and effectively to capture and convey the rhetorical style of Yuanwu for an assembly of Japanese monks largely untrained in reading Chinese classics.[25] That explains why he generally does not use the verse or capping phrase styles from the *Blue Cliff Record*, although there are some prominent exceptions to this rule. From my perspective, the underlying point of demythologization is that Dōgen's expansive prose remarks on Chinese Chan sayings and other Buddhist scriptures feature the ironic, evaluative spirit of capping phrases, even if these were not produced in the strict sense of the *Blue Cliff Record* as in the case of Daitō. Dōgen is a master of the evaluative method in transmitting the legacy of the seminal gongan collection, if not necessarily the text itself or its discursive techniques.

To conclude with a few examples of how Dōgen adopted the evaluative approach of the *Blue Cliff Record*, let us consider some aspects of his interpretative treatment that at times praises and on other occasions criticizes Xuedou and Yuanwu. Xuedou is appreciated in several fascicles of the *Treasury of the True Dharma Eye*, especially "King of Saindhava" ("Ōsaku sendaba"), "Tangled Vines" ("Kattō"), and "Why Bodhidharma Came from the West" ("Soshi seiraii"). However, in a passage from the *Extensive Record* vol. 3.196, Dōgen takes Xuedou's view to task along with four other masters. He opens the sermon by relating the last part of the story, told more extensively in the "Reading Others' Minds" ("Tajinzū") fascicle, in which the National Teacher Nanyang Huizhong (南陽慧忠, 667–775, J. Nanyō Echū) is not visible on a third challenge presented to a Tripitaka Master, who claims to have witnessed Huizhong's activities the first two times he was asked.

Dōgen then cites various interpretations of why the Tripitaka Master failed the third time and finishes the series with Xuedou's ambiguous saying, "Nowhere to be found! Nowhere to be found!" (敗也敗也); this could refer either to Huizhong's ability to escape detection or to the master's inability to see what was right before his eyes. In characteristic evaluative style, or "but here is what I think (or would have said) . . ." fashion, Dōgen concludes,

> These five respected elders have not yet understood the story. If you ask me about it, that would not be the case. Suppose the National Teacher were present now and wished to examine the Tripitaka Master by asking, "Tell me, where is this old monk?" On behalf of the Tripitaka Master I would say, "This autumn morning the frost is cold. I humbly wish that the venerable teacher's health and activities will be filled with blessings."

> 遮五位老人, 未会遮一段因縁在. 若是永平即不然. 而今国師現在欲試驗三蔵, 国師向三蔵道汝道老僧即今在什麼処, 代三蔵道. 即辰季秋霜冷. 伏惟和尚法候動止万福.[26]

On the other hand, Dōgen greatly admires several sayings from Yuanwu's *Record*, including, "Life is the manifestation of total activity, and death is the manifestation of total activity" (生也全機現, 死也全機

現), which is cited in the "Total Activity" ("Zenki") and "Learning the Way through Body-Mind" ("Shinjingakudō") fascicles.[27] In "Summer Retreat" ("Ango") he praises a Yuanwu saying, and in "Arhat" ("Arakan") he eulogizes the authenticity of his monastic lifestyle. Also, in "Spring and Autumn" ("Shunjū") Dōgen appreciates a Yuanwu verse: "The bowl sets the pearl to rolling and the pearl rolls in the bowl. / The absolute within the relative, and the relative within the absolute. / The antelope holds onto a tree branch by its horns, thereby leaving no trace,/ While the hunting dogs circle the forest aimlessly and in vain" (盤走珠珠走盤.偏中正正中偏.羚羊掛角無蹤跡.獵犬遶林空跋踏).[28] Dōgen says, "The expression, 'The bowl sets the pearl to rolling,' is unprecedented and incomparable! It has rarely been heard in past or present. Hitherto people have spoken as if the pearl rolling around in the bowl were something unceasing" (いま盤走珠の道.これ光前絶後.古今罕聞なり.古來はただいはく.盤にはしる珠の住著なきがごとし).[29] However, Dōgen gets the last evaluative word by reversing the meaning of the final two lines, while following the logic of the opening lines, expressing Yuanwu's conventional evocation of a story about how an antelope can escape becoming prey. According to Dōgen, "The antelope is now using his horns to hang onto emptiness, and the forest is now circling the hunting dogs" (羚羊いまは空に掛角せり.林いま獵狗をめぐる).[30]

In conclusion, although it became so important in Japanese Zen, from the Chinese Chan standpoint the *Blue Cliff Record* was largely cast as a niche collection unique to its sociohistorical setting so that, since it can hardly be grasped outside of this original context, its overall significance was relatively short-lived. Retrospectively, the value the collection enjoyed in Japan was applied in a sometimes misleading fashion to the case of China. The collection was, in a sense, a victim of its own later success by standing squarely in the crossfire of profound and pervasive underlying countertendencies in that the same factors that generated a tremendous sense of approval of its literary qualities also resulted in its destruction or, at least, neglect. Therefore, the assertions of detractors could not help but affect the rehabilitative efforts of a long list of enthusiasts, who while praising the collection often acknowledge some element of justification in the claims of its opponents. Nevertheless, while the inspirational qualities of the text's rhetoric and philosophy prevailed on foreign shores to a far greater extent than in its home country, this does not vitiate the fact that the *Blue Cliff Record* was the product of the Northern Song dynasty's emphasis on utilizing poetry and evoking related literary qualities in the service of articulating Chan philosophy that existence must be understood in nondual and, therefore, paradoxical perspectives.

Notes

1. This text is included as T48.2003 in ten volumes, each with ten cases, plus four prefaces and five postscripts. See Thomas Cleary and John C. Cleary, trans., *The Blue Cliff Record*, 3 vols. (Boulder, CO: Shambhala, 1977). Also, some of the materials in this paper have been culled from my monograph, *Chan Rhetoric of Uncertainty in the Blue Cliff Record: Sharpening a Sword at the Dragon Gate* (New York: Oxford University Press, 2016).

2. Wilhelm Gundert trans., *Bi-Yän-Lu: Meister* Yüan-wu›s Niederschrift von der Smaragdenen Felswand, verfasst auf dem Djia-schan bei Li in Hunan zwischen 1111 und 1115 im Druck erschienen in Sïtschuan um 1300, 3 vols. (Munich: Karl Hauser, 1954, 1965, 1973) (includes sixty-eight cases in all with annotations), 1:25; see also Ueda Shizuteru "Wilhelm Gundert, 1880–1971," *Eastern Buddhist* 5, no. 1 (1972): 159–62.

3. Daijōji was an important Sōtō sect temple, but there was a period in the first half of the fourteenth century when it was in the hands of Rinzai monks, adding uncertainty to the question of when and how the text came to land there.

4. John R. McRae, *Seeing Through Zen: Encounter, Transformation, and Genealogy in Chinese Chan Buddhism* (Berkeley: University of California Press, 2003), xix.

5. T48.2003.148c20.

6. T48.2003.160a16–17.

7. Numerous other Edo period monks from both sects wrote their own commentaries on Xuedou's *One Hundred Odes*.

8. T48.2022.1036b19–20.

9. T48.2022.1036b20–22.

10. See T48.2022.1036b21-c3 for this and the above citations of the same passage.

11. T48.2022.1024c07–13.

12. See Thomas Cleary, "Introduction to the History of Zen Practice," in *The Gateless Gate: The Classic Book of Zen Koans*, ed. Yamada Kōun (Boston: Wisdom, 2004), 259–60.

13. The keyword technique Dahui advocates extracts a catchphrase from one of the gongan, such as "No! (無, C. *Wu*, J. *Mu*)," "Three pounds of flax," or "Cypress tree standing in the courtyard," as a shortcut for the practitioner to gain a sudden breakthrough to enlightenment without the need for the embellishments and flourishes of extended literary conceits.

14. T48.2003.139c22–25.

15. Jiang Wu, *Enlightenment in Dispute: The Reinvention of Chan Buddhism in Seventeenth-Century China* (New York: Oxford University Press, 2008), 85.

16. Jih-chang Lin, "A Critique and Discussion of the View That Shi Miyuan Proposed the Five-Mountain, Ten-Monastery System," *Journal of Cultural Interaction in East Asia* 5 (2014): 45–65.

17. Ishii Shūdō (石井修道), *Chūgoku Zenshūshi wa: Mana Shōbōgenzō ni manabu* 中国全集史話: 漢字正法眼蔵に学ぶ (Kyoto: Zen bunka kenkyūjo 1987), 572.

18. See https://www.pref.ishikawa.lg.jp/kyoiku/bunkazai/syoseki/2.html (accessed July 29, 2014).

19. Itō Yūten (伊藤猷典, n.d.), *Hekiganshū teihon,* 碧巌集定本 (Tokyo: Risōsha, 1963); this edition refers to the Dōgen's "One Night" version.

20. Takeuchi Michio (竹内道雄), "Dōgen Zenji *Hekiganroku* shōrai nitsuite," 道元禅師碧巌録招来について, *Indogaku Bukkyōgaku kenkyū* 4, no. 2 (1956): 476–79. See also Tsuchiya Taisuke, "'Ichiya *Hekigan*' " daisan soku yakuchū," 『一夜碧巌』第三則訳注, *Tōyō bunka kenkyūsho kiyō* 171 (2017): 27–56.

21. An exception may be case 31, which corresponds to case 299 in the *300 Cases* and may have been derived from the prose commentary on case 20 in the *Blue Cliff Record* but more likely stems from volume 13 of Yuanwu's *Record*; kōan common in both texts include twenty-seven cases in *Treasury of 300 Cases* (with 29 in Dōgen's verse comments): 26 (99), 46 (9), 52 (49), 81 (86), 95 (14/15), 105 (89), 108 (73), 127 (35), 136 (41), 141 (29), 158 (50), 159 (99), 182 (53), 186 (44), 202 (11), 203 (88), 205 (20), 214 (61), 225 (43), 245 (19), 249 (28), 252 (7), 284 (88), 286 (46), 289 (55), 295 (62), 298 (93).

22. The notion that the Daijōji version has authenticity related to the legend of the "One Night *Blue Cliff*," while disregarded or disputed by some, tends to find its way into many contemporary and otherwise reliable Japanese records of Dōgen's life as well as chronological lists of yearly activities that are appended to scholarly works (other legends also regularly appear); however, noted biographical researcher Nakaseko Shōdō does not deal with the topic, whereas biographer Takeuchi Michio explores in detail its complexity. It is interesting to note that Daitō was said to have memorized an entire, voluminous transmission of the lamp collection in a month.

23. Some of these reflections are based on my visit to the site Jiashan temple in June 2015, and on discussions with representatives there as well as a study of a series of illustrations regarding temple history (or, rather, hagiography) painted on the ceiling of an outdoor structure located near the Blue Cliff Spring.

24. See William Bodiford, *Sōtō Zen in Medieval Japan* (Honolulu: University of Hawai'i Press, 1993), 143–162; John Daido Loori, "Dogen and Koans," in *Sitting With Kōans: Essential writings on the practice of Zen koan introspection*, ed. John Daido Loori (Boston: Wisdom, 2006), 151–162; and Steven Heine, *Dōgen and the Kōan Tradition: A Tale of Two Shōbōgenzō Texts* (Albany: State University of New York Press, 1994).

25. Kagamishima Genryū (鏡島元隆), *Dōgen in'yō goroku no kenkyū*, 道元禅師の引用経典・語録の研究 (Tokyo: Sōtōshūgaku kenkyūsho, 1995).

26. Kawamura Kōdō (河村孝道), et al, eds., *Dōgen Zenji zenshū*, 道元禅師全集) 7 vols. (Tokyo: Shunjūsha, 1988–1993), vol. 3, 132–34.

27. T47.1997.793c6, where Yuanwu refers to this expression as a "gongan."

28. T47.1997.804a29–b1.

29. Kawamura, *Dōgen Zenji zenshū*, vol. 1, 412.

30. Kawamura, *Dōgen Zenji zenshū*, vol. 1, 413.

Chapter 5

Interpreters, Brush-Dialogue, and Poetry
Translingual Communication between Chan and Zen Monks

JASON PROTASS

Introduction

This chapter examines how people from China and Japan communicated with one another, with a focus on Chan and Zen monks during the thirteenth to fourteenth centuries. During this critical period in the shared history of Chan and Zen, hundreds of monks traversed the seas and left records of their encounters with one another. Below, I gather and analyze evidence under four subtopics: abilities to speak and understand spoken language; reliance on third-person bilingual interpreters; the creation and exchange of rhymed, tonally regulated Sinitic poetry between people who could and people who could not speak Chinese; and written vernacular conversations conducted in Sinitic script, or direct dialogue through writing that I call "brush-dialogue" (often rendered "brush talk") after the well-known phrase used across early modern East Asia (C. *bitan*, K. *pildam*, J. *hitsudan* 筆談), and which some medieval sources below more literally refer to as "using the brush to speak." With the exception of polyglottal individuals, Chinese and Japanese monks relied on one or another of these methods to communicate across languages, or "translingually." Chinese and Japanese people who shared writing systems seldom shared a spoken language, and we can more deeply enter the history of Chan and Zen intercultural dialogue once we understand how people communicated.

All later branches of Chinese Chan, Korean Sŏn, and Japanese Zen, even today, view Bodhidharma as the twenty-eighth Indian patriarch of their awakened lineage and the founding patriarch of East Asian traditions. According to Chan scriptures, Bodhidharma, with his awakened mind, recognized the moment his Chinese disciple Huike achieved liberation. Bodhidharma bore witness to the awakened mind of his heir. No words or objects conveyed this ineffable awakening. The teacher confirms the student's realization, but one sees one's Buddha-nature for oneself. Intergenerational recognition means that each accomplished student can trace their own awakened mind, recognized by their teacher, back through generations all the way to Śākyamuni Buddha. Given this religious self-understanding, linguistic communication has a paradoxical place in Chan and Zen. The awakened mind cannot be transmitted by relying on words and letters alone, and yet spoken and written language plays a fundamental role in pedagogy. For this reason, communication barriers sometimes presented practical obstacles to the master-to-disciple transmission of the ineffable awakened mind. Despite the obvious importance of translingual communication in the meeting between Chinese and Japanese monks, the relationship between Chan and Zen has often focused on some kind of pure transmission.

Reflecting on this religious history, some Japanese historians argued for stages of evolution within Japanese Zen, from "joint practice"—a mixing of Zen with Japanese religions—to mature "pure Zen."[1] Generally, this purification process is said to have begun with the "official" transmissions of Rinzai Zen by Eisai (榮西, 1141–1215; alt. Yōsai) and Sōtō Zen by Dōgen (道元, 1200–1253), and to have reached its final stage with the arrival to Kamakura of émigré masters from China, beginning with Lanxi Daolong (蘭溪道隆, 1213–1278; J. Rankei Dōryū), who supposedly established an uncompromising Song style of Chan. In recent decades, however, some Japanese and Western scholars have reconsidered the complexity of contact and reception between Chinese and Japanese Buddhist communities. The evidence recently recovered from the Ōsu Archive at Shinpukuji, Nagoya, has shown how monks in the circles of Eisai, Nōnin (能忍, twelfth century), and Enni Ben'en (円爾辯円, 1202–1280) resituated Chan from the continent within Japanese religious practice and thought, especially that of Japanese esotericism.[2] Enni Ben'en, for example, who traveled to Song China between 1235 and 1241, returned with a copy of the Song Chan rulebook *Rules of Purity for Chan Monasteries* (*Chanyuan qinggui* 禪苑清規, preface 1103), and at Tōfukuji, Kyoto, established Song-style monastic architecture, administration, and rituals. At the same time, however, Enni and some disciples continued to cultivate esoteric Buddhist practices (including transmission rites) and to compose expositions of Chan/Zen practice based on esoteric understandings of the body.[3] Though research is still ongoing, many are beginning to regard Japanese Zen from the perspective of intercultural contact; as the creative recontextualization of Chan within Japanese Buddhist thought and practice, or a fusion of horizons.[4] Moving forward, as scholars continue thinking about the horizons of Chan and Zen (and the relationship that inheres in between), our understanding will be enriched by understanding how translingual communication actually transpired.

Here is one of many cases that warrant further reflection. English language scholarship has known for several decades about language gaps and communication barriers between Chan and Zen monks, though this topic has seldom been treated in a sustained manner.[5] Martin Collcutt, building on work by Tamamura Takeji, noted that when Chinese master Wuxue Zuyuan (無學祖元, 1226–1286; J. Mugaku Sogen) met the powerful Japanese regent Hōjō Tokimune (北条時宗, 1251–1284), they relied upon an interpreter.[6] In this example, the body language of each man could be observed by the other readily enough, but significance still required an interpreter. According to our records, after some verbal back-and-forth through an interpreter, Hōjō Tokimune responded to one of Zuyuan's questions by raising a fist high in the air. Tokimune appears to have mimicked what he imagined a Chan master would do. His gestural response, however, was not a meaningful response to the moment of dialogue and revealed his misunderstanding. Zuyuan wished to give Tokimune a blow, a typical response by a Chan master to guide a student. However, Zuyuan could not assault Tokimune, the de facto ruler of Japan. Instead, Zuyuan "struck the interpreter once and said '[Tokimune] spoke in error'" (師打通事一下，云: 錯下名言).[7] Just as he relied on the interpreter to speak, Zuyuan likewise struck the interpreter to convey his teaching. Zuyuan's response indicates that the regent had failed to understand the ultimate truth that transcends speech and silence, movement and stillness. It is not recorded whether the regent gained any insights from witnessing Zuyuan's physical response. Any oral interpretation for the regent is also not recorded, and we can only wonder whether the interpreter provided Tokimune with an interpretation of Zuyuan's spoken words only, or if he interpreted the meaning of the blow itself. Either way, Zuyuan's striking his interpreter presents us a lovely metaphor for understanding how even shouts and blows (let alone spoken and written language) are not comprehensible beyond the available horizons of meaning. The interpreter here likely was the Zen monk Mukyū Tokusen (無及德詮, n.d.), who had studied in Song China and returned to Japan able to understand and speak Chinese.[8] (Not all interpreters were monks, as discussed later in this chapter.) Interpreters like Mukyū Tokusen played a critical role in explaining Chan to Japanese audiences. In addition to third-person interpreters like Tokusen, some situations in the shared history of Chan and Zen called for translingual writing (including brush-dialogue and poetry exchange) as a supposedly more direct form of communication. However, misunderstanding was still possible even with these forms of untranslated written communication.

Building on recent Japanese scholarship (especially that of Tachi Ryūshi and Enomoto Wataru), I wish to revisit the topic of communication among Chan and Zen monks. My goals are to construct a comprehensive and detailed understanding of the kinds of communication that were most common, as well as to introduce some previously unexamined examples related to poetry (focusing on composition and orality) and thereby consider their potential significance in the history of communication between Chan and Zen monks. Of course, the history of the communication between Chinese and Japanese people is a larger historical topic, one not limited to Chan and Zen monks. The first half of this essay reviews some of this broader context. Given my emphasis on monks, and because interpreters, brush-dialogue, and poetic exchange did not begin with Chan and Zen monks, precedents are drawn from the travelogues of Japanese Tendai monks. After this extensive review of contexts and precedents, the second half of this chapter proceeds to examples of communication between Chan and Zen monks from the thirteenth to the fourteenth century.

Contexts and Precedents

The period between the thirteenth and fourteenth centuries spans multiple political eras: China's latter Southern Song (1127–1279), Yuan (1279–1368), and early Ming (1368–1644), and Japan's Kamakura (1185–1333) and early Muromachi (1336–1573) eras. During this period, Chinese émigré monks traveled to Japan, some by invitation, others to escape deteriorating political conditions; and Japanese travelers went to China to engage in pilgrimage and formal study. Monks also facilitated commerce, engaged in diplomacy, and conveyed texts, objects, and ideas. As a result, new sacred architecture and patronage patterns took root on Japanese soil. Collcutt imagined how the built environments of Zen monastic institutions in the thirteenth century and early fourteenth century, "outposts of Chinese religion and culture," inculcated novel bodily dispositions, active soundscapes, and liturgical routines—new habits to be learned by observation and doing.[9]

Our archive for the hundreds of monks who crossed the seas is fragmentary. Enomoto Wataru recently compiled an inventory of the various detailed records that survive for 106 Chinese or Japanese Buddhist monks who sailed across the sea during the Southern Song and Yuan periods.[10] Many dozens more names are known from the early Ming, too.[11] Even the names of most travelers are, however, lost to us. Nonetheless, we know these monks frequently journeyed on privately owned merchant vessels. Monasteries also managed large amounts of capital, and occasionally Zen temples took stakes in ocean-going vessels to finance temple construction, such as the famous "Kenchōji ship" (建長寺船) that sailed out in 1325 and back the next year. In addition to generating revenue for the temple, this temple-financed ship transported the important émigré monk Qingzhuo Zhengcheng (清拙正澄, 1274–1339) to Japan together with several returning Zen pilgrims.[12]

In many regards, the thirteenth to fourteenth centuries were a lively period of international activity across East Asia. Texts and objects, as well as attendant material cultures, were also in movement in earlier periods. Moreover, the direction of intercultural exchange between Chinese states and their neighbors did not flow in only one direction.[13] The Tendai pilgrim Jōjin (成尋, 1011–1081), for example, brought hundreds of fascicles of texts with him to China, which he presented and lent to Chinese monks; he then purchased hundreds of fascicles to carry back to Japan.[14] Nontextual objects were also significant and could serve as a locus for literary embellishment. The Chinese scholar-official Ouyang Xiu famously composed "Song of the Japanese Sword,"[15] and Chinese tea wares were frequently eulogized in Japanese monks' verse.[16] Monks' poems did not focus exclusively on religious topics. Poetry was a prestige genre and a regular part of social interactions. Poetic competence was a fundamental skill for establishing social standing, and most Japanese monks aspired to master Sinitic verse.

Similarly, the imitation of Song dynasty temple architecture was a significant medium of cultural transmission.[17] The Chinese monastery as a mise-en-scène together with then current poetic practices was extended to Japan, and popular Chinese poetic topics were projected onto the Japanese landscape. Based on the common trope of "ten scenic spots" in Chinese poetry, Qingzhuo Zhengcheng created a Japanese poetic suite, "Ten Scenic Spots of Higashiyama" (J. *Higashiyama jūkyō* 東山十境); likewise, Mingji Chujun (明極楚俊, 1262–1336) wrote "Ten Scenic Spots of Kenchōji" (J. *Dai Kenchōji jūkyō* 題建長寺十境).[18] Similarly, the Japanese reception of the poetic suite "Eight Scenes of Xiao and Xiang" was mediated through Zen monks and proliferated new religio-literary landscapes.[19] Adaptations of Song and Yuan monastic and literary cultures reconfigured Japanese sacred spaces.

This period also marks the spread of an international print culture across East Asia. Among others, Song dynasty woodblock printed "recorded sayings" (C. *yulu*, J. *goroku* 語錄) texts were brought to Japan, where high-fidelity reproductions of *yulu* were issued and indigenous *goroku* were compiled. In some instances, new Zen texts circulated to China.[20] In addition to such orthodox Chan/Zen texts, mainstream Chinese poetry also circulated to Japan, whereupon Zen monks composed religious interpretations.[21] Chinese poems were given "Zen" glosses by Japanese readers—especially poems by Su Shi (蘇軾, 1037–1101) and Huang Tingjian (黃庭堅, 1045–1105)—yet another example of the fusion of horizons. Similarly, Southern Song anthologies of Chinese monks' poems appear to have received more attention in Japan than in China; *Collection of Wind and Moon [Poems] from Rivers and Lakes* (*Jianghu fengyue ji* 江湖風月集) continues to enjoy Japanese commentarial exposition up to today, whereas the text was all but lost in China.[22]

Print culture was important, and its significance can be overstated. Manuscript and print cultures cohabit readily. Manuscript cultures remained ubiquitous in East Asia into the modern period. Further, print culture was geographically uneven. Important Chinese centers of printing during the Song and Yuan were in a few cities, including Hangzhou; in Japan, print culture flourished in the city of Kyoto especially. Finally, the print culture of this period pales in comparison with the seventeenth-century explosion of printed materials, which included new book formats as well as greater varieties of texts, like vernacular Chinese novels.[23]

Commercial, social, and textual histories of the thirteenth to fourteenth centuries provide us context for understanding interpreters, brush-dialogue, and poetic exchange. These broader phenomena also predate the Chan and Zen monks. Precedents can be found in the travelogues of Japanese Tendai monks, which, in part, mitigate against our interpreting translingual communication as a unique Zen phenomenon. The following examples provide points of reference for the second half of this chapter.

A) EXCHANGE POEMS

We turn now to the historical background of cross-cultural and translingual written exchange with a focus on poetry. By "translingual" in the context of exchange poetry I am referring to communication through written Sinitic characters without translation per se; Chinese and Japanese people read the same Sinitic characters but from different language cultures.[24] The shared written system is sometimes referred to as the *scripta franca*, and the region of East Asia in which peoples could read and write in this shared logographic system the "Sinosphere."[25] Comparisons to Latin as a lingua franca shared by people with distinct vernacular languages make for imperfect analogies.[26] Nonetheless, one can readily discern a shared writing system and its entanglements with disparate spoken and written languages.

The exchange of Sinitic poetry was not unique to Buddhist monks. Sets of response poetry were customary in learned society. Murai Shōsuke and others have demonstrated that written Sinitic poetry was a diplomatic language across the East Asian maritime world. Especially without a mutually intelligible spoken language, as Murai artfully explains, "poetry and tea came as a set for mediating friendship."[27] Sinitic poems, known in Japanese as *kanshi* (漢詩), are the same form as standard regulated *shi* (詩) poetry of mainstream Chinese literature. Examples of envoy poetry survive from Japan, Korea, China, Ryūkyū, and Vietnam.[28] Though early examples come from the eighth century, most of the extant envoy poetry and brush-dialogue are from the fifteenth century onward.[29] By contrast, written exchange between monks are numerous and well documented in earlier periods.

Numerous non-Chinese monks traveled to Tang (618–907) China. The Japanese monk Ennin (圓仁, 794–864) in his travel diary records a poem written by another foreign monk Ch'ŏngso (貞素, n.d.) from Balhae Korea (渤海) to commemorate a fallen Japanese pilgrim.[30] At the end of Ennin's expedition, the Chinese monk Qibai (栖白, n.d.) composed the poem "Sending off Tripiṭaka Master Ennin as He Returns to His Country."[31] More examples of ninth-century Chinese poems written to send off Japanese pilgrims can be found in the translations of Edward Schafer.[32]

The first Japanese monk to travel to the Song was Tōdaiji monk Chōnen (奝然, 938–1016), who began his three-year mission in 983 as a personal religious quest to visit Mount Wutai.[33] In Song China, he was twice fêted by the emperor as a state guest, and the second time was gifted with the recently printed 5,048 fascicle Kaibao Buddhist canon plus recently translated texts. During this expedition, Chōnen exchanged written poetry with his hosts—some recorded in his travelogue.[34] Here again we see that the exchange of envoy poetry between Japanese and Chinese monks did not begin with Zen pilgrims. When the Chan and Zen monks of the thirteenth to fourteenth centuries wrote poetry to one another, they were renewing a longer tradition of written poetic exchange.

B) INTERPRETERS AND BRUSH-DIALOGUE: JŌJIN (1011–1081) AND HIS INTERPRETER CHEN YONG

If a Chinese monk and a Japanese monk did not share a mutually intelligible spoken language, they either would rely on an interpreter or engage in "brush-dialogue"—written communication via Sinitic characters. Ennin records at least nine times he engaged in brush-dialogue, which he describes, for example, as "with brushes spoke, and communicated our feelings."[35] To my knowledge, Ennin's diary is the earliest text that purports to record the contents of a face-to-face brush-dialogue between monks.[36]

These two modes of Sino-Japanese translingual communication, interpreters and brush-dialogue, predate the Chan and Zen monks of the thirteenth to fourteenth centuries and also continue today. Regarding Buddhist monks, after a brief lull, international movement suddenly increased in the seventeenth and early eighteenth centuries, and with it also greater translingual communication—including brush-dialogue conversations, acts of interpretation, and spoken Chinese in Japan. Recent studies on interpreters of this latter period offer a useful point of context.

For simplicity, I use "interpretation" to refer to acts across spoken languages and "translation" for acts across written languages (e.g., the translation of Buddhist texts into Chinese). Historically, professional interpreters resided in international port cities, such as Ningbo, China, and Hakata (modern Fukuoka) and Nagasaki, Japan. The history of interpreters in Japan is well documented from the seventeenth century onward, when there was a glut of printed materials.[37] Teams of Japanese interpreters of Chinese language included individuals that specialized in southern dialects, as indicated by a record from 1716 that documents a single team's able handling of Fuzhou 福州, Zhangzhou 漳州, and Nanjing 南京 dialects.[38] The diversity of Japanese dialects—both of region and social class—must be acknowledged, although it will not be of significance to my narrow argument here.[39] Rebekah Clements and Jiang Wu have documented cases in which émigré Chinese Ōbaku school monks relied on interpreters to communicate with their Japanese patrons.[40] The history of interpreters in East Asia before the seventeenth century is not as well documented, but a few examples can illustrate the central role of interpreters in communication between Chan and Zen monks.

Some Japanese Zen pilgrims who lived in China for many years learned spoken Chinese, such as Mukyū Tokusen discussed at the start of this chapter. Other Japanese pilgrims relied on interpreters. An example of the latter, Japanese Tendai pilgrim to Northern Song China, Jōjin (成尋, 1011–1081) in his travelogue *Record of Pilgrimage to Mount Tiantai and Wutai* (*San Tendai-Godaisan ki* 参天台五台山記) recorded numerous details about his Chinese interpreter, a merchant named Chen Yong (陳詠, eleventh century).[41] Jōjin noted his positive first impression of Chen "who had five times traversed the sea to Japan, and excelled in his knowledge of Japanese language" (五度渡日本人也, 善知日本語).[42] During these visits, Chen likely remained in Japan for some duration.[43] Jōjin recorded Chen's handling of official documents (e.g., travel permits), verbal discussions (arranging purchase of newly printed Tiantai texts), and occasionally serving as native informant to explain an unfamiliar Chinese custom. Chen stayed with Jōjin for the entire voyage to Mount Wutai and back. The relationship between Jōjin and his interpreter seems to have been amicable—Jōjin sometimes shared gifts with Chen.[44] Before the end of this expedition, Chen petitioned his government to permit him to ordain as a monk under Jōjin's tutelage.[45] Jōjin records details of the special ordination procedure (because Jōjin was a foreign teacher), that Chen adopted the dharma name Wuben 悟本, and that they then prepared to sail to Japan together.[46]

Although Jōjin relied on interpreters for verbal communication, throughout his journey he also "used his brush to speak." At one memorable encounter early on, he writes that "I had an intelligible discussion through writing with a merchant from Yuezhou [modern Shaoxing]. Later, on account of drunkenness, he and another merchant got into a fight."[47] This is an example of mundane brush-dialogue. Other conversations concerned doctrinal tenets and practice: Jōjin once had "questions and answers piled up, filling nearly two sheets of paper."[48] Jōjin notes how conversing in this manner required materials.

Somewhat unusually, Jōjin's written communications appear to have been almost entirely in prose. This was because Jōjin had sworn off poetry as an idle pursuit. Such vows of abstinence from poetry were not unheard of for monks in China, though not very common.⁴⁹ However, given that Jōjin could not speak in Chinese, his refusal to exchange poetry must have been striking. Jōjin still received numerous poems from Chinese monks, government officials, and other elites—as well as from fellow Japanese pilgrims he encountered. A total of thirty-six poems by twenty-three different people are recorded in the travelogue.⁵⁰ As was customary, these were mostly social poems written by hosts when Jōjin arrived at or departed from a station on his journey (only a few poetic encounters concerned Buddhist teachings). At least twice, when Jōjin was presented poems by Chinese monks, he had his interpreter explain that he, Jōjin, would refrain from writing a poem in response.⁵¹ It is difficult to know if Jōjin's poetic abstinence was perceived as piety or rudeness. We might also wonder if Jōjin was especially untalented at Sinitic poetry, and if this vow was a polite excuse to conceal an inadequacy.

Between Chan and Zen Monks

a) Matched Rhyme Poetry: Zen Monk Mushō Jōshō (1234–1306) in China, Émigré Monks in Japan

In contrast to Jōjin, most Japanese monks who traveled and studied in China, including the Zen pilgrims, participated in the Sinitic poetic culture. To illustrate the dynamics of poetic exchange between monks, I will focus on one among numerous examples, the pilgrim Mushō Jōshō (無象静照, 1234–1306) who traveled to China in 1252, studied with several famous Chan teachers, and returned to Japan in 1265.⁵² After returning to Japan, Mushō Jōshō served as the "head seat" for Zuyuan, and likely was an interpreter—indicative of his proficiency with spoken Chinese.⁵³ A few years before returning, in 1262 Mushō Jōshō climbed Mount Tiantai 天台山. He reached the famous stone bridge where he gave obeisance to the supramundane arhats thought to dwell there. A distinctive, naturally formed stone bridge in the Tiantai mountain range was the subject of intense literary and religious imagination as early as the fourth century CE, and the stone bridge was understood to link this ordinary world to realms of liberation. Veneration of arhats, disciples of the Buddha, expanded greatly in the Song.⁵⁴

Not unique, Mushō was one of many Japanese pilgrims who climbed the mountain to make an offering of tea.[55] After reaching the bridge, Mushō Jōshō rested and soon fell asleep. According to his prefatory note, "I was dreaming of traveling through numinous caves, but the experience was no different from being awake. I suddenly heard the peal of a frosty bell[56] and could not determine from where the sound had come—I stitched together these minor *gāthā* to commemorate this glorious event" (夢遊靈洞, 所歷與覺時無異. 忽聞霜鐘, 不知聲自何發, 因綴小偈以記勝事).[57] A vision was granted to him in a dream, a sure sign that his pilgrimage to Tiantai was a success. He composed two verses that he could later show to others.

In order to discuss the social significance of such verse, I will first illustrate the mechanics of poetry, then analyze each poem's contents. The sequence of tones in each line follows a set pattern. The proper sequence of each subsequent line is derived from the one before. Here, the tones for each word—using ● to mark a word with a "deflected" tone and ○ for a "rising" tone—follow the *Guangyun* (廣韻) rhyme dictionary of Song-era standard phonetics (compiled 1008).[58] The first of Mushō's two verses strictly adheres to standard tonal patterns and sequences.

Amid the crags expressly to offer infused tea, when	崎嶇得得為煎茶	○○●●●○○
Five hundred śrāvaka emerged from dusky clouds,	五百聲聞出晚霞	●●○○○●○
I bow thrice and rise, open my dreaming eyes,	三拜起來開夢眼	○●●○○●●
Then I know dharma after dharma are all sky blossoms.	方知法法總空花	○○●●●○○

The end rhymes above correctly follow a standard pattern (here with optional first-line rhyme) and each individual line internally adheres to a standard tonal sequence. Because Mushō Jōshō arranged these four regulated lines into a regulated sequence, the tones are balanced within each couplet (tones alternating in second, fourth, and sixth positions) and adhere between couplets (in the second, fourth, and sixth positions of lines two and three). Although additional aural considerations also influenced what was considered a mellifluous sonic texture, the correct patterns would generally prevent a jarring sequence of tones. Mushō Jōshō was a competent writer of Sinitic poetry. His Chinese monastic hosts would have noted this foreigner's ability to compose a proper verse.

138 | Jason Protass

Mushō's second poem is technically interesting. The clean execution of the first poem in the pair provided him license to engage in creative tonal violations in the second. Minor tonal violations occur in the latter half of lines two and four (indicated by a square □ or ■). Despite these minor violations within two lines, the overall pattern is still regulated.[59] Moreover, for a listener, the two phrases in lines two and four would stand out as variations from the expected tonal pattern. They also appear to be purposeful. The variations result in phrases that are grammatically parallel (adj. + noun + verb) and situate an echo at the conclusion each couplet (○●○). This artful echo suggests these violations were intentional, and either meant to draw attention to these phrases or to display a further competence.

Waterfall flying from twin brooks, thunderous rush,	瀑飛雙澗雷聲急 ●○○●○○●
Clouds gather in the thousand peaks, Golden Pavilion opens.[60]	雲斂千峰金殿開 ○●○○□●○
The teaching of the worthies is just this!	尊者家風只如是 ○●○○○●●
What was the point of misleading me across the Eastern Sea?	何須賺我東海來 ●○●●□■○

Turning to content, these poems written in the thirteenth century by Mushō join a venerable religio-literary tradition of depicting the environmental wonders—the stone bridge and waterfalls—of the Tiantai range as scenes of revelation. Mushō situates himself as a knowledgeable participant in the living history of the important cultic center. In the first verse, his fleeting vision of arhats in the clouded peaks leads to an insight—all phenomena in this world are like clouds that gather and disperse. "Sky blossoms" refers to seeing spots in one's vision when gazing at the sky, which one should not mistake for being really there. The vision of arhats emerging from mist, the experience of climbing the mountain, all pass like a dream—all are empty.

Mushō's second poem recapitulates his vision, adding a kind of Chan humor. The Buddhist truth revealed to him atop Tiantai is a universal truth, and therefore was equally present and accessible in Japan, too, and might have been revealed to him before he ever set off across the sea. Similar religious humor about a search for "nothing" can be found in Chinese monks' poems written at this time in the Jiangnan region.[61] Mushō's ability to create a poem that properly deployed this Chan humor demonstrated his fluency with the contemporary monastic literary culture. His poems were a performance of literary ability, as well as a demonstration of his thoroughgoing understanding of Buddhist doctrines.

Poems were public texts and would be freely shared with associates. Mushō Jōshō showed his poems to numerous Buddhist monks in China. In the three years before his departure home in 1265, a total of forty-one Chinese monks composed new poems directly in response to Mushō, who collected them on a single long scroll. The Chinese monks' poems also survive today, and all (except one) repeat Mushō's exact rhyme words. This poetic practice of replicating end rhymes from an interlocutor's poem was known as "matched rhyme poetry" 次韻詩. Each new poem responded to the meaning and story behind the original, and responded with either lavish praise, enlightened humor, or a further intellectual challenge. As Mushō traveled home, the scroll of linked poems served as proof that he had met and impressed these Chinese monks.

"Matched rhyme poetry" was the strictest of the three types of response poetry that echoed someone else's rhymes. These widely quoted comments by Liu Ban (劉攽, 1022–1088) give a concise, standard definition:[62]

> As for "extending and responding" in Tang poetry, there is: matched rhyme (the sequence of rhyme-words is unchanged); relying on the rhyme (within the same rhyme-family); and using the rhyme (using the other's rhyme-words, but not necessarily in matching sequence).

> 唐詩賡和有次韻 (先後無易), 有依韻 (同在一韻), 有用韻 (用彼韻不必次).

The earliest extant example of matching sequenced rhyme words, to my knowledge, is a response to Xiao Ziliang's first wife's poem scolding him; his new wife wrote a matched rhyme in his defense.[63] Writers in the Song regarded matching works by Yuan Zhen with Bai Juyi, and Pi Rixiu with Lu Guimeng, to be the model for their practice of matched rhyme poetry. Matched rhyme poetry became extraordinarily popular from the eleventh century onward—constituting roughly one out of every six poems by major poets like Su Shi, Su Zhe, and Huang Tingjian. This form of poetry served important social functions. For these mainstream poets, interlocking rhymes wove together their poems into a textual fabric that recorded relationships. Chinese monks also composed social poems with matching rhymes, often when traveling together, at social gatherings, or in epistolary poetry. These poetic practices were adopted by Japanese Zen monks. Extensive examples survive.[64]

Matched rhyme poetry was also an important vehicle for translingual communication, especially when talking was not possible. Perhaps the repetition of rhyming words felt like a firm handshake. For example, when Chinese émigré monk Dongling Yongyu (東陵永璵, 1285–1365; J. Tōryō/Tōrin Eiyo) came to Japan in 1351, he arrived in Hakata and stayed in Sōfukuji (崇福寺) for nearly three months while waiting for his further travel documents. Yongyu wrote a poem when he met Getsudō Sōki (月堂宗規, 1285–1361), former abbot of Sōfukuji, and then abbot of the newly built Myōrakuji (妙樂寺). Myōrakuji was located directly on the Okinohama port of Hakata, and the site of the Donpekirō (吞碧樓) tower that also served as a lighthouse—a potent metaphoric symbol, and topic of Yongyu's poem. Getsudō offered a friendly poetic response that matched Yongyu's rhyme, followed by eleven other monks. A fourteenth century record noted that poems by Chan monks covered the walls of Donpekirō—a beacon of light covered in poems of friendship.[65]

Japanese monks also adapted a related continental poetic practice, a distinctive form of matched-rhyme poetry that emerged during the Song dynasty: matching rhymes with the dead. The first significant poet to do so was Su Shi, in poems echoing Tao Yuanming (陶淵明, 365?–427).[66] Su, during a period of political exile, engaged Tao, an icon of hermeticism, as his poetic interlocutor. The practice of matching rhymes with the dead was soon adopted by Chan monks. A living master could place himself in direct dialogue with a Chan ancestor, borrowing the latter's charisma by literally echoing his words in new contexts. Poems set to the famous Ten Ox-Herding Pictures were well known for this poetic practice. One set of rhymes was brought to Japan by Yishan Yining (一山一寧, 1247–1317; J. Issan Ichinei), who composed a matching set of ten poems. In his preface he explained: "many worthies wrote verse and matched [rhymes], and now I, though a mere mountain monk not up to the task, append my doggerel after many worthies" (諸老頌者和者頗多，今山僧不揣續貂於諸老之後).[67] Yishan extended the rhyming sounds of Song and Yuan masters into Japan.[68] The practice of rhyming to the words of one's spiritual ancestors proliferated in Japan over centuries.

For example, Ryōkan Taigu (良寛大愚, 1758–1831) composed rhyming responses to his Sōtō Zen ancestor Gida Daichi (祇陀大智, 1290–1366).[69] This kind of poetic dialogue with one's own tradition was learned by imitating Song and Yuan Chan monks.

B) Rhymed Sinitic Poetry without Spoken Chinese in the Diary of Gidō Shūshin (1325–1388)

Although some Japanese Zen monks in the thirteenth to fourteenth centuries understood spoken Chinese, such as the aforementioned Mushō Jōshō, spoken Chinese was not a prerequisite for skillfully composing Sinitic poetry. Virtually all educated Zen monks wrote Chinese-style poetry, but, similar to other medieval Japanese writers of poetry, seldom spoke Chinese. The danger of false cognates—pronunciations that rhymed in medieval Japanese but not in medieval Chinese—was widely understood among the well educated, and so it was not insignificant when Japanese Zen monks wrote Sinitic poems using technically correct Chinese end rhymes. More impressive still, Japanese-authored poems generally adhered to the strict patterns of Chinese tones. The Japanese language is not tonal. For a Zen monk, facility with Chinese tones required effort. It seems that getting both the rhymes and tones right was one criterion for studying and correctly performing Chan/Zen.

Learned Japanese had more than one method for reading and performing a poem written in Sinitic characters. The method known as "reading by gloss" (*kundoku* 訓讀) began by the seventh century and played an important role in the spread of literacy.[70] Put simply, reading by *kundoku* substituted Japanese lexical equivalencies, rearranged the word order to match spoken Japanese, and added Japanese conjugation, particles, and other grammatical elements. This style of reading was closer to colloquial Japanese, nonetheless, excellence in oral *kundoku* performance required talent and training. The oral recitation of Sinitic poetry most often, it is assumed, took the form of "reading by voice" (*ondoku* 音讀), whereby the written characters were recited aloud using a pronunciation that approximated medieval Chinese and in the same order as written. Intoning in an *ondoku* manner could be accompanied by *kundoku*. By the tenth century, the oral performance of Sinitic poetry in the *kundoku* or "reading by gloss" style was widespread, and some sources make clear that a Sinitic poem was prized if it was amenable to both *ondoku* and *kundoku* style performances.[71] The ability to compose Sinitic poetry and perform it aloud in the *ondoku* manner that approximated Chinese pronunciation did not prepare a Japanese person for conversation in spoken Chinese.

Zen monks who traveled to China often gained some degree of fluency in spoken language. Some Zen monks also visited the Chinese sections of port cities to practice conversation—though this was of limited utility. An Edo-period manual for the study of Chinese language insisted that starting at the age of seven or eight was already too late for developing an ear for the colloquial language and that foreign languages education should begin at age two or three.[72] This Edo-era manual, though written some centuries later, provides a sense of the distance between spoken Japanese and spoken Chinese languages. Some Zen monks developed advanced Chinese language skills through years—sometimes decades—of study abroad and language immersion.

Zen monks who did not study abroad could memorize the rhyme category and tones of Sinitic words for the purposes of poetry, even if they could not produce or understand spoken Chinese. This seems to be the purpose of Kokan Shiren's (虎関師錬, 1278–1346) *Shūbun inryaku* (聚分韻略) rhyme dictionary completed in 1306—not the earliest poetic rhyme book in use in Japan but one based largely on the Song dynasty rhyme book. For Zen monks, just as for earlier courtiers, the ability to produce metered Sinitic poetry does not equate to command of the spoken Chinese language. Indeed, this was exactly the case for at least some of the monks in the community of the talented Zen master Gidō Shūshin (義堂周信, 1325–1388). Gidō was a lifelong student of Sinitic poetry and twice produced a personal selection of several thousand quatrains by Song and Yuan monks. His first compilation was lost in a fire, and he spent his remaining years reconstituting the lost collection, stopping work only weeks before his death. Gidō also kept robust diaries, from which his disciples compiled fragments under the title *Excerpts from Master Kūge's Daily Efforts* (*Kūge rōshi nichiyō kufū ryakushū* 空華老師日用工夫略集), from which the following events are drawn.[73]

As the end of the first year of the Eitoku regnal period (永徳, 1381–1384) drew to a close, Gidō busied himself with New Year's rituals and customs, which in the Zen temple included seated meditation. This event called for a poem. In his last diary entry for the year, Gidō records that after he talked about a famous Chan story (summarized below), he then presented a verse to the monk in the "head seat" (J. *shuso* 首座), who seems to have been frantically completing arrangements in the monk's hall. This poem illustrates Gidō's mastery of medieval Chinese tones—as found in the *Guangyun* rhyme dictionary.[74] The rhymes and patterns are technically excellent.

The samādhi of evenly sustaining[75] is our ordinary,	等持三昧是家常 ●○○●●○
As we sit up until midnight, why are you suddenly busy?	分歲何須特地忙 ○●○○●●○
If [Beichan] fried up a white ox, you surely wouldn't discern it.	烹箇白牛應不辨 ○●●○●●
At the deepest moment of the night, try a drop of citrus-peel tincture.[76]	夜深且點橘皮湯 ●○○●●○

This is a technically proficient poem, though it is not especially literary. In terms of diction, Gidō incorporates the name of his own temple and foreign-sounding Buddhist language in line one, then alludes to a Chan story in line three. These allusions display his Zen learning but not the classical learning or refined language of high Sinitic poetry. His end rhymes are correct (with first-line rhyme), and his arrangement adheres to tonal patterns. Gidō has composed a religiously meaningful verse in standard poetic form. Through his command of poetic technique, Gidō establishes himself as a member of the cultural elite and a worthy heir of Song-style Chan.

As for meaning, given the limits of space, I focus on Gidō's allusion to a classic Chan story in line three. This will also illumine his first couplet as a clever recapitulation of the story's pith. This story was especially appropriate for the end-of-year seasonal event. According to our texts, the Northern Song Chan master Beichan Zhixian (北禪智賢, eleventh century) met with his pupils on the last evening of the year, when they would feast and sit together into the night to welcome the new year (a custom known as *fensui* 分歲). Master Zhixian inverted the usual themes of this feast and turned it into a metaphor for the dharma. "Although the year is almost out, I have nothing to share with you to welcome the new year—I, an old monk, have fried up the white ox on the bare ground, cooked a simple local rice, boiled wild vegetable soup, and made fire from meager wood chips—everyone, gather around the hearth and sing local songs. Why are we doing this? I avoid depending on the gates of others and leaning against their walls—and as a result people call me a gentleman." (年窮臘盡，無可與大眾分歲。老僧烹一頭露地白牛，炊土田米飯，煮野菜羹，燒榾柮火。大眾圍爐，唱村田樂。何以如此？免見倚他門戶傍他墻，致使時人

喚作郎。)⁷⁷ This is a sermon about a life of material poverty and spiritual richness. Zhixian had nothing but humble food, and yet offered to his disciples a new year's feast consisting of religious sustenance. A Chinese Buddhist teacher would not cook meat—cooking an ox is an allusion. The images of the white ox and bare ground originate in the *Lotus Sūtra*, and were charged with philosophical meaning in a Tang-era commentary by Li Tongxuan (李通玄, 635–730; alt. 646–740)—the bare ground is the suchness of reality, and the white ox is the manifestation of wisdom and compassion, or the dharma.⁷⁸

Here, Zhixian has stated that his everyday fare—the ordinary vegetables and soup (that is, his instruction throughout the year)—have always been the revelation of ultimate reality (the metaphoric ox). In other words, the realm of awakening is not something special or separate from this present reality—and any ideas about awakening being special belong to deluded thinking. This is the meaning Gidō wished to convey to the "head seat" monk in the above poem's first lines. Although the last night of the year may seem special, one should sustain the same samādhi cultivated every day. Gidō selected this apposite story at the end of the year, sermonized about it, and then further explained its profound relevance to one of his disciples through a Sinitic poem. Several days later, on the third day of the new year, Gidō received guests, and the group composed a total of seventeen more verses with rhymes matching this poem. On that day, he also recognized the "head seat" as a dharma heir. Gidō rightly was celebrated for such religio-literary skillfulness.

Although Gidō composed the above verse with end rhyme and tonal prosody, he does not in his diary allude to his own speaking Chinese. It is unclear, at least to me, the extent of Gidō's comprehension of spoken Chinese—however, it is clear that he did not deliver his sermons in Chinese and that at least some monks in his Zen temple did not understand spoken Chinese. These facts are revealed to us from the subsequent diary entry on the fourth day of the new year. Gidō welcomed three of his disciples back from the Kenninji (建仁寺) Zen temple, where he sent them to listen to a sermon by the abbot Gesshin Kei'en (月心慶圓, fourteenth century). Gesshin Kei'en was a Japanese Zen monk who had traveled to Yuan China to study, where he became proficient in spoken Chinese. After he returned to Japan, he became abbot of several prominent Zen temples.⁷⁹ Gesshin delivered his sermon in the usual format, however, the three monks did not understand it. Gidō recorded this event in his diary.

Fourth day, in a light snow we chanted scriptures and then sat meditation, per usual. I took a bath, and afterward a driving snow arrived suddenly. Those who entered the bath-hall in the two evening sessions likely had cold water. My three students, Bonsei, Shūnan, and Chūshuku,[80] returned from Kenninji. I asked them, "The venerable head of that hall to mark the auspicious start of the year raised an ancient case to instruct the assembly, but you have not yet told me what he said." They replied, "That is because he preached the dharma in Chinese. We could not hear it, and could not retain it."

四日, 小雪、看經・定坐如例. 入浴, 夕後忌風雪, 是夜初後兩次入堂者, 怕浴寒也. 成・南・叔三子自建仁來. 余問, 堂頭和尚歳節示眾古則, 未審有甚麼言句. 答曰, 唐語說法故, 聽不得, 記不得.[81]

Gidō's students had not been able to follow Gesshin's sermon. Only days later, on the ninth day of the year, this same student Chūshuku (中叔) asked for instructions about a poem by Du Fu, and requested Gidō inscribe a poem. Within the space of a single week, Gidō had written a technically perfect Sinitic poem rich with allusions to Song Chan texts, and then three of his students attended a lecture delivered in Chinese and could not understand what was said. At this time, one of those students sought Gidō's explanation of a Tang poem. From this we know that a Zen monk's engagement with Sinitic poetry did not depend on (and is not proof of) the ability to speak Chinese.

It is remarkable that Gesshin, a Japanese monk, delivered Chinese-language sermons to a Japanese audience. Perhaps he and his patrons thought the Chinese language had more ritual efficacy; or perhaps it was a means to distinguish himself as a ritual specialist with rare abilities. Chinese émigré monks delivered their sermons in Chinese, too, addressed in section C.

Before turning to discuss émigré monks, I add here some brief notes regarding Dōgen and his Chinese language skills. Dōgen composed rhymed and tonally regulated Sinitic poetry, but as we have just seen, poetic competence is not sufficient evidence of the ability to speak or comprehend Chinese. According to some of his early biographers, Dōgen had a profound awakening in Song China when his Chinese master Rujing (如淨, 1162–1227) admonished a fellow meditator who had fallen asleep.[82] Dōgen heard Rujing say "slough off body and mind" (C. *shenxin tuoluo*; J.

shinjin datsuraku 身心脱落). Then, it is said, Dōgen sloughed off his body and mind—an event of great significance to Sōtō Zen traditions. However, the erudite Takasaki Jikidō in 1969 noted that the phrase Dōgen heard is not found in writings attributed to Rujing. Today, a search in our databases shows that this phrase Dōgen attributes to Rujing does not appear anywhere in the voluminous collections of Chinese Buddhist writing. At the same time, a suspiciously similar phrase, "the dust of the mind is sloughed off" (C. *xinchen tuoluo*; J. *shinjin datsuraku* 心塵脱落) does appear in the collected teachings of Rujing. These phrases are homophones in Japanese, and Takasaki suggested Dōgen misheard Rujing's "dust of mind" (*shinjin*) as "mind and body" (*shinjin*), which sound the same in modern Japanese.[83] Others countered that while the Japanese *shinjin* suggests these words are homophones, the modern Mandarin initial consonants of *chen* (塵) and *shen* (身) are not identical. Dōgen, of course, was not hearing Mandarin. Rujing, a native of Ningbo, was likely speaking the local dialect (which had been transformed by the southern exodus of Kaifeng residents), which were not identical to the artificially standard pronunciations of the Song-era rhyme tables. Nonetheless, for heuristic purposes, we can see that the reconstructed medieval Chinese pronunciations, *drin* (塵) and *syin* (身), are very close on the rhyme tables.[84] The difference is that one initial is voiced (*zhuo*, 濁), and the other initial is unvoiced (*qing*, 清). In two-word phrases like these, a voicing sandhi transformation may occur to the initial of the second word. In other words, Dōgen could have heard the second word *drin* (as voiced) and assumed that a voicing sandhi transformation had occurred from *syin* (as unvoiced). Nonetheless, if we take these historical pronunciations as a guide, they support the possibility that Dōgen misheard *xinchen* (心塵) as *xinshen* (心身), and sometime later the word order was transposed to the far more common *shenxin* (身心). Though this is possible, phonology will not settle the animated debates about Dōgen and his Chinese language skills. On the one hand, perhaps Dōgen's spoken Chinese was not quite fluent.[85] On the other hand, perhaps Dōgen heard Rujing correctly, and then in an act of profound religious insight thought of a near homophone—a creative act of intentional mishearing.[86]

c) Émigré Monks on the Ground in Japan

Many émigré monks did not learn spoken Japanese. The majority of Japanese monks did not understand Chinese. Recent Japanese scholarship, especially by Tachi Ryūshi, has brought to light the multilingual cultures of early Gozan Zen monasteries. I will introduce some illustrative examples of translingual communication between Chinese Chan monks and Japanese Zen students.

The Zen monastery of Kenchōji (建長寺) in the city of Kamakura became a bastion of Chan/Zen learning administered by Chinese monks. So much Chinese was spoken within the monastery precincts that the Japanese monk Mujū Ichien (無住一円, 1226–1312) wrote that the space of Kenchōji "was like China" (如唐國).[87] The first several émigré abbots negotiated Kenchōji's translingual culture differently.

Lanxi Daolong, the first Chan émigré monk, arrived at Hakata in 1246, was appointed the founding abbot of Kenchōji, under construction from 1249 until 1253, and resided in Japan until his death in 1279. Steffen Döll details Daolong's career in the next chapter. Here I emphasize that Daolong performed rituals and delivered sermons in spoken Chinese, though he was also able to speak Japanese. Another émigré monk, Wuxue Zuyuan, who became abbot of Kenchōji following Daolong's death, memorialized the late Daolong for his being "completely fluent in conversational Japanese" (打盡日本鄉談).[88] Daolong is thought to have given some face-to-face instruction in spoken Japanese.[89] Tachi Ryūshi speculates Daolong may have added Japanese explanations during his sermons delivered in Chinese.[90] (By contrast, Zuyuan once inscribed on a portrait of himself that "My head is short and face narrow, / with three points and five holes; although my belly is full of Buddha-dharma, / I cannot understand spoken Japanese language."[91]) Regardless, Daolong delivered formal sermons and sūtra recitations in Chinese.

Whereas Daolong learned to speak Japanese during his long stay, his successor Wu'an Puning (兀菴普寧, 1198–1276; J. Gotten Funei) was never able to communicate fluently in Japanese. Puning arrived at Hakata in 1260 and there served as abbot of Shōfukuji 聖福寺. In 1262, when Daolong was sent to Kyoto's Kenninji, Puning was summoned to head Kenchōji. After the Shogun died in 1263, Puning sought to retire. He returned home to Song China in 1265 where he served as an abbot again.[92] It seems Puning did not find satisfaction in expatriate religious life. His sermons suggest he was frustrated by language barriers. During one sermon at Kenchōji, first he intoned a verse in Chinese,[93] then said, "When spoken words are not understood, dialogue is even more challenging—for speaker and listener alike, challenge after challenge—so I can only rely on this plain wooden staff. Whether one is from the south or the north, all suffer [a blow from my] staff." (語音未辨, 酬酢猶艱, 説者聽者難復難, 只據一條白棒,

南來者北來者, 俱與痛棒.)⁹⁴ During another lecture, Puning referred to the possibility of body language to communicate. "Although my spoken words are not understood, our stillnesses and movements, comings and goings are silent conversations and are illuminated in our mind's eyes . . . so the mind of the speaker and the mind of listener know one another, their eyes illumine one another's." (雖語音未通, 凡動靜往來, 語默酬酢, 心眼相照 . . . 說者聽者, 心心相知, 眼眼相照.)⁹⁵ Puning acknowledged the things he could recognize by being present with others without resorting to talking. Recently commenting on related phenomena, Steven Heine noted that cases in which Chan teachers revealed a self-awareness of these challenges "could ironically enhance mutual understanding."⁹⁶ This observation may be true in some cases but perhaps not all situations.

Despite Puning resorting to body language, it appears that meaningful communication was often difficult. Another lecture ended with a question to the assembly of monks, and when no one responded, our texts note that "[Puning] used vernacular Japanese to remark, 'o-so-ro-shi.'" (操日本鄉談云, 和蘇嚕之.)⁹⁷ This final phrase was the Japanese word *osoroshii*, "how dreadful," here written out phonetically to show that Puning was able to add one word in Japanese. Presumably, no one present understood his Chinese sermon. In response, he dismissed the assembly in their native tongue.⁹⁸ Puning's own spoken Japanese apparently did not exceed single words like this. Most of the existing correspondence between Puning and others at Kenchōji appears to have taken place through writing and body language.

Another example of a language barrier shows how miscommunication could lead to creative interpretations. According to the mysterious Imai Fukuzan (今井福山, 1854–1945),⁹⁹ a manuscript from Zenkōji (禪興寺) preserved an utterance delivered by Wuxue Zuyuan in response to Hōjō Tokimune. It seems no one present understood what Zuyuan said, and so the sounds of his Chinese were transcribed phonetically (like the "o-so-ro-shi" above). By the nineteenth century, when this written record was viewed by Japanese readers, they thought it was a mysterious kōan (公案), a powerful phrase that could disrupt ordinary discursive thought. Only the rediscovery of a Zen text entitled *Manuscripts from Cold Pine* (*Kanshōkō* 寒松稿), collected writings by Ryūha Zenshu (龍派禪珠, 1549–1636), finally revealed the meaning of Zuyuan's utterance. It read: "Come in, come in! I have something to say to you."¹⁰⁰ This ordinary, mundane greeting through layers of misunderstanding became a site for Zen speculation.

Lest my examples focus only on miscommunication, here is one example that demonstrates multilingual dialogue could succeed. The Chinese émigré monk Zhuxian Fanxian (竺仙梵僊, 1292–1348; J. Jikusen Bonsen) with time was able to engage in spoken Japanese. The following dialogue, a question-and-answer following Zhuxian's sermon, was with Chintei Kaiju (椿庭海壽, 1318–1401). At first, Kaiju asks his question in Chinese, and Zhuxian answers in Chinese. Then, the two men switch to Japanese. The content of the exchange itself concerns the very question of language and is translated here in full.

> Kaiju again stepped out and said, "When Bodhidharma came from the west he could not communicate in spoken language, and yet he transmitted the dharma! I, a student, approach you. What will the master do?"
>
> The master [Zhuxian Fanxian] said, "So, have you already obtained the dharma or not?"
>
> At this point, Kaiju turned to his mother tongue and spoke in a vernacular Japanese, saying "What is the point of Bodhidharma's come from the West?"
>
> The master answered speaking in Japanese, "The cypress in the front of the garden!"
>
> The student continued, "That's the stuff of the ancients, what is your stuff like?"
>
> The master said, "If this is ancient stuff, then how is it coming out of my mouth?" Kaiju then prostrated. The master then said, "The large bell waits to be struck, its sound resonates with the boundless firmament.[101] The precious mirror suspended on high will reflect the ten thousand things that face it. If a Chan/Zen student asks me about Chan in a Chinese manner, I will answer with words in a Chinese manner. If a Chan/Zen student asks me about Zen in a Japanese manner, I will answer with words in a Japanese manner. This matter is now set aside. 'One hauls rock, a second moves earth.'[102] Ha! That

brash fellow [Xuedou] would also leave like this." The master stepped down from the high seat.

壽再出云:「達磨西來言語不通,已曾傳法.學人上來,和尚如何?」

師云:「汝還得法也未.」

是時壽却轉其舌音,作日本鄉談云:「如何是祖師西來意.」

師答亦操日本音云:「庭前柏樹子.」

進云:「此是古人底,如何是和尚底?」

師云:「既是古人底,因甚却在山僧口裏出?」壽乃禮拜.乃云:「洪鐘待扣聲應長空,寶鑑當軒影臨萬像. 禪客唐樣問禪,山僧唐樣答話.禪客日本樣問禪,山僧日本樣答話. 此事且置. 一拽石二搬土. 喝!孟八郎漢又恁麼去.」下座.[103]

In this example, both the Chinese master and his Japanese pupil exhibit bilingual abilities. After Zhuxian's death in 1348, Kaiju set out for Yuan China in 1350 and returned in 1372. He survived the destructive fall of the Yuan dynasty and was called to the new Ming imperial court in Nanjing on account of his excellent bilingual language skills.[104] The above dialogue occurred before his travel to China, however. Although Kaiju may have been an exceptional student, he is proof a Japanese monk could gain some proficiency in spoken Chinese inside the Japanese Zen temple run by an émigré teacher. This lends some credence to the statement by Mujū Ichien that Kenchōji "was like China" and was also an immersive learning environment.

In the examples above, sermons to Japanese audiences were delivered in the Chinese language. Even Gesshin Kei'en, a Japanese Zen monk who had studied in Yuan China, delivered his sermon in Chinese. However, as Wu'an Puning lamented, few people (or no one) in the audience understood what was being said; and the misbegotten transcription of Wuxue's simple statement "Come in!" led to profound miscommunication. We may wonder why sermons to Japanese audiences were delivered in Chinese. Chinese-language sermons may have been culturally desirable to elite Japanese patrons and students. For teachers, perhaps this was a way to be mysterious and generate curiosity in students and patrons. Alternatively, it is also likely that the ritual efficacy of a Chan/Zen sermon depended on the expression of the awakened teacher and not on the understanding of a student. One might compare this to Latin sermons. Closer cultural referents can be found in other Buddhist texts, like *dhāraṇī*. Even discursive content like sūtras were recited in Japan in a manner unlikely to be understood by a listener not already familiar with the text. Future research might show what meaning Japanese audiences attributed to incomprehensible Chinese sermons and whether this is another site for thinking about the fusion of horizons. However, mitigating against a purely functional analysis of Chan/Zen sermons, some records show self-awareness of these communication barriers. If Wu'an Puning was frustrated, it was because he desired his audience to understand. Zhuxian and Kaiju had a seemingly fluent bilingual exchange. Overall, one finds in the records of émigré monks both the ritual expression of awakening as well as a pedagogical attitude toward communication with students. Even clearer evidence of face-to-face pedagogy is found in records of brush-dialogue.

D) Brush-Dialogue: Yishan Yining

A few émigré monks could speak some Japanese. More often, however, émigré monks relied on bilingual interpreters or engaged in brush-dialogue with their Japanese pupils. Some (but certainly not all) of these written exchanges took poetic forms. Written conversations permitted direct communication without relying on an interpreter, but the limitations of this medium are also clear in the historical record.

Following Yishan Yining's appointment to Kenchōji, Zen monks throughout Japan sought to study with him. In 1299, Yishan decided to hold a contest for composing *gāthā* (J. *geju*, C. *jisong* 偈頌) to select the most talented students. I am unaware of any record of such a contest ever taking place in a Song or Yuan Chan monastery—the idea seems to come straight from the *Platform Sūtra*. I would speculate that Yishan creatively devised this contest out of necessity, given his own linguistic situation. Each verse would be short enough to allow Yishan to quickly ascertain the student's capacities for brush-dialogue. Those monks who could compose a Sinitic poem—with proper rhythms and allusions demonstrating their competence as readers and producers of Sinitic text—would be allowed to enter his monastery. This was a requirement because Yishan interacted with students through writing. Yishan at first had only forty or so Japanese students, but soon several hundred were living in his monastery.[105]

Among the initial contestants in 1299 was Musō Soseki (夢窓疎石, 1275–1351).[106] On the day of the contest, several dozen monks entered the abbot's quarters, each presenting a verse. Successful candidates were sorted into three categories, and only two were ranked in the highest category—one of whom was Musō.[107] Following his poetic success, Musō studied Chan texts under Yishan until 1303, when he grew frustrated that he had not progressed beyond book learning. Yishan offered terse comments to assist Musō, who could not grasp their purport. According to his biographers, Musō concluded that "because [Yishan and I] cannot communicate in spoken language I cannot inquire of him in detail (Master Yishan was from Taizhou)." (直是語言不通，故不能子細詳問. 一山乃台州人.)[108] Frustrated with this situation, Musō left Yishan and sought out the Japanese Zen teacher Kōhō Kennichi (高峰顯日, 1241–1316). Kennichi spoke in Japanese and offered Musō constructive interpretations of Yishan's comments. Musō at once had an insight, and a year later Musō reached a profound understanding approved by Kōhō Kennichi, whom Musō then regarded as his teacher. We might say that Musō's years of textual study under Yishan were necessary but insufficient: all preparation for spoken dialogue in his mother tongue with Kōhō Kennichi. Although communication between Musō and Yishan Yining was stymied despite brush-dialogue, by contrast, Kōhō Kennichi's brush-dialogue with his Chinese master is an example of successful communication.

E) BRUSH-DIALOGUE: WUXUE ZUYUAN AND KŌHŌ KENNICHI

In this final example, brush-dialogue culminated in the Chan teacher's recognition of his Zen student's understanding of the dharma. In 1281, the Chinese master Wuxue Zuyuan and his future heir Kōhō Kennichi used brush-dialogue to communicate. Three of the manuscripts from that very dialogue survive today. Kōhō Kennichi's disciple Tengan Ekō (天岸慧廣, 1273–1335) later collected and compiled an edited record of the encounter. Ekō's edited text was included in printed editions of Kōhō Kennichi's teachings, known as *Recorded Sayings of Zen Master Bukkoku* (*Bukkoku zenji goroku* 佛國禪師語録), including the early Gozan editions. Ekō's textual interpolations make it seem as though the Chan teacher and Zen student might have conversed orally with one another—such as adding the ambiguous verb "said" (both 云 and 曰). However, the extant manuscripts show that theirs was a written conversation, passing paper back and forth, lines of brushwork in two different hands. Scholars from

Interpreters, Brush-Dialogue, and Poetry | 153

both Zen studies as well as art history have noted the existence of these manuscripts and at times studied the three pieces together.[109] However, at least one scholar has treated the manuscripts as a secondary document, a record created after a spoken conversation.[110] This is a mistake. One of the manuscripts is reproduced here as figure 5.1.

In his brief review of the manuscripts, Kinugawa Kenji recently concluded that "one can see clearly that these two people are failing to communicate, though it is difficult to say why."[111] Indeed, reading the contents of figure 5.1 only, clearly the two men did not yet have a mutual understanding. Only when we read the more complete record preserved in Ekō's printed edition do we learn that this brush-dialogue culminated with Kōhō Kennichi earning recognition from Zuyuan as his spiritual heir. This manuscript was treasured because it was associated with Kennichi's achievement.[112]

The brush-dialogue between Wuxue Zuyuan and Kōhō Kennichi reminds us that mutual understanding is often arrived at by moving toward miscommunication. According to Ekō's text, a series of written conversa-

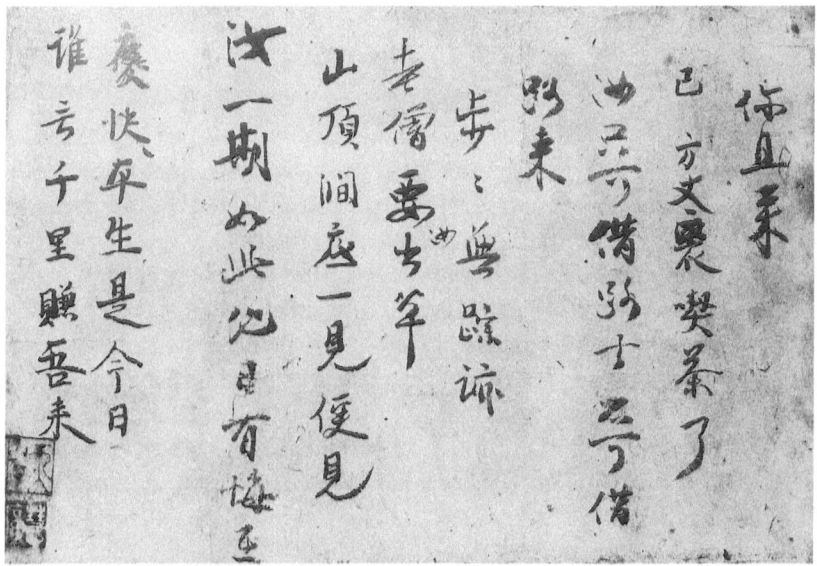

Figure 5.1. Brush-dialogue between Wuxue Zuyuan and Kōhō Kennichi, 1281, collection of Rokuonji. Source: *Kokuhō jūyō bunkazai taizen* 国宝・重要文化財大全, vol. 8 (Mainichi Shinbunsha, 1999).

tions occurred over several days. In the moments before the manuscript reproduced as figure 5.1 was created, Zuyuan invited his student Kennichi to explain the concept "guest and host." When Zuyuan rebuffed Kennichi's explanation, Kennichi grew frustrated and "left with a sweeping jerk of his sleeves." In response, Zuyuan shouted across the room, and Kennichi walked back. Figure 1 picks up at that moment, reading: "Come here you!" From this we glean that brush-dialogue was not a hushed affair. If Kennichi had stood up in a huff, Zuyuan needed to shout to get his attention and beckoned him with exaggerated body language. Only when Kennichi was close enough to see what Zuyuan wrote would he be able to read "Come here you!" Brush-dialogue was not necessarily silent conversation. Due to limits of space, a fuller analysis of the contents of this brush-dialogue must await future research. The example here is of a brush conversation in which Kennichi had an insight that was affirmed by Zuyuan. Zuyuan later wrote that to Kennichi "the way of the dharma has flowed, the true lineage has been extended" (流通法道，接續正宗).[113] This is a complex example in which a historically significant religious transmission between Chan master and Zen student was not only a meeting of minds but also a face-to-face encounter involving their physical presence and written words.

Conclusion

This examination of historical contact between Chan and Zen monks shows the critical roles played by interpreters, brush-dialogue, poetry, and body language. In addition to moments of success, communication barriers and linguistic challenges thwarted students and teachers alike. These numerous acts of communication may have been the necessary grounds for creative interpretations and the birth of Zen as a Japanese religion.

The history of interpreters, brush-dialogue, and poetry among Chan and Zen Monks raises many more questions about both Chan and Zen. For example, we might find instances in which our understanding of Song and Yuan Chan has been influenced by Japanese perspectives. I would underscore how Chinese Buddhist monks' attitudes toward poetry often differed from those of Japanese Buddhist monks. In general, in medieval Japan the way of poetry was not separate from the Buddhist path.[114] The monk Mujū Ichien in his *Shasekishū* calls poetry "a means to religious realization" and says Japanese poetry is itself *dhāraṇī*, or language with salvific power.[115] Even *waka*, short works of the indigenous Japanese poetic tradition seldom associated with Zen were in fact important to the dissemination of difficult continental concepts and incorporated into Zen rituals.[116] Such religious interpretations of poetry were normalized by earlier Tendai traditions, which predated Zen and shaped the distinct landscape within which medieval Zen monks read, thought, and practiced. It is possible that even when Chan and Zen monks met face-to-face, they were reading the same texts within different horizons.

Understanding and reflecting on the details of translingual communication will likely remain critical as we refine our understanding of the horizons of Chan and Zen. The examples in this chapter illustrate different kinds of linguistic abilities for both Chinese and Japanese monks. Some Japanese monks learned spoken Chinese: Mukyū Tokusen traveled to China and returned a competent interpreter; Gesshin Kei'en delivered sermons in Chinese; and an exceptional Japanese monk like Chintei Kaiju learned a significant amount of spoken Chinese from émigré teachers inside a Zen monastery without travel to China. Most Japanese monks, however, did not possess the ability to speak Chinese and yet became talented readers and producers of Sinitic texts, including the written vernacular of Chan sermons and dialogues. Kōhō Kennichi was knowledgeable of Chan texts, able to participate in brush-dialogue and, with effort, communicated meaningfully with his Chinese teacher Wuxue Zuyuan. Gidō Shūshin, a talented Zen monk, was a prolific reader and writer of rhymed and tonally regulated Sinitic poems—even though there is no evidence that he understood spoken Chinese. Similarly, Musō Soseki won a prestigious poetry-writing competition but could not talk directly with Yishan Yining. Medieval Japanese elites prized continental literature, and Sinitic poetry was the most prestigious genre. Chan records, too, enjoyed the allure of continental charisma for Japanese monks and patrons. Turning to Chinese emigrants, some Chan teachers learned spoken Japanese after arriving in Japan and engaged in banter and private instruction in Japanese. Other teachers relied on bilingual interpreters to provide explanation. At the same time, émigré teachers, including Lanxi Daolong, delivered Chinese-language sermons to Japanese audiences, even when few people understood what was said. This raises important questions about sermons as rituals and the Japanese patronage of continental practices. Despite barriers to translingual communication, and differences of understanding and practice, the histories of Chan and Zen are inextricably connected, and our understanding of both traditions is impoverished when we fail to study Chan and Zen together. Our thinking through the realities of translingual communication will allow us to refine our understanding of Chan, Zen, and the relationship that inheres in between.

Notes

My thanks to Kevin Buckelew, Chris Byrne, Steven Heine, Michaela Mross, and Morten Schlütter for their careful reading and discussion of this chapter during a meeting of our Chan Studies Workshop, and to the editors of this volume for including my piece here. I owe a debt of gratitude to Brian Steininger for catching several errors shortly before this chapter went to press and to Jeffrey Niedermaier for advising me on a particular section. My earlier interpretations of materials were refined thanks to feedback from erudite audiences at presentations I delivered to the Shinso Ito Center for Japanese Religions and Culture at University of Southern California, and the Buddhist Studies Forum at Harvard University.

1. Paraphrasing Carl Bielefeldt, "Filling the Zen Shū: notes on the *Jisshū yōdō ki*," *Cahiers d'Extrême-Asia* 7 (1993), 224–25. These terms are dealt with extensively by contributions in Steven Heine, ed., *Dōgen: Textual and Historical Studies* (Oxford: Oxford University Press, 2012).

2. See the explanatory appendices to materials reproduced in the series *Chūsei Zenseki Sōkan* 中世禪籍叢刊 (Kyoto: Rinsen shoten, 2013–2019). For an overview, see Sueki Fumihiko 末木文美士, "Shinpukuji Ōsu bunko shiryō ni miru Nihon Zen no keisei" 真福寺大須文庫資料に見る日本禪の形成, *Indogaku Bukkyōgaku kenkyū* 65, no. 2 (2017): 667–74; and Sueki Fumihiko, "Nihon ni okeru Rinzaishū no keisei—shin shiryō kara mita Zenshū to Darumashū" 日本における臨済宗の形成――新資料から見た禅宗と達磨宗, in *Rinzairoku kenkyū no genzai*「臨済録」研究の現在 (Kyoto: Zen Bunka Kenkyūjo, 2017), 409–28.

3. See especially the essays in *Chūsei Zenseki Sōkan, bekkan*.

4. For more on the significance of situating Zen among its contemporary Japanese intellectual history rather than as a pure extension of Chinese Chan, see Stephen Licha, "Separate Teaching and Separate Transmission: Kokan Shiren's Zen Polemics," *Japanese Journal of Religious Studies* 45, no. 1 (2018): 87–124; Molly Vallor, "*Waka* and Zen in Medieval Japan," *Religion Compass* 10/5 (2016): 101–117; and Molly Vallor, *Not Seeing Snow* (Leiden: Brill, 2019), 1–4.

5. For example, David Pollack, *The Fracture of Meaning* (Princeton, NJ: Princeton University Press, 1986), 122; and Kenneth Kraft, *Eloquent Zen* (Honolulu: University of Hawai'i Press, 1992), 52–53.

6. Martin Collcutt, *Five Mountains* (Cambridge, MA: Harvard University Press, 1981), 66 and 72.

7. "Explanation given to Venerable Kōfuku" (示光福長老), *Bukkō Kokushi goroku* 佛光國師語録 (T80.2549.234c). I have changed the punctuation from *Taishō*

Daizōkyō, and read this four-character phrase as the colloquial expression that appears often in Song Chan texts.

8. I follow Tachi Ryūshi 舘隆志, "Kamakura-ki no Zenrin ni okeru Chūgokugo to Nihongo" 鎌倉期の禅林における中国語と日本語, *Komazawa daigaku bukkyo gaku bu ronshu* 45 (2014), 269 and 283, no. 53. Mukyū Tokusen is named as an interpreter for Tokimune and Wuxue elsewhere in *Bukkō Kokushi goroku* (T80.2549.195b). For a stronger assertion, that Tokusen was Wuxue's regular interpreter until his death, see page 290 of Nishiyama Mika 西山美香 "Nihon gozan to Goetsu-koku, Hokusō, Nansō" 日本五山と呉越国・北宋・南宋, in *Higashi Ajia no naka no Kenchōji* 東アジアのなかの建長寺, ed. by Murai Shōsuke 村井章介 (Tokyo: Bensei Shuppan, 2014), 276–93.

9. Collcutt, *Five Mountains*, 172.

10. Enomoto Wataru 榎本渉, *Nansō Gen-dai Nitchū tokōsō denki shūsei* 南宋-元代日中渡航僧伝記集成 (Tokyo: Bensei shuppan, 2013).

11. An inventory of monks' names and texts corresponding to the Ming period are given in Yu Iji 俞慰慈 [Yu Weici], *Gozan bungaku no kenkyū* 五山文學の研究 (Tokyo: Kyūko shoin, 2004), 153–56.

12. Regarding "Kenchōji bune," see Nishio Kenryū 西尾賢隆, *Chūsei no Nitchū kōryū to Zenshū* 中世の日中交流と禅宗 (Tokyo: Yoshikawa Kōbunkan, 1999), 117; and Enomoto Wataru 榎本渉, "Kenchōji-bune no haken to sono seika" 建長寺船の派遣とその成果, in *Higashi Ajia no naka no Kenchōji*, 200–212. For additional temple-sponsored missions, including the "Tōfukuji bune" to rebuild that Zen temple after a fire in 1319, see Murai Shōsuke 村井章介, "Jishazō eiryō tōsen o minaosu" 寺社造営料唐船を見直す, in *Minatomachi to Kaiki sekai* 港町と海域世界, ed. by Murai Shōsuke (Tokyo: Aoki shoten, 2005), 128–29.

13. Consider the significance of the importation of doctrinal texts from Korea to China, described by Benjamin Brose, "Crossing Thousands of *Li* of Waves: The Return of China's Lost Tiantai Texts," *Journal of the International Association of Buddhist Studies* 29, no. 1 (2008), 21–62.

14. Lending and borrowing texts described on pages 389–90 of Robert Borgen, "Jōjin's Travels from Center to Center (with some periphery in between)," in *Heian Japan: Centers and Peripheries*, ed. Mikael S. Adolphson, Edward Kamens, and Stacie Matsumoto (Honolulu: University of Hawai'i Press, 2007), 384–414.

15. "Riben dao ge" 日本刀歌; Burton Watson's translation plus exposition by Yoshikawa Kōjirō, *An Introduction to Sung Poetry* (Cambridge, MA: Harvard University Press, 1967), 10–11.

16. On the international significance of Jiangnan paintings, tea wares, and other objects, see Ide Seinosuke 井出誠之輔, "Nihon no Sō-Gen butsuka" 日本の宋元仏画, *Nihon no bigaku* 418 (2001), 1–98; and the exhibition catalogue of Nara kokuritsu hakubutsukan 奈良國立博物館 (Nara National Museum), *Seichi Ninpō* 聖地寧波 (Nara: Nara kokuritsu hakabutsukan, 2009).

17. Nomura Shunichi 野村俊一, "*Kenchōji sashizu* to butsuden, hattō, shuryō" 『建長寺指図』と仏殿・法堂・衆寮, in *Higashi Ajia no naka no Kenchōji*, 329–45.

18. *Zengoshū* 禪居集, *Gozan bungaku zenshū* 五山文学全集, vol. 1, 462–63; the latter in *Minki Soshun ikō* 明極楚俊遺稿, *Gozan bungaku zenshū*, vol. 3, 2029–31. For a thorough documentation of the proliferation of topographic poetic suites across Kyoto Zen temples, see Cai Dunda 蔡敦達, "Nihon no Zen'in ni okeru Chūgokuteki yōso no sesshu: Jikkyō o chūshin to shite" 日本の禅院における中国的要素の摂取―十境を中心として, *Nihon kenkyū: Kokusai Nihon bunka kenkyū sentā kiyō* 23 (2001): 13–51.

19. On the Japanese reception and extensive adaptations of "eight scenic spots," see Asakura Hisashi 朝倉尚, *Zenrin no bungaku: Chūgoku bungaku juyō no yōsō* 禅林の文学: 中国文学受容の様相 (Osaka: Seibundō, 1985), 3–58.

20. On Gozan printing, see Kawase Kazuma, *Gozanban no kenkyū* (Tokyo: Nihon koshosekishō kyōkai, 1970). One example of a Zen text in China, known as *Kigen mondo* 機縁問答 and bearing colophons by Chinese masters, is preserved as the final section in a fourteenth-century edition of *Bukkoku roku* 佛國録 (Tochigi-ken, Nasu-gun, Kurobanemachi: Tōzan Unganji, 1965), discussed in more detail below.

21. Asakura Hisashi 朝倉尚, *Shōmono no sekai to Zenrin no bungaku* 抄物の世界と禅林の文学 (Osaka: Seibundō, 1996), 373–92.

22. Numerous editions with commentary include the Edo period *Gōko fūgetsu shū ryakuchū shusha* 江湖風月集略註取捨 and *Gōko fūgetsu shū shō* 江湖風月集抄, and the modern translations by Katsuhiro Yoshizawa, *Gōko fūgetsu shū yakuchū* 江湖風月集訳注 (Kyoto: Zen bunka kenkyūjo, 2003; rpt. 2012).

23. The Edo period Japanese reception of the vernacular story of *Shuihuzhuan* (水滸傳) and its importance for the development of a poetic ear are discussed in Ishizaki Matazō 石崎又造, *Kinsei Nihon ni okeru Shina zokugo bungakushi* 近世日本に於ける支那俗語文學史 (Tokyo: Kōbundō Shobō, 1940; 1967 rpt.), 170–74.

24. A useful review from the perspective of translation studies, Wiebke Denecke, "Worlds Without Translation: Premodern East Asia and the Power of Character Scripts," in *A Companion to Translation Studies*, ed. Sandra Bermann and Catherine Porter (Malden, MA: Wiley-Blackwell, 2014), 204–16. Note that I do not use "translingual" in the same manner detailed by Lydia Liu, *Translingual Practice: Literature, National Culture, and Translated Modernity—China, 1900–1937* (Stanford, CA: Stanford University Press, 1995).

25. See for example, Joshua Fogel, *Articulating the Sinosphere* (Cambridge, MA: Harvard University Press, 2009); and more recent contributions in Nanxiu Qian, Richard J. Smith, and Bowei Zhang, eds., *Rethinking the Sinosphere: Poetics, Aesthetics, and Identity Formation* (Amherst, NY: Cambria, 2020).

26. Benjamin Elman, "Introduction," in *Rethinking East Asian Languages, Vernaculars, and Literacies, 1000–1919* (Leiden: Brill, 2014), 1–28; especially where building on work by Peter Kornicki.

27. Murai Shōsuke, "Poetry in Chinese as a Diplomatic Art in Premodern East Asia," in *Tools of Culture: Japan's Cultural, Intellectual, Medical, and Technological Contacts in East Asia, 1000–1500s* (Ann Arbor: Association of Asian Studies, 2009), 64. This comment about Japanese reception of a Korean envoy also applies well to Song and Yuan China.

28. Examples (excepting Vietnam) found in Murai Shosuke 村井章介, *Higashi Ajia ōkan: kanshi to gaikō* 東アジア往還:漢詩と外交 (Tokyo: Asahi Shinbunsha, 1995).

29. For early envoy poetry, see Wiebke Denecke, "Suffering Everlasting Sorrow in Chang'an's 'Everlasting Tranquility': The Poetics of Japanese Missions to the Tang Court," *East Asian Journal of Sinology* 14 (2020): 253–329. On written exchange from fifteenth to early twentieth centuries, see Wang Yong 王勇, ed., *Dongya de bitan yanjiu* 東亞的筆談研究 (Hangzhou: Zhejiang gongshang daxue chubanshe, 2015).

30. Fascicle 3 of *Nittō guhō junrei kōki* 入唐求法巡禮行記.

31. "Song Ennin Sanzang gui Riben" 送圓仁三藏歸本國, *Quan Tang shi* 全唐詩 (Beijing: Zhonghua shuju, 1960), 9277; *juan* 823.

32. Edward Schafer, "Fusang and Beyond: The Haunted Seas to Japan," *JAOS* 109, no. 3 (1989): 387–95.

33. For Chōnen's itinerary, see Wang Zhenping, "Chōnen's Pilgrimage to China, 983–986," *Asia Major* 7, no. 2 (1994): 63–97. On Chōnen's preparations and goals, see Murai Shōsuke, "Nitchū sōgo ninshiki no naka no Chōnen" 日中相互認識のなかの奝然, in *Nissō kōryūki no Tōdaiji* 日宋交流期の東大寺 (Nara: Todaiji, 2017), 15–16, 25.

34. Two pairs of matched rhyme poems, including the response by Chinese hosts, are preserved in *Nittō shokeden kō* 入唐諸家傳考, 517–518, in *Dainihon Bukkyō Zensho* 大日本佛教全書, vol. 116 (Tokyo: Dainihon Bukkyō Zensho Kankōkai, 1931).

35. I count nine events in fascicle 1 of *Nittō guhō junrei kōki*.

36. Earlier multilateral relations between Chinese, Japanese, and Korean emissaries took place through both interpreters and writing. A convenient table of the first millennium of multilateral East Asian diplomatic exchange can be found in Wang Zhenping, *Ambassadors from the Island of Immortals: China-Japan Relations in the Han-Tang Period* (Honolulu: University of Hawai'i Press, 2005), 229–32.

37. Okada Kesao 岡田袈裟男, *Edo igengo sesshoku: Rango, Tōwa to kindai Nihongo* 江戸異言語接触: 蘭語・唐話と近代日本語 (Tokyo: Kasama shoin, 2006).

38. Ishizaki, *Kinsei Nihon ni okeru Shina zokugo bungakushi*, 15–19.

39. Rebekah Clements, *A Cultural History of Translation in Early Modern Japan* (Cambridge: Cambridge University Press, 2015), 24–25.

40. Rebekah Clements, "Speaking in Tongues? Daimyo, Zen Monks, and Spoken Chinese in Japan, 1661–1711," *Journal of Asian Studies* 76, no. 3 (2017): 603–626. For references to brush-dialogue between Chinese Ōbaku monks and

Edo scholars and officials, see Jiang Wu, *Leaving for the Rising Sun* (Oxford: Oxford University Press, 2015), 183, 200, and 259–61.

41. Borgen, "Jōjin's Travels," provides an overview to the study of Jōjin.

42. STGK 1, 4/19. Given numerous editions of the diary *San Tendai-Godaisan ki* [STGK], I give the traditional fascicle number followed by the date of the entry (e.g., 3/27 refers to third month, twenty-seventh day); based on Wang Liping 王麗萍 ed., *Xinjiao Can Tiantai Wutaishan ji* 新校參天台五台山記 (Shanghai: Shanghai guji chubanshe, 2009).

43. Wang Liping 王麗萍, *Chengxun Can Tiantai Wutai shan ji yanju* 成尋參天台五台山記研究 (Shanghai: Shanghai renmin chubanshe, 2017), 63.

44. When Jōjin received two servings of broth, he gives the second serving to Chen; STGK 7, 3/27.

45. Jōjin's travelogue suggests Song government officials granted Chen permission with the condition he act as an envoy and return to Song China. With hard skepticism, Borgen, "Jōjin's Travels," 402–403, suspects Chen's "true motive" for ordination was "the Chinese government twisted his arm"—and argues Jōjin doubted his religious conviction. By contrast, Wang Liping, *Chengxun*, 75, argues Chen's initial personal motive was commercial activity—but he may have been affected by the pilgrimage with Jōjin. Regardless, it is clear diplomacy, commerce, and religion were intertwined.

46. STGK 8, 4/3, 4/4, and 6/12.

47. STGK 1, 4/8.

48. STGK 8, 4/1.

49. Jason Protass, *The Poetry Demon* (Honolulu: University of Hawai'i Press, 2021), 159–68.

50. Cai Yi 蔡毅, "Cong Riben Hanji kan *Quan Song shi* buyi—yi *Can Tiantai Wutaishan ji* wei lie" 從日本漢籍看《全宋詩》補遺–以《參天台五臺山記》為例, *Yuwai Hanji yanjiu congkan* 2 (2006): 243–62.

51. STGK 2, 6/8, Jōjin wrote that Tendai pilgrim Enchin (円珍, 814–91) regretted the volume of poetry he produced during his six-year journey through China. STGK 4, 10/26, Jōjin decries poetry as a "banquet game."

52. A critical annotated edition with historical introduction of *Mushō Shōkō yumeyū Tendai ge* 無象照公夢游天台偈 in Xu Hongxia 許紅霞, *Wu zhong zhenben Song ji* 五種珍本宋集 (Beijing: Beijing daxue chubanshe, 2013), 209–54.

53. Kokan Shiren (虎関師錬, 1278–1346) in fascicle 8 of *Genkō shakusho* (元亨釋書) records a dialogue between Zuyuan and Mushō Jōshō shortly before Zuyuan's death. See also Tamamura, *Gozan bungaku shinshū* 五山文學新集, vol. 6, 1120–24.

54. Information about the cult of the arhats and further citations can be found in Phillip E. Bloom, "Ghosts in the Mists: The Visual and the Visualized in Chinese Buddhist Art, ca. 1178," *Art Bulletin*, 98, no. 3 (2016): 297–320. On the special role of tea in arhat worship, see n13.

55. Bernard Faure, *Visions of Power* (Princeton, NJ: Princeton University Press, 1996), 91–92.

56. Nine uncanny bells ring with frosty peals in the Central Mountains of the *Shanhai jing* 山海經 (*Siku quanshu Wenyuange* edn.), *juan* 5, 150a.

57. The preface and poems as found in Xu, *Wu zhong zhenben Song ji*, 221.

58. Adapted from Stuart Sargent, *The Poetry of He Zhu (1052–1125)* (Leiden: Brill, 2007), 9–10, who based his system of denotation on the work of Qi Gong 啟功, *Shi wen shenglü lungao* 詩文聲律論稿 (Beijing: Zhonghua shuju, 1977). Per Qi's manual, the cleanly regulated sequence: D2, B1, C1, D2.

59. The sequence of lines follows a standard regulated sequence of A, B, C, D, per Qi's manual: A2; B*4; C3; D*15; the unregulated *lines* marked with * symbol. Minor violations occur in places that do not alter these major qualities.

60. Clouds and golden pavilion may echo an earlier poem about this same site, "Inscribed on the Stone Bridge" by Cishou Huaishen (慈受懷深, 1077–1132), also about offering tea to the arhats; *Cishou Huaishen chanshi guanglu* 慈受懷深禪師廣錄 (ZZ73.1451.111b). Citations to ZZ are to the revised *Shinsan Dainippon Zokuzōkyō* 新纂大日本續藏經 (1975–1989), 90 vols., providing volume, text number, page, register, and line.

61. On similar humor in poems by monks associated with Xutang Zhiyu, with whom Mushō Jōshō also studied, see Jason Protass, "Returning Empty-Handed," *Journal of Chinese Literature and Culture* 4, no. 1 (2017), 402–5.

62. *Zhongshan shihua* 中山詩話 (*Siku quanshu Wenyuange*), *juan* 1, 7b.

63. Fan Xiangyong 范祥雍, ed. *Luoyang qielan ji jiaozhu* 洛陽伽藍記校注 (Shanghai: Shanghai guji chubanshe, 1978), 146–47.

64. Asakura Hisashi 朝倉尚, *Zenrin no bungaku: shikai to sono shūhen* 禅林の文学: 詩会とその周辺 (Osaka: Seibundō, 2004), 339–79.

65. For these poems and background, see Hirowatari Masatoshi 廣渡正利 ed., *Sekijō ihō* 石城遺寶 (Tokyo: Bunken shuppan, 1991), 170–71, 172–75 and 217–22. Another Donpekirō poem is translated by Andrew Goble in Murai Shōsuke, "Poetry in Chinese as a Diplomatic Art in Premodern East Asia," 60.

66. The matched rhymes are presented clearly in Vincent Yang, "A Comparative Study of Su Shi's *He Tao shi*," *Monumenta Serica* 56 (2008): 219–58.

67. *Issan kokushi goroku* 一山國師語錄 (T80.2553.327a-b). Yishan inscribed his poems on paintings for a patron in 1310, per *Nara Kokuritsu Hakubutsukan no meihō* 奈良国立博物館の名宝 (Nara: Nara Kokuritsu Hakubutsukan, 1997), 320, no. 180. Yishan follows the Liangshan Guo'an poems, which became standard in Japan. For more Chinese poetic responses to the Guo'an poems, see *Shiniu tu song* 十牛圖頌 (ZZ64.1269.773b–775a) and *Chanzong zadu hai* 禪宗雜毒海 (ZZ65.1278.98c–99c). In China, another set of ten images and poems by Puming (普明) was more popularly extended through matching. See *Muniu tu song* 牧牛圖頌 in *Jiaxing zang* 嘉興藏, vol. 23 (Taipei: Xinwenfeng, 1987), 347–57, and 357–65.

68. His poems were read and the preface quoted by laity and Zen monks, including Zekkai Chūshin (絶海中津, 1334/36–1405) in *Zekkai oshō goroku* 絶海和尚語録 (T80.2561.759c–760a).

69. Iida Rigyō 飯田利行, *Ryōkan goshaku Daichi geju yaku* 良寛語釈大智偈頌訳 (Tokyo: Daihorin kaku, 1988).

70. David B. Lurie, *Realms of Literacy: Early Japan and the History of Writing* (Cambridge, MA: Harvard University Asia Center, 2011), 185.

71. Brian Steininger, *Chinese Literary Forms in Heian Japan: Poetics and Practice* (Cambridge, MA: Harvard University Asia Center, 2017), 176–81.

72. Ishizaki, *Kinsei Nihon ni okeru Shina zokugo bungakushi*, 13–14.

73. I relied on the Nichibunken edition of *Kūge nikku shū*, published electronically with some annotation: http://rakusai.nichibun.ac.jp/zenseki/. Citations are to the year, month, and day as given in this edition.

74. Per Sargent / Qi Gong, the sequence of lines is cleanly regulated: D1, B4, C1, D1. Gidō mentions having the *Guangyun* as a youth; *Kūge nikku shū*, first entry of 1332.

75. "Evenly sustain" for *tōji* 等持 imperfectly conveys the additional layers of meaning here. First, Tōjiji was the name of Gidō's current monastery. The line could be glossed, "At Tōji Temple, our *samādhi* is just the ordinary and everyday." Second, in translated Buddhist sūtra, *dengchi* (等持) was used to translate into Chinese idiom the Sanskrit word *samādhi*, the meditative concentration. *Sanmei* 三昧 (J. *sanmai* or *zanmai*) transliterates the sound samādhi. The four-character phrase 等持三昧 combines a nativized translation with a foreignizing transliteration. Though semantically redundant, this is a clever way to expand on his temple's name.

76. "Citrus-peel tincture" is a medicinal broth, named in the second- or third-century book of medicine *Jinkui yaolüe* 金匱要略.

77. *Jianzhong jingguo xudenglu* 建中靖國續燈録 (ZZ78.1556.657b). Though that is the earliest anthologized version of this story, it was probably better known from later versions, such as *Wudeng huiyuan* 五燈會元 (ZZ80.1565.323c). I also consulted a related Korean text in English translation by John Jorgensen, ed., *Seon Dialogues* (Seoul: Jogye Order of Korean Buddhism, 2012), 140–41. Following a suggestion from Kevin Buckelew, my translation builds on the interpretation given in *Dachuan Puji chanshi yulu* 大川普濟禪師語録 (ZZ69.1369.765c–766a).

78. Adapted in part from Thomas Kirchner, ed., *The Record of Linji* (Honolulu: University of Hawai'i Press, 2009), 302–3.

79. Tamamura Takeji 玉村竹二, *Gozan Zensō denki shūsei* 五山禪僧傳記集成 (Tokyo: Kodansha, 1983), 161; and *Enpō den tōroku* 延寶傳燈録, fascicle 17.

80. Three monks' names follow those given in Tsuji Zennosuke 辻善之助, *Kūge nichiyō kufū ryakushū* 空華日用工夫略集 (Tokyo: Taiyōsha, 1939), 155.

81. *Kūge nikku shū*, 1382/1/4.

82. Dōgen did not refer to this incident directly in his own writings. He did frequently refer to *shinjin datsuraku* as Rujing's teaching. See Steven Heine, "Dōgen Casts Off 'What': An Analysis of Shinjin datsuraku," *JIABS* 9, no. 1 (1986): 53–70.

83. In Takasaki Jikidō 高崎直道 and Umehara Takeshi 梅原猛, *Bukkyō no shisō 11: Kobutsu no manebi Dōgen* 仏教の思想11: 古佛のまねび道元 (Tokyo: Kadokawa Shoten, 1969; rpt. 1998), 64–66. This topic has been widely written about in English as well, beginning with Takashi James Kodera, *Dogen's Formative Years in China* (Boulder, CO: Prajna, 1980), 106–7.

84. Medieval Chinese pronunciations follow Baxter and Sagart, *Old Chinese: A New Reconstruction* (New York: Oxford University Press, 2014), based on the Song dynasty *Guangyun*. These words *chen* (塵 or *drin*) and *shen* (身 or *syin*) are both in the *zhen* (真) rhyme family; Kokan Shiren's *Shūbun inryaku* rhyme dictionary of 1306, popular in Japan, gives the same information, suggesting a broad continuity that encompassed Rujing and Dōgen.

85. This idea repeated often, such as *Princeton Dictionary of Buddhism*, 263.

86. Heine, "Dōgen Casts Off 'What'"; and Bernard Faure, *Chan Insights and Oversights* (Princeton, NJ: Princeton University Press, 1993), 138–39.

87. Fascicle three of *Zōtanshū* 雜談集, as quoted in Nishio, *Chūsei no Nitchū kōryū to Zenshū*, 129, no. 23.

88. *Bukkō Kokushi goroku* (T80.2549.219b). Inspired by relevant discussion in Tachi, "Kamakura-ki no Zenrin ni okeru Chūgokugo to Nihongo," 264.

89. Tachi Ryūshi, "Kamakura-ki no Zenrin ni okeru Chūgokugo to Nihongo," 264.

90. Tachi Ryūshi 舘隆志, "Kenchōji no kaisan" 建長寺の開山, in *Higashi Ajia no naka no Kenchōji*, 146.

91. *Bukkō Kokushi goroku* (T80.2549.220a).

92. Tachi Ryūshi 舘隆志, "Gotten Funei no rai Nichi o megutte" 兀庵普寧の来日をめぐって, *Kokusai Zen kenkyū* 1 (2018): 63.

93. The verse, in rhymed six-character lines, reads: "Set down the thousand-pound burden, / the only essential is to dwell in pure ease. / Old age comes, and karmic debts remain; / Who stumbles again at this, my single gate?" (卸却千斤重擔, 惟要在處清閑, 老來業債未脫, 復墮建長一關).

94. *Wu'an Puning chanshi yulu* 兀菴普寧禪師語錄 (ZZ71.1404.9b).

95. *Wu'an Puning chanshi yulu* (ZZ71.1404.10a).

96. Steven Heine, *From Chinese Chan to Japanese Zen* (New York: Oxford University Press, 2018), 119. The seeds of this appear in his earlier work, including, "Dōgen Casts Off 'What.'"

97. *Wu'an Puning chanshi yulu* (ZZ71.1404.11c). See also Tachi, "Kamakura-ki no Zenrin ni okeru Chūgokugo to Nihongo," 267.

98. The printed text was likely prepared from the master's own written record, rather than from a student's furtive transcript. An example is not found among Puming's extant calligraphy. For a contemporaneous émigré monk's sermon in his own hand, see Wuxue Zuyuan, in Tayama Hōnan 田山方南, ed., *Zoku Zenrin bokuseki* 續禪林墨蹟 (Kyoto: Shibunkaku, 1981 ed.), no. 121; and corresponding *Bukkō Kokushi goroku* (T80.2549.230a–b).

99. Imai Fukuzan, in his introduction to *Shōnan kattoroku* 湘南葛藤録 (itself likely a spurious collection), as translated in Trevor Leggett, *Zen and the Ways* (London: Routledge and Kegan Paul, 1978), 250. On the dubious reliability of Imai Fukuzan, see Vallor, "*Waka* and Zen."

100. This translation modified from Leggett by Kraft, *Eloquent Zen*, 52.

101. The idea of resonance as demonstrating understanding between two things can be traced back to the *Yijing* 易經, "Things with the same tone resonate with one another; those with the same *qi* seek each other out" (同聲相應同氣相求); translation by Esther Klein, *Reading Sima Qian from Han to Song* (Leiden: Brill, 2018), 198.

102. A quotation of the *Blue Cliff Record* verse in case 44 by Xuedou Chongxian (雪竇重顯, 980–1052), *Biyanlu* 碧巖錄 (T48.2003.181b).

103. *Bonsen oshō goroku* 竺僊和尚語錄 (T80.2554.422a-b).

104. Enomoto Wataru 榎本渉, "Nyū-Gen Nihon sō Chintei Kaiju to Genmatsu Mei-sho no Nitchū kōryū" 入元日本僧椿庭海壽と元末明初の日中交流, *Tōyōshi kenkyū* 70, no. 2 (2011): 260–98.

105. These numbers from Nishio Kenryū 西尾賢隆, *Chūsei no Nitchū kōryū to Zenshū* 中世の日中交流と禅宗 (Tokyo: Yoshikawa Kōbunkan, 1999), 55–56.

106. More details about Musō's training in Vallor, *Not Seeing Snow*, 8–14.

107. "Shō'an gannen" (正安元年) in *Musō kokushi nenpu* 夢窓国師年譜 (1354 edition; Kyoto University Library, no. 30467), 5a; accessed May 2019 from *Kyōto Daigaku Kichō shiryō dejitaru ākaibu* https://rmda.kulib.kyoto-u.ac.jp/. This early text differs slightly from that found in *Zoku gunsho ruijū* 続群書類従 (Tokyo: Zoku gunsho ruijū kanseikai, 1923) 9, 499a-b.

108. *Zoku gunsho ruijū*, 7a-b. This interpolation about Yishan being a person from Taizhou is in the original text.

109. Tayama Hōnan 田山方南, *Zenrin bokuseki* 禪林墨蹟 (Ichikawa: Zenrin Bokuseki Kankai, 1955), speculated these may have been brush-dialogue, and noted the correspondence of manuscript and woodblock text. More significant work sponsored by Unganji from 1965 culminated in a complete annotated modern Japanese translation of the Gozan edition, *Kunchū Bukkokuroku* 訓注仏国録 (Tokyo: Dō kankōkai, 1975); therein the manuscripts are treated as variant texts. In Chinese, the correlation between manuscripts and printed text is noted in Jiang Jing 江靜, *Fu Ri Song seng Wuxue Zuyuan yanjiu* 赴日宋僧無學祖元研究 (Beijing: Shangwu yinshu, 2011), 233–34 and 321–23. The only analysis in a Western language, Steffen Döll, *Im Osten Des Meeres* (Stuttgart: Franz Steiner Verlag, 2010), 159–64, translates one of the three manuscripts and provides insightful reflections on brush-dialogue.

110. Hu Jianming 胡建明 [Ko Kenmei], *Chūgoku sōdai zenrin kōsō bokuseki no kenkyū* 中国宋代禅林高僧墨蹟の研究 (Tokyo: Shunjusha, 2007), 226–231; corrected in the 2011 Chinese edition (however, the manuscripts are still out of sequence).

111. Kinugawa Kenji 衣川賢次, *Chanzong sixiang yu wenxian congkao* 禪宗思想與文獻叢考 (Shanghai: Fudan daxue chubanshe, 2017), 219.

112. The collector's seal located in the corner bears the name of Tengan Ekō, dharma heir of Kōhō Kennichi who compiled the relevant part of *Bukkoku zenji goroku*, known as *Kigen mondo*.

113. This transmission happens that night, per *Bukkoku zenji goroku* (T80.2551.279c–280a). The transmission is recorded both in Zuyuan's record, *Bukkō Kokushi goroku* (T80.2549.234c–235a), and in *Bukkoku zenji goroku*, 282c.

114. For a more comprehensive statement of these differences, see Paul Rouzer, "Early Buddhist Kanshi: Court, Country, and Kūkai," *Monumenta Nipponica* 59, no. 4 (2004), 437–38. One early essay exploring diverse Japanese Buddhist responses is Herbert Plutschow, "Is Poetry a Sin? *Honjisuijaku* and Buddhism versus Poetry," *Oriens Extremus* 25, no. 2 (1978): 206–18. On early evidence for the equivalence of poetic and Buddhist paths, see Michael Jametz, "The Buddhist Affirmation of Poetry," *Japanese Journal of Religious Studies* 34, no. 1 (2016): 55–88.

115. Robert Morrell, trans., *Sand & Pebbles* (Albany: State University of New York Press, 1985), 163–65.

116. Vallor, "*Waka* and Zen," 101–17.

Chapter 6

Doves on My Knees, Golden Dragons in My Sleeves

Emigrant Chan Masters and Early Japanese Zen Buddhism

Steffen Döll

Introductory Remarks

"Zen" has been defined in manifold terms.[1] It has been and still is understood, in no specific order, as an individualized religion,[2] a form of spiritual practice,[3] a type of Eastern philosophy[4] (if not the wellspring of East Asian thought in general), and a specific way to deal with the issue of body and mind (or the absence of this issue).[5] It is also considered to be the foundation of the arts,[6] as well as the unobstructed manifestation of what it means to exist in the first place,[7] especially as manifested in religious heroes such as Linji Yixuan (臨濟義玄, d. 866 or 867), Dōgen Kigen (道元希玄, 1200–1253), or Hakuin Ekaku (白隱慧鶴, 1686–1769).[8] While all these perspectives may offer insights into some of the many facets of Chan/Sŏn/Zen Buddhism, one will advance from a historiographic point of view that these perspectives must be first and foremost related to their respective historical contexts and critically evaluated accordingly—both on the level of the phenomenon as an object of observation and on the meta-level of the observers and the discourses they construct about the object.[9] Indeed, for quite some time now, historical and critical examinations have been the hallmark of contemporary Chan studies.[10]

The paradigm shift in scholarship has significantly contributed to our knowledge about the tradition's development over the centuries, as well as how it was reinterpreted and reinvented in modern times. The growing body of scholarship in European languages, however, typically follows certain topical and geographical tendencies: it has, by and large, Chinese Chan as its object. That the study of Korean Sŏn is treated almost as stepmotherly is an obviously lamentable fact.[11] But it is also not off the mark to state that scholarship on Japanese Zen in the United States and in Europe generally champions much more traditionalist approaches than its Sinological counterparts focusing on the Chan tradition.[12] This is all the more noteworthy since Japanese-language scholarship has long since escaped the narrow confines of sectarianism: it has been steadily producing studies that break new ground in firmly locating Chan/Zen in its historical context and in concrete social, political, and economic formations.[13]

Taking these desiderata in the current state of scholarship into account, this paper addresses a period in time and a group of protagonists that have hitherto received less attention than is warranted by an assessment of the developmental history of Japanese Zen Buddhism. When it comes to the question of how Chan grew roots in Japan, Chinese emigrant monks and masters acted, as this chapter argues, as formative factors in the early phases of Japanese Zen Buddhism (i.e., the thirteenth and fourteenth centuries).[14] Indeed, I suggest, they remain relevant well into the early modern period. I propose an analysis of their biographies not because they are great religious minds and cultural heroes (even though this may have been the case)[15] but because they are inextricably intertwined with their historical situation and played a significant role in developing we are used to calling "Zen." The masters, it appears, made conscious use of their embeddedness in sociopolitical contexts, and spiritual authenticity and social prestige are, to a certain degree, portrayed as coextensive in their biographic materials.

The first task of the following remarks is to provide a general understanding of the institutional framework to East Asian Chan/Zen Buddhism in medieval and early modern times. Cursory considerations on the phenomenon of the so-called Five Mountains (C. *wushan*, J. *gozan* 五山) as Chan/Zen's transnational infrastructure serve to locate biographical sketches of Lanxi Daolong (蘭溪道隆, 1213–1278, J. Rankei Dōryū), Wuxue Zuyuan (無學祖元, 1226–1286, J. Mugaku Sogen), and Yishan Yining (一山一寧, 1247–1317, J. Issan Ichinei), within a context of Sino-Japanese interaction.[16] While the stories of their lives differ significantly with regard to the motives of their decisions and the details of their fortunes, illuminating congruencies come to light with respect to the rationales and teleologies involved. An analysis of their biographical materials shows that they agreed in their understanding of the Japanese situation and its potential for career advancement. Opportunism was the result that held certain risks—as is amply illustrated in the cases of Lanxi and Yishan—but pursued the prospect of betterment within both the secular and the clerical hierarchies. The social and political dimension of Chan/Zen in thirteenth- and fourteenth-century Japan thus complements the identification by lineage so typical of the claim to succession of the Patriarch's dharma transmission.

Historical Context

By the latter half of the 1100s, Japan had changed its isolationist course begun in 894 with the discontinuation of official diplomatic embassies to the Tang (唐) dynasty and had started to reactivate—indeed, expand—its contacts to the mainland.[17] One of the driving forces behind this process was the Buddhist institution: Japanese Monks started traveling to Song (宋) dynasty (960–1279) China as frequently (or sometimes more so) as they had done with Tang China during the Heian (平安) period (794–1185). Reasons for Japanese pilgrimages to the mainland were the pervasive (if not universally accepted) ideologeme of the decline of the dharma (*mappō* 末法) that could be precisely dated to 1052; the perceived fossilization of the established schools and their modes of interacting with society at large as well as the resulting skepticism toward their monastic authenticity and soteriological efficacy; and the reform movements that with time gained momentum, self-confidence, and increasing independence from institutionalized Buddhism, thereby stimulating counterforces from precisely these Buddhist institutions.[18]

The eschatological vector—along which the renewed interest of representatives of Japanese Buddhist schools in the situation on the mainland was oriented—runs counter to the political and diplomatic foreign affairs that characterized the thirteenth century. By 1185, the Kamakura *bakufu* (幕府, *vulgo* Shogunate) had established itself as the center of military power rivaling the symbolic power of the aristocratic court in the imperial city. Throughout the thirteenth and fourteenth centuries, the warrior aristocracy sought paths to distinction that allowed for a balance between the imperial and military capitals also in terms of symbolic capital and cultural prestige. One of the possible venues explored was the patronage—or perhaps, instrumentalization—of the Chan Buddhist tradition that was in vogue on the Chinese mainland and also in Japan in the form of Japanese Zen.

The Chinese mainland was experiencing rapid and thoroughgoing changes in political order from the Jurchen invasion and the loss of the northern territories to the series of definitive defeats of the Southern Song armies in the late 1170s.[19] After a short-lived alliance between the Mongol Khans and the Song dynasty that led to the fall of the Jurchen Empire (i.e., the Jin 金 dynasty, 1115–1234), northern China was attacked by Mongol forces proper in 1235. The border was steadily pushed south until, by the mid-1240s, the Southern Song capital of Hangzhou was occupied. The officially recognized Chan monasteries of the *wushan*—that is the five great Chan monasteries in Eastern Zhejiang province along with their second- and third-tier epigones all over the realm, which was part and parcel of state administration, fell under Mongol control as well. While the Song dynasty nominally lasted a few more decades, and the Yuan (元) dynasty was proclaimed in 1279, every Japanese pilgrim traveling the mainland after 1246 did so under the eyes of Mongol authorities, and that situation persisted until the end of the dynasty in 1368.[20]

Contrary to commonsense expectations, the drastic political overthrows impacted the Buddhist forms of exchange only minimally, and Japanese travelers generally seem to have met with little adversity: reports of Mongolian impediments to the routes and venues of Buddhist exchange are all but absent from historical records. On the contrary, Japanese pilgrimages to China—for the first time since the Heian court in 894 had chosen to discontinue diplomatic embassies to the Tang dynasty—began to flourish: Myōan Eisai (明菴榮西, 1141–1215) dwelled at Mount Tiantai (天臺) and Mount Ayuwang (阿育王) during his travels to China first in 1168 and again from 1185 to 1191. In 1189, Dainichibō Nōnin (大日房能忍, fl. 1189) supposedly commissioned two of his disciples to go to China with letters and donations in order to have their master's enlightenment accredited.[21] Dōgen had been in China between 1223 and 1227,[22] and Enni Ben'en (圓爾辯圓, 1202–1280) followed him, residing in China between 1235 and 1241. Even prolonged sojourns of Japanese monks in China were not an infrequent phenomenon: Sesson Yūbai (雪村友梅, 1290–1347) spent twenty years there before returning to his home country.

In the mid-thirteenth century this direction of exchange was complemented by Chinese monks traveling—and settling—in Japan. What is discussed below is aimed at shedding some light on this part of the entangled history of the Five Mountains. For in the case of Chan/Zen Buddhism we can discern an increase in the number of travelers—both Japanese going West and Chinese crossing the ocean toward the East—during the time of Mongol rule, and indeed quantitative analysis of biographical materials corroborates these findings.[23]

The personal exchange, as well as the sets of cultural techniques and artifacts, religious practices, and texts that made the journey across the Yellow Sea is evidence of the cultural ecumene that was at that time stronger than it had been for centuries and would be for centuries to come. The medieval transfer of knowledge, personnel, and artifacts had a pronounced institutional side as well, and the Chinese *wushan* transformed, over a period of more than a century, into the Japanese *gozan*.[24] Therefore, far-reaching institutional and cultural continuities can be observed between Song dynasty Chan and Kamakura period (1185–1333) Zen: for Japanese pilgrims, these provided a reliable infrastructure and hotspots for Chan/Zen learning, while for Chinese monks Japan became an attractive option when considering one's future career. How such deliberations played out can be witnessed in the biographies that are presented in the following paragraphs.

Lanxi Daolong

Lanxi Daolong was the first Chan master of Chinese origin to arrive in Dazaifu in northern Kyūshū, in the year 1246 or 1247, at age thirty-two or thirty-three. He had begun training in China when he was thirteen years old and studied with Wuzhun Shifan (無準師範, 1178–1249) and Chijue Daochong (癡絕道冲, 1169–1250), among others, before being recognized as dharma heir by Wuming Huixing (無明慧性, 1162–1237). While his masters were of highest renown, Lanxi was not, and he did not hold any office of significance when a monk of the Japanese "School of Monastic Regulations" (*risshū* 律宗), Getsuō Chikyō (月翁智鏡, d.u.), suggested to him that he should effectuate passage to Japan.[25]

Lanxi indeed chose to undertake the voyage and is known to have visited Getsuō at Sennyūji (泉涌寺) in the imperial city (nowadays Kyōto) when he came to Japan. He then traveled to Jufukuji (壽福寺) in Kamakura in 1248 and was bestowed the office of abbot of the newly repurposed Jōrakuji (常樂寺) by regent Hōjō Tokiyori (北条時頼, 1227–1263) himself.[26] At Jōrakuji, Lanxi built a "monks' hall" (*sōdō* 僧堂) typical of Chan monasteries—the first of its kind in the Kantō (關東) area. Tokiyori also decided to have a monastery built in Kamakura that was to be oriented in detail toward Chinese Chan monasteries, especially the compound on Mount Jing (徑山). The result was Kenchōji (建長寺), built in 1246, with two features that are especially noteworthy: first of all, the initial architecture of Kenchōji did not include any syncretistic elements dedicated to the worship of deities and ceremonies according to Shingon (眞言) and/or Tendai (天臺) rites. Instead, it was confined to the so-called *saṃghārāma* in seven halls (*shichidō garan* 七堂伽藍) layout.[27] Secondly, emperor Go-Fukakusa (後深草, 1243–1304, r. 1246–1260) bestowed upon the monastery the title of "Zen Monastery for the Promotion of the Nation of the Kenchō [era] at Kofuku Mountain of Sagami Province" (*Sōyō Kofukuzan Kenchō kōkoku zenji* 相陽巨福山建長興国禪寺). This is the earliest instance of the "Zen monastery" (*Zenji*) denomination in the Kantō area—only Tōfukuji (東福寺) in Kyōto had managed to secure the prestigious title earlier and benefit from the state financing and protection it implied.

Lanxi was installed as founding abbot (*kaisan* 開山) of Kenchōji—and with it, of the first officially sanctioned Zen compound in Kamakura, the seat of military power—after construction was finished in 1253. When Lanxi was called to Kyōto upon the invitation by Emperor Go-Saga (後嵯峨, 1220–1272, r. 1242–1246) in 1262, he was also installed as eleventh abbot of Kenninji (建仁寺). A few months later, in 1263/1264, he returned to Kamakura and to his Kenchōji office, but things started to change: after the death of Tokiyori, with whom Lanxi was closely affiliated, the regent's son Tokimune (時宗, 1251–1284) presided over the Hōjō clan and took over the regency as well. The new shogun's religious inclinations seemed to lie elsewhere at that point, and Lanxi was effectively left without a Hōjō sponsor from 1263 onward. In 1270, when he was relieved of his abbacy at Kenchōji, his outlook and standing deteriorated even further as is evidenced in his biography:

> Among Lanxi's students were those who spread rumors. For this reason, he was transferred to the province of Kō (甲) [that is, today's Yamanashi prefecture]. The small officials and the mob in the northern districts [in and around Kamakura] were pleased that [Lanxi Dao]long was punished with exile, but he himself said: "For the sake of the Buddhist teachings I have crossed the sea and come into this country. I did nothing except travelling back and forth between the imperial

city [of Kyōto] and the princely seat [of Kamakura]. I have no leisure to be directed towards the *hinterlands*. At times I worry about such slander but already have gotten used to the Jie (羯) and the Lao (獠) [i.e., the barbarians to the north and south of China].[28]

His dissatisfaction was alleviated when he was allowed to return from exile finally in 1275 and settle at Jufukuji in Kamakura, but his biography continues that "those among his disciples that were bound together in groups of sixes[29] had still not closed their slanderous lips. That is why Lanxi was sent off to Kō province a second time."[30]

Finally, in 1277, Lanxi was once again allowed back into Kamakura, and first assigned to stay at Jufukuji, but eventually he returned to Kenchōji in 1278 where he died the same year, aged sixty-six. The "poem for leaving the world behind" (*jiseju*, 辭世頌) that he presented to his disciples reads: "I have treated misty eyes for 33 years. With one swing, everything shatters, and the great way runs smoothly once more."[31] Posthumously, Emperor Kameyama (亀山, 1249–1305, r. 1259–1274) conferred upon Lanxi the title of "Zen Master of Great Awakening" (*Daikaku zenji* 大覺禪師), marking the occasion of the first official bestowal of the "Zen teacher" (*zenji*) title in Japan.

Lanxi is sometimes referred to as the first master to introduce "pure" and proper Rinzai-style Zen on Japanese soil. By the same token, both Eisai and Enni are derogatorily counted among the proponents of "syncretical Zen" (*kenshū Zen*, 兼修禪) in which seated meditation is coordinated with esoteric ritual and scholarship.[32] Lanxi, quite differently, is supposed to have established the "pure Chan of the Song dynasty" (*junsui na Sōchō Zen*, 純粋な宋朝禅)[33] in Japan. Upon closer inspection, however, this claim cannot be supported in light of historiographic accuracy and sound philology. In order to prove the point, an indication of an often-quoted passage from the "Records of the Source Mirror" (*Zongjinglu*, 宗鏡錄, 961) speaks to an inclusivist tendency running counter to the fabled image of Chan/Zen's singularity (i.e., the so-called transmission beyond the teachings):

> It is said that the first patriarch of all the schools [of Buddhism] was Śākyamuni. [Accordingly, we may state that] the canonical scriptures are the Buddha's own words (*kyō kore Butsugo nari*, 經是佛語), while meditation is the Buddha's own mind (*Zen*

kore Butsu'i nari, 禪是佛意). How could it be the case that the heart and the mouth of the Buddha contradicted one another?[34]

It was this view that informed the conviction that generally held sway in the Chan/Zen institution of the Song and Yuan dynasty and also those of the Kamakura and Muromachi (1333–1573) eras, namely that while the focus on seated meditation did provide access to an awakening more direct than any other, this did not by any means invalidate other traditions. Compare, for one, these two texts, both titled "Treatise on Seated Meditation" (C. *Zuochanlun,* J. *Zazenron,* 坐禪論); the left one by alleged *kenshū*-style Zen proponent Enni Ben'en, the one to the right by "pure" Zen representative Lanxi Daolong:

Enni's *Zazenron*[35]	Lanxi's *Zuochanlun*[36]
One asked: "One says that seated meditation is the root and source of the manifold teachings. What is the meaning of this?"	One asked: "How about this: Can we say that the school of Chan is the root and trunk of the manifold teachings?"
The master answered: "Zen is the innermost heart (內心) of the Buddha. The monastic discipline is the outer appearance (外相) of the Buddha. The doctrines (教) are the spoken words of the Buddha. And to bear the Buddha in mind (念佛), that is the name of the Buddha. These all come forth from the heart of the Buddha, and it is for this reason that it is their root and trunk."	The master answered: "Chan is the heart of the Buddha. The monastic discipline is his outer appearance. The doctrines are his words. The chanting of his name is his skill-in-means. All these *samādhis* spring forth from the heart of the Buddha. Therefore, one is right to say that it is the root and trunk of these schools."

Even though in both discussions Zen Buddhism is identified as the one Buddhist tradition that must be afforded pride of place—in fact this seems to be coextensive with what it essentially means to be part of Buddhism—other implementations of Buddhist doctrine and practice are not denigrated wholesale. Rather, we may observe a differentiation of roles and strategies that complement, not contradict, one another. The textual continuities between *Zongjinglu* and the respective *Treatises* by Enni Ben'en and Lanxi Daolong paint a picture of the Chinese master that suggests a primarily pragmatic personality: his biography vividly illustrates interactions and interferences between the religious and political spheres. His fortunes fell with Tokiyori's death, that is, with the loss of his patron who promoted and protected him. Simultaneously his relation to the line of emperors is the first instance of Zen Buddhism's representatives gaining a foothold with the court aristocracy—an alliance that would culminate in the figure of Yishan Yining. Far from being the hero that singlehandedly installed pure Rinzai Zen on the Japanese archipelago, we may conclude, Lanxi endeavored—with some success but also with some disappointments—to have a Japanese Zen institution proper officially recognized by the military and courtly authorities.

Wuxue Zuyuan

After Lanxi's death, the abbacy of Kenchōji, with no immediate follow-up in sight, was left vacant until 1279. Tokiyori's son Hōjō Tokimune (北条時宗, 1251–1284, r. 1268–1284), by now having developed a personal interest in Zen Buddhism, dispatched a mission to Yuan China. Despite the ongoing tensions between the two empires, the envoys asked the Mongol authorities for a suitable candidate. They acquiesced, and the required profile was identified in the person of Wuxue Zuyuan who, since 1278, had held the prestigious position of "Head Seat" (*zasu*, 座主), effectively the second in command, at Mount Tiantong (天童).[37]

Wuxue had gained repute when he calmly faced the invasion of Mongolian troops in 1276/1277 at Mount Lingyin (靈隱) where he was staying at the time:

> In the seventh year of his stay [at Mount Lingyin], the pike-armed henchmen and soldiers of the north caused disturbances in the monastery compound [. . .] They had the congregation scurry for cover like rats. Zuyuan alone continued sitting in the hall serenely. When the henchmen's leader was about to lay his blade to Zuyuan's throat, he remained unmoved and intoned a poem: "Between heaven and earth there is not so much as a speck of earth for one to hold high a walking cane. Is it not joyful to see that men are empty and that the law

of the Buddha is empty as well? Take heed with that huge three-feet Mongol sword of yours! In the shadows of a flash of lightning you cut nothing but the spring breeze." At his words, the band of henchmen was contrite. They bowed courteously and made their retreat.[38]

By virtue of this episode—Wuxue's pacifist impassivity versus the open belligerence of the Mongol soldiers—Wuxue has been dubbed an "ardent Song nationalist."[39] While this may indeed have been the case on the level of personal loyalty and emotion, it did not hinder his heeding the authorities' recommendation and accepting the Japanese invitation. His biography outlines the episode as follows:

> In the year of 1279, the seat of Kenchōji was vacated. The governor general Taira no Tokimune had an explanation written to this effect and had it shipped across the ocean in order to ask for a renowned supervisor for the congregation. The [Mongolian] chief-of-staff gave his approval and had Wuxue Zuyuan obey what the petition from afar asked. Huanqi Weiyi (環溪惟一, 1202–1281) left the robe of Fojian (佛鑑)[40] to Wuxue Zuyuan who accepted it and then asked: "What was it that our master and elder brother, the World-Honored One, transmitted apart from the [robe of] gold brocade?"[41] He clicked his tongue and said: "If there is guilt on your part, its consequences will extend to me, as well!" And with these words, he threw the robe over his shoulders.[42]

When Wuxue arrived in Kamakura in 1279, Lanxi was dead and another immigrant monk, Wuan Puning (兀庵普寧; 1197–1276), had returned to China. He had quickly become the most respected personality of Japanese Zen Buddhism at the time. It seems safe to assume that the enormous prestige granted to Chinese Chan masters in early medieval Japan did not go unnoticed and, in fact, may have been helped facilitate Wuxue's decision (as well as the decisions of others): the voyage was dangerous, and the language and customs alien, but the advancement of one's secular and clerical career must have been an obvious benefit. Wuxue himself had the following story to tell in order to rationalize his decision to make the journey to Japan:

In the beginning I had no inclination whatsoever to come hither into this country. But there were certain conditions and causes why things happened that way. When I was among the Song I had once seen a divine man. He had a high-arching crown upon his head and a spectacular gown on, and in his hands, he held a scepter. His whole comport was extraordinary. He told me: "I wish, honorable monk, that you were to descend into my country. There are many there such as me." I did not understand what was going on. But every time he came before me, a single golden dragon slipped up his sleeve. There also was a flock of doves some of which were blue, and some were white, some were flying about or picking the ground, and some were hopping onto my knees. But I did not see any reason for this. When I had then come into this country here there was one who told me: "In our region there is a luminous [i.e., powerful] deity. He is called the Great bodhisattva Hachiman.[43] His majesty and his mystery are unheard of (*iryō hanahada atarashiki nari*, 威靈甚新). Now that you, master, have settled in this our world, would you not pay your respects to his shrine and burn incense there?" When thereupon I went to Hachiman's shrine, I saw a number of doves carved into the wood of the roof beams. I inquired about these and was told that the birds are messengers of this deity. Because of this happenstance I realized that the one with the high-arching crown upon his head was none other than this deity. That this old monk has come here, then, is most assuredly no accident. And all of you are, in accord with my precognition so many years ago, the doves and golden dragons resting upon my miserable knees.[44]

The interpretive frame invoked by Wuxue is one of spiritual destiny: not only is he entreated by a superhuman agency to accept the invitation, but he also gets a congregation that is worthy of his efforts. The precognitive character of his dream is validated by his visit to Hachiman Shrine, and once more the spheres of religious imagination and political pragmatics manifest coextensively.

The importance accorded Wuxue's coming, especially by the regent Tokimune, may be assessed through the fact that a mere three months after his departure from China he became the abbot of Kenchōji. When in

1281 the Mongol invasion attempt was upon the shores of Hakata, Wuxue inquired in private session to what benefit Tokimune studied, practiced, and sponsored Zen Buddhism. Tokimune answered to the effect that he intended for all fear to cease—an intention that Wuxue seemingly turned into a pedagogic device, further instructing the regent to first and foremost determine the origin of his fears:

> When the Taira governor general [i.e., Tokimune] paid a visit to Engakuji (圓覺寺), Zuyuan took his brush in hand and wrote for the governor: "Let not troubles afflict you (*bonnō taru koto nakare*, 莫煩惱)!" The governor said: "What does that mean—let not troubles afflict you?" Zuyuan answered: "Throughout spring and summer, uproar and disorder persisted in Hakata. But then a single wind arose, and tens of thousands of ships were swept away. I would that you, oh Lord, had not troubled yourself about it. The crown of these hundreds of tens of thousands of henchmen rests far off to the West, and at the precise time when the wind and waves had risen, they floundered."[45]

The instrumentalization of Zen methods of training for war in the episode sees the Chan master ready to put his religious insight and spiritual guidance at the warlord's disposal. It seems small wonder that when Wuxue had once declared his intention to go back to the mainland, it was Tokimune who successfully dissuaded him from doing so. The respect in which the regent held his advice also came to bear when he appointed Wuxue as founding abbot of Engakuji in Kamakura. The official appellation of "Zen monastery for the promotion of the sacredness of perfect awakening at the mountain of auspicious deer" (*Zuirokusan engaku kōshō Zenji*, 瑞鹿山圓覺興聖禅寺) selected by the older monk was welcome also because it signaled higher powers' preference for the communal undertaking of establishing a new Zen compound: "On the day of the hall opening, a herd of deer approached the mats [of the festive site]. Zuyuan identified this fact as an auspicious omen and labelled the [location] 'Mountain of the Auspicious Deer.'"[46] Tokimune died in 1284; Wuxue followed within two years. Among his disciples was Kōhō Kennichi (高峰顯日, 1241–1316) and among his second-generation successors, Musō Soseki (夢窓疎石, 1275–1351) stands out as an emblematic figure in whose hands the strands of religious tradition and political ambition were knit together just as tight.[47]

Yishan Yining

The third biography that can be seen as crucial for the development of Zen Buddhism in late thirteenth- and early fourteenth-century Japan is that of Yishan Yining.[48] He was born in 1247 in the district of Linhai in the eastern part of what today is Zhejiang province. His biographical documents start with stereotypical descriptions of his beautiful voice when reading the classics, his intellectual facilities, and his running the gauntlet of Chinese classic education as well as Chan Buddhist training according to family expectations. Individual traits become observable from the time he was accepted into the congregation at Guangli chansi (弘利禪寺, Guangli Chan Monastery) at Mount Ayuwang. These characteristics are grounded less in his reputation as a talented student but rather as an even more talented administrator: The Guangli chansi compound burned down within one year after Yishan's arrival, and a large number of its residents dispersed. Yishan remained behind and assisted the newly arrived Wanji Xingmi (頑極行彌, n.d.) in his reconstruction efforts. His own words illustrate his rationale in doing so:

> Four abbots have I seen come and go, while I remained behind here one time after the other. It is certainly not of my doing [that my talents are disregarded and wasted]! But this honorable monk [Wanji] is not scant with his instructions (*kegon*, 化權). That may [finally] be my fortune! [. . .] [Yishan] decided to stick with Wanji, and their interactions were filled with affection. With ease they handed the cup to one another,[49] but when their conversation had reached the dictum, "I have not a single teaching to give to people,"[50] they suddenly fell into an opaque accord that had no more need for words.[51]

Afterward, Yishan was accepted as dharma heir by Wanji, and he continued to train with half a dozen masters in the Zhejiang area, until in 1285 he was appointed abbot of Zuyinsi (祖印寺) at Mount Siming (四明). For over ten years he filled this post, and his work seems not only to have consisted of the spiritual instruction and social supervision of the congregation but to also have gone a long way toward the restoration of monastery buildings and the procurement of a sound economic basis for the institution. An acquaintance of his—indeed an "old friend from across the mulberry grove" (*ishin no kyū*, 維桑舊)[52]—Yuxi Ruzhi (愚溪如

智, fl. second half of the thirteenth century), asked him to succeed to the abbacy of Guanyinsi (觀音寺) at Mount Putuoluo (普陀落) off the coast of Ningbo when he himself was feeling too frail to carry on:

> "I have grown too old and weary to lead my congregation. May I be permitted to trouble my Elder Brother Yishan with this duty?" But Yishan would not listen and held his hands over his ears. Even so, Ruzhi sent a messenger in secret to the Office of Monastic Matters and made his intention known there to have someone more knowledgeable than himself take over his position. The official document was delivered, and Yishan could refuse no longer. He thus moved into the compounds of Putuoluo, an extraordinary locale on the shores of the ocean.[53]

Undoubtedly the new position meant a significant increase in status and prestige for Yishan: the Guanyin monastery of Putuoluo is special not only because of the beauty of its scenery. Other and more significant factors come into play as well. Guanyinsi had been founded by the Japanese pilgrim Egaku (慧鍔, n.d.) in 858, when he erected a shrine for a statue of Guanyin there that he had brought with him from Mount Tiantai, praying for a safe return passage over the ocean. Putuoluo is also famed for being located at a junction of maritime infrastructures, and it is reported that traders and ship personnel would show their obeisance to Guanyin whenever they berthed at the island. Considering that the Putuoluo Guanyinsi's reputation was known all over East Asia, it seems safe to assume that this was also one of the prime motivators behind Yuxi being chosen by the Yuan authorities for diplomatic missions to Japan twice—although both attempts were frustrated by weather, mutiny, and adverse circumstances. The first diplomatic mission in 1283 was organized in the aftermath of the invasion attempt in 1281 but turned out to be impossible due to weather conditions. A second attempt in the following year saw a confrontation between the accompanying officials and the vessel's crew, resulting in a mutiny and the murder of the secular ambassadors. Ruzhi, however, escaped unharmed and made it back to the mainland and his abbacy:

> In the 21st year of Zhiyuan (至元) [1284], knowing that the people of Japan revered the Buddha, Wang Xiweng (王積翁) [1229–1284] and the monk Ruzhi of Putuoluo were dispatched as emissaries. But on their ship were people that knew no pious

conduct and they murdered Xiweng in cold blood, and the mission did not make it to Japan. In the year 23 the Emperor Kubilai Khan [1215–1294, r. 1260–1294] made it known: "Japan so far has not undertaken to counterattack. And now the Jiaozhi (交趾) are disrespecting our borders. We will set Japan aside and will focus on the Jiaozhi."⁵⁴

Yuxi was asked to take over an embassy to Japan again in 1299. He refused but, as in the case of the Guanyinsi abbacy, suggested a stand-in. Subsequently, it was Guanyinsi's new abbot Yishan who was called upon by the second emperor of the Yuan dynasty, Chengzong (成宗, 1265–1307, r. 1294–1307), to board a Japanese trader and gain passage to the enemy empire:

> The Superintendent and Great Master Yishan from the halls of Putuoluosi is to be made aware of this administrative order. Yen (燕), Minister to the Right, will proclaim the following decree: Yishan Yining is awarded the title of "Grand master of sublime compassion and universal order" (*Myōji kōsai daishi*, 妙慈弘濟大師). At the same time, he is installed as Superintendent of Śākyamuni's teaching (*Shakkyō sōtō*, 釋教總統) in Zhejiang. He is to be compensated with a brocade *kāṣāya* and one hundred rolls of paper money. Subsequently, he will join a five-head delegation to Japan.⁵⁵

Not only did Yishan receive the official honor of being awarded the title of grand master, but he was also installed as superintendent of Zhejiang province, making him the highest clerical authority and the person directly responsible to the state authorities in matters pertaining to Buddhism. He seemed to have reached the pinnacle of his career, but the advancement came with a price: he was to set sail for Japan the following morning. The handsome compensation may go without mention considering what Yishan's biography has to say about the objective of the diplomatic mission he spearheaded:

> The sacred will of our Emperor is enacted by the central government: The master is to be presented with a golden brocade along with the title of "Grand master of sublime compassion and universal order." He is to cross the waves of the ocean

and, having arrived in Japan, effect good-will between the two countries of ours (*nikoku no kō wo tsûzu* (通二國之好).[56]

Such enormous honors related not so much to Yishan's religious insight but to political expediencies. Also, individual proficiency in matters diplomatic can hardly be the one qualification that made Yuxi Ruzhi and Yishan Yining suitable candidates above everyone else. Rather, their position as abbots of Mount Putuoluo was just as decisive, if not more. The administrators of Guanyinsi, located at a crucial point of maritime trade routes connecting large parts of East Asia, were predestined to inspire the Japanese's trust and make any diplomatic offers the Yuan might have had more digestible to their irascible opponents beyond the ocean. And no doubt, offers were to be made: the Yuan Empire was in worse shape in the 1290s than ever before with revolts tying down military forces and resources toward Vietnam in the southeast and the Korean peninsula in the northeast, to say nothing of those conflicts making communication with the other filial Mongol realms across North and Central Asia ever more difficult. It seems a reasonable hypothesis that the Yuan were seeking guarantees from the Japanese that they would not strike back at this most inconvenient point in time.

Given these extraordinary circumstances, there can be no doubt that Yishan's going to Japan was not at all a natural culmination of a brilliant career and unique personality for the Buddhist cause. He was a pawn in political matters of existential significance to the Yuan dynasty. When he arrived in Japan, he did so in the multiple roles of a Chan master, a prestigious abbot, superintendent of the Buddhist institution in eastern China, ambassador, primary representative of the Yuan authorities, and most probably also as an informant maintaining his allegiances to the mainland.

But to merely reduce him to any of these would not only do him personal injustice; it would also be tantamount to disregarding the contemporary perception. For when Yishan arrived in Dazaifu, the Japanese authorities saw him very clearly for what he was, namely a Mongol delegate and informant, but they also recognized him as the genuine Chan master he was and, at least nominally, as one of the most powerful personae in the monastic hierarchy. So why not make use of him?

Accordingly, while Yishan had initially been placed under house arrest at Shuzenji (修禪寺), he was pardoned. Even more, he was prestigiously installed as abbot presiding, at the same time, over Kenchōji and Engakuji and subsequently went on, as abbot of Nanzenji (南禪寺) in the imperial city, and count the Ordained Emperor Go-Uda (後宇多, 1267–1324, r. 1274–1287) among his disciples. All the travels between Kamakura and Kyōto, interactions between the military and the court aristocracy, and the multiple offices at a host of different monasteries unsurprisingly had detrimental effects on Yishan's physical and mental condition. He went so far as to try and steal out of his Nanzenji abbacy in 1317 and flee to the provinces but was caught up by imperial messengers escorting him back to the imperial city. In winter of the same year, he felt his end approaching and wrote a farewell note to his sponsor Go-Uda:

> Your majesty the Ordained Emperor's sacred vehicle favored our gates with its arrival, and that was the pride and splendor of our monastic community. A certain monk has been afflicted with illness for many days now, and while he may attempt to make use of the limbs of his body they refuse to obey. He shall not be permitted to look upon your dragon-like countenance with his own eyes anymore. His time of great transformation has come, and his illusionary appearance is about to shatter. He takes the liberty of assuring you of his most loyal feelings and enters the *samādhi* of being reborn into nothingness.[57]

Yishan's deathbed poem runs along the lines expected from the genre: "A generation of going hither and yon. The Buddhas and Patriarchs hold their breath. Already the arrow has been shot from the bowstring, but emptiness falls down to the earth."[58] He put down the brush and died at age seventy-one. When Go-Uda arrived at the monastery the same day, he found Yishan's deceased body "sitting with legs crossed and awe-inspiring appearance, even as if he were still alive."[59] The next morning the ordained emperor bestowed upon Yishan the posthumous title of national teacher (*kokushi*, 國師) and had the state counselor write an obituary, while he himself contributed an epitaph:

> Internally, he abounded with spiritual vigor. Externally, he was productive in his virtuous dignity. When he swung his staff along the horizon, the winds of his authority moved this *sahā* world. When he threw his gold brocade across his shoulders, clouds of compassion spread across the world unto its very edges. His pioneering work opened the regions of the realms of men and

deities alike and shattered the fences braided by the Buddhas and Patriarchs. In the lands of the Song there may be ten thousand heroes, but in our dynasty, he is the one national teacher.[60]

Yishan's singularity was by no means the natural character of his personality. It was a contested, negotiated, and constructed identity. His biography recounts precisely such a discussion from when he was newly arrived in Japan and suspected of espionage:

> In the government, a discussion was going on: "We will not pardon an emissary being ordered here by the enemy country (*tekikoku no meishi*, 敵國命使)!" But another one said: "Even if we were not to pardon this emissary, what about the dignity of this monk? Let us register him [as if he were a lay person] and detain him at Shuzenji in Izu province."[61] Yet another said: "That a monk [true to] the Song dynasty (*Sōsō*, 宋僧) has travelled to our country means that we have unexpectedly come into possession of vast spiritual powers (*dōjutsu*, 道術). I have heard that Yishan Yining is a gentleman (*bōshi*, 望士) from the realm of the Yuan, and has received manifold benefits from them. But he stays aloof from their coercions. Such a *śramaṇa* is a field of blessings (*fukuden*, 福田), and a gentleman that is conversant with the Way to such a degree is without intentions and obligations even when mingling with the myriad things. When he still was in the country of the Yuan it was their good fortune, but if he has now come into ours, his fortune will be ours, as well. What reason would there be for him to maintain an integrity such as that of Su Wu (蘇武) [140–60 BCE]?[62] If he were to rot away in the impoverished hinterlands, this would imply that our country is hardly of the stuff that could provide a home to great *bhikṣus*."[63]

The rhetorical craftsmanship of the passage is spectacular: in the course of a few bits of discourse Yining is transformed from a Mongol spy (i.e., the enemy personified) to a diplomatic emissary, a venerable monk to be met with respect—even though as an informant he cannot be trusted—to a gentleman scholar and iconic Buddhist master, representative not of the Yuan but the Song dynasty, and finally to a blessing for the whole of the realm. Yishan's coming to Japan is rhetorically turned from a moment of crisis to one of *kairos*.

Concluding Remarks

Why would monks such as Lanxi, Wuxue, or Yishan accept invitations from their Japanese hosts and risk their careers in the *wushan* altogether, or give in to the pressure of Chinese authorities when it was obvious that they were about to risk life and limb in the aftermath of the 1274 and 1281 attacks on Japanese sovereignty? The above indicates that decisions were also motivated by occupational opportunities and career strategies. In the background, there emerges another suggestion: in the *wushan* and proto-*gozan*, the defining factor was not lineage (i.e., the genealogy based upon who one's master was). Yishan's master, for one, was as unknown as he was inconsequential, while Wuxue's biography looks to no less than three masters allegedly responsible for his spiritual maturity. In Five Mountains contexts, literary flourish, rhetorical skill, and cultural prestige were the features that distinguished oneself from one's competition. And these, in the last consequence, translated to social success pure and simple. A Zen monastic proved his mastery by advancing through the hierarchy and being recognized not only by his peers in the religious institution but also by the ruling powers in place. When Yishan became dharma teacher to the retired emperor Go-Uda, he took this as proof of his cultural savoir faire as well as his spiritual superiority and perceived no conflict between these two. In a context in which lineage did not account for as much as it did in the clear-cut factional registers of later times, the lateral, sociopolitical dimension attests to religious authenticity in its stead.

Zen's intimate relation to the high and mighty during medieval Japan provided ample opportunity for competing interpretations of the tradition. Even before the times of the institution's harshest critic Ikkyū Sōjun (一休宗純, 1394–1481), there had been Shūhō Myōchō (宗峰妙超, 1282–1338) and Kanzan Egen (關山慧玄, 1277–1360) who actively positioned themselves and their respective monasteries outside of the Five Mountains administration, forgoing the prerogatives and financial benefits that came with state protection. Their opposition came to play a crucial role in the further development of the tradition. For when the balance of power shifted and the control of the Ashikaga *bakufu* began to slip, the Five Mountains started to diminish in status accordingly, and it was at that point in time that the light shined on the *ōtōkan* (應燈關) lineage:[64] independent of religio-political institutions and largely autonomous, these monasteries—above all, Daitokuji (大德寺) and Myōshinji (妙心寺)—once located at the periphery of the religious landscape gravitated toward the center and displaced the Five Mountains as embodiments of

Zen Buddhist orthodoxy. And while the cultural glories of the *gozan* of times past remained beyond their reach, it is this initially unorthodox part of the tradition from which Hakuin Ekaku, Bankei Yōtaku (盤珪永琢, 1622–1693), and the other Tokugawa era reformers emerged, and a new type of discourse on Zen Buddhist identity and authenticity arose.

That the *gozan* have been almost completely purged from traditionalist memory has had its effect on scholarship, as well. Possibly, this is the Chan/Zen version of the "floating gap"[65] in cultural memory: communities recollect recent occurrences and mythologize events long past. The things in between, however, no longer linger in memory but have not yet entered the mythical pantheon, either. This is one dimension of the "Tang-Tokugawa alliance,"[66] by which Chan/Zen tends to represent itself either with reference to the golden era of great masters of the Tang dynasty or the reformers of the Tokugawa period and their modern-day epigones. The flipside, then, is the collective oblivion of certain parts of early modern Chan and medieval Zen Buddhist history.[67] Therein also lies a reason for responsible and balanced accounts of the "Song-Kamakura continuum" outlined above (i.e., the Kamakura Zen Buddhist tradition and its continuities with Song dynasty Chan).

In a way, then, Chan/Zen Buddhism is also a problem of epistemology. As an object of scholarship, it manifests the inclinations, predispositions, aversions, and blind spots we entertain. These effectively distort and omit certain aspects that once were (and still are) very much part and parcel of a historically conditioned phenomenon: medieval Chan/Zen in all its cultural and social embeddedness. As all objects of knowledge, Chan/Zen Buddhism, too, is doubly conditioned: by the contexts out of which it emerged and through which it was transmitted but also by the lens through which we may attempt to observe it.

Notes

1. I shall employ "Chan" and "Zen" for the parts of the tradition embedded in their respective Chinese and Japanese historical contexts; where transregional phenomena are concerned, these are referred to as "Chan/Zen."

2. See, for example, Shunryu Suzuki, *Zen Mind, Beginner's Mind* (New York: Weatherhill, 1970). This and the following bibliographic data have no intention of being exhaustive (or even impartial, for that matter). References, for the most part, are limited to literature in English and Japanese.

3. See, for example, analyses such as Robert H. Sharf, "Buddhist Modernism and the Rhetoric of Meditative Experience," *Numen: International Review for the History of Religions* 42, no. 3 (1995): 228–83.

4. Such is the case, for example, with James W. Heisig, Thomas P. Kasulis, and John C. Maraldo, eds., *Japanese Philosophy: A Sourcebook* (Honolulu: University of Hawai'i Press, 2011), 135–232.

5. See, for example, Yasuo Yuasa, *The Body: Toward an Eastern Mind-Body Theory*, translated by Shigenori Nagatomo and Thomas P. Kasulis (New York: State University of New York Press, 1987).

6. See, for example, Shin'ichi Hisamatsu, *Zen and the Fine Arts*, trans. Gishin Tokiwa (Tokyo: Kodansha International, 1971).

7. See, notoriously, Eugen Herrigel, *Zen in the Art of Archery*, translated by R.F.C. Hull (New York: Pantheon, 1958).

8. See, for example, Thomas Hoover, *The Zen Experience* (New York: New American Library, 1980).

9. In particular, see the powerful call for a general historiographical awareness in John McRae, *Seeing Through Zen: Encounter, Transformation, and Genealogy in Chinese Chan Buddhism* (Berkeley: University of California Press, 2003).

10. See the archetypical debate between Hu Shi (胡適, 1891–1962) and Suzuki Daisetsu (鈴木大拙, 1870–1966) in *Philosophy East and West* 3, no. 1 (1953): 3–24 (Hu: "Ch'an (Zen) Buddhism in China Its History and Method") and 25–46 (Suzuki: "Zen: A Reply to Hu Shih"). Somewhat more recently, it is Yanagida Seizan (柳田聖山, 1922–2006) who, through his European language students, effected a paradigm shift in the field of European language Chan/Zen studies. The list of contributors in Urs App et al., *Zum Gedenken an Prof. Yanagida Seizan. Volume in Commemoration of Prof. Yanagida Seizan* (Kyoto: Zenbunka Kenkyusho, 2008) reads like a veritable who's who of Chan/Sŏn/Zen studies.

11. Notable exceptions are the works of Robert E. Buswell and A. Charles Muller. See, for example, A. Charles Muller, *Korea's Great Buddhist-Confucian Debate. The Treatises of Chŏng Tojŏn (Sambong) and Hamhŏ Tŭkt'ong (Kihwa)* (Honolulu: University of Hawai'i Press, 2015), and Robert E. Buswell, *Numinous Awareness Is Never Dark: The Korean Buddhist Master Chinul's Excerpts on Zen Practice* (Honolulu: University of Hawai'i Press, 2016).

12. Monographic counterexamples to this claim are few and far between. Wu Jiang, *Leaving for the Rising Sun: Chinese Zen Master Yinyuan and the Authenticity Crisis in Early Modern East Asia* (Oxford: Oxford University Press, 2014), is a most welcome addition that presents a wonderfully detailed study on the beginnings of the Ōbaku (黄檗) school of Zen Buddhism.

13. See, for example, Murai Shōsuke (村井章介), ed., *Higashi Ajia no naka no Kenchōji: Shûkyō, seiji, bunka ga kōsa suru Zen no shōchi*, 東アジアの中の建長寺: 宗教・政治・文化が交叉する禪の聖地 [Kenchōji in the East Asian Context: The sacred site of Chan/Zen where religion, politics, and culture intersect] (Tokyo:

Benseisha, 2014), and Santō Natsuo (山藤夏郎), *"Tasha" toshite no koten: Chūsei Zenrin shigaku ronkō*〈他者〉としての古典: 中世禅林詩学論攷 [The classics as "other:" A treatise on the poetics of medieval Chan/Zen monasteries] (Ōsaka: Izumi shoin, 2015).

14. Cf. Steffen Döll, *Im Osten des Meeres. Chinesische Emigrantenmönche und die frühen Institutionen des japanischen Zen-Buddhismus* [East of the ocean. Chinese emigrant monks and the early institutions of Japanese Zen Buddhism] (Stuttgart: Franz Steiner, 2010).

15. To subscribe to a model of Zen Buddhist historiography oriented to the lives of great masters would be tantamount to falling prey to the so-called string of pearls fallacy. Also termed the "Great Man fallacy," this historiographic model takes personae as protagonists not directly related to their respective historic situations. Rather, it is hagiographic in nature insofar as it aims at proving that the precise opposite is the case: so-called Great Men are not at all products of their respective historic contexts; rather, it is these figures who produce history in the first place. My thanks to Jason Protass for insisting on this issue during conference discussions.

16. The biographies are deliberately taken at face value. Whether the anecdotes factually portray actual situations or fictionally elaborate the background of their protagonists' actions is inconsequential. What is important is that the narratives are based on the premise that the intended audience would find the portrayal convincing. Following McRae's "It's not true, and therefore it's more important" (*Seeing Through Zen*, xix), my point is not that any of the events happened precisely in the way they are narrated but that the way they are narrated allows us to observe the underlying, historically conditioned structures of plausible argument, immediate association, and common sense. The biographies in the later divisions of this paper are culled primarily from vol. 85 of Takakusu Junjirō (高楠順次郎) and Watanabe Kaikyoku (渡辺海旭), eds., *Taishō shinshū daizōkyō* 大正新脩大藏經, 100 vols. (Tokyo: Taishō issaikyō kankōkai, 1924–1932; hereafter referred to as "T" followed by number of text, volume, page count, and column), and the *Genkō shakusho* (元亨釈書), compiled by Kokan Shiren (虎關師錬, 1278–1346) in 1322, as edited in Fujita Takuji (藤田琢司), ed., *Kundoku Genkō shakusho* 訓読元亨釈書 [Transliteration of the Buddhist scripture of the Genkō era] (Kyōto: Zenbunka kenkyūjo, 2011; hereafter referred to as "GKSS" followed by fascicle number, page number, and column).

17. See Charlotte von Verschuer, "Looking from Within and Without: Ancient and Medieval External Relations," *Monumenta Nipponica* 55, no. 4 (2000), 537–66.

18. The contributions collected in Richard K. Payne and Taigen Dan Leighton, *Discourse and Ideology in Medieval Japanese Buddhism* (London and New York: Routledge, 2006), provide an excellent overview of representative parts of these trends.

19. See Hok-Lam Chan, *The Fall of the Jurchen Chin. Wang E's Memoir on Ts'ai-chou Under the Mongol Siege (1233-1234)* (Stuttgart: Franz Steiner, 1993).

20. See the contributions in John D. Langlois (ed.), *China Under Mongol Rule* (Princeton, NJ: Princeton University Press, 1981).

21. Cf. Bernard Faure, "The Daruma-shū, Dōgen, and Sōtō Zen," *Monumenta Nipponica* 42, no. 1 (1987): 25–55.

22. Cf. Steven Heine, *Did Dōgen Go to China? What He Wrote and When He Wrote It* (Oxford: Oxford University Press, 2006).

23. Cf. the detailed study Yu Iji (C. Yu Weici, 俞慰慈), *Gozan bungaku no kenkyū* 五山文學の研究 [A study of Five Mountains literature] (Tokyo: Kyūko shoin, 2004), particularly the discussion 109–182.

24. Cf. Martin Collcutt, *Five Mountains: The Rinzai Zen Monastic Institution in Medieval Japan* (Cambridge: Cambridge University Press, 1981).

25. It seems unlikely for precisely this reason that an invitation by Hōjō Tokiyori (北条時頼, 1227–1263) should be directed specifically at Lanxi's person as, for example, Ishikawa Rikizan (石川力山), *Zenshū kojiten* 禅宗小事典 [A small dictionary of the Chan/Zen school] (Kyōto: Hōzōkan, 1999), 253, suggests.

26. Jōrakuji was rededicated as Zen monastery on this occasion. Initially, the compound had been a family temple of the Hōjō clan known as Awafune midō (粟船御堂) that Yasutoki (泰時, 1183–1242) had built for his stepmother.

27. Cf. Steffen Döll, "Kloster und Konsistenzebene: Das *shichidō garan* im Zen-Buddhismus als sakraler Raum, Kosmos und Körper" [The monastery as level of consistency: The *shichidō garan* in Zen Buddhism as sacred space, cosmos, and body], *Heilige Orte und sakraler Raum in den Religionen Japans*, edited by Michael Wachutka (Munich: Iudicium, forthcoming 2022).

28. GKSS 6:211b.

29. Collections of monastic regulations such as the *Mohe sengqi lü* (J. *Makasōgiritsu*, 摩訶僧祇律, cf. T1425.22.227a–549a; Skt.: *Mahāsāṃghikavinaya*) or the *Wufenlü* (J. *Gobunritsu*, 五分律, cf. T1421.22.1a–194b; Skt.: *Mahīśāsakavinaya*) report of a band of six monks that is supposed to have caused incessant mischief. Many of the *vinaya* regulations are based on their misconduct. Having been convinced by the Buddha to stick to the rules, they became monks of great virtue.

30. GKSS 6:211b.

31. Tamamura Takeji (玉村竹二), *Gozan zensō denki shūsei* 五山禪僧傳記集成 [Collected biographies of Five Mountains Chan/Zen monks] (Kyōto: Shibunkaku, 2003, new edition), 114.

32. See Shinya Mano, "Yosai and Esoteric Buddhism," in *Esoteric Buddhism and Tantras in East Asia*, ed. Charles D. Orzech, Henrik H. Sorensen, and Richard K. Payne (Leiden/Boston: Brill, 2011), 827–834, and Nakao Ryōshin (中尾良信),"Eisai ha Zensō ka Tendaisō ka" 栄西は禅僧か天台僧か [Was Eisai a Zen monk or a Tendai monk?], in *Nihon Zenshū no densetsu to rekishi* 日本禅宗の伝説

と歴史 (The legends and histories of the Zen school in Japan) (Tokyo: Yoshikawa kōbunkan, 2005), 47–70.

33. Ishikawa, *Zenshû kojiten*, 253. For the discussion of "pure" versus "syncretistic" Zen, also cf. Wada Ukiko (和田有希子), "Kamakura chūki no Rinzai Zen: Enni to Rankei no aida" 鎌倉中期の臨済禅: 円爾と蘭渓のあいだ [The framework of the Rinzai sect in the mid-Kamakura period: Enni Ben'en and Rankei Dōryū], *Journal of Religious Studies* 77, no. 3 (2003), 629–53.

34. T2016.48.418b, quoting the *Chanyuan zhuquanji duxu* 禪源諸詮集都序 [Preface to the collection of Chan sources] by Guifeng Zongmi (圭峰宗密, 780–841), cf. T2015.48.397b–413c, here 400b. Cf. Albert Welter, *Yongming Yanshou's Conception of Chan in the* Zongjing lu: *A Special Transmission within the Scriptures* (New York: Oxford University Press, 2011), 79.

35. Quoted from Wada, "Framework," 105.

36. Quoted from *Daikaku zenji zazenron* 大覺禪師坐禪論 in *Kokuyaku zenshū sōsho* (國譯禪宗叢書) [*Collected Texts of the Chan/Zen school in Japanese Translation*], ed. *Kokuyaku zenshū sōsho kankōkai* (國譯禪宗叢書刊行會), vol. 12 (Tokyo: Kokuyaku zenshū sōsho kankōkai, 1985), 579–597 and 603–610, here 579 and 603.

37. The single monograph study on Wuxue to date is Jiang Jing 江靜, *Furi Songseng Wuxue Zuyuan yanjiu* 赴日宋僧无学祖元研究 [A study on the Song dynasty monk Wuxue Zuyuan who traveled to Japan] (Beijing: Shang wu yin shu guan, 2011).

38. GKSS 8:228a.

39. Collcutt, *Five Mountains*, 71.

40. That is the posthumous title of Wuzhun Shifan.

41. A direct quote of *Chuanxin fayao* 傳心法要 [Essentials of the teachings for transmitting the mind] by Huangbo Xiyun (黃檗希運, fl. ninth century), cf. T2012A.48.379c–384a, here 384a.

42. GKSS 8:228a.

43. On Hachiman and his inclusion into a Buddhist framework, see Bernhard Scheid, "Shōmu Tennō and the Deity from Kyushu: Hachiman's Initial Rise to Prominence," *Japan Review* 27 (2014): 31–51.

44. GKSS 8:229a–b.

45. GKSS 8:229b–230a.

46. GKSS 8:228a.

47. For a translation of Musō's *Muchū mondōshū* 夢中問答集 [Collection of questions and answers from a dream], cf. Thomas Yūhō Kirchner, *Dialogues in a Dream* (Kyōto: Tenryu-ji Institute for Philosophy and Religion, 2010). The relation between Kōhō, Musō, and Yishan is vividly evoked in chapter 4, "Chineseness» and «Japaneseness» in Early Medieval Zen: Kokan Shiren and Musō Soseki" in David Pollack, *The Fracture of Meaning. Japan's Synthesis of China from the Eighth through the Eighteenth Centuries* (Princeton, NJ: Princeton University Press, 1986), 111–33. On Musō, see Molly Vallor, *Not Seeing Snow: Musō Soseki*

and Medieval Japanese Zen (Leiden: Brill, 2019), based on her 2013 Stanford University dissertation "No Place Called Home: The Works of Zen Master Musō Soseki (1275-1351)."

48. The biographical analysis in Akabane Yūsaburō (丹羽友三郎), "Issan Ichinei Zenji ni tsuite" 一山一寧禅師について (On the Chan/Zen master Yishan Yining)," *Kōryō joshi tanki daigaku kiyō* 光陵女子短期大學紀要 *Cross Culture* 4 (1986), 1-26, has been updated impressively by Satō Shūkō (佐藤秀考), "Issan Ichinei no denki shiryō" 一山一寧の伝記資料 (Biographic materials of Yishan Yining); and "Kokan Shiren sen «Issan kokushi gyōjō» no yakuchû" 虎関師錬撰『一山国師行状』の訳註 [An annotated translation of Kokan Shiren's biography of national master Yishan], *Komazawa daigaku Bukkyōgakubu kenkyû kiyō* (駒澤大學佛教學部研究紀要) 75 (2017), 37-128.

49. This alludes to a banquet scenario: Wine is enjoyed communally with filled cups being handed from host to guest and back again. Metaphorically, a Chan/Zen exchange in conversation, a so-called question and answer (C. *wenta*, J. *mondō* 問答) session, is indicated.

50. A formula frequently encountered in the "recorded sayings" genre (C. *yulu*, J. *goroku* 語錄). Its *locus classicus* may be identified in the "Records of Linji" (*Linji lu* 臨濟錄): "The mountain monk has not a single teaching to give to people 無一法與人. Only this: to cure their sickness and to release them from their bonds," cf. T1985.47.500b.

51. From the *Issan Kokushi goroku* 一山國師語錄 [Recorded sayings of national master Yishan], T2553.80.331b.

52. T2553.80.331c. Groves of mulberry trees were, in traditional Chinese households, located in the vicinity of the garden fence facing toward neighboring properties. Yishan and Yuxi thus seem to have felt a connection by virtue of coming from the same area.

53. T2553.80.331c

54. "Chronicle of the Yuan dynasty" (*Yuanshi* 元史), fasc. 208 (cf. ctext.org).

55. T2553.80.333b.

56. T2553.80.331c.

57. T2553.80.332b.

58. T2553.80.332b.

59. T2553.80.332b

60. T2553.80.333a.

61. Shuzenji had originally been founded in 798 by Gōrin (杲隣, fl. early ninth century), a disciple of Kūkai (空海, 774-835), as an institution of the Shingon school of Japanese Buddhism. The monastery was converted to the Zen denomination only for Lanxi. When the shogunal succession was in dispute, Minamoto no Noriyori (源範頼, d. 1193) was killed by orders of his elder brother Yoritomo (頼朝, 1147-1199) at Shuzenji. The second shogun Yoriie (頼家, 1182-1204) was put under house arrest there, as well, in all likelihood by the regent Hōjō Tokimasa

(北条時政, 1138–1215), only to be murdered there within the year, as well. Yishan being detained at Shuzenji turns out to be a poorly veiled threat.

62. Su Wu was a general of the Early Han (前漢) dynasty (206–8 BCE). He is remembered for having maintained his integrity even after being captured by enemy troops. His biography records him returning home after nineteen years.

63. T2553.80.332a.

64. Named for the posthumous title of Nanpo Shōmyō (南浦紹明, 1235–1309; also Nanpo Jōmin), Daiō *kokushi* (大應國師), that of his disciple Shūhō Myōchō (Daitō *kokushi* 大燈國師), and his disciple's disciple Kanzan Egen.

65. Cf. Jan Assmann, *Das kulturelle Gedächtnis: Schrift, Erinnerung und politische Identität in frühen Hochkulturen* (Munich: C. H. Beck, 1992); English translation *Cultural Memory and Early Civilization: Writing, Remembrance, and Political Imagination* (Cambridge: Cambridge University Press, 2011).

66. Albert Welter, "Zen Buddhism as the Ideology of the Japanese State: Eisai and the *Kōzen gokokuron*," *Zen Classics. Formative Texts in the History of Zen Buddhism*, ed. Steven Heine and Dale S. Wright (Oxford: Oxford University Press, 2006), 65–112, here 97.

67. This is no hard and fast rule but rather a loose typology of how Chan/Zen is often perceived even academically, and counterexamples may be found—Dōgen, for one; also Dahui Zhonggao (大慧宗杲, 1089–1163).

Chapter 7

The Lute, Lyric Poetry, and Literary Arts in Chinese Chan and Japanese Zen Buddhism

GEORGE A. KEYWORTH

Introduction

Above the entrance to the Meditation Hall at Daiōji (大雄寺), a Sōtō Zen Buddhist temple in rural Tochigi prefecture in eastern Japan, there is a wooden engraving with the seal-script Sinographs for "Study Effortless Action" (*gaku mui*, 學無為, alt. *mui o manabu*, 無爲は学ぶ). Along with another wooden engraving of "Efficacious Vulture" (*ryōju*, 靈鷲) above the main entrance to the monastery compound, these signs were crafted and given as a gift to the temple by a Chinese Caodong lineage Buddhist émigré monk, Donggao Xinyue (東皋心越, 1639–96, J. Tōkō Shin'etsu; also C. Xinyue Xingchou, J. Shin'etsu Kōchū, 心越興儔), when he was in the area to bathe at the nearby hot springs during the seventh lunar month of 1693.¹ Xinyue also gave the abbot, Kakumon Kantetsu (廓門貫徹, d. 1730), a copy of the *Supplement to the Jingshan* (徑山) [printed] edition of the *Chinese Buddhist canon (Jiaxing xu zangjing,* 嘉興藏續藏) to be placed in a revolving sūtra repository (*tenrinzō,* 転輪蔵) at Daiōji.² Remarkably, it took only thirteen years for Kakumon Kantetsu to write a complete commentary to one of the thirty-six Chan texts in this supplement, *Commentary to Stone Gate's Chan of Words and Letters* (*Chū sekimon mojizen,* 註石門文字禪, J.B135), which is the collected works of a Northern Song dynasty Huanglong-Linji lineage poet-monk by the name of Juefan Huihong (覚範惠洪, J. Kakuhan Ekō, 1071–1128). According to a preface to the work composed by contemporary Sōtō Zen master Manzan Dōhaku (卍山道白, 1636–1715), Kantetsu had completed the commentary to every literary piece in the thirty rolls by 1710.10.1 (first day of the tenth month, 1710).³ Because Xinyue was an accomplished poet, artist, and Chinese lute (*qin*, *kin* 琴) player, I speculate that he almost certainly introduced Kantetsu to Huihong's poetry and prose, and quite possibly to some of the other books that Huihong wrote about Northern Song dynasty (960–1127) Chan Buddhism.

Manzan Dōhaku was not the only famous Zen monastic who commended Kantetsu for his commentary to Huihong's collected works; prefaces by Mujaku Dōchū (無著道忠, 1653–1744), a Rinzai-shū monk from Myōshinji (妙心寺) in Kyoto,⁴ an Ōbaku 黃檗宗 monk named Gettan Dōchō (月潭道澄, 1636–1713), and one of Xinyue's disciples, Ranzan Dōchō (蘭山道昶, d. 1756), are included in *Commentary to Stone Gate's Chan of Words and Letters*.⁵ Elsewhere I have argued that together with Kantetsu's commentary to Huihong's collected works, these four prefaces are indicative of esteem for Huihong as a poet and scholar monk in Rinzai, Ōbaku, and Sōtō Zen circles in Edo or Tokugawa period (1603–1866) Japan. In this chapter, first I outline some of the reasons why Xinyue has been virtually ignored by scholars in East Asia or in the West, and provide an overview of him as a poet, artist, lute player and instructor, and scholar monk primarily in seventeenth-century Japan. Next, I examine how Xinyue wrote poetry to express his feelings about homesickness, his exposure to Zen Buddhism and religion in Japan, his many travels, and even his impression of how to use poetry to express the taste of Chan. In this respect there seems to be a literary connection between Huihong and Xinyue to match the tangible evidence in Kantetsu's commentary to Shimen's literary Zen (*Shimen wenzi chan*). But I am afraid that after reading through Xinyue's collected works, there is little direct evidence of him having read Huihong's treatises on poetic criticism, "Evening Talks from a Cold Studio" (*Lengzhai yehua*, 冷齋夜話) and the "Regal Morsels from the Imperial Kitchen" (*Tianchu jinluan*, 天廚禁臠).⁶ I also explore how Xinyue famously [re]kindled an interest in the Chinese lute and the special relationship between Zen and the literary arts among Buddhist monastics and secular intellectuals who were already actively engaged in what would soon become what Benjamin Elman has called a "boom in Chinese studies in Edo and Kyoto in the eighteenth century."⁷ Finally, I ask if we can see Zen and the literary arts as promoted by Xinyue—and

Huihong—as partly responsible for reestablishing strict Zen training in China and Japan during the seventeenth and seventeenth centuries?

Zen and the Literary Arts

In the 1940s, Robert H. van Gulik (1910–67) credited Donggao Xinyue with reintroducing the Chinese lute to Japan, declaring that "[i]n China he is practically unknown; but in Japan abundant materials about him have been preserved. For in Japan he became famous, and had considerable influence on the cultural life of his times."[8] After he was evacuated to Chongqing from Tokyo as a representative of the Dutch foreign service in 1942, Van Gulik even wrote a short treatise about Xinyue that can be difficult to locate.[9] There is little doubt that Xinyue became a renowned lute teacher at the temple that Tokugawa Mitsukuni 徳川光圀 (1628–1701) had constructed for him, Tentokuji (天徳寺) in Mito (水戸), where an anthology of his poetry, prose, a list of the works of art he created in Japan, and even the Pure Rules (*shingi*, 清規) for his novel Chinese-style Jushō (壽昌派, Shouchang) collateral branch of Sōtō Zen were kept until Asano Fuzan (浅野斧山) published *Tōkō zenshū* (東皋全集) in 1911.[10] Because we have the collected works for Juefan Huihong and Donggao Xinyue, which are infrequent in the case of most influential Chinese Chan, Korean Sŏn, or Japanese Zen teachers,[11] let alone Buddhist monastics, it is a far more straightforward process to investigate the historical rather than the religious perspective of a historian of religions. Whereas religion is "that discourse whose defining characteristic is its desire to speak of things eternal and transcendent with an authority equally transcendent and eternal," history, "in the sharpest possible contrast, is that discourse which speaks to things temporal and terrestrial in a human and fallible voice while staking its claim to authority on rigorous cultural practice."[12]

Apart from several sentences about Donggao Xinyue in negligible footnotes to research articles in English, some notes in Japanese, or several fruitful sentences about him in Jiang Wu's study of Yinyuan Longqi (隱元隆琦, J. 1592–1673, Ingen Ryūki, the "founder" of Ōbaku Zen in Japan), *Leaving for the Rising Sun: Chinese Zen Master Yinyuan and the Authenticity Crisis in Early Modern East Asia*, few have followed up with van Gulik's research about Donggao Xinyue.[13] I suspect that despite the manifold strides that scholars working in the field of Chan/Sŏn/Zen studies have made over the past five decades, Philip Yampolsky's (1920–96) declaration (in the otherwise remarkable overview of the history of Zen in medieval, early modern, and modern Japan in the introduction to *The Zen Master Hakuin: Selected Writings*) still rings true for many, though certainly not all, scholars. He writes: "It might not be too much of an exaggeration to say that when Zen flourishes as a teaching it has little to do with the arts and that when the teaching is in decline its association with the arts increases."[14] The teachings of Zen, therefore, are often insulated from expressions about them in literary forms produced by actual people, with the result that the "polemical tools of self-assertion" with "numbers, dates, and other details [to] lend an air of verisimilitude to a story" in discourse records (C. *yulu*, J. *goroku*, 語錄), kōan (C. *gong'an*, 公案) collections, and lamp or flame records (C. *denglu*, J. *tōroku*, 燈錄) are rarely offset with materials more closely tied to the mundane world. Disputed tropes about degeneration and reinvigoration with regard to pure or strict (*junsui*, 純粋) versus syncretic or mixed (*kenshū*, 兼修) teachings, transmission narratives, and monastic regulations are infrequently placed within temporal, terrestrial, and fallible historical contexts.[15]

With a goal of emphasizing the significance of Hakuin Ekaku (白隠慧鶴, 1686–1768), renowned for "reviving" the Rinzaishū from a moribund state,[16] Yampolsky contrasts earlier Zen masters in Japan who "devoted themselves to literary endeavors" by producing and emphasizing the literature of the Five Mountain temples in Kyoto and Kamakura (*Gozan bungaku* (五山文学)) with Hakuin, who saw Zen as a "teaching," rather than as an expression of poetry, art, theater, and the tea ceremony.[17] Yampolsky does not suggest that Zen literature in China and Japan fails to "explicate the teaching of Zen and of Buddhism as a whole."[18] Rather, he proposes that only Hakuin's Ō-Tō-Kan 応灯関 school (or lineage) and the teachings that Yinyuan Longqi brought to Japan from China, "colored with the accretions of Pure Land thought," rejuvenated an "almost dormant Rinzai Zen of Japan" and represent legitimate Zen teachings.[19] With apparently little provocation from members of the other Zen lineage in Japan, Sōtōshū, Yampolsky reveals that "Hakuin returned to the strict koan [kōan] study of the Sung [Song] period [960-1279]."[20] In this rendition, study of Song kōan collections like the *Blue Cliff Record* (C. *Biyan lu*, J. Hekiganroku, 碧巖錄, T.48.2003] and the *Gateless Checkpoint* (alt. *Gateless Barrier*; C. *Wumen guan*, J. Mumonkan, 無門關, T.48.2005]) in the Linji and Rinzai lineages (and, by extension, investigation of Buddhist scriptures and/or meditative techniques for members of the Caodong and Sōtō lineages), necessitate analysis far more than the culturally significant Song expressions of the literary arts.

Donggao Xinyue with Sinophiles and Sinophobes

It is equally possible that a lack of significant attention to Zen and the literary arts may be due to the sources we often use to investigate these East Asian religious traditions. Hakuin is, for example, as famous for his extraordinary paintings as he is for his Zen teachings.[21] Hakuin was only ten when Donggao Xinyue died, but it is possible that he may have seen one of the paintings that Xinyue did of Bodhidharma,[22] or the commemorative portrait of Chan/Zen teachers (*chinzō*, 頂相) Xinyue painted of Ming loyalist Zhu Shunshui (朱舜水, 1600–1682), who was summoned to Mito by Tokugawa Mitsukuni in 1665.[23] Xinyue wrote this poem to Zhu:

> For an old friend who carries the load of combining Confucian and Buddhist [teachings], who truly and especially knows music, a poem to sincerely match the lovely rhyme of your exquisite phrases about the autumn crab apple (begonia) in full bloom.
>
> 熟翁儒釋并擔, 真乃格外知音 為賦海棠, 盛開佳句見贈謹次芳韻。)[24]
>
> 勝地叨居此一方, In this area is a marvelous site where residents chatter away like the sound of clattering knives,
>
> 何多嘉客探幽芳。 What's going on with many fine guests deepening their virtue?
>
> 花容撲面縣奇壁, Like fair flowers[25] caught striking the face of strange wall,
>
> 冶色薰心遶畫廊。 Reeking with amorous thoughts, caught in a painted corridor.
>
> 秉燭夜遊良又似, Truly resembling a candlelit night tour. . . .[26]
>
> 更闌錯認是唐皇。 Mistakenly [taken] late at night by Tang emperor [Xuanzong 玄宗].

從茲愁見遊人醉，Now I have the anxious thoughts of a drunk traveler,

漫掬清泉自滌腸。Selfishly scooping up pure spring water, purifying my intestines.

Donggao Xinyue's personality emerges from poems like this one in his collected works and in the many material objects he crafted that are still extant in Mito and in Nagasaki, where he journeyed to and from along the Tōkaidō to Kyoto from Edo, and by boat from Osaka. Looking back at the life and legacy of Xinyue long after the advent of the Meiji Restoration (1868), the Empire of Japan, and even the broad and sweeping postwar changes within Japanese Buddhist traditions, let me be clear from the onset that Xinyue neither founded a particularly influential branch of Sōtō Zen in Japan, nor does he seem to have been particularly influential in the wake of increasing esteem among intellectuals for the arch-nativist and Sinophobe Motoori Norinaga (本居宣長, 1730–1801).[27] Roughly between the mid-1600s until 1800, however, bidirectional Sino-Japanese exchange of books in classical Chinese (*kanbun* 漢文) imported and exported via the Ningbo-Nagasaki trade prompted a new class of scholars to become literate in classical Chinese to study Confucian teachings and the Chinese literary arts.[28] Primarily Buddhist monastics had been literate in classical Chinese before this, as Chinese scholars and Chan teachers arrived via this trade route. Daozhe Chaoyuan (道者超元, J. Dōsha Chōgen, d. 1660) arrived in 1651, before returning to the continent in 1658. He was followed by Yinyuan Longqi who arrived in Nagasaki in 1654, and within only seven years (1661), and with support from the shōgunate, he and his Chinese and Japanese disciples—lay and monastic—had established a new tradition of Japanese Zen Buddhism with its head temple at Manpukuji (萬福寺) on Mt. Ōbaku (黃檗山) in the small city of Uji, south of Kyoto. It was through a so-called Chinese temple (*karadera* 唐寺) within this network in Nagasaki's Chinatown (*Tōjin yashiki* 唐人屋敷)—Kōfukuji (興福寺)—that Xinyue Xingchou was invited to visit and reached Japan from China in 1677.[29]

Donggao Xinyue was born on August 28, 1639, in Pujiang county (浦江縣) in Jinhua prefecture (金華府) in Zhejiang province. He received tonsure at Baoensi (報恩寺) in Suzhou at seven years old (1646), but he received transmission from Caodong lineage teacher Juelang Daosheng (覺浪道盛, 1592–1659) at Yongansi (永安寺) in Jianchang county, Jiangxi province, in 1658. Juelang Daosheng was a celebrated teacher in his own right who was acquainted with famous Ming literati such as Qian Qianyi (錢謙益, 1582–1664), an incredibly prolific author of commentaries to Buddhist scriptures, especially the Chinese pseudo-Śūraṃgama-sūtra (*Shoulengyan jing*, *Shuryōgongyō*, 首楞厳経, T.18.945).[30] When the Manchu armies attacked and took the city of Hangzhou in 1676, he had moved to Yongfusi (永福寺). Soon thereafter, Xinyue left Hangzhou on a ship bound for Nagasaki; Xinyue was only thirty-eight years old.[31] After only a year in Nagasaki staying at Kōfukuji, Tokugawa Mitsukuni sent a messenger, Imai Kōjirō (今井小四郎), with an invitation for Xinyue. Due to restrictions concerning Chinese traveling outside Nagasaki, it took another five years before he set out for Mito in 1683.[32] Xinyue lived and traveled with Chinese Ōbakushū monks during this time. And we know that he visited Manpukuji and other Ōbaku monasteries.[33]

Not only did Donggao Xinyue befriend fellow Sōtō Zen monks like Dokuan Genkō (独庵玄光, 1630–98) and Manzan Dōhaku while he was waiting in Nagasaki to travel to Mito, he also seems to have read Japanese Zen literature and celebrated some Zen teachers in his poems. We know that, for example, Xinyue read Dōgen's (道元, 1200–1253) Extensive Record of Eihei (Eihei kōroku, 永平廣錄) during the eighth lunar month of 1678 at Shōfukuji (聖福寺) in Nagasaki.[34] Earlier that same spring in Osaka, while visiting the restoration of Zuiryūji (瑞龍寺) as an Ōbaku temple,[35] Xinyue wrote the following poem commending Tetsugen Dōkō (鐵眼道光, 1630–82), who oversaw the production of the first printed Chinese Buddhist canon in Japan in 1681:

For Great Master Tetsugen (*Si Tetsugen daishi* 似鐵眼大師)[36]

扶桑開士幾如公, How many bodhisattvas are there in the land where the sun rises?

幸沐餘光有始終。 Fortunately when one bathes at twilight, there is a beginning and end.

果見為人親切處， To see the fruits one must be kind everywhere,

豈知格外又同風。 How could you know the extraordinary has the same appearance?

言不盡，意無窮。 With incomplete words, meaning is inexhaustible.

總是當年悟性空。All of those years with enlightened awareness of emptiness (śūnyatā).

There is no need to reiterate what Jiang Wu has written about disputes concerning lineage transmission between Ōbaku and Sōtō Zen monks during the late seventeenth and early eighteenth centuries, let alone claims to have conveyed to Japan an "authentic transmission" of Rinzai Zen Buddhism through the publication of Feyin Tongrong's (費隱通容, J. Hiin Tsūyō, 1593–1661) *Strict Transmission of Five Chan Lamps* (*Wudeng yantong* 五灯嚴統, J. *Gotō gentō*, XZJ 1567) in Japan in 1657.[37] But we know that during the fifth lunar month of 1680 a dispute arose while he was still in Nagasaki concerning how the lineage of one of his teacher's teachers in China, Wuming Huijing (無明慧經, 1547–1617), as well as Juelang Daosheng, was recorded in *Strict Transmission of Five Chan Lamps*. Part of the dispute concerned reasons why the Donggao in Donggao Xinyue was not Dongming (東明) instead, following Xingfusi (興福寺) on Mount Dongming in the city of Nanjing.[38] Xinyue opted to seclude himself in meditative retreat to avoid his Ōbaku critics and wrote the following rather odd record for the occasion:

"Maṇḍala pass record" (*Mantuoluo guan ji*, 曼陀羅關記)[39]

Shut off in seclusion on the fourth day of the seventh lunar month during the *gengshen* (庚申, *kanoesaru*) year (29 July, 1680). Because a group of people have been speaking about *mantuoluo* (*mandara*), [I write that] in Chinese the Sanskrit *mantuo luo* (*maṇḍala*) means agreeable (or suitability). But, in fact, it does not mean what is agreeable to oneself or agreeable to others. Instead, [agreeable] is understood as using your own mind with nothing to be ashamed of in front of anyone, to be applied to decisions as they come, like an illusion or a dream. How can I wait for someone to tell me yes or no? One knows by seeing ordinary attachment to phenomena. Because the world is a finite place, [suitability] is not only the realm of important men. Only the mind is boundless. The boundless mind abides in an infinite realm. Therefore, circumstances are always suitable. As for the matter of self-sufficiency or suitability to others here, in this case nothing is suitable. As for the pleasures of simple living, I am not alone in considering wealth to be a floating cloud; this matter is also a floating cloud![40]

I have never encountered this definition of maṇḍala before; usually one thinks of sacred ritual spaces. But it seems intriguing that Xinyue tells us that the word for maṇḍala was used in the dispute about the authenticity of his transmission lineage to mean something like "seal." The original in Xinyue's handwriting was kept in the treasury house of Tentokuji, but it was destroyed during the Great Kantō earthquake on September 1, 1923. A picture of it is preserved in *Tōkō zenshū*.⁴¹

Once he had moved on to enjoy Tokugawa Mitsukuni's patronage in Mito, Xinyue seems to have become a magnet for Chinese lute enthusiasts and eminent Sinophiles. Zen Buddhist transmission disputes behind him, there is instead a Chinese lute transmission chart from Xinyue, *Tōkō kinpu* (東皋琴譜), which lists two principal disciples, doctor of Chinese medicine Hitomi Chikudō (人見竹洞, alt. Hitomi Kakuzan, 鶴山, 1620–88) and Confucian scholar Sugiura Kinzen (杉浦琴川, 1671–1711), and six students who learned the lute from Sugiura.⁴² According to van Gulik, Xinyue's disciples spread the art of playing the Chinese lute across the country, but the "heighday (sic) falls subsequent Kansei [寛政] and Bunka [文化] periods (1789–1817).⁴³ Van Gulik regales his reader with descriptions of three lutes that Xinyue brought with him to Japan: *Yushun* 虞舜 (Gushun), covered with red cement; *Suwang* 素王 (Soō), which he gave to Hitomi Chikudō; and *Wanhesong* (萬壑松, J. Mankakushō), preserved at Tentokuji in Mito.⁴⁴ Xinyue composed songs to be sung to accompany tunes on the lute, and even instructed his disciples about the accessories for lute playing with table, stands, and scholar-musician paraphernalia in a drawing entitled "[Items] to grasp in Japan" (*Fusang sang*, 扶桑操, J. *Fusō tsuau*, literally meaning "items handled in the land where the sun rises").⁴⁵ Xinyue was also well aware of a reference to Huang Tingjia (黃庭堅, 1045–1105) playing a lute and engaging in storytelling to amuse himself beside West Lake in Hangzhou in *Record of Anecdotes from Lake Luo* (*Luohu yelu*, 羅湖野錄, ca. 1155), which he shared with a monk named Genkō (玄光) at Kōtaiji (晧台寺) in Nagasaki.⁴⁶

Expressing Nostalgia and Encountering Japan

Donggao Xinyue was certainly nostalgic about the home he fled when the Manchurian army captured Hangzhou. Hangzhou, West Lake, and remembering the sights and sounds now inaccessible to him are conveyed in this poem about journeying:

"Cherishing travel(s)" (*Huai you* 懷遊)[47]

昔從潮上遊，荏苒今如此。	Past travels on the tides, slip by imperceptibly until now.
眼見春復秋，循環若撚脂。	These eyes have seen spring again pass into fall, in cycles as I twirl my fingers.
山光澹影浮，水色波紋泚。	Tranquil shadows float like dawn light on a mountain, water ripples[48] brilliantly.
楊柳緣侵衣，桃花紅映綺。	The time when poplar and willow [leaves] invade and cover [everything], peach blossoms shine will a red brilliance.
歌聲滿六橋，畫槳盈湖裏。	Sounds of singing covers the six bridges, paintings of many oars in the lake.
潮畔人登樓，笑望來西子。	People on the [lake] shore climb pavilion [stairs], laughingly gaze out to look for Xi Shi (西施) [beauty] coming.[49]
微茫菰藻流，彷彿荷風起。	The water is murky due to wild aquatic plants, seemingly perfect for lotus plants to sprout.
放浪此潮中，半生志猶喜。	Dissolute in this water, half a lifetime's still makes me happy.
故人天一方，目斷雲千里。	The sky is an old friend, clouds cannot be seen for a thousand *li*.
何日復于斯，孤山尋處士。	What a day at that place? Seeking out a recluse on Mount Gu.[50]

Probably written during the twelfth month of 1678, perhaps the clamor of Hangzhou was as distant from him in Nagasaki as Edo and Mito still were.[51] We see no clear allusions to Chan/Zen teachings, Buddhism, nor even the mind of a monastic, but rather the feelings of a fallible individual who we may or may not see as enlightened here.

The same theme of longing is communicated in the following poem, which records the difficult time he spent on [Mount] Putuo island (普陀山), just off the coast from Ningbo, where the bodhisattva of compassion, Avalokiteśvara (C. Guanyin, J. Kannon 観音菩薩), is believed to dwell, and Xinyue landed as he fled Hangzhou:

> "Listening to the tide late at night on Putuoshan" (*Putuo shenye wenchao*, 普陀深夜聞潮)[52]
> 荒齋鎮夜獨無眠， After a meager meal on a cool night, alone, I cannot sleep,
> 靜聽波濤拍岸顛。 Listening quietly to [sound of] waves beating on and toppling the shore.
> 澎匕湃匕聲何似， Splashing[53] and surging, what does the sound resemble?
> 識與鐘山響倍妍。 I identify the beautiful rhythmic sound of a mountain [temple] bell.

I wonder if this is a poem written while on the island or after he had landed in Nagasaki?[54] There is neither any mention of lutes nor of his friend Zhu Shanshui, who we discussed earlier as the individual who arranged an invitation to Mito on his behalf. Once again, there are discernable allusions to his religious orientation as a monk.

How different is the tone of the following poem sent to Mitsukuni sometime in 1680 while still awaiting permission to travel to Edo via Kyoto with Imai Kōjiro?

> "Sent afar" (*Ji yuan* 寄遠)[55]
> 至道猶同日月星， To reach the road still takes many days, months, or even years,
> 君能修治輔朝延。 You can instruct about how to prolong the state by cultivating [good] governance.
> 無為風化殊相合， Conforming to particular manners with effortless action,
> 寓意玄微德自馨。 [Using] deeply hidden allusions to make self-virtue pervasive.

In my reading there is a distinct sense of frustration balanced with praise for the influence Mitsukuni could evidently wield. It is almost certainly not incidental that Xinyue mentions the famous teaching of "effortless action" (*wuwei*, 無為) in the *Laozi Daode jing* (老子道德經); the same Sinographs he would carve in wood for Daiōji twelve years later. Yet this poem expresses another aspect of Xinyue's personality that must have made him an admired lute and presumably Chinese classical literature teacher in Kantō: Xinyue's approach to Chan/Zen made full use of the literary arts.[56] There is even an undated poem he wrote about the flavor—or taste—of Chan/Zen:

> "Characters [to express] the flavor of Chan" (*wei Chan zi* 味禪字)[57]
> 水石出奇清晝永，　Rocks shaped by water[58] constantly emit an unusual purity in daylight,
> 松風淡薄晚生涼。　I am cooled by a slight breeze [that rustles] the pine trees.
> 休稱似隔人間世，　I say that respites [like this] separate [me from] the mundane world,
> 別有乾坤歲月長。　Apart from extensive time on Heaven and Earth.

Where are the allusions to Chan/Zen literature? Where are the bodhisattvas he mentioned in his tribute to Tetsugen? I would like to speculate that the "rustling pine breeze" may be an allusion to playing one of his lutes. This poem seems to confirm that as the foremost literary art, poetry expresses Chan/Zen, perhaps just as Xinyue thought that playing the Chinese lute could as well.

There is an innocence or naiveté in the following poem that Xinyue wrote to remember when he gazed up at Iwashimizu Hachimangū (石清水八幡宮), an eminent shrine near the junction of the Yodo (淀川) and Katsura (桂川) rivers south of Kyoto; Xinyue was probably on a boat heading toward Ōsaka, on his return to Nagasaki, rather than on his way toward Mito:

> "Seeing Mount Hachiman from a boat" (*Zhou zhong jian Hachiman-san*, 舟中見八幡山)[59]
> 崒律南山秀，　An exquisite lofty mountain from the south,
> 春寒曉望時。　I gaze [up] at dawn a spring cold spell.
> 松風常彷彿，　I often reminisce about breezes through pine trees,
> 竹露更漣漪。　or small ripples on dew drops on bamboo at night.

社廟依山古，The temple to earth gods depends on the old mountain,
神宮歷世奇。The *kami* shrine has unusually endured the centuries.
眇餘幽事杳，Far away, I gaze at the peaceful world,[60]
轉覺似還迷。My thoughts turn and are lost in the past.

Several things are striking about these lines. First, although many tourists take a cable car to the top of the hill to visit the shrine precincts today, there is little that makes this site lofty. Second, I am unsure if Xinyue would have been familiar at that time with the indigenous deities of Japan, the *kami*, but as a deity of warfare, the reference to a temple dedicated to the earth or soil god(s) reveals his inexperience in Japan. Xinyue reads the landscape like a Tang or Song poet would: temples endure the centuries encircled by hostilities. Indeed, it seems as if Xinyue was reading Iwashimuzu Hachimangū through the lens of an accomplished Chinese poet.[61]

The final poem for review is one that Xinyue wrote to observe his visit to Zuisenji (瑞泉寺) in Kamakura, where Musō Soseki (夢窗疎石, 1275–1351) is believed to have constructed a garden with a belvedere, the Henkai Ichirantei (遍界一覽亭):

"Rhymed poem about Musō [Soseki's] *Ichirantei*" (*He Musō heshang yilan ting yun* 和夢窗和尚一覽亭韻)[62]
一覽高閣浩氣新，The high 'bird's eye view pavilion' is a refreshing noble spirit,
天高海濶渺無垠。The sky is high, the ocean vast without boundaries.
若將心眼來觀此，If one comes and sees this with a mindful eye,
未舉念時已着塵。Without yet giving [this place] much time for consideration, it stops attachment to this world.

In a departure from the tenor of the other poems examined here, this poem alludes to Buddhist teachings (e.g., impermanence and nonattachment) and may even reflect his experience of the space.[63] Since the site was intended for meditation, Xinyue's reading seems to connect with the place as his views of Iwashimizu Hachimangū did not. But I think there is something much more at stake with this site and in this poem: Xinyue encounters the site of a legendary Japanese Zen literary artist at a time in his life when he was a sought-after teacher of the literary arts in Mito.

Conclusions: Contributions to an Edo Zen "Renaissance"

Chinese learning during the Edo period is typically contrasted with what preceded it during the Kamakura-Muromachi eras (1185–1573) within the system of Five Mountain Zen temples (*Gozan jissatsu*, 五山十刹), an institutional ranking system designed to replicate the Chinese system ostensibly of the same name, established during the Southern Song dynasty (1127–1279) to administer the official Chan temples around Hangzhou. Elman and other historians have even gone so far as to suggest that the Tokugawa government endowment of the Senseiden (先聖殿) college for classical Chinese learning (儒学) established in 1674 in Edo, coupled with altered curricula at Domain schools (*hankō*, 藩校) for warrior elites and their families, or in private, temple schools (*terako-ya*, 寺子屋) is evidence that the Buddhist clergy lost their role as purveyors of Chinese learning.[64] Further evidence of a decline in status and significance for the Buddhist clergy is usually seen with the establishment of the *danka seido* (檀家制度, alt. *jidan seido*, 寺檀制度, or *terauke seido*, 寺請制度) system that made it compulsory for everyone to affiliate—or register—with local Buddhist temples.[65] Yet the meeting between Donggao Xinyue and Kakumon Kantetsu at Daiōji in the late seventeenth century points to another conclusion. I do not think it is coincidental that Kantetsu took such a remarkable interest in working through Juefan Huihong's collected works to produce his *Commentary to Stone Gate's Chan of Words and Letters*. Nor do I think that Xinyue was the only avenue through which Kantetsu could have learned of Huihong and his legacy of literary or scholastic Chan.

Notes

Titles in Japanese and [reconstructed] Sanskrit in the Taishō canon follow Paul Demiéville et al., *Répertoire Du Canon Bouddhique Sino-Japonais, Édition De Taishō* (Paris: Librairie d'Amerique et d'Orient, 1978). Cf. Lewis R. Lancaster and Sung-bae Park, eds., *The Korean Buddhist Canon: A Descriptive Catalogue* (Berkeley: University of California Press, 1979).

1. George A. Keyworth, "'Study Effortless Action' Rethinking Northern Song Chinese Chan Buddhism in Edo Japan," *Journal of Religion in Japan* 6, no. 2 (2017): 1–2; Sugimura Eiji, *Bōkyō No Shisō Tōkō Shin'etsu* (Tokyo: Miki shobō, 1989), 199–201, 29; Takada Shōhei, *Tōkō Shin'etsu: Tokugawa Mitsukuni ga kieshita yūkoku no toraisō* (Tokyo: Ribun shuppan, 2013), 266–69.

2. Xu Xingqing, "Shin'etsu Zenji to Tokugawa Mitsukuni No Shisōhensen Shiron: Shu Shunsui Shisō to No Hikaku Ni Oite," *Nihon kanbungaku kenkyū Nishōgakusha University* 3 (2008). Other names for this canon include: Jiaxing (嘉興版), Wanli (萬曆版), Lenyan monastery (楞嚴寺版), or square-format edition (*Fangce zangjing*, 方冊藏經). Cf. Florin Deleanu, "The Transmission of Xuanzang's Translation of the *Yogācārabhūmi* in East Asia: With a Philological Analysis of Scroll Xxxiii," in *Kongōji Issaikyō No Sōgōteki Kenkyū to Kongōjiseikyō No Kisoteki Kenkyū: Kenkyū Seika Hōkokusho*, ed. Ochiai Tshinori (Tokyo: Kokusai Bukkyōgaku daigakuin daigaku, 2007), 625, no. 8. On the canon at Daiōji, see Kurasawa Yoshihiro, *Kurobanesan Daiōji Shodōhaikan* (2005), 22. A copy of the Chinese Buddhist canon commonly known as the Jingshan edition (徑山版) that first belonged to the fifth *shōgun*, Tokugawa Tsunayoshi 德川綱吉 (1646–1709) and was given to Kantetsu by the would-be eighth *shōgun*, Tokugawa Yoshimune (德川吉宗, 1684–1751). The edition held today by the Tochigi Prefecture Bureau of Cultural Properties (Tochigiken shitei bunkazai, 栃木県指定文化財), once held at Daiōji, has forty-five hundred rolls. On revolving sutra repositories, see L. Carrington Goodrich, "The Revolving Book-Case in China," *Harvard Journal of Asiatic Studies* 7, no. 2 (1942).

3. Kakumon Kantetsu, ed. *Chū sekimon mojizen*, vol. 5, Zengaku Tenseki Sōkan (Kyoto: Rinsen shoten, 2000), 97–99. Shi Huihong et al., eds., *Zhu shimen wenzichan*, 2 vols., Riben Songdai wenxue yanjiu congkan (Beijing: Zhonghua shuju, 2012), 1:5–6.

4. Urs App, "Chan/Zen's Greatest Encylopaedist Mujaku Dōchū (1653–1744)," *Cahiers d'Extrême Asie* 3 (1987).

5. Kakumon Kantetsu, 97–102. Shi Huihong et al., *Zhu shimen wenzichan*, 1:5–13.

6. *Lengzhai yehua*, ten rolls, comp. ca. 1118. Gozan printed edition ca. 1645 in one case (*satsu* [冊]), rpt. of Yuan ed. (ca. 1343) in: Yanagida Seizan and Shiina Kōyū, *Zengaku tenseki sōkan*, vol. 5, Kyoto, 2000, 759–811. Also, *Lengzhai yehua*, Beijing: Zhonghua shuju, 1988. *Tianchu jinluan*, 1 roll. 1670 rpt. of 1507 printed ed. from Komazawa University, Gozan ed. in: Yanagida Seizan and Shiina Kōyū, *Zengaku tenseki sōkan*, vol. 5, Kyoto, 2000, 815–40. *Tianchu jinluan*, Shanghai: Zhonghua shuju, 1958, rpt. of Wang Zongyan ([王宗炎] 1755–1826) ed.

7. Benjamin A. Elman, "Sinophiles and Sinophobes in Tokugawa Japan: Politics, Classicism, and Medicine During the Eighteenth Century," *East Asian Science, Technology and Society: An International Journal* 2 (2008): 107.

8. Robert Hans van Gulik, *The Lore of the Chinese Lute: An Essay in Ch'in Ideology*, Monumenta Nipponica Monographs (Tokyo: Sophia University, 1940), 204–5. Many of van Gulik's propositions about the legendary status of the lute do not stand up quite as well to contemporary scrutiny; see Xiao, "Van Gulik's *the Lore of the Chinese Lute* Revisited," *Monumenta Serica* 65, no. 1 (2017).

9. Robert Hans van Gulik, *Ming Moyiseng Donggao Chanshi Jikan* (Chongqing: Shangwu yinshuguan, 1944).

10. Kōchū and Asano Fuzan, *Tōkō Zenshū: Jō Ge-Kan Betsuroku* [Collected works of Tōkō [Shin'etsu]: two rolls with and additional records] (Tokyo: Ikkatsusha, 1911). The Pure Rules are in the supplemental section (*betsuroku*); there is an outline analysis in *Shouchang lüe qinggui* (*Jushō ryaku shingi*) in Fuzan, *Tōkō Zenshū*, jō: 26–33. There is apparently a Chinese edition published in 2006 by Zhejiang Renmin chubanshe, see Nagai Masashi, "Tōkō Shin'etsu Koto Sekikō," *Komazawa daigaku bukkyō gakubu kenkyū kiyō* 73, no. 1 (2015): 11. These Pure Rules were allegedly promulgated at Shouchangsi (壽昌寺, Jushōji, alt. Yongansi (永安寺) [Eianji]) in Jianchang county (建昌福), Jiangxi province, which is the name of the temple where Xinyue received transmission before he left—or fled—to Japan. Shouchang si was designated an official Chan monastery (*conglin*, J. *sōrin*, 叢林) in 1391; it was rebuilt and received supplemental government funds in 1511 and 1523. See Suzuki Tetsuo, *Chūgoku Zenshū Jimei Sanmei Jiten* (Tokyo: Sankibō busshorin, 2006), 22, 177.

11. There are other collected works, of course, such as *Zibai zunzhe quanji*, 紫柏尊者全集 [Sage of purple cypress tree's collected works] 2 ([1621], XZJ no. 1452, 73:262b, for the early Ming Chan teacher Daguan Zhenke (大觀真可, 1543–1604).

12. No. 2 in "Theses on Method" in Bruce Lincoln, *Gods and Demons Priests and Scholars: Critical Explorations in the History of Religions* (Chicago and London: University of Chicago Press, 2012), 1.

13. Wu Jiang, *Leaving for the Rising Sun: Chinese Zen Master Yinyuan & the Authenticity Crisis in Early Modern East Asia* (Oxford and New York: Oxford University Press, 2015), 86–87, 106, 278n20. See also *Enlightenment in Dispute: The Reinvention of Chan Buddhism in Seventeenth-Century China* (Oxford and New York: Oxford University Press, 2008), 99. An example of a helpful footnote is in Michel Mohr, "Zen Buddhism during the Tokugawa Period: The Challenge to Go Beyond Sectarian Consciousness," *Japanese Journal of Religious Studies* 21, no. 4 (1994): 354 n. 22. Cf. Nagai Masashi, "Tōkō Shin'etsu kenkyū josetsu," in *Zenshū no shomondai*, ed. Imaeda Aishin (Tokyo: Yūzankaku, 1979); "Tōkō Shin'etsu kenkyū satsuki" [Study notes about Tōkō Shin'etsu], *Komazawa daigaku bukkyō gakubu kenkyū kiyō* 75 (2013); *Zengaku Daijiten*, ed. Zengaku Daijiten Hensansho (Tokyo: Taishūkan shoten, 1985), 918. For omissions, see, for example, David E. Riggs, "The Rekindling of a Tradition: Menzan Zuiho and the Reform of Japanese Sōtō in the Tokugawa Era" (PhD, University of California, Los Angeles, 2003); "The Life of Menzan Zuihō, a Founder of Dōgen Zen," *Japan Review* 16 (2004). Unsurprisingly, Donggao Xinyue is not mentioned in Heinrich Dumoulin, James

Heisig, and Paul F. Knitter, *Zen Buddhism: A History Volume 2 Japan* (New York: Macmillan, 1988).

14. Philip B. Yampolsky, *The Zen Master Hakuin: Selected Writings*, Records of Civilization, Sources and Studies, no. 86 (New York: Columbia University Press, 1971), 9. Two exceptions are, one on Chinese Chan, Jason Avi Protass, "Buddhist Monks and Chinese Poems: Song Dynasty Monastic Literary Culture" (PhD diss., Stanford University, 2016). And one on Japan, Joseph D. Parker, *Zen Buddhist Landscape Arts of Early Muromachi Japan (1336–1573)*, SUNY Series in Buddhist Studies (Albany: State University of New York Press, 1999).

15. See "McRae's Rules of Zen Studies" nos. 2–3 in John R. McRae, *Seeing through Zen: Encounter, Transformation, and Genealogy in Chinese Chan Buddhism* (Berkeley: University of California Press, 2003), xix. Steven Heine has addressed a dichotomy in the field in terms of a binary between two often oppositional narrators he refers to as the "Traditional Zen Narrative (TZN)" versus the "Historical and Cultural Criticism (HCC)." In other words, apologists versus scholars, which obligingly encompasses both the rhetorical narratives within premodern Chan/Zen literature and modern scholarly discourse that returns, again and again, to the rhetoric of decline and reinvention, among other things. See Steven Heine, *Zen Skin, Zen Marrow: Will the Real Zen Buddhism Please Stand Up?* (Oxford and New York: Oxford University Press, 2008), 6–30.

16. Robert E. Buswell Jr. et al., eds., *The Princeton Dictionary of Buddhism* (Princeton, NJ: Princeton University Press, 2013), 342.

17. Yampolsky, *The Zen Master Hakuin: Selected Writings*, 8–9. On the Five Mountains monasteries see Ibuki Atsushi, *Zen No Rekishi* (Kyōto: Hōzōkan, 2001; repr., 2005), 218–21. and Martin Collcutt, *Five Mountains: The Rinzai Zen Monastic Institution in Medieval Japan*, Harvard East Asian Monographs, no. 85 (Cambridge, MA: Harvard Council on East Asian Studies, 1981). Morten Schlütter, *How Zen Became Zen: The Dispute over Enlightenment and the Formation of Chan Buddhism in Song-Dynasty China* (Honolulu: University of Hawai'i Press, 2008) provides some discussion of how both Chan and Vinaya monasteries developed within the environment of the *Wushan shicha* 五山十刹 system in China.

18. Yampolsky, *The Zen Master Hakuin: Selected Writings*, 7.

19. Yampolsky, *The Zen Master Hakuin: Selected Writings*, 9–10. Considered to be the only surviving Rinzai Zen lineage in Japan, this is the lineage of [the Rinka (林下) or beyond the Groves] Myōshinji (妙心寺), as well as Daitokuji (大徳寺), in Kyoto. Ō-Tō-Kan stands for Nanpo Jōmyō (南浦紹明, 1235–1308), who received transmission from Xutang Zhiyu (虚堂智愚, J. Kidō Chigu, 1185–1269) in 1265, and returned to Japan in 1267; Shūhō Myōchō (宗峰妙超, 1282–1338); and Kanzan Egen (関山慧玄, 1277–1360), who founded Myōshinji. Ibuki Atsushi, *Zen No Rekishi*, 317.

After the thirty-third abbot of Manpukuji, the Ōbakushū (黄檗宗) head temple, Ryōchū Nyoryū (良忠如隆, 1793–1868), the lineage reverted "back" through Hakuin and the Ō-Tō-Kan; see Wu, *Leaving for the Rising Sun*, 242.

20. Yampolsky, *The Zen Master Hakuin: Selected Writings*, 11.

21. Just one well-known example in English is Stephen Addiss, *The Art of Zen: Paintings and Calligraphy by Japanese Zen Monks* (New York: H. N. Abrams, 1989).

22. Sugimura Eiji, *Bōkyō No Shisō Tōkō Shin'etsu*, 91.

23. van Gulik, *The Lore of the Chinese Lute*, 205. On the *chinzō* Xinyue painted, see Sugimura Eiji, *Bōkyō No Shisō Tōkō Shin'etsu*, 98. On the genre of *chinzō*, see T. Griffith Foulk and Robert H. Sharf, "On the Ritual Use of Ch'an Portraiture in Medieval China," in *Chan Buddhism in Ritual Context*, ed. Bernard Faure (London and New York: Routledge Curzon, 2003).

24. Kōchū and Asano Fuzan, *Tōkō Zenshū* jō: 49–50; Sugimura Eiji, *Bōkyō No Shisō Tōkō Shin'etsu*, 32–33.

25. It is also possible that 容 should be substituted with 客; see 33.

26. 秉燭夜遊 is borrowed from Li Bai's (李白, 701–762) *Chun yeyan congdi taohuayuan xu* (春夜宴從弟桃花園序) [Preface for a Spring evening banquet with cousins in a peach blossom garden].

27. Wu, *Leaving for the Rising Sun*, 254–59, 63; Elman, "Sinophiles and Sinophobes in Tokugawa Japan," 93–102. See also Michele Marra, *The Poetics of Motoori Norinaga: A Hermeneutical Journey* (Honolulu: University of Hawai'i Press, 2007).

28. On the broader history of Sino-Japanese book exchange, see Wang Yong, Chen Xiaofa, and Ge Jiyong, *Zhong-Ri shuji zhi lu yanjiu* (Beijing: Beijing tushuguan chubanshe, 2003).

29. Ibuki Atsushi, *Zen No Rekishi*, 262, 66; Xu Xingqing; Wu, *Enlightenment in Dispute*, 99.

30. *Lengyanjing shu jiemeng chao* 楞嚴經疏解蒙鈔 [Notes to explain the confusion among the commentaries of the Śūraṃgama-sūtra], XZJ 287.13.497a–928a24. See also Ch'oe Changsik [Pŏphye], *Tonkōbon Ryōgongyō no kenkyū* (Tokyo: Sankibō busshorin, 2005), 212–13. See also Wu, *Enlightenment in Dispute*, 96, 131.

31. Sugimura Eiji, *Bōkyō No Shisō Tōkō Shin'etsu*, 224–27; Ibuki Atsushi, *Zen No Rekishi*, 161; van Gulik, *The Lore of the Chinese Lute*, 205.

32. Sugimura Eiji, *Bōkyō No Shisō Tōkō Shin'etsu*, 57.

33. van Gulik, *The Lore of the Chinese Lute*, 205.

34. "[Poem written during] the middle of 1678" *Yanbao liu wuwu zhong* 延宝六戊午仲 (*Enpō roku tsuchinoe chū*) in Sugimura Eiji, *Bōkyō No Shisō Tōkō Shin'etsu*, 40–42. *Eihei kōroku* in *Dōgen zenji zenshū* (道元禅師全集, Collected works of Zen master Dōgen), edited by Kawamura Kōdō (河村孝道) et al. (Tokyo: Shunjusha, 1988–1993), 4:182–297. See also Kagamishima Genryū, *Dōgen zenshi to so no shūhen* (Tokyo: Daitō shuppansha, 1985).

35. Sugimura Eiji, *Bōkyō No Shisō Tōkō Shin'etsu*, 60.

36. Kōchū and Asano Fuzan, *Tōkō Zenshū* jō, 88.

37. Wu, *Leaving for the Rising Sun*, 193–97, 247.

38. Takada Shōhei, *Tōkō Shin'etsu*, 59–168.

39. Kōchū and Asano Fuzan, *Tōkō Zenshū* ge: 12. The text reads: 時歲上章[庚]涒灘[申]夷則[七月]之四日閉關。因名額之曰曼陀羅。梵語曼陀羅者。華言云適意也。蓋以自適其適。非適於此也。但得自心了然。無愧於人。而順逆施來。猶同夢幻。豈待肯人我是非。即為着相凡夫之知見。非大人境界耳。而世間有盡者境也。無盡者心也。以無盡之心。處有盡之境。故處境而適其常。此所以自適其適。非適於此也。如疏水曲肱之樂。不獨以當貴為浮雲即此亦一浮雲而已哉。

40. *Analects* (論語) *Shuer* (述而) 16: The Master said, "With coarse rice to eat, with water to drink, and my bended arm for a pillow; I have still joy in the midst of these things. Riches and honors acquired by unrighteousness, are to me as a floating cloud." 子曰：「飯疏食飲水，曲肱而枕之，樂亦在其中矣。不義而富且貴，於我如浮雲。」https://ctext.org/analects/shu-er (accessed July 2021).

41. Sugimura Eiji, *Bōkyō No Shisō Tōkō Shin'etsu*, 74–75.

42. Kōchū and Asano Fuzan, *Tōkō Zenshū* ge: 61; van Gulik, *The Lore of the Chinese Lute*, 206, 11–12.

43. *The Lore of the Chinese Lute*, 208. On the significance of the reign period name *bunka* in terms of a highpoint in Chinese studies in Edo Japan, see Elman, "Sinophiles and Sinophobes in Tokugawa Japan," 102.

44. van Gulik, *The Lore of the Chinese Lute*, 206–207.

45. Kōchū and Asano Fuzan, *Tōkō Zenshū* ge: 62–63. The Katakana on the text reads *tsu a u* for *cao* Sugimura Eiji, *Bōkyō No Shisō Tōkō Shin'etsu*, 104.

46. Cf. *Luohu yelu* 1, XZJ no. 1577, 83:384, b12-c22.

47. Kōchū and Asano Fuzan, *Tōkō Zenshū* jō: 109–10.

48. Reading 紋 instead of 汶.

49. Xi Shi was a beauty from the Spring and Autumn period (771–476 BCE) in the state of Wu 吳.

50. Gushan ("solitary or lone" hill) is an island in the northwest corner of West Lake in Hangzhou.

51. Sugimura Eiji, *Bōkyō No Shisō Tōkō Shin'etsu*, 79–80.

52. Kōchū and Asano Fuzan, *Tōkō Zenshū* jō, 60.

53. There are two possible characters for the repeated sound of splashing: either 澎々 or 溯々. See Sugimura Eiji, *Bōkyō No Shisō Tōkō Shin'etsu*, 24.

54. Eiji, *Bōkyō No Shisō Tōkō Shin'etsu*, 24.

55. Kōchū and Asano Fuzan, *Tōkō Zenshū* jō, 101.

56. Using this translation of the title I have the translation by Richard John Lynn, *The Classic of the Way and Virtue: A New Translation of the Tao-Te Ching of Laozi as Interpreted by Wang Bi*, Translations from the Asian Classics (New York: Columbia University Press, 1999) in mind. Sugimura Eiji, *Bōkyō No Shisō Tōkō Shin'etsu*, 81.

57. Kōchū and Asano Fuzan, *Tōkō Zenshū* jō, 131.

58. I do not think that these two Sinographs should be read as *suiseki*, as one might were the author Japanese. But the impression does resonate with *gongshi* (供石), so-called scholar's rocks in China.

59. Kōchū and Asano Fuzan, *Tōkō Zenshū* jō, 73–74.

60. Reading 幽事 as 平隱, perhaps indistinct, rather than the world of the dead.

61. Sugimura Eiji, *Bōkyō No Shisō Tōkō Shin'etsu*, 48–49.

62. Kōchū and Asano Fuzan, *Tōkō Zenshū* jō, 136.

63. Sugimura Eiji, *Bōkyō No Shisō Tōkō Shin'etsu*, 142.

64. Elman, "Sinophiles and Sinophobes in Tokugawa Japan," 97–99. Ibuki Atsushi, *Zen No Rekishi*, 253–77.

65. Nam-lin Hur, *Death and Social Order in Tokugawa Japan: Buddhism, Anti-Christianity, and the Danka System*, Harvard East Asian Monographs 282 (Cambridge, MA: Harvard University Asia Center, 2007). Equally relevant to institutional changes to Edo-era Buddhist temples (and shrines devoted to *kami*) were the regulations concerning all sectarian temples (*Shoshū jiin hatto* 諸宗寺院法度) promulgated in the seventh month of 1665. Cf. Miyake Hitoshi, "Japanese Mountain Religion: Shrines, Temples and the Development of Shugendō," *Cahiers d'Extrême Asie* 18 (2009): 82.

Section III
The Korean Sŏn Nexus

Chapter 8

Pure Rules and Public Monasteries in Korea

JUHN Y. AHN

Introduction

On May 29, 1398, a Sŏn (禪) monk named Sangch'ong (尚聰, n.d.) submitted a letter to the king, Yi Sŏnggye (李成桂, 1335–1408), who had just founded the new Chosŏn dynasty six years earlier.[1] The letter caught the king's attention. The king had good reason to take Sangch'ong's letter seriously, for the latter was no ordinary monk. Sangch'ong was the chief monastic officer (K. *kamju* 監主) of Hŭngch'ŏnsa (興天寺), the late Queen Sindŏk's (神德王后, 1356–96) memorial monastery in the new Chosŏn capital.[2] As a monastery commissioned by the dynastic founder himself, needless to say, Hŭngch'ŏnsa and its chief monastic officer carried much political clout. For reasons that he outlines carefully in the letter he submitted to the throne, Sangch'ong decided to put this clout to good use.[3]

The Buddhist establishment, Sangch'ong explained to the king, was in a deplorable state. During the waning years of the last dynasty, Buddhist schools only pursued fame and fortune and fought to gain control over prominent monasteries.[4] This ostensibly left the dynasty with only one or two monasteries where genuine learning and practice took place. To remedy this situation, Sangch'ong recommended that only talented monks of high moral standing be allowed to serve as abbots. Once installed, abbots of Sŏn monasteries should remain true to their specialization and instruct their assemblies with cases and verse comments (K. *yŏmsong* 拈頌) from the transmission of the lamp collections. Similarly, abbots of Kyo (教) monasteries should instruct their assemblies with the words of the

Buddha and authoritative commentaries.[5] In due time, these monasteries could then expect their assemblies to be full of virtuous monks.

For Sangchʼŏng, however, this was not enough. He also urged the king to have all prominent monasteries outside the capital—monasteries that considered themselves to be independent or "head" monasteries (K. ponsa 本寺)—follow the model of Songgwangsa (松廣寺), place themselves under the authority of a single head monastery, and become subject to inspection and monitoring. This, Sangchʼŏng claimed, would prevent any lapse or decline in their observation of monastic rules and ritual obligations to the state.

Sangchʼŏng also had something important to say about monastic rules. Korean monks, he claimed, tend to simply imitate their Chinese counterparts—without fully understanding them—in devising monastic rules. There was, in his opinion, a better alternative. Rather than turn a blind eye to the custom of haphazardly borrowing monastic rules from China, Sangchʼŏng urged the king to have all Korean monasteries study, practice, and permanently observe the regulations (K. che 制) left behind by Pojo Chinul (普照知訥, 1158–1210). What Sangchʼŏng was urging the king to require for all monasteries, it seems, was the use of Chinul's "Admonitions to Beginning Students" (Kye chʼosim hagin mun 誡初心學人文).[6]

If what Sangchʼŏng claims in his letter can be taken for granted, then it seems to be the case that, before 1398, the rules and guidelines that were used to govern Buddhist monasteries in Korea were largely drawn, in haphazard fashion, from texts imported from China. This included, as we shall see, the Pure Rules (or rules of purity) (C. qinggui 清規) texts that outlined the regulations, etiquette, and bureaucratic structures used by official ten directions (C. shifangcha 十方刹) or public Chan monasteries in China. But, curiously, the importation of these influential texts did not entail the establishment of public Sŏn monasteries in Korea. There were, to be sure, state-recognized monasteries in Korea before 1398, but none of them were monasteries where the abbacy remained "public" (i.e., open to monks from different tonsure and transmission lineages). Moreover, none of them were public Sŏn monasteries that required the abbot to possess a transmission certificate from a Chan/Sŏn master. If so, then why did Sŏn monks in Korea import and study Pure Rules texts and, more importantly, how did they make sense and use of them? For the sake of convenience, this chapter will try to answer these questions by focusing on three key phases in the history of the Sŏn tradition when attempts were made to borrow and make sense of Pure Rules texts and the monasticism outlined therein. But first let us confirm that these attempts were made when public Sŏn monasteries did not yet exist in Korea.

Public Monasteries in Korea

Due in large part to the lack of textual information, how individual monasteries were organized, operated, and regulated in pre-Koryŏ (918–1392) Korea is largely unknown. During the Silla period, there was, it seems, a state-sanctioned Buddhist clerical bureaucracy that was modeled on that of the Northern Wei (386–534).[7] Individual monasteries also had a bureaucratic hierarchy. Existing records show that they were run by the three principals (K. *samgang* 三綱), namely the dean, or "top seat" (K. *sangjwa* 上座), prior or "monastery chief" (K. *saju* 寺主), and deacon or "rector" (K. *yuna* 維那).[8] But, as Sem Vermeersch points out, the "three principals" system seems to have been gradually displaced by a new one that privileged the position of the abbot sometime in the late tenth century.[9] This, as Vermeersch also notes, is commonly attributed to the influence of the "Chan monasticism" purportedly invented by Baizhang Huaihai (百丈懷海, 749–814). T. Griffith Foulk and others, however, have shown this claim about Baizhang to be more myth than reality.[10]

Whatever the true provenance of the abbot system in Korea may be, there is no doubt that it became the dominant system during the Koryŏ period. This, however, was not accompanied or followed by the development of public monasteries. In fact, some of the most prominent "Sŏn monasteries" of the early Koryŏ period—monasteries associated with renowned monks who transmitted Chan lineages from China—remained "private." In 971, King Kwangjong, for instance, issued an edict that identified the monasteries Kodalwŏn (高達院), Hŭiyangwŏn (曦陽院), and Tobongwŏn (道峰院, also known as Yŏngguksa 寧國寺) as "unmovable" (*pudong* 不動) monasteries where the abbacies were handed down directly from master to disciple.[11] These influential monasteries founded by early Sŏn pioneers were, in the Chinese parlance of the time, private "disciple-lineage cloisters" (C. *jiayi tudi yuan* 甲乙徒弟院).

Archaeological evidence also suggests that Song dynasty–style public monasteries were never built in the Korean peninsula. There is, indeed, little reason to believe that the monastic structures characteristic of a public monastery such as the dharma hall (K. *pŏptang* 法堂), saṅgha hall

(K. *sŭngdang* 僧堂), abbot's quarters (K. *pangjang* 方丈), and patriarch hall (K. *chosadang* 祖師堂) were present in Korea during the ninth and tenth centuries. Recent archaeological and textual research has shown that the monasteries established or, more commonly, refurbished by the early Sŏn pioneers tended to follow and preserve the structural layout of earlier monasteries in Korea, whose central axis mainly consisted of a front gate, stupa(s), golden hall (K. *kŭmdang* 金堂), and lecture hall (K. *kangdang* 講堂).[12]

The archaeologist Seung-yeon Lee, however, argues that dharma halls, saṅgha halls, abbot's quarters, and patriarch halls, which she mistakenly associates with the Chan monasticism ostensibly invented by Baizhang, did begin to appear in the so-called upper monastic compound (K. *sangwŏn yŏngyŏk* 上院領域) area of monasteries associated with the early Sŏn pioneers.[13] Lee, for instance, cites the funerary epitaph of Sŏkch'o (釋超, n.d.) or Sŏn master Chin'gwan (真觀, 912–964), wherein it is stated that on two different occasions—once at the monastery Chigoksa 智谷寺 (in South Kyŏngsang Province) and again at Pojesa (普濟寺) in the Koryŏ capital—the master "ascended the hall" (K. *sangdang* 上堂). Because Lee assumes that the rite of ascending the hall was only performed in dharma halls, she concludes that Sŏkch'o too must have performed the rite in this hall.[14]

The assumptions that Lee makes, however, are problematic. It must be borne in mind that Chigoksa, the monastery where Sŏkch'o ascended the hall, was a monastery that was established well before Sŏkch'o was born.[15] Other than the reference to Sŏkch'o ascending the hall, there is no other reason to assume that Chigoksa was a Baizhang-style Chan/Sŏn monastery. Moreover, contrary to Lee's belief, the dharma hall (not to mention the saṅgha hall, abbot's quarters, and patriarch hall) was not unique to the Chan/Sŏn tradition.[16] The dharma hall is commonly found in public monasteries, but it is unlikely that Chigoksa was one. When Sŏkch'o left his monastery Chigoksa for another in 959—Sŏkch'o became its abbot in 949—it was inherited by his own disciple Ŏnhŭm (彥欽, d.u.).[17] If Chigoksa was a public monastery, the abbacy would not have been handed down from master to disciple. The hall that Sŏkch'o "ascended," then, was most likely a lecture hall, a common structure in many pre-Koryŏ and Koryŏ monasteries.

Although Lee assumes that the rite of "ascending the hall" was performed only by Chan/Sŏn masters, this too is clearly not the case.[18] In the travel diary of the famous Japanese pilgrim Ennin (圓仁, 794–864),

for instance, we find the same expression being used to describe a ritual that has nothing to do with Chan. Ennin used the expression to describe a sutra lecture ritual (J. *kōkyō gishiki* 講經儀式) performed at the Korean monastery Chŏksanwŏn (赤山院) in Shandong.[19] Both the great assembly and the lecturer "ascended the hall" according to Ennin. After ascending the hall, the lecturer "mounted the high seat" (J. *kōza wo noboru* 登高座). The famous *Platform Sutra* similarly describes the sixth patriarch Huineng mounting the high seat in a lecture hall.[20] We cannot, therefore, simply assume that references to early Sŏn monks "ascending the hall" or "mounting a high seat" denote the kind of Chan-style ascending the hall performance that we see in classical Chan texts such as the *Jingde Era Record of the Transmission of the Lamp* (*Jingde chuandeng lu* 景德傳燈錄). Nor can we assume that these rituals were performed in a dharma hall. Naturally, we also cannot assume that lecture halls were converted into dharma halls for the purpose of providing Sŏn masters with a space to perform the ritual of ascending the hall.[21] If so, then one cannot argue, as Lee does, that the lecture hall and dharma hall began to "overlap" in the early Koryŏ period.[22]

Lee also argues that terms such as "meditation room" (K. *sŏnsil* 禪室) and "meditation hall" (K. *sŏndang* 禪堂), which were also in use during the tenth century, referred to dharma halls. One example of the use of the term "meditation hall" can be found in the funerary epitaph for the Sŏn monk Ch'anyu (璨幽, 869–958). The epitaph states that Ch'anyu's teacher Simhŭi (審希, 855–923), delighted to see his old student, "adorned the *sŏndang* and had [Ch'anyu] mount the lecture seat" (K. *ch'ik sŏndang pisŭng tamjwa* 飭禪堂俾昇譚座).[23] In Simhŭi's own funerary epitaph we also learn that he "passed away at Pongnim *sŏndang*" (K. *myol ŏ Pongnim sŏndang* 滅於鳳林禪堂).[24] But in neither case can it be said with any certainty that the term *sŏndang* refers to a specific hall at the monastery.[25] In fact, it seems more likely that the term was being used in these two sources to refer to the monastery in its entirety. Similarly, the term *sŏnsil*, which appears in the funerary epitaph for Kŭngyang, seems to refer not to a specific room or hall but to the monastery itself.[26]

Although there is no denying the spread and influence of Chan mythology (e.g., mind-to-mind transmission) in Korea during the late Silla and early Koryŏ period, this, as we have seen, was not accompanied by the spread of so-called Chan monasticism. Neither textual nor archaeological evidence support the assumption that monasteries in Korea were converted or newly built to conform to Baizhang's ideal Chan community. When pure rules texts began to make their way to Korea in the late eleventh century these texts therefore found themselves in an environment where they had no obvious institutional or practical use.

Phase I: Tamjin

Efforts were made, indeed, in the eleventh century to introduce new monastic developments taking place in the continent to the peninsula. As before, pilgrims played a key role. It seems worth noting here, however, that these efforts were conditioned not only by individual piety and curiosity but also the Koryŏ court's revived interest in diplomacy with Song China (960–1279).[27] The two states began to formally exchange embassies again after Emperor Shenzong (r. 1067–1085) of Song decreed that diplomatic relations with Koryŏ—then a vassal state of the Khitan Liao—resume in 1068.[28] Koryŏ had severed relations with Song in 1022 after acknowledging Khitan suzerainty. Despite the fierce opposition of Song policymakers like Su Shi (蘇軾, 1036–1101) who feared the possibility of espionage, renewed diplomatic relations presented Koryŏ officials and monks with an opportunity to once again import books, ideas, and new ritual technologies from China.[29] During the reign of King Sŏnjong (r. 1083–1094), the court astrologer Ch'oe Sagyŏm (崔士謙, n.d.) did in fact return from Song China with a new Buddhist mortuary ritual manual known as the *Ritual Text for the Rite of Water and Land* (*Shuilu yiwen* 水陸儀文). Upon his return from China, Ch'oe sought the king's approval to build a water and land hall (K. Suryuktang 水陸堂) at the Sŏn monastery Pojesa in the Koryŏ capital.[30]

Among the monks who traveled to China during this period, arguably the most well known is King Munjong (r. 1046–1083) son, Ŭichŏn (義天, 1055–1101), who defied his brother King Sŏnjong's wishes and embarked on a pilgrimage to China in 1085.[31] But a decade before Ŭichŏn set foot on Chinese soil a monk by the name of Tamjin (曇真, n.d.), also known by his posthumous name Hyejo (慧照/炤), had already accompanied a Koryŏ embassy to China led by the vice-director of public works (K. *kongbu sirang* 工夫侍郎) Ch'oe Saryang (崔思諒, d. 1092) in 1076.[32] Upon arrival, Tamjin headed to Hangzhou.[33] On the ninth of January 1077, Emperor Shenzong summoned Tamjin and two other Koryŏ monks from the monastery (Upper) Tianzhusi (上天竺寺) in Hangzhou to the Song capital where they, perhaps at the emperor's own request, placed themselves in the care of Chan master Daozhen (道臻, 1014–1093), the influential abbot of the grand public monastery Jingyinchansi (淨因禪寺).³⁴ Daozhen, a dharma heir of Fushan Fayuan (浮山法遠, 991–1067) of the Linji branch of Chan, succeeded Dajue Huailian (大覺懷璉, 1009–1090) of the Yunmen branch and became abbot of the monastery in 1065. When the monastery was established in 1049 the prominent statesman Ouyang Xiu (歐陽修, 1007–1072) had recommended Yuantong Ju'ne (圓通居訥, 1010–1071) of the Yunmen branch as its first abbot, but Ju'ne declined the invitation citing poor health. In his place Ju'ne recommended his scribe Huailian who accepted the appointment.³⁵

Not surprisingly, the abbacy of Jingyinchansi proved to be a shortcut to success. Emperor Renzong (r. 1022–1063) and his successor Yingzong (r. 1063–1067) became enthusiastic patrons of Huailian. Daozhen similarly received the warm patronage of Emperor Shenzong whose respect for the abbot was so high that he was even willing to entrust Daozhen with the selection of the abbots of the two Chan cloisters (C. *chanyuan* 禪院)—Huilin (慧林) and Zhihai (智海)—at the new grand public monastery Xiangguosi (相國寺, established in 1082), which was also located in the Song capital Bianjing.³⁶

Jingyinchansi proved to be a shortcut to success for the visiting Korean monk Tamjin as well. Key to Tamjin's success was his knowledge of the new developments taking place in Song China. Again, one key development was the spread of imperially recognized public monasteries and the dominance of Chan Buddhism in these institutions. Tamjin probably acquired at both Upper Tianzhusi and Jingyinchansi firsthand knowledge of the workings of a public Chan monastery. At this hub of Chan learning, Tamjin presumably learned, among other things, how to reproduce the Chan mythology of mind-to-mind transmission, how to perform important Chan rituals such as "ascending the hall," and how to carry himself in a way that was consistent with the pure rules of a Chan monastery.³⁷

But Tamjin's exploration of this new form of monasticism may have been cut short because of what he witnessed outside the walls of the monastery. As the historian Chŏng Su-a points out, Tamjin may have had the chance to observe the implementation of Wang Anshi's (王安石, 1021–1086) New Policies during his sojourn in the Song capital.³⁸ Perhaps for these reasons, after three long years, the emperor finally decided it was time for the three Korean monks to return to Koryŏ. Tamjin and the two other monks were first granted honorary titles and purple robes and then ordered to accompany a Korean embassy back home on March

31, 1080.³⁹ Tamjin, however, returned to China with Ŭich'ŏn in 1085 and made another year-long pilgrimage in southern China.⁴⁰ A few decades later (perhaps in 1105), at the behest of King Yejong (r. 1105–1122), Tamjin seems to have visited China again to purchase a copy of the Khitan canon.⁴¹ The new king was clearly aware of the value of the Sŏn master's knowledge of China and its book market.⁴² For his services to the state, Tamjin was appointed abbot of Kwangmyŏngsa (廣明寺) and Pojesa, two important Sŏn monasteries in the capital associated with the royal cult.⁴³ Not surprisingly, he was named royal preceptor in 1107 and then state preceptor in 1114.⁴⁴

Tamjin was thus in a perfect position to introduce and put into actual use the new monasticism that he personally observed while on pilgrimage in China. He did not, however, go so far as to establish a public monastery. Instead, he introduced some of its customs, practices, and rules to Korea, which monks in his lineage adopted for use in their monasteries. According to one twelfth-century source, Tamjin returned from China with a copy of "a ritual manual for seated meditation" (C. *zuochan yigui* 坐禪儀軌) and instructions on how to lay out bowls and so on. The manuals that Tamjin imported from China were used during a Sŏn grove meeting (K. *ch'ongnim hoe* 叢林會) organized to celebrate the restoration of a monastery named Taehŭngsa (大興寺) near the capital in 1161.⁴⁵ Sŏn master Choŭng (祖膺, n.d.), who received tonsure from Tamjin's disciple (K. *munje* 門第) Yŏngbo (英甫, n.d.), had donated his own private wealth to pay for the restorations.⁴⁶ Choŭng seems to have acquired copies of the manuals imported by Tamjin from his teacher Yŏngbo.⁴⁷

It is, however, unlikely that Taehŭngsa was restored in the form of a public monastery. Choŭng was also involved in the restoration of another monastery named Yongmunsa (龍門寺), but its abbacy was, by royal decree, limited to the heirs in his lineage. The abbacy of Taehŭngsa was also probably limited to monks in Choŭng's lineage. But, like Taehŭngsa, there were signs of change at Yongmunsa. New forms of Chan/Sŏn learning most likely imported by Tamjin were taught there. To celebrate the completion of the restoration, Yongmunsa held a Sŏn debate convocation (K. *tamsŏn pŏphoe* 譚禪法會) with five hundred monks for fifty days. At the convocation, lectures on the *Record of the Transmission of the Lamp* (*Chuandeng lu* 傳燈錄) and Xuedou Chongxian's (雪竇重顯, 980–1052) verse commentaries (C. *niansong* 拈頌) were provided by Sŏn master Hyodon (孝惇, n.d.) from the monastery Tansoksa (斷俗寺), another monastery that belonged to Tamjin's lineage.⁴⁸

What Tamjin introduced to Koryŏ Korea, as we can see, did usher in change, but this change, again, was far from radical or total. This can also be witnessed in his chief disciple T'anyŏn's funerary epitaph.⁴⁹ After receiving tonsure at a relatively obscure monastery named Anjŏksa (安寂寺) near the capital in 1088, T'anyŏn traveled to Kwangmyŏngsa to train under Tamjin who eventually granted him transmission. T'anyŏn passed the monastic exams and served, for just over a decade, as the abbot of several different monasteries. In 1126, four years after he received the title of "Sŏn master" (K. *sŏnsa* 禪師), the second-highest rank for Sŏn monks, he was invited to serve as the abbot of the monastery Chŏnhwasa (天和寺) in the capital. In 1135, T'anyŏn was appointed abbot of Pojesa's Indra Cloister and was granted a concurrent appointment as abbot of Yŏngwŏnsa (瑩原寺) in present-day Miryang. Two years later, he was summoned to the palace; two years after that he, like his teacher Tamjin, received appointment as the abbot of the influential Sŏn monastery Kwangmyŏngsa. After mentioning this appointment, T'anyŏn's funerary epitaph adds that he had some of his verses on the four compartments (K. *sa wiŭi song* 四威儀頌) and sermons prepared for ascending the hall (K. *sangdang ŏgu* 上堂語句) delivered to Chan master Wushi Jiechen (無示介諶, 1080–1148), abbot of Guanglisi (廣利寺) on Mount Ayuwang, to ask for his seal of approval (K. *in'ga* 印可). Jiechen complied with the request and sent the approval in the form of a lengthy letter.⁵⁰ Jiechen sent T'anyŏn, it would seem, an inheritance certificate.⁵¹ Presumably, Tamjin's influence had something to do with T'anyŏn's composition (and perhaps even performance) of ascending the hall sermons and his decision to acquire an inheritance certificate when he assumed the abbacy of Kwangmyŏngsa.

That being said, it is also true that the inheritance certificate had no apparent institutional significance in Korea. What mattered was one's registration (K. *chŏk* 籍). In Korea, a Sŏn monk could register himself as a monk who belonged to one of the so-called Nine Mountain Sŏn lineages. T'anyŏn, for instance, was registered as a Mount Sagul (闍崛山) lineage monk. This enabled him to take the preliminary Sŏn exam (K. *ch'ongsŏk* 叢席) reserved for monks in the Mount Sagul lineage.⁵² And, needless to say, T'anyŏn's relationship with Tamjin, a royal and state preceptor, mattered as well. This is probably why T'anyŏn's funerary epitaph does not identify him as Jiechen's heir. The epitaph explicitly identifies him, instead, as the dharma heir of Tamjin and also a Sagulsan lineage (K. Kulsanha 崛山下) monk.⁵³ Given the lack of a relevant institutional setting such as the public monastery where inheritance certificates were required for incoming abbots, we can only surmise that the significance of the lineage inherited from Jiechen was largely symbolic in nature. Otherwise, it is difficult to explain why T'anyŏn would bother getting an inheritance certificate *after* serving as the abbot of several monasteries.

As I demonstrate elsewhere, before the seventeenth century, Korean Sŏn monks could and did have more than one transmission lineage.[54] T'anyŏn, in other words, was not unique in this regard. If a Korean Sŏn monk was fortunate enough to receive "direct" transmission from a Chan master in China, then this, needless to say, was duly noted. But, like T'anyŏn, it was not uncommon for this monk (or his disciples) to also give due recognition to all of his Korean transmission lineages in his biography and funerary epitaph. The latter, as noted above, was arguably more important. It was a monk's Korean transmission lineage(s) that provided him with the opportunity to take the official saṅgha examination, make the right political connections, and eventually receive the central court's appointment as abbot. All this seems to imply that a direct transmission from China had no institutional purpose whatsoever, but creative uses of direct transmission, as we shall see, enabled Chinul and his lineage to develop a Sŏn monasticism unique to Korea.

PHASE II: SUSŎNSA

Not long after Tamjin's appointment as state preceptor, like other state preceptors before him, he retired to the countryside. He left the capital and, no doubt with handsome state support, founded the monastery Chŏnghyesa (定慧寺) on Mount Kyejok 雞足山 in present-day Sunchŏn.[55] The size and layout of the monastery at the time of its founding are unknown, but sometime in the thirteenth century control over its abbacy had clearly fallen into the possession of Chinul's lineage at Susŏnsa (修禪寺, later renamed Songgwangsa), which was also located in Sunchŏn. With the support of local strongmen and, more importantly, powerful central court officials and the Ch'oe house during the age of military rule, Chinul and the monks in his lineage were able to build a network of monasteries with Susŏnsa—the head monastery—at the center. Within this network we find monasteries such as the aforementioned Tansoksa in nearby Sanchŏng Prefecture, Wŏllamsa (月南寺) in nearby Kangjin Prefecture, Sŏnwŏnsa (禪源寺) on Kanghwa Island, and, of course, Chŏnghyesa.[56]

However, the abbacy of some of these monasteries, most notably Tansoksa and Chŏnghyesa, had once belonged to Tamjin's lineage. This, as shown below, was something that Chinul and the monks in his lineage could not ignore. They clearly made an effort to find a creative way to legitimize their appropriation of what once belonged to Tamjin's lineage. The rules and conventions of public monasteries proved to be particularly useful in addressing this challenge. At a public monastery, the founding abbot was entitled to memorial rites performed by later abbots of the monastery in the portrait hall or patriarch hall.[57] Although Korea still lacked Song-style public monasteries during this period, the writings of Ch'ungji (冲止, 1226–1292), who became the abbot of Chŏnghyesa probably in 1271, reveal that memorial rites were performed for Tamjin, who was honored as the founding patriarch of the monastery.[58] In his official capacity as abbot, Ch'ungji had prepared a sacrificial oration (K. *chemun* 祭文) to be used as part of the memorial rites for the founding patriarch Tamjin.[59] But rather than trace Tamjin's lineage back to Bodhidharma through his Korean Sŏn master or his nine mountain lineage, Ch'ungji made sure to note in the oration that the founding patriarch had "gained Jingyin [Daozhen's] marrow" (K. *tŭk Chŏngin su* 得淨因髓).[60] This is not insignificant. In doing so, Ch'ungji was taking advantage of the fact that the founding patriarch's ("Chinese") lineage was, for lack of a better word, "symbolic"—it stood not for an institutional reality but a mythology that all Sŏn monks shared. Concomitantly, Chŏnghyesa's abbacy stood not for the influence of a particular Korean lineage but for the allure of the Chan/Sŏn mythology that became popular in the Song.

Who succeeded Tamjin as abbot is unfortunately unknown. In his first formal address to the assembly as the new abbot of Chŏnghyesa, Ch'ungji did, however, offer some words of praise to a few former abbots: Tamjin, Mongyŏ (夢如, d. 1252), and Honwŏn.[61] Although likely incomplete, this short list of former abbots reveals a few important things about Chŏnghyesa. First, all three former abbots were state preceptors. As one might expect from a state preceptor's retirement monastery (K. *hasanso* 下山所), Chŏnghyesa clearly presented strong incentives—either economic, symbolic, or perhaps both—for monks of this high stature to assume its abbacy. Second, an intimate relationship clearly developed between Chŏnghyesa and Susŏnsa. Mongyŏ, Honwŏn, and Ch'ungji were all monks who received training at (and eventually served as abbots of) Susŏnsa. And, lastly, although the abbacy of Chŏnghyesa seems to have been dominated by Susŏnsa monks in the thirteenth century, it was not handed down directly from master to disciple. Ch'ungji, for instance, did not inherit the abbacy from his tonsure and dharma master Chŏnyŏng (天英, 1215–1286), who never served as abbot of Chŏnghyesa.[62] Honwŏn also did not inherit the monastery from his tonsure master Chonghŏn (宗軒, n.d.), a ninth-generation heir in Pŏmil's Mount Sagul lineage. Nor did he inherit it from his dharma master, which he did not yet have. He was formally invited to serve as abbot of Chŏnghyesa by the military government leader Ch'oe U (崔瑀, alt. Ch'oe I 崔怡, d. 1249), the de facto ruler of Koryŏ.[63]

In limited but important ways Chŏnghyesa thus resembled a public monastery. This was not a coincidence. The monasteries that belonged to Susŏnsa's network tended to borrow certain elements from Song-style public monasteries. For instance, it was not uncommon for Susŏnsa monks to perform an "opening the hall" (K. *kaedang* 開堂) ritual and formally declare themselves the dharma heir of a particular Sŏn master, which was—institutionally and legally speaking—not necessary in Korea at the time. Not surprisingly, the performance of this ritual did not conform neatly with the rules and conventions of a Song-style public monastery. Before he assumed the abbacy of Sŏnwŏnsa on Kanghwa Island in 1246, Honwŏn (fourth abbot of Susŏnsa) served as abbot of Chŏnghyesa, but according to his funerary epitaph he performed an opening the hall ritual and declared himself the dharma heir of Mongyŏ (third abbot of Susŏnsa) not at Chŏnghyesa but *later* at Sŏnwŏnsa.[64] Ch'ungji similarly served first as abbot of Chŏnghyesa, but he performed the same ritual and declared himself the dharma heir of Chŏnyŏng (fifth abbot of Susŏnsa) when he assumed the abbacy of Susŏnsa later in 1286.[65]

What the Susŏnsa lineage monks did at their monasteries should not, however, be regarded as a "poor imitation" of something more authentic. As noted in the case of Chŏnghyesa, Susŏnsa lineage monks creatively borrowed elements from Song-style public monasteries to establish legitimacy and give themselves a competitive edge. This strategy apparently worked. The Susŏnsa network firmly established itself in the southernmost area of the Korean peninsula—once a Tamjin lineage stronghold—and continued to flourish with the support of military leaders, kings, powerful families, and Mongol sovereigns during the late Koryŏ period.

Phase III: The Fourteenth Century

The monk Sangch'ong, who was mentioned at the beginning of this chapter, clearly wanted to replicate the success of the Susŏnsa network, albeit at a much larger scale. Key to doing so, according to Sangch'ong, was the mandated use of Chinul's *Admonitions to Beginning Students* at all monasteries. This was not a full-blown pure rules text, which may be exactly why Sangch'ŏng deemed it so useful. (It seems worth noting here that Chinul's text was inspired by the *Pure Rules for Chan Monasteries*, which it cites in several places.[66]) Sangch'ŏng had another more recent option. Sŏn master Ch'unggam (冲鑑, 1274–1338), who studied under Chŏnyŏng at Sŏnwŏnsa, is said to have "chosen and put into practice Baizhang's pure rules for the Chan school" at his own monastery Yongch'ŏnsa (龍泉寺).[67] Apparently, full-blown Pure Rules texts—more specifically, the *Imperial Edition of Baizhang's Pure Rules* (*Chixiu Baizhang qinggui* 敕修百丈清規) compiled between the years 1335–1338—had been in use by Susŏnsa lineage monks in the fourteenth century. This was in keeping with Yuan court's desire to make the *Imperial Edition of Baizhang's Pure Rules* standard for all Chan (and Sŏn) monasteries. Not surprisingly, when T'aego Pou (太古普愚, 1301–1383), who learned the Chan public monastery system while on pilgrimage in China, was appointed royal preceptor in 1356 he urged the king to use the same text to standardize monastic rules for Sŏn monasteries in Koryŏ and thus unify the Nine Mountain Sŏn lineages.[68] Following the royal preceptor's advice, the king had the text published and distributed in Koryŏ.[69]

Sangch'ŏng could have also elected to follow the example of the famed monastery Hoeamsa (檜巖寺), which, as Kang Hosŏn points out, was built to look and function exactly like a Chinese public monastery.[70] Like Yongch'ŏnsa, Hoeamsa also seems to have been regulated and structured according to the guidelines found in the *Imperial Edition of Baizhang's Pure Rules*.[71] But Sangch'ŏng chose to recommend to the new Chosŏn king Chinul's *Admonitions to Beginning Students* instead. No doubt this was due in part to the new reality that the Buddhist establishment faced in the Chosŏn dynasty: the waning influence of the Mongols (who authorized the publication of the *Imperial Edition of Baizhang's Pure Rules*) and the growing influence of the new Ming dynasty made it unnecessary to try to establish and maintain large public monasteries in Korea. From Sangch'ŏng's perspective, it clearly made more sense to use a monastic system native to and best suited to the immediate needs of Chosŏn.

Notes

1. The letter can be found in the *T'aejo sillok* 太祖實錄 [Veritable records of T'aejo] 14: 2a–b.

2. *Kamju* (C. *jiansi*) is often regarded as alternative way of referring to the comptroller (K. *kamsa* 監寺), one of the six stewards (K. *yukjisa* 六知事) of a

Chan monastery. But here the term seems to refer the highest-ranking monastic officer at a monastery directly associated with the royal cult such as the Buddhist shrine located within the royal palace (K. naewŏndang 內願堂); for instance, see T'aejo sillok 4: 12b. Hence, my alternative translation, chief monastic officer. It seems worth noting here that Chosŏn sources distinguish the chief monastic officer from the abbot (K. chuji 主持); for instance, see T'aejong sillok 太宗實錄 [Veritable records of T'aejong] 4: 4a, 5: 27a, and 24:7a. The monastic head may be a different name for dean about which I shall have more to say later.

3. This cloud may not have lasted long as the third king to sit on the Chosŏn throne, T'aejong (太宗, 1400–1418), was not particularly fond of his stepmother, Queen Sindŏk, which may explain why he reduced the land grants and slaves of Hŭngch'ŏnsa (T'aejo sillok 5: 5a).

4. The veracity of this rhetorical claim—a claim made frequently in late Koryŏ and early Chosŏn sources—should not be taken for granted; see Juhn Y. Ahn, *Buddhas and Ancestors: Religion and Wealth in Fourteenth-Century Korea* (Seattle: University of Washington Press, 2018).

5. In the early Chosŏn period, the transmission of the lamp texts and a Korean text known as the *Sŏnmun yŏmsong chip* 禪門拈頌集 [Collection of verse comments of the Sŏn tradition] were used to test Sŏn monks. The *Avataṃsaka Sūtra* and its commentary the *Daśabhūmika vibhāśa śāstra* or *Shidi lun* 十地論 (also known as *Shizhu piposha lun* 十住毗婆沙論; *Commentary on the Ten Stages Scripture*) were used to test Kyo monks. See Sem Vermeersch, *The Power of the Buddhas: The Politics of Buddhism During the Koryŏ Dynasty (918–1392)* (Cambridge, MA: Harvard University Asia Center, 2008), 199.

6. The king accepted Sangch'ong's recommendations, but how much of it was actually implemented is unclear. For an English translation of Chinul's *Admonitions*, see Robert E. Buswell Jr., *The Korean Approach to Zen: The Collected Works of Chinul* (Honolulu: University of Hawai'i Press, 1983), 135–39. This is the only text containing a set of "monastic rules" attributed to Chinul. It seems worth noting here that the text functions less as an exhaustive list of monastic rules than as a short moralistic tract.

7. See the discussion in Vermeersch, *The Power of the Buddhas*, 206–213.

8. Vermeersch, *The Power of the Buddhas*, 213–14.

9. Vermeersch, *The Power of the Buddhas*, 217–20.

10. See Foulk, "Myth, Ritual, and Monastic Practice in Sung Ch'an Buddhism," in *Religion and Society in T'ang and Sung China*, ed. Patricia Buckley Ebrey and Peter N. Gregory (Honolulu: University of Hawai'i Press, 1993), 147–208. See also Mario Poceski, "Guishan jingce and the Ethical Foundations of Chan Practice," in *Zen Classics: Formative Texts in Zen Buddhism*, ed. Steven Heine and Dale Wright (New York: Oxford University Press, 2005); and Poceski, "Xuefeng's Code and the Chan School's Participation in the Development of Monastic Regulations," *Asia Major, Third Series* 16, no. 2 (2003): 33–56.

11. "Hyemok san Kodal sŏnwŏn kuksa Wŏnjong taesa chi pi" 慧目山高達禪院國師元宗之碑 (Stele for State Preceptor Great Master Wŏnjong from Kodal Sŏn monastery on Mount Hyemok), *HKC*, 399; cf. Patrick R. Uhlmann trans., *Anthology of Stele Inscriptions of Eminent Korean Buddhist Monks*, Collected Works of Korean Buddhism 12 (Seoul: Jogye Order of Korean Buddhism, 2012), 246; noted in Vermeersch, *The Power of the Buddhas*, 129. Kodalwŏn is associated with the Sŏn monk Hyŏnuk (玄昱, 787–869), whose lineage later came to be known as the Mount Pongnim (鳳林山) lineage. Hyŏnuk received the patronage of King Kyŏngmun (r. 861–875) who granted him the monastery Kodalwŏn on Mount Hyemok (慧目山). Hŭiyangwŏn, also known as Pongamsa (鳳巖寺), was established by Tohŏn (道憲, 824–882) on Mount Hŭiyang (in present-day North Kyŏngsang Province); see "Chijŭng taesa Chŏkcho chi t'ap pimyŏng" 智證大師寂照之塔碑銘 (Chŏkcho stele inscription for Great Master Chijŭng) dated 924, *HKC*, 246–56.

12. See Kim Pongyŏl and Pak Chongjin, "Koryŏ karam ŭi kusŏng hyŏngsik e kwanhan kich'ojŏk yŏn'gu" 고려가람의 구성형식에관한 기초적 연구 [A basic study of the site layout of Koryŏ Buddhist monasteries], *Taehan kŏnch'ukhakhoe nonmunjip* 5, no. 6 (1989): 27–35; Yang Chŏngsŏk, "Kusan sŏnmun karam insik e taehan koch'al" 九山禪門 伽藍 認識에 대한 考察 [An investigation of (scholarly) understandings of Nine Mountain Sŏn monasteries], *Silla munhwa* 40 (2012); and Han Chiman, "Namal Yŏch'o kusan sŏnmun karam kusŏng ŭi ŭimi" 나말여초 구산선문 가람구성의 의미 [The meaning of the building composition of the Nine Mountain Sŏn monasteries of the Late Silla and Early Koryŏ period], *Taehan kŏnch'ukhakhoe nonmunjip* 32, no. 6 (2016). Kim and Pak's article also raises another important point that is worth further investigation. They argue that Koryŏ monasteries tended to cope with the growing demand for space by developing multiple compounds (K. *wŏn* 院) adjacent to the main compound (i.e., the original monastery). These compounds could perhaps be compared to the subtemples (J. *tatchū* 塔頭) that developed around large medieval Japanese monasteries such as Myōshinji (妙心寺) and Daitokuji (大德寺). Although the lecture hall continued to be used during the Koryŏ period, Hong Pyŏng-hwa points out that it tended to grow smaller in scale than the golden hall or main buddha hall over time; Hong, "Urinara sach'al kŏnch'uk esŏ pongbul kwa kangsŏl konggan ŭi pyŏnhwa kwajŏng" 우리나라 사찰건축에서 봉불(奉佛)과 강설(講說) 공간의 변화과정 [The process of the transformation of the space of worshipping the Buddha and preaching the Dharma in monastic construction in our country], *Kŏnch'uk yŏksa yŏn'gu* 19, no. 4 (2010): 109–123. Hong's speculations about the historical conditions that led to this tendency are, in my opinion, too speculative and should be used with caution.

13. Lee, *On the Formation of the Upper Monastic Area of Seon Buddhist Temples from Korea's Late Silla to the Goryeo Era*, Sungkyunkwan University Outstanding Research (Heidelberg: Springer, 2013).

14. Lee, *On the Formation of the Upper Monastic Area*, 46. For the references in Sŏkch'o's funerary epitaph, see the "Sanch'ŏng Chigoksa Chin'gwan sŏnsa Ogong t'appi" 山清智谷寺真觀禪師悟空塔碑 [Ogong Stūpa stele for Sŏn Master Chin'gwan from Chigoksa in Sanch'ŏng], *HKC*, 426 and 427. For more information on Sŏkch'o and his epitaph, see Hŏ Hŭngsik, *Koryŏ Pulgyosa yŏn'gu* (Seoul: Ilchogak, 1986), 598–609.

15. See Ŏm Kip'yo, "Sanch'ŏng Chigok-sa chi ŭi kwibu sŏkcho pudo" 山清 智谷寺址의 龜趺와 石造浮屠 [The stone mortuary stupas and tortoise base at the excavation site of Chigoksa in Sanch'ŏng], *Munhwa sahak* 17 (2002): 357–86.

16. See Foulk, "Myth, Ritual, and Monastic Practice."

17. Sŏkch'o's own lineage is also unclear. His funerary epitaph emphasizes two "Sŏn" encounters. The first is with a certain Great Master Pŏbwŏn (法圓大師) of Yŏhŭng Sŏnwŏn (麗興禪院) in 918. Given that this encounter took place before Sŏkch'o received the full precepts, it seems safe to say that Pŏbwŏn was Sŏkch'o's tonsure master. The other is an unnamed master he met at Longcesi 龍冊寺 in Hangzhou in 940. Although some Korean scholars identify this master as Jingqing Daofu (鏡清道怤, 868–937) for whom the monastery was originally built, this obviously cannot be the case. Aware of this problem, Hŏ Hŭngsik identifies the Chan master as Xiaorong (曉榮, 920–990); see Hŏ, *Koryŏ Pulgyo sa yŏn'gu*, 609. Sŏkch'o's funerary epitaph does not make any explicit mention of Sŏkch'o becoming this Chan master's dharma heir.

18. See also similar arguments made in Okimoto Katsumi, "Zen shisō keiseishi no kenkyū" 禅思想形成史の研究 [A study of the history of the formation of Zen thought], *Hanazono daigaku koksai zengaku kenkyūjo kenkyū hōkoku* 5 (1997): 197–204.

19. Edwin O. Reischauer, *Ennin's Diary: The Record of a Pilgrimage to China in Search of the Law* (New York: Ronald, 1955), 152; cited in Mario Poceski, "Chan Rituals of the Abbots' Ascending the Dharma Hall to Preach," in *Zen Ritual: Studies of Zen Buddhist Theory in Practice*, ed. Steven Heine and Dale S. Wright (New York: Oxford University Press, 2008), 86–87. For the sutra lecture ritual, see Fukui Fumimasa, "Kōkyō gishiki no soshiki naiyō" 経儀式の組織内容 [The structural content of chanted lecture ceremonies] in *Tonkō to Chūgoku bukkyō* 敦煌と中国仏教 (Dunhuang and Chinese Buddhism), ed. Makita Tairyō and Fukui Fumimasa, Kōza Tonkō 7 (Tokyo: Daitō shuppansha, 1984).

20. Philip B. Yampolsky, *The Platform Sūtra of the Sixth Patriarch* (New York: Columbia University Press, 1967), 125; cited in Poceski, "Chan Rituals," 92.

21. It should also be noted here that Yang Chŏngsŏk raised similar concerns; see his "Kusan sŏnmun karam insik e taehan koch'al" 九山禪門 伽藍 認識에 대한 考察 (An investigation of [scholarly] understandings of Nine Mountain Sŏn monasteries), *Silla munhwa* 40 (2012): 195–227. For instance, with regard

to the "refurbished" lecture hall at Sŏngjusa (聖主寺), Lee reads the monastery's enlarged lecture hall as evidence of its transformation into a dharma hall, but Yang cautiously suggests that more evidence is necessary to reach this conclusion; see Yang, "Kusan sŏnmun," 214. I agree with Yang. For similar concerns about Lee's research, see Han, "Namal Yŏch'o," 56.

22. Lee, *On the Formation of the Upper Monastic Area*, 41.

23. See "Hyemok san Kodal sŏnwŏn kuksa Wŏnjong taesa chi pi" (*HKC*, 393–94; cf. Uhlmann trans., *Anthology of Stele Inscriptions of Eminent Korean Buddhist Monks*, 227). Cited in Lee, *On the Formation of the Upper Monastic Area*, 46–47.

24. Yu Tang Sillaguk ko kuksa shi Chin'gyŏng taesa Powŏl nŭnggong chi t'ap pimyŏng 有唐新羅國故國師諡真鏡大師寶月凌空之塔碑銘 [Nŭnggong stele inscription for State Preceptor Great Master Chin'gyŏng from Silla who is in Tang], *HKC*, 260. Pongnim here refers to Pongnimsa (鳳林寺) in Ch'angwŏn.

25. Like Lee, Han Chi-man assumes that there was a separate Sŏn hall at Pongnimsa; see Han, "Namal Yŏch'o," 57.

26. "Chŏngjin taesa pimyŏng" 靜眞大師碑銘 (Stele inscription for Great Master Chŏngjin), *HKC*, 382; noted in Lee, *On the Formation of the Upper Monastic Area*, 46. Here, Lee also mentions Anhwasa (安和寺), a famous monastery located in the capital. Lee mistakenly reads Sŏnbŏp gate 善法門 [Good dharma gate] as Sŏnbŏp gate 禪法門 [Sŏn dharma gate] and the hall behind it, Sŏnbŏp hall 善法堂 [Good dharma hall], as Sŏn bŏptang 禪法堂 [Sŏn dharma hall]. For the correct reading, see Sem Vermeersch trans., *A Chinese Traveler in Medieval China: Xu Jing's Illustrated Account of the Xuanhe Embassy to Koryŏ*, Korean Classics Library (Honolulu: University of Hawai'i Press, 2016), 135. Lee makes the same mistake while reading the "In'gaksa Pojo kuksa chŏngjo t'ap pi" 麟角寺普覺國師靜照塔碑 [Chŏngjo stūpa stele for State Preceptor Pojo from In'gaksa], *HKC*, 1071. Good dharma hall is the name of Indra's dwelling in Tuṣita heaven.

27. See Chŏng Su-a, "Hyejo kuksa Tamjin kwa 'Chŏnginsu': Puk-Song Sŏnp'ung ŭi suyong kwa Koryŏ chunggi Sŏnjong ŭi puhŭng ŭl chungsimŭro" 혜조국사 담진과 '정인수'—북송선풍의 수용과 고려중기 선종의 부흥을 중심으로 [State Preceptor Tamjin and 'Chŏngin's Marrow': The Importation of the Sŏn Style of Northern Song and the revival of the Sŏn school in the mid-Koryŏ period], in *Hanguk sahak nonch'ong: Yi Ki-baek sŏngsaeng kohŭi kinyŏm*, vol. 1., ed. Yi Ki-baek sŏngsaeng kohŭi kinyŏmhoe (Seoul: Ilchogak, 1994); and Chŏng, "Koryŏ chunggi kaehyŏk chŏngch'i wa Puk-Song sinbŏp ŭi suyong" 고려중기 개혁정치 와 북송 신법의 수용 [The reformist policies of mid-Koryŏ and the acceptance of Northern Song's new policies] (PhD diss,. Sŏgang University, 1999). For a brief discussion of the so-called Sŏn-revival during Yejong's reign in English, see Edward J. Shultz, "Twelfth-Century Koryŏ Politics: The Rise of Han Anin and His Partisans," *Journal of Korean Studies* 6 (1988–89): 8–9 and 16.

28. For diplomatic relations between Song and Koryŏ, see Michael Rogers, "Sung-Koryø Relations: Some Inhibiting Factors," *Oriens* 11, no. 1/2 (1958): 194–202; and Rogers, "Factionalism and Koryŏ Policy under the Northern Song," *Journal of the American Oriental Society* 79, no. 1 (1959): 16–25.

29. For more on Su Shi's objections to diplomatic relations with Koryŏ, see Rogers, "Sung-Koryø Relations"; Remco Breuker, *Establishing a Pluralist Society in Medieval Korea, 918–1170*, 247; and also John Jorgensen, "Korea and the Regeneration of Chinese Buddhism: The Evidence of Ch'an and Sŏn Literature," in *Currents and Countercurrents: Korean Influence on the East Asian Buddhist Traditions* (Honolulu: University of Hawai'i Press, 2005), 83–84. Koryŏ envoys were not permitted to socialize with Song scholars; noted in Breuker, *Establishing a Pluralist Society in Medieval Korea, 918–1170*, 234n115 and 247n164.

30. See *KS* 10, 20b; and *KSC* 6, 9b. The text that Ch'oe brought back from China was either the three-fascicle ritual manual of the same name compiled by Yang E (楊鍔, 1032–1098) around 1071 or the expanded four-fascicle edition compiled by Chan master Changlu Zongze (長蘆宗賾, d. 1107?). The water and land hall differed from other Buddhist monastery halls in that it requires an inner and outer altar. For more on the water and land rite, see Daniel B. Stevenson, "Text, Image, and Transformations of the *Shuilu fahui*: the Buddhist Rite for Deliverance of Creatures of Water and Land" in *Cultural Intersections in Later Chinese Buddhism*, ed. Marsha Weidner, 30–70 (Honolulu: University of Hawai'i Press, 2001); Edward L. Davis, *Society and the Supernatural in Song China* (Honolulu: University of Hawai'i Press, 2001), esp. chapter 8; and also Choi Mihwa, "State Suppression of Buddhism and Royal Patronage of the Ritual of Water and Land in the Early Chosŏn Dynasty," *Seoul Journal of Korean Studies* 22, no. 2 (2009): 181–214.

31. For Ŭich'ŏn's pilgrimage to China, see Huang, "Ŭich'ŏn's Pilgrimage and the Rising Prominence of the Korean Monastery in Hang-chou during the Sung and Yüan Periods," in *Currents and Countercurrents: Korean Influence on the East Asian Buddhist Traditions*, ed. Robert E. Buswell Jr., 240–76 (Honolulu: University of Hawai'i Press, 2005).

32. *KS* 9, 15a-b. The Korean embassy left for Song China bearing local tribute items on September 10.

33. Li Tao's (李燾, 1115–1184) *Xu zizhi tongjian changbian* 續資治通鑑長編 [Extended continuation to the comprehensive mirror in aid of governance; Wenyuange siku quanshu edition] simply refers to their location as Tianzhu si in Hangzhou. Since Ŭich'ŏn's first stop was also Upper Tianzhu si, it seems more likely to assume that Tamjin was temporarily residing in the Upper and not the Lower Tianzhusi in Hangzhou. It also seems worth noting here that earlier the Koryŏ court had requested that their port of entry be changed from Dengzhou in present-day Shandong to Mingzhou in present-day Zhejiang; see Rogers, "Sung-Koryø Relations," 195–96.

34. See the *Xu zizhi tongjian changbian* 279, 11; cited in Chŏng, "Hyejo kuksa Tamjin kwa 'Chŏnginsu,'" 618–19. Chŏng incorrectly cites the date as the eleventh lunar month when in fact the text says the Korean monks were asked to leave Tianzhusi on the sixth day of the twelfth lunar month. There is also a record of three Koryŏ monks who came as envoys to China and received dharma transmission from Daozhen in the *Xu chuandeng lu* 續傳登錄 [Continued record of the transmission of the lamp; T51.2077.519c24], and the *Chanlin sengbao zhuan* 禪林僧寶傳 [Biographies of the Saṅgha Jewel from the Chan Grove; ZZ 137.543a13–16]; also cited in Chŏng, "Hyejo kuksa Tamjin kwa 'Chŏng'insu,'" 618.

35. See Chi-chiang Huang, "Elite and Clergy in Northern Sung Hang-chou: A Convergence of Interest," in *Buddhism in the Sung*, edited by Peter N. Gregory and Daniel A. Getz Jr. (Honolulu: University of Hawai'i Press, 1999), 320; and Elizabeth Morrison, *The Power of the Patriarchs: Qisong and Lineage in Chinese Buddhism* (Leiden, Brill, 2010), 105–6. Before his return to Koryŏ in 1086, Ŭich'ŏn had an audience with Huailian at Guanglisi on Mount Ayuwang; see "Chŏnt'ae sijo Taegak kuksa pimyŏng" 天台始祖大覺國師碑銘 [Stele inscription for the founding ancestor of Chŏnt'ae State Preceptor Taegak], *HKC*, 597.

36. Huilin Zongben (慧林宗本, 1020–1099) of the Yunmen branch became the first abbot of the Huilin chan cloister; see Huang, "Elite and Clergy in Northern Sung Hang-chou," 321.

37. For the kinds of teachings and practices that Tamjin may have encountered at Jingyinchansi, see Foulk, "Myth, Ritual, and Monastic Practice." See also Yifa, *The Origins of Buddhist Monastic Codes in China: An Annotated Translation and Study of the Chanyuan Qinggui* (Honolulu: University of Hawai'i Press, 2002).

38. Chŏng, "Hyejo kuksa Tamjin kwa 'Chŏnginsu,'" 621.

39. Tamjin was granted the title of Great Master Fayuan; see *Extended Continuation to the Comprehensive Mirror in Aid of Governance*, 303.1b; cited in Chŏng, "Hyejo kuksa Tamjin kwa 'Chŏng'insu,'" 619. As Chŏng points out, Tamjin seems to have returned to Koryŏ with the embassy led by the minister of taxation (K. *hobu sangsŏ* 戶部尚書) Yu Hong (柳洪, d. 1091). The embassy arrived four months later on the 27th of July (*KS* 9, 27b).

40. Chŏng, "Hyejo Kuksa Tamjin kwa 'Chŏng'insu,'" 630.

41. See Chŏng, "Hyejo Kuksa Tamjin kwa 'Chŏng'insu,'" 630–633. Tamjin's acquisition of three copies of the Khitan canon is mentioned in the *Samguk yusa* 三國逸事 [Memorabilia of the Three Kingdoms]; see T49.2039.994b18–20. For more information on the canon acquired by Tamjin, see O Yong-sŏp, "Hyejo taesa kurae ŭi Yobon taejang ŭi pongan" 혜조대사 구래의 요본대장의 봉안 [A Study on the enshrinement of the Khitan Buddhist canon brought by Master Hyejo], *Sŏjihak yŏn'gu* 27 (2004): 5–26.

42. Often, Koryŏ kings entrusted envoys with the acquisition of books from China; see Chŏng Su-a, "Koryŏ chunggi tae-Song oegyo ŭi chaegae wa kŭ ŭiŭi 고려중기 대송 외교의 재개와 그 의의" [The renewal of trade with Northern Song

in the mid-Koryŏ period and its significance], *Kuksakwan nonch'ong* 61 (1995), esp. 116–22.

43. Tamjin served as abbot of Kwangmyŏngsa, it seems, from the late 1080s to probably 1107; see "Taegam kuksa pimyŏng" 大鑑國師碑銘 [Stele inscription for State Preceptor Taegam, dated 1172], *HKC*, 820–824. Tamjin returned to Korea in 1086 and probably assumed the abbacy of Kwangmyŏngsa shortly thereafter (Daozhen passed away a few years later in 1093). Tamjin may have moved to Pojesa from Kwangmyŏngsa when he received the title of royal preceptor in 1107. He would have then overseen the king's visit to Pojesa in the summer of 1108. There, the king prayed for the success of his troops led by assistant supreme commander (K. *pyŏngma puwŏnsu* 兵馬副元帥) O Yŏnch'ong (吳延寵, 1055–1116) in the suppression of the Jurchen incursions; see *KS* 12, 37a and *KSC* 7, 26b.

44. See *KS* 12, 27b and *KS* 13, 32b respectively.

45. See the "Chungsu Yongmunsa ki" 重修龍門寺記 [Restoration record of Yongmunsa] written by the Hallim academician Yi Chi-myŏng (李知命, 1127–91) in 1188 (*HKC*, 874). Yongmunsa was first established by the Koryŏ founder T'aejo for a monk named Tuun (杜雲, d.u.) who had traveled to China with Pŏmil (梵日, 810–89). According to the monastery's restoration record, the abbacy was continuously held by dharma heirs in Tuun's lineage (K. *chŏnbŏp chason kyegye sangju* 傳法子孫繼繼相住). But the monastery seems to have become dilapidated by the twelfth century. The last in Tuun's lineage to hold the abbacy, Yŏngnyŏn (英繼, n.d.), invited Choŭng to take his place. Choŭng used his own private wealth to restore the monastery, which was entrusted with the task of caring for the crown prince's placenta in 1171. For more information on Yongmunsa and the stele, see Han Kimun, "Yech'ŏn 'Chungsu Yongmun-sa ki' pimun ŭro pon Koryŏ chunggi sŏnjonggye ŭi tonghyang—ŭmgi ŭi sogae rŭl chungsimŭro" 醴泉 "重修 龍門寺記" 碑文으로 본 高麗中期 禪宗界의 動向 [A study of the tendencies of the Sŏn school the mid-Koryŏ period as observed in the Yongmunsa Restoration Record Stele at Yech'ŏn], *Munhwa sahak* 24 (2005): 73–105. In his study of the introduction of Pure Rules texts to Korea Ven. Chŏngmyŏl also notes Tamjin's pioneering role, but his study is riddled with errors; see Chŏngmyŏl, "Han'guk esŏŭi ch'oech'o chŏnggyu toip e kwanhan koch'al 韓國에서의 最初 清規導入에 관 한 考察" [An investigation of the earliest example of pure rules in Korea], *Taegak sasang* 8 (2005): 283–313.

46. The "Chungsu Yongmunsa ki" makes no mention of dharma transmission in its summary of Choŭng's life, which seems to imply that he had but one master, namely Yŏngbo. According to the reverse side inscription of the "Chungsu Yongmunsa ki," Choŭng had several dharma heirs (K. *sabŏp cheja* 嗣法弟子). Some of them, however, are recorded as heirs in Iŏm's (and hence Yunju Daoying's) Mount Sumi (須彌山) transmission lineage; see Han, "Yech'ŏn 'Chungsu Yongmun-sa ki' pimun," 75–79. Han Kimun believes this is evidence of conversion, but more research to substantiate this belief seems necessary.

47. It seems worth noting that the *Chanyuan qinggui* 禪苑清規 [Pure Rules for Chan monasteries], first published in 1103 (which is *after* Tamjin returned from China in 1086), was carved and printed in Koryŏ in 1254. The edition used as the base text for the Koryŏ carving (currently in the possession of Kosaka Kiyū) is dated 1111; for a Korean translation of this edition, see Ch'oe Pŏphae trans., *Koryŏp'an Sŏnwŏn chŏnggyu yŏkchu* 고려판 선원청규 역주 [An annotated translation of the Koryŏ edition of the *Chanyuan qinggui*] (Seoul: Kasan pulgyo munhwa yŏn'guwŏn ch'ulp'anbu, 2001). The edition more commonly known and used today is a recurving of the *Chanyuan qinggui* dated 1202; see Kagamishima Genryū, Satō Tatsugen, and Kosaka Kiyū eds., *Yakuchū Zenen shingi* 訳註禪苑清規 [An annotated translation of the *Chanyuan qinggui*] (Tokyo: Sōtōshū shūmuchō, 1972). Chŏngmyŏl argues that the Chan manual imported by Tamjin was the *Chanyuan qinggui* or some earlier version of it, but this seems unlikely given the date of Tamjin's return to Koryŏ; see Chŏngmyŏl, "Han'guk esŏŭi ch'oech'o chŏnggyu." New rules and regulations for public monasteries such as Baiyun Shouduan's (白雲守端, 1025–1072) rules for the patriarch hall (C. *zutang gangji* 祖堂綱紀, dated 1070) were being written in the eleventh century; see Foulk and Sharf, "On the Ritual Use of Ch'an Portraiture in Medieval China," *Cahiers d'Extrême-Asie* 7 (1993–1994): 181. What Tamjin brought back could be a manual like Baiyun's.

48. Tansoksa had been chosen by Tamjin's disciple T'anyŏn (坦然, 1070–1159) as his *hasanso* (下山所). Royal and state preceptors, like Tamjin and T'anyŏn, were entitled to build or restore a monastery where they could enjoy retirement. Such a monastery was known as the preceptor's *hasanso*; see Han Kimun, *Koryŏ sawŏn ŭi kujo wa kinŭng* (Seoul: Minjoksa, 1998), 372–97; and also Pak Yunjin, "Koryŏ sidae wangsa-kuksa e taehan taeu 고려시대 王師 國師에 대한 대우" [Attitude towards the royal and state preceptors during the Koryŏ period], *Yŏksa hakpo* 190 (2006): 6–11.

49. See "Taegam kuksa pimyŏng" (*HKC*, 820–24).

50. The fact that T'anyŏn already possessed a record of his *sangdang* (or *shangtang* in Chinese) sermons at this point in his career is not without significance as he did not yet have an inheritance certificate and had not yet performed an ascending the hall ceremony.

51. For inheritance certificates, see Morten Schlütter, *How Zen Became Zen: The Dispute Over Enlightenment and the Formation of Chan Buddhism in Song-Dynasty China* (Honolulu: University of Hawai'i Press, 2008), 63–65.

52. During the Koryŏ period, to gain the abbacy of a monastery a monk had to receive the *taedŏk* (大德, lit. "great virtue") rank by successfully passing the official saṅgha examination in the capital, and to sit for this exam the monk had to first pass a preliminary exam administered by his school or lineage. In order to take the preliminary Sŏn exam a Sŏn monk had to be registered with one of the recognized Sŏn lineages. In Sŏn master Hŏnwŏn's (混元, 1191–1271) funerary epitaph there is mention of monks of royal birth who, out of respect for Honwŏn,

"transferred their registration" (K. *ijŏk* 移籍) to the Sagulsan lineage and "became P'umil's [i.e., Pŏmil's] descendants" (K. *wi P'umil son* 為品日孫), that is, Sagulsan lineage holders. For preliminary clerical exams, see Hŏ Hŭngsik, *Koryŏ ŭi kwagŏ chedo* (Seoul: Ilchogak, 2005), 232. See also the discussion in Vermeersch, *The Power of the Buddhas*, 192–94.

53. The term Kulsanha ("belonging to Sagulsan") can be found in the funerary epitaph's title. T'anyŏn's funerary epitaph also states: "In terms of his lineage the master is a ninth-generation grandson of Linji" (*i chongp'a ko chi sa nae Imje kudaeson ya* 以宗派考之師乃臨濟九代孫也); see *Taegam kuksa pimyŏng* (*HKC*, 821). This can only be interpreted to mean that T'anyŏn inherited Linji's dharma through Tamjin. For T'anyŏn to be counted as a ninth-generation heir of Linji, he would have to be recognized as Tamjin's dharma heir (Linji > 1. Zunjiang > 2. Huiyong > 3. Yanzhao > 4. Shengnian > 5. Guisheng > 6. Fayuan > 7. Daozhen > 8. Tamjin). Jiechen's lineage would place T'anyŏn in the twelfth generation (Linji > 1. Zunjiang > 2. Huiyong > 3. Yanzhao > 4. Shengnian > 5. Shanzhao > 6. Chuyuan > 7. Huinan > 8. Zuxin > 9. Weiqing > 10. Shouzhuo > 11. Jiechen). The funerary inscription also emphasizes the fact that T'anyŏn received transmission from Tamjin. It makes no mention of the transmission from Jiechen.

54. See Juhn Y. Ahn, "Have a Korean Lineage and Transmit a Chinese One Too: Lineage Practices in Seon Buddhism," *Journal of Chan Buddhism* 1 (2019): 1–32.

55. Tamjin is said to have remained in retirement there for a decade; see *Wŏn'gam kuksa chip* 圓鑑國師集 [State Preceptor Wŏn'gam's collected writings], *HPC* 6, 398b18–19.

56. Honwŏn and his teacher Hyesim (惠諶, 1178–1234) had both served as abbots of Tansoksa.

57. See Foulk and Sharf, "On the Ritual Use of Ch'an Portraiture," 179. It seems worth noting here that there was a portrait hall for T'anyŏn at Tansoksa; see No Sasin, et al. *Sinjŭng Tongguk yŏji sŭngnam* 新增東國輿地勝覽 [Revised and expanded edition of the survey of the geography of Chosŏn], vol. 30, 15a (Seoul: Sŏgyŏng Munhwasa, 1994), 514.

58. For Ch'ungji's move to Chŏnghyesa, see "Wŏn'gam kuksa pimyŏng" 圓鑑國師碑銘 [Stele inscription for State Preceptor Wŏn'gam], HKC: 1116.

59. *Wŏn'gam kuksa chip* (*HPC* 6, 398b6-c13).

60. *Wŏn'gam kuksa chip* (*HPC* 6, 396b12).

61. *Wŏn'gam kuksa chip* (*HPC* 6, 398b18–22).

62. Ch'ungji did, however, succeed Chŏnyŏng as the sixth abbot of Susŏnsa.

63. "Chaunsa chinmyŏng kuksa pimyŏng" 慈雲寺真明國師碑銘 [Stele inscription for State Preceptor Chinmyŏng from Chaunsa], *CKS*, 593.

64. Honwŏn's tenure as abbot of Chŏnghyesa—his first appointment in this capacity—is noted in his funerary epitaph; see Yi Nŭnghwa, *Chosŏn Pulgyo t'ongsa, ha* 朝鮮佛教通史 下 [A comprehensive history of Chosŏn Buddhism, II] (Kyŏngsŏng: Sinmun'gwan, 1918), 356.

65. "Wŏn'gam kuksa pimyŏng" *HKC*, 1116.

66. See Ch'oe Pŏphae, *Koryŏp'an chungch'ŏmjokpon Sŏnwŏn ch'ŏnggyu* 고려판 重添足本 禪苑淸規 [Expanded Koryŏ edition of the *Chanyuan qinggui*] (Seoul: Minjoksa, 1987), 481–83 (who cites Satō Tatsugen's *Chūgoku Bukkyō ni okeru kairitsu no kenkyū* [Tokyo: Mokujisha, 1986]); also noted in Chŏngmyŏl, "Han'guk esŏŭi ch'oech'o ch'ŏnggyu," 305–307.

67. "Pogwangsa chungch'ang pi" 普光寺重刱碑 [Stele inscription for State Preceptor Chinmyŏng from Chaunsa], *HKC*, 1190; cited in Hŏ, *Koryŏ pulgyosa yŏn'gu*, 482. For attempts to more thoroughly adopt Chan pure rules in the late Koryŏ period, see Kang Hoseon, "Koryŏ mal sŏnsŭng ŭi ip Wŏn yuryŏk kwa Wŏn ch'ŏnggyu suyong" 고려말 선승(禪僧)의 입원유력(入元遊歷)과 원(元) 청규(淸規)의 수용 [Late Koryŏ Sŏn pilgrims in Yuan and the importation of Yuan's *Chanyuan qinggui*], *Han'guk sasangsahak* 40 (2012): 30–64.

68. *T'aego hwasang ŏrok* [Venerable T'aego's recorded sayings], *HPC* 6, 698–699; cited in Kang "Koryŏ mal sŏnsŭng ŭi ip Wŏn yuryŏk," 41–42.

69. *T'aego hwasang ŏrok* (*HPC* 6, 694); cited in Kang "Koryŏ mal sŏnsŭng ŭi ip Wŏn yuryŏk," 44.

70. Kang "Koryŏ mal sŏnsŭng ŭi ip Wŏn yuryŏk," 44–51.

71. Kang, "Koryŏ mal sŏnsŭng ŭi ip Wŏn yuryŏk," 49–51.

Chapter 9

Gender and Dharma Lineage

Nuns in Korean Sŏn Buddhism

JIN Y. PARK

Introduction

Prior studies on nuns in Korean Buddhism have been done without sectarian distinctions.[1] The lack of relevant materials must have been the main reason for such an integrated approach to Buddhist nuns' lives and practice. Along with the emergence of women's studies and the increase in female Buddhist scholars, a broad topic such as women and Buddhism began to attract scholars' attention. What followed were examinations of Buddhist nuns in specific periods in Korean history, the status of Buddhist nuns in Korean society or within the monastic order, and the reasons for women joining the monastery. Research on nuns in Sŏn Buddhism has yet to be done, and this chapter launches such a study. When and under what circumstances did Korean Buddhist nuns practice Sŏn, and what is the current situation of nuns in the Sŏn order? What kind of records are available to answer these questions? And what can we learn from studying Korean nuns in Sŏn Buddhist tradition about the nature of Chan/Sŏn/Zen Buddhism and some of Korean Sŏn Buddhism's issues? These are main questions that I hope to address in this chapter.

With these goals in mind, I will discuss materials from three different periods in Korean Buddhism and consider what these materials tell us about nuns' practice and position in Sŏn Buddhism. In that context, I will also consider the implicit and explicit influences of Chinese Buddhism on Korean Buddhism.

Korean Nuns' Practice of Hwadu Meditation under Master Hyesim

The earliest evidence regarding Korean Buddhist nuns' participation in Sŏn meditation appears in the records of Chin'gak Hyesim (眞覺慧諶, 1178–1234).[2] Hyesim is known as the successor of Pojo Chinul (普照知訥, 1158–1210), the founder of Korean Sŏn Buddhism,[3] but the relationship between the two and the process of succession have been topics of debate among scholars. Some say that Hyesim in a way completed Chinul's work on Kanhwa meditation by publishing gongan collections and spreading the practice widely.[4] Others argue that Hyesim was more interested in political power than Chinul, and the spread of Kanhwa Sŏn was part of his goal to obtain power.[5] Hyesim became the second abbot of Susŏnsa (修禪社), succeeding Chinul as the first abbot, but he did so by following the king's command, not by accepting Chinul's invitation to be his successor. These issues require a larger scale of research and is not the chapter's aim. What is relevant to our discussion is that Hyesim's *Recorded Sayings* shows that he encouraged nuns to practice *hwadu* meditation.[6] This in itself could be considered as evidence that Hyesim's approach to Kanhwa Sŏn was different from that of Chinul, since, for Chinul, Kanhwa Sŏn was reserved for people with higher capacity, and women could not have been considered a part of such a group during Chinul's time.

As far as I know, no research has been done on Chinul's view on women's practice, but it has been pointed out that in his *Essentials of the Exposition on the Huayan Sūtra* (*Hwaŏm non chŏryo* 華嚴論節要), Chinul mentions the story of the Dragon Girl in the *Lotus Sūtra* and the sudden awakening in the *Huayan jing* several times.[7] The *Exposition* here refers to Li Tongxuan's (李通玄, 635–730 or 646–740) *Exposition on the New Translation of the Huayan jing* (*Xin Huayan jing lun* 新華嚴經論). In a frequently cited passage from Chinul's stele, the composer of the stele inscription Kim Kunsu (金君綏, ?–?) identified three major influences on Chinul's Buddhism, namely, the *Platform Sūtra of the Sixth Patriarch*, Li Tongxuan's *Exposition*, and Dahui Zonggao's (大慧宗杲, 1089–1163) *Recorded Sayings of Chan Master Dahui Pujue* (*Dahui Pujue Chansi yulu* 大慧普覺禪師語錄).[8]

These three sources demonstrate the core of Chinul's Buddhism: Sŏn tradition, Hwaŏm teaching, and Kanhua Chan or Kanhwa Sŏn. Chinul's admiration of Li Tongxuan's *Exposition* is clearly articulated in his preface to the *Essentials*. In the preface, Chinul states that after a conversation with a certain Huayanist, he struggled to find a balance or compatibility between the Huayan teachings and Sŏn meditation and eventually found a resolution through Li Tongxuan's statements that "the minds [of the sentient being] are the Buddha of Immovable Wisdom,"[9] and that "the body is the reflection of wisdom. This land [phenomenal world] is also the same. When wisdom is pellucid and its reflection clear, large and small are mutually intersecting, as in the realm of Indra's net."[10] As I have discussed elsewhere, at the core of Li Tongxuan's teaching in his *Exposition* is the conviction that there is not an infinitesimal difference between the sentient being and the Buddha.[11] Through these statements Chinul concluded that Sŏn meditation of the mind and Huayan emphasis on the phenomenal world should not be two separate practices.

Another noticeable aspect of Li's *Exposition* is his comparison of the *Lotus Sūtra* with the *Huayan jing* by comparing the Dragon Girl of the former to Sudhana in the latter. Li argues that the Dragon Girl had to change her body to a male form and then move to the southern region; to Li, this indicates that the Dragon Girl's awakening was not for everybody. She was not part of the audience who watched her body transform; hence, there was a gap between the awakened and those who were not. Also, awakening was not for all beings, since the Dragon Girl had to change her body. In comparison to the Dragon Girl, whose awakening took place at a distance from unenlightened beings, Li argues that the Sudhana of the *Huayan jing*, in the "Entering the Realm of Reality Chapter" (Rufajie pin 入法界品), meets all types of beings: men and women, children and adults, monastics and laypeople. One does not need to transform one's body, since every being is capable of attaining awakening, despite the ways in which they exist. Chinul's *Essentials* mirrors Li's position on this, and as a result it is not clear whether the section on the Dragon Girl in Chinul's *Exposition* can be counted as Chinul's position on women's bodies. In the *Exposition*, Chinul offered his own comments, but these are rare, and he did not comment on the issue of body transformation. And even if Chinul had commented on body transformation, it would not be of much help to us, since we are trying to discover Chinul's view on nuns' practice of Sŏn, not just how women were treated in Korean Buddhism.

A more relevant case with regard to Chinul and Korean nuns' Sŏn Buddhism could be his relation to Dahui. Chinul's Kanhwa Sŏn was heavily influenced by Dahui's Kanhua Chan, and we can clearly see Dahui's influence in Chinul's *Treatise on Resolving Doubts about the Hwadu Meditation* (*Kanhwa kyŏrŭi ron* 看話決疑論). As Miriam Levering's pioneering works show, Dahui encouraged his female practitioners to practice Chan meditation.[12] We don't see the same record with Chinul. Based on the lack of evidence, if we conclude that Sŏn meditation was not extended to Buddhist nuns during Chinul's time, the fact that Hyesim, who was only twenty years younger than Chinul, openly encouraged nuns' practice of *hwadu* meditation deserves our attention.

The discovery of a piece of Hyesim's stele by historian Min Hyŏn'gu offers us important information on this topic. In 1974, Min found a piece of broken stele at the ruins of a temple named Wŏllamsa (月南寺) in Gangjin, Chŏlla province, South Korea. Through archeological examination, Min confirmed that the discovered fragment was part of Hyesim's stele. Hyesim's stele had been said to exist in Songgwangsa, where Chinul's stele also exists. It turned out that Songgwangsa only had a broken piece of Hyesim's stele. Min claimed that the stele must have originally been erected at Wŏllamsa, which Hyesim established, but a piece of the broken stele was taken to Songgwangsa at some point. How the broken piece traveled from Wŏllamsa to Songgwangsa is yet to be revealed.

The broken piece that Min identified as part of Hyesim's stele contains sections of the inscription on the back. In an article discussing his discovery, Min offers some details about the inscription's content. The words on the front side of the stele were composed by Yi Kyubo (李奎報, 1168–1241), a well-known writer during the Koryŏ period (高麗, 928–1392). The inscription on the back of the stele was composed by Ch'oe Cha (崔滋, 1188–1260), another celebrated writer of Koryŏ. The inscription contains information about the people who composed it and inscribed it, a list of Hyesim's disciples, and another of those who were involved in the stele's establishment. What is relevant to our discussion is that among Hyesim's disciples on the stele appear the names of four nuns: Min (敏), Chŏngwŏn (淸遠), Hŭiwŏn (希遠), and Chŏngsim (正心).[13] According to the historian Kim Youngmi, this is the earliest record of a Korean Buddhist nun's involvement with Sŏn practice.[14]

What do we know about these nuns' Sŏn practice? In the *Recorded Sayings of National Master Chin'gak of Jogye* (*Chogye Chin'gak kuksa ŏrok* 曹溪眞覺國師語錄, published in 1526),[15] we find Hyesim's dharma talks given to nuns, including Chongmin (宗敏),¹⁶ Chŏngwŏn, Hŭiwŏn, and Yoyŏn (了然).¹⁷ Yoyŏn was not listed in the stele inscription, and Young Mi Kim suggests that was probably because Yoyŏn died before the stela was erected.¹⁸

As is well known, recorded sayings contain dialogues between a Chan master and a disciple. According to the Korean Buddhist scholar Yi Tongjun, Hyesim's recorded sayings are the oldest in Korean Buddhism.¹⁹ In his *Recorded Sayings*, Hyesim writes that in the summer of 1213, Hŭiwŏn, Chŏngwŏn, Chongmin, and Yoyŏn had a ninety-day retreat at Susŏnsa (currently Songgwangsa). At the end of the retreat, these nuns requested dharma talks, and Hyesim gave lessons to each of them.²⁰ After writing about the circumstances of his dharma talks to these four nuns, Hyesim states that he wishes they would work hard so they can quickly attain awakening.²¹

In his dharma talk to Chongmin, Hyesim emphasizes the importance of awakening to the emptiness of nature. Referencing Mazu (馬祖, 709–788) and Huangbo (黃檗, d. 850), Hyesim tells Chongmin to hold on to Zhaozhou's *wu hwadu* (無話頭). He also teaches her that one should hold on to *hwadu* all the time but not separate oneself from daily activities. Separating *hwadu* from daily activities, Hyesim tells Chongmin, would be like separating water from waves. If the principle (K. *li* 理) becomes quiet, the activities (K. *sa* 事) naturally become quiet, Hyesim teaches. Hyesim also says that she should not fall into the various maladies of *wu* and that if she continues to practice in this manner, suddenly she will have an experience of getting through the *hwadu*. He ends his dharma talk by expressing his wish that Chongmin would rapidly attain awakening.²²

In his talk to Yoyŏn, Hyesim references diverse gongans in the history of Buddhism. This time, the reference to Zhaozhou is not *wu gongan* but the gongan of "All the things return to one, to where does the one return?" In this talk, Hyesim mentions the *Sūtra of Sturdy Lady* (*Fúshuō Jiangunü jing* 佛說堅固女經).²³ In this sutra, Sturdy Lady wishes to practice bodhicitta, and Śāriputra asks her how she might practice attaining perfect enlightenment (K. *anyoktabori* 阿耨多菩提). Sturdy Lady outwits Śāriputra by saying that since perfect enlightenment does not have a fixed form, one cannot attain it, but she will still practice bodhicitta by helping sentient beings. The Buddha confirms the awakening of Sturdy Lady and predicts that when Maitreya comes, she will become a buddha.²⁴

Finishing his story about Sturdy Lady with the confirmation that Sturdy Lady will be a great teacher, Hyesim turns his talk to the Chinese bhikṣuni Liaoran (了然; K. Yoyŏn). Bhikṣuṇī Liaoran was a disciple of Chan Master Gaoan Dayu (高安大愚), who lived during the time of Mazu. One day, Liaoran received a visit by bhikṣu Guanxi Zhixian (灌溪志閑). The latter asks, "What is Mount Mo?" Liaoran responds, "It does not have the peak." Guanxi asks, "Who is the head of Mount Mo?" and Liaoran responds, "Neither man's shape nor woman's shape." The former asks Liaoran why she does not transform herself. Liaoran responds: "[She is] Neither a deity nor a ghost."[25] Guanxi gives in. With this story, Hyesim asks Yoyŏn, "The Yoyŏn (Liaoran) of the past was like this, and what should Yoyŏn of today do?"[26] This is clear encouragement that Yoyŏn can attain awakening like Chinese female Chan Master Liaoran. In this dharma talk, Hyesim found topics closely related to women's practice and encouraged his female disciple to rapidly attain awakening.

In his dharma talk to Bhikṣuṇī Chŏngwŏn, Hyesim highlights Huangbo's teaching that the minds of the Buddha and the sentient being are the same. Hyesim tells Chŏngwŏn that one might think that the Buddha's works are all pure and those by sentient beings are all contaminated, but the differences exist only at the phenomenal level. Once one lets go of attachment to the dualism of good and bad, purity and impurity, right at that moment the mind will open wide. Hyesim emphasizes that there is nowhere to find the Buddha outside of the mind. When a thought arises, one should be careful not to hold on to it nor discard it. Hyesim encourages Chŏngwŏn to practice *hwadu* with such a mind as he advises: "There is also the single gateway of *kanhwa* (看話, "examination of the story") that is very marvelous and profound, such as "the dog has no Buddha-nature" and "the bamboo rod" and so on. Please, investigate them in detail at your convenience. In speaking of the faults (lit. illnesses) involved in this effort, they are all as you heard during the summer retreat, so I will not bother to describe them here."[27] Here we see that Hyesim is explicitly encouraging Chŏngwŏn to practice *kanhwa* meditation.

In his dharma talk to Hŭiwŏn, Hyesim teaches that one should overcome the distinction between good and bad, secular and sacred. If one liberates oneself from such distinctions and realizes that the mind is originally empty, one will realize wisdom, which would be like the sun appearing through an opening in the clouds.

In sum, in the dharma talk to Chongmin, Hyesim emphasized *wu hwadu*, the emptiness of nature, warned against the malady of meditation, and taught that awakening is not different from everyday activities. In his talk to Yoyŏn, Hyesim told the story of Sturdy Lady and Chinese Chan

Master Liaoran and showed that one's gender should not be an obstacle to awakening. In the talk to Chŏngwŏn, he highlighted the identity of the mind of the sentient being as being the same as that of the Buddha and emphasized that there is no Buddhahood outside of one's mind. In the final talk to Hŭiwŏn, Hyesim again emphasized the nonduality of the opposites in dualism and the emptiness of the mind.

In all four cases, Hyesim encouraged his female disciples that nuns could also attain enlightenment. His use of the *Sūtra of Sturdy Lady* is also relevant. In the entire *Collected Works of Korean Buddhism*, Hyesim is the only figure who uses this sutra.

The fact that nuns' names were listed in the inscription on the back of Hyesim's stele and that Hyesim encouraged nuns to quickly attain Buddhahood shows that nuns were not completely excluded from Sŏn tradition during Hyesim's time, even though nothing of their lives and practices other than what appeared in the *Recorded Sayings* of Hyesim are yet known.

Jikji (直指) and Bhikṣuṇī Myodŏk (妙德)

Another occasion that a nun's name appears in Korean Sŏn tradition occurs over a hundred years after Hyesim's time. *Essentials of the Buddhist Patriarchs' [Teaching] Directly Pointing at the Essence of the Mind Selected by Master Paeg'un* (Paeg'un hwasang ch'orok Pulcho chikchi simch'e yojŏl 白雲和尙抄錄佛祖直指心體要節, 1377), better known in Korea as "Jikji" (直指), reveals another aspect of Korean nuns' activity in Sŏn Buddhism.

As the title says, this is a text that compiled selected teachings by Buddhist masters. In the context of Korean culture, the text became better known for its importance as a piece of Korean cultural heritage. The text was composed in two volumes in 1372 by Sŏn Master Paeg'un Kyŏnghan (白雲景閑, 1299–1375) and was printed in 1377 and 1378. The 1377 version was printed by using movable metal characters, while the 1378 version is a wooden block printing. The former has been recognized as the oldest extant movable metal character printing in history. Currently, only the second volume of the metal character print version is extant, located in the French National Museum (Bibliotéque Nationale de France).

What is relevant to our discussion is that the name of Bhikṣuṇī Myodŏk (妙德) appears at the end of the second volume of the metal character version as the sole financier of the printing. Her name also appears as a financial supporter for the wooden block printing of the *Essentials* and the printing of the *Recorded Sayings of Master Paeg'un* (*Paek'un hwasang ŏrok* 白雲和尙語錄) in 1378, though in both cases she was not the sole financier. Who was this nun, and how was she able to offer financial support to the degree that her name was listed as the sole contributor to the metal character printing and to the other two printings?

Despite the high visibility of her name at the end of Paeg'un's *Essentials* and *Recorded Sayings*, not much is known about Myodŏk. One might assume that she did not practice Sŏn but was merely a donor, as was typically the case in the involvement of aristocratic women with Buddhism in Korea during the Koryŏ and especially the neo-Confucian Chosŏn dynasties. However, those female aristocrats were not monastics, whereas Myodŏk was. Still, one might assume that Myodŏk joined the monastery late in life, perhaps after the death of her husband, as was common for nuns in the Koryŏ and Chosŏn periods;[28] therefore, one would conclude that she did not practice Sŏn.

Paeg'un Kyŏnghan (白雲景閑, 1299–1375), the composer of *Essentials*, is one of three well-known Sŏn masters during the late Koryŏ period, together with Naong Hyegŭn (懶翁惠勤, 1320–1376) and T'aego Pou (太古普愚, 1301–1382). All three of them traveled to China and received recognition of their awakening and came back to Koryŏ to play a major role in the Korean Buddhist world.

According to the preface to the 1378 edition of the *Essentials*, written by Yi Saek (李穡, 1328–1396), Paeg'un went to China in 1351 and visited Chinese Chan Master Shiwu Qinggong (石屋清珙, 1272–1352), who recognized Paeg'un's awakening. Paeg'un returned to Koryŏ in 1353. Shiwu died in 1352 and left a deathbed poem to Paeg'un, which was delivered to Paeg'un in 1353. The poem states: "In order to buy white clouds [*paeg'un*], I have sold out even blue winds// The entire house is empty, I'm cold to my bones// All that is left is this shabby house// While getting ready to leave, I will leave it to you."[29] In this manner, Shiwu once again confirmed the transmission of dharma to Paeg'un. The original *Essentials* was given to Paeg'un by Shiwu, while Paeg'un was in China and Paeg'un expanded it into two volumes, as in the current form.

While Paeg'un was in China, he also visited Zhikong (指空, 1300?–1361), an Indian monk who traveled to China and from there to Korea. Zhikong came to Korea in March 1326 and returned to China in September 1328.[30] As an envoy of Jinzong (晉宗, Taiding Di, 泰定帝, r. 1323–1328) of Yuan China and at the same time as a descendent of Śākyamuni Buddha and Bodhidharma,³¹ Zhikong enjoyed great respect and success in Korea with his dual position of an emperor's envoy in the secular world and a renowned monk in the sacred world. Zhikong was revered to the extent that he was considered to be a reappearance of Śākyamuni Buddha. Soon after his arrival in Koryŏ, Zhikong earned a large number of followers. His teaching seems to have involved a mixture of Sŏn and precepts.

One of the major events that happened during his stay in Koryŏ was the issuance of Certificates of Ordination (K. *kyechŏp* 戒牒). Only four of them are currently extant, even though it was recorded that he issued thousands of them. Zhikong's ordinance is known to have been based on the teaching of the precept of no-birth (K. *musaenggye* 無生戒). By realizing no-mind (K. *musim* 無心), one learns that there is neither birth nor death; thus, one should not give rise to either good or bad. The teaching of the precept of no-birth does not discriminate between men and women or monastics and laypeople, which was enthusiastically received by the people of Koryŏ.

Zhikong is also known as the one from whom Naong received recognition. Naong had an awakening experience in 1347 and traveled to China in November of that year, where he would spend the next ten years until returning to Koryŏ in March 1358.³² A major reason for Naong's journey to Yanjing was to receive recognition from Zhikong. Naong arrived in Fayuansi (法源寺) in Yanjing in March 1348 and met with Zhikong. He had dharma dialogue with him at the first meeting and eventually received recognition from Zhikong in 1353.³³

Zhikong's recognition of Naong's awakening gave Naong the legitimacy and authenticity he needed to emerge as a leading figure in Koryŏ during the mid- and late thirteenth century. Zhikong died in 1361. Six years later, in the winter of 1367, Naong receives his robe and a note that Zhikong had left behind for him. In the note, Zhikong addressed Naong as his disciple.³⁴ All of these circumstances supported Naong's ascendance as a major figure in Koryŏ Buddhism.³⁵

With regards to Zhikong's Certificates of Ordination, one clue that helps us learn about Bhikṣuṇī Myodŏk is a Certificate of Ordination for Myodŏk (K. *Myodŏk kyech'ŏp* 妙德戒牒) that was discovered in 1988, one of the four extant certificates issued by Zhikong during his stay in Korea from 1326 to 1328. The certificate is dated 1326 and addresses the recipient as lay practitioner Myodŏk (Ubai Myodŏk 優婆夷妙德), not Bhikṣuṇī Myodŏk. Since the metal character printing of *Essentials* happened in 1377, a fifty-one-year gap exists between the two events. Given that the last activities of

Myodŏk that we know about happened in 1378, when she offered financial support for the wooden printing of the *Essentials*[36] and *Recorded Sayings of Paeg'un*,[37] it is not likely that the fifty-one-year gap should be a reason to distrust that the two Myodŏks are the same individual.[38]

As I mentioned, Myodŏk appears as the sole financial contributor for the metal printing, whereas other aristocratic ladies appear as financial supporters for the wooden block printing. Metal character printing was costly at the time, so how was it possible for Myodŏk to take care of such expenses on her own? Scholars assume that she must have been from a high aristocratic family or even a royal family. Did she practice Sŏn with Paeg'un or in another way, or was she involved with Buddhism only as a donor, as most women were at the time? We don't have direct information on this, but the visibility of her contribution to the printings of the *Essentials* and *Recorded Sayings* of Paeg'un offers a fragment about a possible linkage to the engagement of Korean nuns with Sŏn Buddhism.

Nuns in Modern Korean Sŏn Buddhism

Scholars attested that during the Chosŏn period (1392–1910), nuns' practices must have been limited to chanting, sutra reading, and sutra copying.[39] At the beginning of the twentieth century, around 1909, according to the *Hwangsŏng Newspaper*, the number of monks was 5,218, nuns 563, and total monastics 5,781.[40] According to a report by the Jogye Order, in 2006 the number of bhikṣu was 5,120 and bhikṣuṇī 5,033. In a hundred years' time, the number of bhikṣuṇī increased exponentially, but the number of bhikṣu remained almost the same.

Nuns' participation in Sŏn practice in Korea made visible advances in the modern period with the establishment of nuns' meditation halls. The first nun's meditation hall was the Kyŏnsŏngam (見性庵) at Sudŏksa, which officially opened in 1928.[41] As soon as it did, the Kyŏnsŏngam began to play a significant role in boosting Sŏn meditation among Korean nuns.[42]

Myori Pŏphŭi (妙理法喜, 1887–1975) is credited as a pioneer in the Sŏn lineage of Korean nuns in modern times. Pŏphŭi was born in the southern part of Korea. Her father died when she was three, and the next year her grandmother sent her to Mit'aam (彌陀庵, Amitābha Cloister) at Tonghaksa.[43] Her mother joined the monastery the following year. Mother and daughter stayed at Mit'aam for about a year together, but then the mother moved to Kapsa, thinking that to stay with her daughter would impede her practice. She died when Pŏphŭi was eight.⁴⁴ Pŏphŭi received the śramaṇa precepts in 1901 and the full precepts in 1910 at Haeinsa, when she was twenty-three years old. She studied Buddhist scriptures with the lecturer Manu (萬愚) at Tonghaksa and studied the *Lotus Sutra* with Sŏn Master Kobong at Chŏngamsa. Sŏn Master Kobong advised Pŏphŭi to practice Sŏn meditation with Man'gong (滿空, 1871–1946) at Sudŏksa, which Pŏphŭi did.

Under Man'gong, Pŏphŭi practiced with the *hwadu*, "All things return to one, and to where does the one return?" (K. *Manpŏp kwiil kwiil hachŏ* 萬法歸一歸一何處). After five years of practice, she attained awakening and received recognition from Man'gong, who gave her the dharma alias "Myori." Her name "Myori Pŏphŭi" means "Since the mysterious principle is all understood, the happiness of Buddhist teaching is complete."

Few records remain of Myori Pŏphŭi's awakening or activities. She left behind no record of her awakening experiences or her practice, and her disciples made no such records. Pŏphŭi, however, has been recognized as the founder of the nuns' Sŏn tradition and as the first bhikṣuṇī to start a bhikṣuṇī Sŏn dharma lineage in modern Korean Buddhism.⁴⁵ This shows a visible difference with the premodern period, when a dharma lineage for the bhikṣuṇī Sŏn tradition was probably unthinkable. How was it possible that the nuns' Buddhist practice, which had been suppressed for hundreds of years during the Chosŏn period, suddenly revived, and nuns became involved with Sŏn meditation at the beginning of the twentieth century? Diverse factors seem to have worked through synergy to create this situation.

Elsewhere I discussed three characteristics of modern Korean Buddhism: revival of Sŏn Buddhism, Buddhist reform movements, and Buddhist encounter with new intellectualism.⁴⁶ All three aspects are closely related to the nuns' engagement with Sŏn Buddhism in modern times. In that context, below I will list several conditions that I believe played significant roles in the emergence of Korean nuns' practice of Sŏn Buddhism.

The first is the Sŏn revival movement in modern Korea. This movement began in the mid-nineteenth century. Yi Nŭnghwa (李能和, 1869–1943), a modern Korean historian and folklorist, published *History of Korean Buddhism* (*Chosŏn Pulgyo t'ongsa* 朝鮮佛敎通史 1918), the first comprehensive book on the history of Korean Buddhism. In the section that discusses Buddhism in the modern period, Yi describes Taech'i Yu Honggi (大致 劉鴻基, 1831–?) and the emergence of meditation practice in Seoul among the reformists who led the Kapsin Coup (Kapsin chŏngbyŏn

甲申政變) of 1884. Around 1882, a small group of young Korean intellectuals created the Enlightenment Party (Kaehwadang 開化黨). According to Yi, the members of the Enlightenment Party followed Yu Taech'i, who loved to engage in discussion about Sŏn Buddhism. His efforts created a boom of Sŏn meditation in Seoul.[47] Yi also points out that the members of the Enlightenment Party tried to put the teachings of Buddhism into practice, which party members learned from Yu Taech'i. The revival of Sŏn Buddhism among the monastics became clearer with Kyŏnghŏ Sŏngu (鏡虛惺牛, 1849–1912), who is credited as the founder of the modern Korean Sŏn tradition.

The second factor, which is related to the first, is Buddhist reform movements. In reaction to the influx of Western culture into Korean society in the name of modernity, Korean Buddhism proposed various changes to make it more relevant to the new social environment. Buddhist reformists claimed that Buddhism should relate itself to the general public and their daily lives. To do so, they demanded that Buddhist monasteries, then mostly located in the mountains, should come to the city center, and Buddhists should actively engage with society. Some of these reformers were critical of women's Buddhism at the time, degrading it as a Buddhism of fortune-bringing (K. *kibok Pulgyo* 祈福佛教).[48] These reformists also proposed that one should guide women practitioners to help others and learn about Buddhism instead of praying for personal fortune.

Through the movements to popularize Buddhism, people gained more opportunities to participate in Sŏn practice, and Sŏn practice became an alternative to the popular women's practice of fortune-bringing Buddhism. It became a way for women to lead lives outside the domestic sphere that had defined their position in Korea.

Unlike the premodern period when Sŏn meditation was mostly a forbidden realm for nuns, at the beginning of the twentieth century it became a major practice for them.[49] The Sŏnhakwŏn (禪學院), or Sŏn Center, that opened in 1921 at the center of Seoul played an important role in spreading Sŏn practice to the general public and also female practitioners both lay and monastic.

In the context of nuns' Sŏn practice in modern Korea, Sŏn Master Man'gong earns credits. Myori Pŏphŭi was not the only nun to practice under Man'gong. He guided nuns at both Kyŏnsŏngam at Sudŏksa and Yunp'ilam in Munkyeung, Gyeongbuk province. Since the distance between the two was quite far to travel, Man'gong encouraged nuns to send him letters to report their progress in meditation while he was not around.[50]

Hwasan Suok (華山守玉, 1902–66), Mansŏng (萬性, 1897–1975), Kim Iryŏp (金一葉, 1896–1971), and Pon'gong Kyemyŏng (本空戒明, 1907–1965), all practiced under Man'gong.

As the Buddhist scholar Kang Munsŏn pointed out, one notable aspect of nuns' Sŏn tradition in modern Korea is that not all of them go through the typical stages of studying sutras and Buddhist texts, receiving a *hwadu* from a master, and attaining recognition. Some did, like Myori Pŏphui, but others didn't have a background in doctrinal Buddhist studies at all, and exclusively practiced *hwadu*, and received recognition, as in the case of Mansŏng. Yet there is still a group of Sŏn nuns who neither studied doctrinal Buddhism nor received a *hwadu* from a master. Instead, they came up with their own existential question that functioned as a *hwadu*. They received some recognition from Sŏn masters for their efforts but not a final recognition; such was the case with Iryŏp and Pon'gong, two well-known nuns in modern Korean Buddhism.[51] In current nuns' society, they are not taken less seriously because of that.

It is possible to consider that this practice could destabilize the core of the Sŏn tradition. I mean this in a positive way. One reason nuns have had difficulty engaging with Sŏn was that it was based on a mind-to-mind transmission tradition, and this mind was patriarchal. The Sŏn tradition of dharma lineage made it more difficult for nuns to participate. Loosening up the dharma lineage and recognition tradition for modern Korean nuns is in fact one of the reasons Sŏn Buddhism became a major form of practice for nuns. This loosening of tradition and recognition in nuns' Sŏn practice shows a good contrast with the mainstream (or monks') Sŏn practice in modern Korean Buddhism.

Center and Margin in Sŏn Buddhism

T'oeong Sŏngchŏl (退翁性徹, 1912–1993) is one of the most influential Sŏn masters of the twentieth century in South Korea. In his *Dharma Lineage of Korean Buddhism* (*Han'guk Pulgyo ŭi pŏpmaek* 韓國佛敎의 法脈, 1976), Sŏngchŏl made a claim that would lead Korean Buddhism into debates for the next two decades. He said that the legitimate founder of the Jogye Order should be T'aego Pou, not Pojo Chinul.[52] There were at least two reasons for Sŏngchŏl to deny Chinul's position in Korean Buddhism. First, Chinul did not receive an authentic dharma transmission, whereas Pou did. Second, Chinul followed the gradualism of Zongmi, which from

Sŏngchŏl's perspective makes Chinul a heretic to Sŏn Buddhism because for him the authentic teaching of Sŏn Buddhism should be based on sudden awakening.

T'aego Pou (太古普愚, 1301–1382) was a contemporary of Paeg'un and Naong, who were discussed earlier. Pou had an awakening in 1338 and traveled to China in 1346, met with Shiwu the next year, and received recognition from him in 1347.[53] Pou returned to Koryŏ in 1348. From the beginning, Pou's practice was always that of Kanhwa Sŏn in the tradition of Linji. He started with the *hwadu* of "all the things return to one, and where does the one return to?" at the age of nineteen. From there, he practiced Zhaozhou's *wu hwadu* and then went through all seventeen hundred *hwadus*. After he returned from Yuan China, he also taught Kanhwa Sŏn.

During the late Koryŏ period, recognition trips to China became popular. Chinul never went to China, nor did he have verbal recognition from any masters. For Chinul, the mind-to-mind transmission of Chan Buddhism did not mean that one should actually find a teacher to confer a recognition of awakening on them. Rather, Buddhist scriptures and Buddhist masters' dharma talks were his teachers, and awakening through the study of those materials was more important than finding a teacher to recognize one's awakening.

In the late Koryŏ, the situation changed. Along with the influence of Deyi (德異, 1231–?), getting recognition after the awakening (K. *ohu in'ga* 悟後印可) became widespread. In this case, the awakening experience happened first in Korea, and Korean monks would then travel to Yuan China to earn recognition from Chinese Chan masters.[54] Dharma lineage was essential not only to ascertain the authenticity of one's awakening but to exercise influence in the Buddhist world and society in general in Koryŏ. As scholars have noted, this trend led to a tendency to emphasize the Sŏn lineage and the legitimacy of certain Sŏn lineages, which became an obstacle to the free and creative development of Sŏn Buddhism.[55]

The rigidity of the Sŏn spirit and closed discussion of the legitimacy of dharma lineage are exactly what we see in Sŏngchŏl's claim for Pou. Sŏngchŏl deemed Pou the legitimate descendent of the Jogye (Linji) Order and the authentic founder of Korean Sŏn Buddhism, based on the fact that Pou received the recognition of Chinese Chan master Shiwu, the eighteenth descendent of Linji and making Pou the nineteenth descendent. Sŏngchŏl severely criticized Chinul for claiming that he had received the teachings of Huineng and Dahui without actually receiving recognition from them.[56]

For Sŏngchŏl, Chinul is guilty of assuming the recognition of teachers from whom he never received it. In *Authentic Path of Sŏn School* (*Sŏnmun chŏngro* 禪門正路, 1981), Sŏngchŏl blamed Chinul for renouncing the sudden teaching of Sŏn Buddhism and practicing the gradualism of Hwaŏm Sŏn (華嚴禪).[57] This issue is taken up in detail in a following chapter by Bernard Senécal.

The position of nuns in Sŏn Buddhism and Sŏngchŏl's enthronement of Pou as a legitimate founder of Korean Sŏn Buddhism might look like two separate issues, but I argue that the patriarchal nature of the Sŏn lineage tradition has been a serious obstacle for nuns' involvement in Sŏn Buddhism. The Korean Sŏn Buddhist tradition claims its identity through Kanhwa Sŏn and *hwadu* practices, which in most cases were limited to monks. Nuns' practices focused on non-*hwadu* meditation such as sutra chanting or sutra copying. Sŏn masters such as Hyesim and Man'gong encouraged nuns to practice *hwadu* meditation,[58] but they were rather exceptions in Korean Sŏn tradition.

Gender and Dharma Lineage: Nuns in Korean Sŏn Buddhism

The creation of the bhikṣuṇī dharma lineage in modern Korea reveals that a new phase in the relationship of nuns to Sŏn Buddhism has emerged. The history of nuns' meditation halls in Korea began in January 1916 when Kyŏnsŏngam began to function as a bhikṣuṇī meditation hall. Since then, more than thirty meditation halls for Buddhist nuns have opened their doors.[59] The rapid increase of the number of meditation halls for nuns in Korea during the twentieth century was made possible by several social shifts, and it reflects a transformation in the membership of Korea's monastic community. This change also resulted in the formation of the bhikṣuṇī dharma lineage in the 1970s. Ha Ch'unsaeng, a Korean Buddhist scholar, reports that at least eleven major bhikṣuṇī dharma lineages (K. *piguni munjung* 比丘尼門中) and over five smaller bhikṣuṇī dharma lineages exist in contemporary Korea.[60]

Based on his research on the formation and characteristics of these dharma lineages, Ha tells us that bhikṣuṇī dharma lineages work differently in comparison to the traditional Sŏn dharma lineages. In Sŏn Buddhism, the foundational elements include the recognition of awakening by a Sŏn master, the mind-to-mind transmission that follows the recognition, which confirms one's position in a dharma lineage. These elements are related to the nature of Sŏn Buddhism. But they also have functioned to consolidate the power of those who have attained the recognition of awakening and dharma transmission. Ha reports that unlike such traditional format of the dharma lineage, Korean nuns' dharma lineages started in an effort to create a practice community and propagate their masters' teachings. Members of the same lineage also gather together to perform ceremonies for their founders.[61] Eun-su Cho, a scholar of Korean Buddhism, observes that the emergence of nuns' organizations for the past fifty or so years in Korea indicates that nuns' minority position in traditional Sŏn Buddhism has been reinterpreted according to the sociohistorical and even political context of our time.[62]

Both Ha and Cho credit the women's movements of the twentieth century as one of the most influential factors that led nuns to establish their own dharma lineages. Women's issues have become some of the pressing social, historical, and political issues of our time, and this was reflected in the rapid increase of Buddhist nuns in Korea during the twentieth century.[63] Still, materials that can help us understand the lives and practices of nuns in Korean Sŏn Buddhism are seriously limited. To understand nuns in the premodern period, we need to put together pieces of the puzzle and create possible narratives; most likely, we will not find all of the pieces needed to solve the puzzle. And with the limited knowledge we have, which I have presented in this chapter, many questions remain unanswered.

First, were there specific periods when nuns' practice of Sŏn was more permissible? In the premodern period, Hyesim was the first Sŏn master with whom nuns practiced *hwadu* meditation. The second "wave" occurred about 130 years later at the end of the Koryŏ period with the teachings of Paeg'un, Naong, and Pou. What made this phenomenon possible? Was it the ambience of the time, Sŏn masters' personalities, or something else? In the context of Chinese Chan or Japanese Zen Buddhism, more searches on female Chan or Zen masters' direct engagement with the issue of gender are available, as I mentioned in an earlier note.[64] In Korean Buddhism, such research is still lacking.

Second, the beginning of the modern period (that is, the early twentieth century), when Korean Buddhism was in its weakest state, it was a vibrant time for Korean nuns' practice of Sŏn Buddhism. Buddhist nuns eventually founded their own meditation halls where they could focus on Sŏn practice. Research shows that Buddhist reform movements that tried to appeal to the general public led to opportunities for nuns to participate in Sŏn practice.⁶⁵ Were there any other specific Buddhist movements or trends that were conducive to the visibility of nuns in Sŏn Buddhism at that time?

Third, what does our examination of nuns in Sŏn Buddhism tell us about Chan/Sŏn/Zen Buddhism itself? In theory, Chan/Sŏn/Zen Buddhism can be said to represent one of the most liberal interpretations of Buddhism. Chan is the school that teaches the killing of its founder and patriarchs, if only rhetorically, in order to prevent a reified understanding of the Buddha's and the patriarchs' teachings. On the other hand, Chan/Sŏn/Zen has been one of the most authoritarian and patriarchal Buddhist traditions. How do we reconcile these two factors?

Sŏn authoritarianism is closely related to the school's original claim of the mind-to-mind transmission, which led to the requirements of dharma lineage and recognition by a Sŏn master in order to confirm the authenticity of awakening. In Sŏn Buddhism, knowledge production and the legitimacy and value of that knowledge or wisdom need to be confirmed by patriarchs, which makes the confirmation patriarchal, linear, and authoritarian in nature. This process has also created a power imbalance between bhikṣuṇī and bhikṣu in Sŏn Buddhism and also between Chinese Chan and Korean Sŏn Buddhism.

In the records I have presented in this chapter, nuns' Sŏn practice is almost always related to Sŏn masters who are monks. Without masters and without receiving *hwadu* from them, it was difficult for nuns to practice Sŏn. Nuns' positions in Sŏn became doubly marginalized because the dharma lineage was patriarchal and because of the Buddhist teaching that women cannot attain awakening.

The power dynamics of the center and margin are repeated in Korean Sŏn Buddhism's efforts to obtain recognition from Chinese Chan masters during the middle and late periods of the Koryŏ dynasty. One cannot ignore the political rapport between Yuan China and Koryŏ when we consider Koryŏ Buddhists' desire to be recognized by Chinese Chan masters.

Correspondence between the power relation in the secular world and that in the religious sphere has been a common theme in the history of religion, but that does not mean that such a practice is not disturbing, especially when the practice is related to the very core of defining the authenticity and legitimacy of a religious practice. It should be even more unsettling to see the practice continue in the twentieth century when the power relationship of China and Korea shouldn't be a part of religious discourse. Sŏngchŏl's attempt to confirm Pou as the legitimate founder of the Jogye Order because he attained recognition in Yuan China by a Chinese master seems like evidence to me of the authoritarian aspects of Sŏn Buddhism that suppress more creative engagement with Sŏn teaching, as some have argued was the case with Chinul.

The Sŏn Buddhist school is still dominated by patriarchal power, and the nuns' Sŏn practice in the modern period was made possible because of male masters who allowed and encouraged nuns to practice Sŏn meditation. In recent years, however, Korean nuns have begun to develop their own sects, as I have briefly discussed. The trend has not yet completely changed the centuries-old patriarchal tradition in Sŏn Buddhism, but we can hope that this development may open a new chapter on gender issues and women's position in Buddhism.

Notes

1. In the context of women in Chinese Chan Buddhism, research has been well under way. See Beata Grant, *Eminent Nuns: Women Chan Masters of Seventeenth-Century China* (Honolulu: University of Hawai'i Press, 2009); Beata Grant, *Zen Echoes: Classic Kōans with Verse Commentaries by Three Female Chan Masters* (Boston: Wisdom, 2017). Miriam Levering has done extensive research on women in Chan Buddhism: "Dōgen's *Raihaitokuzui* and Women Teaching in Sung Ch'an," *Journal of the International Association of Buddhist Studies* 21, no. 1 (1998): 77–110; "The Dragon Girl and the Abbess of Mo-shan: Gender and Status in the Ch'an Buddhist Tradition," *Journal of the International Association of Buddhist Studies* 5, no. 1 (1982): 19–35; "Lin-chi (Rinzai) Ch'an and Gender: The Rhetoric of Equality and the Rhetoric of Heroism," in *Buddhism, Sexuality and Gender*, ed. Jose Ignacio Cabezon, 137–58 (Albany: State University of New York Press, 1992); "Miao-tao and Her Teacher Ta-hui," in *Buddhism in the Sung Dynasty*, ed. Peter Gregory and Daniel Getz, 188–219 (Honolulu: University of Hawai'i Press, 1999); "Women Ch'an Masters: The Teacher Miao-tsung as Saint," in *Women Saints in World Religions*, ed. Arvind Sharma, 180–204 (Albany: State University of New York Press, 2000).

Grace Jinn Schireson, *Zen Women: Beyond Tea Ladies, Iron Maidens, and Macho Masters* (Boston: Wisdom, 2009) offers women in Buddhism beginning from the time of the Buddha. For women in the gongan tradition, see Zenshin Florence Caplow and Reigetsu Susan Moon, eds., *The Hidden Lamp: Stories from Twenty-Five Centuries of Awakened Women* (Boston: Wisdom, 2013).

2. The first known Buddhist nun in the history of Korean Buddhism was Lady Sa (Sassi 史氏), who lived in the sixth century (Iryŏn 一然, *Samguk yusa* 三國遺事 [The Memorabilia of the Three Kingdoms], T48.2039.986a. About

brief discussions of bhikṣuṇīs in premodern Korea, see Kim Yŏngmi 김영미, "Samguk, Koryŏ sidae piguni ŭi salm kwa suhaeng," 삼국, 고려시대 비구니의 삶 과 수행 [Bhikṣuṇīs' lives and practice during the Three Kingdoms' and Koryŏ periods], in *Han'guk piguni ŭi suhaeng kwa salm* 한국 비구니의 수행과 삶 [Korean Bhikṣuṇī's lives and practices], ed. Chŏn'guk pigunihoe (Seoul: Yemoonseowon, 2007), 23–58. Lady Sa was the sister of a person named Morok (毛祿 or Morye 毛禮) who helped Master Ado (阿道) to spread Buddhism in the Kingdom of Silla. Lady Sa was the first person to be ordained in Silla. For a general discussion of Korean Buddhist nuns, see Eun-su Cho, "Female Buddhist Practice in Korea—A Historical Account," in *Korean Buddhist Nuns and Laywomen: Hidden Histories, Enduring Vitality*, ed. Eun-su Cho (Albany: State University of New York Press, 2011), 14–43.

3. The Jogye Order, the largest order in contemporary Korean Buddhism, takes Toŭi (道義: fl. 821) as the founding father (K. *chongjo* 宗祖) of Korean Sŏn Buddhism and Chinul as the one who clarified the school's teaching (K. *chungch'ŏnjo* 重闡祖). http://www.buddhism.or.kr/jongdan/sub1/sub1-1-t1.php (accessed on July 10, 2021).

Toŭi went to China and brought Bodhidharma's practice to Silla and is thus considered the first Korean monk to practice Sŏn Buddhism. In between Toŭi's returning from China around the ninth century and Chinul's time in the late eleventh and early twelfth centuries, a number of Korean monks went to China to learn the new type of Buddhism (i.e., Chan Buddhism), which eventually created what is known as the Nine Mountains of Sŏn school (K. *kusan Sŏnmun* 九山禪門). The historical accuracy of the Nine Mountains has been debated. In this context, Chinul can be reasonably counted as the founder of Korean Sŏn Buddhism. For a detailed discussion of the Nine Mountains of Sŏn school, see Robert, E. Buswell Jr., *The Korean Approach to Zen: Collected Works of Chinul* (Honolulu: University of Hawai'i Press, 1983), 9–12.

4. Kwŏn Kijong 權奇悰, "Hyesim ŭi Kanhwa Sŏn sasang yŏn'gu: Chinul ŭi Sŏn sasang kwa pigyo hamyŏnsŏ 慧諶의 看話禪思想 研究–知訥의 선사상과 比較하면서 [Study on Hyesim's Kanhwa Sŏn thought: In comparison with Chinul's Sŏn thought], *Pojo sasang* 7 (1993): 13–37, 14.

5. Park Jae-Hyeon, 박재현, "Hyesim ŭi Sŏn sasang kwa Kanhwa" 혜심 (慧諶)의 선사상과 간화 [Study on Hyesim's Sŏn thought and Kanhwa], *Chŏrhak* 78 (2004): 29–49.

6. Kim Yŏngmi 김영미, "Koryŏ sidae piguni ŭi hwaldong kwa Chin'gak Kuksa Hyesim ŭi yŏsŏng sŏngpulron" 高麗時代 比丘尼의 활동과 眞覺國師 慧諶의 女性成佛論 [Bhikṣuṇī's activities during the Koryŏ period and National Master Chin'gak Hyesim's theory of women's attainment of Buddhahood], in *Tong Asia ŭi Pulgyo chŏnt'ong esŏ pon Han'guk piguni ŭi suhaeng kwa salm* 동 아시아 불교 전통에서 본 한국 비구니의 수행과 삶 [Life and practice of Korean bhikṣuṇī in the context of East Asian Korean Buddhism], ed. Hanmaeum Seonweon, 37–52 (Anyang, Korea: Hanmaeum Seonweon, 2004).

7. For the relevant pages in Chinul's work, see *Hwaŏm non chŏryo*, *HPC* 4, 775, 777, 808.

8. Kim Kunsu, "Pojo Kuksa pimyŏng" 普照國師碑銘 [Stele inscription of National Master Pojo], *Pojo chŏnsŏ* 普照全書 [Complete works of Pojo], ed. Pojo sasang yŏn'guwŏn (Chŏnam: Puril ch'ulp'ansa, 1989), 419–20; for an English translation, see "Stele Inscription of Pojo Chinul," in *Anthology of Stele Inscriptions of Eminent Korean Buddhist Monks*, ed. John Jorgensen, trans. Patrick R. Uhlmann (Seoul: Jogye Order of Korean Buddhism, 2012), 367–71.

9. Chinul, "Hwaŏm non chŏryo sŏ" 華嚴論節要序 [Preface to the *Exposition of the Huayan jing*], *HPC* 4, 767c; Robert E. Buswell Jr., trans. *Chinul: Selected Works* (Seoul: Jogye Order of Korean Buddhism, 2012), 357. Translation modified.

10. *HPC* 4, 767c; Buswell, *Chinul*, 357; [phenomenal world] added.

11. See Jin Y. Park, "Temporality and Non-temporality in Li Tongxuan's Huayan Buddhism," *Dao Companion to Chinese Buddhist Philosophy*, ed. Youru Wang and Sandra Wawryko (New York: Springer, 2019), 325–47; "A Huayanist Reading of the Lotus Sūtra: The case of Li Tongxuan," *Journal of the International Association of Buddhist Studies* 35 (2012): 295–328.

12. Levering, "The Dragon Girl and the Abbess of Mo-Shan," 26–27.

13. Min Hyŏn'gu 민현구, "Wŏllan-sa ji Chin'gak Kuksa pi ŭi ŭmgi e taehan ilgoch'al" 月南寺址 眞覺國師碑의 陰記에 대한 一考察 [Study of the inscription on the monumental stone for National Master Chin'gak at the ruins of Wŏllam-sa], *Chindan Hakpo* 36 (December 1973): 7–38.

14. Kim, "Koryŏ sidae piguni ŭi hwaldong kwa Chin'tak Kuksa Hyesim ŭi yŏsŏng sŏngpulron," 38.

15. Chin'gak Hyesim 眞覺慧諶, *Chin'gak Kuksa ŏrok* 眞覺國師語錄 [Recorded sayings of National Master Chin'gak], *HPC* 6, 47c.

16. I follow Kim Young Mi and assume that Chongmin is the same person who appeared as Min (敏) in the stele inscription. See Kim Young Mi 김영미, "Koryŏ sidae yŏsŏng ŭi ch'ulga" 高麗時代 여성의 出家 [Women's joining the monastery during the Koryŏ period], *Ihwa sahak* 26 (December 1999): 49–74.

17. Young Mi Kim also mentions Sŏnan, Chŏngsin, Chŏngyŏn, and Wang doin as Buddhist nuns who appear in Chin'gak's *Recorded Sayings*. See Young Mi Kim, "Male Sŏn Masters' Views on Female Disciples in Later Koryŏ," in *Korean Buddhist Nuns and Laywomen: Hidden Histories, Enduring Vitality*, ed. Eun-Su Cho (Albany: State University of New York Press, 2011), 51.

18. Kim, "Male Sŏn Masters' Views on Female Disciples in Later Koryŏ," 51.

19. Yi Tongjun 李東埈, "*Jogye Chin'gak Kuksa Ŏrok* ŭi kusŏng kwa naeyongsang t'ŭksŏng" <曹溪眞覺國師語錄>의 구성과 내용상 특성 [The structure and characteristics in the contents of the *Recorded Sayings of National Master Chin'gak of the Jogye Order*], *Pojo sasang* 7 (1993): 140–71, 146. Kim "Male Sŏn Masters' Views on Female Disciples in Later Koryŏ," 45–46.

20. *HPC* 6, 28b.

21. For English translation of Hyesim's teaching to these four nuns, see John Jorgensen, "Koryŏ Buddhist Nuns and the Practice of the Kanhwa Meditation of Non-Duality: The Recorded Sayings of National Teacher Chingak of Chogye by Hyesim," in *Korean Buddhism Reader*, ed. Jin Y. Park and Sumi Lee, forthcoming. Young Mi Kim's article "Male Sŏn Masters' Views on Female Disciples in Later Koryŏ" also offers these cases in some detail.

22. *HPC*, vol. 6, 24c–25c. The ending of this dharma talks reflects Chinul's teaching on *hwadu*. See Chinul, *Kanhwa kyŏrŭi ron* 看話決疑論 [Treatise on resolving doubts about hwadu meditation], *HPC* 4, 732c–737c.

23. T14.574.946c–948b.

24. In fact, there is not just one Sturdy Lady. The Buddha states that there were thousands of them in the past, and thousands of them will attain the recognition of their awakening at the time of the arrival of Maitreya (Naliantiyeshe, T14.574.948a). But then at the end of the sutra, Buddha says that when the life comes to an end, Sturdy Lady will discard the woman's body and become a man. So after all, the body transformation theory does not change here (*Naliantiyeshe* (Narêndrayaśas) 那連提耶舍, trans 1924–1935. *Fúshuō jiāngùnǚ jīng* 佛說堅固女經 [Sutra of the sturdy lady]. T14.574, 948b.

25. "Moshanni Liaoran Chanshi" [Chan Master Liaoran of Mount Mo], X84.1565, 107a.

26. *HPC* 6, 26c.

27. *HPC* 6, 27b; English translation, John Jorgensen, "Koryŏ Buddhist Nuns and the Practice of the Kanhwa Meditation of Non-Duality."

28. Ch'u Pokyŏng 추보경, "Koryŏ sidae piguni sach'al ŭi chonjae wa unyŏng" 고려시대 비구니 사찰의 존재와 운영 [The existence and management of bhikṣuṇī monasteries during the Koryŏ period] (Master's thesis, Yongnam University, 2014).

29. *HPC* 6, 637b.

30. See Hŏ Hŭngsik 許興植, *Koryŏ ro olmkin Indo ŭi tŭngbul* 高麗로 옮긴 印度의 등불 [The India lamp that migrated to Koryŏ] (Seoul: Iljogak, 1997).

31. About Zhikong's family line, see Yŏm Chungsŏp 염중섭, "Chigong ŭi kagye chujang e taehan kŏmt'o: Koryŏ esŏ Chigong ŭi sŏnggong yoin ŭl chungsim ŭro: Koryŏ esŏ Zhikong ŭi sŏnggong yoin ŭil chungsim ŭiro" 지공의 가계 주장에 대한 검토: 고려에서 지공의 성공요인을 중심으로 [Examination of the claims about Zhikong's family lineage: With a focus on the elements of Zhikong's success in Koryŏ], *Chindan Hakpo* 4 (2014): 31–53.

32. Kakkoeng 覺宏, *Naong hwasang haengjang* 懶翁和尙行狀 [An account of Master Naong's life], *HPC* 6, 703b.

33. *HPC* 6, 705bc and 710b. Naong in fact received a recognition from Pyŏngsan in 1350. *HPC* 6, 704bc.

34. *HPC* 6, 711a.
35. For a detailed discussion on Zhikong and Naong, see Yŏm, "Chigong ŭi kagye chujang e taehan kŏmťo."
36. *HPC* 6, 636.
37. *HPC* 6, 668.
38. For a detailed discussion on the issue, see Lee Seyŏl 이세열, "Chikji wa piguni Myodŏk e kwanhan yŏn'gu." 직지와 비구니 묘덕에 관한 연구 [Study on Chikji and bhikṣuṇī Myodŏk] *Chungwŏn Munhwawŏn* 4 (2000): 67–95.
39. See Yi Hyangsun이향순, "Chosŏn sidae piguni ŭi salm kwa suhaeng" 조선시대 비구니의 삶과 수행 [Bhikṣuṇī's life and practice during the Chosŏn period], in *Han'guk Piguni ŭi suhaeng ka salm*, ed. Chŏn'guk pigunihoe, 103–127 (Seoul: Yemoonseowon, 2007); John Jorgenson, "Marginalized and Silenced: Buddhist Nuns of the Chosŏn Period," in *Korean Nuns within the Context of East Asian Buddhist Traditions*, 88–105 (Anyang: Hanmaum Seonwon 2004); Kang Hee-jung 강희정, "Chosŏn chŏn'gi Pulgyo wa yŏsŏng ŭi yŏkhal" 조선 전기 불교와 여성의 역할 [Buddhism during the early Chosŏn and Women's role], *Ase'a yŏsŏng yŏn'gu* 41 (2002): 269–98.
40. *Hwangsŏng sinmun* 황성신문, 1909, cited in Pak Huisŭng 박희승, *Ije sŭngnye ŭi ipsŏng ŭl hŏham i ŏttŏlrunjiyo* 이제, 승려의 입성을 허함이 어떨는지요? [How about now allow the monastics to enter the capital city?] (Seoul: Tŭlnyŏk. Pak 1999), 256–57.
41. Kyŏnsŏngam functioned as a nuns' meditation hall beginning January 1916. See Haeju 해주, "Han'guk kŭnhyŏndae piguni ŭi suhaeng" 한국 근현대 비구니의 수행 [Bhikṣuṇī's practice in modern and contemporary Korea], in *Han'guk Piguni ŭi Suhaeng kwa salm*, ed. Chŏn'guk pigunihoe (Seoul: Yemoonseowon, 2007), 132.
42. Haeju, "Han'guk kŭnhyŏndae piguni ŭi suhaeng," 132.
43. Hyoťan 효탄, "Piguni Sŏnp'ung ŭi chunghŭngja, Myori Pŏphŭi sŏnsa," 비구니 선풍의 중흥자 묘리법희 선사 [Sŏn Master Myori Pŏphŭi, the revivalist of piguni Sŏn tradition], in *Han'guk piguni ŭi suhaeng kwa salm*, ed. Chŏn'guk pigunihoe (Seoul: Yemoonseowon, 2007), 201.
44. Ha Ch'unsaeng하춘생, *Kkaedalŭm ŭi kkok: Han'guk kŭnse rŭl pitnaen piguni* 깨달음의 꽃: 한국 근세를 빛낸 비구니 [Flowers of enlightenment: Celebrated Buddhist nuns in modern Korea], vol. 1 (Seoul: Yŏrae, 1998), 30.
45. Ha, *Kkaedalŭm ui kkok*, vol. 1, 28. For a discussion on the bhikṣuṇī dharma lineage in Korea, see Ha Ch'ungsaeng 하춘생, *Han'guk ŭi piguni munjung* 한국의 비구니 문중 [Dharma lineages of Korean Buddhist nuns] (Seoul: Hajoum, 2013).
46. Jin Y. Park, ed., *Makers of Modern Korean Buddhism* (Albany: State University of New York Press, 2010), 1–10.
47. Yi Nŭnghwa 李能和, *Chosŏn Pulgyo T'ongsa* 朝鮮佛敎通史 [History of Korean Buddhism]. (Seoul: Sinmun'gwan, 1918), 898–99.

48. See Cho Seung Mee 조승미, "Yŏsŏngjuŭijŏk kwanjŏm esŏ pon Pulgyo suhaengron yŏn'gu: Han'guk yŏsŏng Pulja ŭi kyŏnghyŏm ŭl chungsim ŭro" 여성주의적 관점에서 본 佛敎修行論 연구: 한국 여성 불자의 경험을 중심으로 [Study on the theory of Buddhist practice from the Womanist perspective: With a focus on the experiences of Korean women Buddhists] (PhD diss., Dongguk University, 2005).

49. For a discussion of lay Buddhist women's Sŏn practice, see Cho, "Yŏsŏngjuŭijŏk kwanjŏm esŏ pon Pulgyo suhaengron yŏn'gu," 120-33.

50. Kang Munsŏn (Hyewŏn) 강문선 (혜원), "Kŭndae Han'guk piguni Sŏn suhaeng yangsang kwa in'ga e taehan munje" 근대 한국 비구니 선 수행 양상과 印可에 대한 문제 [The mode of Sŏn practice of bhikṣuṇī in modern Korea and the issue of recognition], *Taegak sasang* 23 (2015): 355.

51. For research on Kim Iryŏp, see Jin Y. Park, trans. *Reflections of a Zen Buddhist Nun: Essays by Zen Master Kim Iryŏp* (Honolulu: University of Hawai'i Press, 2014); *Women and Buddhist Philosophy: Engaging Zen Master Kim Iryŏp* (Honolulu: University of Hawai'i Press, 2017); "An Examined Life: Women, Buddhism, and Philosophy in Kim Iryŏp," *World Philosophy* 5, no. 2 (Winter 2020): 176-82; "Gendered Response to Modernity: Kim Iryŏp and Buddhism," in *Makers of Modern Korean Buddhism,* edited by Jin Y. Park, 109-127. Albany: State University of New York Press.

52. T'oeong Sŏngch'ŏl 退翁性徹, *Han'guk Pulgyo ŭi pŏmmaek* 韓國佛敎의 法脈 [Dharma lineage of Korean Buddhism] (Hapch'ŏn, Korea: Changgyŏnggak, 1976), 18.

53. For a critical evaluation of Pou's Buddhism in the context of his relation to Linji Chan and dharma lineage in Korean Buddhism, see Ch'oe Pyŏnghŏn 최병헌, "T'aego Pou ŭi Pulgyo sa chŏk wich'i" 태고보우의 불교사적 위치 [T'aego Pou's position in the history of (Korean) Buddhism], *Korean Culture* 7 (December 1986): 97-132.

54. About the popularity of the trip to China to attain recognition, see Kang Hoseon 강호선, "Muja hwadu ŭi hwaksan kwa ipwŏn in'ga ŭi yuhaeng" 무자화두의 확산과 입원 인가의 유행 [The spread of *mu hwadu* and the trend of attaining recognition in Yuan China], *Han'guksa ron* 46, 95-99.

55. Ch'eo Pyŏnghŏn was especially critical about Pou in that context. Ch'oe, "T'aego Pou ŭi Pulgyo sa chŏk wich'i," 113-15.

56. Sŏngch'ŏl, *Han'guk Pulgyo ŭi pŏmmaek*, 347-349.

57. T'oeong Sŏngch'ŏl 退翁性徹, *Sŏnmun chŏngro* 禪門正路 [The Orthodox path of Sŏn Buddhism], (Hapch'ŏn, Korea: Changgyŏnggak, 1981), 209.

58. Ha Ch'unsaeng proposes that one reason Man'gong was enthusiastic about promoting nuns' practice and playing a pivotal role in opening the first bhikṣuṇī meditation hall at Kyŏnsŏngam in Sudŏksa was because his mother received precepts at Sudŏksa. Ha, *Han'guk ŭi piguni munjung,* 235.

59. Ha, *Han'guk ŭi piguni munjung,* 86.

60. Ha, *Han'guk ŭi piguni munjung,* 96-263.

61. Ha, *Han'guk ŭi piguni munjung*, 100–101.

62. See Cho Eunsu 조은수, "Han'uk ŭi piguni kyodan e taehan yŏsŏng chuŭijŏk koch'al" 한국의 비구니 교단에 대한 여성주의적 고찰 [Feminist examination of Korean bhikṣuṇī organization], *Pulgyo p'yŏngnon* 24 (2010).

63. According to statistics, the numbers of bhikṣu and bhisuni were 6,133 and 869, respectively, in 1925. In 2008, the numbers were 7,335 and 6,525 (Ha, *Han'guk ŭi piguni munjung*, 102).

64. See note 1.

65. For example, scholar of Korean literature Pang Minho states that Buddhist movements that reached out to the general public made it possible for a layperson like Kim Iryŏp to participate in Sŏn meditation, and she eventually joined the monastery. See Pang Minho 방민호, "Kim Iryŏp munhak ŭi sasangjŏk pyŏnmo kwajŏng kwa Pulgyo sŏnt'aek ŭi ŭimi" 김일엽 문학의 사상적 변모과정과 불교 선택의 의미 [Evolution of Kim Iryŏp's literary thoughts and the significance of her engagement with Buddhism], *Han'guk hyŏndae munhak yŏn'gu* 20 (2006): 357–403.

Chapter 10

Mindful Interactions and Recalibrations
From Chinul to T'oegye

Kevin N. Cawley

Introduction

Religious and philosophical traditions often generate intercultural interactions that cross-fertilize different traditions. Some of these "after-effects," as I refer to them, are often underplayed or ignored between traditions and at times even attacked. In this regard, Sŏn Buddhism in Korea owed much to the development of Chan Buddhism during the Tang (唐朝, 618–907) and Song (宋朝 960–1279) dynasties. However, these Sinitic meditational Buddhist developments also influenced the recalibration of Neo-Confucianism, which focused on the mind, even shaping its own concept of "quiet-sitting" (C. *jingzuo*, K. *chŏngjwa* 靜坐),[1] though Confucian scholars typically denied and renounced these impure "after-effects." If we examine the broader intellectual "history of effect," to draw on Gadamer's term "effectual history" (G. *Wirkungsgeschichte)* in *Truth and Method*,[2] it becomes necessary to examine the "after-effects" of Chan Buddhism that have cross-fertilized the sophisticated spiritualism of Neo-Confucianism, especially its "study of the mind" (C. *xinxue*, K. *simhak* 心學), which was recalibrated toward Confucian spiritual practices.[3] Quiet sitting is described by William Theodore de Bary as "a definite spiritual exercise that could be programmed into one's life. It provided a specific discipline and regimen in matters of conscience and spiritual direction," which would lead to better regulation of external affairs.[4] In this sense, it was a secular spiritual practice that guided one's mental disposition toward moral action.

The "history of effect" insinuates itself into the consciousness of anyone thrust into a particular tradition, and the tradition affects their interpretation of ideas. Hence, the Confucian cannot escape projecting Confucian meanings onto ideas, even onto ideas that were not "originally" Confucian, in a sense "Confucianizing" meaning, which inevitably leads to a recalibration of the "original" meaning(s) toward a new goal or purpose. New meanings are already shaped by the traditions we grew up in—even if we later reject them (a lapsed Catholic has still been shaped by Catholic culture, for example). Hans-Georg Gadamer highlights that "a person who is trying to understand a text is always projecting," and is therefore "reading the text with particular expectations in regard to a certain meaning."[5] Such ideas were influenced by Martin Heidegger who noted that we interpret based on what we have in advance (G. *Vorhabe*), in what we see in advance (G. *Vorsicht*) and that our way of conceiving ideas was already based on fore-conceptions (G. *Vorgriff*) shaped by the traditions and the cultural world we live in.[6] Traditions and cultures sometimes cover over their "original" sources, and this is the case of the "mindful practices" that we recognize in Neo-Confucianism, which made itself master of orthodoxy, particularly in the Korean context of the Chosŏn dynasty (朝鮮, 1392–1910). Heidegger warns that

> when tradition thus becomes master, it does so in such a way that what it "transmits" becomes so inaccessible, proximally for the most part, that it rather becomes concealed. Tradition takes what has come down to us and delivers it over to self-evidence; it blocks our access to those primordial "sources" from which the categories and concepts handed down to us have been in part quite genuinely drawn. Indeed it makes us forget that they have had such an origin.[7]

This leads us to the deconstruction, or rather the dis-enclosure[8] of traditions that shape one another, opening practices up to different possibilities by unfixing the boundaries between traditions, retracing their constitutive elements, and thereby understanding how they modified each other.

This chapter will briefly outline the intercultural trajectory of ideas and traditions that tie together the emergence of meditational Buddhism with the development of Neo-Confucian ideas in China, and subsequently in Korea. It will examine the emergence of Chan in China and its eventual consolidation in Korea as Sŏn. Then it addresses the dis-enclosure of Confucianism and its own recalibrated understanding of the mind, which would emphasize the need for seriousness, restraint, and mindfulness, incorporated into an ongoing daily moral practice. Specifically, it will focus on the ideas of the Koryŏ (高麗, 918–1392) Buddhist monk Chinul (知訥, 1158–1210) related to continued gradual cultivation. Finally, it links this morally refining process with the ideas of one of Korea's greatest Neo-Confucian scholars, Yi Hwang (李滉, 1501–1570), known by the penname T'oegye (退溪), who considered self-cultivation (C. *xiuji*, K. *sugi* 修己) as the alpha and the omega of sage learning (C. *shengxue*, K. *sŏnghak* 聖學).

The Emergence of Chan Buddhism

The origin of Chan is often linked to several unverifiable records of, depending on accounts, a Persian or Indian monk, Bodhidharma (c. 470–543), who is said to have transmitted a meditative form of Buddhism to China, and who allegedly meditated in front of a wall for nine years.[9] Though little is known about the historical Bodhidharma, he is considered the first patriarch of the school in China, while Chan owes its name to the Chinese phonetic transliteration of the Sanskrit term dhyāna, translated as "meditation," pronounced Sŏn in Korean, and Zen in Japanese.[10] The teachings of the earliest Chan schools had already been brought to the peninsula with the Silla Monk Pŏmnang (632–?), who had studied in China, returning during the reign of Queen Sŏndŏk.[11] However, it was the sixth patriarch of Chan Buddhism, Huineng (638–713), whose ideas would significantly impact the Sŏn tradition there, especially with regard to his belief in a "sudden enlightenment" experience that opened the mind up to the true nature of reality. *The Platform Sūtra of the Sixth Patriarch*, which is attributed to Huineng, has been considerably influential in East Asia, linking together teachings on ethical behavior, sudden enlightenment, and meditation.[12] Huineng's selection as successor to the fifth patriarch of Chan, Hongren (601–674), rather than an elder disciple Shenxiu (c. 606–706), who taught that the mind needed to be well prepared for an enlightenment experience, led to a split into two different schools of Chan. Southern Chan followed Huineng, while Northern Chan followed Shenxiu.[13] Once again, there is little authentic information on Huineng, but different sources recount that he was an illiterate young monk who succeeded his master Hongren (601–674), who was impressed by his belief that anyone could have a "sudden enlightenment" experience, illuminating the mind, and transforming one's understanding of the reality of the universe.¹⁴

For Koreans, this elicits the experience of great Silla monk Wŏnhyo (元曉, 617–686), one of the greatest intellectuals in East Asian history. All Koreans have heard the famous story of the monks Wŏnhyo and his friend Ŭisang (義湘, 625–702), whose initial journey to study in Tang China was derailed by a terrible storm.¹⁵ The two monks sought shelter from a typhoon and found themselves in what appeared (in the darkness) to be a cave. Being thirsty, they drank water that tasted fresh from a smooth vessel they had found and then had a peaceful sleep. However, when they awoke the next morning, they realized (in the light) that they had spent the night in a tomb and that the water was actually muddy, and it had been scooped up in a human skull. Despite clearly having slept well the first night, due to the continued stormy weather they had to remain a second night—and this time ghosts appeared! This experience led to Wŏnhyo's "sudden enlightenment."¹⁶ In his biography, he reflects upon this awakening experience, which left an indelible mark on his ideas:

> When a thought arises, the myriad dharmas arise. When thoughts subside [a cup and] a skull are not different. The Tathāgata thus said: "The three worlds are only mind; how can I be deceived!" Then he gave up on seeking a master, and immediately returned to his country.¹⁷

This teaching emphasized that the mind could "spontaneously" achieve enlightenment given the right experience, without the need for doctrinal study, as the mind alone holds the key to achieving its own liberation. This tale also highlights that Koreans were already open to ideas that were later linked with the Chan teachings from China. Additionally, these teachings do not diverge far from the Daoist teachings of Laozi and Zhuangzi, and partly explain why this form of Buddhism is sometimes described as an indigenous form of "Chinese" Buddhism, reorienting the Indian Buddhist traditions.

As is often the case, many diverging schools of the tradition formed, but two were of great importance: the Caodong school and the Linji school.¹⁸ The Caodong line advocated silent meditation under the guidance of a master, which is what many people associate with seated meditation. Meanwhile, the Linji school, "aims at sudden enlightenment through the use of shouting, beating, and riddles called *gongan* (K. *kongan*, J. *kōan*) to provoke an experience of enlightenment," adding that the *gongan*, "by posing an insoluble [seemingly illogical and idiosyncratic] problem to reason and the intellect [. . .] is supposed to lead to the dissolution of the boundary between the conscious and the unconscious in the human psyche" ultimately revealing the true nature of the mind.[19] This form of Buddhism clearly moved away from textual analysis of scriptures and commentaries—dis-enclosing a new path*way* for those seeking enlightenment who no longer needed to be scholars with a great knowledge of classical Chinese (at least in theory). In Korea, Chinul would much later advocate these new techniques, while emphasizing "sudden enlightenment" accompanied by a rigorous form of gradual moral self-cultivation, not unlike that prescribed by Neo-Confucians.

Such new Buddhist ideas gained prominence toward the end of the Tang dynasty, which experienced political and social degeneration and decline, just as they would during similar circumstances at the end of the Unified Silla period during the ninth century. In 821, monk Toŭi (道義, ?-?) returned after a period of thirty-seven years study and practice in China and established one of the first temples that exemplified the teachings of the Southern Chan tradition at Chinjŏnsa (陳田寺). Cho Myong-gi notes that "after this time, [monks] of Silla who studied in China brought back Southern Chan in successive journeys while domestically, a group of nine large temples came to occupy a focal position in the promulgation of the Chan sect."[20] These are known as the Nine Mountain schools of Sŏn (K. *kusan Sŏnnum* 九山禪門). It is noteworthy that Japanese Zen, well known in name at least to Westerners, did not develop its Five Mountain system until the twelfth century. Advocates of Sŏn Buddhism in Korea were also often followers of Hwaŏm (C. Huayan, J. Kegon, 華嚴) Buddhism and were deeply intellectual. It is this form of Sŏn Buddhism, infused with Hwaŏm doctrinal interests, which would shape Buddhism in Korea during the subsequent Koryŏ period, influencing both Ŭichŏn (1055–1101) and Chinul, who would attempt to unify the doctrinal and Sŏn schools.

By the end of the Tang dynasty Buddhism had lost its patronage from the emperor, having grown exponentially until the mid-ninth century when the number of monasteries amounted to some 44,600. This led to a rise in regional patronage after the collapse of the central government and in a way was instrumental to the growth and success of Chan in different regions, as examined by Albert Welter and Ben Brose. Both Welter and Brose describe that the political rivalries led to positions of power for certain monks and their lineages.²¹ Needless to say, such growth of an "alien" religion did not please the Confucian scholars who criticized the economic impact of such a large number of monasteries and nunneries draining revenue from the state, as well as their failure to adhere to their own moral codes. Influenced by Daoist priests, Emperor Wuzong (r. 841–847) issued a decree that dramatically reduced the number of monasteries. The aristocratic families who had been promoted due to social connections were later replaced by an educated, trained bureaucracy not necessarily beholden to aristocratic pedigrees. This meant that the emperor himself required counselors from this new bureaucracy to advise him, and hence their role had a more practical function than anything the Buddhists had to offer. Chan Buddhism could not compete on a pragmatic level with the new surge of interest in Confucianism, which its proponents boasted, could revive the poor sociopolitical situation of the state.²²

The Emergence of Sŏn in Korea

One of the most important monks of this period was Ŭichŏn (義天, 1055–1101), the fourth son of King Munjong (r.1046–83), who had been to China during the Song dynasty. He believed in the compatibility of the doctrines of the major doctrinal schools, which Wŏnhyo himself had been eager to reconcile, but Ŭichŏn also acknowledged the importance of the meditational schools. This growing issue of disunity among the different Buddhist schools distracted monks from developing the philosophical views initiated in China and could have escalated completely out of control, if we think about it along the lines of Protestants and Catholics in Christianity after Luther.²³ Ŭichŏn made Kukchŏngs the center of this new consolidated Buddhism and hoped to encourage other leading monks from the Nine Mountain schools of Sŏn to join and help him achieve his vision of "concurrent cultivation of doctrinal study and meditation" (K. *kyokwan kyŏmsu* 教觀兼修), recalibrating both traditions to form a new pathway of self-cultivation.²⁴ Though Ŭichŏn died at a young age, unable to see his dream realized, he considered this new development as a Sŏn school, not a doctrinal one, something that would continue to shape the tradition in Korea. His influence led several schools to converge to become known as the Chogye (曹溪) order, the name of the largest order of Korean Buddhism today, founded in the twentieth century (now usually written as Jogye). Ŭichŏn was also interested in collecting the various Buddhist scriptures in order to compile a comprehensive collection that would be a precursor to the mammoth *Tripitaka Koreana,* printed using over eighty thousand wooden blocks.[25]

The most significant monk of this era who again tried to unify the different schools was Chinul, known also by his posthumous title of National Preceptor (K. *kuksa* 國師) Puril Pojo (佛日普照). It must not go unrecognized that Chinul was "very much indebted to Zongmi (780–841), the ninth-century Chinese Huayan and Chan patriarch who wanted to harmonize Chan with doctrinal Buddhism."[26] Chinul came to a conclusion much like that of Zongmi who said "Sūtras are the word of the Buddha, whereas Ch'an is the mind of the Buddha; the mind and the mouth of the Buddha should not be divergent."[27] For both scholars, while "Kyo" (敎) represents what the Buddha said, what is transmitted to the mind is "Sŏn," therefore they interpenetrated each other. Chinul's focus on Sŏn "permeated the subsequent development of the Korean Sŏn tradition."[28]

For Chinul, the internal machinations of the mind should be one's major concern, and this is reflected in his guiding discourse, an intellectually internalized one, which was coupled with very practical advice and guidance. Chinul was also deeply aware of the negative reputation that the Buddhist monastic community had acquired and realized that unless this was changed, Buddhism would face an inevitable crisis, which he saw in no small way linked to state sponsorship. In fact, some of the leaders of the military coup in 1170, such as Ch'oe Ch'unghŏn (1149–1219), actually supported the meditation monasteries, as they had previously been in conflict with the doctrinal schools.[29] Such a precarious sociopolitical situation may have motivated Chinul to emphasize a retreat community, away from the luxuries of life, with insistence on the necessity of practice (an idea also emphasized by the Confucians and Wŏnhyo), outlined in his first work written in 1190, *Encouragement to Practice: The Compact of the Concentration [Samadhi] and Wisdom [Prajñā] Society* (K. *Kwŏnsu chŏnghye kyŏlsa mun* 勸修定慧結社文). It was composed shortly after he had established his own retreat community at Kŏjosa (居祖寺). He reached out to leading monks to join his new community and criticized the search of certain monks for riches and fame (as would T'oegye in relation to Confucians), as well as the degenerate state of Buddhism where he felt some followers overly relied on chanting the Buddha's name, possibly a snub at Pure Land Buddhism. This, he feared, could lead people to depend on external worship and adulation of a Buddha rather than looking into their own minds to recover their Buddha Nature (C. Fóxìng, K. Pulsŏng, J. Busshō 佛性).[30]

Chinul and the Pathway to *Mindful Sŏn*

Sŏn masters, though dedicated to meditation, nonetheless collected and composed a huge body of literature. In 1205 Chinul composed his influential text *Admonitions to Beginning Students* (K. *Kye ch'osim hakin mun* 誡初心學人文), which coincided with his latest attempt to consolidate Sŏn in Koryŏ through his Society for Cultivating Sŏn (K. *Susŏnsa* 修禪社). It was also established at Mount Chogye, one of the reasons why Chinul is considered the founder of the order of the same name today, the Chogye (Jogye) order. Though some of Wŏnhyo's teachings reverberate in Chinul's texts, he was greatly influenced by Changlu Zongze's (?–ca. 1107) *Rules of Purity for the Chan Monastery* (C. *Chanyuan qinggui* 禪苑清規), which was composed in 1103. This "rulebook" emphasizes the modes of conduct monks were expected to adhere to, and the great Neo-Confucian scholar Zhu Xi (1130–1200) would similarly draw up a set of rules for his White Deer Grotto Confucian Academy (later emulated in Korea). Students had to learn the rules, but more importantly, they were expected to keep to them, possibly showing the influence of Buddhist order (and discipline) on later Neo-Confucian developments. Robert Buswell emphasizes the importance of Chinul's *Admonitions* in Korea: "*Admonitions* came to be adopted by Korean Buddhists as the standard of conduct at almost every major monastery, helping to ensure uniformity of conduct and decorum across the Korean Sŏn monastic tradition. It was so popular that an early Korean vernacular translation into the *Han'gŭl* writing system was made in 1612. [It]was so widely used in Korean Buddhism, in fact, that during the middle of the Chosŏn dynasty (1392–1910) it was included in a primer of three short texts used to train Korean postulants and novices in the basics of Buddhist morality and daily practice."[31]

This primer, *Personal Admonitions to Neophytes Who Have First Aroused the Mind* (K. Ch'obalsim chagyŏngmun 初發心自警文), consists of only three texts, the first of which is Chinul's, followed by Wonhyo's *Awaken Your Mind and Practice* (K. Palsim suhaengjang 發心修行章). Only the third text in this primer, called *Personal Admonitions* (K. Chagyŏng mun 自警文), was composed during the Chosŏn dynasty, by Yaun Kagu (fl. ca. 1376). These texts are still studied by Buddhist monks in Korean monasteries today.

Despite the ubiquitous importance of Chinul's texts, probably his greatest contribution to Sŏn thought in general, but in particular within the Korean context, is his text *Secrets of Cultivating the Mind* (K. *Susim kyŏl* 修心訣). This outlines his teachings on sudden awakening followed by gradual cultivation, as well as the practice of meditation and its cardinal focus on wisdom. Buswell describes how this "sudden" enlightenment experience (known as "subitism") makes students lucidly and incontestably aware of their inherent Buddha Nature, which he describes as "tracing the radiance emanating from the mind back to its source," which helps them to lift the clouds that have hidden even unto themselves that they are already enlightened beings.[32]

One's own "mind" needs to be cleansed of impurities, which cloud one's Buddha Nature, and enlightenment is necessary before attempting to lead others to their own salvation. This required a pathway of cultivation to recover one's original Buddha Nature, which is already contained in one's mind, though people search for it outside themselves, even in the sages from the past, detailed by Chinul in *Secrets of Cultivating the Mind*.[33] Chinul underlines the need for people to look into their own minds in order to find their Buddha Nature:

> It is so tragic. People have been deluded for so long. They do not recognize that their own minds are the true buddhas. They do not recognize that their own natures are the true dharma. Wanting to search for the dharma, they still look in the distance for all the sages. Wanting to search for the Buddha, they will not observe their own minds. [. . .] I hope all of you who cultivate the path will never search outside. "The nature of the mind is untainted; it is originally consummate and complete in and of itself. If you will only leave behind false conditioning, you will be a 'such-like' buddha."[34]

A salient feature of Chinul's thought, that of "sudden enlightenment and gradual cultivation," is also discussed in this text. This method, he suggests, is much more accessible than "sudden enlightenment and sudden cultivation," which was only "for people of extraordinary spiritual faculties."[35] But why the need for gradual cultivation if one is enlightened? Robert Buswell clarifies that "just because students understand that they are inherently Buddhas does not mean that they will be able to act as buddhas."[36] This may explain why Chinul had an ambivalent attitude toward "radical subitism" and that a singular awakening experience was enough to make you permanently act in an enlightened manner.[37] This is an idea (and lesson) that could easily be transferred to T'oegye and other Confucians but also to Daoists, Christians, Muslims, and so on—practice what you preach, but *practice it every day*—and this is what T'oegye is emphatic about in his *Ten Diagrams on Sage Learning* (*Sŏnghak sipdo* 聖學十圖).

Chinul's approach recognises the mind as the essence (K. *che* 體) of one's Buddha Nature, while continual practice and cultivation aids in refining its function (K. *yong* 用), bringing together the important essence-function (K. *che-yong* 體-用) feature of Korea's Buddhist tradition, which also features strongly in T'oegye's work.[38] While also encouraging students to study texts as a precursor to a successful introduction to the practice of meditation, this synthesizes both strands of Buddhism, doctrine (K. *kyo* 教) and meditation (K. *Sŏn* 禪) into a holistic guide and practice. It is not some ideal "out there," but something emanating from within, where it already exists perfectly (though clouded) and that requires practice to transform our (heart and) mind so that we *become* our own truth.

This idea resembles the idea of truth espoused by the American philosopher John D. Caputo in his text *Truth*, where it is described as an "event" that can transform (us/everything), which he describes as "the process of trying to *become*-true," or related to this chapter, trying to become a Buddha, or a sage in the Confucian sense: a continuous pathway.[39] Caputo underscores that it "is the passionate search for the things we most care about, the restlessness of our heart [and mind] in the midst of a mysterious world."[40] It requires us to think of the world and ourselves in a dramatically different way, not based on knowledge predicated through "reason," but rather it requires us to suspend all conceptual understanding, which brings us to Chinul's encounter with the study of *kongan* (公案, J. *kōan*).

It was only in his final years that Chinul engaged with the *kongans* and the meditational techniques related to them. Nevertheless, his teachings and writings on the subject would greatly impact his disciples, and Korean Buddhism in general, through the technique known as Kanhwa Sŏn (看話禪). This study of the *kongan* developed from the great Chinese Chan master Dahui Zonggao (1089–1163) of the Linji school. In Korea, "[it] is the predominant technique cultivated in meditation halls, and almost all masters advocate its use for students at all levels."[41] This practice, carried out today in temples all over Korea, developed on the peninsula before the kōan achieved its iconic importance within the Japanese Rinzai Zen tradition. Chinul collected various *kongan*, publishing them in *On the Resolution of Doubts in Kanhwa* (*Kanhwa kyŏrŭi ron* 看話決疑論). The title itself highlights an integral part of the practice, which revolves around generating doubt, even in Buddhist ideas and teachings. Great doubt, it was understood, was necessary for great enlightenment, reflected in a recent publication on *Kanhwa Sŏn* in English: *Great Doubt, Great Enlightenment: The Tradition and Practice of Ganhwa Seon in Korean Buddhism* by Seon Masters Gou, Muyeo, Hyeguk, Uijeong and Seoru.

Kanhwa Sŏn deemphasizes the scriptures and dis-encloses the centrality of the text. For the Buddhists in East Asia, this move away from dependence on the textual tradition led Neo-Confucians contemporaneous with Chinul in China to criticize it as something esoteric and too abstract to be effective. Before too long, this negative attitude toward Buddhism would reach the peninsula itself, foreshadowing an extended period of decline.

Before this crisis would reach its peak due to the new intellectual influence of Yuan China, some influential monks did emerge. Hyesim (慧諶, 1178–1234), an important disciple of Chinul, would carry on and develop his master's ideas, especially the meditational *kanhwa* practice, collecting well over a thousand *kongan* published in his *Collection of the Meditation School's Explanatory Verses* (*Sŏnmun yŏmsong chip* 禪門拈頌集), one of the largest collections in East Asia, highlighting how seriously their study became for the Korean Buddhist tradition. Hyesim asserted the compatibility of Confucianism and Buddhism, noting that they had similar teachings, and that many Confucians had become Buddhists, like Kihwa (己和, 1376–1433), who was then able to comfortably refute Confucian criticisms of Buddhism.[42] Of incontestable importance is Iryŏn (1206–1289), author of the *Legends and History of the Three Kingdoms* (*Samguk yusa* 三國遺事) whose text is of tantamount cultural importance for his collection of myths and legends but also as a source of information on the contributions of Korea's early Buddhist monks.

The Emergence of Neo-Confucianism

Often scholars who were interested in Buddhism also had an interest in Confucianism and Daoism (The three teachings). Such intertraditional scholarship would open a new pathway for Confucians to revitalize their own tradition by engaging with Buddhist and Daoist ideas. This is an irony, perhaps, for those coming from monotheistic backgrounds, but not so much in East Asia, where interest across traditions was far from unusual, at least until the rise of Neo-Confucianism. Later Neo-Confucians would turn against and attack these intertraditional "after-effects" vehemently, lacking the inclusivist approach of the Buddhists, even refuting and denying the "history of effect" of important cultural and intellectual interactions. For example, Liang Su (梁肅, 753–793), though a proponent of the Tiantai school and a practitioner of Chan, is still referred to as a Confucian. Charles Hartman points out how Liang Su

> re-affirmed the school's basic eclectic and syncretistic tendencies, which made it possible for thinkers to interpret certain passages in Confucian texts as rudimentary expositions of Buddhist metaphysical principles, thus laying the ground for Neo-Confucian philosophy.[43]

Confucian scholars, accused of having a rudimentary metaphysical basis for their ethical codes, sought to "offer a cosmology that could compete with the Buddhists," leading them to construct a more sophisticated hermeneutical approach to their own tradition.[44]

Han Yu (韓愈, 768–824) is an important figure who advocated a "rejuvenated traditionalism," or the renewed interest in Confucianism.[45] He traced the transmission of Confucian *Dao* from the ancient sage kings to Confucius, then Mencius, rejecting Xunzi and his legalist lineage from the "pure" Confucian genealogy. He is also responsible for the initial attacks against Buddhism, mainly criticizing it as being of "barbarian origin," suggesting the Buddha did not appreciate the important Confucian relationships, arguing that it "shortened the duration of those dynasties which embraced it."[46] His work relies deeply on *The Great Learning* and reflects its call for sincerity and self-cultivation. There is also an influence from *The Mencius* in his important essay "An Inquiry on Human Nature," and he has helped shape the guiding discourse that encapsulates the Confucian cultivation of one's moral being and its interrelationship with a moral society. In his essay "An Inquiry on the Way (*Dao*)" he has even further highlighted the unseen *way* and its inextricable link with humaneness (仁). He rejects the Buddhists as they "insist on discarding the relationship between ruler and ministers, doing away with the relationship between ruler and ministers."[47]

Li Ao (died ca. 844), one of Han Yu's disciples, and a forerunner of his reoriented Confucianism, presented sagehood as a practical path*way* in his essay "Returning to the Nature": "(i) a general discussion on the nature (K. *song* 性), the feelings (K. *chŏng* 情), and the sage (K. *song*

聖); (ii) the process of self-cultivation whereby one may become a sage; (iii) the necessity for self-exertion in this process," which focused on the elimination of negative and selfish desires.[48] What we can notice is the attempt at formulating a guiding discourse to enable one "to become a sage" to recover the original mind, which urges one to continuously practice as part of a gradual process (echoing both Chinul and T'oegye). His writings are somewhat indebted to Buddhist ideas about the recovery of the inherent good nature or Buddha Nature, though he has recalibrated Buddhist notions of self-cultivation and self-exertion in order to lead one to Confucian sagehood.

However, the greatest elaboration of Neo-Confucianism appeared during China's Song dynasty (960–1279). The development of this new ideology was a Southern Song phenomenon and initiated by the writings of "The Five Sages of Song": Shao Yong (1011–1077), Zhou Dunyi (1017–1073), Zhang Zai (1020–1077), and two brothers, Cheng Hao (1032–1085) and Cheng Yi (1033–1107). However, these five thinkers were less influential than Zhu Xi (1130–1200) who synthesized their ideas in *Reflections on Things at Hand* (*Jinsilu* 近思錄), a text that was compiled along with Lu Zuqian (1137–1181). Zhu Xi was particularly influenced by the philosophy of the Cheng brothers, in particular their ideas on a universal *Principle* (C. *li*, K. *i* 理) and its relation to the mind (K. *sim* 心) and [human] nature (K. *sŏng* 性).[49] Later their combined ideas even became known as the "Cheng-Zhu school," or "the school of *Principle*" and regarded as orthodoxy. Wm Theodore de Bary points out that in Japan and Korea, orthodox Neo-Confucianism "[centred] often upon the [*Jinsilu*] as an inspiration and guide to the attainment of sagehood, and on quiet-sitting, mind-control, and scholarly study as complementary ingredients in its spiritual and cultural discipline."[50] Zhu Xi refers to the practice of quiet sitting (translated as meditation by Wing-tsit Chan) in *Reflections on Things at Hand*, noting the advice of Cheng Hao on the matter:

> When there is nothing to put into practice, go and sit in meditation. For while sitting in meditation, we can cultivate our original mind [inherent good nature] and become calm to some degree. Although we are still not free from chasing after material things, when we come to an awakening, we can collect and concentrate on the mind and then there will be a solution.[51]

Zhu Xi does not devote any long discussion to quiet sitting in his main opus, and here it is discussed as a way to calmly guide practitioners toward a solution for problems in their external life. So Zhu Xi was interested in quiet-sitting but not if it became "a practice as an end unto itself, and not simply a subsidiary element in the investigation of things and the cultivation of seriousness [mindfulness]," then he feared, "it ran the risk of becoming a Buddhist practice."⁵² Hence quiet sitting had its place and was a tool for the mastery of the mind, but its idea of mental stillness was inextricably linked with eliminating desires that could negatively impact external action and daily affairs. These ideas were later emphasized and developed by T'oegye in his own quest for becoming a sage, further disinfecting it of Buddhist techniques (in his own view), while reorienting their focus on the mind toward a daily self-refining practice, which would help Confucians conduct affairs in a morally responsible manner.

What had initially started as a Southern Song (1127–1279) phenomenon would, due to the unified Mongol kingdom (1271–1368), gradually be used to construct a new dynasty with Neo-Confucianism as its guiding ideology on the Korean peninsula. Zhu Xi had reanimated an unprecedented interest in Confucianism, which had greatly influenced all Chinese sociopolitical spheres through his intertextual reappraisal of the works of the Song scholars. However, a divided China made the interchange of ideas initially problematic, and issues with the Jurchens and Khitans in Northeast Asia also severed contact with China from within Koryŏ. Internally, military regimes started by General Chŏng Chungbu in 1170, which consequently led to a Ch'oe clan military dictatorship, forced scholars from the capital. Many Confucian scholars, ironically, fled to Buddhist temples where they encountered the intricate Buddhist doctrines, inspiring some scholars to develop a moral discourse that could rival such intricate issues as the metaphysics of Buddhism.⁵³

As the end of the Koryŏ dynasty drew near, the royal household had virtually lost all credibility, and the state had seriously degenerated. Chŏng Tojŏn (鄭道傳, 1342–1398) bolstered his friend General Yi Sŏnggye (李成桂, 1335–1408), assisting him to form a military alliance with the Neo-Confucian scholars after ousting the Koryŏ king from power in 1388 and establishing the Chosŏn dynasty and becoming King T'aejo (太祖, r.1392–1398). The philosophical underpinnings of the new king's reign were masterminded by Chŏng, who vehemently rejected Buddhism and adopted Neo-Confucianism as the state ideology. Chŏng would formulate a moral polity that would lead to the Confucianization of the state through the use of rites, which shape social norms in a more cohesive manner than the use of laws and the threat of punishment. These social norms were guided through adherence to the Five Relationships,[54] which advocated absolute loyalty (K. *ch'ung* 忠) toward the higher ranks in social relationships, and within the family, *hyo* (K. *hyo* 孝), or filial piety, underpinned this ideology. These patterns of behavior were inculcated through *ritual* sourcebooks, especially *Zhu Xi's Family Rites* (*Zhuzi jiali*, K. *Chuja karye* 朱子家禮), which fostered the development of propriety, or *ye* (禮), through four specific secular rites: capping (or coming of age), wedding, mourning, and ancestor memorial rites.[55] The most important of these rites are the memorial rites, known as *chesa* (祭祀) in Korea, and still conducted by many Korean families today but enshrined in law during the early Chosŏn period, whereby refusal to comply led to punishment (and brutal executions for later converts to Catholicism). Ancestor memorial rites had great significance as they reinforced patrilineality, contributing to the hypermasculinization of Korean society.[56] A patriarchal and hierarchical metamorphosis of both living and dying was ordained by a meticulously prescribed sociocultural Neo-Confucian order.

T'oegye's Gradual Guide to Become a Sage: *Mindfulness and Practice*

T'oegye's ideas represent the maturity of Cheng-Zhu orthodoxy in Korea and his ideas dominated intellectually, especially those concerning sagehood—sagehood being "one of the essential components, if not the essence, of Korean Confucianism."[57] These ideas influenced those of Yi I (李珥, 1536–1584), *nom de plume* Yulgok (栗谷), the other great Neo-Confucian from the early Chosŏn period, who considered the elder scholar as the one who "explained the learning of the Way" adding that his scholarship "is unmatched by any other scholars in Korea."[58] T'oegye's influence is most noticeable in Yulgok's *Essentials of the Learning of the Sages* (*Sŏnghak chipyo* 聖學輯要), written in 1575, which is also based on the Cheng-Zhu school of meta-ethics and philosophy, and the goal of this work echoes T'oegye's in *The Ten Diagrams on Sage Learning*. Edward Chung describes him as "arguably the most eminent thinker in Korean Neo-Confucianism," going on to highlight his influence in Japan by scholars such as Fujiwara Seika (1561–1619), Hayashi Razan (1583–1657) and Yamasaki Ansai (1618–1682), garnering him the reputation as the "Korean champion of

Cheng-Zhu orthodoxy."⁵⁹ A feature of this scholarship was its rejection of Buddhism and Daoism, highlighted in Zhu Xi's *Reflections on Things at Hand*, especially chapter 13, "Sifting the Heretical Doctrines." It suggests Buddhists were not interested in life and did not understand the mind in relation to *principle* (理), though there is no evidence that Zhu had a deep knowledge of Buddhist ideas and doctrines, and his criticism merely relies on the fact that Buddhists did not follow the sages of Confucianism and so could not understand Heaven. What needs to be stressed here is that Confucians and Buddhists had become rivals, something that shaped the later reception of these ideas in Korea.

To unlock T'oegye's ideas and his emphasis on the learning of the Confucian sages, it is key to note that from the late fifteenth century until the mid-sixteenth century, while Confucian ideology had transformed the state, there had also been several purges of scholar officials (known as *sahwa* 士禍). During this same time, Buddhism even had a brief revival led by the influential monk Hŏhŭng Pou (虛應普雨, 1515–1565), and during the reign of King Myŏngjong (r. 1545–67) the government was swayed by his mother, Queen Regent Munjong (r. 1546–53), a devout Buddhist. Not only was the Buddhist examination system revived, but monk Hyujŏng (休靜, 1520–1604) was an adviser to the royal family and the anti-Buddhist policy of the previous reigns was somewhat reversed. These facts must have directed Toegye's own intellectual trajectory toward the teachings of the Confucian masters and the sage Kings of the past, reflected in the sense of urgency in his seminal text, *The Ten Diagrams on Sage Learning* (*Sŏnghak sipto* 聖學十圖). Toegye presented *The Ten Diagrams on Sage Learning* to King Sŏnjo prior to his retirement, just two years before his own death, and intellectually it represents the culmination of his life's study. This text revolves around the importance of teaching and the practice of self-cultivation, his final manual on 'Sage Learning' (K. *sŏnghak* 聖學) which teaches and instructs, rather than just recapitulating the ideas of his important Chinese predecessors. It is a philosophy for living a better life and signifies hope for humanity.

The first two diagrams in T'oegye's work rely on the diagrams of two Song dynasty greats: (1) Zhou Dunyi's "The Diagram of the Supreme Ultimate" (*Tiaji zhitu*, K. *T'aegŭk chi to* 太極之圖), itself influenced by Daoist cosmology, and (2) Zhang Zai's "The Diagram of Western Inscription" (*Ximingtu*, K. *Sŏmyŏng to* 西銘圖), which provide the ontologico-cosmological substructure of Neo-Confucianism. The first diagram identifies the Supreme Ultimate as *principle*, which generates yin and yang, which then materialize through the Five Elements. The second diagram describes Heaven as the father and Earth as the mother of all things (drawing on the first two trigrams of the *Book of Changes,* or *I Ching*), linked by a universal organizing principle that reflects an interdependent and interrelated microcosmic reflection of the macrocosmic universe. It is this view that greatly distinguishes T'oegye's view of "humanity" from Buddhist ideas by what he considered their lack of understanding of *principle,* also pointed out by Zhu Xi.

The next three diagrams are all concerned with Confucian education, guiding readers along a pathway of continual study of the Confucian Way, a gradual process of cultivation that required adherence to rules and regulations, not completely dissimilar to those prescribed by Chinul. "The Diagram of Elementary Learning" "The Diagram of the Great Learning," and "The Diagram of Rules of the White Deer Hollow Academy" embody Confucian morality, which is the basis for understanding more complex issues of the mind and the nature. "The Diagram of Elementary Learning," an original diagram by T'oegye himself, synthesizes Zhu Xi's ideas of the learning process and reflects his focus on "The Five Relationships." "The Diagram of the Great Learning" was by Kwŏn Kŭn (1352–1409), an important Neo-Confucian who supervised editions of the Confucian Classics and whose "Diagram of Heaven and Man, Mind and Nature, Combine as One" (Chŏnin simsŏng habil to 天人心性合一圖) influenced T'oegye greatly.[60] By including Zhu Xi's "Rules of the White Deer Hollow Academy," T'oegye was probably hoping to gain the king's endorsement of such academies (known as *sŏwŏn* 書院) in Korea. Indeed, by the end of King Sŏnjo's reign, there were more than one hundred *sŏwŏn,* which had become renowned places of learning, occupying a similar place of esteem, as had the Buddhist temples during the Koryŏ dynasty, but also highlighting the more reclusive nature of scholars such as T'oegye who shunned official positions and who enjoyed the quiet life in the midst of the beauty of nature.[61]

The previous diagrams may be perceived as propaedeutic instructions that represent the basic steps of a much more complicated process that lasts throughout one's lifetime. Similar ideas were espoused in T'oegye's *Record of Self-Reflection* (*Chasŏngnok* 自省錄) and were reiterated in his letters to other scholars (including Yulgok himself). These teachings represented "true learning" for T'oegye, which could potentially transform one's wayward mind and lead to sagehood along a complex and arduous pathway. The complexities of this process are encompassed in the meta-psychological theories of the Cheng-Zhu school, mentioned previously, concerning the mind (K. *sim*) and nature (K. *sŏng*), and the sixth diagram elaborates this theoretical framework. This may be interpreted as the fruit of the "Four-Seven Debate," which Michael Kalton refers to as "the single most important intellectual controversy of the Yi dynasty."[62] The "Four" Beginnings are referred to by *Mencius* (2A:6) and the "Seven" Feelings are referred to in the ninth chapter of the *Book of Rites*.[63] The Four-Seven Debate originated from two cycles of correspondences between T'oegye and Ki Taesŭng (1527–1572) and later between Yulgok and Sŏng Hon (1536–1598)—and not directly between T'oegye and Yulgok. The sixth diagram corresponds with T'oegye's final evaluation of the Four-Seven Debate consisting of three sections: diagrams A, B, and C, relating to the saying "The Mind Combines and Governs the Nature and the Feelings" (*Simt'ong sŏngjŏng to* 心統性情圖). The first of the three diagrams was by Cheng Fuxin (1279–1368), a Yuan dynasty scholar, while the other two diagrams were by T'oegye himself, summarizing his views of *principle* and material force or *ki* (氣) in relation to the Four Beginnings and the Seven Feelings. Diagram A describes two aspects of the mind and presents human nature "as the not yet aroused state" linked to the Four Beginnings (and *principle*), and the Seven Feelings linked to "the aroused state" and interaction with the material force. Diagrams B and C then develop these meta-psychologies; however, it is important to note that the different aspects of the mind are interrelated and only phenomenologically exclusive—the mind was ultimately one but required a gradual process of cultivation to help it focus and function to the best of its innate and naturally good potential.[64] T'oegye has in fact incorporated Zhang Zai's notion of the combination of "physical nature" with "original nature," and it is this physical or *ki* nature that gives rise to the occasion for evil, clouding one's innate moral purity, misdirecting *principle* as such.[65]

The seventh diagram is entitled "The Diagram of the Explanation of Humaneness" (*Insŏl to* 仁說圖) and represents a focal point of Cheng-Zhu orthodoxy, which warns how one's "good" inborn "nature" may become impaired, hampering the operation of the original mind, and then negatively impacting our character in action. Humanity embodies the gradual realization of our optimum level of perfection that already exists in our mind but that depends on how we think about things and how we relate that to others in a social context. Humanism by definition is concerned with "human rather than divine or supernatural matters,"[66] and T'oegye is deeply concerned with the human condition within a social context. Through propounding a process of cultivation that is humanistic in essence, it strives to ameliorate the place of (wo)man in society, society in (wo)man (while adhering closely to Confucian teachings), because the outside world shapes our interior one and vice versa. Social beings penetrate the consciousness of others, and so humans are linked externally (through conduct) and internally (through thought). Humanity is a unifying approach that holds the potential to solve human problems, internally and externally, as well as help people realize the perfection that is innately theirs, similar to the Buddhist idea of the Buddha Nature.

The eighth "Diagram of the Study of the Mind" (*Xinxuetu*, K. *Simhak to* 心學圖) was originally by Cheng Fuxin. It depicts two aspects of the mind: the Mind of Tao/Original Mind and the Physical Mind/Human Mind. Yet, at the center of the lower part of the diagram is "mindfulness" or *kyŏng* (C. *ching*, K. *kyŏng* 敬). Transforming the concept of "seriousness" was needed to control one's feelings and to focus on one's good nature, eliminating selfish desires. Often "*kyŏng*" is translated as "seriousness" or "reverence," but in *To Become a Sage: The Ten Diagrams of Sage Learning* (1988), Michael Kalton translates it as "mindfulness," which underscores the reverential nature of the term as well as identifies the constant effort needed to control one's mind. Kim Hyoungchan translates the term as "reverent mindfulness," combining the notion of an ongoing reverent seriousness with mindfulness, ideas that interpenetrate each other.[67] Such ideas in T'oegye's text have been profoundly influenced by the *Classic of the Heart and Mind* (*Xinjing*, K. *Simgyŏng* 心經) by Zhen Dexiu (1178–1235), which deals almost exclusively with inward cultivation and emphasizes "mindfulness." T'oegye, one might surmise, was responsible for the important place Zhen's text held in the Korean Neo-Confucian textual corpus, where it was printed over twenty-five times before the end of the Chosŏn dynasty.[68] It may also be viewed as the nexus in understanding T'oegye's ideas on this subject, described by Chung as "arguably the most important topic in his entire system of ethics and spirituality."[69] The Buddhist influence, though not entirely repressed, is recalibrated in T'oegye's practical pathway toward sagehood, being able to focus the mind and prevent it from being distracted from *the things at hand*. Mindfulness has also been worked into T'oegye's discussion on "Learning" in diagrams 3–5, making it central to his holistic guiding discourse and gradual pathway toward becoming a sage. Thus, while T'oegye depends greatly on Zhu Xi's writings, one must note that his spiritual dynamism is deeply indebted to Zhen Dexiu, hence, for T'oegye, mindfulness is as serious as meditation is for the Buddhists but focuses on recovering the "original mind," which was calm and not agitated, ultimately benefiting one's decision-making skills in external affairs. Chung highlights how Zhen's *Classic of the Heart and Mind* "inspired T'oegye in his daily reading and contemplative practice. Through his reading of [it] together with quiet sitting, he found a deeper meaning of self-cultivation."[70] Such contemplative forms of self-cultivation are the focus of the final two diagrams where the "practice" of mindfulness is a tool to transform our thoughts and to guide them toward appropriate "moral" actions.

The final diagrams (9) "The Diagram of the Admonition for Mindfulness Studio" (Kyŏngjae cham to 敬齋箴圖) and (10) "The Diagram of the Admonition on Rising Early and Retiring Late" (Sukhŭng yamae cham to 夙興夜寐箴圖), reinforce the need for a daily practice of Confucian mindfulness. In these diagrams the meaning of mindfulness is linked to the internal and external aspects of cultivation and self-refinement: it links interior calm thoughts (or tranquillity) to exterior moral actions, guiding one gradually toward sagehood, where the complementary constituents of the one's mind are freed of selfish desires and other negative mental detritus. There is no short-cut or subitist entry to this lifelong method of self-cultivation, whereby a daily practice helps us to transform ourselves, leading us to become better versions of who we are, without the need for faith in anything beyond our own refined and polished innate abilities and potential. T'oegye summarizes the overall thesis of the final five diagrams in his last comments on the tenth diagram: "The above five diagrams are based on considerations of the mind and the nature; their essential theme is the exercise of diligence in cultivating oneself in the course of daily life, and esteem for the practice of mindfulness and reverent fear."[71]

This final comment and its curious reference to "reverent fear" alludes to the statement in the ninth diagram, warning readers to "recollect your mind and make it abide, as if you were present before the Lord on High"[72] (C. *shangti*, K. *sangje* 上帝), leaving us with an almost agnostic anecdote that the Lord on High might be watching you! It exudes a lingering sense of moral intensity and underscores the spiritual reverence T'oegye applied to his mindfulness practice: the same sort of intensity Chinul and Sŏn Buddhists applied to their own spiritual practice of gradual cultivation, shaped by their faith in the Buddha but also ultimately dependent on their own mental cultivation.

Conclusion

Sŏn Buddhism does not lack a deep study of Buddhist doctrine, nor does it lack a textual history of its own in the form of manuals for practice and collections of *kongan*. Especially in the Korean context, monks such as Ŭich'ŏn compiled remarkable collections of the Buddhist Tripitaka and drew together the doctrinal schools. They even attempted to incorporate Sŏn, an intellectual trajectory that culminated in the assimilation of Kyo and Sŏn under the great Koryŏ master Chinul. Chinul organized retreat societies to reinvigorate the Buddhist clergy and to draw practitioners away from material temptations by setting up Sŏn centers in the mountains. Drawing on Changlu Zongze's (長蘆宗賾, d. 1107?) rules of purity, Chinul emphasized a series of rules for Buddhists who had to take their meditational practices seriously, just as his Neo-Confucian Chinese contemporary Zhu Xi would assign rules to his own rural academy where quiet sitting was considered as part of a new approach to purify the mind. Chan Buddhism's "after-effects" on Neo-Confucian mental practices are far from negligible. Both traditions sought to remove desires and selfish thoughts: for the Buddhists, it was an aid to uncloud and recover one's inherent Buddha Nature, while for the Neo-Confucians it meant recovering the errant mind to uncover one's inherently good nature, as explained in the *Mencius*.

For the Neo-Confucians, there was no moment of sudden enlightenment as taught by adherents of Chan in China, Sŏn in Korea, Zen in Japan. Sagehood was a journey, a rather hopeful destination after a lifelong practice that continually refined how one thought and therefore could lead to humane behavior and good moral actions, and possibly "enlightened leadership" if the king himself were to engage in this practice daily. This latter idea is underscored by T'oegye in his *Ten Diagrams on Sage Learning*, and this point encapsulates the Buddhist recalibration of mindful practices; these transformative Neo-Confucian practices were to shape how people were ruled and how they lived and engaged with one another. T'oegye's practice is a secularized one, but his "reverent mindfulness" is a serious matter with agnostic undertones, not requiring a temple and could be practiced in any place at any time. Just as Ch'en argues that "certain aspects of Philosophic Taoism unquestionably played some part in the development of the [Chan] movement,"[73] so too would I argue that Chan/Sŏn/Zen has been a dynamic force of great propensity, animating the redirection of Neo-Confucianism toward mindful practices that were to be incorporated into one's daily secular life—even if the Neo-Confucians were the last to acknowledge it. Chinul's ideas shaped the Sŏn tradition on the Korean peninsula, just as T'oegye's ideas recalibrated the peninsular trajectory of Neo-Confucian ideas, guiding them toward sagehood (rather than Buddhahood) and mindfulness, emphasizing a daily practice and the ability of each of us to transform ourselves and thereby our world. Both Chinul and T'oegye were shaped by different "history of effects," which animated their own desire to transform our mental lives into more enriched moral experiences. Their different practices share similar psychologico-philosophic ramifications, ultimately culminating in the belief that we can transform our lives by focusing on how we cultivate our minds.

N\otes

1. This was also known as "to sit quietly and preserve the mind" (K. *chŏngjwa chonsim* 靜坐存心). See James B. Palais, *Confucian Statecraft and Korean Institutions: Yu Hyŏngwŏn and the Late Chosŏn Dynasty* (Seattle: University of Washington Press, 1996), 181.

2. See Hans-Georg Gadamer, *Truth and Method*, trans. Joel Weinsheimer and Donald G. Marshall (London: Continuum, 2006), 299–302.

3. This school of *Simhak* should not be confused with the alternative to the Cheng-Zhu school of Neo-Confucian thought represented by Lu Hsiang-shan (1139–1192), and subsequently by Wang Yang-ming which was also called the "school of the mind."

4. Wm Theodore de Bary, *The Unfolding of Neo-Confucianism* (New York and London: Columbia University Press, 1975), 17.

5. de Bary, *The Unfolding of Neo-Confucianism*, 269.

6. Martin Heidegger, *Being and Time*, trans. John Macquarrie and Edward Robinson (New York: Harper Perennial, 2008), 191.

7. Heidegger, *Being and Time*, 43.

8. This term draws on the work of Jean-Luc Nancy, *Dis-Enclosure: The Deconstruction of Christianity*, trans. Bettina Bergo, Gabriel Malefant, and Michael B. Smith (New York: Fordham University Press, 2008).

9. Kenneth Ch'en, *Buddhism in China: A Historical Survey* (Princeton, NJ: Princeton University Press, 1964), 351–52. For a more in-depth look at the Boddhidarma and early Chan Buddhism, see Jeffrey L. Broughton, *The Bodhidharma Anthology: The Earliest Records of Zen* (Berkeley: University of California Press, 1999); Bernard Faure, *Le Traité de Bodhidharma: Première Anthologie du Chan* (Paris: Le Seuil, 2012); For an examination of the development of the Chan tradition from its origins ascribed to the Bodhidharma, see John McRae, *Seeing*

through Zen: Encounter, Genealogy, and Transformation in Chinese Chan Buddhism (Berkeley: University of California Press, 2003).

10. Joseph Adler, *Chinese Religions* (London: Routledge, 2002), 86–87.

11. James Grayson, *Korea—A Religious History* (New York: Routledge Curzon), 69–70.

12. English translation, see John McRae, *The Platform Sutra of the Sixth Patriarch* (Berkeley: Numata Center for Buddhist Translation and Research, 2017).

13. Julia Ching, *Chinese Religions* (London: Macmillan), 140.

14. For a very extensive examination of the historical construction of Huineng based on Chinese, Korean, and Japanese sources, see John Jorgensen, *Inventing Hui-neng, the Sixth Patriarch Hagiography and Biography in Early Ch'an* (Leiden: Brill, 2005).

15. Ŭisang would eventually travel to China, studying alongside the great Huayan monk Fazang (643–712), considered one of the great intellectual pioneers of the Huayan school. The school focused on the *Avataṃsaka* or *Flower Garland Sūtra* (*Huyang jing* 華嚴經, K. *Hwaŏmgyŏng*) and developed the "all-in-one and one-in-all theory" emphasizing the interpenetration of all things/realities/views. It identifies principle (C. *li*, K. *i* 理) with the mind, or rather, the 'One-Mind' (K. *ilsim* 一心), which permeates and connects all things. See Kevin N. Cawley, *Religious and Philosophical Traditions of Korea* (New York: Routledge, 2019), 35–36.

16. Charles Muller, *Wonhyo, Selected Works*, ed. Charles Muller, tans. Charles Muller, Sem Vermeersch and Jin Y. Park, *Collected Works of Korean Buddhism*, vol. 1 (Seoul: Jogye Order of Korean Buddhism, 2012), 302–7.

17. Muller, *Wonhyo, Selected Works*, 305.

18. Morten Schlütter examines the disputes between these different lineages in detail in *How Zen Became Zen: The Dispute over Enlightenment and the Formation of Chan Buddhism in Song-Dynasty China* (Honolulu: University of Hawai'i Press, 2008).

19. Ching, *Chinese Religions*, 141.

20. Cho Myong-gi, "Ch'an Buddhist Culture in Korea," in *Korean and Asian Religious Tradition*, ed. Chai-Shin Yu, trans. Kenneth L. Richard (Toronto: University Toronto Press, 1977), 208–24.

21. Albert Welter, *Monks, Rulers, and Literati: The Political Ascendancy of Chan Buddhism* (Oxford: Oxford University Press, 2006); Ben Brose, *Patrons and Patriarchs: Regional Rulers and Chan Monks during the Five Dynasties and Ten Kingdoms* (Honolulu: University of Hawai'i Press, 2015).

22. See Herlee Creel, *Chinese Thought from Confucius to Mao Tse-tung* (Chicago: University of Chicago Press, 1971), 203, and J. K. Fairbank and Merle Goldman, *China: A New History* (Cambridge, MA: Harvard University Press, 1999), 83–85.

23. See Grayson, *Korea: A Religious History*, 85–86, and Hee-Sung Keel, "Word and Wordlessness: The Spirit of Korean Buddhism," *Korean Philosophy:*

Its Tradition and its Modern Transformation, ed. Korean National Commission for UNESCO (Seoul: Hollym, 2004) 172–73.

24. Hee-Sung Keel, *Chinul: The Founder of the Korean Sŏn Tradition* (Berkeley: University of California Press, 1984), 4.

25. For a discussion on the impressive printing achievements of Koryŏ monks, see Cawley, *Religious and Philosophical Traditions*, 61–63.

26. Cawley, *Religious and Philosophical Traditions*, 7.

27. Cawley, *Religious and Philosophical Traditions*, 60–61.

28. Sim Chae-ryong. "Seon Buddhist Tradition in Korea as Reflected in Jinul's Seon," *Korean Philosophy: Its Tradition and its Modern Transformation*, ed. Korean National Commission for UNESCO (Seoul: Hollym, 2004), 221.

29. Keel, "Word and Wordlessness," 174; Peter H. Lee and Wm Theodore De Bary, eds., *Sources of the Korean Tradition: From the Sixteenth to the Twentieth Century* (New York: Columbia: University Press, 1997), 224–26.

30. Robert E. Buswell Jr., ed., *Chinul, Selected Works*, Collected Works of Korean Buddhism, vol. 2 (Seoul: Jogye Order of Korean Buddhism, 2012), 90–93.

31. Buswell, *Chinul*, 93.

32. Buswell, *Chinul*, 94.

33. Buswell, *Chinul*, 205–46.

34. Buswell, *Chinul*, 206–7.

35. Buswell, *Chinul*, 213.

36. Buswell, *Chinul*, 95.

37. See Robert E. Buswell Jr., "Chinul's Ambivalent Critique of Radical Subitism in Korean Sŏn Meditation," *Journal of the International Association of Buddhist Studies* 12, no. 2 (1989): 20–44.

38. For a discussion on *ch'e-yong*, see Charles Muller, "The Key Operative Concepts in Korean Buddhist Syncretic Philosophy; Interpenetration and Essence-Function in Wŏnhyo, Chinul and Kihwa," *Bulletin of Toyo Gakuen University* 3 (1995): 33–48.

39. John D. Caputo, *Truth: The Search for Wisdom in the Postmodern Age* (New York: Random House, 2013), 52–53.

40. Caputo, *Truth*, 53.

41. Robert E. Buswell Jr., *Tracing Back the Radiance: Chinul's Way of Korean Zen* (Honolulu: University of Hawai'i Press, 1991), 68–69.

42. On Kiwha, see Charles Muller, "The Buddhist-Confucian Conflict in the Early Chosŏn and Kihwa's Syncretic Response: The Hyŏn chŏng-non," *Review of Korean Studies* 2 (1999): 183–200. Also by Charles Muller, *The Sutra of Perfect Enlightenment: Korean Buddhism's Guide to Meditation (with Commentary by the Sŏn Monk Kihwa)* (Albany: State University of New York Press, 1999).

43. William H. Nienhauser, ed., *The Indiana Companion to Traditional Chinese Literature* (Bloomington: Indiana University Press, 1986), 562.

44. Creel, *Chinese Thought*, 205.

45. Nienhauser, *The Indiana Companion to Traditional Chinese Literature*, 397.
46. Ch'en, *Buddhism in China*, 225.
47. Wing-Tsit Chan, *A Sourcebook in Chinese Philosophy* (Princeton, NJ: Princeton University Press, 1973), 452–55.
48. Fung Yulan, *A History of Chinese Philosophy*, vol. I, trans. Derk Bodde (Princeton, NJ: Princeton University Press, 1983), 414.
49. This term, *principle*, refers to the original ideal governing source of all principles of reality in the Neo-Confucian world. Everything has its own individual principle that is a part of this one greater immaterial and universally organizing *principle*. See Fung, *A History of Chinese Philosophy*, vol. 2, 444.
50. De Bary, *The Unfolding of Neo-Confucianism*, 19.
51. Wing-tsit Chan, *Reflections on Things at Hand* (New York: Columbia University Press, 1967), 151.
52. Rodney L. Taylor, "The Sudden/Gradual Paradigm and Neo-Confucian Mind-Cultivation," *Philosophy East and West* 33, no. 1 (1983): 20.
53. See Martina Deuchler, *The Confucian Transformation of Korea* (Cambridge, MA: Harvard University Press, 1992), 16; and Andrew Nahm, *Korea: Tradition and Transformation* (Seoul: Hollym, 1986), 59–88.
54. The "Five Relationships" indicates: between father and son, there should be affection; between ruler and minister, there should be righteousness; between husband and wife, there should be attention to their separate functions; between old and young, there should be proper order; and between friends, there should be faithfulness. See Chan, *A Sourcebook*, 69–70. The "Five Relationships" appear in the *Mencius* (3A:4).
55. This manual has been translated and edited by Patricia Ebrey, see *Chu Hsi's Family Rituals: A Twelfth-Century Manual for the Performance of Cappings, Weddings, Funerals, and Ancestral Rites* (Princeton, NJ: Princeton University Press, 1991).
56. Deuchler, *The Confucian Transformation of Korea*, 110–111.
57. Oh Kangnam, "Sagehood and Metanoia: The Confucian-Christian Encounter in Korea," *Journal of American Academy of Religion* 61, no. 2 (1993): 313.
58. Edward Y. J. Chung, *A Confucian Way of Life and Thought: The Chasŏngnok (Record of Self-Reflection) by Yi Hwang (T'oegye)* (Honolulu: University of Hawai'i Press, 2015), 4.
59. Chung, *A Confucian Way of Life and Thought*, 4–5.
60. See Michael Kalton, "The Writings of Kwŏn Kŭn: The Context and Shape of Early Yi Dynasty Neo-Confucianism," in *The Rise of Neo-Confucianism in Korea*, ed. Wm. Theodore de Bary and JaHyun Kim Haboush (New York: Columbia University Press, 1985), 89–124.
61. Michael Kalton, *To Become a Sage* (New York: Columbia University Press, 1988), 119.

62. Kalton, *To Become a Sage,* 119. For an in-depth analysis of the Four-Seven Debate see Edward Y. J. Chung, *The Korean Neo-Confucianism of Yi Toegye and Yi Yulgok: A Reappraisal of the "Four-Seven Thesis" and Its Practical Implications for Self-Cultivation* (Albany: State University of New York Press, 1995).

63. The Four Beginnings: humanity, righteousness, propriety, and wisdom; The Seven Feelings: joy, anger, sadness, fear, love, dislike, and liking.

64. Ro Young-Chan, *The Korean Neo-Confucianism of Yi Yulkok* (Albany: State University of New York, 1989), 50.

65. Chan, *A Sourcebook of Chinese Philosophy*, 511.

66. Richard Nelson-Jones, *Cognitive Humanistic Therapy* (London: Sage, 2004), 3.

67. See Kim Hyoungchan, *Korean Confucianism: The Philosophy and Politics of Toegye and Yulgok* (London: Rowman and Littlefield, 2018), 27–32.

68. See Chung, A Korean Confucian Way, 150n30.

69. Chung, *A Korean Confucian Way*, 39.

70. Chung, *A Korean Confucian Way*, 12.

71. Kalton, *To Become a Sage,* 196.

72. Kalton, *To Become a Sage,* 178.

73. Ch'en, *Buddhism in China*, 361.

Section IV
Chan, Zen, and Sŏn in the Modern Period

Chapter 11

Taixu's History of the Chan Tradition

Eric Goodell

Introduction

Unlike the "Zen boom" in America in the 1950s, Chan Buddhism in China in the early and mid-twentieth century faced a future that was ambiguous at best. Although Chan monks such as Xuyun, Laiguo, and Yuexi had sizeable followings, for many Buddhists, Chan held limited interest. During this period, figures such as Yang Wenhui criticized the antilearning stance of Chan monks in the late imperial period. Buddhist modernizers chose Yogācāra, not Chan, as the Buddhist tradition most suited to the new China.[1] In the 1950s, Chan "was destroyed, while still alive" by political policies according to Holmes Welch.[2] Unsurprisingly, Chan is almost invisible in the Humanistic Buddhism of the religious modernizer Taixu (太虛, 1890–1947).[3] This changed in 1944, when he published *Chinese Buddhist Learning*,[4] a history of Chinese Buddhism linking Chan with Humanistic Buddhism. The present chapter discusses Taixu's change of approach through an examination of that work's second chapter, his history of the Chan tradition.

Taixu's own relationship with the Chan tradition has multiple dimensions. As a young monk, he trained under the eminent Chan master Jichan (寄禪, 1852–1912; also known as "Eight Fingers").[5] The two long-term retreats in his life both involved daily meditation. In the 1920s, in response to interest in Yogācāra and Tantric Buddhism, Taixu remarked that Chinese Buddhism could only be revived through Chan. Once he founded his own Buddhist academies, however, Taixu used the Maitreya Pure Land tradition to structure the religious training of his monastic students.⁶ Taixu further held that Humanistic Buddhism was gradual, not sudden, effectively declaring its separation from Chan.⁷ In a 1938 proposal for reform, Taixu provided a rare hint that Chan might have a significant role in Humanistic Buddhism. This work describes a monastery where a limited number of monks would live, work, study, and do four hours of meditation and chanting daily. Those who spent twelve years there and had the aspiration for enlightenment would be qualified to serve as the core leaders of Humanistic Buddhism.⁸ Although Chan played a significant role in Taixu's own training and his vision for reformed monasticism, he excluded it from the content of Humanistic Buddhism.

This changed in 1943 when Taixu delivered *Chinese Buddhist Learning* as a lecture series to students at his Sino-Tibetan Doctrinal Institute in Chongqing. The content was then published serially in Taixu's Buddhist magazine *Haichaoyin* from 1944–45. As a whole, *Chinese Buddhist Learning* presents Taixu's argument that meditation, and subsequently Chan (the word "*chan*" 禪 can mean both), played a central role in the history of Chinese Buddhism. Like Zürcher's *Buddhist Conquest of China* published fifteen years later, Taixu argued that the historical development of Buddhism in China was imprinted by a strong social force: the literati. Whereas Zürcher examines the literati's reception of, or "conquest" by Buddhism, Taixu argues that literati interest in meditation shaped Buddhism's development in China. Their interest gave Chan a special status in Chinese Buddhism.

The present analysis focuses on the second chapter of Taixu's *Chinese Buddhist Learning*, a history of the Chan tradition in China. I look at the questions of how Taixu saw the literati shaping Chan history and why Taixu shifted to a stance of promoting the Chan tradition. In the context of these two questions, I argue that Hu Shih's research on Chan was a significant factor in Taixu's shift, despite the fact that Taixu does not mention Hu Shih in this work.

Taixu's second chapter presents a coherent trajectory of Chan history in China, ending in the present. This contrasts sharply with the work of most Chan historians, whose studies end with the Song dynasty.⁹ Although Taixu does not claim to be a scholar, Jan Yün-hua has remarked that researchers of Chan history have not fully utilized Taixu's *Chinese Buddhist Learning*.¹⁰ Therefore my analysis includes a summary of Taixu's second chapter, albeit without most of his quotations from Chan texts. This is additionally valuable as an emic presentation of the Chan tradition in the modern period.

Taixu's perspective is not neutral. For example, he sees Chan as being compatible with Pure Land practice, and argues that Chan training should be linked with systematic doctrinal learning, positions that are not universally held in Chan circles. At the same time, he cites the historical precedents for these positions, which may be of value to students of Chan history.

For convenience, I have prepared a list of the subsections of Taixu's second chapter and brief descriptions of their contents:

Section 1 Introduction. Taixu's analysis of how meditation came to be the most prominent aspect of Indian Buddhism for Chinese encountering the tradition.

Section 2 Chan as Mental Cultivation Based on the Teachings. A summary of meditation traditions in Chinese Buddhism before Bodhidharma's arrival.

Section 3 Chan as Attaining Buddhahood through Insight into Mind. Tathāgata Chan. Bodhidharma up to the sixth patriarch, Huineng.

Section 4 Chan of the Patriarchs that Supersedes the Buddha. Patriarch Chan. Huineng's disciples Huairang and Xiqian, as well as figures from the next three generations.

Section 5 Chan of the Lamp Traditions that Supersedes the Patriarchs. This includes the Five Houses of Guiyang, Linji, Caodong, Yunmen and Fayan.

Section 6 Song, Yuan, Ming, and Qing. Historical treatment of the ten topics that follow.
6.1 Commenting on Gongans
6.2 Investigating the *Huatou* with Doubt
6.3 Dual Practice of Chan and Pure Land
6.4 Reintegrating Chan and the Teachings
6.5 Silent Illumination
6.6 Compiling and studying recorded sayings
6.7 The Practice of Alternating Sitting Meditation and Running
6.8 The State of Affairs in the Sangha
6.9 Coattail Taoism
6.10 Influence on Confucianism

1. Introduction

In this section, Taixu addresses the question of how meditation and Chan came to have such an important role in Chinese Buddhism. He argues that two factors were involved: the demeanor of the foreign monks and the predispositions of Chinese literati culture. The first is evident from the fact that Indian and central Asian monks were able to inspire Chinese people to devote their lives to Buddhism. Taixu writes, "Chinese culture was already highly developed when the Indian monks came to China. Dignified and serene, these monks demonstrated mysterious abilities and captivating wisdom. This created in their [Chinese] admirers an extremely strong desire to further explore the truths they could sense but not fully fathom. After Bodhidharma arrived in China, this became the Chan school's style of teaching. Students used meditation to investigate Buddhism's deeper truths. As a result, meditation/Chan became the most prominent feature of Chinese Buddhist learning." In other words, the charismatic wisdom of the Indian monks inspired some Chinese to devote their lives to the methods of gaining that wisdom, prominently meditation. However, if this were the only factor, Chinese Buddhism could become purely a "religion of mystical faith. Therefore it is necessary to discuss another factor."[11]

The second factor, according to Taixu, is literati trends and interests, which predisposed Chinese scholars to be interested in meditation. Literati of that time valued "subtle truths" (a reference to *xuanxue* 玄學, dark learning) and plain language, preferring concise poetry to lengthy treatises. They had high standards of personal virtue, and valued self-reliance, seclusion, and cultivation. Taixu cites the seven sages of the Bamboo Grove as well as Zhuge Liang and Tao Yuanming as representative examples. Their interests determined which texts were translated, such as the *Sutra in Forty-Two Chapters* (trans. first or second century CE) and *The Eight Kinds of Mindfulness of Great People* (trans. 148–70).

Taixu further depicts an image that appealed to the literati of that period: a cultivator leading a simple life, living in a cave, doing meditation, and giving "instructions that were true and to the point" when people came with questions about life. This is very much related to the Chinese ideal of the recluse (*yinshi* 隱士), wise hermits who live at a distance from society. This description recalls a vignette from Chan history that Taixu recounts in section 2: one day, while Bodhidharma was meditating in his cave, a well-educated, middle-aged gentleman visited him for instruction. As a result of their conversations, this man devoted the next six years of his life to studying with Bodhidharma. This was Huike (慧可), Bodhidharma's dharma heir. Thus literati cultural trends were the second factor.

Taixu addresses the question of why meditation rather than other aspects of Indian Buddhism became prominent. In the early centuries of Buddhist history in China, there were efforts to make Vinaya central, for example with Fadu (法度), a disciple of Dharmayaśas. There were also efforts to emphasize analytical treatises, such as Abhidharma, Satyasiddhi, Madhyamaka, Yogācāra, or Buddhist logic: "But because the literati found themselves unable to grasp their basic principles, these [other aspects of Buddhism] did not flourish."[12]

To add what Taixu has not stated, this was not due to the literati's lack of intelligence. Rather, their involvement with China's highly sophisticated intellectual tradition, generally referred to as Confucianism, made it difficult for literati to commit to an alternative discourse. Fortunately, Chan did not require a doctrinal or philosophical commitment and further offered something appealing not found in Confucian philosophy. In other words, literati interests and commitments made them very amenable to Chan as something that did not rely on words and was transmitted separately from the teachings.

Chan's close relationship to literary culture is explored by other chapters in this volume. John Jorgensen argues that outside of China, Chan was most appreciated by those with knowledge of the Chinese literary tradition. Jason Protass shows how poetic writing served as a medium in the transmission of Chan from China to Japan. George Keyworth explores the relationship between the Chinese literary arts and Chan through the activities of the Chinese monk Donggao Xinyue (Tōkō Shin'etsu) in Japan.

2. Chan as Mental Cultivation Based on the Teachings

This section deals with meditation (*chan*) before the time of Bodhidharma, which was still firmly based on the sutra teachings (*jiao*). This period includes four stages: *ānāpāna* meditation (mindfulness on breathing), meditation on the five gates, *nianfo chan* (which includes *pratyutpanna* meditation), and Kumārajīva's meditation on the true characteristic.

Taixu then quotes Daoxuan's criticisms that Bodhidharma and his followers not only broke Vinaya rules but also claimed to have ended afflictions, completed the ten *bhūmis,* and attained Buddhahood despite the fact that they did not even understand the term "*chan*."[13] This, Taixu says, shows that mainstream Buddhism was critical of meditation methods that did not rely on the Vinaya and sutra teachings.

Taixu does not follow the Chan school's traditional method of tracing its history back to Bodhidharma and Śākyamuni. Instead, he takes a historical approach, looking at traditions of Buddhist meditation in China before Bodhidharma. This approach is found in an earlier article published by Hu Shih in 1935. Hu writes, "It is often said that there was no Chan in China before Bodhidharma, but this is wrong" and then argues that the Chan tradition should be traced to the meditators in the *Eminent Monk* biographies of Huijiao and Daoxuan rather than to the twenty-eight patriarchs.[14]

The difference between Hu Shih's and Taixu's accounts is twofold. First, Hu argues that the Chan tradition of Huineng and Shenhui was a "revolution" against Indian Buddhism,[15] while Taixu presents a more continuous sequence based on historical developments. Second, Taixu's analysis is more systematic, presenting four stages of development beginning with *ānāpāna* meditation, naming their major figures, and outlining their meditation methods. Although Hu names some important figures, he argues that Chinese people did not truly understand the meditation teachings. Instead, they misinterpreted them in terms of the Taoist ideal of the immortal or saw their ultimate purpose as the attainment of supernormal powers.[16]

3. Chan as Attaining Buddhahood through Insight into Mind

This section looks at the Chan tradition from Bodhidharma to Huineng, but also includes some pre-Bodhidharma figures. For example, Daosheng (道生) is mentioned for his theory of attaining Buddhahood with sudden enlightenment.[17] This period is characterized by encounters and interactions that stimulate insight into the nature of mind. By contrast, the previous period emphasized insight into sutra teachings.

Taixu also cites cases of transcending the teachings that occurred before Bodhidharma or did not belong to the Chan tradition. This includes exchanges between Daosheng and Buddhabhadra, Emperor Wu of Liang (梁武帝) and Baozhi (寶誌), Huisi (慧思) and Baozhi, as well as passages in Huiyuan (慧遠), Sengzhao (僧肇), Daosheng, Fu Dashi (傅大士), Dushun (杜順), and Li Tongxuan (李通玄). Taixu concludes, "These are all contributing factors that occurred before Bodhidharma's Chan became popular. Their remarks contain simple yet profound interpretations of ideas from the sutras and sastras, or ideas not found in the sutras, or even references to what is beyond language."[18] The remaining subsections, not summarized here, deal with Bodhidharma up to Huineng.

During this period, Taixu remarks that Chan's methodology was still controversial. Citing the *Eminent Monks* account of an assassin sent after Huike, Taixu says this act was inspired by the jealousy of mainstream clergy who prioritized sutra teachings. A similar theme occurs in the *Platform Sutra*, when Huineng is pursued after his dharma transmission from the fifth patriarch. Taixu identifies the episode with Huike as an important event marking the division between Chan and sutra teachings.

Taixu concludes with a quote from Zongmi summarizing this period: "If you have a sudden awakening realizing that your mind was always pure and without afflictions, that taintless wisdom-nature was always complete within yourself, that this very mind is buddha and there is ultimately no difference between the two, and then continue to cultivate on this basis, then this is the highest vehicle of Chan. It is also known as the pure Chan of the tathāgatas."[19] This period is therefore synonymous with the traditional name, tathāgata Chan.

4. Chan of the Patriarchs that Supersedes the Buddha

Whereas the previous period emphasized the attainment of Buddhahood by seeing the nature of mind, this period focuses on transcending attachments to the Buddha. In other words, tathāgata Chan becomes patriarch Chan. Taixu quotes several figures. Danxia (丹霞) said, "I don't like to hear the word 'Buddha'"; Zhaozhou (趙州) said, "If you invoke the Buddha's name once, rinse your mouth for three days"; and Nanquan (南泉) said, "Mazu teaches identity of mind and Buddha, but for me it isn't mind, Buddha, or anything."[20] The shift to Bodhidharma and the patriarchs is represented by a famous *gongan* (公案, J. *kōan*). Taixu writes, "At this time it was common to ask about the meaning of Bodhidharma's arrival. From this we can see that the Buddha had already been pushed aside, and the significance of the patriarchs had become central."[21]

The remaining subsections are as follows. Section 4.1 deals with Xingsi (行思) and Huairang (懷讓), the two main figures after Huineng. Section 4.2 covers Xiqian (希遷) and Mazu (馬祖), the subsequent generation after Xingsi and Huairang respectively. Section 4.3 includes Baizhang

(百丈), who was Mazu's heir, as well as Daowu (道悟) and Weiyan (惟儼) who both studied under Xiqian. Section 4.4 includes Yunyan (雲岩), who studied under Weiyan, Chongxin (崇信), the Dharma heir of Daowu, as well as Huangbo and Guishan (潙山), who studied under Baizhang.

Taixu follows tradition in his assessment of Baizhang and Mazu. Baizhang "did not establish a Buddha Hall, in order to show reverence for the current master.[22] There was a special emphasis on establishing a Dharma Hall, with the senior monk teaching the Dharma before monks standing in two rows. Once Mazu created the Chan monastery (*conglin*), and Baizhang created the Pure Regulations, Chan monks had a proper mode of living, and the Chan school entered a new stage of development."[23]

Taixu concludes with an episode showing that the categories of tathāgata Chan (described in section 3 above) and patriarch Chan (section 4) were used early in the tradition. Guishan asked Zhixian (智閑) about his original face before his parents were born. The question shook Zhixian, who left to do further practice. Later, while Zhixian was clearing away an area at Xiangyansi (香嚴寺), he picked up a tile and threw it. The tile hit a stalk of bamboo, and the sound stimulated a great awakening in him. He wrote a verse to Guishan, who judged him to be fully awakened. Yangshan, however, argued that Zhixian understood tathāgata Chan but not patriarch Chan. Zhixian composed another verse, this time for Yangshan, who recognized that he had now understood patriarch Chan.

5. Chan of the Lamp Traditions that Supersedes the Patriarchs

Chan of the lamp traditions includes a new development. Students were expected to surpass their masters. Taixu remarks, "To those who ask about the meaning of Bodhidharma, the reply would be, 'Why don't you ask yourself about the meaning?'" This includes the five houses of Guiyang, Linji, Caodong, Yunmen, and Fayan. It also includes subdevelopments such as the Yangqi lineage under Linji.

Taixu compares the five houses with the five highest yoga tantras in Tibet after Langdarma's (r. 838–841) persecution.[24] Taixu says, "Subsequent developments in Vajrayāna occurred within the context of the five highest yoga tantras. Similarly, the five Chan houses arose after Wuzong's (r. 840–846) persecution in the Tang dynasty. Subsequent developments in the Chan tradition occurred within the context of the five houses."[25] Taixu therefore recognizes this period as an important pinnacle in the

Chan tradition. Although some scholars argue that subsequent periods were inauthentic and characterized by decline, Taixu's work presumes that Chan masters strived to maintain the high standards of the five houses in the centuries that followed.

Taixu's mention of tantric Buddhism raises the question of why he was using Tibetan Buddhism to explain Chan. After the Japanese invasion of China in 1937, the KMT government moved to Chongqing (Chungking) in Sichuan. Taixu and many other public figures also moved to Chongqing. Taixu stayed at his Sino-Tibetan Doctrinal Institute, which he had established there in 1932. Sichuan had long been a place with easy access to Tibetan Buddhism. Because of these factors, Taixu's institute offered more lectures and had more visitors. One may surmise that Taixu found himself in an environment where Buddhism, especially the Tibetan tradition, was a topic of interest for more people than usual.[26] This may explain why he used Tibetan Buddhism to explain Chan.

6. Song, Yuan, Ming, and Qing

In the preceding sections, Taixu presents an evolutionary development of the Chan tradition. Each new period is worded in a way that shows progress over the previous stage. On the surface, this demonstrates Taixu's reception of the modern concept of evolutionary thought. This idea of progressive development was also present in the tradition itself, with patriarch Chan superseding tathāgata Chan (see section 4). Taixu also identifies a continuity: "Each period of Chan connects with the others in a single network. On the basis of each one's specific traits, however, we can provisionally establish names as distinguishing markers."[27] Beginning with the Song, however, Taixu's history of the Chan tradition becomes thematic rather than chronological. The ten themes, listed in the introduction above, are discussed individually, in terms of their developments from the Song to Qing dynasties.

6.1. Commenting on Gongans

This subsection introduces commentarial literature composed for the lamp records and recorded sayings. According to Taixu, commentary on public cases (*gongan* 公案) comes in the form of comments on old cases (*niangu* 拈古) and verses on old cases (*songgu* 頌古). Verse commentary emerged after prose commentary. Taixu quotes a Ming dynasty text: "In the Chan school, there are four traditions of verses on old cases: those of Hongzhi Zhengjue, Xuedou Chongxian, Touzi Yiqing, and Danxia Zichun. [Versified comments] began with Fenyang Shanzhao."[28] Important texts include Xuedou's *Verses on One Hundred Old Cases*,[29] Hongzhi Zhengjue's *Verses on One Hundred Old Cases*, and Puhui's *Pearl String Collection of Verses on Old Cases*. Later, Yuanwu Keqin's *Blue Cliff Record* quotes and comments on Xuedou's work to become an important work in the Linji tradition, and Wansong Xingxiu's (萬松行秀) *Congrong lu* (從容錄, Serenity records) does the same for Zhengjue's work in the Caodong.

Taixu attributes the earliest example of commenting on old cases to Yunmen. For example, Yunmen commented on a passage describing how Śākyamuni, as a child, took several steps, pointed one finger up and one finger down, and said, "I alone am worthy in this world." This stimulated comments by many subsequent Chan masters.[30] While Yunmen was the earliest example of prose comments on old cases, Fenyang is the earliest for versified comment. Fenyang wrote verses on topics such as Linji's "three mysteries and three essentials" and the meeting of Bodhidharma and Huike.

Taixu also remarks on Dahui's (大慧) critique of Keqin (克勤), his master. He does not mention that Dahui burned Keqin's *Blue Cliff Record*, but he does mention the reason: some of Keqin's students had simply memorized the answers. Taixu comments that Keqin's purpose in composing the text was to stimulate enlightenment. Therefore the blame lies not with Keqin but with those who believed that just being clever was the proper approach.

Taixu concludes this section with a remark that the practice of commenting on *gongans* has two purposes: providing subtle hints and inspiring contemplative investigation. This practice began in the Song, and continued to be an important "dharma gate," a method of instruction and practice that leads to enlightenment.

6.2. Investigating the *Huatou* with Doubt

For Taixu, *huatou* (話頭, topic of meditative inquiry) practice is central to Chan. He remarks, "The Chan school, from start to finish, is one big *huatou*."[31] The most important model for *huatou* practice before Dahui is Xiangyan Zhixian (香嚴智閑). Guishan asked him, "Without talking about what you have learned or what you remember, what was your original face before your parents were born?" After doing ascetic practice for several years, Zhixian came to experience great enlightenment (see section 4).

Taixu then observes that at this time, *huatou* practice was not promoted on a wide scale, nor was it the central practice of Chan practitioners. For Taixu, it is important to distinguish between practices done by a few individual masters and practices that are promoted on a wide scale.

Taixu continues that Dahui was the most effective proponent of *huatou* practice. Later in his lineage, Gaofeng Yuanmiao (高峰原妙) and Zhongfeng Mingben (中峰明本) became enlightened through *huatou* practice and taught it to others. During the Yuan and Ming, the most popular *huatou* was, "The myriad dharmas can be traced back to the one, but what can the one be traced back to?" Tianqi Benrui (天琦本瑞) was the first to propose a "who" *huatou*, prior to "Who is the one doing *nianfo?*" Tianqi writes, "Every hour of the day and night, and with every thing, bring the light inward and invert your gaze, then see who is doing this. Don't fixate on a single thing, it should be every thing. Follow it up and down, don't worry about being wrong, don't let even a single hair pass by. When you're walking, see who is doing the walking. When you're standing, see who is doing the standing. When you're sitting, see who is doing the sitting. When you're lying down, see who is doing the lying down. . . . If you can't speak, see who it is that can't speak. Then when you have the sense of doubt, see who it is that is doubting. If you keep looking in this way, the ground will suddenly explode with a boom, and you will know you have stopped seeking externals."[32] During the late Ming and early Qing, once Zhuhong's (袾宏) practice of reciting "Amituofo" became popular, the *huatou* "Who is the one doing *nianfo?*" became the most widespread.

Thus in Taixu we can see a continuity of Chan practice up through the Qing. The significance of the earlier recorded sayings lies not in emulating or performing them but in finding them genuinely puzzling and working hard to figure them out in a context of meditative practice.

6.3. Dual Practice of Chan and Pure Land

This section outlines the main developments in the history of the dual practice of Chan and Pure Land. Taixu takes the unusual stance of dating the earliest instance of joint practice to the fourth century.[33] The rationale is that Daoan practiced *ānāpāna* meditation (*chan*) but also had faith in the Maitreya Pure Land tradition. He was thus a very early figure doing both *chan* (meditation) and Pure Land practices.³⁴ Lushan Huiyuan also fits in a similar way.³⁵

According to Taixu, once Bodhidharma arrived, Chan and Pure Land became separate. It was not until Yongming Yanshou (永明延壽) that Chan and Pure Land practices were reunited. Yanshou, a patriarch in the Fayan house of the Chan tradition, did tens of thousands of verbal *nianfo* invocations daily. After Yanshou, the Fayan school stopped after just one more generation and shifted to Pure Land practice. Yanshou wrote a text dedicated to rebirth in the Pure Land, his *Wanshan tonggui ji* (萬善同歸集, Anthology on the common end of myriad good deeds). The verse, "With Pure Land and Chan / You are like a tiger with horns" was attributed to Yanshou. After Yanshou, many did dual practice.

Taixu mentions several later figures doing dual practice. The first is the Linji Chan monk Chushi Fanqi (楚石梵琦), who wrote verses on Pure Land. Zhongfeng Mingben wrote a manual on Pure Land ritual.³⁶ The Yuan dynasty Chan monk Tianru Weize (天如惟則) wrote a work on questions about the Pure Land tradition that discusses a model of first attaining enlightenment through Chan and then doing Pure Land practice after that.³⁷ In addition, Hanshan Deqing (憨山德清) of the late Ming has many discussions of *nianfo* and supports the idea of Chan followed by Pure Land. Yunqi Zhuhong, who promoted exclusive Pure Land practice, started his practice with Chan.³⁸ The one who has the highest understanding of joint practice is the Chan master Chewu (徹悟).³⁹ He had a unique perspective treating Chan and Pure Land as equals in his recorded sayings.

6.4. Reintegrating Chan and the Teachings

This section addresses the relationship between Chan and the sutra teachings (as represented in the Tiantai and Huayan traditions). We can see Taixu's preference for a Chan that is integrated with, rather than separate from, the teachings. Taixu attributes the distinction between Chan and teachings to the *Laṅkāvatāra sūtra*, which distinguishes between realization (*zong* 宗) and verbal explanation (*yanshuo* 言說).⁴⁰ Realization refers to "witnessing the supreme state," or as Suzuki translates, the "inner attainment." The teachings include the ninefold division of Buddhist literature, as well as the ability to skillfully create Buddhist teachings.⁴¹ Taixu remarks that Bodhidharma's transmission was concerned with realization rather than teachings, with verified personal experience, or "witness" (*zheng* 證)

as the main criterion. Therefore, Bodhidharma represents "the beginnings of the sudden method (*zong*) transmitted separately from the teachings."[42]

After this, some figures worked to integrate Chan realization with the teachings. Huineng, Huizhong (慧忠), and Dazhu (大珠) utilize important ideas from sutras and treatises. Later figures strived to create a more conscious re-integration of Chan and teachings. These include Zongmi, Yanshou, Zibo Zhenke (紫栢真可), Hanshan Deqing, as well as lay figures Zeng Fengyi (曾鳳儀)[43] and Qian Qianyi (錢謙益). Taixu concludes the list with mention of the Qing emperor Yongzheng (雍正), who claimed Chan enlightenment, greatly admired Yanshou's project, and attempted to integrate the teachings with Chan. Nonetheless for Taixu, their efforts fall short of the larger systematization that he envisions.

Taixu then suggests that an ideal system should be created which integrates the Vinaya, sutra teachings, and Chan in a graduated scheme. He mentions the Gelugpa system of Tsongkhapa, which is based on the bodhisattva path and integrates the various divisions of sutra and Vinaya in a graduated manner for people of ordinary, middling, and great capacities, with Tantra in the highest position. Taixu remarks that so far the Chan school has been unable to firmly establish itself upon a graduated foundation of Vinaya and teachings, to its detriment.

Finally, Taixu names emperors whose policies went in the direction of Taixu's desired system. The first is the Ming emperor Taizu (r. 1368–1398), who "had a good understanding of Chan and teachings, and strongly wished to renew Buddhism."[44] His policies established five categories of monastery: Chan, teachings (*jiang* 講), discipline (*lü* 律), Pure Land (*jing* 淨), and esoteric ritual (*jiao* 教).[45] Taixu remarks that this hierarchical system included esoteric Buddhism and placed Chan at the top. Unfortunately, Taixu remarks, there were no fully enlightened clergy who created a matching doctrinal system. The second emperor is Yongzheng of the Qing dynasty, who understood the teachings and Chan. He resolved to spend ten years on improving governance and reviving Buddhism but died before this was carried out.

6.5. SILENT ILLUMINATION

According to Taixu, silent illumination (*mozhao* 默照) is a valid Chan practice that historically has brought about enlightenment for some people. However, if promoted on a broad scale, it is easily misunderstood. He cites a critique of silent illumination made by Zhenjing Kewen (真淨

克文).⁴⁶ Kewen remarked that many people's Chan practice and enlightenment were inauthentic, and therefore they could not understand the ancient adage, "Countless corpses lie on the flat ground; good is the one who can pass through the thicket of thorns."⁴⁷ Kewen goes on to remark that many just want eternal quietude, or they are attached to the idea of ordinary mind being the Way, passing their entire lives in this manner. Taixu then cites Dahui's criticism of "heretical silent illumination Chan," which appealed to literati because their normally overactive minds benefitted from a quietistic meditation method.⁴⁸ Taixu concludes that genuine silent illumination practice has indeed resulted in the enlightenment of some monks, but very often it is not properly understood and results in attachment to quietistic attitudes.

6.6. Compiling and Studying Recorded Sayings

If we ask the question of what practice Taixu recommends for his readers, the answer may be surprising. The only practice explicitly recommended is compiling or studying the recorded sayings literature. This practice, outlined in this section, provides a way for interested intellectuals to contribute to the tradition by sorting through Chan literature produced after the seventeenth century.

Taixu first discusses the history of the compilation of Chan literature. The *Platform Sutra* marks an important beginning for recorded sayings texts. There were a few recorded sayings texts before it; however, significantly, there were many after it. Taixu identifies several collections of recorded sayings beginning with the *Baolin zhuan* (寶林傳, Transmission of the Baolin [Temple]) and the *Jingde chuandeng lu* (景德傳燈錄, Jingde era lamp transmission record). However, for Taixu, the most systematic of these is the *Zhiyue lu* (指月錄, Records of pointing at the moon), compiled in 1602 by the lay Buddhist Qu Ruji (瞿汝稷)⁴⁹ and the *Xu zhiyue lu* (續指月錄, Further records of pointing at the moon) compiled in the Qing by Nie Xian (聶先).

Although scholars have generally not attached a great deal of importance to the *Zhiyue lu* due to its late date, three factors make it important for Taixu. First, it was a text that he studied while doing Chan training during his early years as a monk.⁵⁰ Second, it is a highly systematic collection of Chan literature. It is arranged chronologically, with biographies and encounter dialogues for important figures in each generation. It differs from previous works by including both the chronological structure of lamp records as well as the comments of multiple later masters. Each encounter dialogue is followed by comments from several masters but none from the editor. Taixu holds this up as a model for modern scholars to follow because the *Zhiyue lu* only goes up to Dahui, and the *Xu zhiyue lu* only goes up to 1678. Third, the compiler of the *Zhiyue lu* was a lay Buddhist. This matches the intended audiences of Taixu's *Chinese Buddhist Learning*: lay intellectuals. The fact that a lay Buddhist could contribute to the Chan literary tradition would be important to Taixu's readers.

Taixu provides instructions for working on the texts: "The key to compiling and studying recorded sayings lies in deeply studying the words of the ancient masters. When you can't figure out what they mean, then you have a doubt (*yi* 疑), which you investigate (*can* 參). In this way, you begin investigating a *huatou*. Therefore the most crucial thing in compiling and studying recorded sayings is your effort to figure out the places you can't understand."[51] This important passage takes the Buddhist intellectual's interest in studying Chan literature and links it with the beginnings of *huatou* practice.

Taixu further stipulates that the researcher or compiler must know about the three stages (*guan* 關, "barriers") of Chan practice. He remarks that enlightenment is thorough and without stages for those of the highest capacity, but because the Chan tradition later included practitioners with a broad range of abilities, the division into stages (*jieci* 階次) is necessary. There are three stages, but different texts have different versions. Taixu presents quotes from Huanglong Huinan (黃龍慧南), Doushuai Congyue (兜率從悅), Yongzheng's preface in the *Yuxuan yulu* (御選語錄, Imperial selection of recorded sayings), and others. Taixu first describes the three levels in Huanglong: "When Huanglong encountered someone, he extended his hand and asked, 'How is my hand like the Buddha's hand?' If you answered this question, he extended his foot and asked, 'How is my foot like a donkey's foot?' Then he would ask, 'Where, venerable one, do you come from?'"[52]

Taixu then quotes Congyue (從悅): "This is like the three questions of Doushuai Congyue: 'Travelling against the wind and crossing fields, you just want to see the nature. But how about right now, where sir is your enlightened nature?' This is the first question. The second is 'Seeing self-nature is the only way to gain liberation from birth and death. But when your vision drops to the ground, how do you get liberated?' The third question is 'Knowing birth and death means knowing where you are going, but when the four elements disperse, where do you go?'"[53]

Taixu then quotes the classic passage from Yongzheng's *Yuxuan yulu* describing the three stages. This is the first stage:[54]

> In the preface to his *Yuxuan yulu,* Yongzheng writes, "When a student of Chan first walks over the threshold of liberation, they are suddenly and temporarily released from the suffering of karmic bondage. They perceive that mountains, rivers, earth, and space in the ten directions disappear or fall away. They are no longer deceived by the words of ancient masters. . . . [They become] completely pure, without a single attachment. This is called the breaching of past and future." This is the initial investigative breakthrough, which is the first stage.

The second stage:

> This is the next step: "After the initial investigative breakthrough, one knows that mountains are mountains, rivers are rivers, and earth is earth. [The same is true for] space in the ten directions, . . . earth, water, fire and wind . . . even ignorance, . . . afflictions, . . . colors, sounds, smells, tastes, and objects of touch. Everything is part of one's path. Everything awakens." After the initial investigative breakthrough, when one sees "every single thing is the Dharmakaya; every single thing is oneself,"[55] one has broken through the second pass, which is "great death and great life."

The third stage:

> This is the third stage: "After one has crossed the second pass, home is being on the way, and being on the way is home. In brightness one accords and in darkness one accords. Tranquility is illumination and illumination is tranquility. It is walking and it is standing. It is *ti* and it is *yong*. It is emptiness and it is existence. It is ancient and it is new. Non-arising and non-cessation sustain it forever. . . . [Then] one steps into the final difficult pass."

From these three stages in the *Yuxuan yulu,* we can see detachment from physical afflictions, then a realistic understanding of the world, and finally an ability to embrace dualities. Taixu simply wants his readers to become aware of these three stages.

Taixu remarks that the main point of the Chan tradition is to evoke the first breakthrough. If one attains that but does not know about the second, one will be a naturalistic (Taoistic) non-Buddhist practitioner. One who attains the second but does not know about the third will be content with "Hinayana nirvana." The reader thus becomes implicated in a layered system culminating with the Mahayana ideal of universal awakening.

This section contains three different subtexts. First, for intellectuals interested in the Chan tradition, Taixu provides a goal: continuing the work of the *Zhiyue lu*. Second, those who wish to work on that goal, and those who just want to study Chan literature, become implicated in Chan's religious system.

The third subtext relates to Hu Shih. Taixu was undoubtedly familiar with Hu Shih's works on Buddhism, such as his study of Shenhui's recorded sayings published in 1930. Taixu's insistence on the expression "compile and study" above now comes into clearer focus: was Taixu putting forth an alternative to Hu's method of researching Buddhism?

This question can be addressed through a comparison with part of Hu Shih's 1935 article "Zhongguo chanxue de fazhan" (中國禪學的發展, The development of Chan learning in China). At the end of this article, Hu describes five stages in the career of the Chan practitioner: 1. being taught by the method of "not speaking plainly" (*bu shuo po* 不說破); 2. the arising of doubts (*yi* 疑) due to hardships in learning; 3. Chan encounters (*chanji* 禪機); 4. itinerant learning (*xingjiao* 行腳); and 5. enlightenment (*wu* 悟), with the student suddenly gaining a new understanding and feeling gratitude to his teacher.[56] Hu's five stages and Taixu's three stages present competing understandings of the Chan career.

Where Hu's model is transparent and intelligible, Taixu's engages. Hu Shih uses plain language to describe his model. By contrast, Taixu's model is only partially accessible, placing most readers in a context of incomplete understanding. The reader is now faced with the limits of his or her rational faculties. In addition, the reader may be inspired to seek deeper meaning. This recalls Taixu's analysis of the early Indian monks in China, who inspired in their followers an "extremely strong desire to further explore the truths they could sense but not fully fathom."[57] Hu's model is purely historical, while Taixu's incorporates soteriological goals into a historical analysis.

308 | Eric Goodell

6.7. The Practice of Alternating Sitting Meditation and Running

In this subsection, Taixu relates an interesting anecdote about the origins of the practice of running rather than walking between meditation periods. In the Qing dynasty, the emperor Yongzheng was seeking a successor to Yulin Tongxiu (玉林通琇), a national preceptor. The monk Tianhui Shiche (天慧實徹) was recommended. The emperor summoned him and said, "You belong to the lineage of the national preceptor [Yulin Tongxiu]. Do you know his main teaching?" Shiche replied, "I have a mangy head." Yongzheng prodded him with a sword and said, "How will it be when I cut off your mangy head?" Shiche was unable to say anything. The emperor gave him seven days to respond, allowing him use of the imperial Chan hall. Each day an attendant outside the hall announced how many days had passed and how many remained. Under this pressure, Shiche did not sit in meditation but ran. On the seventh day, he ran into a pillar and suddenly awakened. He asked to see Yongzheng. Yongzheng replied, "I am pleased to see that you now understand the main teaching of the national preceptor." Taixu remarks that this case was the origin of Gaomin si's (高旻寺) policy of alternating sitting and running.

Taixu refers to this episode as an "orally transmitted account from the Chan tradition." It indeed cannot be found in texts. The earliest source, a biography of Shiche by his disciple Jisheng, says that Shiche was summoned to meet with Yongzheng in 1733 and they had an engaging conversation; in 1734 he was awarded the purple robe, and later imperially appointed as abbot of Gaomin.[58] The *Foguang* Buddhist dictionary says that Shiche was summoned to meet the emperor in 1733 and given a purple robe, and later became abbot of Gaomin.[59] According to Laiguo's (來果) work on the rules and regulations for Gaomin si, Shiche was enlightened in the imperial grounds and received the purple robe in the palace of Yongzheng. Further, Shiche and Yongzheng had a conversation of deep mutual understanding in which both were equals. The emperor appointed Shiche to serve as abbot of Gaomin si.[60]

6.8. The State of Affairs in the Sangha

This section outlines the situation in Chan monasteries (*conglin* 叢林) during the Ming and Qing dynasties. For information on this period, Taixu quotes three passages in the *Zongtong biannian* (宗統編年, Chronicle of orthodox Chan lineages), compiled by the Sanfeng monk Jiyin (紀蔭) in 1689.[61] The first passage begins with a brief mention of four figures in the Song and Yuan who were most influential on later generations: Gaofeng Yuanmiao, Zhongfeng Mingben, Wansong Xingxiu, and Xueting Fuyu (雪庭福裕).[62]

The second quote states that during the period from 1621 to 1644, the Chan tradition was greatly revived by the two patriarchs Miyun Yuanwu (密雲圓悟) and Hanyue Fazang (漢月法藏). The three great masters Yunqi Zhuhong, Zibo Zhenke, and Hanshan Deqing were active around the same time. Other important figures from this period include Zhenji [Guang]yin (真寂廣印), Ehu [Guang]xin (鵝湖廣心), Yifeng Fangtuan (儀峰方彖), and Wunian Shenyou (無念深有). Jiyin, the editor, remarks, "During these decades, there was a revival that approached the flourishing of the Tang and Song."[63] For Jiyin, the golden age includes not only the Tang dynasty but also the Song.

The third quote summarizes developments during the period from 1615 to 1689. The Linji school was revived when Miyun Yuanwu and Tianyin Yuanxiu (天隱圓修) expanded the teachings of their master Yumen Zhengchuan (禹門正傳). The Caodong school was strengthened when Yunmen Yuancheng (雲門圓澄) popularized the teachings of his master Dajue Fangnian (大覺方念), and Boshan Yuanlai (博山元來) popularized the teachings of his master Shouchang [Hui]jing (壽昌慧經). Hanyue Fazang dedicated himself to teaching Chan (*gangzong* 綱宗). Those who continued his tradition include Tuiweng Hongchu (退翁弘儲) and Lingyin [Hongli] (靈隱弘禮). Muchen Daomin (木陳道忞) was a very important disciple of Miyun. Feiyin Tongrong (費隱通容) and Muyun Tongmen (牧雲通門) were also excellent disciples of Miyun. Zhuhong promoted the Pure Land tradition. Additionally, the Vinaya, Tiantai, and Yogācāra traditions also saw important activity.[64]

Although the Sanfeng lineage belonged to the Linji school, Jiyin makes a distinction between the two by referring to his own Sanfeng lineage as "Chan," in contrast to his mentions of the Linji and Caodong schools. On one hand, this reflects the tension between the lineages of Miyun, a Linji monk, and his Dharma heir Hanyue, the founder of the Sanfeng lineage. On the other, Sanfeng did emphasize all five Chan houses rather than Linji alone.[65]

Taixu remarks that although Jiyin has grasped the important developments of this period, his work contains several deficiencies. It does not mention emperor Yongzheng's praise of the national preceptor Yulin, his criticism of Muchen Daomin, or his oppression of the Sanfeng tradition. This is to be expected, as Jiyin's work was compiled in 1689 and Yongzheng's criticisms occurred in 1733. Additionally, Jiyin's work does not mention a number of Qing dynasty Caodong monks who were Ming loyalists before their renunciation under Tianran Hanshi (天然函昰) and built several monasteries in Guangdong. It also omits important figures in Sichuan, such as Zhaojue Zhangxue (昭覺丈雪)[66] and other disciples of Poshan Haiming (破山海明), a disciple of Miyun. Taixu allows that Jiyin probably did not have access to information from those two regions. Finally, it omits mention of Ouyi Zhixu (藕益智旭).

Taixu then discusses the system of five types of monastery developed by emperor Ming Taizu—Chan, teachings, discipline, Pure Land, and esoteric ritual. He remarks that in the late Ming and early Qing, monasteries that were Chan in name began replacing the other types. "Chan" monasteries thus came to have sutra lectures, precept ordinations, and *nianfo* halls. By the mid-Qing, ownership of monastery property became the central issue, with dharma transmissions taking on the function of identifying successors. Taixu remarks that unfortunately this situation has continued to the time of his writing. Holmes Welch's long article on dharma scrolls demonstrates the complexity of the situation.[67] Taixu further laments that some of the strictest Chan monasteries of his day have lost their focus. He writes that the true Chan monasteries did not do rituals for laity during the Qing dynasty but suggests that was changing in the Republican period. He quotes a monk who says, "Chan, the teachings, discipline, and Pure Land are for seeking the truth, while repentance rituals, vegetarian feasts and Yankou (焰口) rituals are for the laity. Tiantong has both." Taixu concludes that even some of the true Chan monasteries had become empty shells. This ends the discussion of Chan as the most prominent feature of Chinese Buddhism. The remaining two sections discuss the influence of Chan on Taoism and Confucianism.

6.9. Coattail Taoism

The term "coattail" is used to translate "*pangfu*" (旁附), a term Taixu uses to indicate that this type of Taoism borrows heavily from Buddhism, especially the silent illumination (*mozhao*) tradition. Taixu first describes some areas in which Taoism has borrowed from Buddhism then discusses the Taoist idea of the dual cultivation of nature (*xing* 性) and vitality (*ming* 命).

An early Taoist figure who relied heavily on Buddhism is Zhang Ziyang (張紫陽, 984–1082). He was so influential that Yongzheng's *Yuxuan yulu* includes some of his writings.⁶⁸

The Qing dynasty figure Liu Huayang (柳華陽) also propounded the idea of dual cultivation of nature and vitality. He held that Buddhism had good methods for cultivating nature, which resulted in the pacification of all taints (or "outflows," *loujin tong* 漏盡通). At the same time, Buddhism was deficient in the cultivation of vitality, which extends one's lifespan. Liu stated, "If you cultivate nature but not vitality, your soul will be weak and sagehood will be difficult to obtain. If you cultivate vitality but not nature, it is like having a family treasure but being unable to take ownership of it."

Taixu remarks that dual cultivation does not actually originate in Taoism. In the Qin and Han, Taoists used inner alchemy to cultivate *qi*, and outer alchemy to make medicine. There was no such thing as cultivating nature in early alchemy. The dual cultivation of nature and vitality began with Lü Dongbin (呂洞賓, a.k.a. Lü Chunyang 呂純陽), who was influenced and inspired by the Chan master Huanglong. He took the Chan idea of cultivating nature as the starting point of his method for cultivating longevity, just as Confucian literati used Chan enlightenment as "capital" to bolster their credentials.

Taixu cites a passage in Chan literature demonstrating Huanglong's influence on Lü Dongbin:⁶⁹ "One day, master Meiji of Huanglong shan (Huanglong) ascended the hall. [He said, 'A thief of the Dharma sits nearby.']⁷⁰ Lü Chunyang (Dongbin) stepped forward and said, 'The world can be contained in one grain of rice. What is it like when mountains and rivers are cooking in the half-*sheng* crucible?' Huanglong replied, 'You are a ghost watching over a corpse.' Lü said, 'I just want to know if there is medicine for everlasting life in this hall.' Huanglong said, 'Even after eighty thousand kalpas, you'll end up dying in empty futility.' Lü threw daggers at him but Huanglong remained untouched. Thereupon Lü bowed down before him and asked to become his disciple. Huanglong asked him, 'What is it like to hold the world in a grain of rice?' With this, Lü had a great awakening. He then spoke a verse indicating that Huanglong helped him see that his previous practice was incorrect, and as a result he was giving up Taoist practices."⁷¹ Taixu concludes that this type of Taoist dual cultivation of nature and vitality not only fails to realize Chan ideals but also does not attain the goals it sets for itself.

6.10. Influence on Confucianism

Taixu first includes a brief catalog of Buddhist influences on the Confucian world, such as intellectual influences on Neo-Confucianism and emperors who had gone forth to become monks. He then names Confucian figures who used Buddhist ideas but criticized the Buddhist tradition. For example, Li Ao (李翱) borrowed Buddhist ideas when he wrote, "Nature (性) is what enables sagehood, and the passions (情) are what confuses nature."[72] Li further argues that Confucian morality is the true middle way and criticizes Buddhist monks for eating but not growing food. Taixu responds that this perspective is based on "agrarian economics," which demands that everyone engage in agriculture.

Taixu discusses the modern historian Fung Yu-lan, who cites the Chan tradition to illustrate his philosophical methodology of "transcending" (*chaoyue* 超越). We can find this theme in the English translations of Fung's works. He writes, "I would say that the craving for something beyond the present actual world is one of the innate desires of mankind, and the Chinese people are no exception to this rule. . . . [The function of Chinese philosophy is] the elevation of the mind—a reaching out for what is beyond the present actual world, and for the values that are higher than the moral ones."[73] Then Fung criticizes Buddhism for requiring people to renounce the family life, study precepts, and do meditation, a lifestyle he claims to be inferior to that of the Confucian who serves as a moral paragon and carries out his worldly responsibilities.

In reply, Taixu remarks that Buddhism does not require this of anybody, and cites a passage from Dahui.[74] Dahui names three lay scholar-officials who had either attained enlightenment or gained a true understanding of Chan. Dahui then asks, "If they had given up their wives and children and quit their positions in order to be vegetarian and do austerities that weakened their body and mind, if they avoided excitement in favor of quietude, and ended up obsessing over their thoughts doing dry meditation in a 'ghost cave,' would they have become enlightened?"[75]

Taixu ends this section, which concludes his history of Chan, with an implicit challenge. Historically, he remarks, Confucians who compile and study Chan recorded sayings have generally been unable to cross the threshold of Chan. Most have only attained the level of Hanyue Fazang before his enlightenment. After a period of study, Hanyue said, "According to ancient books and Buddhism, one must begin one's seeking in a place beyond language. This is verified by the Four Books and Five Classics. One day I was disappointed to make the following realization: I have asked myself if I understand things in Chan—and I do. I can also explain them. But one thing is missing: liberation from samsara."[76] Then according to the text, Hanyue stopped what he was doing and did *huatou* practice for several years, after which he attained great enlightenment. This passage, in contrast with Dahui's, provides a model for readers interested in a more monastic lifestyle.

Taixu concludes his work by saying, "The key to studying recorded sayings lies in the hard work of investigating them to attain enlightenment. If your study only allows rational explanations, you will be far from the mark."[77]

Conclusion

Three factors contribute to Taixu's decision to include Chan as an explicit component of his program of Humanistic Buddhism. The first is Tibetan Buddhism. Ten years before his *Chinese Buddhist Learning*, in 1934, Taixu had identified Chan and Tantra as the "twin peaks" among all Buddhist traditions, suggesting that both are equally viable for people interested in Buddhism.[78] But the present work adds a cultural perspective: Chinese culture shaped Chan and continues to be suited to Chan. An earlier statement reflects this: "If Chinese Buddhism is going to be revived, it will be through Chan rather than Tantra or Yogācāra."[79] Despite evidence that Taixu saw Chan as being in a competitive relationship with Tantra, I cannot but wonder if Taixu was heartened by his exposure to Chinese intellectuals interested in tantric Buddhism while in Chongqing. In contrast to figures like Hu Shih and Fung Yu-lan, these intellectuals would have embraced Buddhist practice. The possibility that Chan could play the same role as Tantra for Chinese intellectuals is reflected in Taixu's call to construct Chinese Buddhism after the Gelugpa model, but with Chan rather than Tantra at the top. In other words, underlying the competition was a flourishing that benefited both traditions. Taixu's *Chinese Buddhist Learning* represents Taixu's hope for the future of the Chan tradition.

The second factor is Hu Shih. Although Taixu does not mention him at all, it is clear that he is responding to Hu's work. As John McRae remarks, Hu's studies of Shenhui were "a major stimulus in the emergence of an international field of Zen and Ch'an studies."[80] Growing scholarly interest in Chan is one factor in Taixu's decision to bring Chan into Humanistic Buddhism.

The third factor lay in the ambiguity of Chan's future. Chan's state of affairs warranted new efforts to inspire interest in the Chan tradition. For Taixu, continuity in the Chan tradition is maintained by the living tradition of *huatou* practice, which includes the creation of new *huatous*, and the preservation of all five houses. This requires the existence of Chan monasteries dedicated to Chan practice and study, where the clergy are not called upon to do extra rituals. In addition, Chan's identity was closely related to literati involvement. Taixu hoped to create not just a passing fascination but also a long-term engagement with its core texts and practices. His call for scholars to study and compile texts on the model of the *Zhiyue lu* served four purposes. First, intellectuals would increase their exposure to the Chan tradition. Second, they might begin to understand their own lives in terms of the Chan religious path. Taixu did not explicitly call for his audience to seek out Chan masters, but this could be one effect. Third, it would inspire Buddhist clergy to increase their intellectual sophistication, either by relying on his work as a teaching guide or by doing their own research. Fourth, it would help bring Chan into the rapidly growing realm of intellectual discourse. As Taixu remarked in the beginning of his second chapter, intellectuals (or literati) were a key force in shaping the Chan tradition. As he looked to the future, he hoped they would continue to make important contributions.

Notes

1. John Makeham, ed., *Transforming Consciousness: Yogācāra Thought in Modern China* (New York: Oxford University Press, 2014).

2. Holmes Welch, *The Practice of Chinese Buddhism, 1900–1950* (Cambridge, MA: Harvard University Press, 1973), 47.

3. For an introduction to Taixu's Humanistic Buddhism, see the subsection entitled "Humanistic Buddhism," in Eric Goodell, "Taixu," *Oxford Research Encyclopedia of Religion*, (accessed April 24, 2022) https://oxfordre.com/religion/view/10.1093/acrefore/9780199340378.001.0001/acrefore-9780199340378-e-1018.

4. Taixu, *Zhongguo foxue* 中國佛學 (Chinese Buddhist learning), TDQ 2:531–760, in *Taixu dashi quanshu* 太虛大師全書 (Collected works of Master Taixu), 32 vols., ed. Yinshun (Taipei: Shandao si, 1980). Abbreviated as TDQ. "Learning"

is a translation of *xue* 學, a general term in Chinese indicating a pedagogically structured body of knowledge, for example in "Confucian learning" or "Western learning." It signals that Taixu intends his work for a well-educated audience.

5. Eric Goodell, "Taixu's Youth and Years of Romantic Idealism, 1890–1914," *Chung-Hwa Buddhist Journal* 21 (2008): 91–93.

6. Justin Ritzinger, *Anarchy in the Pure Land: Reinventing the Cult of Maitreya in Modern Chinese Buddhism* (New York: Oxford University Press, 2017), chap. 3.

7. Taixu, "Fuotuoxue gang" 佛陀學綱 (An outline of Buddhology), TDQ 1:250; TDQ 3:208–209.

8. Taixu, "Jiren chengfo de zhen xianshi lun" 即人成佛的真現實論 [True realism: Buddhahood in this very life], TDQ 24, 462–463.

9. For example Abe Chōichi 阿部肇一, *Chūgoku zenshūshi no kenkyū* 中國禪宗史の研究 [A history of the Chan school in China], rev. ed. (Tokyo: Seishin shobō, 1987) ends in the Song. A notable exception in the form of a micro history is Jiang Wu, *Enlightenment in Dispute* (New York: Oxford University Press, 2008).

10. Jan Yün-hua, *Zhongguo chanxue yanjiu lunji* 中國禪學研究論集 [Studies in Chinese Chan] (Taipei: Dongchu, 1990), 2.

11. Taixu, *Zhongguo foxue*, 551–52.

12. Taixu, *Zhongguo foxue*, 553.

13. Taixu, *Zhongguo foxue*, 564, citing Daoxuan, *Xu gaoseng zhuan* 續高僧傳, CBETA T50.2060.597b7–15.

14. Hu, "Zhongguo chanxue de fazhan" 中國禪學的發展 (The development of Chan learning in China), in *Hu Shi wenji* 胡適文集, vol. 12, ed. Ouyang Zhesheng (Beijing: Peking University Press, 1998), 311–12. This is the Chinese version of his 1932 English article, "Development of Zen Buddhism in China," in *English Writings of Hu Shih*, vol. 2, ed. Chih-p'ing Chou and Hu Shih (New York: Springer, 2013), 109–121. Hu would have encountered this idea in Nukariya Kaiten's 忽滑谷快天 1925 history of Chan Buddhism (*Zengaku shisōshi* 禪學思想史), which Hu mentions in his introduction, 301.

15. Hu, "Zhongguo chanxue de fazhan," 317 and 332.

16. Hu, "Zhongguo chanxue de fazhan," 312–13; "Development of Zen Buddhism in China," 107.

17. Taixu, *Zhongguo foxue*, 567.

18. Taixu, *Zhongguo foxue*, 566–69.

19. Zongmi, *Chanyuan zhuquanjidu xu* 禪源諸詮集都序 [Chan preface], CBETA T48.2015.399b16–19.

20. Taixu, *Zhongguo foxue*, 588.

21. Taixu, *Zhongguo foxue*, 588.

22. From *Chixiu Baizhang qinggui* 敕修百丈清規, CBETA T48.2025.1158a9.

23. Taixu, *Zhongguo foxue*, 599. For a historical analysis of Baizhang and the Pure Regulations, see T. Griffith Foulk, "*Chanyuan qinggui* and Other 'Rules

of Purity' in Chinese Buddhism," in *The Zen Canon: Understanding the Classic Texts,* ed. Steven Heine and Dale S. Wright (New York: Oxford University Press, 2004), 280–83, 307.

24. The five highest yoga tantras 五大金剛 in the Gelugpa tradition are the *guhyasamāja* 集密 (or 密集), *yamāntaka* 大威德, *hevajra* 歡喜, *cakrasaṃvara* 勝樂, and *kālacakra* 時輪 tantras.

25. Taixu, *Zhongguo foxue,* 618.

26. Brenton Sullivan, "Venerable Fazun at the Sino-Tibetan Buddhist Institute (1932–1950) and Tibetan Geluk Buddhism in China," *Indian International Journal of Buddhist Studies* 9 (2008): 210–13.

27. Taixu, *Zhongguo foxue,* 588.

28. *Qiongjue laoren tianqi zhizhu xuedouxian heshang songgu* 聱絕老人天奇直註雪竇顯和尚頌古, CBETA X67.1302.255a5–6. For a fuller historical analysis, see Griffith Foulk, "The Form and Function of Koan Literature: An Overview," in *The Koan: Texts and Contexts in Zen Buddhism,* ed. Steven Heine and Dale S. Wright (New York: Oxford University Press, 2000), 26–33.

29. This text is not found in the Taishō canon. Extant versions are found in the Gozan collection and the Taiwan National Library. See Yi-hsun Huang, *Xuedou qiji zhi yanjiu* 雪竇七集之研究 [A study of Xuedou's seven works] (Taipei: Fagu wenhua, 2015), 209.

30. See for example *Zongmen niangu huiji* 宗門拈古彙集, CBETA X66.1296.7b19–8a20, which lists twenty-three other comments after Yunmen's.

31. Taixu, *Zhongguo foxue,* 652.

32. Taixu's quotation abridges the full passage in *Xu zhiyue lu* 續指月錄, CBETA X84.1579.112b11–c2.

33. This is described in section 2.1, *Zhongguo foxue,* 555.

34. On Daoan and the Maitreya cult, see Kenneth Ch'en, *Buddhism in China* (Princeton, NJ: Princeton University Press, 1973), 99.

35. Taixu, *Zhongguo foxue,* 558.

36. Taixu is probably referring to his *Sanshi xinian yijie* 三時繫念儀範, X74.1465.

37. Weize, dharma heir of Zhongfeng Mingben, wrote *Jingtu huowen* 淨土或問 [Questions on the Pure Land], T74.1972.

38. See Chün-fang Yü's excellent study, *The Renewal of Buddhism in China: Chu-Hung and the Late Ming Synthesis* (New York: Columbia University Press, 2021).

39. Chewu is also recognized as a twelfth patriarch in the Pure Land lineage.

40. Technically they are both aspects of realization: 二種宗法相. See *Dasheng ru lengqie jing* 大乘入楞伽經, CBETA T16.672.609a20–21.

41. *Dasheng ru lengqie jing* 大乘入楞伽經, 609a20–28; For Suzuki's translation of the Sanskrit text, see *The Lankavatara Sutra* (London: Routledge and Kegan Paul, 1956), 128.

42. Taixu, *Zhongguo foxue,* 657.

43. Jennifer Eichman, *A Late Sixteenth-Century Chinese Buddhist Fellowship: Spiritual Ambitions, Intellectual Debates, and Epistolary Connections* (Leiden and Boston: Brill, 2016), 303. Red Pine's translation of the *Laṅkāvatāra sūtra* makes particular usage of Zeng Fengyi's commentary. Red Pine, *The Lankavatara Sutra: A Zen Text* (Berkeley: Counterpoint, 2012), 296.

44. Taixu, *Zhongguo foxue*, 659.

45. According to Chün-fang Yü, Ming Taizu only had three categories for monasteries: *chan, jiang*, and *jiao*. See her "Buddhism in the Ming Dynasty," chap. 14 in vol. 8 of *The Cambridge History of China*, edited by Dennis Twitchett and Frederick Mote (Cambridge and New York: Cambridge University Press, 1998), 906.

46. See for example *Guzun suyu lu* 古尊宿語錄, CBETA X68.1315.296a6–14.

47. This adage is from Yunmen's *Guanglu* 雲門匡真禪師廣錄, CBETA T47.1988.554b22–23. Yunmen lived before the silent illumination controversy.

48. For a more sophisticated discussion of the intended target of Kewen's critiques, see Morten Schlütter, *How Zen Became Zen* (Honolulu: University of Hawai'i Press, 2008), 138–39. On Dahui's critique, see pp. 125–26.

49. Wu, *Enlightenment in Dispute*, 60–61; for more on Qu, see p. 365.

50. Goodell, "Taixu's Youth and Years of Romantic Idealism," 92.

51. Taixu, *Zhongguo foxue*, 663.

52. Taixu, *Zhongguo foxue*, 663–64. This appears to be a reference to the *Zhiyue lu* 指月錄, CBETA X83.1578.677b10–c20, which identifies Huanglong's three questions as three stages or levels of understanding (*guan*); also compare with Huanglong's recorded sayings, CBETA T47.1993.636c16–20.

53. Taixu, *Zhongguo foxue*, 664. See also *Yuxuan yulu* 御選語錄, CBETA X68.1319.714a9–12.

54. My translation is from Taixu, *Zhongguo foxue*, 664–65, which has some differences from the original passage in *Yuxuan yulu*, 523c11–524a1. The ellipses in these passages are also found in Taixu's text. For the first and second stages, I have relied on the translation in Jiang Wu, *Enlightenment in Dispute*, 169–70, but with modifications.

55. Taixu emends Yongzheng's text, which reads, "every single thing is myself; no single thing is my self." In a 1945 talk two years later, Taixu places the Dharmakaya in the third stage (TDQ 28:499, "Jueyuan ying wei xiu qijue zhi yuan" 覺苑應為修七覺之苑).

56. "Zhongguo chanxue de fazhan," 328–332. The English version only discusses two stages on pp. 120–121. The five-stage version is similar to the version in Hu's 1953 article, "Ch'an (Zen) Buddhism in China: Its History and Method."

57. The full quote is discussed in Taixu's introduction.

58. *Tianhui che chanshi yulu* 天慧徹禪師語錄, ed. Jisheng 際聖 (1906, held at Inner Mongolia Library), fasc. 2, 65–66.

59. The biography in *Zhengyuan lüeji* 正源略集, cited by the *Foguang dacidian*, also contains nothing about this incident, CBETA X85.1587.87a17–c3.

60. Laiguo 來果, *Gaomin si guiyue* 高旻寺規約 (Rules and regulations for Gaomin si), CBETA B18.98.415b2–4. A twentieth-century biography makes no mention of this episode. See *Xin xugaosengzhuan* 新續高僧傳, CBETA B27.151.218b8–219a7.

61. This was composed by Xiangfu Jiyin 祥符紀蔭, who belonged to the Sanfeng lineage founded by Hanyue. The text is a history of the Chan school starting with Śākyamuni, then going through the Indian and Chinese patriarchs. The final two fascicles include important events in Buddhist history from 1615–1689.

62. Jiyin, *Zongtong biannian* 宗統編年, CBETA X86.1600.290c16–291a4.

63. Jiyin, *Zongtong biannian*, 298b7–8.

64. Jiyin, *Zongtong biannian*, 316b18–c2; Taixu, *Zhongguo foxue*, 668–69.

65. Hanyue's *Wuzong yuan* 五宗源 (X69.1279) is a treatise on the five houses of Chan. Several newly discovered texts composed by Hanyue have been studied in Yi-hsun Huang 黃繹勳, *Hanyue Fazang chanshi zhenxi wenxian xuanji 1* 漢月法藏禪師珍稀文獻選輯(一) (Kaohsiung: Foguang wenhua, 2019).

66. I have emended 大雪 to 丈雪.

67. Welch, "Dharma Scrolls and the Succession of Abbots in Chinese Monasteries," T'oung-pao 50, 1–3 (1963): 93–149.

68. *Yuxuan yulu*, 528c7–532a12.

69. This is found under the biography of Huanglong in the Qing dynasty work *Bu xu gaoseng zhuan* 補續高僧傳, CBETA X77.1524.405b6–14.

70. Taixu's text omits the bracketed passage.

71. Taixu, *Zhongguo foxue*, 672–73.

72. Li Ao, *Fu xing shu* 復性書, in the *Zibu* 子部 section of the *Siku quanshu*.

73. Fung Yu-lan, *A Short History of Chinese Philosophy*, edited by Derk Bodde (New York: Free Press, 1948), 4 and 5.

74. Taixu, *Zhongguo foxue*, 676–77.

75. *Zhiyue lu*, CBETA X83.1578.738c12–17; Taixu, *Zhongguo foxue*, 676. Taixu's text has minor differences from the *Zhiyue lu*.

76. *Xu zhiyue lu*, 132b18–21. This differs in many ways from the account in Hanyue's chronological biography in *Sanfeng Zang heshang yulu* 三峰藏和尚語錄, CBETA J34.B299.204c1ff.

77. Taixu, *Zhongguo foxue*, 678.

78. "Fofa yiweilun zhi shizong pianmian guan" 佛法一味論之十宗片面觀, TDQ 1:344.

79. "Ping Baoming jun Zhongguo Fojiao zhi xianshi" 評寶明君中國佛教之現勢, TDQ 25:103.

80. John McRae, "Religion as Revolution in Chinese Historiography: Hu Shih (1891–1962) on Shen-hui (684–758)," *Cahiers d'Extrême-Asie* 12 (2001): 61–62.

Chapter 12

Zen Internationalism, Zen Revolution

Inoue Shūten, Uchiyama Gudō, and the Crisis of (Zen) Buddhist Modernity in Late Meiji Japan

JAMES MARK SHIELDS

Introduction

In his foreword to Paul Carus's *Gospel of Buddhism* (1894), Donald Lopez Jr. provides a summary of the essential features of "modern Buddhism":[1]

> Modern Buddhism seeks to distance itself from those forms of Buddhism that immediately precede it and even those that are contemporary with it. Its proponents viewed ancient Buddhism, especially the enlightenment of the Buddha 2,500 years ago, as the most authentic moment in the long history of Buddhism. It is also the form of Buddhism, they would argue, that is most compatible with the ideals of the European Enlightenment, ideals such as reason, empiricism, science, universalism, individualism, tolerance, freedom, and the rejection of religious orthodoxy. It stresses equality over hierarchy, the universal over the local, and often exalts the individual over the community.[2]

While Lopez's understanding of modern Buddhism clearly resonates with the work of a great number of Asian and Western Buddhist reformers, from Anagarika Dharmapala (1864–1934) through B. R. Ambedkar (1891–1956) to Stephen Batchelor, in a Japanese context it is in fact more reflective of the early period of Buddhist modernism—characterized by the figures of the so-called Buddhist Enlightenment, including Inoue Enryō (井上円了, 1858–1919) and Kiyozawa Manshi (清沢満之, 1863–1903)—than of the middle and late periods as represented by the more politically progressive and doctrinally experimental New Buddhist Fellowship and Youth League for Revitalizing Buddhism, respectively. This is especially true of Lopez's final feature: the exaltation of the individual over the community.

Here, Juliane Schober's more recent remarks are pertinent:

> Many theorists writing on modernity and civil society presume that the western model of religion in modern, civil society applies equally to non-western cultures and their religious traditions. Yet modernizing reforms of religion do not inevitably engender individualism, a Protestant ethnic [sic], the development of capitalism, and the relegation of religion to the private sphere.[3]

In fact, religious modernism in Asia (and perhaps elsewhere) seems to lead to a "maximalist" understanding, in which religion is "the central domain of culture, [and] deeply involved in ethical and aesthetic practices constitutive of the community," in contrast to a "minimalist" approach, whereby religion is restricted, in Weberian and archetypically "modern" fashion, "to the private sphere and metaphysical concerns."[4] It goes without saying that the minimalist approach is well-suited to liberal understandings of the separation of "church and state" as well as—if somewhat less evidently—neoliberal capitalist injunctions to self-define through production and consumption (i.e., work and leisure). The "maximalist" perspective is, on the other hand, resonant with both conservative (especially fascist) views and those of the far left, which either dismiss religion or subsume it within broader categories of feeling and behavior. It is certainly the case that in Japan, this expansion/dissolution of the religious *imaginaire* was true of both "reactionary" and "progressive" modernisms. In short, we might say that while Lopez's summary applies, to some extent, to all forms of Buddhist modernism, it remains heavily inflected with assumptions that are more specifically germane to Buddhist modernism as constructed by Western Buddhists—and thus we must be cautious in applying it to "indigenous" forms of Buddhist modernism (while acknowledging that all forms of Buddhist modernism are, to some extent, "hybrid").

With this important caveat in mind, this chapter examines the lives and thought of two rather different radical Buddhists of late Meiji Japan, both of whom were affiliated with the Zen tradition, in order to discern whether and in what ways their progressive political ideals were influenced by Chan/Zen thought and practice. It will also contextualize progressive Zen thought within contemporary debates, particularly the lay-oriented Zen modernism emerging at the same time in the line that runs from Imakita Kōsen (今北洪川, 1816–1892) through Shaku Sōen (釋宗演, 1860–1919) to D. T. Suzuki (aka Suzuki Daisetsu 鈴木大拙, 1870–1966).

The New Buddhist Fellowship

The best example of an early and "moderate" form of Buddhist modernism in Japan is the New Buddhist Fellowship (J. Shin Bukkyō Dōmei, 新仏教同盟; hereafter, NBF). Established in 1899, in the wake of the first Sino-Japanese War and the emergence of new social forces and contradictions brought on by several decades of Westernization as well as industrial capitalism, the NBF was made up of a dozen young scholars and activists, many of whom had studied under Buddhist Enlightenment figures Murakami Senshō and Inoue Enryō.[5] The New Buddhists were fiercely critical of the "old Buddhism," which they believed had been complicit in the conservative forces that had thus far inhibited progress in Japan, particularly in the areas of education and ethics. While the fellowship was overtly lay-oriented, several of the New Buddhists had been ordained as Buddhist priests, and most had some sort of Buddhist educational background, especially via the Nishi Honganji branch of the Shin (Pure Land) sect. Although he spent a large part of the period of the NBF's existence abroad in the United States, one member of the group would come to have tremendous influence on postwar Zen: Suzuki Teitarō (Daisetsu), known to the West as D. T. Suzuki.

While many of the New Buddhists were, like the young Suzuki, moderately liberal in their political views, the final few years of the journal reveal an increasing attention to the thought and practice of socialism. In addition, these years saw contributions to the journal from many of the leading radicals of the day, including Kōtoku Shūsui (幸徳秋水, 1871–1911), Sakai Toshihiko (堺利彦, 1871–1933), Ishikawa Sanshirō (石川三四郎, 1876–1956), and Shirayanagi Shūko (白柳秀湖, 1884–1950). Of all the New Buddhists, those who were sympathetic to socialist thinking were Takashima Beihō (高嶋米峰, 1875–1949), Mōri Saian (毛利柴庵, 1872–1938), Sugimura Sojinkan (杉村楚人冠, 1872–1945), and Inoue Shūten.[6] Of these, Inoue most strongly identified with the Zen tradition and thus provides the first of our two cases of "progressive Zen modernism."

Inoue Shūten: Buddhism, Socialism, and Pacifism

Born in 1880 into a merchant family in Tottori prefecture, Inoue was sent to Sōtō Zen temple at the age of nine.[7] After learning English at a young age from American missionaries, in 1895, while most of his eventual New Buddhist confreres were gravitating toward Inoue Enryō's Tetsugakkan (哲学館), he entered Sōtōshū Daigakurin (曹洞宗大学林; today, Komazawa University), beginning a course of study in Indian philosophy under the direction of Riku Etsugan (陸鉞巖, dates unknown), with whom he soon undertook an extensive series of travels throughout south China, Ceylon, Burma, and India. In 1903 he published his journal of these experiences, entitled *Conditions in India* (J. *Indo jijō*, 印度事情). While in Ceylon, Inoue met with Sinhalese Buddhist reformer Anagarika Dharmapala. After a brief stint serving as an army interpreter at the outbreak of the Russo-Japanese War (from which he was discharged due to tuberculosis), he took a teaching position at a Christian women's university, Kobe College. This was the same period (1905) in which he joined the New Buddhist Fellowship. In later years, Inoue would be employed by both the American and British consulates-general and helped to translate several books written by British diplomats on Japanese religions.

Like his fellow NBF travelers Watanabe Kaikyoku (渡辺海旭, 1872–1933) and Suzuki Daisetsu, Inoue's thought and activities drew heavily on his experiences abroad, but whereas Watanabe and Suzuki spent most of their time in Western Christian countries (Germany and the United States, respectively), Inoue visited primarily Buddhist nations in East, South, and Southeast Asia. These travels, in concert with his studies under Riku, led to a sustained interest in Theravāda Buddhist traditions and particularly the virtue of *ahimsa* or nonviolence, which would become foundational to his lifelong commitment to pacifism.[8]

While Inoue's pacifism thus appears to be rooted in a combined personal and academic interest in South and Southeast Asian Buddhist traditions, it was bolstered by the writings of the fledgling socialist movement, which by the time of the Russo-Japanese War had become virtually the only antiwar voice remaining in Japan. In 1906, not long after joining the NBF, Inoue became a member of a socialist organization, the Kobe People's Club (J. Heimin Kurabu, 神戸平民倶楽部). Through this affiliation he would become well connected to various radicals, establishing personal contact with Taixu (太虚, 1890–1945), the well-known Chinese Buddhist reformer (and erstwhile anarchist sympathizer), as well as Uchiyama Gudō, the Zen monk who was arrested and executed in 1911 for his alleged role in the plot to assassinate the Meiji emperor known as the "High Treason Incident" (J. Taigyaku jiken, 大逆事件). As a result, Inoue was classified as a key witness regarding the incident and was, along with the other New Buddhists, put under government surveillance for a period.[9]

In his writings, Inoue is strongly critical of late Meiji and Taishō government policy, particularly what he viewed as Japanese imperial aggression in Asia. At the same time, he denounces the emergence of so-called Imperial Way Buddhism, associated especially with the Zen sect, but emerging as the dominant way of thinking about the ideal relationship between Buddhism and the modern Japanese state. This would lead Inoue to criticize fellow New Buddhist Suzuki Daisetsu, who, in his acceptance of the necessity of state censorship and allowance that Buddhists could be effective soldiers, arguably helped pave the way for the spread of Imperial Way Buddhism in the succeeding decades.[10] While it is beyond the scope of this chapter to examine Imperial Way Buddhism or Suzuki's role in its development (following, it is often argued, the lead of his mentor Shaku Sōen), the growing split between progressive Buddhists like Inoue and those like Suzuki who, while also adhering to modernist ideals and frequently espousing liberal and even socialist principles, were far more supportive of the emerging imperialist ideology, bears our attention. In the case of Inoue, at least, it seems clear that in addition to studies of principles such as *ahimsa* in Theravāda Buddhism, his personal experience of war played a significant role in his unwavering commitment to a pacifist stance. As Moriya Tomoe writes: "Unlike Suzuki's abstract notions of warfare and the 'spiritual' soldier, Inoue critically reports the cruelty and lack of spirituality among military officers as well as the fallacies of politicians during the Russo-Japanese War."[11] In addition, however, an argument can be made that Inoue shared a more properly "maximalist" understanding of Buddhism that transcended not only sectarian distinctions but the lines between religion, philosophy, morality, and politics.

The most representative of Inoue's essays is "Ordinary, Extreme Pacifism" (J. "Heibon kiwamaru heiwaron," 平凡極まる平和論), published in the December 1911 edition of *New Buddhism* (J. *Shin bukkyō*, 新仏教), in the immediate aftermath of the High Treason Incident. After noting the difficulties of advocating for peace during times of conflict, amid heightened feelings of nationalism (as anyone doing so is quickly labeled a "socialist" or "anarchist"), Inoue provides his own view of war:

> No matter what name is given to it, war is the greatest sin (J. *mujō no zaiaku*, 無上の罪悪). If we were to euphemize war by placing upon it the crown of righteousness, then we might as well praise a whore for her chastity. Since the act of war is an evil vocation in and of itself, we have no need to distinguish between just and unjust wars on the basis of such things as objectives or intentions. That is to say, the inhumane (J. *fujin*, 不仁) act of war, with its massacres and carnage—performed only to make a profit—is in fact millions of miles removed from the path of humanity (J. *jindō*, 人道).[12]

These remarks show that Inoue's pacifism emerges from a moral, religious, or humanist ideal rather than a purely pragmatic or utilitarian one—a perspective that distinguishes him from the well-known American Unitarian pacifist (and eugenicist) David Starr Jordan (1851–1931), the so-called Doctor of Peace (J. *heiwa no hakase*, 平和の博士) who plays the role of a foil for Inoue in this essay. Jordan was well known for the argument that warfare causes literal, physical "degeneration" among the citizens of a militaristic nation. While agreeing that war does cause "decay" in the "nobility" (J. *seiei*, 精英) of a nation's people, Inoue charges Jordan with "superficiality" on this point: "It is not the fact that warfare robs a nation of its nobility that makes war evil. War would still be evil even if it did not have that effect."[13] And yet, despite the clear moral grounds, Inoue here fails to situate his moral critique of warfare in specific Buddhist ideas or doctrines. The closest he comes is to argue in the conclusion that "peace" is, in fact, the final goal of all religion and that any pacifist theory that does not root itself in religion is of little value to the real world.[14] In fact, while Inoue does make an explicit call for Buddhist monks, along with Christian priests, to join his peace crusade, the only "religious" ideas he cites are from the Confucian tradition: a passing reference to *jin* (仁), benevolence or humaneness; and an extended quote from Mencius on the connection of war to a mindset focused on profit rather than virtue.[15]

At the same time, beyond the perceptive and quasi-Marxist understanding of the intricate connection between war and an expansionist economy, the most striking aspect of Inoue's argument for "extreme pacifism" is his "universalist" (i.e., explicitly anti-imperialist and antinationalist) conception of human brotherhood, one he insists is shared by both Buddhism and Christianity (not to mention most modern anarchists and socialists). As Moriya has argued, Inoue utilizes religion in a critical capacity; his "harsh criticism of structural injustice shows that he considered the existing socio-political authority as secondary to the Buddhist teachings."[16] Once again, this distinguished him from Suzuki, who had by this time begun to formulate an understanding, akin to that of Shin sect reformer Kiyozawa Manshi, of religious experience that leaves little room for a distinction between religion and "reality"—and thus allows little space for criticism.[17] This raises the question of the limits to "maximalism"—one that seems to have political resonance. In short, if a maximalist understanding is pushed toward a metaphysical monism, it becomes very difficult to critical perspective on the actions of individuals or groups, let alone construct a politics of resistance. Inoue, like most of the New Buddhists and all later Buddhist progressives, did not extend their maximalism toward what more recent Critical Buddhists would call "totalism," a religio-philosophical stance that *assumes* a fundamental harmony or unity that is often manifested in the nation-state. Along these lines, it is surely no coincidence that the very issue of New Buddhism in which Inoue's above article appeared was one of those banned by the government.[18]

Uchiyama Gudō: Self-Awakening to Freedom

Of all the radical Buddhists of the prewar era, Sōtō Zen priest Uchiyama Gudō (内山愚童, 1874–1911) is probably the best known in the West, not least because he is discussed as the most striking exception to the rule of Zen collaboration with twentieth-century militarism in Brian Victoria's *Zen at War* (1997).[19] Among Japanese scholars, too, Uchiyama's case has long fascinated, due both to its tragic ending and, one suspects, to the character of the protagonist, who seemed well suited to the role of heroic martyr.[20]

Born in 1874 in the village of Ojiya, Niigata prefecture, in his youth Uchiyama apprenticed to his father as a carver of wooden statues, including Buddha statues and family altars. A bright student, he showed an early indication of his later political leanings by identifying strongly with the semilegendary tale of Sakura Sōgorō (佐倉惣五郎; also known as Sōgo-sama 佐倉様, 1605–1653), the early Edo-period "martyr" who was executed after appealing to the shogun for help to ease the hardship of the peasants in his village.[21] Indeed, the area in which Uchiyama was raised (former Echigo province) had a long tradition of rural poverty, as well as a deeply ingrained tradition of peasant revolt.[22] Upon the death of his father in 1890, Uchiyama set off on a series of travels throughout the country, looking to further his education, which had been cut short at the elementary level. He spent some time in Tokyo, where he may have stayed at the house of Inoue Enryō, the Meiji Buddhist Enlightenment reformer who was a distant relative of Uchiyama's mother.[23]

While Inoue Shūten was undergoing a course of study that would lead him to South and Southeast Asia, in 1897 Uchiyama ordained as a Sōtō Zen monk. Achieving the rank of abbot in 1904 at the age of twenty-nine, he took up the position of head monk at Rinsenji (林泉寺), a temple in the mountains of Hakone, Kanagawa prefecture, where he immediately focused his attention on helping his mostly poor parishioners. It was at this time that Uchiyama began to develop his ideas about Buddhist social organization, looking back to an idealized Chinese Chan sangha as a model of simplicity and communal lifestyle.[24] Around the same time, Uchiyama encountered the anarchist and socialist ideas that were beginning to spread on the eve of the Russo-Japanese War. In particular, he was inspired by the ideology of the left-wing *People's Paper* (J. *Heimin shimbun* 平民新聞), to which he contributed his own declaration of principles in a piece entitled "How Did I Become a Socialist?" which was published in the January 17, 1904 issue. In this brief essay, citing various Buddhist texts, including the *Diamond Sutra* and *Lotus Sutra*, Uchiyama insists on a fundamental link between (Mahāyāna) Buddhist teachings and socialism.

Through his contact with the *People's Paper* and his acquaintance with Dr. Katō Tokijirō (加藤時次郎, 1858–1930), chief editor of the short-lived but influential *Straight Talk* (J. *Chokugen*, 直言) newspaper, Uchiyama was introduced to leading socialists Kōtoku Shūsui and Sakai Toshihiko. In the five-year period between 1901, when the first socialist party was established in Japan, to 1906, when the Japan Socialist Party (J. *Nihon Shakaitō*, 日本社会党) was founded, socialists had gained considerable public support, due in no small part to their firm antiwar stance during the Russo-Japanese War. Despite, or perhaps because of this growth in support, the factions within the broader progressive movement were growing stronger, represented by Abe Isoo (阿部磯雄, 1865–1949) and Katayama Sen (片山潜, 1859–1933) in the Christian, "idealist" and more reform-minded faction (J. *gikai seisakuha*, 議会政策派) on the one hand, and Kōtoku and Sakai in the antireligious, materialist, and more openly revolutionary—but also more abstract and intellectual—wing (J. *chokusetsu kōdōha*, 直接行動派).[25] Despite being a religionist with close ties to poor farmers, Uchiyama sympathized more strongly with the Kōtoku faction. Facing pressure from the government crackdown on left-wing movements following the Red Flag Incident (J. *Akahata Jiken*, 赤旗事件) in June 1908, he purchased equipment to set up his own underground press within Rinsenji (under the altar of *shumidan*, 須弥壇), with which he produced socialist pamphlets and tracts in addition to his own writings. As a result, in May 1909 he was arrested for violating publication laws, and, upon a search of Rinsenji, police claimed to have discovered a cache of materials used to make explosive devices. Implicated, along with twenty-five others, in the Kōtoku or High Treason Incident, Uchiyama was convicted and executed on January 24, 1911. According to witnesses, he was serene and even smiling as he climbed the scaffold.

Uchiyama's priestly status was rescinded by the Sōtō Zen leadership in June 1910, five months after his death, and the sect took great pains to distance themselves from Uchiyama and his ideas, organizing a series of meetings in the months following the renegade priest's death in which over one hundred Sōtō sect leaders, government administrators, and prominent intellectuals (including Inoue Tetsujirō, 井上哲次郎) denounced both the man and his work, pledging themselves to the principle of "revere the Emperor, protect the nation" (J. *sonnō gokoku*, 尊皇護国).[26] This decision was eventually reversed and an apology issued by the organization—eight decades later, in 1993.

Off all four Buddhist priests convicted in the High Treason Incident, Uchiyama was the most actively involved in "subversive" (i.e., socialist and antigovernmental) activities—thus his punishment was harsher than the others. Moreover, he left behind more writings on his beliefs than they did. Unlike Suzuki, Inoue, and many of the New Buddhist Fellowship, Uchiyama was not a scholar of Buddhism, sociology, politics, or economic theory. Yet, like his Buddhist modernist contemporaries and epigones, Uchiyama struggled to establish doctrinal links and reinterpretations of Buddhist teachings to suit the perceived needs of his times.[27] Here I turn to a brief analysis of two representative works by Uchiyama: *In Commemoration of*

Imprisonment: Anarcho-communist Revolution (J. *Nyūgoku kinen museifu kyōsan kakumei*, 入獄紀念・無政府共產・革命) and *Ordinary Self-awakening* (J. *Heibon no jikaku*, 平凡の自覚).

Anarcho-communist Revolution was the first work published by Uchiyama's secret press. Uchiyama made a thousand copies, which were distributed throughout Japan. It was this work, more than any other, that would lead to his arrest and implication in the High Treason Incident. Regardless of Uchiyama's direct involvement, the tract apparently inspired Miyashita Takichi (宮下太吉, 1875–1911), one of the apparent ringleaders of the High Treason Incident, to carry out his plans.[28]

The main theme of the pamphlet is the problem of rural poverty, a central concern of Uchiyama's work. While this was also a problem addressed by some of the New Buddhists—including Inoue Shūten—the difference in both the tone and the structure of the argument quickly become apparent, as Uchiyama moves quickly into a scathing critique of the economic and political system, given that it allows for a very few to monopolize the labor of the vast majority, who work with no hope of reward. The subtitle *Why do Tenant Farmers Suffer?* (J. *Kosakunin wa naze kurushiika*, 小作人ハナゼ苦シイカ) indicates the implicit connections between Uchiyama's chosen theme and his Buddhist commitments. As a Buddhist, he felt compelled to seek the causes and conditions of suffering in order to eliminate them by whatever means necessary.

What were these conditions? Marius Jansen gives the following account of the life of a typical tenant farmer during the Edo period—circumstances that despite the Meiji Restoration and incipient industrialization, had changed little by Uchiyama's time:

> The tenant . . . shared few of the public rights and the duties of his landlord, and he lived under severe economic dependence. His plot was usually too small to give him the opportunity of accumulating anything, and the house in which he lived, and the tools he used, were probably not his own. Paternalism, vital for his life, was expressed in language, deportment, and deference summed up in his status as *mizunomi*, or "water drinking," farmer. The landlord was his "parent person," *oya-kata*, and he the landlord's *kokata* or child.[29]

Here we see that the suffering of tenant farmers was both material and psychological—as they were reduced to near total dependence on their *oya-kata* (親方).³⁰ Yet, while Uchiyama was a staunch advocate of land reform, this alone would not be enough to solve the dire problem of rural penury. Decisive actions must be taken by the oppressed themselves to cut off the source of suffering at its roots. To this end, Uchiyama advises tenant farmers to actively resist by refusing to deliver rice and pay taxes. Later in the tract, he goes even further, recommending that farmers refuse military conscription and encouraging them to denounce the emperor system based as it is on a "superstition" rooted in "mistaken ideas."

What, if anything, can we find in Uchiyama's vision that is specifically "Zen," as opposed to more generally Mahāyāna Buddhist? Is there any evidence that Uchiyama saw Zen as particularly well suited to anarcho-communism? Uchiyama often invoked catchphrases that implicitly draw connections between Buddhism and socialism, though these tend to be broad doctrines rooted in the early Mahāyāna texts, and thus to a large degree foundational for all East Asian Buddhist sects. If we were to choose a single text that brings together these themes, it would be the *Lotus Sutra*—a foundational text for several East Asian schools such as Tiantai/Tendai and Nichiren but also deeply respected within other Mahāyāna streams, including Zen.³¹ Thus, while we might argue that Uchiyama's vision is one with roots in Zen doctrine, we have to admit that it is not by any means a vision exclusive to Zen (though, given the manifest hybridity of Japanese Buddhism, even prior to modernity, this should hardly come as a surprise).³² Although Uchiyama makes no direct reference in this pamphlet to any specific Buddhist text or doctrine, we can interpret Buddhist connections from several of his expressions and ideas. Perhaps the most conspicuous of these is the unusual phrase *anraku jiyū* (安楽自由; lit., comfort and freedom), which appears at several key points in the piece and may be understood as a motto for Uchiyama's Buddhist-socialist vision.

There may also be "Zen" significance to Uchiyama's close identification with anarchism and the Kōtoku faction of the progressive left. Though it would remain loosely defined from its first appearance in late Meiji through the 1920s, the appeal of anarchism—as opposed to Marxism or other forms of socialism—to young Japanese radicals of the period can be best understood in terms of: (a) its focus on individual freedom and liberty from all constraints—moral or political; and (b) its emphasis on "direct action"—as opposed to social reform.³³ John Crump defines "anarchist-communism" as it developed in Japan in the Taishō period as "a revolutionary theory and practice which seeks to establish, by means which from the outset transcend the state, a society where individual freedom is reinforced by communal solidarity and mutual aid."[34] Though it requires some measure of interpretive verve, one can see how a Buddhist—and particularly a Zen—case could be made for these priorities as well.[35] In time, as anarchism and Marxist socialism eventually split (albeit much later in Japan than in Europe and the United States), it was the anarchists who held more closely to an ideal of restructured consciousness as part and parcel of a revolutionary state (in strict Marxist terms, they were thus guilty of clinging to "utopian" as opposed to "scientific" socialism).[36]

At the same time, as noted above, Uchiyama's vision for a better world is also heavily informed by the monastic tradition—specifically, the simple and communal life of the (idealized) *sangha*. Here again, we could argue that the monastic ideal is shared by virtually all forms of Buddhism, though it appears that Uchiyama's inspiration was the Chinese Chan tradition(s) that gave birth to Japanese Zen.[37] Around the time he became an abbot, in 1904, Uchiyama avers:

> I reflected on the way in which priests of my sect had undergone religious training in China in former times [and] I realized how beautiful it had been. Here were two or three hundred persons who, living in one place at one time, shared a communal lifestyle in which they wore the same clothing and ate the same food. I held to the ideal that if this could be applied to one village, one county, or one country, what an extremely good system would be created.[38]

As Inagaki notes, Uchiyama's insight into the fundamental similarity between the idealized Buddhist *sangha*—rooted in dedication to simple, communal living and, most significantly, a rejection of private property— and the basic assumptions of socialism, was one that would not appear again within Japanese Buddhist thought for nearly three decades, in the work of Senoʾo Girō and the Youth League for Revitalizing Buddhism.[39]

Uchiyama's *Ordinary Self-awakening* is different in both style and content from *Anarcho-communist Revolution*. Here the manifesto-like rhetoric is toned down considerably, and Uchiyama makes a more deliberate case for freedom and democracy using the leitmotif of *jikaku* (自覚). While this term can be reasonably translated into English as "self-awareness" or "self-consciousness," it also has deep Buddhist roots and associations as a synonym for a variety of terms connected to awakening, such as *nirvāṇa, bodhi, kenshō* (検証), and *satori* (悟り)—thus I have chosen to render it as "self-awakening." As with his use of the compound *anraku jiyū* in *Anarcho-communist Revolution*, the term *jikaku* in this piece implies both a Buddhist awakening (i.e., an existential awareness that entails a fundamental person transformation and encompasses or leads to liberation from suffering) and the more overtly Western philosophical sense of gaining "autonomy" (and political "freedom") through liberation from the constraints of tradition, authority, and personal ignorance. Reading this essay, with its emphasis on "freedom," the libertarian aspect of Uchiyama's vision becomes apparent, and we can see why he identified with anarchism as much as communism as a political ideal.[40] While communal living and the abandonment of private property remain a future ideal, Uchiyama's immediate concern was the destruction of the semifeudal system that denied farmers the use of what is theirs by "natural right" (J. *tōzen no kenri*, 當然の權利). On one level, *Ordinary Self-awakening* reads as much like a work by classical liberal writers such as John Locke (1632-1704) or Thomas Paine (1737-1809)—or Fukuzawa Yukichi (福澤諭吉, 1835-1901)—as it does one by Marx or Bakunin. And yet, as with Inoue Shuten, Uchiyama's invocation of the term *heibon* (平凡; ordinary, commonplace or even vulgar) is resonant of both the secular left discourse of "the people" (J. *heimin* 平民) as well as the Chan/Zen emphasis on the mundane or everyday as the vehicle or mode of awakening.

Finally, let us return to Uchiyama's declaration of his commitment to socialism, published in the January 17, 1904 edition of the *People's Paper*. However brief, this remains his clearest expression of the link between classical Buddhist teachings and early twentieth-century left-wing politics. Here is the declaration in its entirety:

> As a propagator of Buddhism I teach that "all sentient beings possess Buddha nature" [J. *issai shujō shitsū busshō*, 一切衆生悉有仏性] and that "within this Dharma there is equality, with neither superior nor inferior" [J. *kore hō byōdō mu kōge*, 此法平等無高下]. Furthermore, I teach that "all sentient beings are my children" [J. *issai shujō mina kore ako*, 一切衆生的(皆)是吾子]. Having taken these golden words as the basis of my faith, I discovered that they are in complete agreement with the principles of socialism. It was thus that I became a believer in socialism.[41]

In short, here we see Uchiyama seeking Buddhist foundations for equality in the early (and admittedly controversial) Mahāyāna teaching of Buddha Nature, which, via Tiantai/Tendai, would eventually provide a shared foundation for virtually all East Asian Buddhist sects, including Zen, Pure Land (both Jōdo and Shin), and Nichiren. While it remains an open question as to whether the doctrine of Buddha Nature can provide a sure foundation for a modern Buddhist conception of social and political equality, this is certainly a feature of East Asian Mahāyāna teachings that has been upheld by socially engaged Buddhists in recent decades.[42] Working against the egalitarian interpretation favored by Uchiyama and socially engaged Buddhists, however, is the question of to which "realm" these statements apply. For instance, the well-known teaching of *sabetsu byōdō* (差別平等)—usually translated as "differentiation is equality"—was taken by prominent Meiji Buddhist figures like Shimaji Mokurai (島地黙雷, 1838–1911) to imply that distinctions in social status and wealth are simply natural givens like age, sex, and so on, and have nothing whatsoever to do with the fundamental equality of the "absolute" realm.

Rather than try to resolve the "problem" of inequality in the here and now, Buddhists—according to Shimaji and others of his ilk—must focus on reaching the realm of undifferentiated being, by which all such superficial distinctions are recognized as illusory. Thus socialists, whether of the revolutionary or reformist hue, are mistaken in taking the material (i.e., contingent) world to be the fundamental reality, missing the forest for the trees, as it were.[43] Of course, Uchiyama, like most other Buddhist progressives and radicals, turned this around to ask Shimaji and his compatriots why they are fixated on establishing a ("conventional") duality between this world and some other—what Ketelaar has termed "the bifurcation of form [J. *yūkei*] and formless [J. *mukei*]"—when in fact no "ultimate" distinction can be made.[44] The world in which we live, and suffer, is nothing less than the "transcendent" realm in its imperfect, "unawakened" state. The fundamental or "transcendent" equality asserted in the Mahāyāna sutras is, for Uchiyama, a call to action, to bring about the transformation of this world of inequality and suffering into a perfected "Buddha land" in which there is "comfort and freedom" (J. *anraku jiyū*). After all, the key here for Uchiyama is the logical chain that: (a) suffering exists in this world; (b) social inequality is a primary cause for suffering and thus must be eliminated; and (c) to eliminate social inequality, the system that creates such inequality must be replaced—even at the risk of one's life.

Meiji Zen Currents: Universalism and the State

Given their unabashed eclecticism—freely mixing social democracy, libertarianism, anarchism, socialism, communism, various forms of Buddhism (both Mahāyāna and Theravāda) and even progressive interpretations of Christianity and Confucianism—it would seem neither the Zen-trained layman Inoue nor the Zen priest Uchiyama was particularly beholden to Chan/Zen ideas or practices. And yet, in their commitment to basic principles of universalism as well as the possibility of a direct, potentially radical transformation of being, which may begin with the individual consciousness but must irrevocably transcend the self-other divide, one detects hints of a contemporaneous stream of Zen thought, traceable to the archetypal Zen modernist lineage of Imakita Kōsen, Shaku Sōen, and D. T. Suzuki. At the same time, as we see above, there are important distinctions that create a clear political separation between these two "wings" of Zen modernism. The following section examines these distinctions by tracing the roots of "mainstream" Zen modernism in Japan (and by extension, the postwar West).

Imakita Kōsen was a Rinzai Zen priest who, on the heels of the 1868 Meiji Restoration, became the first leader of the influential lay Zen society Association for the Abandonment of Concepts of Objectivity and Subjectivity (J. Ryōmō Kyōkai, 両忘協会).[45] Inspired by his early studies with Confucian scholar Fujisawa Togai (藤沢東垓, 1794–1864), Imakita became convinced that Buddhism must expand beyond the monasteries and beyond funeral services to engage the everyday lives of ordinary men and women. At the same time, against the beliefs of many prominent mid-Meiji intellectuals, in the 1880s Imakita insisted that the modern Japanese state *required* religion—specifically, Buddhism—in order to develop in a progressive fashion, since only religion could provide both clear ethical guidelines and engender "faith," a dual task that neither Confucian nor Western learning could match, at least not on the level of the ordinary person.[46] As such, as with many of his Buddhist Enlightenment peers but in contrast to the later New Buddhists—and particularly progressives such as Inoue and Uchiyama—he called for active government support for the dharma, if not the sangha.[47]

The Ryōmō Kyōkai was however more than simply a place for lay Buddhists to engage in the practice of meditation. It also served as an intellectual society for a discussion of Zen and Buddhist thought, as well as a place where participants could engage in cultural activities such as poetry, music, calligraphy, and the game of *go*. And yet, the first of the four simple "rules" of the society states that "members could discuss anything they wanted *except* politics and 'worldly affairs.'"⁴⁸ That is to say, the point of the society was *personal* moral cultivation (J. *jitsugaku*, 實学), which must extend outward to others in active compassion but should not intrude upon political concerns. This is a good example of the way that morality, ethics, and culture were frequently disconnected from politics (and economics) in the discourse, if not practice, of Meiji Buddhist modernism.⁴⁹

While very much a product of the conflicting streams of modernity that coursed through Japan in the late Edo and early Meiji periods, as we have seen in both examples cited above, lay Buddhist movements of the period also had roots in (often eclectic) interpretations of Confucian and Neo-Confucian dictates on the importance of moral cultivation and "practical wisdom." In addition, while priestly advocates like Imakita Kōsen clearly wished to preserve the traditional monastic lifestyle, others such as Nagamatsu Nissen (長松日扇, 1817–1890), were less sanguine when it came to institutional Buddhism. A few leading lay—or *koji* (居士)—Buddhists modeled themselves along the lines of the image of the traditional Mahāyāna bodhisattva (e.g., Vimalakīrti), whose overwhelming compassion required a commitment to secular life that kept them voluntarily attached to this world. For reformers like Takada Dōken (高田道見, 1858–1923), author of the influential *Koji shinron* (居士新論, 1891), this lay orientation, coupled with a nonsectarian "unified (or universal) Buddhism" (J. *tsū bukkyō*, 通仏教), was the wave of the future for Japanese Buddhism.⁵⁰ Though Takada himself does not seem to go quite so far, it is possible to read this scenario as one in which the priests—like the fully awakened buddhas—could be left to their contemplations and otherworldly realms because the *bosatsu-koji* were the ones engaged in the active work of compassion. This contrast fits well with the lingering Meiji discourse on Buddhist "degeneration"—and indeed, the anticlerical flavor one finds in some remarks by *koji* of the period would find a home in the New Buddhist movements of late Meiji and beyond.

Shaku Sōen (1859–1919), Rinzai Zen master, chief abbot of Engakuji in Kamakura was, among other things, de facto leader of the Japanese delegation at the 1893 Chicago World Parliament of Religions. In addition, as Imakita's dharma heir, Sōen carried on his teacher's work by instructing lay Buddhists in Kamakura and Tokyo in the practice of meditation.⁵¹ Here I focus my remarks on some distinctive elements of Sōen's modernistic and internationalist vision for Buddhism, which extend the lay initiatives of Imakita and others and lay the foundations for Suzuki's distinctive brand of "existential" Zen that has had a defining influence on Western Buddhism since World War II.

Sōen advocated Buddhist unity (e.g., in his collaborative multivolume project, *Essentials of the Buddhist Sects*) as well as hegemony—he proclaimed Japanese Mahāyāna the "universal" religion of the modern world.[52] A theme that recurs in many of Sōen's lectures and writings is that of evolution, which is in turn intricately connected with a conception of "progress." As with most of his Parliament or religious colleagues, Sōen viewed Buddhism—more specifically, Mahāyāna Buddhism as it existed in modern Japan—as the pinnacle of Buddhist (if not more generally religious or "spiritual") evolution. While he admits that even contemporary Japanese Buddhism is not free from "superstition, error [and] prejudice," he quickly notes that this is an inevitable by-product of a dynamic, "ever-living faith[,] which knows no ossification or fossilization."[55] Moreover, despite the fact that some believers understand their faith in terms of a "fixed and unchanging" essence, this is a mistake. Religion does (and must) "evolve" with the times and conditions.

For Sōen, as for most New Buddhists who followed him, a key feature of Buddhism—as opposed to most (if not all) other forms of religion—is its "tendency . . . toward intellectuality."[53] This does not imply, he quickly adds, that Buddhism is solely defined by logic or rationality but simply that it "is always ready to stand before the tribunal of science." The danger that haunts most religious systems, he insists, is not intellectual error so much as "sentimentalism," which in turn leads to "mysticism." In short, while Buddhism embraces compassion as a guiding principle, Buddhist love is always tempered by "spiritual insight and intellectual discrimination." Furthermore, in picking up the Meiji discourse of practical wisdom, Sōen argues that Buddhism is, first and foremost, inclined toward aims that are "pre-eminently practical and spiritual." By this he means that all metaphysical speculation, while valuable, must be considered as preparatory for "ethics."

In considering Buddhist metaphysics, Sōen is quick to point out (against the perceptions of many Westerners) that Buddhists are fundamentally empiricists and realists, that is, they accept and affirm the reality of the world itself: "This life as we live it, is true, and not a dream." He also affirms (on, it must be said, more selective doctrinal grounds) the a priori existence of one "ultimate source which is all-powerful, all-knowing, and all loving," of which the entire world is a "manifestation." Citing the authority of American writer and Transcendentalist Ralph Waldo Emerson (1803–1882), Sōen goes on to paint a pantheistic, Spinozistic, or possibly Neoplatonic vision of the universe, in which all existence (both sentient and nonsentient) emerges from the creative force of "Original Reason." And yet, while this creative and moral force is inherent, Sōen rejects a strict pantheism, since "God is greater than the totality of things."

Once again, all this speculation must be connected to the practice of ethics, which he proceeds to summarize in the following remarkably succinct passage:

> Stop doing anything wrong, which is against the reason of things; do whatever is good, which advances the course of reason in this and finally help those who are still behind and weary of life to realize enlightenment: and here is Buddhism in a nutshell. It has nothing to do with prayer and worship and singing and so on. Our simple everyday life of love and sympathy is all that is needed to be a good Buddhist.[54]

While we must keep in mind that this essay was written for the purpose of proselytizing Buddhism to a Western audience—and filtered through the Westernized lens of Sōen's interpreter Suzuki—it displays a fascinating combination of elements of Buddhist and Zen modernism, especially the clear Unitarian inflections, some of which come via Emerson. Here, Sōen is quite explicit that the "religious life" is meaningless outside of everyday, ethically oriented activity. Indeed, as with Spinoza and the New Buddhists, there does not seem to be a "secular" realm to speak of—only a life that is or is not lived according to Buddhist ideals. Having said that, notice that Sōen, like Imakita before him and Suzuki after him, does not extend his argument about Buddhist engagement into the realm of politics or social activism. In this sense, however modern he may be in many respects, and however undeniably cosmopolitan in others, he remains a true "conservative" in the Burkean sense of being convinced that "evil" or "ignorance" is rooted in individuals and their behaviors, not in social structures. Thus, as with most of the reformist figures discussed thus far, even while "awakening" is firmly set within the context of this world and human relationships, and the point of Buddhism (and any religion) reaffirmed as "the promotion of general welfare and . . . the realization of Reason," the focus remains on spiritual and moral cultivation, rather than a critique of economic or political structures or social activism.[55]

This also comes through clearly in Sōen's remarks on materialism. Though in the same essay cited above he notes that Buddhism "never forgets the fact that our religious consciousness ever demands something concrete, that which is visible to our senses, that which is observable in our everyday life," the Rinzai Zen priest certainly does not accept the doctrine of materialism, in any of its various forms. Part of this no doubt emerges from his Hegelian sympathies, as seen above and elsewhere, where he asserts the following, rather disarming doctrine of individual destiny: "This corporeal existence, this particular temporary combination of feelings and thoughts and desires, may dissolve, may not last forever as it is, for it is no more than an agent in the hands of the world-soul to execute its own end. When it decrees that its agent must put on a new garment, this will take place as it is willed."[56]

We will not dwell here on the contentious issue of Shaku Sōen's nationalism, though the short essay under analysis here clearly provides Buddhist support for self-sacrifice in times of national conflict. More significant for my purposes is, once again, the rejection of a materialist perspective in favor of something more clearly Hegelian and idealist, framed here in terms of both religious evolution and individual awakening. As Ketelaar has argued, Sōen, along with other members of the Japanese Buddhist delegation, aimed to present "Eastern Buddhism" as a spiritual antidote for the crisis of (Western) modernity, and thus as an alternative to Christianity. Only a spirituality that is at once "non-contingent yet immanent" can rein in a purely secular materialism, which is here assumed to be inherently immoral and hedonistic.[57][61] This antimaterialist strain would provide a key foundation to the Buddhist response to and critique of socialism in the final decade of Meiji, when most Buddhists—including the leading figures of Buddhist modernism discussed here—would join forces with their erstwhile foes, Japanese Christians, to do battle against the "common enemy" of irreligious materialism.[62]

Conclusions: Is There Any Zen There?

Returning to our case studies of Inoue Shūten and Uchiyama Gudō, once we set their work into the context of contemporary movements in Japanese Buddhism—particularly the lay and philosophical developments occurring beyond the monasteries—the "Zen" connections become somewhat more apparent. Both men remained Buddhists throughout their lives. Uchiyama (at least by his own understanding, if not that of his Sōtō sect), died in the robes of a Zen priest. While Inoue's pacifism was certainly inspired by *ahimsa* and socialist ideals, his universalist inclinations and residual naturalism (if not materialism) have Zen roots. As for Uchiyama, while his ideas appear to be more explicitly grounded in Mahāyāna themes—including, as noted above, the *Lotus Sutra*—he looks to the (idealized) Chan/Zen monastery as a model of simplicity, equality, democracy, and virtue. Both men worked within a Buddhist modernist discourse shaped by scholars and scholar-priests such as Inoue Enryō, Murakami Senshō, Kiyozawa Manshi, and the New Buddhist Fellowship, as well as the more specific Zen modernist line extending from Imakita Kōsen through Shaku Sōen and D. T. Suzuki. And yet, due to the distinctive form of maximalism at work, the Zen modernism(s) of Inoue and Uchiyama set a distinctive, progressive course.

Where the two men differed most, of course, was on the question of violence. A brief anecdote serves to make this point. As previously mentioned, at some point Inoue contacted fellow socialist Uchiyama. While most scholars today absolve Uchiyama of any complicity in a plot to assassinate the Meiji emperor, he was certainly no pacifist, as a perusal of his scathing *Anarcho-communist Revolution* makes plain. Uchiyama affirmed his belief in the use of explosives for fomenting revolution in speeches made while touring the Kansai region in 1910, not long before his arrest and incarceration.[58] While staying with friends in Kobe, he made plans to visit Inoue, presumably to solidify their connection. When he arrived at Inoue's door, however, the latter pretended to be out (after which Uchiyama decided to take a stroll around Minatogawa Shrine, dedicated, ironically, to a military commander).[59] While it is impossible to know Inoue's motivations, a reasonable conclusion is that he, like other New Buddhists, was uncomfortable associating with the more radical fringe of the socialist movement and, more specifically in the case of Inoue and Uchiyama, with someone who clearly did not share his views about the renunciation of violence, even as a means toward establishing "social justice."

Notes

1. Sections of this essay have been previously published in modified form in chapters 1, 3, and 4 of my monograph, *Against Harmony: Progressive and Radical Buddhism in Modern Japan* (Oxford, 2017).

2. Donald S. Lopez Jr., "Foreword," in *The Gospel of Buddhism: According to Old Records by Paul Carus* (LaSalle, IL: Open Court, 2004), 8.

3. Juliane Schober, *Modern Buddhist Conjunctures in Myanmar: Cultural Narratives, Colonial Legacies, and Civil Society* (Honolulu: University of Hawai'i Press, 2011), 148.

4. Bruce Lincoln, *Holy Terrors: Thinking about Religion after September 11*, 2nd ed. (Chicago: University of Chicago Press, 2006), 59; see also Schober, *Modern Buddhist Conjunctures*, 72.

5. See Yoshinaga Shin'ichi, *Shin bukkyō* to wa nani mono ka? "jiyū tōkyū" to "kenzen naru shinkō,"『新仏教』とはなにものか？―「自由討究」と「健全なる信仰」 (What is *New Buddhism*? From "free investigation" to "sound faith"). In *Kindai Nihon ni okeru chishikijin shūkyō undō no gensetsu kūkan: "Shin Bukkyō" no shisōshi, bunkashiteki kenkyū*, 近代日本における知識人宗教運動の言説空間 ―『新佛教』の思想史・文化史的研究 [The discursive space of intellectual religious movements in modern Japan: A study of the intellectual and cultural history of "New Buddhism"]. Grants-in-Aid for Scientific Research, no. 20320016, 2011, 35.

6. Takashima Beihō, *Takashima Beihō tsuioku* 高嶋米峰―追憶 [Recollections of Takashima Beihō], (Tokyo: Ōzorasha, 1993), 11.

7. For more on Inoue Shūten, see Akamatsu Tesshin (赤松連城), "Inoue Shūten no shisō: Sono shōgai to heiwaron oyobi zen shisō" 井上秀天の思想―その生涯と平和論及び禅思想 [The thought of Inoue Shūten: His life, peace theory, and Zen thought], *Ryūkoku daigaku ronshū* 434-35 (1989): 517-53; Fukushima Hirotaka (福嶋寛隆), "Mō hitotsu no hisenron: Nihon teikokushugi kakuritsuki ni bukkyōsha toshite" もう一つの非戦論―日本帝国主義確立期に仏教者として [Another antiwar theory: From a Buddhist during the establishment of Japanese imperialism], *Dendōin kiyō* 18 (1976): 54-71; Moriya Tomoe (守屋友江), "Inoue Shūten" (井上秀天), in *Kindai Nihon ni okeru chishikijin shūkyō undō*, 近代日本における知識人宗教運動の言説空間 ―『新佛教』の思想史・文化史的研究, 283-86; Moriya, "Social Ethics of 'New Buddhists' at the Turn of the Twentieth Century: A Comparative Study of Suzuki Daisetsu and Inoue Shūten," *Japanese Journal of Religious Studies* 32, no. 2 (2005): 283-304; Sahashi Hōryu (佐橋法龍), *Inoue Shūten* (井上秀天). Tokyo: Meicho Fukyūkai, 1982.

8. See Moriya, "Social Ethics of 'New Buddhists,'" 293.

9. Moriya, "Social Ethics of 'New Buddhists,'" 296.

10. For Inoue's critique of Suzuki, see Inoue Shūten (井上秀天), *Bukkyō no gendaiteki hihan* 仏教の現代的批判 [Contemporary criticism of Buddhism], (Tokyo: Hōbunkan, 1925); Suzuki, D[aisetsu] T[eitarō], "Gendai shin'yaku hekiganroku shōkai" o yomu,「現代新訳碧巖録詳解」を読む [On reading "A New, Modern Translation and Interpretation of the *Blue Cliff Record*"], *Zendō* 97 (1918): 13-21.

11. Moriya, "Social Ethics of 'New Buddhists,'" 293.

12. SB 12, 12 (December 1911), 1380-87; Akamatsu Tesshin (赤松徹真) and Fukushima Hirotaka (福嶋寛隆), eds., *Shin bukkyō*, 新仏教 (New Buddhism). 4 vols. (Kyoto: Nagata Bunshōdō, 1982). Cited as SB, by volume and date of original publication.

13. SB 12, 12 (December 1911), 1384.

14. SB 12, 12 (December 1911), 1386.
15. SB 12, 12 (December 1911), 1386.
16. Moriya, "Social Ethics of 'New Buddhists,'" 294.
17. Moriya, "Social Ethics of 'New Buddhists,'" 296. For more on Suzuki's views of society and the state, see Kirita Kiyohide, "D.T. Suzuki on Society and the State." In *Rude Awakenings: Zen, the Kyoto School, and the Question of Nationalism*, edited by James W. Heisig and John C. Maraldo (Honolulu: University of Hawai'i Press, 1994), 52–74.
18. See Yoshida Kyūichi, Nihon *kindai bukkyōshi kenkyū*, 日本近代仏教史研究 [A study of modern Japanese Buddhist history], (Tokyo: Yoshikawa kōbunkan, 1992), 340–41.
19. See Brian Victoria, *Zen at War* (New York: Weatherhill, 1997), chap. 3: "Uchiyama Gudō: Radical Soto Zen Priest," 38–48; Ishikawa Rikizan, "The Social Response of Buddhists to the Modernization of Japan: The Contrasting Lives of Two Sōtō Zen Monks," *Japanese Journal of Religious Studies* 25 (1998), 87–115, for a treatment of Uchiyama and the nationalist Sōtō Zen priest Takeda Hanshi 竹田範之 (1864–1911).
20. See, for example, Yoshida, *Nihon kindai bukkyōshi kenkyū*, 402–408. For more on Uchiyama, see Inagaki Masami, *Kindai bukkyō no henkakusha*, 近代仏教の変革者 [Modern Buddhist radicals], (Tokyo: Daizō shuppan, 1975); Kashiwagi Ryūhō (柏木隆法), *Taigyaku jiken to Uchiyama Gudō* 大逆事件と内山愚童 [Uchiyama Gudō and the High Treason Incident], (Tokyo: JCA shuppan, 1979); Morinaga Eizaburō (森長英三郎). *Uchiyama Gudō* (内山愚童) (Tokyo: Ronsōsha, 1984).
21. See Ann Walthall, "The Sakura Sōgorō Story," in *Peasant Uprisings in Japan: A Critical Anthology of Peasant Histories*, ed. and trans. Anne Walthall (Chicago: University of Chicago Press, 1991), 35–76.
22. According to the collective research and statistical work of Aoki Kōji, Yokoyama Toshio, and Yamanaka Kiyotaka, Echigo was one of only six provinces (out of seventy-one) to experience more than 100 *ikki* (armed peasant revolts) between 1590 and 1867; see Herbert P. Bix, *Peasant Protest in Japan, 1590–1884* (New Haven: Yale University Press, 1986), xxiv–xxv.
23. Ishikawa notes in particular the "germination of the idea of the 'self' of 'self-awakening'" in Uchiyama's *Ordinary Self-awakening*, which may have come from Inoue; "Social Response of Buddhists," 99.
24. See Griffith T. Foulk, "Myth, Ritual and Monastic Practice in Sung Ch'an Buddhism," in *Religion and Society in Tang and Sung China*, ed. Patricia Buckley Ebrey and Peter N. Gregory (Honolulu: University of Hawai'i Press, 1993), esp. 147–49, for an analysis of the rhetoric of Chan monastic practice as developed in Song China.
25. Stefano Bellieni, "Notes on the History of the Left-Wing Movement in Meiji Japan." *Supplemento n. 21 agli Annali* 39, fasc. 4 (1979): 23.
26. See Ishikawa, "Social Response of Buddhists," 102–103.

27. Whereas Victoria is somewhat dismissive of the intellectual work of Uchiyama and similar activist monks, Yoshida Kyū'ichi goes to the other extreme, proclaiming that "Uchiyama Gudō was not a thinker like Kōtoku [Shūsui]. His socialist and anarchist ideas emerged from his experience" (*Nihon kindai bukkyōshi kenkyū*, 402). In his work (originally published in 1959), Yoshida called for more research on the theoretical connections between Buddhism and political theories such as socialism and anarchism (401); see Ishikawa, "Social Response of Buddhists," 104.

28. Ishikawa, "Social Response of Buddhists," 102.

29. Marius B. Jansen, *The Making of Modern Japan* (Cambridge, MA: Belknap, 2002), 114.

30. Bix notes the increase in the power of landlord families over tenants throughout the eighteenth and nineteenth centuries, citing it as the primary reason for the growth of peasant riots during the same period; *Peasant Protest*, xx.

31. In a recently published article, Asai Endo has argued that the *Lotus Sutra* should be considered the very foundation of Japanese Buddhism; see Asai Endō. "The Lotus Sutra as the Core of Japanese Buddhism: Shifts in Representations of its Fundamental Principle," *Japanese Journal of Religious Studies* 41, no. 1 (2014): 45–64.

32. On this issue, Yoshida argues that both Uchiyama and Itō Shoshin shared a fundamental belief in the difference between "the way of original Buddhism" (J. *bukkyō honrai no michi*, 仏教本来の道) and the forms of sectarian Buddhism existent in Meiji Japan; *Nihon kindai bukkyōshi kenkyū*, 406.

33. Uchiyama seems to have arrived at his preference for anarchism prior to Kōtoku Shūsui's famous lecture at Kinkikan Hall in Kanda, Tokyo, on June 28, 1906, entitled "Sekai kakumei undō no chōryū," 世界革命運動の潮流 [The tide of the world revolutionary movement], in which the founder of the Heiminsha announced his break with social democratic (i.e., parliamentary) tactics in favor of revolutionary syndicalism, effecting an irrevocable split in Japan's young socialist movement; see Frederick G. Notehelfer, *Kōtoku Shūsui, Portrait of a Japanese Radical* (New York: Cambridge University Press, 1971), 133–37.

34. John Crump, *Hatta Shūzō, and Pure Anarchism in Interwar Japan* (New York: St. Martin's Press, 1993), 1.

35. In an essay on "Nakae Chōmin and Buddhism," Eddy Dufourmont discusses the possibility of a connection between materialist and atheistic thinking and Zen by focusing on the impact of Buddhism on mid-Meiji thinker Nakae Chōmin (中江兆民, 1847–1901). Certainly, despite the fact that Inoue Enryō was his blood relation, Uchiyama seems to have far more in common with the politically liberal Chōmin, Enryō's rival and Kōtoku Shūsui's teacher; see Dufourmont, "Nakae Chomin and Buddhism: Reconsidering the Controversy between Nakae Chomin and Inoue Enryō," *International Inoue Enryō Research* 1 (2013): 63–75.

36. See Stephen Filler, "Chaos from Order: Anarchy and Anarchism in Modern Japanese Fiction, 1900–1930" (PhD diss., Ohio State University, 2004), 73–74.

37. It bears reiterating that Uchiyama's vision of a simple Chan monastic community is filtered through centuries of "myth-making" by Chan/Zen Buddhists, and bears little connection to historical reality; see Foulk, "Myth, Ritual."

38. Inagaki, *Kindai bukkyō no henkakusha*, 112–13; trans. Victoria, *Zen at War*, 40–41, with modifications by the author.

39. Inagaki, *Kindai bukkyō no henkakusha*, 113.

40. Although it is often said that Uchiyama, following the lead of Kōtoku Shūsui and Sakai Toshihiko, abandoned socialism for anarchism, in fact he never makes a clear theoretical distinction between anarchism, socialism, or communism—just as he never makes a clear distinction between Buddhism and these economic and political theories; see Yoshida, *Nihon kindai bukkyōshi kenkyū*, 405.

41. Originally published in *People's Paper* 10 (January 17, 1904); reprinted in Kashiwagi, *Taigyaku jiken to Uchiyama Gudō*, 29; trans. Brian Victoria, with my modifications.

42. Ishikawa notes the similarities between Uchiyama and Dr. B. R. Ambedkar (1891–1956) on the issue of employing Buddhist teachings to battle discrimination and promote social equality, as well as the struggle to connect Marxism and Buddhism. Of course, as Ishikawa rightly notes, Ambedkar was working on the basis of Theravāda (as Ishikawa has it, "original" or *gensho* 原初) Buddhism, and thus could not appeal to the specific doctrine of Buddha Nature. Also, whereas Ambedkar clearly favored Buddhism over Marxism, Uchiyama, like Seno'o Girō after him, saw them as perfectly compatible—perhaps even, if understood and practiced correctly, perfectly identical; Ishikawa, "Social Response of Buddhists," 100.

43. Shimaji Mokurai, *Shimaji Mokurai zenshū*, 島地黙雷全集 [Complete works of Shimaji Mokurai], vol. 3 (Kyoto: Honganji shuppan, 1973), 285–96.

44. James Edward Ketelaar, *Of Heretics and Martyrs in Meiji Japan: Buddhism and Its Persecution* (Princeton, NJ: Princeton University Press, 1990), 134.

45. Ryōmō (also read ryōbō; lit. "neglecting both") is a traditional Buddhist term implying "detachment from dichotomies." In this context it can be taken to mean "abandonment of objectivity and subjectivity."

46. Suzuki, *Imakita Kōsen*, 184–85.

47. At the same time, it should be noted that Imakita—as with most Buddhist leaders of the day—opposed the 1872 Council of State decree that Buddhist monks could now get married and eat meat (J. *nikujiki saitai*, 肉食妻帯).

48. Sawada, *Practical Pursuits*, 159, my emphasis.

49. Sawada argues that the idealization of the lay practitioner in Imakita's group represents a larger coalescence of two distinctive East Asian models of human fulfillment: "the Confucian gentleman official and the Buddhist lay bodhisattva"; see Sawada, *Practical Pursuits*, 6.

50. Ikeda Eishun (池田英俊), *Meiji no shin bukkyō undō*. 明治の新仏教運動 [The Meiji New Buddhist movement] (Tokyo: Yoshikawa kōbunsha, 1976), 123; also see Ketelaar, *Of Heretics and Martyrs*, 185. Sawada notes that despite his enthusiasm for lay Buddhism, Takada was wary of appropriation or misuse of the term *koji* by "dilettantes" (*Practical Pursuits*, 181–82).

51. The original organization, which had flourished in the 1870s and 1880s, had long since lapsed. Sōen encouraged his student Shaku Sōkatsu (釈宗活, 1870–1954) to restart the Ryōmō Kyōkai around 1900. In 1906, Sokatsu and Sasaki Shigetsu (佐々木指月; also known as Sōkei-an 曹渓庵, 1882–1945) brought the newly reformed group to San Francisco. In Japan, Ryōmō Kyōkai would have a postwar reincarnation with Ningen Zen Kyōdan (人間禅教団), founded by Koun-an Tatsuta Eizan (耕雲庵立田英山, 1893–1971). See Sawada, *Practical Pursuits*, 161.

52. It is for the latter, as well as for various remarks on the positive connection between Zen and warfare, that Sōen is targeted by Brian Victoria for his complicity in the early development of "Imperial Way Zen" in Japan.

53. All quotes in the following section are from Shaku, "What is Buddhism?," 37–40.

54. Shaku, "What is Buddhism?," 40.

55. Shaku, "What is Buddhism?," 41.

56. Shaku, "Buddhism and Oriental Culture," 44.

57. Ketelaar, *Of Heretics and Martyrs*, 165–66.

58. Yoshida, *Nihon kindai bukkyōshi kenkyū*, 421–24.

59. Yoshida, *Nihon kindai bukkyōshi kenkyū*, 423.

Chapter 13

The Struggle of the Jogye Order to Define Its Identity as a Meditative School in Contemporary Korea

BERNARD SENÉCAL (SEO MYEONGWEON)

Introduction

The Jogye Order (Jogyejong 曹溪宗) is the most powerful Buddhist order in Korea. Nevertheless, confronted with both Buddhist and non-Buddhist competition on the national and international stages, as well as with an image problem due to a series of historical setbacks and scandals, it is struggling to define its identity and retain its supremacy within South Korea. Judging from recent statistics, despite massive efforts to recruit more monks, nuns, and followers, numbers remain stagnant, at best. When considered from a doctrinal viewpoint, on the one hand, the Jogye Order claims to be exceptionally faithful to the supposedly bibliophobe and iconoclastic practice of key phrase meditation[1] (C. *Kanhua Chan*, K. *Kanhwa Sŏn* 看話禪) taught by Dahui Zonggao (大慧宗杲, 1089–1163). On the other hand, below the surface, it often displays undying signs of attachment to the sudden/gradual doctrine (K. *tono chŏmsu sasang* 頓悟漸修思想) advocated by Pojo Chinul (普照知訥, 1158–1210), who is generally believed to have recognized the value of Dahui's key phrase meditation, albeit he remained, until the end of his life, an outstanding scholiast. Even though these two tendencies are not necessarily incompatible, T'oeong Sŏngchŏl (退翁性徹, 1912–1993), perhaps the most towering figure of Korean Buddhism in the second half of the twentieth century, radically contrasted them with one another by advocating an unconditional sudden/sudden approach of awakening and practice (K. *tono tonsu* 頓悟頓修), thus giving rise to the contemporary Korean sudden/gradual debate (K. *Han'guk Pulgyo tonjŏm nonjaeng* 韓國佛教頓漸論爭).

Dealing with these issues, this chapter is composed of three parts. The first one focuses on Pojo Chinul and his successor Chin'gak Hyesim (眞覺慧諶, 1178–1234) and comprises three sections. After briefly describing who Chinul was, a first one focuses on an analysis of his so-called three awakening experiences, including their impact on his life, his writings and teachings, as well as their sequence. A second one focuses on the research of Park Keonjoo (朴健柱),[2] which not only strongly challenges the traditional attribution to Chinul of the *Treatise on Resolving Doubts about Observing the Key Phrase* (*Kanhwa kyŏrŭi ron* 看話決疑論) but also questions the origin of the four insertions on key phrase meditation found in *Excerpts* (*Chŏryo* 節要).[3] Chinul's magnum opus, which was finished—but not published—in 1209, just a few months before his death. A last one focuses on Cho Myungje's (趙明濟) research that, based on an in-depth analysis of Hyesim's *Compilation of Handpicked Stanzas of the Sŏn School* (*Sŏnmun yŏmsongjip* 禪門拈頌集; hereafter *Compilation*)[4] and other works, calls into question the traditional understanding of Chinul's successor's thought.[5]

The second part of the essay focuses on the political background of the Sino-Korean Connection (i.e., the dharma connection that was established between masters of the Chinese Linji school and Korean monks in the fourteenth century). It describes how this transmission fared at the end of the Koryŏ period, at the beginning of the Chosŏn dynasty, in the aftermath of the Imjin (壬辰, 1592–1598) and Pyŏngja (丙子, 1636–1637) Japanese and Manchu invasions, and in the nineteenth century.

The third part of the chapter is a critical evaluation of Sŏngchŏl's life, works, and influence. Besides providing a description of his life as a layman and as a monk, this part draws attention to some aspects of the contemporary Korean sudden/gradual debate that are seldom underscored: the fact that the hermeneutics Sŏngchŏl used to reform Korean Buddhism from the mid-1960s until the late 1980s were deeply influenced, not only by modern Japanese Buddhist scholarship but also by the socioeconomic and geopolitical context of South Korea during the Cold War. When acknowledged and taken into account, these factors singularly add to the complexity of the Jogye Order's identity quest.

Part I
Pojo Chinul and Chingak Hyesim

Chinul, also known as the Oxherder (Moguja 牧牛子) or State Preceptor (*kuksa* 國師) Puril Pojo, is generally accepted as the outstanding Buddhist of the Koryŏ period (高麗, 918–1392).[6] A scholiast (*kyoga* 教家) and a meditation master (*sŏnsa* 禪師, *sŏn'ga* 禪家) endowed with an exceptionally eclectic mind, Chinul dedicated his energies to creating harmony between two bitterly conflicting sectarian positions, those who emphasized meditation (*sŏn* 禪) to achieve an awakening unmediated by language versus those who were dedicated to the study of doctrine (*kyo* 教) to become awakened. Demonstrating through his writings, teachings, and his life the essential congruence of these two approaches (*sŏngyo ilch'i* 禪教一致), that is, their interpenetration (*sŏngyo hoet'ong* 禪教會通) or unity (*sŏngyo habil* 禪教合一), Chinul became a major reformer of Korean Buddhism. His position could accommodate three apparently antagonistic claims: that of the necessity of a thorough understanding of doctrine prior to the practice of meditation (*hoegyo kuisŏn* 會教歸禪); that of the necessity of a complete abandonment of doctrine to enter fully into the practice of meditation (*sagyo ipsŏn* 捨教入禪);[7] and the claim that a pervasive and all-inclusive understanding of doctrine is only possible as a result of a thorough breakthrough in the practice of meditation (*t'ongsŏn hoegyo* 通禪會教). Chinul's eclecticism, known as *tono chŏmsu sasang* (頓悟漸修思想, a doctrine advocating a sudden enlightenment, that is, an awakening experience[8] presumably not mediated by language,[9] followed by gradual or language mediated cultivation), has been influential ever since and remains so in Korea today.

However, the strong but subtle balance that Chinul championed between *sŏn* and *kyo* has proven both difficult to maintain at times and somewhat controversial. It is generally believed that soon after Chinul's death—because of the personal preference of his student and successor Chingak Hyesim—an exclusive focus on *Kanhwa Sŏn* typical of the Linji school (臨濟宗 K. Imjejong, J. Rinzaishū) began to gain influence, adversely affecting the equilibrium and eventually eclipsing his carefully fashioned eclecticism. It is also assumed that this exclusivism persisted till the end of the Koryŏ period, toward the end of which a direct line of transmission was established between Linji masters of the Mongol Yuan Dynasty (元, 1271–1368) and Korean monks such as Paegun Kyŏnghan (白雲京漢,

1299–1375), T'aego Pou (太古普愚, 1301–1382), Naong Hyegŭn (懶翁惠勤, 1320–1376), Muhak Ch'acho (無學自超, 1327–1405), etc.[10]

In the first section of this first part, I demonstrate that such a view may be an oversimplification of the more nuanced course of historical events which finally led, indeed, to the establishment of a Linji-style Sino-Korean connection and to the predominance of *Kanhwa Sŏn*. I begin with analyses of Chinul's three awakening experiences.

The *Funerary Inscription* Account of Chinul's Three "Awakenings"

The most complete source of information on Chinul's life is the "Funerary Inscription and Epitaph for State Preceptor Puril Pojo of the Society for Cultivating Sŏn on Mount Chogye" (Chogyesan Susŏnsa Puril Pojo Kuksa pimyŏng 曹溪山修禪社佛日普照國師碑銘, hereafter "Funerary Inscription"), composed by the literatus Kim Kunsu (金君綏, fl. ca. 1210–1220) on the basis of a no-longer extant "Account of Conduct" (*Haengjang* 行狀), a detailed account of Chinul's life and career written and provided to the court by Chinul's student and successor, the aforementioned Hyesim.[11]

The Funerary Inscription describes what are generally understood to be Chinul's three awakenings or experiences of enlightenment,[12] although Chinul himself only ever mentioned the second one. The first event is said to have taken place in 1182 while Chinul was staying at Ch'ŏngwŏnsa (清源寺, South Chŏlla province, near Naju, exact location unknown):

> By chance one day . . . as he was looking through the *Platform Sūtra of the Sixth Patriarch* (C. *Liuzu tanjing*, K. *Yukcho tangyŏng* 六祖壇經), he came across [the following passage]: "The self-nature of suchness generates thoughts. Although the six sense-faculties may see, hear, sense, and know, they do not taint the myriad sensory objects and the true nature remains constantly autonomous."[13] Astonished and overjoyed, he gained what he had never experienced before; getting up, he walked around the Buddha hall, reflecting on the passage while continuing to recite it, until he understood its meaning for himself. From that time on, his mind was disillusioned with fame and profit; he desired only to dwell in seclusion in the mountain ravines [forest caves]. Bearing hardships joyfully, he aspired to the path; even in moments of haste, he cleaved to it.[14]

The second experience is said to have taken place in 1185, while he was at Pomunsa (普門寺) on Mount Haga (下柯山) in North Kyŏngsang province.

> As he was reading through the canon, he came across Li [Tongxuan]'s (李通玄, 635–730) *Exposition of* [the New Translation of] *the Avataṃsaka sūtra* (*Xin Huayan jing lun* 新華嚴經論),[15] and this gave new impetus to his faith. Searching through [the text], he dug out its hidden meaning, and, chewing away on it, he relished its essence, until his previous understanding became even clearer. He then immersed his mind in the approach to contemplation of the complete and sudden teaching (K. *wŏndon kwanmun* 圓頓觀門), for he also wanted to steer students in this degenerate age away from their delusions so they would be able to . . . [overcome the grasping at both self and the dharmas].[16]

The third experience is said to have taken place between 1198 and 1200, while Chinul was living on Mount Chiri (智異山) at Sangmujuam (上無住庵) in South Kyŏngsang province.

> [Chinul] said, "More than ten years had passed since I came from Pomunsa. Although . . . I had cultivated diligently and not wasted my time, I had still not forsaken passions and views—it was as if something were blocking my chest, or as if I were dwelling together with an enemy. While sojourning on Mount Chiri, I obtained the *Records* of the Sŏn Master Dahui Pujue (大慧普覺, 1089–1163), which said: "Sŏn does not consist in quietude; it does not consist in bustle. It does not consist in the activity of daily life; it does not consist in ratiocination. Nevertheless, it is of first importance not to investigate [Sŏn] while rejecting quietude or bustle, the activities of daily life or ratiocination. Unexpectedly, your eyes will open and you then will know that these are all things taking place inside your own home."[17] I understood . . . and naturally nothing blocked my chest again and I never again dwelt together with an enemy. From then on I was at peace." Thanks to this [experience], [Chinul's] wisdom and understanding increased dramatically and he became a master revered by the entire congregation.[18]

CHINUL'S OWN ACCOUNT OF THE SECOND "AWAKENING"

Chinul's account of the second "awakening" is found in the preface to his *Condensation of the Exposition of the New [Translation of the] Avataṃsakasūtra* (*Hwaŏm non chŏryo* 華嚴論節要) of 1207.[19] This account is much more detailed than the *Funerary Inscription* in two respects.[20] Firstly, Chinul claims it occurred not in 1185 but rather between 1185 and 1188, most probably toward the end of that period. Indeed, he explains that he dedicated those three years to the reading of the canon because he wanted to find an answer to the criticism of Sŏn often made by Hwaŏm (C. Huayan 華嚴) scholar-monks who dedicated themselves to the study of the *Avataṃsakasūtra*. They claimed that the Sŏn school's exclusive focus on seeing Buddha Nature (K. *kyŏnsŏng* 見性) and recognizing that one's own mind is the Buddha produced only introspective awareness, not the consummate, holistic knowledge of the "unimpeded interpenetration between all phenomena" (K. *sasa muae* 事事無礙).[21] Secondly, he seems to describe two successive experiences. Indeed, before quoting twice from Li's *Exposition*, Chinul begins with two quotations from the chapter of the sutra entitled "Manifestation of the Tathāgata" (Rulai chuxian pin 如來出現品): "The simile of one dust mote containing rolls of scriptures as numerous as the world systems of the trichiliocosm" and "The wisdom of the tathāgatas is also just like this: . . . it is fully present in the bodies of all sentient beings. It is merely all these ordinary, foolish people . . . who are not aware of it and do not recognize it." Then, Chinul says: "I put the roll of scriptures on my head in reverence and, unwittingly, began to weep."[22]

He immediately adds: "Nevertheless, as I was still not fully clear about the initial access to faith that was appropriate for ordinary people of today, I reread the explanation of the first level of the ten faiths (K. *sinsim* 信心) in the Exposition of the New [Translation of the] Avataṃsakasūtra." It explains that Buddhahood exists in ordinary sentient beings at the first level of faith, that is, the first of the fifty-two degrees of awakening, in three different forms: as the dharmadhātu (K. *pŏpkye* 法界), which can be understood as both thusness (K. *pŏp* or *pŏpsin* 法身) and the phenomenal world (K. *kye* 界)[23] as well as their mutual interpenetration; as the Buddha of Immovable Wisdom (K. Pudongji Pul 不動智佛), the eponymous figure representing the mind's original freedom from the subject-object dichotomy; and lastly as Mañjuśrī, who embodies wisdom in action because he readily distinguishes the genuine from the distorted. The text adds that as soon as the first degree of faith is achieved, an ordinary sentient being becomes awakened to these three different forms of Buddhahood and that therefore this sentient being becomes the Bodhisattva chief of enlightenment (Kaksu Posal 覺首菩薩). Chinul adds:

> I set down the volume and, breathing a long sigh, said: "What the World-Honored One said with his mouth is Kyo (教, teaching). What the Patriarchs transmitted with their mind is Sŏn (禪, meditation). The mouth of the Buddha and the minds of the Patriarch can certainly not be in contradiction with one another. How can [the students of both the Sŏn and Kyo schools] not plumb the fundamental source but instead, complacent in their own training, wrongly foment disputes and squander all their time?"[24]

In other words, Chinul understood that the Sŏn school's "seeing the buddha nature and recognizing that one's own mind is the buddha" could be defined as producing far more than mere introspective awareness. Indeed, thanks to Li Tongxuan, he discovered that it could not only involve an awakening to the unimpeded interpenetration between all phenomena as described by the Hwaŏm perspective but that it could also take place at the first level of faith. This discovery is the cornerstone of Chinul's sudden/gradual doctrine. Based as it is on the harmonization of Sŏn and Kyo, it may be defined as an "already but not-yet" paradoxical paradigm, in the sense that one has to become gradually, in the phenomenal world, what one has suddenly discovered to already be at a transcendental level.

POINTS OF CONVERGENCE

Despite these differences between Chinul and the Funerary Inscription regarding this second experience, they both recognize that the triggering factor was one or more scriptural loci. In other words, none of the three awakenings was the result of meditation pure and simple, albeit meditation was clearly part and parcel of the overall context in which the third reading experience took place: "The site was isolated and quiet—first in all the realm as a peaceful place that was ideal for the practice of Sŏn. There, the Master . . . fully devoted himself to introspective contemplation."[25]

Moreover, the Funeral Inscription underscores that in the case of the first and second experiences, time and effort, sometimes involving memorization and recitation, were required to fully assimilate the meaning of each locus and let it fully awaken his mind. As we have seen, Chinul also strongly insisted on this important aspect of the only experience that he describes, even adding that further readings were required for full attainment. In other words, these experiences, mediated as they are by textual studies, time, and effort, seem to be only relatively sudden rather than immediate. Since no such need for time and effort before assimilation is mentioned in the description of Chinul's third and last experience, it appears to have been somewhat more sudden than the first two. However, that experience was only one in a series of others, albeit perhaps the most conspicuous one. Indeed, even though the account pinpoints the specific scriptural locus that triggered Chinul's so-called final awakening, it adds that "there were several occasions when there were auspicious signs that he had attained the dharma, but these have not been recorded in such detail."[26] Considering that Chinul stayed at Sangmuju hermitage for some three years (1198–1200), it is possible that he had time to experience a number of such enlightenment events.

The fact that a few scriptural loci triggered Chinul's awakenings is all the more important because, according to Kim Kunsu, these loci and their corresponding experiences appear to have provided Chinul with the entire structure of his thought and teachings. As the *Funeral Inscription* explains: "When he exhorted people to recite and keep [scriptures], he always recommended the *Diamond Sūtra*. When he established the dharma and expounded on its import, his preference was necessarily for the *Platform Sūtra of the Sixth Patriarch*, and when he expanded on it, he used Li [Tongxuan's] *Exposition* or the *Records of Dahui*, which were inseparable like wings and feathers."[27]

The *Funerary Inscription* goes on to explain how each of the above texts correspond to one of Chinul's three methods of teaching (K. *mun* 門). The "balanced maintenance of alertness and calmness" (K. *sŏngjŏk tŭngji mun* 惺寂等持門) corresponds to his first awakening triggered by the *Platform Sūtra*; "Faith and understanding according to the complete and sudden teaching" (K. *wŏndon sinhae mun* 圓頓信解門) corresponds to his second awakening, triggered by Li's *Exposition*; and the "shortcut approach" (K. *kyŏngjŏl mun* 徑截門) corresponds to his last awakening, triggered by the reading of Dahui's *Records*. However influential this summation has been, it definitely tends to give—as we shall see—the false impression that Chinul's last awakening was triggered by the practice of *Kanhwa Sŏn*, the kind of practice developed and promoted by Dahui, and that without it Chinul could not have achieved a supreme, correct,

The Struggle of the Jogye Order | 353

perfect enlightenment (S. *anuttarā-samyak-saṃbodhi*, K. *musang chŏngdŭng chŏnggak* 無上正等正覺).

THE IMPACT OF THE THREE "AWAKENINGS" ON CHINUL'S LIFE

The *Funeral Inscription* briefly describes the result of each experience. The first one (1182) strengthened Chinul's intent on seeking awakening; the second (ca. 1188) one generated his desire to help sentient beings. It also marked the beginning, at Kŏjosa (居祖寺), of the Samādhi and Prajñā Society (Chŏnghyesa 定慧社), which he had vowed to found in 1182. The last awakening, or, more exactly, the last series of enlightenment experiences, took place sometime between 1198 and 1200. By freeing Chinul from all his afflictions and deluded conceptualizations (K. *pŏnnoe mangsang* 煩惱妄想), this awakening dramatically increased his wisdom and understanding, and transformed him to such a point that he became a universally acknowledged meditation master.

THE SEQUENCE OF THE THREE "AWAKENINGS"

Despite its accuracy, the *Funeral Inscription* makes no systematic attempt to see the three experiences as forming a definite sequence, but one may investigate whether or not they follow the sudden enlightenment followed by gradual practice model that Chinul later so strongly advocated. It seems possible, even though it was triggered by an excerpt from the *Platform Sūtra*, to liken the first experience (1182) to a sudden awakening that prompted gradual cultivation; this would then be a matter of understanding (K. *haeo* 解悟), not of realization (K. *chŭngo* 證悟). However, since there is less suddenness in Chinul's second experience (1185) than in the first one, it can hardly be called a "sudden awakening" but appears closer to a gradual practice followed by gradual awakening (K. *chŏmsu chŏmo* 漸修漸悟) pattern, where practice consists in reading scriptures thoroughly during a long period, and awakening amounts to understanding them better as well as desiring to help others along the path to awakening. Chinul's second experience undoubtedly contributed to reinforce the gradual cultivation that led him to his final experience.

Judging from what Kim says, the last experience (1198–1200) definitely freed Chinul from all his afflictions and deluded conceptualizations and transformed him into a universally acknowledged meditation master. It seems to qualify as sudden awakening with sudden cultivation (K. *tono tonsu* 頓悟頓修), namely, implying simultaneous completion of cultivation and awakening (K. *suo tongsi* 修悟同時), thus encompassing both understanding and realization awakenings. Since this transformation took place before Chinul moved to Kilsangsa (1200), it can be understood as the ultimate preparation needed to assume his duties as a *dhyāna* master there. It is probably because of this need that he stayed three years in Sangmujuam. Otherwise, it is difficult to understand why Chinul left Kŏjosa, where he was in charge of the retreat society he had founded, for such a long period.

CHINUL'S *EXCERPTS* AND POSTHUMOUS WORKS

Chinul spent the last decade of his life in Kilsangsa, which was later renamed Susŏnsa (修禪社), in South Chŏlla province, teaching, writing, meditating, founding other institutions,[28] and enjoying royal support. In 1209, a few months before his death, Chinul finished the writing of his magnum opus *Excerpts from the "Dharma Collection and Special Practice Record" with Inserted Personal Notes* (*Pŏpchip pyŏrhaengnok chŏryo pyŏngip sagi* 法集別行錄節要并入私記, hereafter *Excerpts*), based on excerpts from Guifeng Zongmi's (圭峰宗密, 780–841) *Dharma Collection and Special Practice Record* (*Faji biexing lu* 法集別行錄), to which Chinul added notes.[29] Here Chinul examined the practice of four representative traditions of early Chan: the Beizong (北宗), Niutou (牛頭宗), Hongzhou (洪州宗), and Heze (荷澤宗) schools, and concluded—with Zongmi—that the cultivation of sudden awakening/gradual practice of the Heze school was ideally suited to the needs of the majority of Buddhist practitioners.

Two works that were attributed to Chinul, *Straight Talk on the True Mind* (*Chinsim chiksŏl* 眞心直說) and *Essentials on Pure Land Practice* (*Yŏmbul yomun* 念佛要門), may be found, together with annotated translations and an introduction, in Robert E. Buswell's *Korean Approaches to Zen: Collected Works of Chinul*,[30] but these attributions are no longer accepted.[31] *Treatise on the Complete and Sudden Attainment of Buddhahood* (*Wŏndon sŏngbullon* 圓頓成佛論) and *Treatise on Resolving Doubts about Observing the Key Phrase* (*Kanhwa kyŏrŭi ron* 看話決疑論) are posthumous works, generally believed to have been discovered after Chinul's death and published in 1215 by Hyesim.[32] *Treatise on the Complete and Sudden Attainment of Buddhahood* demonstrates "that Hwaŏm thought can be deployed to provide the doctrinal underpinnings of Sŏn soteriology." As such, it "may be considered one of Chinul's most important contributions to East Asian Buddhist thought."[33]

Park Keonjoo's Challenge to the Traditional Attribution of *Treatise on Resolving Doubts about Observing the Key Phrase* to Chinul

The traditional attribution of the *Treatise on Resolving Doubts about Observing the Key Phrase*—a seemingly powerful defense of *Kanhwa Sŏn*—to Chinul, invites the following comments. Even though Chinul is considered to have discovered the thought of Dahui and introduced it with *Kanhwa Sŏn* in Korea, there is no significant mention of it in *Encouragement to Practice: The Compact of the Samādhi and Prajñā Society* (*Kwŏnsu chŏnghye kyŏlsa mun* 勸修定慧結社文, 1190), *Moguja's Secrets on Cultivating the Mind* (*Moguja susim kyŏl* 牧牛子修心訣, 1205), *Excerpts from the Exposition of the Avataṃsakasūtra* (1207), nor the posthumous *Treatise on the Complete and Sudden Attainment of Buddhahood*. Even though *Excerpts* evokes *Kanhwa Sŏn*, it does so only four times, mostly briefly, and chiefly at the very end of the work. Moreover, according to what available sources say, none of Chinul's awakening experiences are connected to the practice of *Kanhwa Sŏn*, and nowhere is it said that he ever practiced it. In any case, what need would he have had for it after his final series of awakenings at Sangmujuam? And how could he have gone through the kind of direct dialogue between a certified master and a disciple (K. *sŏnmundap* 禪問答) required to train in the practice of *Kanhwa Sŏn*? "Tracing back the radiance emanating from the mind back to its source (K. *hoegwang panjo* 廻光返照)"[34] clearly is "the process fundamental to all meditative practice" in Chinul's thought.[35] In other words, *Kanhwa Sŏn* seems to be a rather late love, at best, in Chinul's life, and the systematization of its use as advocated in the *Treatise on Resolving Doubts about Observing the Key Phrase* may well have been deeply influenced by Hyesim, if not entirely written by him and attributed to Chinul, as Park Keonjoo does not hesitate to claim. Park adds, in good measure with a number of academics, that most of the work's contents have been "directly inspired" by that of Dahui's *Records*.[36]

Park also underscores that the aforementioned classification of Chinul's teachings into three parts, provided by the *Funerary Inscription* and crowned by the shortcut approach (K. *kyŏngjŏl mun* 徑截門)—supposedly corresponding to his last awakening triggered by the reading of Dahui's *Records*—has considerably helped to instill the idea that Chinul was an adept of the practice of *Kanhwa Sŏn*.[37] Let us recall that it was on the basis of information Hyesim provided to the royal court as the detailed account of Chinul's life and career in the no-longer extant "Account of Conduct" that Kim Kunsu wrote the *Funerary Inscription*. Be this as it may, let us underscore that the *Treatise on Resolving Doubts about Observing the Key Phrase* acknowledges the value of two types of practice:[38] the conceptual investigation of the meaning of a *kongan*'s (公案) "dead words" (K. *sagu ch'amŭi* 死句參意); and the nonconceptual investigation of a *hwadu*'s (話頭) "live words" (K. *hwalgu ch'amgu* 活句參句).[39] The work thus maintains a balance between the use of words and the silence that transcends them, that is, between a kataphatic approach and an apophatic one. Moreover, it sees in the practice of *Kanhwa Sŏn* a means to trigger a sudden understanding-awakening or sudden understanding (K. *haeo* 解悟) as awakening (K. *tono* 頓悟),[40] which will be followed by gradual cultivation (K. *chŏmsu* 漸修) until the achievement of a realization-awakening (K. *chŭngo* 證悟). Keeping this in mind should prevent one from falling into the temptation of an "excessively sudden" interpretation of the final stage of Chinul's thought,[41] as Master Sŏngch'ŏl tends to, as we shall see, even when it appears to have been markedly influenced by his successor Hyesim, who was strongly inspired by Dahui.

Park Keonjoo claims not only that the *Treatise on Resolving Doubts about Observing the Key Phrase* is a work entirely written by Hyesim and attributed to Chinul but also that the four specific allusions to the practice of *Kanhwa Sŏn* that can be found in *Excerpts* are all additions inserted by Hyesim into Chinul's magnum opus in order to promote that kind of practice. Since it is not Chinul but Hyesim who published *Excerpts* after his master's demise, inserting those additions into the work was not difficult.[42] According to Park, Hyesim was inspired by an ancient Chinese practice of mixing one's thoughts into the writings of a famous master, or attributing one's own writings to them to promote one's ideas.[43] Park underscores that the technique of insertion used by Hyesim in the *Treatise on Resolving Doubts about Observing the Key Phrase* is simply an imitation of the technique used by Heze Shenhui's (荷澤神會, 670–762) disciples to discredit the Northern school, or by Dahui Zonggao to promote *kanhua chan*.[44] It consisted in adding an explicit reference to the practice of *Kanhwa Sŏn* immediately after either an old master's or Chinul's very words, for instance on the kind of practice capable of allowing one to achieve the ultimate goal of Buddhism.

As a typical example of this technique, Park takes the question found at the beginning of the *Treatise on Resolving Doubts about Observing the Key Phrase* where someone asks the Oxherder:

Since the teachings of the Hwaŏm school explain the unimpeded conditioned arising of the *dharmadhātu* [K. *pŏpkye muae yŏngi* 法界無礙緣起]⁴⁵ and eschew any semblance of grasping or rejecting [when such a realm has been reached], with what purpose in mind does the Sŏn school observe the *hwadu* while still analyzing the ten defects of practice?⁴⁶

Beginning to talk about *Kanhwa Sŏn* after having made the description of realization of "the unimpeded conditioned arising of the *dharmadhātu*," an achievement that clearly is as great as one can be, is a technique of quotation frequently used by Dahui Zonggao.⁴⁷ In other words, at the risk of contradicting themselves, Dahui and other users of this technique literally "build a house on a roof top (K. *oksang kaok* 屋上架屋)," that is, they say something that can only sound completely useless when considering what they had said before.

PARK KEONJOO'S UNDERSTANDING OF THE FOUR ALLUSIONS TO KANHWA SŎN FOUND IN *EXCERPTS*

Similarly, according to Park, Hyesim also inserted the four allusions to key phrase meditation found in *Excerpts*, all tending to claim, in a way or another, that *Kanhwa Sŏn* is the ultimate means to achieve the supreme goal of Sŏn: no-mind, which conforms with the path (K. *musim hapdomun* 無心合道門).⁴⁸

Firstly, Park sees in the description of Heze Shenhui found at the beginning of *Excerpts*, which depicts the latter as an "eminent master of intellectual understanding (K. *chihae chongsa* 知解宗師), who was not a formal successor of Liuzu Huineng," a disparaging remark toward Heze inserted by Hyesim, in complete contradiction with Chinul, who considered Heze an outstanding Sŏn master.⁴⁹

Secondly and thirdly, Hyesim made a brief insertion in the introduction of *Excerpts* to announce a longer critique, located immediately before the conclusion of the work, a full chapter on Zhaozhou's dog (C. *Zhaozhou gouzi*, K. Choju *kuja* 趙州狗子), and the ten defects (C. *shibing*, K. *sippyŏng* 十病) to be avoided when investigating the *hwadu mu* (無).

> Furthermore, as I fear that meditators who are not yet able to forget the passions and keep their minds empty and bright

might stagnate in theoretical interpretations, at the end of my exposition [i.e., of *Excerpts*] I briefly quote some statements by original masters of our school who followed the shortcut approach. My purpose there is to remove the defects of conceptual understanding so that you may know that there is a living road which leads to salvation."[50]

Park underscores that the content of this paragraph is often found in Dahui's writings and corresponds to his style. By inserting it in *Excerpts*' introduction, Hyesim clearly intended to establish a correspondence between the beginning of the work and its last chapter, the introductory part of which ends with the following paragraph.

For the sake . . . of those . . . who have the capacity to enter the path after leaving behind words, I will briefly cite some passages from the records of the patriarchs and masters. These shortcut expedients (K. *kyŏngjŏl pangp'yŏn* 徑截方便) . . . should allow accomplished meditators to know that there is one living road which leads to salvation (*chi yu ch'ulsin ilcho hwallo i* 知有出身一條活路耳).[51]

Park adds that the contents of the last chapter of the *Excerpts* are entirely borrowed from Dahui.

Fourthly, even though Chinul repeated carefully, time and again, that *samādhi* and *prajñā* (K. *chŏnghye* 定慧) are the two sine qua non pillars of practice in order to achieve "no-mind which conforms with the path (K. *musim hapdomun* 無心合道門)," a sentence of *Excerpts* suddenly and abruptly declares that "this no-mind which conforms with the path also is the entrance employed by the shortcut approach."[52] This unexpected sentence gives the impression that because it dispenses with the combined practice of *samādhi* and *prajñā* (K. *chŏnghye ssangsu* 定慧雙修), the shortcut approach is superior to the traditional approach of patriarchal Sŏn, which, on the contrary, is entirely based on that practice. Park also sees a contradiction in the fact that *Kanhwa Sŏn* practice is not based on no-mind but on *hwadu* investigation.[53]

According to Park, Hyesim did all the aforementioned falsification because *Kanhwa Sŏn* completely lacked the credentials that it needed to become recognized as part and parcel of Koryŏ's Sŏn tradition.[54] Park also underscores that in doing so, Hyesim was encouraged by the sociopolitical and religious context of Koryŏ since the 1170 coup d'état.⁵⁵ Indeed, in order to firmly establish their political power, the military officials were in serious need of a new kind of Buddhism. They were repeatedly confronted with, and therefore had to respond to, the strong criticisms of them by the Buddhist establishment affiliated with the scholastic school (K. *kyomun* 教門),⁵⁶ which could not accept submission to their rule. It is not easy to determine how much Hyesim's endeavor was motivated by his personal preferences, and how much it was motivated by a desire to match the expectations of military officials in power in order to secure the position of Susŏnsa within Korean Buddhism. Cho Myŏngje's research may help to answer this question.

Cho Myungje's Research on Hyesim's *Compilation* and Other Works

According to Cho Myungje, contrary to what is generally believed, Hyesim did not have much interest in *Kanhwa Sŏn*. Indeed, Hyesim's magnum opus *Compilation*,⁵⁷ composed in 1226 but published later, does not express any interest in Dahui's *Correspondence* (*Shuwen* 書問), *General Sermons* (*Pushui* 普說), *Sermons in the Hall* (*Shangdang* 上堂⁵⁸), etc., that is, all the works in which Dahui Zonggao emphasized the practice of *Kanhua Chan*.⁵⁹ Moreover, *Compilation* does not evoke either the criticism of Trouble Free Chan (C. *wushi Chan* 無事禪) raised by Letan Kewen (泐潭克文, 1025–1102) and Yuanwu Keqin (圜悟克勤, 1063–1135) at the intersection of the Northern (960–1127) and Southern (1127–1279) Song dynasties.⁶⁰ By contrast, judging from the number of times Hyesim quotes Dahui's "brief critiques" (C. *zheyu*, K. *ch'akŏ* 著語) of *kongans*, one may conclude that *Compilation* was chiefly interested in the kind of literary Sŏn (C. *wenzi Chan*, K. *munja Sŏn* 文字禪) that focuses on making "comments and remarks" (C. *piping*, K. *pip'yŏng* 批評) on those *kongans*.⁶¹ This is confirmed by the twenty-four *kongans* to which Hyesim attached his own "verse" (K. *songgo* 頌古) in *Tales on Handpicked Stanzas* (*Yŏmsong Sŏlhwa* 拈頌說話, hereafter *Tales*), a work based on the contents of *Compilation* but attributed to Hyesim's disciple Kagun (覺雲, ?–?). Cho underscores that Hyesim hardly ever talked about *Kanhwa Sŏn* as he wrote his verses.⁶²

Cho also suggests that Hyesim's understanding of Sŏn was not without affinities with the so-called Trouble Free Chan of the Tang dynasty (618–907), which rested on the idea that "mind is Buddha" (C. *jixin jifo*, K. *chŭksim chŭkpul* 卽心卽佛) and later became an object of criticism by advocates of *Kanhua Chan*. Indeed, in answer to a disciple who asks him for a stanza, Hyesim writes in his *Collection of Poems of the Naked Son* (*Muŭija sijip* 無依子詩集, hereafter *Collection*) that "awakening is not the result of much learning and strenuous efforts but of just letting one's mind rest quietly and go back to its original face (K. *pollae myŏnmok* 本來面目)."[63]

Cho does not deny that Hyesim attached significant importance to the practice of *Kanhwa Sŏn*, or that he recommended to his followers the detection of the ten potential defects when investigating the *mu hwadu* (K. *kuja mu pulsŏng hwa kanbyŏng non* 狗子無佛性話揀病論), the technique he himself used to achieve final awakening according to his funerary inscription. But, at the same time, Cho makes it clear that Hyesim's interests went beyond the *mu hwadu* and the "sole gate of *Kanhwa Sŏn*" (K. *kanhwa ilmun* 看話一門)."[64] In contrast with Dahui's preference for Zhaozhou's Wu (K. *mu* 無), Hyesim did not hesitate to use others like, for instance, "the bamboo clapper" (K. *chukpija* 竹篦子), "what is this?" (K. *si kae simma* 是箇甚麼), or Qingliang Taiqin's (清涼泰欽, d. 974) "letter A" (C. *ya zi*, K. *a cha* 啞字).[65] According to Cho, the reason why Hyesim is interpreted as essentially focused on *Kanhwa Sŏn* resides in the fact that, until recently, only his *Recorded Sayings* (Ŏrok 語錄)[66] have been studied, to the detriment of research on *Compilation*, *Tales*, *Collection* and other works.[67]

If Park's and Cho's research results are combined, it not only becomes quite clear that Hyesim, not Chinul, promoted *Kanhwa Sŏn* at Susŏnsa but also that Hyesim retained at least as much interest in Literary Sŏn, and even in Trouble Free Sŏn, as in *Kanhwa Sŏn*. In other words, even though Hyesim promoted the practice of *Kanhwa Sŏn* as the head of Susŏnsa, he did not drop his interest in more traditional forms of Sŏn. According to Cho, Hyesim's attitude plainly reflects the sociopolitical situation he was in, which was between tradition and transformation. On the one hand, as the writing of *Compilation* and other works proves, he was well aware that monks in Susŏnsa and elsewhere in the peninsula had no reason to suddenly give up the kinds of Sŏn practice they were accustomed to;[68] on the other hand, he had to take into account the expectations of military rulers, like Ch'oe'u (崔瑀, r. 1219–1249), who were in need of a new kind of Buddhism—like the one that *Kanhwa Sŏn* could provide—to back them politically and secure their economic interests.[69] Cho adds that safe traveling to southern Song China was virtually impossible during the thirteenth century, thus rendering impossible the kind of direct dialogue between a master and disciple (C. *chanwenda*, K. *sŏnmundap* 禪問答)

required by the training leading to a certification (C. *yinke*, K. *inga* 印可) in the practice of *Kanhwa Sŏn*. As mentioned in the introduction, it is only in the fourteenth century that Korean monks managed to travel to China and get the certification that allowed them to establish a connection between the Linji school and their homeland.[70]

HOW DID HYESIM INFLUENCE THE INTERPRETATION OF HIS MASTER'S THOUGHT?

In view of those conclusions, and in answer to the question raised above, it may be inferred that Hyesim's falsification work, as described by Park, was at least partly motivated by a desire to match the expectations of the military officials in power, in order to secure the position of Susŏnsa within Korean Buddhism. One may also infer that personal preferences contributed to Hyesim's motivation. Nevertheless, in view of Cho's conclusion, which is based on an overall and thorough analysis of Hyesim's works, Hyesim's thought is in no way reducible to the sole content of his *Recorded Sayings* and thus to the practice of *Kanhwa Sŏn*.

One sometimes hears that Chingak Hyesim betrayed the eclectic mind of Pojo Chinul regarding language and soteriology by overemphasizing the practice of *Kanhwa Sŏn*. It is hoped that the research presented here has successfully demonstrated that Hyesim was endowed with a broad, clever, and complex mind, at least as eclectic as that of his master, the Oxherder Chinul.

Part II
The Sociopolitical Background of the Sino-Korean Connection

An essential aspect of the Sino-Korean Connection is its sociopolitical background, to which few scholars have paid attention.

In the fourteenth century, when King Kongmin (恭愍王, 1351–1374) ascended the throne, he wanted to reduce the influence of the Yuan (元, 1271–1368) on Koryŏ's international relations. In order to succeed, he had to suppress the pro-Yuan factions domestically, especially the most influential clans (K. *kwŏnmun sejok* 權門勢族), which were closely connected to the Nine Schools (Kusanmun 九山門) of Sŏn, and to favor the growth of new ones capable of backing him. To apply that policy to Buddhism, Kongmin chose to promote the development of the Sino-

Korean connection. To achieve that goal, he appointed T'aego Pou royal preceptor and entrusted him with the responsibility of all appointments within Buddhism, thus making him supervisor of the whole tradition, and created the Department of Complete Interpenetration (Wŏnyungbu 圓融府) to assist him. Notwithstanding a conspicuous lack of contact with the rising gentry, T'aego was astonishingly well connected to the rest of the polity. Besides the influential families to which he was naturally related by birth, his network encompassed Empress Qi (奇皇后, 1301–1369) and a number of power-oriented public servants, some of them disreputable. T'aego's activities significantly weakened the Nine Schools of Sŏn, and he, as well as Naong Hyegŭn, became influential representatives of Buddhism with a large following, to the extent that their lineages became the mainstream of the tradition. This strong trend was maintained by their disciples Hwan'am Honsu (幻庵混修, 1320–1392) and Mogam Ch'anyŏng (木庵粲英, 1328–1390) during the reign of King U (禑王, 1374–1388); however, it was not powerful enough to set in motion an overall reform of Buddhism, the general decay of which is inseparable from the downfall of Koryŏ.[71] It seems that T'aego's failure may be attributed to the following weaknesses: the ambiguity of his sociopolitical position as a Sŏn master; the inadequacy of the *Kanhwa Sŏn* doctrine he was advocating to face challenges raised by the historical context the kingdom was in; and his lack of influence with the rising gentry looking for an entirely new sociopolitical paradigm.

At the beginning of the Chosŏn (朝鮮, 1392–1910) dynasty, after King T'aejo (太祖王, 1393–1398), with the overwhelming influence of the Neo-Confucians at the court, T'aego and Naong's legacy lost its support. However, Chinul's teaching resurfaced later during the Chosŏn period, albeit in the context of the Policy of Repression of Buddhism and Promotion of Confucianism (K. ŏkpul sungyu chŏngch'aek 抑佛崇儒政策). Indeed, Chinul's thought made decisive comebacks, exerting strong influence on monks such as Kihwa (己和, 1376–1433, also known as Hamhŏ Tŭkt'ong 涵虛得通) and, later on, Chŏnghŏ Hyujŏng (淸虛休靜), alias Sŏsan Taesa (西山大師, 1520–1604), the most towering Buddhist figure of the Chosŏn dynasty. It also attracted a number of important commentaries.[72]

In the aftermath of the Imjin (壬辰, 1592–1598) and Pyŏngja (丙子, 1636–1637) Japanese and Manchu invasions, the Sino-Korean connection made another major comeback. Indeed, the participation of armies of monks in repelling the invaders created a political climate favorable to a partial rehabilitation of Buddhism. But the two wars had thrown the peninsula into a state of chaos; to face the resulting crisis, the Neo-Confucians were actively compiling genealogical records in an effort to create a strict social order based on clans. In order to revive itself in such a context, not only did the saṃgha (K. sŭngga 僧伽) have to redefine its identity, but it also had to do this in line with the Neo-Confucians' endeavors. To do so it began by proclaiming, despite a total lack of historical grounds, that all Chosŏn's monks belonged to the dharma lineage of Sŏsan Taesa who was famous for having levied an army of monks during the Imjin invasion. Afterward, it proclaimed that Sŏsan was a sixth-generation disciple of T'aego and that the transmission of the lamp (K. *chŏndŭng* 傳燈), or, of the dharma (K. *chŏnbŏp* 傳法) between the former and the latter had taken place over time without any physical interruption of the lineage. That amounted to claiming—despite a conspicuous lack of historical evidence—a continuous human succession (K. *injŏk kyesŭng* 人的繼承) instead of a purely doctrinal one (K. *sasangjŏk kyesŭng* 思想的繼承). By doing so, the *saṃgha* intended to accumulate not only the prestige of Sŏsan and T'aego but also of the Linji school's Yangqi (K. Yangki) branch as well as, beyond, through the Sixth Patriarch and Bodhidharma, the Buddha Śākyamuni himself. If that Dharma Transmission Doctrine (K. *pŏpt'ongsŏl* 法通說) had the advantage of allowing Korean Buddhism to recover its patent of nobility—by putting forward a match to the Neo-Confucians' Transmission of the Dao Doctrine (K. *tot'ongsŏl* 道通說)—it had the serious disadvantage of reducing its horizon to the Sino-Korean connection, thus marginalizing or excluding the lineages and the teachings of masters like Pojo Chinul.[73]

A debate over the identity of Korean Buddhism flared up again in the nineteenth century and lasted until the beginning of the twentieth. It was sparked by the rising influence of doctrinal studies that challenged the supremacy of key phrase meditation as promoted by the text-phobic heirs of the Sino-Korean connection. Paekp'a Kŭngsŏn (白坡亙璇, 1767–1852), a lapsed adept of textual studies, was its principal protagonist; in his *Hand Mirror of the Sŏn School* (*Sŏnmun Sugyŏng* 禪文手鏡), he presented a new *doctrinal taxonomy* (K. *kyosang p'ansŏk* 教相判釋) that he systemized under the Imje school—to which he belonged—thus introducing an unheard-of gradation in the quality of the teaching provided by the Chinese Five Houses (C. *wujia*, K. *oga* 五家). The controversy is peppered with regional feelings of animosity (K. *chiyŏk kamjŏng* 地域感情) toward the geographical areas within which dwelled adversaries and readily resorts to the Confucian sense of seniority (K. *sŏnbae hubae kwangye* 先輩後輩關係) to find fault with younger opponents at the expense of a real debate. Although those who took part in it were generally well qualified, most of their arguments boiled down to hammering out truths that were already known without bringing about any doctrinal breakthroughs. However, it is worth mentioning that Ch'usa Kim Chŏnghŭi (秋史 金正喜, 1786–1856), a layman, criticized Paekp'a's "key phrase meditation absolutism," saying that in order to be properly understood *Kanhwa Sŏn* had to be put back into the historical context from which it was born.[74]

All of the aforementioned examples demonstrate that the sudden/gradual debate has never been a purely doctrinal matter in Korean history; on the contrary, just like in Chinese history, it has always been closely connected to the sociopolitical background against which it was occurring.

Part III
A Critical Evaluation of T'oeong Sŏngch'ŏl's Influence

In the second half of the twentieth century, inspired again by Linji-style exclusivism, the influential Sŏn Master T'oeong Sŏngch'ŏl (退翁性徹, 1912–1993, hereafter Sŏngch'ŏl) attempted to debunk Chinul's sudden/gradual paradigm, criticizing it sharply and relentlessly throughout his life, trying to demonstrate, to no avail, that Chinul revised his position during his final years, favoring the doctrine of sudden awakening/sudden practice (K. *tono tonsu sasang* 頓悟頓修思想).[75]

As a reformer of the Jogye Order, Sŏngch'ŏl is one of the most outstanding figures of Korean Buddhism in the twentieth century. Interestingly, he never received systematic training in Buddhist studies. In fact, he did not receive much of an education at all, in either public or private institutions, prior to becoming a monk. Indeed, because of his poor health, he had to stop attending classes with his peers after graduating from primary school. Once he became a mountain monk (K. *sansŭng* 山僧), and despite never having attended classes in any of the Korean monasteries' lecture halls (K. *kangwŏn* 講院), Sŏngch'ŏl rapidly acquired a reputation for having thoroughly read all of the Buddhist canon. Chŏnche (闡提, b. 1939), his eldest disciple, says that he spent a considerable amount of time translating Sanskrit Buddhist texts into Korean, encouraging reputable academics to do the same and trying to relate Buddhist doctrine to contemporary science. However, Sŏngch'ŏl's knowledge always remained that of a self-taught, chiefly practice-oriented meditation monk (K. *sŏnsŭng* 禪僧); he never became an academic trained in Buddhist scholarship, which helps us understand why he was good neither at teaching nor at writing. According to Wŏnt'aek (圓澤, b. 1944), his best known disciple and promotor, Sŏngch'ŏl was adamant that "theory ruins Sŏn" (K. *iron i Sŏn ŭl mangch'inda* 理論이 禪을 망친다).⁷⁶

Sŏngch'ŏl's Life

Sŏngch'ŏl's Life as a Layman until 1936⁷⁷

Sŏngch'ŏl was born Yi Yŏngju (李英柱) in Mukkogni (默谷里), a village in northwestern South Kyŏngsang Province, in 1912, two years after Japan's formal colonization of the Korean peninsula (1910–1945). The first-born son of a landowner, at age fourteen, he married seventeen-year-old Yi Tŏgmyŏng (李德明, 1909–1982). In his early twenties, while living as a married layman and now with a daughter, three events marked his change of circumstance.

Firstly, a Buddhist monk introduced him to the *Song of Enlightenment* (*Zhengdaojia*, K. *Chŭngdoga* 證道歌) of Yongjia Xuanjue (K. Yŏngga Hyŏn'gak 永嘉玄覺, 665–713). According to tradition, Yongjia was nicknamed "overnight awakening" (C. *yisujue*, K. *ilsuk'kak* 一宿覺) in memory of the sudden awakening that he achieved overnight after his first encounter with the Sixth Patriarch Liuzu Huineng (K. Yukcho Hyenŭng, 六祖惠能, 638–713). Before, Yongjia had enjoyed a reputation for having mastered all the scholastic teachings of both the Tiantai (K. Chŏnt'ae 天台) and Huayan (K. Hwaŏm 華嚴) schools but without ever reaching full awakening. As a result, Yongjia's *Song of Enlightenment* very powerfully extols the sudden and complete realization of the Way (C. *zhengdao*, K. *chŭngdo* 證道) through the practice of Chan (K. Sŏn 禪), thus proclaiming the absolute superiority of the meditative school's teachings over those of the scholastic ones. The influence the *Song of Enlightenment* exerted upon Yi Yŏngju helps explain the powerful anti-intellectual drive that pervades his thought.

Secondly, as he was reading a Buddhist periodical, Yi Yŏngju fortuitously discovered key phrase meditation and Dahui Zonggao (K. Taehye Chonggo). Let us recall that Dahui was the most decisive Chinese promoter of *Kanhua Chan*, and that as a disciple of Yuanwu Keqin, he belonged to the Yangqi branch (K. *Yanggip'a* 楊岐波) of the Linji school. According to Dahui, *Kanhua Chan* was the means par excellence to achieve sudden awakening, in conformity with the teachings of the Buddhas and Patriarchs.

Thirdly, Yi Yŏngju started practicing *Kanhwa Sŏn* by himself at Taewŏnsa (大源寺) in Mount Chiri (智異山), receiving guidance from the *Records of Chan Master Dahui Zonggao* (*Dahui Zonggao chansi yulu*, K. *Taehye Chonggo sŏnsa ŏrok* 大慧宗杲 禪師語錄). After over five weeks of deep and intense practice, he achieved "sameness of movement and stillness" (K. *tongjŏng iryŏ* 動靜一如), a state of consciousness such that the *hwadu* keeps resounding extremely clearly (K. *sŏngsŏng* 星星) in a meditator's mind, whether standing still or moving around. Reaching this first of three stages (K. *sammungwan* 三門關) along the path to full awakening, Yi was strongly emboldened to make the decision to leave his home and become a monk (K. *ch'ulga* 出家). He acquired the dharma name (K. *pŏbmyŏng* 法名) Sŏngch'ŏl (性徹), which means "thoroughly manifested Buddha Nature."

SŎNGCH'ŎL'S LIFE AS A SŎN MONK (1936 TO 1993)

In 1936, Yi Yŏngju departed from his home village, leaving behind a first daughter and a wife who was pregnant with a second one—the future and well-known Buddhist nun Pulp'il (不必, "useless")—saying that he would come back in ten years. Although he never returned, it seems that he never divorced either. He went to Haeinsa (海印寺) in order to begin living as a Sŏn monk with the then very famous Tongsan Hyeil (東山慧日, 1890–1965) as his benevolent master (K. *ŭnsa* 恩師). From then on, Sŏngch'ŏl started to live as a meditation monk.[78] He spent the summer and winter annual retreat seasons (K. *ha dong an'gŏ* 夏冬安居), lasting roughly three months each, practicing *Kanhwa Sŏn* in meditation halls (K. *sŏnwŏn* 禪院) located mostly within Kyŏngsang province. He spent the rest of his time reading Buddhist scriptures and books. He did not return to his home monastery until 1967, the year he was appointed Sŏn master (K. *pangjang* 方丈) there. Thus, Sŏngch'ŏl's monastic life can be divided into two main periods: before and after the beginning of his public life in 1967.

The first period lasted thirty years, from 1936 to 1966. Between 1936 and 1946, Sŏngch'ŏl lived as an itinerant monk (K. *unsu* 雲水, lit. "cloud and water," another name given to Sŏn monks). In 1940, at age twenty-nine and while taking part in the winter retreat at Tonghwa monastery's (桐華寺) Kŭmgang sŏnwŏn (金剛禪院) in Mount P'algong (八公山, North Kyŏngsang province), he recited and wrote an awakening stanza (K. *odosong* 悟道頌). Following that enlightenment, to receive confirmation in the form of a dharma seal (K. *in'ga* 印可), he met the most famous Sŏn masters of the day, Hyobong Hagnul (曉峰學訥, 1888–1966) and Man'gong

Wŏlmyŏn (滿空月面, 1871–1946), from Songgwangsa (松廣寺) and Sudŏksa (修德寺) respectively (South Chŏlla and South Ch'ungchŏng provinces). These encounters left him deeply disappointed. At about the same time, he discovered the sudden awakening/gradual practice (K. *tono chŏmsu* 頓悟漸修) doctrine of State Preceptor Pojo Chinul, Songgwangsa's standard bearer, but he found it irrelevant to the sudden awakening/sudden practice (K. *tono tonsu* 頓悟頓修) experience that he had just achieved. From then on, he stopped looking for confirmation of his awakening.

Sŏngch'ŏl's dissatisfaction evokes that of Siddhārtha Gautama with the teachings of the famous *dhyāna* Masters Ālāra Kālāma and Udakka Ramaputta, which led him to start threading a new path on his own. But, according to an unofficial story (K. *yasa* 野史), Sŏngch'ŏl was humiliated by Hyobong's unexpectedly cold reception, and he rapidly left Songgwangsa empty-handed.[79] Some see in this episode one of the main reasons—if not the chief one—why Sŏngch'ŏl spent his public life attempting to debunk Chinul's teachings. Be this as it may, from a historical viewpoint, the fact that Sŏngch'ŏl never received a dharma seal (nor transmitted one) leaves entirely open the question of his awakening, albeit many consider him a living Buddha.

From 1947 to 1949, following the liberation of Korea in 1945, a number of monks headed by Sŏngch'ŏl organized the Pongamsa religious community (Pongamsa *kyŏlsa* 鳳巖寺結社, North Kyŏngsang province), which promoted the reformation of Korean Buddhism under the motto "Let's live according to the Buddha [Śākyamuni's] Dharma" (*Puchŏnim pŏptaero salja* 부처님 法대로 살자). The outbreak of the Korean War on June 25, 1950, put an end to this endeavor. Even though this religious community was short-lived, its spirit has exerted (perhaps not always for the best) a long-lasting influence on the destiny of contemporary Korean Buddhism. For instance, because of its fundamentalist tendencies, its influence is sometimes perceived as controversial. As an example of those tendencies, Sŏngch'ŏl wanted Korean monks to use bowls and robes that were exact replicas of the ones used by *bhikkhus* in early Buddhism. Moreover, some members of the community, like Chŏngdam (青潭 1902–1971), and Sŏ Ŭihyŏn (徐義玄, b. 1935), were to develop strong ties to political circles under the dictatorship. Sŏ, the youngest member of the group, became the Jogye Order's infamous head administrator in the late 1980s and early 1990s, under Sŏngch'ŏl's patriarchate.

During most of the war and the year that followed, Sŏngch'ŏl lived as a hermit in the shanty that he built and named "the hut of the *icchan-*

tika"[80] (K. Chŏnjaegul 闡提窟) in the vicinity of Anjŏngsa (安靜寺) in the South Kyŏngsang province. From then on, he started requiring three thousand prostrations—in front of the Buddha—from anyone requesting to meet him. It is also during those years that Sŏngchŏl started to read a considerable number of books written by Japanese Buddhist scholars.[81]

From 1955 till 1964, Sŏngchŏl confined himself (K. *tonggu pulch'ul* 洞口不出) at P'agyesa's (把溪寺) Sŏngjŏnam (聖殿庵) in the North Kyŏngsang province, which he had surrounded by barbed wire. There, he is believed to have remained seated in meditation without ever lying down (K. *changjwa purwa* 長座不臥). A sign on a huge tree in front of Sŏngjŏnam claims that that very tree witnessed Sŏngchŏl's tireless practice. Even so, Master Chin'gwan (眞寬, b. 1948), corepresentative of the Buddhist Committee for Human Rights and director of Mujinjang [Sŭnim] (無盡藏, 1932–2013) Buddhist Culture Research Institute, insisted that no one can remain seated in meditation for so long without lying down.

To understand the meaning of that period in Sŏngchŏl's life, we should note the many transformations that occurred in Buddhism under Japanese rule, including that most Buddhist monks were married. In the aftermath of the Korean War (1950–1953), between 1954 and 1962, that is, during the later years of Syngman Rhee's presidency (1948–1960) and the early years of that of Pak Chung-hee (1960–1979), a dramatic and bloody schism occurred between the married monks (K. *taechŏsŭng* 帶妻僧) and the few still upholding celibacy (K. *pigu* 比丘). Out of seven thousand monks, approximately three hundred were celibate (i.e., slightly more than 4 percent). Out of those three hundred, a mere seventy were practicing Sŏn monks. Although begged by other Buddhist monks—including his benevolent master Tongsan—to take part in the movement for the purification of Buddhism from its Japanese elements (K. *waesaek Pulgyo chŏnghwa undong* 倭色佛教淨化運動) instigated by President Rhee, Sŏngchŏl, to their dismay, adamantly refused to do so. Instead, he took refuge in solitude for a decade. It is perhaps because even though he lived as a Sŏn monk, he was still married from a legal viewpoint and had no intention of asking for a divorce.

The second period of Sŏngchŏl life as a monk, from 1967 to 1993, corresponds to the era of sociopolitical stability and economic growth, which culminated in the so-called Miracle on the Han River. These are the years of Sŏngchŏl's career within Haein comprehensive training monastery (K. *ch'ongnim* 叢林) and the Jogye Order. From 1967 on, nicknamed "Tiger of Mount Kaya" (*Kayasan* ŭi *horangi* 伽倻山의 호랑이), he dwelled in Paengnyŏnam (白蓮庵) as the highly respected and fearsome *dhyāna* master of the Haein *ch'ongnim*. Sŏngch'ŏl had been close to Master Chaun (慈雲, 1911–1992) and the aforementioned Chŏngdam since the 1940s. He highly praised the role played by the latter in the Buddhist purification ordered by President Rhee, although he himself refused to take part in it. Chŏngdam was directly connected to President Pak's wife, Yuk Yŏngsu Yŏsa (陸英修 女史, 1925–1974), a devout Buddhist with the dharma name Taedŏkhwa Posal (大德華 菩薩). Chŏngdam took advantage of his connection to the Blue House to appeal in favor of the celibate monks against the married monks. As a result, all the rulings made by the judiciary in favor of the latter were nullified. With the help of Chaun, Chŏngdam also played a leading role in the appointment of Sŏngch'ŏl as Haein *ch'ongnim*'s Sŏn master.[82] It is noteworthy that the time at which Sŏngch'ŏl was appointed corresponds—perhaps not coincidentally—with the death of Tongsan (1965) and Hyobong (1966).

Although Sŏngch'ŏl added the pseudonym "retired old man" (T'oeong 退翁) to his monastic name on his sixtieth birthday (K. *hwangap* 還甲), it is during these later years that he wrote all his works, starting with the *Dharma Lineage of Korean Buddhism* (*Han'guk Pulgyo ŭi pŏmmaek* 韓國佛敎의 法脈) in 1976, the year when Sŏong (西翁, 1912–2003), the fifth patriarch of the Jogye Order announced the beginning of a revitalizing reform (K. *yusin* 維新) of Korean Buddhism. Spearheaded by Sŏngch'ŏl, the Buddhist reform started four years after President Pak made his famous political Yusin declaration. The reform of Buddhism was to be based on the exclusive promotion of the practice of *Kanhwa Sŏn* and the sudden/sudden (K. *tono tonsu*) doctrine transmitted by the Yangqi branch of the Linji school. Moreover, Sŏngch'ŏl was appointed Jogye Order's sixth supreme patriarch (K. *chongjŏng* 宗正) in 1981—one year after Chŏn Tuhwan's (全斗煥, b. 1931) coup d'état—and the seventh in 1991. Although he retained this responsibility until his death in 1993, Sŏngch'ŏl's capacity to work was considerably diminished after 1987.

SŏNGCH'ŏL'S WORKS AND THOUGHT[83]

Sŏngch'ŏl's works comprise eleven volumes, called *Sŏngch'ŏl's Dharma Talk Collection* (*Sŏngch'ŏl sŭnim pŏbŏjip* 法語集), and are divided into two bodies. The first one, comprising seven books, was not written by Sŏngch'ŏl but is a compilation of his dharma talks collected by his disciples; the second comprises four books mostly written by Sŏngch'ŏl himself. Because their content sometimes seems to have been significantly altered by Sŏngch'ŏl's disciples, the publications of the first part cannot always be considered as reliable as those from the second. In addition, modern Korean translations of classical Chinese and Korean master's Dharma talks established by scholars at Sŏngch'ŏl's and Wŏnt'aek's request, the thirty-seven volumes of the *Library of Old Mirrors of the Groove of Meditation* (*Sŏllim kogyŏng ch'ongsŏ* 禪林古鏡叢書) cannot be considered part of Sŏngch'ŏl's writings.

THE FIRST PART OF SŎNGCH'ŎL'S WORKS

Among the volumes of the first part, the first two comprise the *Sermon of One Hundred Days*[84] (*Paegil pŏmmun sang ha* 百日法門上下) published in 1987, which are the best known. They deserve special attention since they contain the teachings transmitted by Sŏngch'ŏl at Haeinsa during the winter retreat of 1967, just after he commenced his public life. These teachings amount to an introduction to Buddhism understood as the religion of enlightenment, which is defined as an actual, complete and definitive awakening to the Middle Path (Skt. *madhyama pratipad*, K. *chungdo* 中道). In his postface to this work, Wŏnt'aek describes it as a masterly attempt to demonstrate the relationship between the various doctrines contained in major sutras and the whole of Buddhism, by examining them from the standpoint of the Middle Path, an ideal that vivifies each of them. For Sŏngch'ŏl, what the Buddha Śākyamuni discovered through his awakening, and taught during his lifetime, is nothing but the Middle Path. Sŏngch'ŏl's *Sermon of One Hundred Days* was deeply inspired and thoroughly influenced by the Japanese Buddhist scholar Miyamoto Shoson's (宮本正尊, 1893–1983) magnum opus *Madhyamaka Thought and Its Developments* (*Chūdō shisō oyobi sono hattatsu* 中道思想及びその發達),[85] which accepted Japanese imperialism and nationalism centered on the emperor.[86] Whatever the reason, the English translation of *Paegil pŏmmun* does not acknowledge and take into account these strong hermeneutical influences.

Above all, the *Sermon of One Hundred Days* is well known because it sparked the Korean sudden/gradual debate, which remains one of the major ongoing debates within Korean Buddhism. This debate saw Sŏngch'ŏl publicly criticize the sudden/gradual approach of awakening and practice by stating that Chinul, its main protagonist, cannot be honored as the Jogye Order's founder. For Sŏngch'ŏl, awakening is entirely sudden (K. *tono* 頓悟), and he who is awakened suddenly becomes a Buddha (K. *tonsu* 頓修). Such is the meaning of the sudden awakening and sudden practice doctrine that he then started to advocate openly and that he championed without compromise throughout his public life. For Sŏngchŏl, as for Dahui Zonggao, the best practice to achieve the same experience in one's present life is none other than *Kanhwa Sŏn*.

As a result, Sŏngchŏl radically rejects any understanding of the concept of sudden awakening if it implies a follow-up with gradual practice (K. *chŏmsu* 漸修). While Sŏngchŏl's sudden awakening implies the complete and sudden achievement of Buddhahood, Chinul's sudden awakening would merely correspond to entering the stream (K. *imryu* 入流) at the level of the eleventh of the fifty-two degrees of awakening described by the Tiantai and Huayan schools—albeit, in fact, for Li Tongxuan this entering takes place at the level of the first degree, not the eleventh one. Consequently, Chinul's *tono* would be nothing but an understanding-awakening (K. *haeo* 解悟), a partial destruction of one's passions (K. *punp'a* 分破) and, accordingly, a partial awakening (K. *punjŭng* 分證). For Sŏngchŏl, the highest and correct awakening (K. *musang chŏnggak* 無上正覺) requires a thorough purification of the eighth consciousness, or storehouse consciousness (Skt. *ālayavijñāna*, K. *aroeyasik* 阿賴耶識). Even the bodhisattvas that have reached the fifty-first degree of awakening (K. *tŭnggak* 等覺) have not freed themselves from the three subtle conceptions (K. *samse* 三細) dwelling in their eighth consciousness. In other words, according to Sŏngchŏl, Chinul's sudden awakening is nothing but a misnomer that has caused a considerable amount of confusion within the Korean Sŏn tradition.

Sŏngchŏl attributed Chinul's mistakes to the influence of Guifeng Zongmi (K. Kyubong Chongmil, 圭峰宗密, 780–841), himself influenced by Heze Shenhui (K. Hat'aek Sinhoe 荷澤神會, 668–760 or 670–762). Heze was a first-generation disciple of the sixth patriarch but was subsequently dismissed by the Chan school for being a master with an excessive propensity to learn and conceptualize (K. *chihae chongsa* 知解宗師). As the putative patriarch of both the Heze (K. Hat'aek) and the Huayan schools, Guifeng worked at harmonizing the meditative and the doctrinal approaches (K. *Sŏn kyo ilch'i* 禪教一致). Sŏngchŏl categorically rejected all such attempts as "double-dealing or sitting on the fence" (K. *yangdari kŏlch'igi* 兩다리 걸치기).

In the postface of the *Sermon of One Hundred Days*, Wŏnt'aek explains that it was published so late because Sŏngchŏl's lectures as recorded on tapes in 1967 required a considerable amount of work in order to be reshaped into readable books. One may wonder why, even though

Sŏngchŏl stated that "theory ruins Sŏn," some of his followers worked so hard at transforming dharma talks into books that—far from being destined to become writings—were addressed to Sŏn monks involved in the practice of deep meditation during a three-month retreat. Moreover, a new version of these talks—in three volumes now instead of two—saw publication in 2014.[87] A comparison of the old and new editions reveals that the language has been significantly transformed and the contents considerably amplified. In other words, in order to become publishable, the contents of the original tapes have undergone even more reworking.[88]

Among the many transformations noticeable in the new edition, the most important one is the clear effort made to soften the harsh tone used by Sŏngchŏl to condemn Chinul. Indeed, Wŏnt'aek declares in his preface that Sŏngchŏl did not in fact criticize Chinul, but the monks who did not understand that late in his life Chinul gave up the sudden/gradual teaching in favor of the sudden/sudden one.[89] Accordingly, Chinul is clearly presented as having (wisely) rejected the sudden/gradual approach and acknowledged the superiority of the sudden/sudden one in his posthumously published works.

Such an interpretation will be contested by the many who consider the fundamental congruence of the meditative and doctrinal approaches (K. *Sŏn kgyo ilch'i* 禪教一致) to be part and parcel of Chinul's thought. Indeed, beyond time and space and in absentia, it tends to transform State Preceptor Pojo Chinul into someone who—in the end—completely agrees with Sŏngchŏl. In other words, Chinul's rehabilitation is conditional. To be sure, to prove that he is acceptable from the sudden/sudden viewpoint, Chinul had to abandon all his earlier writings, including his magnum opus *Excerpts*, the study of which was—and remains—forbidden by Sŏngchŏl at the lecture hall in Haeinsa. In the end, since this amounts to stripping Chinul of his identity as a scholiast, his rehabilitation boils down to his disguised neutralization. All this reinforces Sŏngchŏl's dominating position in the history of Korean Buddhism. Beyond Sŏngchŏl's superficial befriending, the radical hostility toward Chinul as he was otherwise understood remains unchanged. In the end, there is no significant difference between the old and the new versions of the *Paegil pŏmmun*. In other words, we wind up just where we started (K. *toro* Amit'abul 도로 阿彌陀佛).

One often hears that Sŏngchŏl's biggest contribution to Korean Buddhism in the twentieth century is his relentless endeavor to provide a clear definition of complete awakening, as if Chinul had not done the same. Be this as it may, Sŏngchŏl's antagonizing of Chinul constitutes, if not the cornerstone of his teachings, certainly one of the main keys required to understand them. When examined from the perspective of the political background of the Chinese and Korean sudden/gradual debates throughout history, Sŏngch'ŏl's radical criticism of Chinul can be understood as a full-fledged "doctrinal *coup d'état.*"⁹⁰ The attempt made in the new edition of the *Sermon of One Hundred Days* to soften Sŏngch'ŏl's harsh tone regarding Chinul clearly appears to be an answer to recent research that "examines the socio-political underpinnings of his [Sŏngch'ŏl's] reformation and defines six points of structural resonance between it and the way of the authoritarian [anticommunist] state under which it was carried out."⁹¹ Judging from the overall contents of the second part of Sŏngch'ŏl's works, Wŏnt'aek's claim to the contrary hardly seems to be sustainable.

THE SECOND PART OF SŎNGCH'ŎL'S WORKS

The first work on the list of those written by Sŏngch'ŏl himself is an annotated translation of the Dunhuang manuscript of the *Platform Sūtra of the Sixth Patriarch* (*Yukcho Tan'gyŏng Tonhwang-bon hyŏnt'o pŏnyŏk* 六祖壇經敦惶本 縣吐飜譯).⁹² Published as his last work in 1987, six years before his death, it represents Sŏngch'ŏl's ultimate attempt to prove that orthodox Sŏn (i.e., Sixth Patriarch Huineng's Chan) is exclusively founded on the sudden awakening/sudden practice doctrine. Sŏngch'ŏl truly believed—despite strong evidence to the contrary—that the Dunhuang manuscript amounted to Huineng's *ipsissima verba* (very words). Although Sŏngch'ŏl's translation is the first in Korean history, it has been followed by a number of others, mostly characterized by diametrically opposed interpretations.⁹³ Judging from Sŏngch'ŏl's preface, a few sentences of the *Platform Sūtra* are of considerable importance to grasp how he understood himself and his role in the history of Korean Buddhism.

> To know the mind, see the nature and [suddenly] accomplish the Buddha-Way by oneself (K. *siksim kyŏnsŏng chasŏng Pul to* 識心見性自成佛道).⁹⁴
>
> Unless you know your fundamental mind, studying the Dharma is futile (K. *pulsik ponsim hakpŏp mu'ik* 不識本心學法無益).⁹⁵
>
> After awakening, one's deeds are the deeds of a Buddha (K. *ohu suhaeng Pul haeng* 悟後修行佛行).⁹⁶

Only hand down the sudden teaching. Enter into the world and destroy erroneous doctrine[s] (K. *yujŏn tonʼgyobŏp chʼulse pʼasajong* 唯傳敦教法 出世破邪宗).[97]

This last quote points to the task that Sŏngchŏl dedicated his entire life to, the heterodox school (K. *sajong* 邪宗) to be destroyed, which obviously refers to Chinul's sudden/gradual paradigm. Accordingly, Wŏnʼtaek attempted to connect Sŏngchŏl to the emblematic figure of Sixth Patriarch Huineng, if not to identify the latter with the former.[98] By publishing an annotated translation of the *Platform Sūtra*, Sŏngchŏl wanted to place his teachings under the authority of the sixth patriarch.[99]

The *Correct Path of Sŏn* (*Sŏnmun chŏngno* 禪門正路),[100] Sŏngchŏl's second work and best known, is considered his magnum opus. It is the compilation of Dharma talks made at Haeinsa at the end of the 1960s and during the 1970s. As clearly expressed in the preface of the work, those talks aimed at demonstrating that the Buddhas and patriarchs of the past exclusively advocated the sudden/sudden doctrine, not the sudden/gradual one. To that end, the *Correct Path of Sŏn* is composed of 326 quotations, extracted from some eighty-eight classical Buddhist sutras, treaties, and records, loosely organized and distributed unevenly in nineteen chapters.[101] Thus, Sŏngchŏl's methodology consisted in gathering as many scriptural testimonies as possible because, for him, orthodoxy and strict fidelity to past masters' words—as he understood them—were synonymous. As a result, the *Correct Path of Sŏn* leaves no room at all for debate. Perhaps some will claim that Sŏngchŏl's genius consists in the way he meticulously gathered various extracts to emphasize his point and condemn his adversaries. However, many have pointed to problems with the way Sŏngchŏl interprets Buddhist texts, drawing water to his own mill, so to speak.[102] Moreover, almost everybody has complained that the work is difficult to understand, to the point that it seems to have been written in an idiolect: a language spoken only by the individual who makes use of it. Nevertheless, Sŏngchŏl claimed that if someone wanted to inherit his dharma transmission, they should master the contents of this magnum opus. Therefore, the *Commentary of the Correct Path of Sŏn* (*Sŏnmun chŏngno pʼyŏngsŏk* 禪門正路評釋) was published as a more accessible alternative in 1993. Actually, this commentary is also difficult to understand, which led to the publishing of *Smash the Old Mirrors and Come* (*Yet kŏul rŭl pusuʼgo onŏra* 옛 거울을 부수고 오너라) in 2006.

The third work is *Magnificence of the Origin* (*Ponji p'unggwang* 本地風光). Published in 1982, one year after the *Correct Path of Sŏn*, it is a collection of nearly a hundred *kongan*, collected and commented on by Sŏngchŏl and to which were added a few poems composed at the end of long meditation retreats, making for an even one hundred in all. This number was probably inspired by the *Book of the Two Cliffs* (C. *Shuangbishu*, K. *Ssangbyŏksŏ* 雙壁書), which comprises the *Blue Cliff Record* (*Biyanlu*, K. *Pyŏgamnok* 碧巖錄)[103] of the Linji school, and the *Guidance record* (*Congronglu*, K. *Chongyongnok* 從容錄)[104] of the Caodong (K. Chodong, J. Sōtō 曹洞) school, which each contained a hundred *kongan* as well. This is even more probable since Sŏngchŏl knew the *Book of the Two Cliffs* and included its translation in the *Old Mirrors of the Groove of Meditation's Library*.[105] Perhaps, sometime in the future, the next generations of the Sŏn school will refer themselves to the *Book of the Three Cliffs* (*Sambyŏksŏ* 三壁書), instead of the *Book of the Two Cliffs*. Be this as it may, Sŏngchŏl considered the *Magnificence of the Origin* and the *Correct Path of Sŏn* to be his two masterpieces, through which he "paid back to the Buddha the price of all the rice he had eaten during his monastic life." However, one may wonder if the contents of the *Magnificence of the Origin* are not directly related to that of literary Chan or Sŏn.

The fourth and last of the works (although the first to be published in 1976) is the aforementioned *Dharma Lineage of Korean Buddhism*. It consists of an essay demonstrating that the Jogye Order belongs to the Yangqi branch of the Linji school and thus only follows its sudden awakening/sudden practice teaching. The "Sino-Korean Connection"[106] was established by the aforementioned T'aego Pou who, toward the end of the Koryŏ dynasty, went to China to earn a dharma seal from the Yangqi branch. Moving upstream from Linji, Sŏngchŏl connects Korean Buddhism to Sixth Patriarch Huineng, Bodhidharma, Nāgārjuna and, ultimately, to the Buddha Śākyamuni's peerless correct perfect enlightenment (K. *musang chŏngdŭng chŏnggak* 無上正等正覺).

Apparently, Sŏngchŏl believed that Imje's Dharma seal had been transmitted from T'aego down a continuous human succession (K. *in chŏk kyesŭng* 人的 繼承)—not through a purely doctrinal one (K. *sasang chŏk kyesŭng* 思想的 繼承)—until contemporary Korea. However, as aforementioned, the tracks of that new lineage were lost at an early stage of the Chosŏn dynasty. By exclusively emphasizing the importance of Imje's lineage (i.e., the lineage of Tongsan, his benevolent master) to the point of absolutizing it—and himself with it, even though he never received a dharma seal nor transmitted one—Sŏngch'ŏl obviously discarded all the others, especially Chinul's, thus reinforcing the antagonizing mechanism that pervades all his thought.

A CRITICAL APPROACH TO SŎNGCH'ŎL'S THOUGHT

Sŏngch' ŏl and his teachings have been criticized by both Buddhist monks and scholars.[107] Even though he acted within a specific institutional frame, well connected to the sociopolitical context of a given time in Korean history, and his dharma talks rest on well-defined Buddhist hermeneutics, his sudden/sudden approach consistently denied all of these, that is, the overall gradualness underlying the suddenness that he so unconditionally emphasized. Sŏngch'ŏl provided—unknowingly—a full-fledged reenactment of "the rhetoric of immediacy [of awakening]," described by Faure[108] and "the rhetoric of experience [of awakening]," described by Sharf.[109] As Sŏngch'ŏl did so, just as he was unable to be fully aware of his own historical situation and therefore unable to clearly take it into account, he failed to acknowledge Chinul's context during the Koryŏ dynasty. In other words, Sŏngch'ŏl never understood Chinul as the latter understood himself and as he can be understood from a historical standpoint.

But it is perhaps at the level of active ethics that Sŏngch'ŏl's sudden/sudden awakening doctrine elicits the most criticism. Many (and probably history as well) will not forget Sŏngch'ŏl's three great silences: at the time of the October 27, 1980 crackdown on Buddhism (K. *sip i ch'il pŏmnan* 十二七法難); at the peak of the democratization movement in 1987; and when he gave the aforementioned and infamous Sŏ Ŭihyŏn free rein as the Jogye Order's twenty-fifth and twenty-sixth head administrator (K. *ch'ongmu wŏnjang* 總務院長), August 25, 1986–April 8, 1994. Insofar as Sŏngch'ŏl occupied a very central leadership position within Korean Buddhism, most people—and even more so Buddhists—expected at least a statement from him.

But Sŏngch'ŏl's promoters are undeterred by those criticisms.[110] If ever in doubt, they can look to the powerful mediations put in place to enhance their belief that Sŏngch'ŏl was a living Buddha: the numerous relics that came out of his cremation (S. *śarīra*, K. *sari* 舍利); the sheer size of the Indian granite stupa—crafted in Japan—enshrining them, built in the midst of a 430m² square at the entrance of Haeinsa and mostly paid for by Samsung family; the more than eighty books already published, not to mention the ones that continue to appear; Kŏboesa (却外寺), a monastery built on the spot of Sŏngchŏl's birth home, with a museum dedicated to his life; the yearly academic conferences on Sŏngchŏl's thought; and the fact that the main hall Buddha statue at Paengnyŏnam has been replaced by a bronze one representing Sŏngchŏl.

Nevertheless, judging from the result of opinion polls, Sŏngchŏl is no match for Cardinal Kim Suhwan's (金壽煥, 1922–2009) unabated popularity,[111] perhaps because the overall tendency of his hermeneutics reflects more of a predemocratization spirit than a postdemocratization one.[112] Sŏngchŏl's adamant rejection of Pojo Chinul's sudden/gradual paradigm has inadvertently locked major parts of Korean Buddhism in a kind of Tower of Babel, light years away from the diversity that it could boast of during its Golden Age (CE 540–780). As Chin'gwan says, "In order to adapt itself to contemporary Korea and play the role that it deserves, the Jogye Order needs a thousand monks with doctorates."[113] This obviously requires a relation between theory and scholarship to practice as well as allowing a diversity of discourses. The continued effort by the White Lotus Buddhist Cultural Foundation (Paengnyŏn Pulgyo munhwa chedan 白蓮佛教文化財團) to promote Sŏngchŏl by relegating to second-class positions other makers of Korean Buddhism in the last century, appears to have done a disservice to the latter.

Notes

1. Often translated by "keyword meditation" and abbreviated KWM, which is inaccurate when the principal theme (C. *huatou*, K. *hwadu* 話頭) of a public case (C. *gongan*, K. *kongan* 公案) of meditation contains more than one word.

2. Park Keonjoo 박건주, "*Chŏryo sagi* wa *Kanhwa kyŏrŭi ron* esŏ ŭi Kanhwa Sŏn pŏbmun kwa kŭ munje chŏm" 『節要私記』 와 『看話決疑論』 에서의 간화선 법문과 그 문제점 [The dharma talks on key phrase meditation and their problems in *Excerpts with Personal Notes* and the *Treatise on Resolving Doubts about Observing the Hwadu*]. *Chindan hakpo* 116 (2012): 1–28.

3. Abbreviation of Excerpts from the "Dharma Collection and Special Practice Record" with inserted personal notes (Pŏpchip pyŏrhaengnok chŏryo pyŏngip sagi 法集別行錄節要幷入私記, hereafter Excerpts), based on excerpts from Guifeng Zongmi's (圭峰宗密, 780–841) Dharma Collection and Special Practice Record (Faji biexing lu 法集別行錄), to which Chinul added notes. HPC 4, 740–68.

4. Or "Compilation of examinations of verses on ancient precedents of the Sŏn school." It consists of "a massive collection of edifying ancient precedents

from Chan or pre-Chan Buddhist literature that comprises the entire fifth volume of the *Han'guk Pulgyo Chŏnsŏ* (韓國佛教全書 [The complete works of Korean Buddhism])." Charles Muller, *A Korean-English Dictionary of Buddhism* (Seoul: Unjusa, 2014), 825.

5. Cho Myungje, *Sŏnmun yŏmsong jip yŏn'gu—12-13 segi Koryŏ ŭi kongan Sŏn kwa Song ŭi sŏnjŏk* 禪門拈頌集研究—12-13 世紀 高麗의 公案禪과 宋의 禪籍 [A study of the *Sŏnmun yŏmsong jip*—Koryŏ dynasty *kongan* Sŏn and Chan texts of the Song dynasty in the twelfth and thirteenth centuries] (Seoul: Kyŏngjin, 2015).

6. Some of the contents of the introduction to this part and its first section can be found, either slightly or substantially modified, in Bernard Senécal (Seo Myeongweon), "Chinul," *Brill's Encyclopedia of Buddhism*, vol. 2 (Leiden and Boston: Brill, 2019), 853–59.

7. Kim Taljin 金達鎮, trans. and ed., *Pojo Kuksa chŏnsŏ* 普照國師全書 [The complete works of Chinul] (Seoul: Koryŏwŏn, 1987), 17.

8. Throughout this essay, "awakening" and "enlightenment" are used synonymously.

9. Considering that all Chinul's awakenings were triggered by the reading of Buddhist scriptures, it is difficult to claim that they were "absolutely sudden" (i.e., not mediated by language).

10. Robert. E. Buswell Jr., *Numinous Awareness is Never Dark: The Korean Buddhist Master Chinul's Excerpts on Zen Practice* (Honolulu: University of Hawai'i Press, 2016), 76–77.

11. Robert. E. Buswell Jr., trans., *Chinul: Selected Works* (Paju, Korea: Chun'il Munhwasa, 2012), 109–111, 367–86.

12. Buswell, *Chinul: Selected Works*, 370–75.

13. T2008.48.353b4–5.

14. Buswell, *Chinul: Selected Works*, 371–72.

15. T36.1739.

16. Buswell, *Chinul: Selected Works*, 372.

17. T47.1998.893c28–894a2.

18. Buswell, *Chinul: Selected Works*, 374.

19. Buswell, *Chinul: Selected Works*, 107.

20. Buswell, *Chinul: Selected Works*, 355–58.

21. Buswell, *Chinul: Selected Works*, 18.

22. Buswell, *Chinul: Selected Works*, 356–57.

23. That is, as the eighteen compositional elements of cognition (K. *sipp'algye* 十八界).

24. Buswell, *Chinul: Selected Works*, 358.

25. Buswell, *Chinul: Selected Works*, 374.

26. Adapted from Buswell, *Chinul: Selected Works*, 374.

27. Buswell, *Chinul: Selected Works*, 376.

28. Buswell, *Chinul: Selected Works*, 28, 376–77.
29. See note 3.
30. Robert E. Buswell Jr., trans. *The Korean Approach to Zen—The Collected Works of Chinul* (Honolulu: University of Hawai'i Press, 1983), 160–90, 191–97.
31. Buswell, *Chinul: Selected Works*, 89–90.
32. Buswell, *Chinul: Selected Works*, 96–102, 103–107, 247–314, 315–354.
33. Buswell, *Chinul: Selected Works*, 96.
34. "To withdraw and reflect on one's original nature" (Muller, *A Korean-English Dictionary of Buddhism*, 1675).
35. Buswell, *Chinul: Selected Works*, 62–63.
36. Keonjoo, "Chŏryo sagi wa kanhwa kyŏrŭi ron," 13.
37. Keonjoo, "Chŏryo sagi wa kanhwa kyŏrŭi ron," 24.
38. Buswell, *Chinul: Selected Works*, 80.
39. *Ch'amgu* (參句): investigating (K. *ch'am* 參) the key phrase or keyword (K. *gu* 句) is a meditation technique that requires exclusive focus on the *hwadu* (話頭) of a *kongan* (公案), without any conceptualization; *ch'amgu* (參究): to concentrate on breaking or penetrating the doubt mass (K. ŭidan 疑團): solidification of the doubt [question or puzzlement] mass aroused at the bottom of one's mind by the investigation of the *hwadu* in order to achieve awakening (Muller, *A Korean-English Dictionary of Buddhism*, 1240, 1493, 1494).
40. A means to trace the radiance emanating from the mind back to its source.
41. As if ultimately Chinul had completely rejected the significance and necessity of an understanding-awakening experience prior to gradual practice and thus exclusively focused on the achievement of realization-awakening.
42. Keonjoo, "Chŏryo sagi wa kanhwa kyŏrŭi ron," 3, 24.
43. Keonjoo, "Chŏryo sagi wa kanhwa kyŏrŭi ron," 22, 25.
44. Keonjoo, "Chŏryo sagi wa kanhwa kyŏrŭi ron," 22, 25.
45. Dharma realm of unimpeded dependent origination.
46. "Hok mun Moguja Hwaŏm kyo gi myŏng pŏpkye muae yŏn'gi mu so ch'uisa ha'go Sŏnmun kan sipchong pyŏng i kanhwa ya" 或問牧牛子 華嚴教 既明法界無礙緣起 無所取捨 何故 禪門 揀十種病 而看話耶? in *HPC* 4, 732c. Translation adapted from Buswell, *The Korean Approach to Zen*, 239.
47. Keonjoo, "Chŏryo sagi wa kanhwa kyŏrŭi ron," 15.
48. Keonjoo, "Chŏryo sagi wa kanhwa kyŏrŭi ron," 24.
49. Keonjoo, "Chŏryo sagi wa kanhwa kyŏrŭi ron," 24.
50. "Mihu yagin ponbun chongsa kyŏngjŏlmun ŏngu yoryŏng ch'ŏkche chigyŏn chi pyŏng chi yu ch'ulsin hwallo i" 末後略引本分宗師徑截門言句 要令滌除知見之病 知有出身活路爾, HPC 4, 741a-b. Transl. adapted from Buswell, The Korean Approach to Zen, 264.
51. *HPC* 4, 764a. Translation adapted from Buswell, *The Korean Approach to Zen*, 334.

52. "*Ch'a musim hapdomun yŏksi kyŏngjŏlmun tŭgip ya*" 次無心合道門 亦是徑截門得入也," HPC 4, 749a. Translation from Buswell, *The Korean Approach to Zen*, 287.

53. Keonjoo, "Chŏryo sagi wa kanhwa kyŏrŭi ron," 5–6, 11.

54. Keonjoo, "Chŏryo sagi wa kanhwa kyŏrŭi ron," 22.

55. Keonjoo, "Chŏryo sagi wa kanhwa kyŏrŭi ron," 22–23.

56. Lee Pyŏnguk, *Koryŏ sidae ŭi Pulgyo sasang* 高麗時代의 佛敎思想 [Buddhist thought during the Koryŏ period] (Seoul: Hyean, 2002), 69. Lee also quotes research suggesting that the military needed Susŏnsa's influence to strengthen their economic control on the agriculturally rich southwestern part of the peninsula.

57. See note 4.

58. Lit. "going to the hall to expound the doctrine."

59. Cho Myungje, *Sŏnmun yŏmsong jip yŏn'gu*, 313. See note 1.

60. Cho Myungje, *Sŏnmun yŏmsong jip yŏn'gu*, 316–17.

61. Cho Myungje, *Sŏnmun yŏmsong jip yŏn'gu*, 313.

62. Cho Myungje, *Sŏnmun yŏmsong jip yŏn'gu*, 318.

63. Cho Myungje, *Sŏnmun yŏmsong jip yŏn'gu*, 321.

64. Cho Myungje, *Sŏnmun yŏmsong jip yŏn'gu*, 316–17.

65. Cho Myungje, *Sŏnmun yŏmsong jip yŏn'gu*, 319.

66. Chogye Chingak Kuksa Ŏrok 曹溪眞覺國師語錄.

67. Cho Myungje, *Sŏnmun yŏmsong jip yŏn'gu*, 314.

68. Cho Myungje, *Sŏnmun yŏmsong jip yŏn'gu*, 324, 327.

69. Cho Myungje, *Sŏnmun yŏmsong jip yŏn'gu*, 346–47.

70. Cho Myungje, *Sŏnmun yŏmsong jip yŏn'gu*, 346–47.

71. Ch'oe Pyonghŏn 최병헌, "T'aego Pou ŭi Pulgyo sa chŏk wich'i" 태고 보우의 불교사적 위치 [T'aego Pou's position in Buddhist history], *Han'guk munhwa* 4, no 7–8 (1986): 97–132; Ch'oe Kyŏnghwan 최경환, "T'aego Pou ŭi inmaek kwa Kongmin wangdae ch'o chŏngch'i hwaltong" 태고 보우의 인맥과 공민왕대 초 정치 활동 [T'aegu Pou's dharma seal and King Kongmin's reign's early political activity], MA thesis, Seoul, Seoul National University (2010): i–ii, 67–68; Ch'oe Yŏnsik, "How did *Ganhwa Seon* Practice Became Predominant over the Other Buddhist Traditions of the Late Goryeo Dynasty?" (Seoul: Tongguk Institute for Buddhist Studies Research, 2011), 154–55.

72. Buswell, *Numinous Awareness is Never Dark*, 77–80.

73. Ch'oe Yŏnsik 최연식, "Sŏngch'ŏl ŭi pŏmmaek ron e taehan pip'anjŏk kŏmt'o rŭl ilkko" 성철의 법맥 론에 대한 비판적 검토를 읽고 [An answer to "A critical examination of Sŏngch'ŏl's Dharma transmission doctrine"]," in *T'oeong Sŏngch'ŏl ŭi kkaedarŭm kwa suhaeng* 퇴옹성철의 깨달음과 수행 [T'oeong Sŏngch'ŏl's enlightenment and practice], edited by Cho Sŏngt'aek (Seoul: Yemoon, 2006), 392–400.

74. Pak Haedang, "The *Seon* dispute of the Late Joseon Era," *Conference Proceedings of Tongguk Institute for Buddhist Studies Research*, day 2 (2011), 225–26, 243–44.

75. Bernard Senécal, "The Philosophy of Sŏn Master T'oeong Sŏngch'ŏl (1912–1993)," *Journal of Korean Religions* 7, no. 1 (2016), 104–5; Seo Myeongweon (Bernard Senécal) *Kaya-san ho'rang'i ŭi ch'ech'wi rŭl mat'atta* 가야산 호랑이의 체취를 맡았다. [I have picked up the scent of the Tiger of Kaya Mountains], new ed. (Seoul: Sogang University Press, 2017), 271–76.

76. Senécal, "The Philosophy of Sŏn Master T'oeong Sŏngch'ŏl (1912–1993)," 94–95.

77. Senécal, "The Philosophy of Sŏn Master T'oeong Sŏngch'ŏl (1912–1993)," 95–97.

78. Senécal, "The Philosophy of Sŏn Master T'oeong Sŏngch'ŏl (1912–1993)," 97–99.

79. Kim T'aek'kŭn 김택근, "Kim T'aek'kŭn ŭi Sŏngch'ŏl sŭnim p'yŏngjŏn—honja ka'nŭn kir i chung ŭi kir'ida" 김택근의 성철스님 평전-혼자 가는 길이 중의 길이다 [Kim T'aek'kŭn's critical biography of Sŏngch'ŏl Sŭnim—going alone is the way of a monk]. *Pŏppo sinmun*, July 27, 2015.

80. A sentient being forever deprived of the capacity to achieve Buddhahood.

81. Myungje Cho and Bernard Senécal S. J. (Myeongweon Seo), "Japanese Buddhist Modernism and the Thought of Sŏn Master Toeong Sŏngch'ŏl 退翁性徹禪師 (1912–1993)," *Journal of Korean Religions* 12, no. 1 (2021), 40.

82. Wŏnt'aek 원택, *Sŏngch'ŏl sŭnim haengjang* 성철스님행장 [Records of Sŏngch'ŏl sŭnim's life], (Seoul: Kŭlsi midiŏ, 2012), 115, 127, 129.

83. A more detailed version of the contents of this section may be found in Senécal, "The Philosophy of Sŏn Master T'oeong Sŏngch'ŏl (1912–1993)," 99–110.

84. Translated by Hwang Soon-Il and edited by Linda Covill (Oxford: Oxford Center for Buddhist Studies Monographs, 2014).

85. Kyoto: Hozokan, 1944.

86. Cho Myungje 조명제, "1910 nyŏndae singminji Chosŏn ŭi Pulgyo kŭndaehwa wa chapchi midiŏ" 1910년대 식민지 조선의 불교 근대화와 잡지 미디어 [Periodicals and modernization of Buddhism in colonial Chosŏn in the1910s], *Chonggyo munhwapip'yŏng* 30 (2016), 58–59. Myungje Cho and Bernard SENÉCAL S.J. (Myeongweon Seo), "Japanese Buddhist Modernism and the Thought of Sŏn Master Toeong Sŏngch'ŏl 退翁性徹禪師 (1912–1993)," 40–41, 62–65.

87. Sŏngch'ŏl, Sŏngch'ŏl Sŭnim Paegil pŏmmun, sang, chung, ha 성철 스님 백일법문, 상중하 [Sermon of one hundred days, vols. I, II, III], (Paengnyŏnam: Changgyŏnggak, 2014).

88. For a translation of the puzzling explanation provided by Wŏnt'aek to justify this new edition and its striking characteristics, see Senécal, "The Philosophy of Sŏn Master T'oeong Sŏngch'ŏl," 103–4.

89. Sŏngch'ŏl, Sŏngch'ŏl Sŭnim Paegil pŏmmun, II, 354, 364.

90. Bernard Senécal, "Sŏn Master T'oeong Sŏngch'ŏl's Legacy: A Reflection on the Political Background of the Korean Sudden/Gradual Debate," *Seoul Journal of Korean Studies* 25, no. 1 (2012), 108–9.

91. Senécal, "Sŏn Master T'oeong Sŏngch'ŏl's Legacy," 89.
92. Senécal, "The Philosophy of Sŏn Master T'oeong Sŏngch'ŏl (1912–1993)," 106–10.
93. Bernard Senécal, "Le *Sūtra de l'Estrade* dans la Corée contemporaine," *Archives de Sciences Sociales des Religions* 147 (July/September 2009), 222–23.
94. T48.2007.338a12.
95. T48.2007.337c3.
96. T48.2007.342a16.
97. T48.2007.341c18.
98. Bernard Senécal (Seo Myeongweon), "T'oeong Sŏngch'ŏl kwa Yukcho Hyenŭng: Sŏngch'ŏl sŭnim ŭi Tonhwang-bon Yukcho Tan'gyŏng hyŏnt'o p'yŏnyŏk ŭl koch'al ha'myŏnsŏ" 퇴옹 성철과 육조 혜능: 성철 스님의 동황본 육조단경 현토 번역을 고찰하면서 [T'oeong Sŏngch'ŏl and the Sixth Patriarch Huineng: studying Sŏngch'ŏl sŭnim's annotated translation of the *Liuzu Tanjing Dunhuang-ben*]." In [Proceedings of] *Yukcho Hyenŭng kwa T'oeong Sŏngch'ŏl, kŭrigo Han'guk Pulgyo* (*Yukcho Hyenŭng sŭnim yŏlban 1300 chugi/T'oeong Sŏngch'ŏl sŭnim yŏlban 20 chugi ch'umo haksul p'orŏm*) [Sixth Patriarch Huineng and T'oeong Sŏngch'ŏl memorial academic event to commemorate the thirteen-hundredth anniversary of the Sixth Patriarch Huineng's Nirvāṇa and the twentieth anniversary of T'oeong Sŏngch'ŏl sŭnim's Nirvāṇa], 119~149 (Hanam: Taehan Pulgyo Chogyejong Paengnyŏn Pulgyo munhwa chaedan, 2013).
99. Senécal, "Le *Sūtra de l'Estrade* dans la Corée contemporaine," 216–22.
100. Paengnyŏnam: Changgyŏnggak, 1981.
101. Bernard Senécal (Seo Myeongweon) *Kayasan horangi ŭi ch'ech'wi rŭl mat'atta*, 42–54.
102. Senécal, "Sŏn Master T'oeong Sŏngch'ŏl's Legacy," 111.
103. T48.2003.
104. T48.2004.
105. Vol. 32–37. "The high importance held by the *Blue Cliff Record* in the contemporary Korean Buddhist community . . . as the 'foremost text of the Chan school' or the 'climax of Chan texts' . . . tells about the great influence exerted by the Japanese Zen school on it since the modern Meiji era (1868–1912)." In Myungje Cho and Bernard Senécal (Myeongweon Seo), "Japanese Buddhist Modernism and the Thought of Sŏn Master T'oeong Sŏngch'ŏl 退翁性徹禪師 (1912–1993)," 44.
106. Bernard Senécal, "A Critical Reflection on the Chogye Order's Campaign for the Worldwide Propagation of Kanhwa Sŏn," *Journal of Korean Religions* 2, no. 1 (2011): 77–78.
107. Senécal, "The Philosophy of Sŏn Master T'oeong Sŏngch'ŏl (1912–1993)," 114–18.
108. Bernard Faure, *The Rhetoric of Immediacy: a Cultural Critique of Chan/Zen Buddhism* (Princeton, NJ: Princeton University Press, 1991).

109. Robert H. Sharf, "The Rhetoric of Experience and the Study of Religion," *Journal of Consciousness Studies: Controversies in Science & the Humanities* 7, no. 11-12 (2000), 267-87.

110. Senécal, "The Philosophy of Sŏn Master T'oeong Sŏngch'ŏl (1912-1993)," 116-17.

111. Senécal, "The Philosophy of Sŏn Master T'oeong Sŏngch'ŏl (1912-1993)," 117.

112. Senécal, "Sŏn Master T'oeong Sŏngch'ŏl's Legacy, 120.

113. Senécal, "The Philosophy of Sŏn Master T'oeong Sŏngch'ŏl (1912-1993)," 118.

Bibliography

Abbreviations

CBETA   Chinese Buddhist Electronic Text Association, http://www.cbeta.org.

CKS   *Chōsen kinseki sōran* (朝鮮金石総覧). Chōsen sōtokufu, ed. Reprint. Seoul: Chungang Munhwa Ch'ulp'ansa, 1968.

CSW   *Chinul: Selected Works*, ed. and trans., Robert E. Buswell, Jr., In *Collected Works of Korean Buddhism*, Vol. 2., Paju: Chun'il Munhwasa, 2012. http://www.acmuller.net/kor-bud/collected_works.html#div-2. Contains revised trans. of five texts from Buswell 1983, with further additions.

HPC   *Han'guk Pulgyo chŏnsŏ* 韓國佛教全書 [Complete works of Korean Buddhism]. Togguk Taehakkyo Han'guk Pulgyo Chŏnsŏ p'yŏnch'an wiwŏnhoe 東國大學校韓國佛教全書編纂委員會, ed. Seoul: Tongguk taehakkyo ch'ulp'anbu, 1994.

HKC   *Han'guk kŭmsŏk chŏnmun* 韓國金石全文 [Complete collection of Korean epigraphy]. 3 vols. Hŏ Hŭng-sik 許興植, ed. Seoul: Asea Munhwasa, 1984.

JIABS   *Journal of the International Association of Buddhist Studies*

KS   *Koryŏsa* 高麗史 3 vols. [History of Koryŏ Korea]. Chŏng In-ji, et al. ed. Seoul: Asea Munhwasa, 1972.

KSC   *Koryŏsa chŏryo* 高麗史節要 [Excerpts from the history of Koryŏ Korea]. Minjok munhwa ch'ujinhoe 민족문화추진회, trans. Seoul: Sinsŏwŏn, 2004.

PC   *Pojo chŏnsŏ* 普照全書, ed. Pojo Sasang Yŏn'guwŏn 普照思想研究院, Sŭngjugun: Puril ch'ulp'ansa 佛日出版社, 1989.

SKQS   *Siku quanshu Wenyuange* 四庫全書文淵閣.

STGK   *San Tendai-Godaisan ki* 参天台五台山記.

T   *Taishō shinshū dai zōkyō* 大正新修大藏經 [Taishō edition of the Buddhist canon], edited by Takakasu Junjirō 高楠順次郎 et al., 100 vols. Tokyo: Taishō Issaikyō Kankōkai, 1924–1935.

TDQ	*Taixu dashi quanshu* 太虛大師全書 [Collected works of Master Taixu]. 32 vols. plus index. Edited by Yinshun. Taipei: Shandao si, 1980.
TMS	*Tongmunsŏn* 東文選 [Anthology of Korean Literature]. Sŏ Kŏ-jŏng et al. Seoul: Minjok Munhwasa, 1994.
X	CBETA version of XZJ & ZZ.
XZJ	*Xuzangjing* 續藏經 [Taiwan reprint of *The Kyoto Supplement to the Buddhist Canon* (*Dai Nihon zokuzōkyō* 大日本續藏經) Kyoto, 1905–1912], 150 vols. Taipei: Xinwenfeng.
ZZ	*Shinsan dainihon zokuzōkyō* 新纂大日本續藏經 [*The Kyoto Supplement to the Buddhist Canon*], 90 vols. Kawamura Kōshō henshu shunin ed. Tokyo: Kokusho kankōkai, 1975–1989.

Primary Sources

Baizhang qinggui. 敕修百丈清規. CBETA T48 no. 2025.
Baolin zhuan 寶林傳. CBETA B14, no. 81.
Biezhuan xinfa yi 別傳心法議. CBETA X57 no. 953.
Biyanlu 碧巖錄. CBETA T48 no. 2003
Bonsen oshō goroku 竺僊和尚語錄. CBETA T80 no. 2554.
Bu xu gaoseng zhuan 補續高僧傳. CBETA X77 no. 1524.
Bukkō Kokushi goroku 佛光國師語錄. CBETA T80 no. 2549.
Bukkoku roku 佛國錄. Tochigi-ken Nasu-gun Kurobanemachi: Tōzan Unganji, 1965.
Chanlin sengbao zhuan 禪林僧寶傳. CBETA X79 no. 1560.
Chanyuan zhuquanjidu xu 禪源諸詮集都序. CBETA T48 no. 2015.
Chanzong zadu hai 禪宗雜毒海. CBETA X65 no. 1278.
Chū sekimon mojizen 註石門文字禪. Yanagida Seizan 柳田聖山 and Shiina Kōyū 椎名宏雄, eds. Vol. 5, Zengaku Tenseki Sōkan 禪学典籍叢刊. Kyoto: Rinsen shoten, 2000.
Chūsei Zenseki Sōkan 中世禪籍叢刊. 12 volumes. Abe Yasuro 阿部泰郎, et al., eds. Kyoto: Rinsen shoten, 2013–2019.
Chuanxin fayao 傳心法要. CBETA T48 no. 2012A
Cishou Huaishen chanshi guanglu 慈受懷深禪師廣錄. CBETA X73 no. 1451.
Cixiu Baizhang qinggui 敕修百丈清規. CBETA T48 no. 2025.
Dachuan Puji chanshi yulu 大川普濟禪師語錄. ZZ 69 no. 1369.
Dahui Pujue Chanshi yulu 大慧普覺禪師語錄, CBETA T47 no. 1998A.
Daikaku zenji zazenron 大覺禪師坐禪論. Kokuyaku zenshū sōsho kankōkai 國釋禪宗叢書刊行會, ed. *Kokuyaku zenshū sōsho* 國釋禪宗叢書, vol. 12. Tokyo: Kokuyaku zenshū sōsho kankōkai, 1985: 579–597 and 603–610.
Dainihon Bukkyō Zensho 大日本佛教全書. Tokyo: Dainihon Bukkyō Zensho Kankōkai, 1931.

Dasheng ru lengqie jing 大乘入楞伽經. CBETA T16 no. 672.
Dengyō Daishi shōrai Etchū roku 傳教大師將來越州錄. CBETA T55 no. 2160.
Dōgen zenji zenshū 道元禪師全集. Kawamura Kōdō 河村孝道 et al., eds. Tokyo: Shunjusha, 1988–1993.
Edo jidai Tōwahen 江戶時代唐話篇, 5 vols. *Chūgokugo kyōhonrui shūsei*. 中国語教本類集成. Tokyo: Fuji shuppan, 1998.
Enpō den tōroku 延寶傳燈錄.
Foshuo jiangunü jing 佛說堅固女經. CBETA T14 no. 574.
Gaomin si guiyue 高旻寺規約. CBETA B18 no. 98.
Genkô shakusho 元亨釋書. In Fujita Takuji 藤田琢司, edited by *Kundoku Genkō shakusho*, 訓読元亨釈書. Kyōto: Zenbunka kenkyūjo, 2011.
Guzun suyu lu 古尊宿語錄. CBETA X68 no. 1315.
Huanglong Huinan chanshi yulu 黃龍慧南禪師語錄. CBETA T47 no. 1993.
Issan Kokushi goroku 一山國師語錄. T80 no. 2553.
Jianfu Chenggu Chanshi yulu 薦福承古禪師語錄. CBETA X73 no. 1447.
Jianzhong jingguo xudenglu 建中靖國續燈錄. CBETA X78 no. 1556.
Jingde chuandeng lu 景德傳燈錄. CBETA T51 no. 2076.
Jingtu huowen 淨土或問. CBETA T47 no. 1972.
Jinkui yaolüe 金匱要略. https://ctext.org/jinkui-yaolue/zh
Kūge nikku shū. http://rakusai.nichibun.ac.jp/zenseki/
Kunchū Bukkokuroku 訓注仏国録. Tokyo: Dō kankōkai, 1975.
Lengyanjing shu jiemeng chao 楞嚴經疏解蒙鈔. XZJ13 no. 287.
Lengzhai yehua 冷齋夜話. Beijing: Zhonghua shuju, 1988.
Liandeng huiyao 聯燈會要. CBETA X79 no. 1557.
Linji lu 臨濟錄. CBETA T47 no. 1985.
Luoyang qielan ji jiaozhu 洛陽伽藍記校注. Edited by Fan Xiangyong 范祥雍. Shanghai: Shanghai guji chubanshe, 1978.
Minki Soshun ikō 明極楚俊遺稿. *Gozan bungaku zenshū* 3.
Mohe sengqi lü 摩訶僧祇律. CBETA T22 no. 1425.
Moshanni Liaoran Chanshi 末山尼了然禪師. CBETA X84 no. 1565.
Muniu tu song 牧牛圖頌. In *Jiaxing zang* 嘉興藏. Taipei: Xinwenfeng, 1987, vol. 23.
Musō kokushi nenpu 夢窓国師年譜. 1354 edition; Kyoto University Library, no. 30467.
Naong hwasang haengjang 懶翁和尚行狀. *Han'guk Pulgyo chŏnsŏ* vol. 6, 703.
Nittō guhō junrei kōki 入唐求法巡禮行記. CBETA B18 no, 95.
Qiongjue laoren tianqi zhizhu xuedouxian heshang songgu 筇絕老人天奇直註雪竇顯和尚頌古. CBETA X67 no. 1302.
Quan Tang shi 全唐詩. Beijing: Zhonghua shuju, 1960.
Samguk yusa 三國遺事. CBETA T48 no. 2039.
Sanfeng Zang heshang yulu 三峰藏和尚語錄. CBETA J34 no. B299.
Sanshi xinian yijie 三時繫念儀範. X74 no. 1465.

Sekijō ihō 石城遺寶. Tokyo: Bunken shuppan, 1991.
Shanhai jing 山海經. SKQS edition.
Shi wen shenglü lungao 詩文聲律論稿. Beijing: Zhonghua shuju, 1977.
Shiguo qunchiu 十國春秋. Beijing: Zhonghua shuju, 1983.
Shiniu tu song 十牛圖頌. CBETA X64 no. 1269.
Song Gaoseng zhuan 宋高僧傳. CBETA CBETA T50 no. 2061.
Tianchu jinluan 天廚禁臠. Shanghai: Zhonghua shuju, 1958. Reprint of Wang Zongyan 王宗炎 (1755–1826) edition.
Tianhui che chanshi yulu 天慧徹禪師語錄, ed. Jisheng 際聖. 1906. Held at Inner Mongolia Library.
Tōfuku kaizan Shōichi Kokushi nenpu 東福開山聖一國師年譜. Bussho kankōkai 仏書刊行会. Edited by *Dai Nippon Bukkyō zensho* 大日本佛教全書, vol. 95. Tokyo: Bussho kankōkai, 1912: 129–150.
Wei shi yue pu 魏氏樂譜. Compiled by Wei Hao 魏皓 (a.k.a. Gi Shimei 魏子明. *Xu xiu siku quan shu* 續修四庫全書 vol. 1096. Shanghai: Shanghai guji chubanshe, 1995.
Wu zhong zhenben Song ji 五種珍本宋集. Xu Hongxia 許紅霞. Beijing: Beijing daxue chubanshe, 2013.
Wu'an Puning chanshi yulu 兀菴普寧禪師語錄. CBETA X71 no. 1404.
Wudeng huiyuan 五燈會元. CBETA X80 no. 1565.
Wufenlü 五分律. CBETA T22 no. 1421.
Wuzong yuan 五宗源. CBETA X69 no. 1279.
Xin xugaosengzhuan 新續高僧傳. CBETA B27 no. 151.
Xinjiao Can Tiantai Wutaishan ji 新校參天台五台山記. Shanghai: Shanghai guji chubanshe, 2009.
Xu gaoseng zhuan 續高僧傳. CBETA T50 no. 2060.
Xu chuandeng lu 續傳登錄. CBETA T51 no. 2077.
Xu zhiyue lu 續指月錄. CBETA X84 no. 1579.
Xu zizhi tongjian changbian 續資治通鑑長編. *Wenyuange siku quanshu* edition.
Xuedou qiji zhi yanjiu 雪竇七集之研究. Edited by Huang Yi-hsun. Taipei: Fagu wenhua, 2015.
Yuanshi 元史. Wuyingdian ershisi shi 武英殿二十四史.
Yunmen Kuangzhen chanshi guanglu 雲門匡真禪師廣錄. CBETA T47 no. 1988.
Yuxuan yulu 御選語錄. Yongzheng. CBETA X68 no. 1319.
Zekkai oshō goroku 絕海和尚語錄. CBETA T80 no. 2561.
Zengoshū 禪居集. *Gozan bungaku zenshū* 五山文學全集 1.
Zenrin bokuseki 禪林墨蹟. Tayama Hōnan 田山方南. Ichikawa: Zenrin Bokuseki Kankai, 1955.
Zhengyuan lüeji 正源略集. CBETA X85 no. 1587.
Zhiyue lu 指月錄. CBETA X83 no. 1578.
Zhongshan shihua 中山詩話. SKQS edition.

Zhu shimen wenzichan 注石門文字禪. Shi Huihong 釋惠洪, Zhang Bowei 張伯偉, Guo Xing 郭醒, and Tong Ling 童嶺, eds. 2 vols. Riben Songdai wenxue yanjiu congkan 日本宋代文学叢刊. Beijing: Zhonghua shuju, 2012.

Zibai zunzhe quanji 紫柏尊者全集. XZJ73 no. 1452.

Zoku gunsho ruijū 続群書類従. Tokyo: Zoku gunsho ruijū kanseikai, 1923.

Zoku zenrin bokuseki 續禪林墨蹟. Tayama Hōnan 田山方南. Kyoto: Shibunkaku, 1981 edition.

Zongmen niangu huiji 宗門拈古彙集. CBETA X66 no. 1296.

Zongtong biannian 宗統編年. CBETA X86 no. 1600.

Zōtanshū 雜談集. http://base1.nijl.ac.jp/iview/Frame.jsp?DB_ID=G0003917KTM&C_CODE=0001-003302

Secondary Sources

Abe Chōichi 阿部肇一. *Chūgoku zenshūshi no kenkyū* 中国禅宗史の研究 [A History of Chinese Zen]. Tokyo: Seishin shobō, 1987. Revised edition.

Addiss, Stephen. *Obaku: Zen Painting and Calligraphy*. Lawrence, Kansas: Helen Foresman Spencer Museum of Art., 1978.

———. *The Art of Zen: Paintings and Calligraphy of Japanese Monks, 1600-1925*. New York: H. N. Abrams, 1989.

Adler, Joseph. *Chinese Religions*. London: Routledge, 2002.

Ahn, Juhn Y. *Buddhas and Ancestors: Religion and Wealth in Fourteenth-Century Korea*. Seattle: University of Washington Press, 2018.

———, trans. *Gongan Collections 1*, Collected Works of Korean Buddhism, vol. 7-1. Seoul: Jogye Order of Korean Buddhism, 2012.

———. "Have a Korean Lineage and Transmit a Chinese One Too: Lineage Practices in Seon Buddhism," *Journal of Chan Buddhism* 1, no. 1/2 (2019): 178–209.

Akabane Yūsaburō 丹羽友三郎. "Issan Ichinei Zenji ni tsuite 一山一寧禪師について" [On the Chan/Zen Master Yishan Yining]. *Kōryō joshi tanki daigaku kiyō* 光陵女子短期大学紀要 *Cross Culture* 4 (1986): 1–26.

Akamatsu Tesshin 赤松連城. "Inoue Shūten no shisō: Sono shōgai to heiwaron oyobi zen shisō" 井上秀天の思想―その生涯と平和論及び禅思想 [The Thought of Inoue Shūten: His Life, Peace Theory, and Zen Thought]. *Ryūkoku daigaku ronshū* 434–35 (1989): 517–53.

Akamatsu Tesshin 赤松徹真 and Fukushima Hirotaka 福嶋寛隆, eds. *Shin bukkyō* 新仏教 [New Buddhism]. 4 vols. Kyoto: Nagata Bunshōdō, 1982.

App, Urs. "Arthur Schopenhauer and China." *Sino-Platonic Papers* Nr 200. April, 2010.

———. "Chan/Zen's Greatest Encylopaedist Mujaku Dōchū (1653–1744)." *Cahiers d'Extrême Asie* 3 (1987): 155–87.

———. *The Cult of Emptiness: The Western Discovery of Buddhist thought and the Invention of Oriental Philosophy*. Rorshach and Kyoto: University Media, 2012.

———, et al. *Zum Gedenken an Prof. Yanagida Seizan. Volume in Commemoration of Prof. Yanagida Seizan*. Kyoto: Zenbunka Kenkyusho, 2008.

Arnold, Sir Edwin. *The Light of Asia: Being the Life and Teaching of Gautama, Prince of India and Founder of Buddhism*. London: Donohue bros, 1879.

Asai Endō. "The Lotus Sutra as the Core of Japanese Buddhism: Shifts in Representations of its Fundamental Principle." *Japanese Journal of Religious Studies* 41, no. 1 (2014): 45–64.

Asakura Hisashi 朝倉尚. *Shōmono no sekai to Zenrin no bungaku* 抄物の世界と禅林の文学 [The world of commentarial works and the literature of Zen monasteries]. Osaka: Seibundō, 1996.

———. *Zenrin no bungaku: Chūgoku bungaku juyō no yōsō* 禅林の文学: 中国文学受容の様相 [Zen Monastery Literature: Aspects of the incorporation of Chinese literature]. Osaka: Seibundō, 1985.

———. *Zenrin no bungaku: shikai to sono shūhen* 禅林の文学: 詩会とその周辺 [Zen Monastery Literature: Poetry Societies and their environs]. Osaka: Seibundō, 2004.

Asami Ryūsuke 浅見龍介. "Nihon bunka to Zenshū 日本文化と禅宗" [Zen and Japanese culture]. In *Kyōto Gozan Zen No Bunka Ha: Ashikaga Yoshimitsu Roppyakunen Gyokikinen* [Zen treasures from the Kyoto Gozan temples]. Tokyo National Museum, Kyushu National Museum and Nikkei Inc, edited by Nihon Bunka to Zenshū, 14–35. Tokyo: Nihon keizai shimbunsha, 2007.

Assmann, Jan. *Das kulturelle Gedächtnis: Schrift, Erinnerung und politische Identität in frühen Hochkulturen*. Munich: C.H. Beck, 1992. English translation. *Cultural Memory and Early Civilization: Writing, Remembrance, and Political Imagination*. Cambridge: Cambridge University Press, 2011.

Barnes, Gina. *China, Japan, Korea: The Rise of East Asian Civilization*. London: Thames & Hudson, 1997.

Baroni, Helen. *Obaku Zen: The Emergence of the Third Sect of Zen in Tokugawa Japan* Honolulu: University of Hawai'i Press, 2000.

Baskind, James. "Ming Buddhism in Edo Japan: the Chinese Founding Masters of the Japanese Obaku School." PhD diss., Yale University, 2006.

Baxter, William H., and Laurent Sagart, *Old Chinese: A New Reconstruction*. New York and Oxford: Oxford University Press, 2014.

Bellieni, Stefano. "Notes on the History of the Left-Wing Movement in Meiji Japan." *Supplemento n. 21 agli Annali* 39, fasc. 4 (1979).

Berger, Louis Jacques Willem. "The Overseas Chinese in Seventeenth Century Nagasaki." PhD diss., Harvard University, 2003.

Bielefeldt, Carl. "Filling the Zen Shū: Notes on the *Jisshū yōdō ki*." *Cahiers d'Extrême-Asia* 7 (1993): 221–48.

———. "Recarving the Dragon: History and Dogma in the Study of Dōgen." In *Dōgen Studies*, edited by William R. LaFleur, 21–53. Honolulu: University of Hawai'i Press, 1985.
Bix, Herbert P. *Peasant Protest in Japan, 1590–1884*. New Haven, CT: Yale University Press, 1986.
Bloom, Phillip E. "Ghosts in the Mists: The Visual and the Visualized in Chinese Buddhist Art, ca. 1178." *Art Bulletin* 98, no. 3 (2016): 297–320.
Blumenthal, James. "Śāntarakṣita." In *Stanford Encyclopedia of Philosophy* https://plato.stanford.edu/entries/saantarak-sita/)
Bodiford, William. *Sōtō Zen in Medieval Japan*. Honolulu: University of Hawai'i Press, 1993.
———. "Zen and Esoteric Buddhism." In *Esoteric Buddhism and the Tantras in East Asia*, edited by Charles D. Orzech, Henrik H. Sørensen and Richard K. Payne, 924–35. Leiden and Boston: Brill: E. J. Brill, 2011.
Borgen, Robert. "Jōjin's Travels from Center to Center (with Some Periphery in Between)." In *Heian Japan: Centers and Peripheries*, edited by Adolphson, Kamens, and Matsumoto. Honolulu: University of Hawai'i Press, 2007.
Bourdieu, Pierre. "The Forms of Capital." In *Handbook for Theory and Research for the Sociology of Education*, edited by J.G. Richardson, 241–58. New York: Greenwood, 1986.
Breuker, Remco E. *Establishing a Pluralist Society in Medieval Korea, 918–1170: History, Ideology and Identity in the Koryŏ Dynasty*. Leiden and Boston: Brill, 2010.
Brock, Erland J., ed. *Swedenborg and His Influence*. Bryn Athyn, Pennsylvania: The Academy of the New Church, 1988.
Brose, Benjamin. "Crossing Thousands of *Li* of Waves: The Return of China's Lost Tiantai Texts," *JIABS* 29, no. 1 (2008): 21–62.
———. *Patrons and Patriarchs: Regional Rulers and Chan Monks during the Five Dynasties and Ten Kingdoms*. Honolulu: University of Hawai'i Press, 2015.
Broughton, Jeffrey Lyle. *Zongmi on Chan*. New York: Columbia University Press, 2009.
Brown, Kendall H. *The Politics of Reclusion: Painting and Power in Momoyama Japan*. Honolulu: University of Hawai'i Press, 1997.
Bryson, Megan. *Goddess on the Frontier and Religion: Ethnicity and Gender in Southwest China*. Stanford: Stanford University Press, 2017.
———. "Southwestern Chan: Lineage and Texts and Art of the Dali Kingdom (937–1253)." *Pacific World*, 3rd Series no. 18 (2016): 67–96.
Buswell, Robert E., trans. *Chinul: Selected Works*. In *Collected Works of Korean Buddhism*, Vol. 12. Seoul: Jogye Order of Korean Buddhism, 2012.
———. "Chinul's Ambivalent Critique of Radical Subitism in Korean Sŏn Meditation." *Journal of the International Association of Buddhist Studies* 12, no. 2 (1989): 20–44.

———. "Patterns of Influence in East Asian Buddhism: The Korean Case." In *Currents and Countercurrents: Korean Influences on the East Asian Buddhist Traditions*, edited by Robert E. Buswell. Honolulu: University of Hawai'i Press, 2005.

———, trans. *Numinous Awareness is Never Dark: The Korean Buddhist Master Chinul's Excerpts on Zen Practice* [from the "Dharma Collection and Special Practice Record" with Inserted Personal Notes on Zen Practice]. Honolulu: University of Hawai'i Press, 2016.

———. *Tracing Back the Radiance: Chinul's Way of Korean Zen*. Honolulu: University of Hawai'i Press, 1991.

———. *The Korean Approach to Zen: Collected Works of Chinul*. Honolulu: University of Hawai'i Press, 1983.

Buswell, Robert E. Jr., and Donald S. Lopez Jr., eds. *The Princeton Dictionary of Buddhism*. Princeton, NJ and Oxford: Princeton University Press, 2013.

Cai Dunda 蔡敦達, "Nihon no Zen-in ni okeru Chūgoku-teki yōso no sesshu: Jikkyō o chūshin to shite" 日本の禅院における中国的要素の摂取―十境を中心として [Incorporation of Chinese elements in Japanese Zen: Focus on the ten objects]. *Nihon kenkyū: Kokusai Nihon bunka kenkyū sentā kiyō* 23 (2001): 13–51.

Cai Yi 蔡毅, "Cong Riben Hanji kan *Quan Song shi* buyi—yi *Can Tiantai Wutaishan ji* wei lie" 從日本漢籍看《全宋詩》補遺—以《參天台五臺山記》為例. [Supplements to the *Complete Compendium of Song Poetry* from Chinese records in Japan—using the *Can Tiantai Wutaishan ji* as an example]. *Yuwai Hanji yanjiu congkan* 2 (2006): 243–62.

Caplow, Zenshin Florence and Reigetsu Susan Moon. *The Hidden Lamp: Stories from Twenty-Five Centuries of Awakened Women*. Boston: Wisdom, 2013.

Caputo, John D. *Truth: The Search for Wisdom in the Postmodern Age*. Milton Keynes, UK: Penguin Random House, 2013.

Carioti, Patrizia. "Focusing on the Overseas Chinese in Seventeenth Century Nagasaki: The Role of *Tōtsūji* in Light of the Early Tokugawa Foreign Policy." In *Large and Board: The Dutch Impact on Early Modern Asia—Essays in honor of Leonard Blussé*, edited by Nagazuni Yōko, 62–75. Tokyo: Tōyō Bunko, 2010.

———. The International Role of the Overseas Chinese in Hirado (Nagasaki) during the First Decades of the 17(th) Century." In *New Studies on Chinese Overseas and China*, edited by Cen Huang, Zhuang Guotu, and Tanaka Kyōko, 31–45. Leiden and Boston: Brill: International Institute for Asian Studies, 2000.

———. "The Origin of the Chinese Community of Nagasaki, 1571–1635." *Ming Qing Yanjiu* (Napoli) 2006: 1–34.

Cawley, Kevin N. *Religious and Philosophical Traditions of Korea*. New York: Routledge, 2019.

Ch'ae Sangsik 蔡尙植. *Koryŏ hugi Pulgyosa yŏn'gu* 高麗後期佛教史研究 [Study of the Buddhist history of the later Koryŏ period]. Seoul: Ilchogak, 1991.
Chan, Hok-Lam. *The Fall of the Jurchen Chin. Wang E's Memoir on Ts'ai-chou Under the Mongol Siege (1233–1234)*. Stuttgart: Franz Steiner, 1993.
Chan, Wing-tsit. *Reflections on Things at Hand*. New York: Columbia University Press, 1967.
———. *A Sourcebook in Chinese Philosophy*. Princeton, NJ: Princeton University Press, 1973.
Chandra, Lokesh. *Life of Lord Buddha from Chinese Sutras Illustrated in Ming Woodcuts*. New Delhi: International Academy of Indian Culture and Aditya Prakashan, Sata-Pitaka Series, Indo-Asian Literatures Volume 627, 2010.
Chang, Aloysius. "The Nagasaki Office of the Chinese Interpreters in the Seventeenth Century." *Chinese Culture* 8, no. 3 (1972): 3–19.
———. "The Chinese Community of Nagasaki in the First Century of the Tokugawa Period (1603–1688)." PhD diss., St. John's University, 1970.
Chen Huan 陳垣. *Mingji Dian Qian Fojiaoshi* 明季滇黔佛教史 [History of Buddhism in Southwest China in the Ming period]. 2 vols. Shijiazhuang: Hebei jiaoyu chubanshe, 2000.
Ch'en, Kenneth. *Buddhism in China: A Historical Survey*. Princeton, NJ: Princeton University Press, 1964.
Chin'gak Hyesim 眞覺慧諶. *Chin'gak Kuksa ŏrok* 眞覺國師語錄 [Recorded sayings of National Master Chin'gak]. *HPC* 6, 1–49.
Ching, Julia. *Chinese Religions*. London: Macmillan Press Ltd., 1993.
Chinul 知訥. "Hwaŏm non chŏryo sŏ" 華嚴論節要序 [Preface to the *Exposition of the Huayan jing*]. *HPC* 4, 767c–768b.
———. *Kanhwa kyŏrŭi ron* 看話決疑論 [Treatise on resolving doubts about hwadu meditation] *HPC* 4, 732c–737c.
Cho Eunsu 조은수. "Han'uk ŭi piguni kyodan e taehan yŏsŏng chuŭijŏk koch'al" 한국의 비구니 교단에 대한 여성주의적 고찰 [Feminist examination of Korean bhikṣuṇī organization]. *Pulgyo p'yŏngnon* 42 (2010): 167–196.
Cho, Eun-su. "Female Buddhist Practice in Korea—A Historical Account." In *Korean Buddhist Nuns and Laywomen: Hidden Histories, Enduring Vitality*, edited by Eun-su Cho, 14–43. Albany: State University of New York Press, 2011.
Cho Myŏngje 趙明濟. *Koryŏ hugi kanhwaSŏn yŏn'gu* 高麗後期 看話禪 研究 [Studies on Kanhua Sŏn of the later Koryŏ period]. Seoul: Hyean, 2004.
Cho, Myong-gi. "Ch'an Buddhist Culture in Korea." In *Korean and Asian Religious Tradition*, edited by Chai-Shin Yu, translated by Kenneth L. Richard, 228–224. Toronto: University Toronto Press, 1977.
Cho Myungje 조명제. "Kŭnd'ae Pulgyo hak ŭi yŏnghyang kwa *Paegil pŏmmun*." 근대 불교학의 영향과 백일법문. In [proceedings of] *1960 nyŏndae chŏnhu sanghwang kwa Sŏngch'ŏl sŭnim ŭi yŏkhal* 1960 년대의 전후 상황과 성철 스님의 역할 [The situation before and after the 1960s and Sŏngch'ŏl's role],

edited by Sŏngch'ŏl sŭnim yŏlban 13 chu'gi ch'u'mo haksul hoeŭi. 30–38. Seoul: Taehan Pulgyo Chogyejong Paengnyŏn Pulgyo munhwa chaedan, 2006.

———. "*Sŏnmun yŏmsongjip* yŏngu—12–13 segi Koryŏ ŭi kongan Sŏn kwa Song ŭi Sŏnjŏk" 禪門拈頌集研究-12-13 세기 高麗의 公案禪과 宋의 禪籍 [A research on the *Sŏnmun yŏmsongjip* [Compilation of handpicked stanzas of the Sŏn school]—Koryŏ's Kongan Sŏn and Song's Chan Writings of the twelfth and thirteenth centuries]. Seoul: Kyŏngjin Publishing, 2015.

———. Sŏngch'ŏl ŭi Pulgyo kwan kwa Ilbon kŭndae Pulgyo hak" 성철의 불교학 과 일본 근대 불교학 [Sŏngch'ŏl's view of Buddhism and modern Japanese Buddhology]. In [Proceedings of] *Ilsang saenghwal kwa suhaeng ŭn hana* 일상생활과 수행은 하나 [Daily life and practice are non-dual]. Sogang University for the Study of Religion, 2016.

———. "Sŏnsa T'oeong Sŏngch'ŏl ŭi yusan—Han'guk tonjŏm nonjaeng e taehan sukko" e kwanhan nonp'yŏngmun" 선사 퇴옹 성철의 유산-한국 돈점논쟁에 대한 숙고에 관한 논평문 [Comments on the Legacy of Sŏngch'ŏl T'oeong—a reflection on the Korean Tonjŏm controversy]. In *Proceedings of Saenghwal kwa suhaeng ŭn hana*, 47–66. Seoul, Sŏgang taehakkyo chonggyo yŏn'guso, 2018.

Cho Myungje and Bernard Senécal (Myeongweon Seo). "Japanese Buddhist Modernism and the Thought of Sŏn Master T'oeong Sŏngch'ŏl 退翁性徹禪 師 (1912–1993)." *Journal of Korean Religions* 12, no. 1 (April 2021): 39–71.

Cho Pŏmhwan 조범환. *Silla Sŏnjong yŏn'gu* 新羅禪宗研究 (신라선종연구) [Study of the Silla Sŏn school]. Seoul: Ilchogak, 2001.

Cho Seung Mee 조승미. "Yŏsŏngjuŭijŏk kwanjŏm esŏ pon Pulgyo suhaengnon yŏn'gu: Han'guk yŏsŏng pulja ŭi kyŏnghŏm ŭl chungsim ŭro "여성주의적 관점에서 본 佛教修行論 연구: 한국 여성 불자의 경험을 중심으로 [Study on the theory of Buddhist practice seen from the feminist perspective: with a focus on the women Buddhist practitioners' experience]. PhD diss., Dongguk University, Seoul, Korea, 2005.

Cho Sŏngt'aek 조성택, ed. *T'oeong Sŏngch'ŏl ŭi kkaedarŭm kwa suhaeng* 퇴옹 성 철의 깨달음과 수행 [Awakening and practice of T'oeong Sŏngch'ŏl]. Seoul: Yemoon Seowon, 2006.

Ch'oe Ch'angsik [Pŏphye] 崔昌植 [法慧]. *Tonkōbon Ryōgongyō no kenkyū* 敦煌本 楞嚴經の研究 [Study of the Dunhuang editions of the *Śūraṃgama-sūtra*]. Tokyo: Sankibō busshorin, 2005.

Ch'oe Kyŏnghwan 최경환. "T'aego Pou ŭi inmaek kwa Kongmin Wang tae ch'o chŏngch'i hwaltong 太古普愚의 人脈과 恭愍王代初 政治活動 [T'aego Pou's personal connection and political activities during the early period of King Kongmin]. MA thesis, Seoul National University, 2010.

Ch'oe Pyŏnghŏn 최병헌. "Chosŏn sidae ŭi Pulgyo pŏpt'ongsŏl ŭi munje" 朝鮮時 代의 佛教法統說의 問題 [On the dharma lineage during the Chosŏn period]. In *Han'guksa ron* 19, Pyŏlch'aek 別冊, 1988.

———. "Han'guk Pulgyo sasang ŭi Chogyejong" 韓國佛教思想의 曹溪宗 [Jogye Order in the context of Korean Buddhist thought]. In *Proceedings* of the

25th Biennial AKSE Conference. Moscow, June 17–20, 2011, vol. 2 (2011): 613–25.

———. "Koryŏ chunggi Yi Chahyŏn ŭi Sŏn kwa kŏsa-Pulgyo ŭi sŏnggyŏk." 高麗中期 李資玄의 禪과 居士佛教의 性格 [The Sŏn of Yi Chahyŏn and the nature of lay Buddhism in the Mid-Koryŏ]. Reprinted in *Koryŏ chunghugi Pulgyo saron*. Compiled by Pulgyosa hakhoe, 189–210. Seoul: Minjoksa, 1986.

———. "T'aego Pou ŭi Pulgyosa chŏk wich'i" 太古普愚의 佛教史的 位置 [T'aego Pou's position in the history of (Korean) Buddhism]. In *Han'guk munhwa*, 7 (Winter 1986): 97–132.

Ch'oe Yŏnsik 최연식. "Sŏngch'ŏl ŭi pŏbmaegnon e taehan pip'anjŏk kŏmt'o rŭl ilkko" 性徹의 法脈論에 대한 批判的 檢討를 읽고 [After reading a critical examiniation of Sŏngch'ŏl's theory of dharma lineage]. In *T'oeong Sŏngch'ŏl ŭi kkaedarŭm kwa suhaeng*, edited by Cho Sŏngt'aek, 392–400. Seoul: Yemoon Seowon, 2006.

———. "How did Ganhwa Seon Practice Became Predominant over the Other Buddhist Traditions of the Late Goryeo Dynasty." *Conference Proceedings*. Tongguk Institute for Buddhist Studies Research 2011: day 2 (2011): 136–58.

Ch'oe Pŏphae 최법해. *Koryŏp'an chungch'ŏmjokpon Sŏnwŏn ch'ŏnggyu*. 고려판 重添足本 禪苑淸規 [Expanded Koryŏ edition of the *Chanyuan qinggui*]. Seoul: Minjok-sa, 1987.

———, trans. *Koryŏp'an Sŏnwŏn ch'ŏnggyu yŏkchu* 고려판 선원 청규 역주. Seoul: Kasan Pulgyo munhwa yŏn'guwŏn ch'ulp'anbu, 2001.

Choi, Mihwa. "State Suppression of Buddhism and Royal Patronage of the Ritual of Water and Land in the Early Chosŏn Dynasty." *Seoul Journal of Korean Studies* 22, no. 2 (2009): 181–214.

Chŏn'guk pigunihoe, ed. *Han'guk piguni ŭi suhaeng kwa salm* 한국 비구니의 수행과 삶 [Korean Bhikṣuṇī's lives and practices]. Seoul: Yemoonseowon, 2007.

Chin'gak Hyesim 眞覺惠諶. *Chin'gak Kuksa Ŏrok* 眞覺國師語錄 [Recorded sayings of National Master Chin'gak]. *HPC* 6, 1–49.

Chŏng Sŏngbon 鄭性本. *Silla Sŏnjong ŭi yŏn'gu* 新羅禪宗의 硏究 [Studies of the Sŏn school in Silla]. Seoul: Minjoksa, 1995.

Chŏng Su-a 정수아. "Hyejo kuksa Tamjin kwa 'Chŏnginsu': Puk-Song Sŏnp'ung ŭi suyong kwa Koryŏ chunggi Sŏnjong ŭi puhŭng ŭl chungsimŭro" 혜조 국사 담진과 '정인수': 북송 선풍의 수용과 고려 중기 선종의 부흥을 중심으로 [State Preceptor Tamjin and 'Chŏngin's Marrow': The Importation of the Sŏn Style of Northern Song and the revival of the Sŏn School in the mid-Koryŏ Period]. In *Han'guk sahak nonch'ong: Yi Ki-baek sŏnsaeng kohŭi kinyŏm*, vol. 1. Yi Ki-baek sŏnsaeng kohŭi kinyŏmhoe, 616–639. Seoul: Ilchogak, 1994.

———. "Koryŏ chunggi kaehyŏk chŏngch'i wa Puk-Song Sŏnbŏp ŭi suyong" 고려 중기 개혁 정치와 북송 선법의 수용 [The reformist policies of mid-Koryŏ and the acceptance of Northern Song's New Policies]. PhD diss., Sŏgang University, 1999.

Chŏngmyŏl 정멸. "Han'guk esŏŭi ch'oech'o ch'ŏnggyu toip e kwanhan koch'al" 韓國에서의 最初 淸規導入에 관한 考察" [An investigation of the earliest example of pure rules in Korea]. *Taegak sasang* 8 (2005): 283–313.

Chou, Chih-p'ing, and Hu Shih. *English Writings of Hu Shih*. New York: Springer, 2013.

Chōsen Sōtokufu 朝鮮総督府, comp. *Chōsen kinseki sōran* 朝鮮金石総覧 [Complete survey of Korean epigraphy]. 2 vols. Seoul: Asea munhwasa, 1976 reprint of 1920 edition.

Ch'u Pokyŏng 추보경. "Koryŏ sidae piguni sach'al ŭi chonjae wa unyŏng" 고려시대 비구니 사찰의 존재와 운영 [The existence of Bhikṣuṇī monastery during the Koryŏ dynasty and its management]. MA thesis, Yongnam University, 2014.

Chung, Edward Y. J. *A Confucian Way of Life and Thought: The Chasŏngnok (Record of Self-Reflection) by Yi Hwang (T'oegye)*. Honolulu, University of Hawai'i Press, 2016.

———. *The Korean Neo-Confucianism of Yi Toegye and Yi Yulgok: A Reappraisal of the "Four-Seven Thesis" and Its Practical Implications for Self-Cultivation*. Albany: State University of New York Press, 1995.

Cleary, Thomas. "Introduction to the History of Zen Practice." In *The Gateless Gate: The Classic Book of Zen Koans*. Yamada Kōun, Translation and Commentary. Boston: Wisdom, 2004.

Cleary, Thomas, and John C. Cleary, trans. *The Blue Cliff Record*, 3 vols. Boulder, CO: Shambhala, 1977.

Clements, Rebekah. *A Cultural History of Translation in Early Modern Japan*. Cambridge: Cambridge University Press, 2015.

———. "Speaking in Tongues? Daimyo, Zen Monks, and Spoken Chinese in Japan, 1661–1711." *Journal of Asian Studies* 76, no. 3 (2017): 603–26.

Coleman, James. "Social Capital in the Creation of Human Capital." *American Journal of Sociology* 94 (1988): S95–S120.

Cogan, Gina. *The Princess Nun: Bunchi, Buddhist Reform, and Gender in Early Edo Japan* Cambridge, MA: Harvard University Asia Center, 2014.

Collcutt, Martin. *Five Mountains: The Rinzai Zen Monastic Institution in Medieval Japan*. Harvard East Asian Monographs, 1981.

———. "Lanxia Daolong (1213–1278) at Kenchōji: Chinese Contributions to the Making of Medieval Japanese Rinzai Zen." In *Tools of Culture: Japan's Cultural, Intellectual, Medical, and Technological Contacts in East Asia, 1000s–1500s*. Ann Arbor, MI: Association for Asian Studies, 2009: 135–62.

Creel, Herrlee. *Chinese Thought from Confucius to Mao Tse-tung*. Chicago: University of Chicago Press, 1971.

Crump, John. *Hatta Shūzō, and Pure Anarchism in Interwar Japan*. New York: St. Martin's Press, 1993.

Davis, Edward L. *Society and the Supernatural in Song China*. Honolulu: University of Hawai'i Press, 2001.

De Bary, Wm. Theodore. *The Unfolding of Neo-Confucianism*. New York and London: Columbia University Press, 1975.

Dean, Britten. "Mr Gi's Music Book, an Annotated Translation of Gi Shimei's *Gi-shi gakufu*. *Monumenta Nipponca* 37, no. 3 (Autumn, 1982): 317–32.

Deleanu, Florin. "The Transmission of Xuanzang's Translation of the *Yogācārabhūmi* in East Asia: With a Philological Analysis of Scroll XXXiii." In *Kongōji issaikyō no sōgōteki kenkyū to Kongōjiseikyō no kisoteki kenkyū: kenkyū seika hōkokusho* 金剛寺一切経の総合的研究と金剛寺聖教の基礎的研究: 研究成果報告書 [General research on the Kongōji manuscript canon and a basic survey of the Kongōji sacred texts]. Edited by Ochiai Tshinori, 1-44/632-589. Tokyo: Kokusai Bukkyōgaku daigakuin daigaku, 2007.

Demiéville, Paul. *Concile de Lhasa: Une controverse sur le quiétisme entre bouddhistes de l'Inde et de la Chine au VIIIe siècle de l'ère chrétienne*. Paris: Institut des hautes études chinoises, 1952.

Demiéville, Paul, Hubert Durt, Anna K. Seidel, and Académie des inscriptions & belles-lettres (France). *Répertoire Du Canon Bouddhique Sino-Japonais, Édition De Taishō [Fascicule Annexe Du Hōbōgirin]*. Éd. rev. et augm. ed. Paris: Librairie d'Amerique et d'Orient, 1978.

Denecke, Wiebke. "Suffering Everlasting Sorrow in Chang'an's 'Everlasting Tranquility': The poetics of Japanese Missions to the Tang Court." *East Asian Journal of Sinology* 14 (2020): 253–329.

———. "Worlds Without Translation: Premodern East Asia and the Power of Character Scripts." In *A Companion to Translation Studies*, edited by Sandra Bermann and Catherine Porter, 204–16. Malden, MA: Wiley-Blackwell, 2014.

Deuchler, Martina. *The Confucian Transformation of Korea*. Cambridge, MA: Harvard University Press, 1992.

Döll, Steffen. *Im Osten des Meeres. Chinesische Emigrantenmönche und die frühen Institutionen des japanischen Zen-Buddhismus* [East of the ocean: Chinese emigrant monks and the early institutions of Japanese Zen Buddhism]. Stuttgart: Franz Steiner, 2011.

———. "Kloster und Konsistenzebene: Das *shichidō garan* im Zen-Buddhismus als sakraler Raum, Kosmos und Körper" [The monastery as level of consistency: The *shichidō garan* in Zen Buddhism as sacred space, cosmos, and body]. In *Heilige Orte und sakraler Raum in den Religionen Japans*, edited by Michael Wachutka. Munich: Iudicium, forthcoming 2022.

Duan Jinlu 段金録 and Zhang Xilu 張錫禄. Comp. *Dali lidai mingbei* 大理歷代名碑 [Famous Stelae of Dali through the ages]. Kunming: Yunnan minzu chubanshe, 2000.

Dufourmont, Eddy. "Nakae Chomin and Buddhism: Reconsidering the Controversy between Nakae Chomin and Inoue Enryō." *International Inoue Enryō Research* 1 (2013): 63–75.

Dumoulin, Heinrich. *Zen Buddhism: A History, vol. 2: Japan*. Translated by James Heisig and Paul Knitter. New York: Macmillan, 1990.

Eichman, Jennifer. *A Late Sixteenth-Century Chinese Buddhist Fellowship: Spiritual Ambitions, Intellectual Debates, and Epistolary Connections*. Leiden and Boston: Brill, 2016.

Elman, Benjamin A. "Introduction." In *Rethinking East Asian Languages, Vernaculars, and Literacies, 1000–1919*, edited by Benjamin Elman, 1–28. Leiden and Boston: Brill, 2014.

———. "Sinophiles and Sinophobes in Tokugawa Japan: Politics, Classicism, and Medicine During the Eighteenth Century." *East Asian Science, Technology and Society: An International Journal* 2 (2008): 93–121.

Enomoto Wataru 榎本渉. "Kenchōji-bune no haken to sono seika" 建長寺船の派遣とその成果 [The dispatch of the Kingchōji ship and its effects]. In *Higashi Ajia no naka Kenchō-ji* 東アジアのなかの建長寺, edited by Murai Shōsuke. Tokyo: Bensen shuppan, 2014.

———. *Nansō Gen-dai Nitchū tokōsō denki shūsei* 南宋-元代日中渡航僧伝記集成 [Collection of Buddhist monks' biographies who travelled between China and Japan in the Southern Song and Yuan dynasties]. Tokyo: Bensei shuppan, 2013.

———. "Nyū-Gen Nihon sō Chintei Kaiju to Gen-matsu Mei-sho no Nitchū kōryū" 入元日本僧椿庭海壽と元末明初の日中交流 [Japanese monk Chintei Kaiju who traveled to Yuan and Japan-China relations in the late Yuan and early Ming]. *Tōyōshi kenkyū* 70 no. 2 (2011): 260–98.

Fairbank, J. K., and Merle Goldman. *China: A New History*. Cambridge, MA: Harvard University Press, 1999.

Faure, Bernard. *Chan Insights and Oversights*. Princeton, NJ: Princeton University Press, 1993.

———. "The Daruma-shū, Dōgen, and Sōtō Zen." *Monumenta Nipponica* 42, no. 1 (1987): 25–55.

———. *The Rhetoric of Immediacy: A Cultural Critique of Chan/Zen Buddhism*. Princeton, NJ: Princeton University Press, 1991.

———. *Visions of Power*. Princeton, NJ: Princeton University Press, 1996.

Filler, Stephen. "Chaos from Order: Anarchy and Anarchism in Modern Japanese Fiction, 1900–1930." PhD diss., Ohio State University, 2004.

Fogel, Joshua. *Articulating the Sinosphere*. Cambridge, MA: Harvard University Press, 2009.

Foulk, T. Griffith. "The 'Ch'an School' and Its Place in the Buddhist Monastic Tradition." PhD diss., University of Michigan, 1987.

———. "*Chanyuan qinggui* and Other 'Rules of Purity' in Chinese Buddhism." In *The Zen Canon: Understanding the Classic Texts*, edited by Steven Heine and Dale S. Wright, 275–312. New York and Oxford: Oxford University Press, 2004.

———. "The Form and Function of Koan Literature: An Overview." In *The Koan: Texts and Contexts in Zen Buddhism*, edited by Steven Heine and Dale S. Wright, 15–45. New York and Oxford: Oxford University Press, 2000.

———. "Myth, Ritual, and Monastic Practice in Sung Ch'an Buddhism." In *Religion and Society in T'ang and Sung China*, edited by Patricia Buckley Ebrey and Peter N. Gregory, 147–208. Honolulu: University of Hawai'i Press, 1993.

———. "The Spread of Chan (Zen) Buddhism." In *The Spread of Buddhism*, edited by Ann Heirman and Stephan Peter Bumbacher, 433–56. Leiden and Boston: Brill, 2007.

———. "Sung Controversies Concerning the "Separate Transmission" of Ch'an." In *Buddhism in the Sung*, edited by Peter N. Gregory and Daniel A. Getz, 220–94. Studies in East Asian Buddhism, No. 13. Honolulu: University of Hawai'i Press, 1999.

Foulk, T. Griffith, and Robert H. Sharf. "On the Ritual Use of Ch'an Portraiture in Medieval China." *Cahiers d'Extrême-Asie* 7 (1993–1994): 149–220; reprinted in *Chan Buddhism in Ritual Context*, edited by Bernard Faure, 74–150. London and New York: Routledge Curzon, 2003.

Franklin, J. Jeffrey. "The Life of the Buddha in Victorian England." *ELH (English Literary History)* 72 (Winter 2005): 941–74.

Fujita Takuji 藤田琢司, ed. *Kundoku Genkô shakusho* 訓読元亨釈書 [Transliteration of the Buddhist scripture of the Genkô era]. Kyoto: Zenbunka kenkyujo, 2011.

Fukui Fumimasa 福井文雅. "Kōkyō gishiki no soshiki naiyō" 経儀式の組織内容 [The structural content of chanted lecture ceremonies]. In *Tonkō to Chūgoku bukkyō* 敦煌と中国仏教 [Dunhuang and Chinese Buddhism], edited by Makita Tairyō and Fukui, 359–82. Fumimasa. Kōza Tonkō 7. Tokyo: Daitō shuppansha, 1984.

Fukushima Hirotaka 福嶋寛隆, "Mō hitotsu no hisenron: Nihon teikokushugi kakuritsuki ni bukkyōsha toshite" もう一つの非戦論―日本帝国主義確立期に仏教者として [Another antiwar theory: From a Buddhist during the establishment of Japanese imperialism]. *Dendōin kiyō* 18 (1976): 54–71.

Fung Yu-lan, *A History of Chinese Philosophy*. Translated by Derk Bodde. Princeton, NJ: Princeton University Press, 1983.

———. *A Short History of Chinese Philosophy*. Edited by Derk Bodde. New York: The Free Press, 1948.

Furuse Tamami 古瀬珠水. "*Kenshō jōbutsu ron* no kihonteki seikaku ni kansuru ichikōsatsu." 見性成佛論」の基本的性格に関する一考察 [An examination of the fundamental character of the *Kenshō jōbutsu ron*]. *Sengokuyama ronshū* 仙石山論集 4 (2008): 154–73.

Gadamer, Hans-Georg. *Truth and Method*. Translated by Joel Weinsheimer and Donald G. Marshall. London: Continuum, 2006.

Gethin, Ruthert. *The Foundations of Buddhism*. Oxford and New York and Oxford: Oxford University Press, 1998.

Gimello, Robert M. "Mārga and Culture: Learning, Letters, and Liberation in Northern Sung Ch'an." In *Paths to Liberation: The Mārga and Its Transformations in Buddhist Thought*, edited by Robert E. Buswell Jr. and Robert

M. Gimello, 371–437. Studies in East Asian Buddhism no. 7. Honolulu, Hawaii: University of Hawai'i Press, 1992.

Glaze, Shyling. "Muan Xingtao: An Obaku Zen Master of the Seventeenth Century in China and Japan." MA thesis, University of Arizona, 2011.

Goodell, Eric. "Taixu." *Oxford Research Encyclopedia of Religion*. 23 Mar. 2022; Accessed 24 Apr. 2022. https://oxfordre.com/religion/view/10.1093/acrefore/9780199340378.001.0001/acrefore-9780199340378-e-1018

———. "Taixu's Youth and Years of Romantic Idealism, 1890–1914." *Chung-Hwa Buddhist Journal* 21 (2008): 77–121.

Goodrich, L. Carrington. "The Revolving Book-Case in China." *Harvard Journal of Asiatic Studies* 7, no. 2 (1942): 130–61.

Granoff, Phyllis. "A Modern Border Crossing: Fakir Mohan Senapati's Life of the Buddha." In *Buddhist Transformations and Interactions: Essays in Honor of Antonino Forte*, edited by Victor H. Mair, 121–40 Amherst, NY: Cambria, 2017.

Grant, Beata. *Eminent Nuns: Women Chan Masters of Seventeenth-Century China*. Honolulu: University of Hawai'i Press, 2009.

———. *Zen Echoes: Classic Kōans with Verse Commentaries by Three Female Chan Masters*. Boston: Wisdom, 2017.

Grayson, James. *Korea—A Religious History*. New York: Routledge Curzon, 2002.

Gregory, Peter N. "The Vitality of Buddhism in the Sung." In *Buddhism in the Sung*, edited by Gregory and Daniel Getz, 1–20. Honolulu: University of Hawai'i Press, 1999.

Groner, Paul. "Ryōō Dōkaku 了翁道覚 (1630–1707), Ascetic, Philanthropist, Bibliophile, and Entrepreneur: the Creation of Japan's First Public Library (Part I)." *Sange gakkai kiyō* 山家学会紀要 (9) (2007): 1–35.

———. "Ryōō Dōkaku 了翁道覚 (1630–1707), Ascetic, Philanthropist, Bibliophile, and Entrepreneur: the Creation of Japan's First Public Library (Part II)." *Tada Kōshō hakushi koki kinen ronbunshū kankōkai*. Edited by *Bukkyō to bunka* 仏教と文化. 1–33. Tokyo: Sankibō Busshōrin, 2009. A revised version published in *Images, Relics, and Legends: The Formation and Transformation of Buddhist Sacred Sites*, edited by James Benn, James Robson, and Jinhua Chen, 248–72. Oakville, ON: Mosaic, 2012.

van Gulik, Robert Hans. *The Lore of the Chinese Lute: An Essay in Ch'in Ideology*. Monumenta Nipponica Monographs. Tokyo: Sophia University, 1940.

———. *Ming Moyiseng Donggao Chanshi Jikan* 明末義僧東皋集刊 [Ch'an Master Tung-Kao: A loyal monk of the end of the Ming period]. Chongqing: Shangwu yinshuguan, 1944.

Gundert, Wilhelm. Translated by *Bi-Yän-Lu: Meister* Yüan-wu›s Niederschrift von der Smaragdenen Felswand, verfasst auf dem Djia-schan bei Li in Hunan zwischen 1111 und 1115 im Druck erschienen in Sïtschuan um 1300, 3 vols. Munich: Karl Hauser, 1954, 1965, 1973.

Ha Ch'unsaeng 하춘생. *Han'guk ŭi piguni munjung* 한국의 비구니 문중 [Dharma lineages of Korean Buddhist nuns]. Seoul: Hajoŭm, 2013.

———. *Putda ŭi cheja piguni* 붓다의 제자 비구니 [Bhikṣuṇīs, the Buddha's disciples]. Seoul: Kukche munhwa chedan, 2016.

———. *Kkaedarŭm ŭi kkok: Han'guk kŭnse rŭl pitnaen piguni* 깨달음의 꽃: 한국 근세를 빛낸 비구니 [Flowers of enlightenment: Bhiksunis who rightened up modern Korea]. Vol. 1. Seoul: Yoerai, 1998.

Haeju 해주. "Han'guk kŭnhyŏndae piguni ŭi suhaeng" 한국 근현대 비구니의 수행 [Bhikṣuṇī's practice in modern and contemporary Korea]. In *Han'guk piguni ŭi suhaeng kwa salm*, edited by Chŏn'guk pigunihoe, 129–164. Seoul: Yeomoon seoweon, 2007.

Han Chiman 한지만. "Namal Yŏch'o kusan sŏnmun karam kusŏng ŭi ŭimi" 나말 여초 구산선문 가람구성의 의미 [The meaning of the building composition of the Nine Mountain Sŏn monasteries of the Late Silla and Early Koryŏ period]. *Taehan kŏnch'ukhakhoe nonmunjip* 32, no. 6 (2016): 49–58.

Han Kimun 한기문. "Yech'ŏn 'Chungsu Yongmun-sa ki' pimun ŭro pon Koryŏ chunggi sŏnjonggye ŭi tonghyang" 醴泉 "重修龍門寺記" 碑文으로 본 高麗中期 禪宗界의 動向 [A study of the tendencies of the Sŏn school the mid-Koryŏ period as observed in the Yongmunsa Restoration Record Stele at Yech'ŏn]. *Munhwa sahak* 24 (2005): 73–105.

———. *Koryŏ sawŏn ŭi kujo wa kinŭng* 고려 사원의 구조와 기능 [The structure and function of Koryŏ temples]. Seoul: Minjoksa, 1998.

Harada Masatoshi 原田正俊. *Nihon chūsei no Zenshū to shakai* 日本中世の禅宗と社会 [The Zen school and society in medieval Japan]. Tokyo: Yoshikawa Hirobumi kan, 1998.

Hatanaka Jōen 畑中浄圜, "Goetsu no bukkyō—toku ni Tendai Tokushō to sono shi Eimei Enju ni tsuite" 呉越の仏教—特に天台德韶とその嗣永明延寿について [Buddhism in Wuyue: With special reference to Tiantai Deshao and his heir, Yongming Yanshou]. *Ōtani daigaku kenkyu nenpō* 大谷大学研究年報 7 (1954): 305–365.

Hayashi Rokurō 林陸朗, *Nagasaki Tōtsūji: daitsūji Hayashi Dōei to sono shūhen* 長崎唐通事:大通事林道榮とその周邊 [Nagasaki Chinese interpreters: Chief interpreter Lin Daorong and his environs]. Tokyo: Yoshikawa kōbunkan, 2000.

Hayashi Yukimitsu 林雪光. Et al. *Ōbaku bunka jinmei jiten* 黃檗文化人名辞典 [Dictionary of person's names in Ōbaku culture]. Kyoto: Shibunkaku, 1988.

Heidegger, Martin. *Being and Time*. John Macquarrie and Edward Robinson. Translated New York: Harper Perennial, 2008.

Heine, Steven. *Chan Rhetoric of Uncertainty in the Blue Cliff Record: Sharpening a Sword at the Dragon Gate*. New York and Oxford: Oxford University Press, 2016.

———. *Did Dogen Go to China? What He Wrote and When He Wrote It*. Oxford [et al.]: Oxford University Press, 2006.

---. *Dōgen and the Kōan Tradition: A Tale of Two Shōbōgenzō Texts.* Albany: State University of New York Press, 1994.
---. "Dōgen Casts Off 'What': An Analysis of Shinjin datsuraku," *JIABS* 9.1 (1986): 53–70.
---. *Dōgen: Textual and Historical Studies.* New York and Oxford: Oxford University Press, 2012.
---. *From Chinese Chan to Japanese Zen.* New York and Oxford: Oxford University Press, 2018.
---. *Zen Skin, Zen Marrow: Will the Real Zen Buddhism Please Stand Up?* New York and Oxford: Oxford University Press, 2008.
Heisig, James W. Thomas P. Kasulis, and John C. Maraldo, eds. *Japanese Philosophy: A Sourcebook.* Honolulu: University of Hawai'i Press, 2011.
Heller, Natasha. *Illusory Abiding: The Cultural Construction of the Chan Monk Zhongfeng Mingben.* Cambridge, MA: Harvard University Asia Center, 2014.
Henderson, William E. *A History of Korea.* New York: The Free Press, 1971.
Herrigel, Eugen. *Zen in the Art of Archery.* Translated by R.F.C. Hull. New York: Pantheon Books, 1958.
Hirakubo Akira 平久保章. *Ingen* 隱元 [Yinyuan]. Tokyo: Yoshikawa Kōbunkan, 1962.
---, ed. *Shinsan kōtei Ingen zenshū* 新纂校訂隱元全集 [The newly collated complete collection of Ingen]. 12 vols. Kyoto: Kaimei shoin, 1979.
Hirowatari Masatoshi 廣渡正利, ed. *Sekijō ihō* 石城遺寶 [Remains from Ishijō]. Tokyo: Bunken shuppan, 1991.
Hisamatsu, Shin'ichi. *Zen and the Fine Arts.* Translated by Gishin Tokiwa. Tokyo: Kodansha International, 1971.
Hŏ Hŭngsik 許興植, ed. *Han'guk kŭmsŏk chŏnmun: kodae* 韓國金石全文: 古代 [Complete epigraphy of Korea: ancient period]. Seoul: Asea munhwasa, 1987.
---. "Koryŏ chunggi Sŏnjong ŭi puhŭng kwa kanhwa Sŏn ŭi chŏn'gae." 高麗中期 禪宗의 復興과 看話禪의 展開 [The Revival of the Sŏn school and the development of Kanhwa Sŏn in the mid-Koryŏ period]. Reprinted in *Pulgyosa hakhoe*, compiled by *Koryŏ chunghugi Pulgyo saron.* Seoul: Minjoksa, 1986.
---. *Koryŏ Pulgyosa yŏn'gu* 고려 불교사 연구 [Study on the history of Koryŏ Buddhism]. Seoul: Ilchogak, 1986.
---. *Koryŏ ro olmkin Indo ŭi tŭngbul* 高麗로 옮긴 印度의 등불 [The Indian lamp that migrated to Koryŏ]. Seoul: Iljogak, 1997.
---. *Koryŏ ŭi kwagŏ chedo.* 고려의 과거 제도 [Civil service exam system in Koryŏ]. Seoul: Ilchogak, 2005
Hong Pyŏng-hwa 홍병화. "Uri nara sach'al kŏnch'uk esŏ pongbul kwa kangsŏl konggan ŭi pyŏnhwa kwajŏng" 우리나라 사찰건축에서 봉불(奉佛)과 강설(講說) 공간의 변화과정 [The process of the transformation of the space of worshipping the Buddha and preaching the Dharma in monastic construction in our country]. *Kŏnch'uk yŏksa yŏn'gu* 19, no. 4 (2010): 109–123.

Hoover, Thomas. *The Zen Experience*. New York: New American Library, 1980.
Hu Jianming 胡建明 [Ko Kenmei]. *Chūgoku sōdai zenrin kōsō bokuseki no kenkyū* 中国宋代禅林高僧墨蹟の研究 [A Study of the Calligraphy and Painting of Chinese Eminent Monks at Chan Monasteries in the Song Dynasty]. Tokyo: Shunjusha, 2007.
Hu, Shih. "Ch'an (Zen) Buddhism in China: Its History and Method." *Philosophy East and West* 3, 1 (April 1953): 3–24.
———. "Development of Zen Buddhism in China." In *English Writings of Hu Shih*, vol. 2, ed. Chih-p'ing Chou and Hu Shih, 109–121. New York: Springer, 2013.
———. "Zhongguo chanxue de fazhan" 中國禪學的發展 [The development of Chan learning in China]. In *Hu Shi wenji* 胡適文集 12, edited by Ouyang Zhesheng, 301–333. Beijing: Peking University Press, 1998.
Huang, Chi-chiang. "Elite and Clergy in Northern Sung Hang-chou: A Convergence of Interest." In *Buddhism in the Sung*, edited by Peter N. Gregory and Daniel A. Getz Jr., 295–339. Honolulu: University of Hawai'i Press, 1999.
———. "Canfang mingshi: nansong qiufa riseng yu jiangzhe fojiao conglin" 參訪名師: 南宋求法日僧與江浙佛教叢林 [Searching for Inspiring Masters: Japanese Pilgrims and Buddhist Monasteries in the Jiang-Zhe Region during the Southern Song Dynasty]. *Fojiao yanjiu zhongxin xuebao* 10 佛教研究中心學報, 第十期 (2005 年): 185–233.
———. "Ŭichŏn's Pilgrimage and the Rising Prominence of the Korean Monastery in Hang-chou during the Sung and Yüan Periods." In *Currents and Countercurrents: Korean Influence on the East Asian Buddhist Traditions*, ed. Robert E. Buswell Jr., 240–76. Honolulu: University of Hawai'i Press, 2005.
Huang, Yi-hsun 黃繹勳. *Xuedou qiji zhi yanjiu* 雪竇七集之研究 [A study of Xuedou's seven works]. Taipei: Fagu wenhua, 2015.
———. *Hanyue Fazang chanshi zhenxi wenxian xuanji 1* 漢月法藏禪師珍稀文獻選輯 (一) [Rare texts of the Chan master Hanyue Fazang 1] (Kaohsiung: Foguang wenhua, 2019).
Hur, Nam-lin. *Death and Social Order in Tokugawa Japan: Buddhism, Anti-Christianity, and the Danka System*. Harvard East Asian Monographs 282. Cambridge, MA: Harvard University Asia Center, 2007.
Hyot'an 효탄. "Piguni Sŏnp'ung ŭi chunghŭngja, Myori Pŏphŭi sŏnsa" 비구니 선풍의 중흥자 묘리법희 선사 [Sŏn Master Myori Pŏphŭi, the Revivalist of Sŏn Tradition]. Edited by Chŏn'guk pigunihoe 199–219. *Han'guk piguni ŭi suhaeng kwa salm*, 2007.
Ibuki Atsushi 伊吹敦. *Zen no rekishi* 禅の歴史 [History of Chan/Zen]. Kyoto: Hōzōkan, 2001.
Ide Seinosuke 井出誠之輔. "Nihon no Sō-Gen butsuka" 日本の宋元仏画 [Song and Yuan dynasties Buddhist painting in Japan]. *Nihon no bigaku* 418 (2001): 1–98.

Iida Rigyō 飯田利行. *Ryōkan goshaku Daichi geju yaku* 良寛語釈大智偈頌訳 [Translations of gathas and verses on great wisdom in the words of Ryōkan]. Tokyo: Daihorin kaku, 1988.

Iioka Naoko 飯岡直子. "Literati Entrepreneur: Wei Zhiyan in the Tonkin-Nagasaki Silk Trade." Ph.D. diss., National University of Singapore, 2009.

Ikeda Eishun 池田英俊. *Meiji no shin bukkyō undō* 明治の新仏教運動 [The Meiji New Buddhist Movement]. Tokyo: Yoshikawa kōbunsha, 1976.

Imaeda Aishin 今枝愛真. *Chūsei Zenshūshi no kenkyū* 中世禅宗史の研究 [Study of the History of the Zen School in Medieval Japan]. Tokyo: Tōkyō Daigaku shuppankai, 1970.

Inagaki Masami 稲垣真美. *Kindai bukkyō no henkakusha* 近代仏教の変革者 [Modern Buddhist Radicals]. Tokyo: Daizō shuppan, 1975.

Inoue Shūten 井上秀天. *Bukkyō no gendaiteki hihan* 仏教の現代的批判 [Contemporary Criticism of Buddhism]. Tokyo: Hōbunkan, 1925.

Iriya Yoshitaka 入矢義高. "Mujaku Dōchū no Zengaku." 無著道忠の禅学 [The Zen Studies of Mujaku Dōchū]. In *Kūgeshū: Iriya Yoshitaka tanpenshū* 空華集: 入矢義高短編集 [Collection of spots before the eyes: Collection of short essays by Iriya Yoshitaka]. Iriya Yoshitaka. Kyoto: Shibunkaku, 1992.

Ishii Shūdō 石井修道. *Chūgoku Zenshūshi wa: Mana Shōbōgenzō ni manabu* 中国全集史話:漢字正法眼蔵に学ぶ [Discussions on the history of Chinese Chan: Studying the treasury of 300 cases]. Kyoto: Zen bunka kenkyūjo, 1987.

———. *Sōdai Zenshūshi no kenkyū* 宋代禅宗史の研究 [Studies in the history of the Song Dynasty Chan school]. Tokyo: Daitōshuppansha, 1987.

Ishikawa Rikizan 石川力山. "The Social Response of Buddhists to the Modernization of Japan: The Contrasting Lives of Two Sōtō Zen Monks." *Japanese Journal of Religious Studies* 25 (1998): 87–115.

———. *Zenshū kojiten* 禅宗小事典 [A Small Dictionary of the Chan/Zen School]. Kyoto: Hôzôkan, 1999.

Ishizaki Matazō 石崎又造. *Kinsei Nihon ni okeru Shina zokugo bungakushi* 近世日本に於ける支那俗語文學史 [History of Chinese vernacular literature in early modern Japan]. Tokyo: Kōbundō Shobō, 1940; 1967 reprint.

Itō Yūten 伊藤猷典. *Hekiganshū teihon* 碧巌集定本 [The Authentic Text of the Blue Cliff Record]. Tokyo: Risōsha, 1963.

Ivanhoe, Philip J. *Readings from the Lu-Wang School of Neo-Confucianism*. Indianapolis/Cambridge: Hackett, 2009.

Jackson, Peter, and David Morgan, eds. *The Mission of Friar William of Rubruck: His Journey to the Court of the Great Khan Möngke, 1253–1255*. London: Hakluyt Society, 1990.

James, William. *Varieties of Religious Experience*. London: Longmans, Green & Co., 1902.

Jametz, Michael. "The Buddhist Affirmation of Poetry." *Japanese Journal of Religious Studies* 34.1 (2016): 55–88.

Jan Yün-hua 冉雲華. "Tsung-mi: His Analysis of Ch'an Buddhism." *T'oung Pao* 58 (1972): 1–54.

———. *Zhongguo chanxue yanjiu lunji* 中國禪學研究論集 [Studies in Chinese Chan]. Taipei: Dongchu, 1990.

Jansen, Marius B. *China in the Tokugawa World*. Cambridge, MA: Harvard University Press., 1992.

———. *The Making of Modern Japan*. Cambridge, MA: Belknap, 2002.

Jiang Boqin 姜伯勤. *Shilian Dashan yu Ao'men Chanshi: Qingchu Lingnan Chanxue yanjiu chubian* 石濂大汕與澳門禪史: 清初嶺南禪學研究初編 [Shilian Dashan and Chan History in Macau: First series of Chan studies in Guangdong during the early Qing period]. Shanghai: Xuelin chubanshe, 1999.

Jiang Jing 江静. *Furi Songseng Wuxue Zuyuan yanjiu* 赴日宋僧无学祖元研究 [A study on the Song dynasty monk Wuxue Zuyuan who travelled to Japan]. Beijing: Shang wu yin shu guan, 2011.

Jorgensen, John. *Inventing Hui-neng, the Sixth Patriarch*. Leiden and Boston: Brill, 2005.

———. "Korea as a Source for the Regeneration of Chinese Buddhism: The Evidence of Ch'an and Sŏn Literature." In *Currents and Countercurrents; Korean Influences on the East Asian Buddhist Traditions*, edited by Robert E. Buswell Jr., 73–152. Honolulu: University of Hawai'i Press, 2005.

———. "Marginalized and Silenced: Buddhist Nuns of the Chosŏn Period." In *Korean Nuns within the Context of East Asian Buddhist Traditions: Conference Proceedings*. Yanyang: Hanmaum Seonwon, 2004: 88–105.

———, ed. *Seon Dialogues*. Seoul: Jogye Order of Korean Buddhism, 2012.

Kagamishima Genryū 鏡島元隆. *Dōgen in'yō goroku no kenkyū* 道元禅師の引用経典・語録の研究 [Studies of Dōgen's citations of sūtras and recorded sayings]. Tokyo: Sōtōshūgaku kenkyūjo, 1995.

———. *Dōgen zenshi to so no shūhen* 道元禅師とその周辺 [Zen Master Dōgen and his environs]. Tokyo: Daitō shuppansha, 1985.

Kagamishima Genryū, Satō Tatsugen, and Kosaka Kiyū, eds. *Yakuchū Zenen shingi* 訳註禪苑清規 [An annotated translation of the *Chanyuan qinggui*]. Tokyo: Sōtōshū shūmuchō, 1972.

Kakkoeng 覺宏. *Naong hwasang haengjang* 懶翁和尙行狀 [An account of Master Naong's life]. *HPC* 6, 703.

Kakumon Kantetsu 廓門貫徹, ed. *Chū sekimon mojizen* 註石門文字禪 [Commentary to the *Shimen wenzichan*]. Yanagida Seizan 柳田聖山 and Shiina Kōyū 椎名宏雄, eds. Vol. 5, *Chū sekimon mojizen* 禪学典籍叢刊 [Collection of (rare) published books for Zen studies]. Kyoto: Rinsen shoten, 2000.

Kalton, Michael. *To Become a Sage*. New York: Columbia University Press, 1988.

———. "The Writings of Kwŏn Kŭn: The Context and Shape of Early Yi Dynasty Neo-Confucianism." In *The Rise of Neo-Confucianism in Korea*, edited by

Wm. Theodore de Bary and JaHyun Kim Haboush, 89–124. New York: Columbia University Press, 1985.

Kang Hee-jung 강희정. "Chosŏn ch'ogi Pulgyo wa yŏsŏng ŭi yŏkhal" 조선 초기 불교와 여성의 역할 [Buddhism during the Early Chosŏn and women's role]. *Ase'a yŏsŏng yŏn'gu* 41 (2002): 269–98.

Kang Hoseon 강호선. "Muja hwadu ŭi hwaksan kwa ip Wŏn in'ga ŭi yuhaeng" 무자화두의 확산과 입원 인가의 유행 [The Spread of mu hwadu and the trend of attaining recognition in Yuan China]. *Han'guk sasangsahak* 40 (2012): 29–66.

———. "Koryŏ mal sŏnsŭng ŭi ip Wŏn yuryŏk kwa Wŏn ch'ŏnggyu suyong" 고려말 선승(禪僧)의 입원유력(入元遊歷)과 원(元) 청규(淸規)의 수용 [Late Koryŏ Sŏn pilgrims in Yuan and the importation of Yuan's *Chanyuan qinggui*]. *Han'guk sasangsahak* 40 (2012): 30–64.

Kang Munsŏn (Hyewŏn) 강문선 (혜원). "Kŭndae Han'guk piguni Sŏn suhaeng yangsang kwa in'ga e taehan munje" 근대 한국 비구니 선 수행 양상과 印可에 대한 문제 [The Mode of bhikṣuṇī's Sŏn practice in modern Korea and the issue of recognition]. *Taegak sasang* 23 (June 2015): 317–355.

Kashiwagi Ryūhō 柏木隆法. *Taigyaku jiken to Uchiyama Gudō* 大逆事件と内山愚童 [Uchiyama Gudō and the High Treason Incident]. Tokyo: JCA shuppan, 1979.

Kawamoto Kunie 川本邦衛. "Vetonamu no Bukkyō." ヴェトナムの仏教 [Vietnamese Buddhism]. In *Ajia Bukkyōshi: Chūgoku hen IV: Higashi Ajia sho chi'iki no Bukkyō* アジア仏教史: 中国編 IV: 東アジア諸地域の仏教 [The History of Buddhism in Asia: China IV: The Buddhism of various regions of Asia]. Edited by Nakamura Hajime, et al. Tokyo: Kōseisha, 1979.

Kawamura Kōdō 河村孝道, et al., eds. *Dōgen Zenji zenshū* 道元禅師全集 [Dōgen's collected works]. 7 vols. Tokyo: Shunjūsha, 1988–1993.

———. *Eihei kaisan Dōgen Zenji Gyōjō Kenzeiki* 永平開山道元禅師行状建撕記 [The *Gyōjō* and *Kenzei* records of Zen master Dōgen, founding abbot of Eihei (Monastery)]. Tokyo: Taishūkan, 1975.

Kawase Kazuma 川瀬一馬. *Gozanban no kenkyū* 五山版の研究 [Studies in Five Mountains editions]. Tokyo: Nihon koshosekishō kyōkai, 1970.

Keel Hee-sŏng. "Word and Wordlessness: The Spirit of Korean Buddhism." In *Korean Philosophy: Its Tradition and its Modern Transformation*, edited by Korean National Commission for UNESCO, 169–84. Seoul: Hollym, 2004.

———. *Chinul: The Founder of the Korean Sŏn Tradition*. Berkeley: University of California Press, 1984.

Ketelaar, James Edward. *Of Heretics and Martyrs in Meiji Japan: Buddhism and Its Persecution*. Princeton, NJ: Princeton University Press, 1990.

Keyworth, George A. "'Study Effortless Action': Rethinking Northern Song Chinese Chan Buddhism in Edo Japan." *Journal of Religion in Japan* 6, no. 2 (2017): 75–106.

Kim, Hee-Jin. 1989. "'The Reason of Words and Letters': Dōgen and Kōan Language." In *Dōgen Studies*, edited by William R. LaFleur, 54–82. Honolulu: University of Hawai'i Press.

Kim Hyoungchan. *Korean Confucianism: The Philosophy and Politics of Toegye and Yulgok*. London: Rowman and Littlefield, 2018.

Kim Kunsu 김군수. "Pojo Kuksa pimyŏng" 普照國師碑銘 [Stele inscription of National Master Pojo]. *Pojo chŏnsŏ* 普照全書 [Complete works of Pojo]. Edited by Pojo sasang yŏn'guwŏn, 419–20. Chŏnam, Korea: Puril ch'ulpa'nsa, 1989.

———. "Stele Inscription of Pojo Chinul." In *Anthology of Stele Inscriptions of Eminent Korean Buddhist Monks*, edited by John Jorgensen and translated by Patrick R. Uhlmann, 367–371. Seoul: Jogye Order of Korean Buddhism, 2012.

Kim Kwangsik 金光植. *Koryŏ muin chŏnggwŏn kwa Pulgyogye* 高麗武人政權과 佛敎界 [The Koryŏ military regime and the Buddhist world]. Seoul: Minjoksa, 1995.

Kim Mungyŏng 金文經. *Tangdae ŭi sahoe wa chonggyo* 唐代의 社會와 宗教 [Society and religion in the Tang dynasty]. Seoul: Sŭngsil taehakkyo ch'ulpanbu, 1984.

Kim Pongyŏl and Pak Chŏngjin 김봉열, 박정진. "Koryŏ karam ŭi kusŏng hyŏngsik e kwanhan kich'ojŏk yŏn'gu" 고려 가람의 구성 형식에 관한 기초적 연구 [A basic study of the site layout of Koryŏ Buddhist monasteries]. *Taehan kŏnch'ukhakhoe nonmunjip* 5, no. 6 (1989): 27–36.

Kim T'aek'kŭn 김택근. "Kim T'aek'kŭn ŭi Sŏngch'ŏl sŭnim p'yŏngjŏn—honja ka'nŭn kir i chung ŭi kir'ida" 김택근의 성철스님 평전-혼자 가는 길이 중의 길이다 [Kim T'aek'kŭn's critical biography of Sŏngch'ŏl Sŭnim—going alone is the way of a monk]. *Pŏppo sinmun*, July 27, 2015.

Kim, Taljin 金達鎭, trans and ed. *Pojo Kuksa chŏnsŏ* 普照國師全書 [Complete works of National Master Chinul]. Seoul: Koryŏwŏn, 1987.

Kim Young Mi 김영미. "Koryŏ sidae piguni ŭi hwaldong kwa Chin'gak Kuksa Hyesim ŭi yŏsŏng sŏngpulron" 高麗時代 比丘尼의 활동과 眞覺國師 惠諶의 女性成佛論." [Bhikṣuṇī's activities during the Koryŏ period and National Master Chin'gak Hyesim's theory of Women's attainment of Buddhahood]. In *Tong Asia ŭi Pulgyo chŏnt'ong esŏ pon Han'guk piguni ŭi suhaeng kwa salm* 동아시아 불교 전통에서 본 한국 비구니의 수행과 삶 [Life and practice of Korean bhikṣuṇī in the context of East Asian Buddhism], edited by Hanmaeum Seonweon, 37–52. Anyang, Korea: Hanmaeum Seonweon, 2004.

———. "Koryŏ sidae yŏsŏng ŭi ch'ulga" 高麗時代 여성의 出家 [Women's joining the monastery during the Koryŏ period]. *Ihwa sahak* 26 (December 1999): 49–74.

———. "Samguk, Koryŏ sidae piguni ŭi salm kwa suhaeng" 삼국, 고려시대 비구니 의 삶과 수행 [Bhikṣuṇīs' lives and practice during the Three Kingdoms' and

Koryŏ periods]. In *Han'guk piguni ŭi suhaeng ka salm*, edited by Chŏn'guk pigunihoe, 79–102. Seoul: Yemoonseowon, 2007.

———. "Male Sŏn Masters' Views on Female Disciples in Later Koryŏ." In *Korean Buddhist Nuns and Laywomen: Hidden Histories, Enduring Vitality*, edited by Eun-su Cho, 45–68. Albany: State University of New York Press, 2011.

Kinugawa Kenji 衣川賢次. *Chanzong sixiang yu wenxian congkao* 禅宗思想与文献丛考. Shanghai: Fudan daxue chubanshe, 2017.

Kirchner, Thomas Yūhō, trans. *Dialogues in a Dream*. Kyōto: Tenryu-ji Institute for Philosophy and Religion, 2010.

———, ed. *The Record of Linji*. Honolulu: University of Hawai'i Press, 2009.

Kirita Kiyohide. "D.T. Suzuki on Society and the State." In *Rude Awakenings: Zen, the Kyoto School, and the Question of Nationalism*, edited by James W. Heisig and John C. Maraldo, 52–74. Honolulu: University of Hawai'i Press, 1994.

Klein, Esther. *Reading Sima Qian from Han to Song*. Leiden and Boston: Brill, 2018.

Kōchū 興儔, and Asano Fuzan 浅野斧山. *Tōkō zenshū: jō ge-kan betsuroku* 東臯全集上下卷別錄 [Collected works of Donggao (Xinyue): two rolls with and additional records]. Tokyo: Ikkatsusha, 1911.

Kodera, Takashi James. *Dogen's Formative Years in China*. Boulder: Prajna, 1980.

Komazawa Daigaku Zengaku daijiten hensansho 駒澤大學禪學大辞典編纂所, ed. *Zengaku Daijiten* 禪學大辞典 [Great dictionary of Zen studies]. 3 vols. Tokyo: Daishūkan shoten, 1977.

Kornicki, Peter. *The Book in Japan: A Cultural History from the Beginnings to the Nineteenth Century*. Leiden and Boston: E. J. Brill, 1998.

Kraft, Kenneth. *Eloquent Zen: Daitō and Early Japanese Zen*. Honolulu: University of Hawai'i Press, 1992.

Kurasawa Yoshihiro 倉沢良裕. *Kurobanesan Daiōji Shodōhaikan* 黒羽山大雄寺諸堂拝観 [Guide to the various buildings at Great Hero Temple on Mt. Kurobane]. Shūkyō hōnin Daiōji, 2005.

Kwŏn Kijong 權奇悰. "Hyesim ŭi Kanhwa Sŏn sasang yŏn'gu: Chinul ŭi Sŏn sasang kwa pigyo hamyŏnsŏ 慧諶의 看話禪思想 硏究-知訥의 선사상과 比較하면서 [Study on Hyesim's Kanhwa Sŏn thought: In comparison with Chinul's Sŏn thought]. *Pojo sasang* 7 (1993): 13–37.

Hok-Lam Chan. *The Fall of the Jurchen Chin. Wang E's Memoir on Ts'ai-chou Under the Mongol Siege (1233–1234)*. Stuttgart: Franz Steiner, 1993.

Lancaster, Lewis R., and Sung-bae Park, eds. *The Korean Buddhist Canon: A Descriptive Catalogue*. Berkeley: University of California Press, 1979.

Langlois, John D., ed. *China Under Mongol Rule*. Princeton, NJ: Princeton University Press, 1981.

Lee Kit-wah 李潔華. "Tang Song Chanzong zhi dili fenbu" 唐宋禪宗之地理分佈 [Geographical istribution of the Chan school in the Tang and Song]. *Xinya xuebao* (1979) 13: 211–362.

Lee, Peter H., and Wm Theodore De Bary, eds. *Sources of the Korean Tradition: From the Sixteenth to the Twentieth Century*. New York: Columbia University Press, 1997.

Lee Pyŏnguk 이병욱. *Koryŏ sidae ŭi Pulgyo sasang* 高麗時代의佛敎思想 [Buddhist thought during the Koryŏ period]. Seoul: Hyean, 2002.

Lee, Seung-yeon. *On the Formation of the Upper Monastic Area of Seon Buddhist Temples from Korea's Late Silla to the Goryeo Era*. Sungkyunkwan University Outstanding Research. Heidelberg: Springer, 2013.

Lee Seyŏl 이세열. "Chikji wa puguni Myodŏk e kwanhan yŏn'gu." 직지와 비구니 묘덕에 관한 연구 [Study on Chikji and bhikṣuṇī Myodŏk]. *Chungwŏn munhwawŏn* 4 (2000): 67–95.

Lee, Yeon-Ju and Laurent Sagart. "No Limits to Borrowing: The Case of Bai and Chinese." *Diachronics* 25, no. 3 (2008): 357–85.

Leggett, Trevor. *Zen and the Ways*. London: Routledge & Kegan Paul, 1978.

Levering, Miriam. "Dōgen's *Raihaitokuzui* and Women Teaching in Sung Ch'an." *Journal of the International Association of Buddhist Studies* 21, no. 1 (1998): 77–110.

———. "The Dragon Girl and the Abbess of Mo-shan: Gender and Status in the Ch'an Buddhist Tradition." *Journal of the International Association of Buddhist Studies* 5, no. 1 (1982): 19–35.

———. "Lin-chi (Rinzai) Ch'an and Gender: The Rhetoric of Equality and the Rhetoric of Heroism." In *Buddhism, Sexuality and Gender*, edited by Jose Ignacio Cabezon, 137–58. Albany: State University of New York Press, 1992.

———. "Miao-tao and Her Teacher Ta-hui." In *Buddhism in the Sung Dynasty*, edited by Peter Gregory and Daniel Getz, 188–219. Honolulu: University of Hawai'i Press, 1999.

———. "Women Ch'an Masters: The Teacher Miao-tsung as Saint." In *Women Saints in World Religions*, edited by Arvind Sharma, 180–204. Albany: State University of New York Press, 2000.

Li Hui 李輝 and Feng Guodong 馮国棟. "E-zang Heishuicheng wenxian 'Cijue Chanshi quanhua ji' kao." 俄藏黑水文献「慈覚禪師勸化集」考 [Study of the *Collection of Encouragements to Practice by Chan Master Cijue*, a document from Heishuicheng (Khara-Khoto) kept in Russia]. *Dunhuang yanjiu* 84, no. 2 (2004): 104–6.

Li Xiaoyou 李孝友. "Nanzhao Dali xiejing shulue" 南詔大理寫經述略 [A brief description of sutra-copying in the Dali of the Nanzhao period] In *Yunnan Dali Fojiao lunwen ji* 雲南大理佛教論文集 [Collection of essays on the Buddhism of Dali in Yunnan]. Lan Jifu et al. Gaoxiong: Foguang chubanshe, 1991.

Liang Wuzhen (Yang Ojin) 梁伍鎮. *Hanhaksŏ yŏn'gu* 漢學書研究 [Researches on Chinese studies textbooks for Koreans]. Seoul: Pangmunsa, 2010.

Licha, Stephen. "Separate Teaching and Separate Transmission: Kokan Shiren's Zen Polemics." *Japanese Journal of Religious Studies* 45, no. 1 (2018): 87–124.

Lin Guanchao 林觀潮. "Ingen Ryūki to Nihon Kōshi: Tōzuihen o megutte" 隱元隆琦と日本皇室: 桃蕊編を巡って [Yinyuan Longqi and Japanese imperial house: A survey of *Tōzuihen*]. Ōbaku bunka 黃檗文華 123 (2002–2003): 31–55.

Lin, Jih-chang. "A Critique and Discussion of the View That Shi Miyuan Proposed the Five-Mountain, Ten-Monastery System." *Journal of Cultural Interaction in East Asia* 5 (2014): 45–65.

Lincoln, Bruce. *Gods and Demons Priests and Scholars: Critical Explorations in the History of Religions*. Chicago and London: University of Chicago Press, 2012.

———. *Holy Terrors: Thinking about Religion after September 11*, 2nd ed. Chicago: University of Chicago Press, 2006.

Liu, Lydia. *Translingual Practice: Literature, National Culture, and Translated Modernity—China, 1900–1937*. Palo Alto: Stanford University Press, 1995.

Long, Darui. "The *Yongle Northern Canon* and its donors." *Studies in Chinese Religions* 2, no. 2 (2016): 173–85.

Loori, John Daido. "Dogen and Koans." In *Sitting With Kōans: Essential Writings on the Practice of Zen koan Introspection*, edited by John Daido Loori. Boston: Wisdom, 2006.

Lopez, Donald S. Jr. "Foreword." In *The Gospel of Buddhism: According to Old Records by Paul Carus*. LaSalle, IL: Open Court, 2004.

———. *Prisoners of Shangri-La*. Chicago: University of Chicago Press, 1999.

———. *Curators of the Buddha: The Study of Buddhism under Colonialism*. Chicago: University of Chicago Press, 1995.

Lu Cheng 呂澂. *Zhongguo Foxue yuanliu lüejiang* 中國佛學源流略講 [A brief account of the origins and development of Chinese Buddhist studies]. Beijing: Zhonghua shuju, 1979.

Lynn, Richard John. *The Classic of the Way and Virtue: A New Translation of the Tao-Te Ching of Laozi as Interpreted by Wang Bi*. Translations from the Asian Classics. New York: Columbia University Press, 1999.

Makeham, John, ed. *Transforming Consciousness: Yogācāra Thought in Modern China*. New York and Oxford: Oxford University Press, 2014.

Malm, William P. "Chinese Music in the Edo and Meiji Periods in Japan." *Asian Music* 6, no. 1/2 (1975): 147–72.

Mano, Shinya. "Yosai and Esoteric Buddhism." In *Esoteric Buddhism and Tantras in East Asia*, edited by Charles D. Orzech, Henrik H. Sorensen, and Richard K. Payne, 827–34. Leiden and Boston: Brill, 2011.

Marra, Michele. *The Poetics of Motoori Norinaga: A Hermeneutical Journey*. Honolulu: University of Hawai'i Press, 2007.

McRae, John R., trans. *Platform Sutra*. Tokyo: Bukkyō Dendō Kyōkai (BDK) English Translation Project, 2000.

---. "Religion as Revolution in Chinese Historiography: Hu Shih (1891–1962) on Shen-hui (684–758)." *Cahiers d'Extrême-Asie* 12 (2001).

---. *Seeing through Zen: Encounter, Transformation, and Genealogy in Chinese Chan Buddhism*. Berkeley: University of California Press, 2003.

de Meyer, Jan. "Confucianism and Daoism in the Political Thought of Luo Yin." *T'ang Studies* 10–11 (1992–93): 67–80.

Min Hyŏn'gu 민현구. "Wŏllamsa ji Chin'gak Kuksa pi ŭi ŭmgi e taehan ilgoch'al" 月南寺址 眞覺國師碑의 陰記에 대한 一考察 [Study of the inscription on the monumental stone for National Master Chin'gak at the ruins of Wŏllamsa]. *Chindan hakpo* 36 (December 1973): 7–38.

Miya Noriko 宮紀子. *Mongoru jidai no shuppan bunka* モンゴル時代の出版文化 [The Publication Culture of the Mongol Period]. Nagoya: Nagoya Daigaku shuppankai, 2006.

Miyake Hitoshi 宮家準. "Japanese Mountain Religion: Shrines, Temples and the Development of Shugendō." *Cahiers d'Extrême Asie* 18 (2009): 73–88.

Miyata Yasushi 宮田安. *Tōtsūji kakei ronkō* 唐通事家係論攷 [Investigations of the genealogy of Chinese interpreters]. Nagasaki: Nagasaki bunkensha, 1979.

Mohr, Michel. "Zen Buddhism during the Tokugawa Period: The Challenge to Go Beyond Sectarian Consciousness." *Japanese Journal of Religious Studies* 21, no. 4 (1994): 341–72.

Morinaga Eizaburō 森長英三郎. *Uchiyama Gudō* 内山愚童 [Uchiyama Gudō]. Tokyo: Ronsōsha, 1984.

Moriya Tomoe. "Social Ethics of 'New Buddhists' at the Turn of the Twentieth Century: A Comparative Study of Suzuki Daisetsu and Inoue Shūten." *Japanese Journal of Religious Studies* 32, no. 2 (2005): 283–304.

Moriya Tomoe 守屋友江. "Inoue Shūten" 井上秀天 [Inoue Shūten]. In *Kindai Nihon ni okeru chishikijin shūkyō undo* 近代日本における知識人宗教運動の言説空間 — 『新佛教』の思想史・文化史的研究 [The discursive space of intellectual religious movements in modern Japan: A study of the intellectual and cultural history of New Buddhism]. Grants-in-Aid for Scientific Research, no. 20320016 (2011): 283–86.

Morrell, Robert, trans. *Sand & Pebbles*. Albany: State University of New York Press, 1985.

Morrison, Elizabeth. *The Power of the Patriarchs: Qisong and Lineage in Chinese Buddhism*. Leiden and Boston: Brill, 2010.

Muller, Charles. "The Buddhist-Confucian Conflict in the Early Chosŏn and Kihwa's Syncretic Response: The Hyŏn chŏng non." *Review of Korean Studies* 2 (1999): 183–200.

---. *Collected Works of Korean Buddhism, Vol. 1: Wonhyo, Selected Works*. Translated by Charles Muller, Sem Vermeersch, and Jin Y. Park. Seoul: Jogye Order of Korean Buddhism, 2012.

---, ed. *Digital Dictionary of Buddhism* (DDB). http://buddhism-dict.net/ddb.

———. "The Key Operative Concepts in Korean Buddhist Syncretic Philosophy; Interpenetration and Essence-Function in Wŏnhyo, Chinul and Kihwa." 1995. https://philpapers.org/rec/MULTKO

———. *A Korean-English Dictionary of Buddhism*. In Collaboration with Ockbae Chun, Seoul: Unjusa, 2014.

———. *Korea's Great Buddhist-Confucian Debate. The Treatises of Chŏng Tojŏn (Sambong) and Hamhŏ Tŭkt'ong (Kihwa)*. Honolulu: University of Hawai'i Press, 2015.

———. *The Sutra of Perfect Enlightenment: Korean Buddhism's Guide to Meditation (with Commentary by the Sŏn Monk Kihwa)*. Albany: State University of New York Press, 1999.

Müller, Max, ed. *The Sacred Books of the East* (SBE) series. 50 vols. Oxford: Oxford University Press, 1879–1910.

Murai Shōsuke 村井章介. "Chūsei no gaikō to Zenji Zensō" 中世の外交と禅寺。禅僧[Medieval diplomacy and Zen monasteries and Zen monks]. In *Chūsei ji'in no sugata to kurashi—Mikkyō, Zensō, yuya* 中世寺院の姿とくらし：密教、禅僧、湯屋 [The forms and livelihood of Medieval monasteries; Esoteric Buddhism, Zen monks, and bathhouses]. Kokuritsu rekishi minzoku hakubutsukan. Comp. Tokyo: Yamakawa shuppansha, 2004.

———. *Higashi Ajia ōkan: kanshi to gaikō* 東アジア往還:漢詩と外交 [Coming and going in East Asia: Chinese poetry and diplomacy]. Tokyo: Asahi Shinbunsha, 1995.

———, ed. *Higashi Ajia no naka no Kenchô-ji Shûkyô: seiji, bunka ga kôsa suru Zen no shôchi* 東アジアの中の建長寺。宗教・政治・文化が交叉する禅の聖地 [Kenchōji in the East Asian Context: The sacred site of Chan/Zen where religion, politics, and culture intersect]. Tokyo: Benseisha, 2014.

———. "Jishazō eiryō tōsen o minaosu" 寺社造営料唐船を見直す[A review of temple and shrine construction fees in the China ships]. In *Minatomachi to Kaiki sekai* 港町と海域世界, edited by Murai Shōsuke. Tokyo: Aoki shoten, 2005.

———. "Nitchū sōgo ninshiki no naka no Chōnen" 日中相互認識のなかの奝然 [Chōnen's mutual knowledge of Japan and China]. In *Nissō kōryūki no Tōdai-ji* 日宋交流期の東大寺. Nara: Todaiji, 2017.

———. "Poetry in Chinese as a Diplomatic Art in Premodern East Asia." In *Tools of Culture: Japan's Cultural, Intellectual, Medical, and Technological Contacts in East Asia, 1000s–1500s*, edited by Andrew Goble et al., 46–69. Translated by Haruko Wakabayshi and Andrew Goble. Ann Arbor, MI: Association for Asian Studies, 2009.

Nagai Masashi 永井政之. *Chūgoku Zenshū kyōdan to minshū* 中国禅宗教団と民衆 [The Chinese Chan School Order and the Masses]. Tokyo: Uchiyama shoten, 2000.

———. "Tōkō Shin'etsu kenkyū josetsu" 東皋心越研究序説 [Introduction to research on Donggao Xinyue]. In *Zenshū no shomondai* 禅宗の諸問題, edited by Imaeda Aishin 今枝愛真, 365–85. Tokyo: Yūzankaku, 1979.

———. "Tōkō Shin'etsu kenkyū satsuki" 東皋心越研究札記 [Study notes about Donggao Xinyue]. *Komazawa daigaku bukkyō gakubu kenkyū kiyō* 駒沢大学仏教学部研究紀要 75 (2013): 1–23.

———. "Tōkō Shin'etsu koto sekikō" 東皋心越事蹟考 [Textual reserch on Donggao Xinyue]. *Komazawa daigaku bukkyō gakubu kenkyū kiyō* 駒沢大学仏教学部研究紀要 73, no. 1 (2015): 1–27.

Nahm, Andrew. *Korea: Tradition and Transformation*. Seoul: Hollym: Seoul, 1996.

Nakamura Sōichi 中村宗一. *Zenyaku Shōbōgenzō* 全訳正法眼蔵 [Complete Translation of the *Store of Appreciations of the Correct Dharma*], 4 vols. Tokyo: Shōshin shobō, 1971.

Nakao Ryōshin 中尾良信. "Eisai ha Zensô ka Tendaisô ka" 栄西は禅僧か天台僧か [Was Eisai a Zen monk or a Tendai monk?]. In *Nihon Zenshû no densetsu to rekishi* 日本禅宗の伝説と歴史 [The legends and histories of the Zen school in Japan], edited by Nakao Ryōshin, 47–70. Tokyo: Yoshikawa kôbunkan, 2005.

Nakata Yoshikatsu 中田喜勝. "Sorai to Chūgokugo: Eppō oshō to sono hitsugo" 徂徠と中国語—悦峯和尚とその筆語 [Sorai and Chinese language: the monk Yuefeng and their brush conversations]. *Kyūshū Chūgoku gakkai hō* 九州中国学会報 15 (June 1969): 52–68.

Nancy, Jean-Luc. *Dis-Enclosure: The Deconstruction of Christianity*. Translated by Bettina Bergo, Gabriel Malefant, and Michael B. Smith. New York: Fordham University Press, 2008.

———. "Rise and Fall of the Tonkin-Nagasaki Silk Trade during the 17th Century." In *Large and Board: The Dutch Impact on Early Modern Asia—Essays in Honor of Leonard Blussé*. 46–61. Tokyo: Tōyō Bunko, 2010.

———. "Wei Zhiyan and the Subversion of the '*Sakoku*.'" In *Offshore Asia*, edited by Anthony Reid and Momoki Shiro. Singapore: National Singapore University Press, 2013.

Nara kokuritsu hakubutsukan 奈良國立博物館, ed. *Nara Kokuritsu Hakubutsukan no meihō* 奈良国立博物館の名宝 [Famous treasures of Nara National Museum]. Nara: Nara Kokuritsu Hakubutsukan, 1997.

———, ed. *Seichi Ninpō* 聖地寧波 [Sacred Ningbo]. Nara: Nara kokuritsu hakabutsukan, 2009.

Narita Kōtarō 成田鋼太郎, ed. *Sakai Tadakatsu kō nenpu narabini genkōshō* 酒井忠勝公年譜並言行抄 [Chorological biography and sayings of Mr. Sakai Tadakatsu]. Tokyo: Tōkyōkyūgikai, 1911.

Nelson-Jones, Richard. *Cognitive Humanistic Therapy*. London: SAGE, 2004.

Newell, Catherine. "Approaches to the Study of Buddhism." In *The New Blackwell Companion to the Sociology of Religion,* edited by Bryan S. Turner. Hoboken, NJ: Wiley-Blackwell, 2010.

Nguyen, Cuong Tu. *Zen in Medieval Vietnam: A Study and Translation of the Thiền Uyển Tập Anh.* Honolulu: University of Hawai'i Press, 1997.

Nienhauser, William H., ed. *The Indiana Companion to Traditional Chinese Literature.* Bloomington: Indiana University Press, 1986.

Nishiguchi Yoshio 西口芳男. Comp. *Zenmon hōzōroku no kisoteki kenkyū*「禪門寶藏錄」の基礎的研究 [Fundamental studies of the *Sŏnmun pojang nok*]. In *Kenkyū hōkoku* vol. 7, Kyoto: Kokusai Zengaku kenkyūsho, 2000.

Nishio Kenryū 西尾賢隆. *Chūsei no Nitchū kōryū to Zenshū* 中世の日中交流と禅宗 [Medieval Japan-China relations and Zen Buddhism]. Tokyo: Yoshikawa Kōbunkan, 1999.

Nishiyama Mika 西山美香. "Nihon gozan to Goetsu-koku, Hokusō, Nansō" 日本五山と呉越国・北宋・南宋 [Japan's Five Mountains and Wuyue, Northern Song, and Southern Song]. In *Higashi Ajia no naka no Kenchōji* 東アジアのなかの建長寺, edited by Murai Shōsuke 村井章介. Tokyo: Bensei Shuppan, 2014.

No Sasin, et al. *Sinjŭng Tongguk yŏji sŭngnam* 新增東國輿地勝覽 [Revised and expanded edition of the survey of the geography of Chosŏn]. Seoul: Sŏgyŏng Munhwasa, 1994.

Noguchi Yoshitaka 野口善敬. *Gendai Zenshūshi kenkyū* 元代禅宗史研究 [Study of the history of the Chan school in the Yuan period]. Kyoto: Zenbunka kenkyūsho, 2005.

Nomura Shunichi 野村俊一. "*Kenchōji sashizu* to butsuden, hattō, shuryō" 『建長寺指図』と仏殿・法堂・衆寮 [Guide to Kenchōji and the Buddha Hall, Dharma Hall, and Dormitory]. In *Higashi Ajia no naka no Kenchōji*, edited by Murai Shōsuke 村井章介, 329–345. Tokyo: Bensei shuppan, 2014.

Notehelfer, Frederick G. *Kōtoku Shūsui, Portrait of a Japanese Radical.* New York: Cambridge University Press, 1971.

Nukariya Kaiten's 忽滑谷快天. *Zengaku shisōshi* 禪學思想史 [History of Chan Buddhism]. 2 vols. Tokyo: Genkōsha, 1925.

O Yong-sŏp 오용섭. "Hyejo taesa kurae ŭi Yobon taejang ŭi pongan" 혜조대사 구래의 요본대장의 봉안 [A Study on the enshrinement of the Khitan Buddhist Canon brought by Master Hyejo]. *Sŏjihak yŏn'gu* 27 (2004): 5–26.

Ōba Osamu 大庭修. *Books and Boats: Sino-Japanese Relations and Cultural Transmission in the Eighteenth and Nineteenth Centuries.* Translated by Joshua A Fogel. Honolulu: University of Hawai'i Press, 2012.

———. *Edo jidai no Nit-Chū biwa* 江戸時代の日中秘話 [Secret history of Japan and China during the Edo period]. Tokyo: Tōhō shoten, 1980. Partially translated by Joshua A. Fogel as "Sino-Japanese Relations in the Edo Period." *Journal of Sino-Japanese Studies*, 8, no. 1 (October 1995): 40–52; 8, no. 2 (May 1996): 50–61; 9, no. 1 (October 1996): 56–74; 9, no. 2 (November 1996):

3–12; 10, no. 1 (October 1997): 33–55; 10, no. 2 (April 1998): 43–59; 11, no. 1 (October 1998): 21–37; 11. no. 2 (May 1999): 50–68; 12.1 (November 1999): 47–64; 12, no. 2 (April 2000): 51–64; 13, no. 1 (October 2000): 34–53.

Obeyesekere, Gananath. "Religious Symbolism and Political Change in Ceylon." *Modern Ceylon Studies* 1, no. 43 (1970): 43–63.

Oh Kangnam. "Sagehood and Metanoia: The Confucian-Christian Encounter in Korea." *Journal of American Academy of Religion* 61, no. 2 (1993): 303–20.

Okada Kesao 岡田袈裟男. *Edo igengo sesshoku: Rango, Tōwa to kindai Nihongo* 江戶異言語接触: 蘭語・唐話と近代日本語 [Contact between different languages in Edo: Dutch, Chinese and Modern Japanese]. Tokyo: Kasama shoin, 2006.

Okimoto Katsumi. "Zen shisō keiseishi no kenkyū" 禅思想形成史の研究 [Studies on the formative history of Chan/Zen thought]. *Hanazono daigaku koksai zengaku kenkyūjo kenkyū hōkoku* 5 (1997): 1–451.

Oldenberg, Hermann. *Buddha, sein Leben, seine Lehre, seine Gemeinde*. Berlin, 1881; English translation, *Buddha, His Life, His Doctrine, His Order*. London: Williams, 1882.

Ŏm Kip'yo 엄기표. "Sanch'ŏng Chigok-sa chi ŭi kwibu sŏkcho pudo" 山清 智谷寺 址의 龜趺와 石造浮屠 [The stone mortuary stupas and tortoise base at the excavation site of Chigoksa in Sanch'ŏng]. *Munhwa sahak* 17 (2002): 357–86.

Ouyang, Xiao. "Van Gulik's *the Lore of the Chinese Lute* Revisited." *Monumenta Serica* 65, no. 1 (2017): 147–74.

Paengnyŏn Mundohoe 백년 문도회, ed. *Sŭnim, Sŏngch'ŏl kŭn sŭnim* 스님, 성철 큰 스님 [Sŭnim, the great Sŭnim Sŏngch'ŏl]. Haein-sa Paengnyŏn-am, 1995.

Pak Haedang. "The *Seon* dispute of the Late Joseon Era." *Conference proceedings* of Tongguk Institute for Buddhist Studies Research, day 2 (2011).

Pak Huisŭng 박희승. *Ije sŭngnye ŭi ipsŏng ŭl hŏham i ŏttŏlrŭnjiyo* 이제, 승려의 입성을 허함이 어떨는지요? [How about now allowing monastics to enter the capital city?]. Seoul: Tŭlnyŏk, 1999.

Pak Yunjin 박윤진. "Koryŏ sidae wangsa-kuksa e taehan taeu" 고려시대 王師 國師에 대한 대우 [Attitude toward the royal and state preceptors during the Koryŏ period]. *Yŏksa hakpo* 190 (2006): 1–32.

Palais, James B. *Confucian Statecraft and Korean Institutions: Yu Hyŏngwŏn and the Late Chosŏn Dynasty*. Seattle: University of Washington Press, 1996.

Pang Minho 방민호. "Kim Iryŏp munhak ŭi sasangjŏk pyŏnmo kwajŏng kwa Pulgyo sŏnt'aek ŭi ŭimi" 김일엽 문학의 사상적 변모 과정과 불교 선택의 의미 [Evolution of Kim Iryŏp's literary thoughts and the significance of her engagement with Buddhism]. *Han'guk hyŏndae munhak yŏn'gu* 20 (2006): 357–403.

Park Haedang 박해당. "Sŏngch'ŏl ŭi pŏbmaegron e taehan pip'anjŏk kŏmt'o" 性徹의 法脈論에 대한 批判的 檢討 [Critical examination of Sŏngch'ŏl's theory of dharma lineage]. In *T'oeong Sŏngch'ŏl ŭi kkae'darŭm kwa suhaeng* [Awakening and practice of T'oeong Sŏngch'ŏl], edited by Cho Sŏngt'aek, 157–89. Seoul: Yemoon Seowon 2006.

———. "The Seon Dispute of the Late Josoen Era." *Proceedings* of the Tongguk Institute for Buddhist Studies Research: day 2 (2011): 224–46.

Park Jae-Hyeon 박재현. "Hyesim ŭi Sŏn sasang kwa Kanhwa" 혜심 (慧諶)의 선사상과 간화 (Study on Hyesim's Sŏn thought and Kanhwa). *Chŏrhak* 78 (2004): 29–49.

Park, Jin Y. "Temporality and Non-temporality in Li Tongxuan's Huayan Buddhism." In *Dao Companion to Chinese Buddhist Philosophy*, edited by Youru Wang and Sandra Wawryko, 325–47. Dordrecht: Springer, 2018.

———. "A Huayanist Reading of the *Lotus Sūtra*: The case of Li Tongxuan." *Journal of the International Association of Buddhist Studies* 35 (2012): 295–328.

———. *Women and Buddhist Philosophy: Engaging Zen Master Kim Iryŏp*. Honolulu: University of Hawai'i Press, 2017.

———. "An Examined Life: Women, Buddhism, and Philosophy in Kim Iryŏp." *Journal of World Philosophies* 5, no. 2 (Winter 2020): 176–82.

———. "Gendered Response to Modernity: Kim Iryŏp and Buddhism." In *Makers of Modern Korean Buddhism*, edited by Jin Y. Park, 109–27. Albany: State University of New York Press, 2010.

———. ed. *Makers of Modern Korean Buddhism*. Albany: State University of New York Press, 2010.

———, trans. *Reflections of a Zen Buddhist Nun: Essays by Zen Master Kim Iryŏp*. Honolulu: University of Hawai'i Press, 2014.

Park Keonjoo 박건주. "Chŏryo sagi wa Kanhwa kyŏrŭiron esŏ ŭi Kanhwa Sŏn pŏmmun kwa kŭ munje chŏm" 節要私記와看話決疑論 에서의 간화선 법문과 그 문제점 [The dharma talks on Kanhwa Sŏn in Chŏryo sagi and Kanhwa kyŏrŭiron and their problems]. *Chin-tan hakpo* 116 (2012): 1–28.

Parker, Geoffrey. *Global Crisis: War, Climate Change and Catastrophe in the Seventeenth Century*. New Haven, CT, and London: Yale University Press, 2003.

Parker, Joseph D. *Zen Buddhist Landscape Arts of Early Muromachi Japan (1336–1573)*. State University of New York Series in Buddhist Studies. Albany: State University of New York Press, 1999.

Payne, Richard K., and Taigen Dan Leighton. *Discourse and Ideology in Medieval Japanese Buddhism*. London and New York: Routledge, 2006.

Peng, Hao. *Trade Relations between Qing China and Tokugawa Japan 1685–1859*. Studies in Economic History. Singapore: Springer:2019

Peterson, C. A. "Court and Province in Mid- and Late T'ang." In *The Cambridge History of China, volume 3, Sui and T'ang China, 589–906, Part I*, edited by D. Twitchett, 464–560. Cambridge: Cambridge University Press, 1979.

Phạm Thị Huệ, ed. *Mộc Bản Chùa Vĩnh Nghiêm: Thiềm Tông Bản Hạnh* [Woodblocks from Vĩnh Nghiêm monastery: Basic practices of the Chan school]. Hà Nội: Nhà Xuât Bản Văn Hóa Dân Tộc, 2018.

Piggot, Joan. *The Emergence of Japanese Kingship*. Palo Alto: Stanford University Press, 1997.

Pine, Red. *The Lankavatara Sutra: A Zen Text*. Berkeley: Counterpoint, 2012.
Plutschow, Herbert. "Is Poetry a Sin? *Honjisuijaku* and Buddhism versus Poetry." *Oriens Extremus* 25, no. 2 (1978): 206–218.
Poceski, Mario. "Chan Rituals of the Abbots' Ascending the Dharma Hall to Preach." In *Zen Ritual: Studies of Zen Buddhist Theory in Practice*, edited by Steven Heine and Dale S. Wright, 83–111. New York and Oxford: Oxford University Press, 2008.
——. "Guishan jingce and the Ethical Foundations of Chan Practice." In *Zen Classics: Formative Texts in Zen Buddhism*, edited by Steven Heine and Dale Wright, 15–42. New York and Oxford: Oxford University Press, 2005.
——. "Xuefeng's Code and the Chan School's Participation in the Development of Monastic Regulations," *Asia Major, Third Series* 16, no. 2 (2003): 33–56.
Pollack, David. *The Fracture of Meaning. Japan's Synthesis of China from the Eighth through the Eighteenth Centuries*. Princeton, NJ: Princeton University Press, 1986.
Polo, Marco, and Rustichello of Pisa. Henry Yule annotated translation as revised by Henri Cordier. *The Travels of Marco Polo*. London: John Murray, 1920.
Protass, Jason Avi. "Buddhist Monks and Chinese Poems: Song Dynasty Monastic Literary Culture." PhD diss., Stanford University, 2016.
——. *The Poetry Demon: Song Dynasty Monks on Poetry and the Way*. Honolulu: University of Hawai'i Press, 2021.
——. "Returning Empty-Handed." *Journal of Chinese Literature and Culture* 4, no. 2 (2017): 383–419.
Prothero, Stephen. "Henry Steel Olcott and 'Protestant Buddhism.'" *Journal of the American Academy of Religion* 63, no. 2 (1995): 281–302.
Qian, Nanxiu, Richard J. Smith, and Bowei Zhang, eds. *Rethinking the Sinosphere: Poetics, Aesthetics, and Identity Formation*. Amherst, NY: Cambria, 2020.
Qing, Chang. "Feilaifeng and the Flowering of Chinese Buddhist Sculpture From the Tenth to the Fourteenth Centuries." PhD diss., University of Kansas, 2005.
Reischauer, Edwin O. *Ennin's Diary: The Record of a Pilgrimage to China in Search of the Law*. New York: Ronald, 1955.
Riggs, David E. "The Life of Menzan Zuihō, a Founder of Dōgen Zen." *Japan Review* 16 (2004): 67–100.
——. "The Rekindling of a Tradition: Menzan Zuiho and the Reform of Japanese Sōtō in the Tokugawa Era." PhD diss., Universoty of California, Los Angeles, 2003.
Ritzinger, Justin. *Anarchy in the Pure Land: Reinventing the Cult of Maitreya in Modern Chinese Buddhism*. New York and Oxford: Oxford University Press, 2017.
Ro Young-Chan. *The Korean Neo-Confucianism of Yi Yulkok*. Albany: State University of New York, 1989.

Rockhill, William Woodville. *The Journey of William of Rubruck to the Eastern Parts of the World, 1253–55*. London: Hayklut Society, 1900.

Rogers, Michael. "Sung-Koryŏ Relations: Some Inhibiting Factors," *Oriens* 11, no. 1/2 (1958): 194–202.

———. "Factionalism and Koryŏ Policy under the Northern Song," *Journal of the American Oriental Society* 79, no. 1 (1959): 16–25.

Rokkaku Tsunehiro 六角恒広. *Chūgokugo kyōikushi no kenkyū* 中国語教育史の研究 [Research on the history of Chinese language instruction]. Tokyo: Tōhō Shoten, 1988.

———. ed. *Edo jidai Tōwahen* 江戸時代唐話篇 [Series of Chinese language textbooks during the Edo period]. 5 vols. In the supplementary volumes of *Chūgokugo kyōhonrui shūsei*. 中国語教本類集成 [Collection of Chinese language textbooks]. Tokyo: Fujishuppan, 1998.

Rossabi, Morris. *From Yuan to Modern China and Mongolia: The Writings of Morris Rossabi*. Leiden and Boston: Brill, 2014.

———. "The Muslims in the Early Yüan Dynasty." In *China under Mongol Rule*, edited by John D. Langlois Jr., 257–95. Princeton, NJ: Princeton University Press, 1981.

Rouzer, Paul. "Early Buddhist Kanshi: Court, Country, and Kūkai." *Monumenta Nipponica* 59.4 (2004): 431–61.

Nishigori Ryōsuke 錦織亮介. "Itsunen Shōyū Nempō" 逸然性融年譜 [Chronological biography of Yiran Xingrong]. *Kitakyūshū Daigaku Bungakubu kiyō* 北九州大學文學部紀要, no. 59 (1997): 45–64.

Sahashi Hōryu 佐橋法龍. *Inoue Shūten* 井上秀天 [Inoue Shūten]. Tokyo: Meicho Fukyūkai, 1982.

Santō Natsuo 山藤夏郎. *"Tasha" toshite no koten: Chūsei Zenrin shigaku ronkô* 〈他者〉としての古典：中世禅林詩学論攷. [The classics as "other": A treatise on the poetics of medieval Chan/Zen monasteries]. Ōsaka: Izumi shoin, 2015.

Sargent, Stuart. *The Poetry of He Zhu (1052–1125)*. Leiden and Boston: Brill, 2007.

Sasaki Kōzō 佐佐木剛三. *Manpukuji* 萬福寺 [Manpukuji]. Tokyo: Chuo koron Bijutsu, 1964.

Satō Shūkō 佐藤秀考. "Issan Ichinei no denki shiryō" 一山一寧の伝記資料 [Biographic materials of Yishan Yining], and "Kokan Shiren sen «Issan kokushi gyōjô» no yakuchū" 虎関師錬撰『一山国師行状』の訳註." [An annotated translation of Kokan Shiren's «Biography of National Master Yishan»]. *Komazawa daigaku Bukkyōgakubu kenkyū kiyō* 駒澤大學佛教學部研究紀要 75 (2017): 37–128.

Satō Tatsugen. *Chūgoku Bukkyō ni okeru kairitsu no kenkyū* 中国仏教における戒律の研究 [Studies on the precepts in Chinese Buddhism]. Tokyo: Mokujisha, 1986.

van Schaik, Sam. *Tibetan Zen: Discovering a Lost Tradition*. Boston: Snow Lion, 2015.

Schafer, Edward. "Fusang and Beyond: The Haunted Seas to Japan." *JAOS* 109, no. 3 (1989): 387–95.

Scheid, Bernhard. "Shōmu Tennō and the Deity from Kyushu: Hachiman's Initial Rise to prominence." *Japan Review* 27 (2014): 31–51.

Schireson, Grace Jill. *Zen Women: Beyond Tea Ladies, Iron Maidens, and Macho Masters*. Boston: Wisdom, 2009.

Schlütter, Morten. *How Zen Became Zen: The Dispute over Enlightenment and the Formation of Chan Buddhism in Song-Dynasty China*. Honolulu: University of Hawai'i Press, 2008.

Schober, Juliane. *Modern Buddhist Conjunctures in Myanmar: Cultural Narratives, Colonial Legacies, and Civil Society*. Honolulu: University of Hawai'i Press, 2011.

Schopen, Gregory. "Archaeology and Protestant Presuppositions in the Study of Indian Buddhism." *History of Religions* 31, no. 1 (1991): 1–23.

Schopenhauer, Arthur. *The World as Will and Idea*. Translated by K. B. Haldane and J. Kemp. London: Kegan Paul, Trench, Trubner & Co., 2016.

Sen, Tansen. "The Travel Records of Chinese Pilgrims Faxsian, Xuanzang, and Yijing." *Education About Asia* 11, no. 3 (2006). http://www.columbia.edu/itc/eacp/japanworks/special/travel_records.pdf

Senécal, Bernard (Sŏ, Myŏngwŏn or Seo, Myeongweon).

———. "Chinul." In *Brill's Encyclopedia of Buddhism*, Vol. 2, edited by Jonathon A. Silk. Leiden and Boston: Brill, 2019, 853–59.

———. "A Critical Reflection on the Chogye Order's Campaign for the Worldwide Propagation of Kanhwa Sŏn." *Journal of Korean Religions* 2, no. 1 (2011 March): 75–105.

———. *Kayasan horangi ŭi ch'ech'wi rŭl mat'atta* 가야산 호랑이의 체취를 맡았다 [I have picked up the scent of the Tiger of Kaya Mountains,]. Seoul: Sogang University Press, 2017.

———. "The Philosophy of Sŏn Master T'oeong Sŏngch'ŏl (1912–1993)." *Journal of Korean Religions* 7, no. 1 (April 2016): 93–132.

———. "Sŏn Master T'oeong Sŏngch'ŏl's Legacy: A Reflection on the Political Background of the Korean Sudden/Gradual Debate." *Seoul Journal of Korean Studies* 25, no. 1 (June 2012): 89–126.

———. "Le *Sūtra de l'Estrade* dans la Corée contemporaine." *Archives de Sciences Sociales des Religions* 147 (July–September 2009): 209–27.

———. "T'oeong Sŏngch'ŏl kwa Yukcho Hyenŭng: Sŏngch'ŏl sŭnim ŭi Tonhwang-bon Yukcho Tan'gyŏng hyŏnt'o p'yŏnyŏk ŭl koch'al ha'myŏnsŏ 퇴옹 성철과 육조혜능: 성철 스님의 돈황본 육조단경 현토편역을 고찰하면서 [T'oeong Sŏngch'ŏl and the Sixth Patriarch Huineng: studying Sŏngch'ŏl sŭnim's annotated translation of the *Liuzu Tanjing Dunhuang-ben*]." In [Proceedings of] *Yukcho Hyenŭng kwa T'oeong Sŏngch'ŏl, kŭrigo Han'guk*

Pulgyo (Yukcho Hyenŭng sŭnim yŏlban 1300 chugi/T'oeong Sŏngch'ŏl sŭnim yŏlban 20 chugi ch'umo haksul p'orŏm) [Sixth Patriarch Huineng and T'oeong Sŏngch'ŏl memorial academic event to commemorate the thousand and three hundredth anniversary of the Sixth Patriarch Huineng's Nirvāṇa and the twentieth anniversary of T'oeong Sŏngch'ŏl sŭnim's Nirvāṇa]. 119-149. Hanam: Taehan Pulgyo Chogyejong Paengnyŏn Pulgyo munhwa chaedan, 2013.

Seo, Myeongweon. See Senécal, Bernard.

Seon Masters Gou, Muyeo, Hyeguk, Uijeong and Seoru. *Great Doubt, Great Enlightenment: The Tradition and Practice of Ganhwa Seon in Korean Buddhism*. Seoul: Jogye Order, 2014.

Sharf, Elizabeth Horton. "Obaku Zen Portrait Painting: A Revisionist Analysis." PhD diss., University of Michigan, 1994.

Sharf, Robert H. "Buddhist Modernism and the Rhetoric of Meditative Experience" *Numen. International Review for the History of Religions* 42, no. 3 (1995): 228-83.

———. "The Rhetoric of Experience and the Study of Religion." *Journal of Consciousness Studies: Controversies in Science & the Humanities* 7, no. 11-12 (2000): 267-87.

———. "Suzuki, D. T." In *Encyclopedia of Religion*, edited by Lindsay Jones, 257-95. New York: Macmillan, 2005.

———. "The Zen of Japanese Nationalism." In *Curators of the Buddha: The Study of Buddhism under Colonialism*, edited by Donald S. Lopez Jr., 107-160. Chicago: University of Chicago Press, 1995.

Shields, James Mark. *Against Harmony: Progressive and Radical Buddhism in Modern Japan*. New York: Oxford, 2017.

Shimaji Mokurai 島地黙雷, *Shimaji Mokurai zenshū* 島地黙雷全集 [Complete works of Shimaji Mokurai], vol. 3. Kyoto: Honganji shuppan, 1973.

Shultz, Edward J. "Twelfth-Century Koryŏ Politics: The Rise of Han Anin and His Partisans." *Journal of Korean Studies* 6 (1988-1989): 3-38.

Sim Chae-ryong. "Seon Buddhist Tradition in Korea as Reflected in Jinul's Seon." *Korean Philosophy: Its Tradition and its Modern Transformation*, edited by Korean National Commission for UNESCO, 201-24. Seoul: Hollym, 2004.

Skilton, Andrew. *A Concise History of Buddhism*. Birmingham, England: Windhorse Publications, 2004.

Smidt, Corwin, ed. *Religion as Social Capital: Producing the Common Good*. Waco, TX: Baylor University Press, 2003.

Snellgrove, David L. "Śākyamuni's Final nirvāṇa." *Bulletin of the School of Oriental and African Studies* 36, no. 2 (1973): 399-411.

Snodgrass, Judith. *Presenting Buddhism to the West: Orientalism, Occidentalism and the Columbian Exposition*. Chapel Hill and London: University of North Carolina Press, 2003.

Sŏ, Myŏngwŏn. See Senécal, Bernard.

Solonin, Kirill (see also Suoluoning 索羅寧). "The Chan Teaching of Nanyang Huizhong (?-775) in Tangut Translation." In *Medieval Tibeto-Burmese Linguistics, IV*, edited by N. Hill, 274–352. Leiden and Boston: Brill, 2012.

———. "Local Literatures: Tangut/Xixia." In *Brill Encyclopedia of Buddhism*, vol. 1, edited by Jonathan A. Silk, 844–859. Leiden and Boston: Brill, 2015.

———. "The 'Perfect Teaching' and Liao Sources of Tangut Chan Buddhism: A Study of *Jiexing zhaoxin tu*." *Asia Major* 26 no. 1 (2013): 79–120.

———. "Tangut Identity and the Three Teachings in Tangut State." (Unpublished article).

———. "The Teaching of Daoshen in Tangut Translation: *The Mirror of Mind*." In *Avatamsaka Buddhism in East Asia: origins and Adaptation of a Visual Culture*, edited by Robert Gimello, Frédéric Girard, Imre Hamar, 137–87. Weisbaden: Harrasowitz, 2012.

Song Ki-joong. *The Study of Foreign Languages in the Chosŏn Dynasty*. Seoul: Jimoondang, 2001.

Sŏngch'ŏl 성철. *Kogyŏng, Chogye Sŏnjong soŭi ŏrok chip* 고경, 조계 선종 소의 어록집 [Old mirrors, the collection of the recorded sayings serving as the foundation of the Jogye Order]. Paengnyŏnam, Korea: Changgyŏng-gak, 1993.

———. *Sermon of One Hundred Days*. Translated by Hwang Soon-Il. Edited by Linda Covill. Oxford Center for Buddhist Studies Monographs, 2010.

———. *Sŏllim kogyŏng ch'ongsŏ* 선림 고경 총서 [Collected works of old mirrors of the Sŏn school]. 37 vols. Edited by Wŏnt'aek. Paengnyŏn-am, Korea: Changgyŏng-gak, 1987–1993.

———. *Sŏngch'ŏl sŭnim Paeg'il pŏmmun* 성철 스님 백일 법문 [Sŏn Master Sŏngch'ŏl's one hundred day sermons]. 3 vols. Paengnyŏn-am, Korea: Changgyŏng-gak, 2014.

———. *Sŏngch'ŏl sŭnim pŏbŏjip che 1 jip* 성철 스님法語集 第一集 [The collection of Sŏn Master Sŏngch'ŏl's dharma talks, part 1]. Paengnyŏn-am, Korea: Changgyŏng-gak, 1986–1993.

———. *Sŏngch'ŏl sŭnim pŏbŏjip che 2 ljip* 성철 스님法語集第二集 [The collection of Sŏn Master Sŏngch'ŏl's dharma talks, part 2]. Paengnyŏn-am, Korea: Changgyŏng-gak, 1976–1988.

———. *Sŏnmun chŏngno p'yŏngsŏk* 선문정로 평석 [Commentary on the correct path of Sŏn School]. Paengnyŏn-am, Korea: Changgyŏng-gak, 1993.

———. *Yet Kŏul ŭl pusugo onŏra* 옛 거울을 부수고 오너라 [Smash the old mirrors and come]. Paengnyŏn-am, Korea: Changgyŏng-gak, 2006.

Soper, Alexander C., and Helen B. Chapin. "A Long Roll of Buddhist Images, I." *Artibus Asiae* 32, no. 1 (1970): 5–41.

Stevenson, Daniel B. "Text, Image, and Transformations of the *Shuilu fahui*: the Buddhist Rite for Deliverance of Creatures of Water and Land." In *Cultural Intersections in Later Chinese Buddhism*. Edited by Marsha Weidner, 30–70. Honolulu: University of Hawai'i Press, 2001.

Sueki Fumihiko 末木文美士. "Nihon ni okeru Rinzaishū no keisei—shin shiryō kara mita Zenshū to Darumashū" 日本における臨済宗の形成——新資料から見た禅宗と達磨宗 [Formation of the Rinzai School in Japan: the Zen school and Bodhdharma school as seen from new materials]. In *Rinzairoku kenkyū no genzai* 「臨済錄」研究の現在, 409–428. Kyoto: Zen Bunka Kenkyūjo, 2017.

———. "Shinpukuji Ōsu bunko shiryō ni miru Nihon Zen no keisei" 真福寺大須文庫資料に見る日本禅の形成 [Formation of Japanese Zen as seen in materials of Ōsu bunko at Shinpukuji]. *Indogaku Bukkyōgaku kenkyū* 65, no. 2 (2017): 667–74.

Suganuma Akira 菅沼晃. "Chibetto ni okeru Indo Bukkyō to Chūgoku Bukkyō to no tairon" チベットにおけるインド仏教と中国佛教との対論 [The debates between Indian Buddhism and Chinese Buddhism in Tibet]. *Bukkyō shisōshi* 4 (1981): 175–208.

Sugimura Eiji 杉村英治. *Bōkyō no shisō Tōkō Shin'etsu* 望郷の詩僧東皐心越 [Homesick poet-monk Donggao Xinyue]. Tokyo: Miki shobō, 1989.

Sullivan, Brenton. "Venerable Fazun at the Sino-Tibetan Buddhist Institute (1932–1950) and Tibetan Geluk Buddhism in China." *Indian International Journal of Buddhist Studies* 9 (2008): 199–241.

Suoluoning 索羅寧 (K. Solonin). "Heishuicheng Xixiawen Hongzhou Chan wenxian chubu fenxi: yi 'Hongzhou zongshi jiaoyi' ji 'Hongzhou zongqu zhujie ji' wei lie," 黑水城西夏文洪州禪文獻初步分析:以「洪州宗師教儀」及「洪州宗趣注解記」為例 [An initial analysis of Hongzhou Chan literature in Tangut from Huishuicheng (Khara-Khoto)], *Zhongguo Chanxue* 6 (2012): 1–18. https://www.academia.edu/5051986/151231504-Study-of-the-Tangut-text-pertaining-to-the-lineage-of-Mazu-Daoyi-Hongzhou-school.

Suzuki, Daisetsu (D.T.). "Gendai shin'yaku hekiganroku shōkai" o yomu 「現代新訳碧巌録詳解」を読む [On reading A new, modern translation and interpretation of the *Blue Cliff Record*]. *Zendō* 97 (1918): 13–21.

———. *An Introduction to Zen Buddhism*. Kyoto: Eastern Buddhist Society, 1934.

———. *Japanese Spirituality*. Translated by Norman Waddell. Tokyo: Japan Society for the Promotion of Science, Ministry of Education, Japan, 1972. Originally published as *Nihonteki reisei* 日本的霊性. Tokyo: Iwanami bunko, 1944.

———. *The Lankavatara Sutra*. London: Routledge & Kegan Paul, 1956.

———. *Mysticism: Christian and Buddhist*. London: George Allen & Unwin, 1957.

———. *Swedenborg: Buddha of the North*. West Chester, PA: Swedenborg Foundation, 1996.

———. "Zen: A Reply to Hu Shih." *Philosophy East and West* 3, no. 1 (1953): 25–46.

Suzuki, Shunryu. *Zen Mind, Beginner's Mind*. New York: Weatherhill, 1970.

Suzuki Tetsuo 鈴木哲雄. *Tō Godai Zenshūshi* 唐五代禅宗史 [History of the Chan school in the Tang and Five Dynasties]. Tokyo: Sankibō busshorin, 1985.

———. *Chūgoku Zenshū jimei sanmei jiten* 中国禅宗寺名山名辞典 [Dictionary of famous Chan Temples and mountains in China]. Tokyo: Sankibō busshorin, 2006.

Tachi Ryūshi 舘隆志. "Gotten Funei no rai Nichi o megutte" 兀庵普寧の来日をめぐって [On the visit of Wu'an Puning to Japan]. *Kokusai Zen kenkyū* 1 (2018).

———. "Kamakura-ki no Zenrin ni okeru Chūgokugo to Nihongo" 鎌倉期の禅林における中国語と日本語 [Chinese language and Japanese language in Zen monasteries of the Kamakura period]. *Komazawa daigaku bukkyo gaku bu ronshu* 45 (2014), 269 and 283, no. 53.

———. "Kenchōji no kaisan" 建長寺の開山 [The founding of Kenchōji]. In *Higashi Ajia no naka Kenchō-ji*. Edited by Murai Shōsuke. Tokyo: Bensen shuppan, 2014.

Taixu 太虛. "Fofa yiweilun zhi shizong pianmian guan" 佛法一味論之十宗片面觀. TDQ 1.

———. "Fuotuoxue gang" 佛陀學綱 [An outline of Buddhology]. TDQ 1.

———. "Jiren chengfo de zhen xianshi lun" 即人成佛的真現實論 [True Realism: Buddhahood in this very life]. TDQ 24.

———. "Jueyuan ying wei xiu qijue zhi yuan" 覺苑應為修七覺之苑. TDQ 28.

———. "Ping Baoming jun Zhongguo Fojiao zhi xianshi" 評寶明君中國佛教之現勢 [Comments on Bao Minghun's essay "The Current Situation of Chinese Buddhism"]. TDQ 25.

———. *Zhongguo foxue* 中國佛學 [Chinese Buddhist learning]. TDQ 2:531–760.

Takada Shōhei 高田祥平. *Tōkō Shin'etsu: Tokugawa Mitsukuni ga kieshita yūkoku no toraisō* 東臯心越: 徳川光圀が帰依した憂国の渡来僧 [Donggao Xinyue: A Patriotic Immigrant Monk who was Devoted to Tokugawa Mitsukuni]. Tokyo: Ribunshuppan, 2013.

Takahashi, Hara. "Shin bukkyō-to to wa dare ka?" 新仏教徒とは誰か [Who are the new Buddhists?]. In *Kindai Nihon ni okeru chishikijin shūkyō undo no gensetsu kūkan: "Shin Bukkyō" no shisōshi, bunkashiteki kenkyū* 近代日本における知識人宗教運動の言説空間 —『新佛教』の思想史・文化史的研究 [The discursive space of intellectual religious movements in modern Japan: A study of the intellectual and cultural history of new Buddhism]. Grants-in-Aid for Scientific Research, no. 20320016, 2011.

Takai Kyōko 高井恭子. "Minmatsu Kika Chūgokusō no gakushiki nit suite" 明末帰化中国僧の学識について [On the learning of naturalized Chinese monks during the late Ming period]. *Indogaku Bukkyōgaku kenkyū* 印度学仏教学研究 49, no. 1 (December 2000).

Takasaki Jikidō 高崎直道 and Umehara Takeshi 梅原猛. *Bukkyō no shisō 11: Kobutsu no manebi Dōgen* 仏教の思想11: 古佛のまねび道元 [Buddhist thought 11: The Old Buddha Imitator Dōgen]. Tokyo: Kadokawa Shoten, 1969; reprint 1998.

Takashima Beihō 嶋米峰. *Takashima Beihō tsuioku* 高嶋米峰—追憶 [Recollections of Takashima Beihō]. Tokyo: Ōzorasha, 1993.

Takeuchi Michio 竹內道雄. "Dōgen Zenji *Hekiganroku* shōrai nitsuite" 道元禪師碧巖錄招来について ["On the origins of Dōgen's *Blue Cliff Record*"]. *Indogaku Bukkyōgaku kenkyū* 4, no. 2 (1956): 476–79.

Tamamura Takeji 玉村竹二. *Gozan Zensō denki shūsei* 五山禪僧傳記集成 [Collected biographies of Five Mountains Chan/Zen Monks]. Kyōto: Shibunkaku, 2003.

Tan Zhici 譚志詞. "Qingchu Guangdongji qiaoseng Yuanshao chanshi zhi yiju Yuenan ji xiangguang wenti yanjiu" 清初廣東籍僑僧元韶禪師之移居越南及相關問題研究 [Research on the Chan monk Yuanshao who migrated to Vietnam from Guangdong during the early Qing period and related issues]. *Huaqiao Huaren lishi yanjiu* 華僑華人歷史研究 2 (2007).

———. "Shiqi shiba shiji Lingnan yu Yuenan de Fojiao jiaoliu" 十七十八世紀嶺南與越南的佛教交流 [The Buddhist exchange between Guangdong and Vietnam during the seventeenth and eighteenth centuries]. *Shijie zongjiao yanjiu* 世界宗教研究 3 (2007): 42–52.

Tanaka Ryōshō 田中良昭. *Tonkō Zenshū bunken no kenkyū* 敦煌禅宗文献の研究 [Studies on Chan school literature from Dunhuang]. Tokyo: Daitō shuppansha, 1983.

Taylor, Rodney L. "The Sudden/Gradual Paradigm and Neo-Confucian Mind-Cultivation." *Philosophy East and West* 33, no. 1 (1983): 17–34.

Thich Thien-An. *Buddhism and Zen in Vietnam: In Relation to the Development of Buddhism in Asia*. Rutland, VT, and Tokyo: Charles E. Tuttle, 1975.

T'oeong Sŏngchŏl 退翁性徹. *Han'guk Pulgyo ŭi pŏmmaek* 韓國佛教의 法脈 [Dharma lineage of Korean Buddhism]. Hapchŏn, Korea: Changgyŏnggak, 1976.

———. *Sŏnmun chŏngro* 禪門正路 [The authentic path of Sŏn Buddhism]. Hapchŏn, Korea: Changgyŏnggak, 1981.

Trainor, Kevin. Review of Reginald Ray, *Buddhist Saints in India: a Study of Buddhist Values and Orientations*. *History of Religions* 37, no. 1 (1997): 96–98.

Tsuchiya Taisuke 土屋太祐. "'Ichiya *Hekigan*'" daisan soku yakuchū," 『一夜碧巌』第三則訳注) [Annotated translation of Case 3 of the One Night *Blue Cliff*]. *Tōyō bunka kenkyūsho kiyō* 171 (2017): 27–56.

Tweed, Thomas A. "American Occultism and Japanese Buddhism: Albert J. Edmunds, D. T. Suzuki, and Translocative History." *Japanese Journal of Religious Studies* 32, no. 2 (2005): 249–81.

Ueda, Shizuteru. "Wilhelm Gundert, 1880–1971." *The Eastern Buddhist* 5, no. 1 (1972): 159–62.

Uhlmann, Patrick R., trans. *Anthology of Stele Inscriptions of Eminent Korean Buddhist Monks*. Collected Works of Korean Buddhism 12, edited by John Jorgensen. Seoul: Compilation Committee of Korean Buddhism Through, Jogye Order of Korean Buddhism, 2012.

Vallor, Molly. *Not Seeing Snow: Musō Soseki and Medieval Japanese Zen*. Leiden and Boston: Brill, 2019.

———. "*Waka* and Zen in Medieval Japan," *Religion Compass* 10, no. 5 (2016): 101–117.

Vermeersch, Sem. *The Power of the Buddhas: The Politics of Buddhism During the Koryŏ Dynasty* (918–1392). Cambridge, MA: Harvard University Asia Center, 2008.

———, trans. *A Chinese Traveler in Medieval China: Xu Jing's Illustrated Account of the Xuanhe Embassy to Koryŏ*, Korean Classics Library. Honolulu: University of Hawai'i Press, 2016.

von Verschuer, Charlotte. "Looking from Within and Without: Ancient and Medieval External Relations." *Monumenta Nipponica* 55, no. 4 (2000): 537–66.

Viallé, Cynthia, and Leondard Blussé. *The Deshima Dagregisters, Volume XII (1650–1660.)*. Brill: Institute for the History of European Expansion, 2005.

Victoria, Brian. *Zen at War*. New York: Weatherhill, 1997.

Wada Ukiko 和田有希子. "Kamakura chūki no Rinzaizen: Enni to Rankei no aida" 鎌倉中期の臨済禅: 円爾と蘭渓のあいだ [The Framework of the Rinzai sect in the mid-Kamakura period: Enni Ben'en and Rankei Doryu]. *Journal of Religious Studies* 77, no. 3 (2003): 629–53.

Walthall, Ann. "The Sakura Sōgorō Story." In *Peasant Uprisings in Japan: A Critical Anthology of Peasant Histories*, edited and translated by Anne Walthall. Chicago: University of Chicago Press, 1991.

Wang Ha 王霞, Yu Chaewŏn 柳在元 and Ch'oe Chaeyŏng 崔宰榮. *Yŏkchu Pak T'ongsa ŏnhae* 譯註[朴通事諺解] [Annotated translation of the Korean glosses on *Pak the Translator*]. Seoul: Hakkobang, 2012.

Wang Haitao 王海濤. *Yunnan Fojiao shi* 雲南佛教史 [History of Buddhism in Yunnan]. Kunming: Yunnan Meishu chubanshe, 2001.

Wang Liping 王麗萍. *Chengxun Can Tiantai Wutai shan ji yanju* 成尋參天台五台山記研究 [Studies on Jōjin's visits to Mt. Tiantai and Mt. Wutai]. Shanghai: Shanghai renmin chubanshe, 2017.

———, ed. *Xinjiao Can Tiantai Wutaishan ji* 新校參天台五台山記 [Newly revised Record of visits to Mts. Tiantai and Wutai]. Shanghai: Shanghai guji chubanshe, 2009.

Wang Yong 王勇, ed. *Dongya de bitan yanjiu* 東亞的筆談研究 [Studies on brush-dialogue in East Asia]. Hangzhou: Zhejiang gongshang daxue chubanshe, 2015.

Wang Yong 王勇, Chen Xiaofa 陳小法, and Ge Jiyong 葛继勇. *Zhong-Ri shuji zhi lu yanjiu* 中日「书籍之路」研究 [Study of the Sino-Japanese "Book Road"]. Beijing: Beijing tushuguan chubanshe, 2003.

Wang Yueting 王月珽. "Liaochao Huangdi de chongfo jiqi shehui yingxiang" 遼朝皇帝的崇佛及其社會影響 [The veneration of Buddhism by the Liao emperors and their social influence]. *Neimenggu Daxue xuebao (Zhexue shehuikexue pan)* 1 (1994): 49–57.

Wang Zhenping. *Ambassadors from the Island of Immortals: China-Japan Relations in the Han-Tang Period*. Honolulu: University of Hawai'i Press, 2005.

———. "Chōnen's Pilgrimage to China, 983–986." *Asia Major* (3rd series) 7.2 (1994): 63–97.
Watsuji Tetsurō 和辻哲郎. *Shōbōgenzō zuimonki* 正法眼蔵随聞記 [Record of what was heard about the *Eye of Appreciations of the Correct dharma*]. Tokyo: Iwanami shoten reprint, 1976.
Welch, Holmes. "Dharma Scrolls and the Succession of Abbots in Chinese Monasteries." *T'oung-pao* 50, nos. 1–3 (1963): 93–149.
———. *The Practice of Chinese Buddhism, 1900–1950*. Cambridge, MA: Harvard University Press, 1973.
Welter, Albert. *The Meaning of Myriad Good Deeds: A Study of Yung-ming Yenshou and the Wan-shan t'ung-kuei chi*. New York: Peter Lang, 1993.
———. *Monks, Rulers and Literati: The Political Ascendancy of Chan Buddhism*. Oxford and New York and Oxford: Oxford University Press, 2006.
———. "The Problem with Orthodoxy in Zen Buddhism: Yongming Yanshou's Notion of *Zong* in the *Zongjing lu* (Records of the Source Mirror)." *Studies in Religion/ Sciences Religieuses* 31, no. 1 (2002): 3–18.
———. *Yongming Yanshou's Conception of Chan in the* Zongjing lu*: A Special Transmission within the Scriptures*. New York and Oxford: Oxford University Press, 2011.
———. "Zen Buddhism as the Ideology of the Japanese State: Eisai and the *Kōzen gokokuron*." In *Zen Classics: Formative Texts in the History of Zen Buddhism*, edited by Steven Heine and Dale S. Wright, 65–112. New York and Oxford: Oxford University Press, 2006.
Wheeler, Charles. "Buddhism in the Re-ordering of an Early Modern World: Chinese Missions to Cochinchina in the Seventeenth Century." *Journal of Global History* 2 (2007): 303–24.
Wills, John E. Jr. "Maritime China from Wang Chih to Shih Lang: Themes in Peripheral History." In *From Ming to Ch'ing: Conquest, Region, and Continuities in 17th Century China*, edited by Jonathan Spence and John E. Wills, 201–238. New Haven: Yale University Press, 1979.
Wu, Jiang. "Building a Dharma Transmission Monastery: The Case of Mount Huangbo." *Journal of East Asian History* 31 (June 2006): 29–52.
———. *Enlightenment in Dispute: The Reinvention of Chan Buddhism in Seventeenth-Century China*. New York and Oxford: Oxford University Press, 2008.
———. "Huangbo canxue ji" 黄檗參學記. Ōbaku bunka 黄檗文華 134 (2014): 278–67 (reverse pagination). Reprint. *Hanyu Fojiao Pinglun* 漢語佛教評論 6(2018): 250–74. Japanese translation, "Ōbaku sangaku ki: Ingen zenji yukari no jiin wo megutte" 黄檗参学記：隠元禅師ゆかりの寺院を巡って. Yang Kuei Hsiang 楊桂香, Hayashi Masako 林正子, and Tanaka Shōzō 田中昭三, trans. Ōbaku bunka 黄檗文華 135 (2015): 223–204 (reverse pagination).
———. *Leaving for the Rising Sun: Chinese Zen Master Yinyuan & the Authenticity Crisis in Early Modern East Asia*. New York and Oxford: Oxford University Press, 2015.

———. "Leaving for the Rising Sun: The Historical Background of Yinyuan Longqi's Migration to Japan in 1654." *Asia Major* (3rd series) 17, pt. 2 (2004): 89–120.
Wu Zhou 吳洲. *Zhongwan Tang Chanzong dili kaoshi* 中晚唐禪宗地理考釋 [Philological study of the geography of the Chan school in mid-to-late Tang]. Beijing: Zongjiao wenhua chubanshe, 2012.
Xu Xingqing 徐興慶. "Shin'etsu Zenji to Tokugawa Mitsukuni no shisōhensen shiron: Shu Shunsui shisō to no hikaku ni oite" 心越禅師と德川光圀の思想變遷試論: 朱舜水思想との比較において [Zen Master Shin'etsu and Tokugawa Mitsukuni's theory of the transformation of thought: Comparison with the thought of Shu Shunsui (Zhi Zhiyu)]. *Nihon kanbungaku kenkyū* 日本漢文学研究. *Nishōgakusha University* 二松学舎大学 3 (2008): 356–13 (reverse pagination).
*———. *Tianxianlaoren Dulixingyi quanji* 天閑老人獨立性易全集. Taibei: Taida chuban zhongxin, 2015.
Yamaguchi Zuihō 山口瑞鳳. "Chibetto Bukkyō to Shiragi no Kin Oshō" チベット仏教と新羅金和尚 [Tibetan Buddhism and Reverend Kim of Silla]. In *Shiragi Bukkyō kenkyū* 新羅佛教研究 [Studies of Silla Buddhism], edited by Kim Chigyǒn 金知見 and Chae Inhwan 蔡印幻 Tokyo: Sankibō Busshorin, 1973: 1–36(L).
Yamawaki Teijirō 山脇悌二郎. *Nakasaki no Tōjin bōeki* 長崎の唐人貿易 [The Chinese trade at Nagasaki]. Tokyo: Yoshikawa Kōbunkan, 1964.
Yampolsky, Philip B. *The Zen Master Hakuin: Selected Writings*. Records of Civilization, Sources and Studies, No. 86. New York: Columbia University Press, 1971.
Yanagida Seizan 柳田聖山, trans. *Kōzen gokokuron* 興禪護國論 [On Promoting Zen to protect the country]. In *Chūsei Zenge no shisō* 中世禅家の思想 [The thought of Medieval Zen masters], edited by Ichikawa Hakugen 市川白弦, Iriya Yoshitaka 入矢義高 and Yanagida Seizan 柳田聖山, 7–122. Tokyo: Iwanami shoten, 1972.
———. *Sodōshū sakuin* 祖堂集索引 [Index to the *Anthology of the Hall of the Patriarchs*], 3 vols. Kyoto: Kyoto Daigaku Jinbunka kenkyūjo, 1984.
———. *Zen no Jidai: Eisai, Musō, Daitō, Hakuin* 禅の事大: 栄西、夢窓、大燈、白隠 [Zen's greats: Eisai, Musō, Daitō, Hakuin]. Tokyo: Chikuma Shobō, 1987.
———. *Zen goroku: Sekai no meicho zoku 3*. 禅語録: 世界の名著 [Chan recorded sayings: Famous works of the world]. Tokyo: Chūōkōronsha, 1974.
Yang Chǒng-sǒk 양정석. "Kusan sǒnmun karam insik e taehan koch'al" 九山禪門 伽藍 認識에 대한 考察 [An investigation of (scholarly) understandings of Nine Mountain Sǒn monasteries]. *Silla munhwa* 40 (2012): 195–227.
Yang, Vincent. "A Comparative Study of Su Shi's *He Tao shi*," *Monumenta Serica* 56 (2008): 219–58.
Yi Chigwan 李智冠, ed. and trans. *Yǒktae kosǔng pimun: Silla p'yǒn* 歷代高僧碑文: 新羅編 [The Stelae inscriptions for eminent monks through the ages: Silla collection]. Rev. ed. Seoul: Kasan mun'go, 1994.

———, ed. and trans. *Yŏktae kosŭng pimun: Koryŏ p'yŏn 1* 歷代高僧碑文: 高麗編 1 [The stelae inscriptions for eminent monks through the ages: Koryŏ collection 1]. Seoul: Kasan Pulgyo munhwa yŏn'guwon, 2004. Revised edition.

Yi Hyangsun 이향순. "Chosŏn sidae piguni ŭi salm kwa suhaeng" 조선시대 비구니의 삶과 수행 [Bhikṣuṇī's life and practice during the Chosŏn period]. In *Han'guk Piguni ŭi Suhaeng ka salm* 한국 비구니의 수행과 삶 [Korean bhikṣuṇī's lives and practice], edited by Chŏn'guk pigunihoe, 103–127. Seoul: Yemoonseowon, 2007.

Yi Nŭnghwa 李能和. *Chosŏn Pulgyo T'ongsa* 朝鮮佛教通史 [History of Korean Buddhism]. Seoul: Sinmun'gwan, 1918.

Yi Tongjun 李東埈. "Jogye Chin'gak Kuksa Ŏrok ŭi kusŏng kwa naeyongsang t'ŭksŏng" <曹溪眞覺國師語錄>의 구성과 내용상 특성 [Recorded sayings of National Master Chin'gak of the Jogye Order]. *Pojo sasang* 7 (1993): 140–71.

Yifa. *The Origins of Buddhist Monastic Codes in China: An Annotated Translation and Study of the Chanyuan Qinggui*. Honolulu: University of Hawai'i Press, 2002.

Yŏm Chungsŏp 염중섭. "Naong ŭi puch'im kwa kwallyŏndoen Zhikong ŭi yŏnghyang: Zhikong e taehan insik ŭi pyŏnhwa rŭl chungsim ŭro" 나옹의 浮沈과 관련된 지공의 영향: 지공에 대한 인식의 변화를 중심으로 [Zhikong's influence on Naong's rise and fall: with a focus on the changing recognition of Zhikong]. *Korean Studies* 24 (2014): 93–127.

———. "Zhikong ŭi kagye chujang e taehan kŏmt'o: Koryŏ esŏ Zhikong ŭi sŏnggong yoin ŭl chungsim ŭro" 지공의 가계 주장에 대한 검토: 고려에서 지공의 성공요인을 중심으로 [Examination of the claims about Zhikong's family lineage: With a focus on the elements of Zhikong's success in Koryŏ]. *Chindan hakpo* 4 (2014): 31–53.

Yoshida Kyūichi 吉田久一. *Nihon kindai bukkyōshi kenkyū* 日本近代仏教史研究 [A study of modern Japanese Buddhist history]. Tokyo: Yoshikawa kōbunkan, 1992.

Yoshikawa Kōjirō. *An Introduction to Sung Poetry*. Translated by Burton Watson. Cambridge, MA: Harvard University Press, 1967.

Yoshinaga Shin'ichi 吉永進一. "*Shin bukkyō* to wa nani mono ka? "jiyū tōkyū" to "kenzen naru shinkō" 『新仏教』とはなにものか？—「自由討究」と「健全なる信仰」 [What is *New Buddhism*? From "free investigation" to "sound faith"]. In *Kindai Nihon ni okeru chishikijin shūkyō undō no gensetsu kūkan: "Shin Bukkyō" no shisōshi, bunkashiteki kenkyū* 近代日本における知識人宗教運動の言説空間 —『新佛教』の思想史・文化史的研究 [The discursive space of intellectual religious movements in modern Japan: A study of the intellectual and cultural history of new Buddhism]. Grants-in-Aid for Scientific Research, no. 20320016, 2011.

Yoshizawa Katsuhiro 芳澤勝弘. *Gōko fūgetsu shū yakuchū* 江湖風月集訳注 [Annotated translation of *Gōko fūgetsu shū*]. Translation of *Gōko fūgetsu shū ryakuchū shusha* 江湖風月集略註取捨 and *Gōko fūgetsu shū shō* 江湖風月集抄. Kyoto: Zen bunka kenkyūjo, 2003; reprint 2012.

Yü, Chün-fang. *The Renewal of Buddhism in China: Chu-Hung and the Late Ming Synthesis*. New York: Columbia University Press, 1981.

Yü, Chün-fang. "Buddhism in the Ming Dynasty." In *The Cambridge History of China*, edited by Dennis Twitchett and Frederick Mote, 893–952. Vol. 8. Cambridge and New York: Cambridge University Press, 1998.

Yu Iji 俞慰慈 [Yu Weici]. *Gozan bungaku no kenkyū* 五山文學の研究 [Studies of Five Mountains Literature]. Tokyo: Kyūko shoin, 2004.

Yuasa, Yasuo. *The Body: Toward an Eastern Mind-Body Theory*. Translated by Shigenori Nagatomo and Thomas P. Kasulis. Albany: State University of New York Press, 1987.

Zheng, Aihua. "A Portrait of an Ōbaku Monk: The Life and Religion of Jifei Ruyi (1616–1671)." MA thesis, University of Arizona, 2009.

Zieme, Peter. "Local Literatures: Uighur." In *Brill Encyclopedia of Buddhism*, edited by Jonathan A. Silk, 871–82. Leiden and Boston: Brill, 2015.

Contributors

Juhn Y. Ahn is associate professor of Buddhist and Korean studies at the University of Michigan and author of *Buddhas and Ancestors: Religion and Wealth in Fourteenth-Century Korea*, which focuses on the relationship between Buddhist mortuary practices and elite identity formation in fourteenth-century Korea, when a small but growing number of families that belonged to the late Koryŏ elite began to abandon Buddhist mortuary practices in favor of Neo-Confucian ones. He is currently working on two research monographs concerning reading practices in Song-dynasty Chan Buddhism and seventeenth-century Korean Buddhism, economic history, and climate change.

Kevin N. Cawley is the former head of the Department of Asian Studies at University College Cork and current director of the Irish Institute of Korean Studies. He is the author of *Religious and Philosophical Traditions of Korea* (2019), which examines Korea's intellectual history. He has multiple publications relating to interactions between various traditions, in particular between Neo-Confucianism and early Catholicism during the Chosŏn dynasty, examined from a translational and transcultural point of view and engaging with contemporary critical theory.

Steffen Döll is Numata Professor of Japanese Buddhism at the University of Hamburg, Germany. His research focuses on Buddhist philosophy and history, the processes of cultural transfer in East Asia, and Japanese intellectual and literary traditions. He is author of *Im Osten des Meeres: Chinesische Emigrantenmönche und die frühen Institutionen des japanischen Zen-Buddhismus* [East of the ocean: Chinese emigrant monks and the early institutions of Japanese Zen Buddhism] (2010) and several articles on historical issues related to East Asian religions and cultures.

432 | Contributors

Eric Goodell is an adjunct assistant professor in the Department of Buddhist Studies at Fo Guang University in Taiwan. He specializes on the Chinese Buddhist monk Taixu and his efforts to modernize Buddhism in the early to mid-twentieth century. His recent publications include "Conservative and Progressive Models for Buddhism under the Republic of China" and "Taixu" in the *Oxford Research Encyclopedia of Religion*. He is also translating the Dharmaguptaka Vinaya with Bukkyo Dendo Kyokai (BDK) of Japan which will appear in the BDK Tripiṭaka English translation series.

Steven Heine is professor and director of Asian studies at Florida International University. A specialist in the spread of Zen Buddhism from Song-dynasty China to Kamakura-era Japan, Heine is author of more than thirty books on East Asian religion and society, including most recently *Chan Rhetoric of Uncertainty in the* Blue Cliff Record (2016) and *From Chinese Chan to Japanese Zen* (2017), in addition to *Flowers Blooming from a Withered Tree: Giun's Verse Comments on Dōgen's Treasury of the True Dharma Eye* (2020) and *Dogen: Japan's Original Zen Teacher* (2021). He has lectured extensively on these and related topics at leading institutions worldwide and was the recipient of the Order of the Rising Sun award from the government of Japan for a lifetime of service promoting Japanese culture.

John Jorgensen, now senior research fellow in the China Studies Research Centre, La Trobe University, Australia, taught Japanese studies for twenty years. His research covers East Asian Buddhism and Korean new religions. His publications include *Inventing Hui-neng* (2005), *A Handbook of Korean Zen Practice* (2015), *The Foresight of Dark Knowing: Chŏng Kam nok and Insurrectionary Prognostication in Pre-Modern Korea* (2018), five volumes of translations of the Korean Sŏn masters (2005, 2012, 2016), plus numerous chapters and articles, most recently on medieval Chan, modern Chinese Yogācāra, and Korean new religions.

George A. Keyworth is an associate professor in the History Department at the University of Saskatchewan. Keyworth received his BA (Honors) and MA in Chinese and Asian studies from the University of California, Santa Barbara (UCSB). He received his PhD in Chinese Buddhist studies from the University of California, Los Angeles (UCLA). He has published several articles on topics ranging from Chinese Chan Buddhism and the figure of Juefan Huihong (1071–1128); Japanese pilgrims to Song China (e.g., Jōjin [1011–1081]); apocryphal Chinese Buddhist scriptures using sources from Dunhuang; esoteric Buddhism in Tang and Song China; Zen Buddhism in Edo (1603–1868) Japan; and old Japanese manuscript Buddhist canons (*issaikyō*), especially from the Nanatsudera and Matsuo shrine canons.

Jin Y. Park is a professor and the Department Chair of Philosophy and Religion at American University. Park specializes in East Asian Buddhism, Buddhist ethics, intercultural philosophy, and modern East Asian philosophy. She has published numerous journal articles and book chapters on these topics. Her books include *Women and Buddhist Philosophy* (2017); *Reflections of a Zen Buddhist Nun* (2014); *Makers of Modern Korean Buddhism* (2010); *Merleau-Ponty and Buddhism* (coedited, 2009); *Buddhism and Postmodernity* (2008), *Buddhisms and Deconstructions* (2006).

Jason Protass is William A. Dyer Jr. Assistant Professor of the Humanities at Brown University. He specializes in Chinese Buddhism of the Song dynasty (960–1279). His first book is entitled *The Poetry Demon: Song-Dynasty Monks on Verse and the Way* (2021). Recent essays include "The Flavors of Monks' Poetry: On a Witty Denigration and its Influences" (2021), and "A Geographic History of Song Dynasty Chan Buddhism: The Decline of the Yunmen Lineage" (2019).

Bernard Senécal, SJ (Sŏ Myŏngwon 徐明源) received his PhD from Denis Diderot University in 2004 with a dissertation on the Sŏn Master Seongcheol (Sŏngchŏl). He is a qualified Dhyāna master in the Sŏndohoe 禪道會 (Imjejong 臨濟宗) and chairman of the board of the Way's End Stone Field Community, specializing in Buddhist-Christian encounter and organic farming. His recent publications include, "Chinul" (2019), "A Comparative Study of Sudden and Gradual in Sŏn 禪 and the New Testament" (2019), the edited volume *San ŭn san, mur ŭn mul: Sŏngchŏl Pulgyo ae taehan kŏmt'o* (2019), "Chonggyo chŏk tayang sŏng e kwanhayŏ" (2020), and "Japanese Buddhist Modernism and the Thought of Sŏn Master Toeong Seongcheol 退翁性撤禪師 (1912–1993)" (2021).

James Mark Shields is professor of comparative humanities and Asian thought and inaugural director of the Humanities Center at Bucknell University (Lewisburg, PA). Educated at McGill University (Canada), the University of Cambridge (UK), and Kyoto University (Japan), he conducts research on modern Buddhist thought, Japanese philosophy, comparative ethics and philosophy of religion. He is author of *Critical Buddhism: Engaging with Modern Japanese Buddhist Thought* (2011), *Against Harmony: Progressive and Radical Buddhism in Modern Japan* (2017), and coeditor of *Teaching Buddhism in the West: From the Wheel to the Web* (2003), *Buddhist Responses to Globalization* (2014), and *The Oxford Handbook of Buddhist Ethics* (2018).

Albert Welter is professor and head of the Department of East Asian Studies, University of Arizona. His research focuses on the study of Buddhism in the transition from the late Tang (ninth century) to the Song dynasty (tenth to thirteenth centuries). In recent years, he has published *Monks, Rulers, and Literati: The Political Ascendancy of Chan Buddhism* (2006), *The Linji lu and the Creation of Chan Orthodoxy: The Development of Chan's Records of Sayings Literature* (2008), and *Yongming Yanshou's Conception of Chan in the* Zongjing lu*: A Special Transmission within the Scriptures* (Oxford, 2011). His most recent book, *The Administration of Buddhism in China: A Study of Zanning and the Topical History of the Buddhist Clergy* (2018). He recently received funding from the Khyentse Foundation for a project, "The Hangzhou Region and the Creation of East Asian Buddhism."

Jiang Wu is professor in the Department of East Asian Studies, University of Arizona, and director of the Center for Buddhist Studies. He received his master's degree from Nankai University (1994) and PhD from Harvard University (2002). His research interests include seventeenth-century Chinese Buddhism, especially Chan/Zen Buddhism, the role of Buddhist canons in the formation of East Asian Buddhist culture, and the historical exchanges between Chinese Buddhism and Japanese Buddhism. Other interests include Confucianism, Chinese intellectual history and social history, and the application of electronic cultural atlas tools in the study of Chinese culture and religion. He has published articles in *Asia Major, Journal of East Asian History, Journal of Chinese Philosophy*, and *Monumenta Serica* on a variety of topics. His first book, *Enlightenment in Dispute: The Reinvention of Chan Buddhism in Seventeenth-century China* was published in 2008. Recent publications include *Leaving for the Rising Sun: Chinese Zen Master Yinyuan and the Authenticity Crisis in Early Modern East Asia* (2015); *Spreading Buddha's Word in East Asia: The Formation and Transformation of the Chinese Buddhist Canon* (2016), and *Reinventing the Tripitaka: Transformation of the Buddhist Canon in Modern East Asia* (2017).

Index

Note: References in *italic* and **bold** refer to figures and tables.
References followed by "n" refer to endnotes.

Abe Iso'o, 327
Abhidharma, 295
Account of Conduct, 348, 355–56
Admonitions to Beginning Students
 (Chinul), 5, 216, 226, 227
ahimsa, 322–23, 338. See also pacifism
Ahn, Juhn, 57
Ālāra Kālāma, 367
Ambedkar, B. R., 319, 342n42
ānāpāna meditation, 295, 296, 301
anarchism, 329, 341n33; appeal of,
 329–30; and Buddhism, 323, 324,
 326, 331, 333
Anarcho-communist Revolution, 330,
 331, 338
Andō Seian, 82
Anhwasa, 231n26
Anjŏksa, 223
Anjŏngsa, 368
*Annotated Record of Kenzei (Teiho
 Kenzeiki)*, 119
anraku jiyū, 329, 331, 332
anti-Christian policy, 73, 74, 80
antinomian Chan/Zen: in Japan, 22;
 in Tibet, 13
Aoki Kōji, 340n22

App, Urs, 37
aristocratic Zen, 22
Arnold, Edwin, 37, 38
Asai Endo, 341n31
Asano Fuzan, 195
Ashikaga *bakufu*, 185
*Authentic Path of Sŏn School (Sŏnmun
 chŏngro)*, 253
Avalokiteśvara, 203
Avataṃsaka, 285n15
Avataṃsaka sūtra, 349, 350
Awafune midō, 66n59
awakening: partial, 371; self-
 awakening, 331; sudden. *See*
 sudden awakening
Ayuwang si (temple), 53, 119
azhali, 17

Bach Lien, 17
Bai, 16–17
Bai Juyi, 139
Baizhang Huaihai, 217–19, 227, 298
Bankei Yōtaku, 186
Baoensi, 198
Baolin zhuan, 304
Baozhi, 296

Batchelor, Stephen, 320
Beichan Zhixian, 143–44
Beizong school, 354
bhikkhus, 367
Bhiksuni Liaoran, 244, 245
Bhiksuni Myodŏk, 245–48
bhūmis, 295
bilingual monasteries, Japan, 24, 25
Blavatsky, Helen, 38
Blue Cliff Record (Yuanwu Keqin), 4, 196, 300, 375; and capping phrases, 97, 99, 101, 115, 121; destruction of, 108; history of, 98, 101–5; and "One Night Blue Cliff," 100, 104, 119; One-Night version *vs.* Taishō version, **114,** 114–16, **115;** overview, 97–101; structure of, 98, 101–5; translation of, 99; versions of, 104–5, **106**
bodhi, 331
Bodhidharma, 120, 128, 265, 294–95, 297, 375; Tamjin's lineage back to, 225; and Vinaya rules, 295
Bodiford, William, 121
Book of Rites, 280
Book of the Two Cliffs, 375
Borgen, Robert, 157n14
bosatsu-koji, 334
Boshan Yuanlai, 309
Bourdieu, Pierre, 86
Brose, Benjamin, 157n13, 267
brush-dialogue, 127, 133, 134–36; Wuxue Zuyuan and Kōhō Kennichi, 152–54; Yishan Yining, 151–52
Buddhabhadra, 296
Buddha Nature, 269, 280–81, 342n42; Buddhist idea of, 281; and equality, 331–32; inherent, 271, 283; Mahāyāna teaching of, 332; mind and, 272; original, 271; Sŏn school focus on, 350
Buddha of Immovable Wisdom, 350

Buddhism: Ceylonese, 38; Chinese, 35–36; cultural capital, as source of, 86–88; discovery, 37; East Asian, 35–59; forms of, 333; human capital, as source of, 80–83; Imperial Way, 323; Indian, 35, 36, 38, 41, 42, 45; Indo-centric, 43–45; Japanese, 35–36, 52, 80–88; Ōbaku, 88; as "Oriental philosophy," 37; pilgrims to India, 44, 45; Pure Land, 269; purification of, 368; rehabilitation of, 362; social capital, as source of, 83–86; spread of, 43–45; stages in development of Buddhism in China, 43–44; Tang dynasty, 267–68; Theravāda, 61n10, 322, 323
Buddhist Committee for Human Rights, 368
Buddhist Conquest of China, 292
Buddhist Culture Research Institute, 368
Buddhist Enlightenment, 320, 321; peers, 333
Buddhist Hybrid Sinitic, 11, 14, 24
Buddhist modernism, 319–22, 333, 336, 337, 338; indigenous forms of, 320; in Japan, 321; Meiji, 334. *See also* Zen modernism
Buddhist Saints in India: A Study of Buddhist Values and Orientations (Ray), 40
Buswell, Robert, 58, 270, 271; *Korean Approaches to Zen: Collected Works of Chinul,* 354

Caodong, 53, 56, 375; lineage, 72–73; school, 266, 309
capitalism, 320, 321
Caputo, John D., 272
Carus, Paul, 319
Cawley, Kevin, 6

Index | 437

Ceylonese Buddhism, 38
Ch'amgu, 379n39
Chan: attaining Buddhahood, 296–97; discourse, 104, 105; dual practice of, 301–2; esoteric understandings of body, 129; history of, Taixu's, 291–314; of lamp traditions, 298–99; and Lanxi Daolong, 128; literary style, 99; as mental cultivation based on teachings, 295–96; of patriarchs that supersedes Buddha, 297–98; radicals, 11–12; realization, 303; reintegrating of teachings and, 302–3; relationship to literary culture, 295; scholasticism, 49; sermons, 101; Song. *See* Song Chan; syncretism, 48–49; tathāgata, 298, 299; temples in Zhejiang, 102; translingual writing, 130; Wuyue, 48
Chan Buddhism, 1, 7, 42, 57, 59, 167, 170–71, 186; after-effects, 6, 263, 283; dominance of, 221; emergence of, 265–68; mind-to-mind transmission of, 252; monk-travelers, 71–73
Changlu Zongze, 232n30, 270, 283
Chan koine, 11, 14; and Dōgen, 24; and Enni Ben'en, 24; in Japan, 22; in Khitan and Jurchen, 15; in Korea, 19–20; in Vietnam, 18; and Yōsai, 23; in Yunnan, 16–17
Chan monastery, 221, 298, 310; Chinese, 172; in Eastern Zhejiang, 170; Lingyin, 50; during the Ming and Qing dynasties, 308; public, 5
Chan monasticism, 217, 218, 219
Chan monks, 11, 17, 132, 291, 298; Bai Gao clan and, 16; communication with Zen monks, 129, 130, 136–54; poems of, 140; Sanping Yizhong, 12; Song and Yuan, 141

Chan of Zongmi, 13, 14
Ch'anyu, 219
Chanyuan qinggui, 24, 128, 235n47, 270
Chanlin sengbao zhuan, 233
Chan *yulu*, 19
Chaoran, 76, 77
Ch'en, Kenneth, 283
Cheng Fuxin, 280, 281, 282
Cheng Hao, 275
Cheng Yi, 275
Cheng-Zhu: orthodoxy, 280; school, 277, 280, 284n3
Chengzong, 180, 181
Chen Yong, 135
chesa, 277
Chewu, 302, 316n39
Chicago World Parliament of Religions (1893), 334–35
Chigoksa monastery, 218, 230n14
Chijue Daochong, 171
China: Chan Buddhism in, 291; Dōgen in, 170; geographical spread of Chan in, 12; Japanese pilgrimages to, 170; Jurchen invasion, 170; Mushō Jōshō in, 136–41; Paegun Kyŏnghan in, 246; Song. *See* Song China; stages in development of Buddhism in, 43–44; Tang, 13, 18, 133, 169, 266; Yuan. *See* Yuan China; Zen literature in, 196
Chinese Buddhism, 3, 6, 294, 313; linking Chan with Humanistic Buddhism, 291; in Nagasaki, 79, 83
Chinese Buddhist Learning, 291, 313
Chinese Chan: and *Blue Cliff Record*, 123; discourse, 111; Dōgen's remarks on, 121; sangha, 326; teachers, 104
Chingak Hyesim, 19, 57, 254, 273, 347, 354–59; approach to Kanhwa

438 | Index

Chingak Hyesim *(continued)*
Sŏn, 240; *Collection of Poems of the Naked Son,* 360; *Compilation of Handpicked Stanzas of the Sŏn School,* 346, 359–61; dharma talks to nuns, 242–43; disciples, 242; falsification work, 361; interpretation of master's thought, influence on, 361; Korean nuns' practice of *hwadu* meditation, 240–45; and military, 20–21; *Recorded Sayings,* 240, 243; stele, 242; *Sūtra of Sturdy Lady,* 243–44, 245
Chin'gwan, 218, 368
Chinjŏnsa, 267
Chinsim chiksŏl, 354
Chintei Kaiju, 149, 150, 151, 155
Chixiu Baizhang qinggui, 227
Ch'oe Cha, 242
Ch'oe Ch'unghŏn, 269
Ch'oe I, 226
Ch'oe Sagyŏm, 220
Ch'oe Saryang, 57, 220
Ch'oe U, 226, 360
Chogye, 268
Chŏksanwŏn monastery, 219
Cho Myungje, 267, 346; research on *Compilation of Handpicked Stanzas of the Sŏn School,* 359–61
Chŏnche, 364
Chōnen, 134
Chŏng Chungbu, 276
Chŏngdam, 367, 369
Chŏnghŏ Hyujŏng, 362
Chonghŏn, 226
Chonghwi, 20
Chŏnghyesa monastery, 224–26, 353
Chongmin, 243, 258n16
Chongqing (Chungking), 299
Chongsheng Monastery, 16
Chŏngsim, 242
Chŏngso, 133

Chŏng Su-a, 221
Chŏng Tojŏn, 276–77
Chŏngwŏn, 242, 243, 244, 245
Chŏngwŏnsa, 348
Chongxin, 298
Chŏnhwasa, 223
Chŏn Tuhwan, 369
Chŏnyŏng, 225, 226, 227, 236n62
chosadang, 218
Chosŏn dynasty, 215, 227, 228n5, 248, 249, 264, 270, 276, 346, 375; beginning of, 362; Buddhist establishment in, 227; neo-Confucian, 246
Choŭng, 222, 234n45, 234n46
Chūdō shisō oyobi sono hattatsu, 370
chuji, 228n2
Chung, Edward, 277
Ch'unggam, 227
Ch'ungji, 225, 226
Ch'usa Kim Chŏnghŭi, 364
Chushi Fanqi, 302
Chūshuku, 145
Classic of the Heart and Mind, 281, 282
Clements, Rebekah, 135
coattail Taoism, 310–11
Cold War, 346
Coleman, James, 83
Collcutt, Martin, 129, 131
Collection of Outstanding Figures in Chan Monasteries, 17
Collection of Wind and Moon [Poems] from Rivers and Lakes (Jianghu fengyue ji), 132
colloquial language, 2–3, 11–12; of Chan master, 15; Chinese, 82, 83; Chinese and Bai, 12, 17; and Yishan Yining, 25
Commentary to Stone Gate's Chan of Words and Letters (Chū sekimon mojizen), 193, 194

Index | 439

Compilation of Handpicked Stanzas of the Sŏn School, 346, 359–61
Conditions in India, 322
Confucianism, 6, 50, 265, 273, 274, 278, 324. *See also* Neo-Confucianism
conservative Chan, 11; and Dainichi Nōnin, 22; in Tangut empire, 14; and Yōsai, 23; and Zongmi, 13
Crump, John, 329
cultural capital: Buddhism as source of, 86–88; definition, 86

Dahui Pujue, 349
Dahui Zonggao, 56, 98, 252, 272, 300, 357, 358, 365, 371; and Bai Chan, 16, 18; and Chinul, 20; criticism, 304; and Daruma-shū, 23; disciple of, 109; and Dōgen, 24; as follower of Yuanwu, 111; and *huatou,* 301; incineration legend, 105–12; Kanhua Chan, 242, 359; *kanhua chan,* promote, 356; and military, 20–21; phrase meditation taught by, 345; practice of *Kanhwa Sŏn,* 352; *Precious Lessons,* 105, 108, 109; *Recorded Sayings of Chan Master Dahui Pujue,* 240, 355
Dahui Zonggao chansi yulu, 366
Dai Andao, 91n19
Daigenshūri Bosastsu, 119
Dai Jingqiao, 91n19
Daijōji temple, 100, 113, 124n3, 193, 206
Dai Li, 91n19
daimyō, 92n27; Fudai, 84; Japanese, 70, 84
Dainichibō Nōnin, 170
Dainichi Nōnin, 22, 170
Daiō, 100
Daiōji, 204, 206
Daitō, 99, 100, 121, 125n22

Daitokuji temple, 100, 185, 209n19, 229n12
Dajue Fangnian, 309
Dajue Huailian, 221
Dali kingdom, 16
danka seido, 206
Danxia Zichun, 297, 300
Daoism, 50, 273. *See also* Taoism
Daolin temple, 105, **106,** 114
Daoshen, 14–15
Daowu, 298
Daoxuan, 296
Daoyuan, 51
Daozhe Chaoyuan, 72, 76, 198
Daozhen, 220–21
Daozong, 15
Dapeng Zhengkun, 87
Daruma-shū, 22–24
Dasabhūmika vibhāsa śāstra, 228n5
Dazhu, 303
de Bary, William Theodore, 263, 275
demythologization, 99, 109, 113, 121
Denecke, Wiebke, 158n24
dengchi, 162n75
Department of Complete Interpenetration, 362
Deshao, 48, 49
Deyi, 252
dhāranī, 151, 154
dharmadhātu, 350, 357
dharma hall, 217, 218–19, 231n21, 298
dharma lineage: nuns', 5–6
Dharma Lineage of Korean Buddhism, 251, 369
Dharmapala, Anagarika, 37, 319, 322
Dharmarakṣa, 44
dharma seal, 366, 375
dharma talks, 370, 372, 374, 376
Dharma Transmission Doctrine, 363
Dharmayasas, 295
dhyāna, 265, 354, 367, 369

Dialogues of Buddha, 40
Diamond Sutra, 326, 352
Dōgen, 22–23, 24, 53, 98, 99, 128, 170, 199; Chinese language skills, 145–46; citations to *Biyanlu*, **117**; commentarial techniques used by, 113; and Daigenshūri Bosastsu, 119; *Extensive Record*, 116, 117, 121, 199; "One Night" legend, 112–20; *Record of Kenzei*, **118**, 118–19; and *shinjin datsuraku*, 162n82; *Treasury of 300 Cases*, 116, 117; *Treasury of the True Dharma Eye*, 116, 117, 121; *Verse Comments*, 117
Dōgen Kigen, 167
dojishin, 119
Dokuan Genkō, 199
Döll, Steffen, 4, 56
Domain schools, 206
Donggao Xinyue, 4–5, 78, 195, 295; birth place of, 198; émigré monk, 193; expressing nostalgia and encountering Japan, 201–6; final poem of, 205; handwriting, 201; invited to Kōfukuji, 198; landed in Nagasaki, 73; *Laozi Daode jing*, 204; left Hangzhou, 199; personality, 198, 204; with Sinophiles and Sinophobes, 197–201; wrote poetry, 5, 194
Dongling Yongyu, 140
Donpekirō, 140
Doushuai Congyue, 305
Du Fu, 145
Duhou Xingshi, 77
Duli Xingyi, 81, 82
Dunhuang, 13–14, 45–47
Dushun, 296
Duzhen Xingying. *See* Lin Shoudian

East Asian Buddhism, 35–59; creation of, Wuyue kingdom and, 47–51; Hangzhou as new center of, 51–56; search of, 35–43; sects, 329; spread of, 58–59
eclecticism, 347
Edo period, 86, 194, 198, 202, 203, 206; commentary of, 158n22; *Shuihuzhuan*, reception of, 158n23
Egaku, 180
Ehu [Guang]xin, 309
The Eight Kinds of Mindfulness of Great People, 294
Eiheiji temple, 113, 119
Eihei kōroku, 116
Eisai (Yōsai), 51–56, 128
Elman, Benjamin, 194, 206
Emerson, Ralph Waldo, 336
émigré monks, 56, 76, 80; Chinese, 121, 130, 140; Donggao Xinyue, 193; Dongling Yongyu, 140; and Huqiu-based lineage, 111–12; in Japan, 136–41, 146–51; Lanxi Daolong, 147; Qingzhuo Zhengcheng, 131; Wuxue Zuyuan, 147; Yishan Yining, 99; Zhuxian Fanxian, 149
Eminent Monks, 296, 297
Empress Qi, 362
Engakuji, 121, 182
Enlightenment Party, 250
Enni Ben'en, 24, 53–54, 128, 170, 174
Ennin, 133, 134, 218–19
Enomoto Wataru, 131
equality: in Buddhism/Zen, 319, 321, 332, 338; political, 332; social, 332, 342n2; transcendent, 332
Esoteric Buddhism: and *azhali*, 17; and Bai, 16; in Dunhuang, 13; and Khitan, 15; and Tangut, 14
Essentials of the Learning of the Sages (Sŏnghak chipyo), 277
Essentials on Pure Land Practice, 354
Etsugan, Riku, 322

Eun-su Cho, 254
exceptionalist Chan, 15; and Dōgen, 24; and Khitan, 15; and Yōsai, 23
Excerpts from Master Kūge's Daily Efforts (Kūge rōshi nichiyō kufū ryakush), 142
exchange poems, 133–34
exclusivism, 347; Linji-style, 364

Fadu, 295
Faji biexing lu, 354
Fajing si, 53
farming, 11–12. *See also* paddy-rice agriculture
Faxi si, 53
Fayuansi, 247
Fazang, 285n15
Feilaifeng, 52–53
Feiyin Tongrong, 69–70, 72, 309
Fenyang Shanzhao, 105, 299
Feyin Tongrong, 200
Five Mountains, 54, **54**, 55, **55**, 100, 170; as embodiments of Zen Buddhist, 185–86; in Kyoto and Kamakura, 196; Rinzai-based temples, 120; Zen temples, 206
Five Relationships, 277, 279, 287n54
Floating Yuanwu. *See* Daitokuji temple
Flower Garland Sūtra (Huyang jing), 285n15
Foguang, 308
Foulk, T. Griffith, 217
freedom: individual, 329–30; political, 331
Fudai daimyō, 84
Fu Dashi, 296
Fujisawa Togai, 333
Fujiwara Seika, 277
Fukusaiji, 74, *75*
Fukushūji. *See* Sōfukuji monastery
Fukuzawa Yukichi, 331

Fumonji monastery, 70, *70*
Funerary Inscription, 348–49, 350, 351–52, 353, 356
Fung Yu-lan, 312, 313
Fuqing: merchants, 76, 85, 93; native, 76, 78; Wanfu monastery in, 69
Fushan Fayuan, 221
Futaki Jinbee. *See* Lin Fenggao
Fuzhou, 135

Gadamer, Hans-Georg, 6, 263, 264
Gaoan Dayu, 244
Gao clan, Bai, 16
Gaofeng Yuanmiao, 17, 111, 301, 309
Gaomin si, 308
Gaoquan Xingdun, 82
Gateless Checkpoint, 196
gāthā, 21, 137, 151
Gelao people, 12
Gelugpa system of Tsongkhapa, 303
gengshen, 200
Genkō, 201
Genyō, Princess, 84
Gesshin Kei'en, 144–45, 150, 155
Getsudō Sōki, 140
Getsuō Chikyō, 171
Gettan Dōchō, 194
Gida Daichi, 141
Gidō Shūshin, 141–46, 155
Golden Age, 377
Gomizunoo (emperor), 84, 93n29
gongan, 17, 57, 267, 297; commentary on, 299–300; failure to understand, 25; in Japan, 22; in Korea, 19; in Vietnam, 18
Gong Tingxian, 81
Goodell, Eric, 6
Go-Saga (Emperor), 172
Gospel of Buddhism (Carus), 319
Gou, 273
Go-Uda (Emperor), 183, 185
gozan, 171, 186

Great Kantō earthquake (1923), 201
Groner, Paul, 88n1
Grove, Bamboo, 294
Guangli chansi, 179
Guanglisi, 223, 233n35
Guangyun, 137, 143
Guanxi Zhixian, 244
Guanyinsi, 180, 181, 182
Guidance record, 375
Guifeng Zongmi, 371; *Dharma Collection and Special Practice Record*, 354
Guishan, 298, 300
Gundert, Wilhelm, 99
gwanhwa, 57

Hachiman Shrine, 177
Ha Ch'unsaeng, 253, 254, 261n58
Haeinsa, 366, 370, 372, 374, 376
Haengjang, 348
Hag'il, 20
Hakata (port city), 134, 140, 178
Hakuin Ekaku, 97, 102, 167, 186, 196
Hakusan Gongen, 119
Hakusan Myōri Gongen, 119
Hamhŏ Tŭkt'ong, 362
Hand Mirror of the Sŏn School, 363
Han'gŏl writing system, 270
Han'guk Pulgyo ŭi pŏmmaek, 369
Hangzhou (Qiantang), 45, 47, 170, 202, 203; Korean Sŏn connection to, 57; Longcesi, 230n17; Lower Tianzhusi in, 232n33; Manchu armies, attacked by, 199; as new center of East Asian Buddhism, 51–56; print culture in, 132; Southern Song capital in, 55; spread of East Asian Buddhism, 58–59; Tianzhu si, 232n33; West Lake in, 201
Hanshan Deqing, 72, 302, 303, 309

Han Yu, 274
Hanyue Fazang, 72, 309, 312–13
Haorui, 47
Hartman, Charles, 273
hasanso, 235n48
Hayashi Razan, 277
He Gaocai, 76; moved to Nagasaki, 78; plaque donated by, 79
Hegel, G. W. F., 337
heibon, 331
Heidegger, Martin, 264
Heine, Steven, 4, 148
Henkai Ichirantei, 205
Heze Shenhui, 354, 356, 357, 371
He Zhaojin, 78
High Treason Incident, 322, 324, 327, 328
History of Korean Buddhism (Chosŏn Pulgyo t'ongsa), 249
Hitomi Chikudō, 201
Hoeamsa monastery, 227
hoegyo kuisŏn, 347
Hŏhŭng Pou, 278
Hŏ Hŭngsik, 230n17
Hŭiyang, Mount, 229n11
Hōjō clan, 66n59
Hōjō Tokimune, 54, 129, 148, 172, 175, 178
Hōjō Tokiyori, 54, 56, 171–72, 175
Hōnan, Tayama, 164n109
Hongren, 265, 266
Hongzhi Zhengjue, 300
Hongzhou Chan, 13, 354; in Japan, 22, 23; and Tanguts, 14–15; in Tibet, 13
Honwŏn, 225–26, 235n52, 236n64
Huairang, 297
Huaishen, Cishou, 161n60
Huangbo, 243, 298
Huanglong Huinan, 16, 305
Huang Tingjian, 132, 139, 201

Huanqi Weiyi, 176
huatou, 17, 57, 300–301, 305; practice of, 313, 314
Huayan Buddhism, 44, 365, 371; and Bai, 17; and Khitan, 15; and Sŏn meditation, 241; and Tanguts, 14. *See also* Zongmi
Huijiao, 296
Huike, 295, 297
Huilin Zongben, 221, 232n36
Huineng, 15, 252, 265, 296, 297, 303, 375; *ipsissima verba,* 373; in *Platform Sutra,* 219. See also *The Platform Sūtra of the Sixth Patriarch*
Huiri Monastery, 47
Huisi, 296
Hŭiwŏn, 242, 243, 244, 245
Hŭiyangwŏn monastery, 217, 229n11
Huiyuan, 296
Huizhong, 303
human capital, Buddhism as source of, 80–83
humanism, 280
Humanistic Buddhism, 6, 7, 292, 313, 314
Hŭngch'ŏnsa, 215, 228n3
Huqiu Shaolong, 100, 111
Hu Shih, 292, 296, 313; language used by, 307; "Zhongguo chanxue de fazhan," 307
hwadu, 249, 251–55, 366, 379n39; investigation, 358; Korean nuns' practice of, 240–45
hwadu mu, 357
Hwan'am Honsu, 362
Hwaŏm, 267, 350, 351
Hwaŏm non chŏryo, 350
Hwasan Suok, 251
Hyeguk, 273
Hyejo, 19, 20, 220. *See also* Sŏn revival

hyo, 277
Hyobong Hangul, 366, 367, 369
Hyodon, 222
Hyujŏng, 278

icchantika, 367–68
Ieom, 56
Ikkyū Sōjun, 185
Illustrated Annotated Record of Kenzei (Teiho Kenzeiki zue), 119
Imai Fukuzan, 148, 164n99
Imai Kōjiro, 203
Imakita Kōsen, 333–34, 335, 336; as Zen modernist, 321, 333, 338
Imje school, 363
Imjin, 346, 362
Imperial Edition of Baizhang's Pure Rules, 227
Imperial Way Buddhism, 323
Inagaki Masami, 330
Inari deity, 118, 119
Indra Cloister, 223
Inoue Enryō, 320, 321, 326; criticized Suzuki Daisetsu, 323; "Ordinary, Extreme Pacifism," 323–24; and Tetsugakkan, 322
Inoue Shūten, 7, 322–25, 326, 328, 331, 333, 337–38; contrasted with D. T. Suzuki, 323, 325, 327; as New Buddhist, 322, 323, 325; and pacifism, 322–24; and socialism, 323, 325
ipsissima verba, 373
Iryŏn, 273
Ishii Shūdō, 117
Ishikawa Sanshirō, 321, 342n42
Itakura Shigemune, 84
Itō Shoshin, 341n32
Itō Yūten, 113, 114
Iwashimizu Hachimangū, 204, 205

James, William, 41

Jansen, Marius, 86
Jan Yün-hua, 292
Japan, 21–25; Chinese Buddhist canon in, 199; dialects of, 135; émigré monks in, 136–41, 146–51; Japanese Zen monks, 25, 99, 113, 140, 141, 144, 150; Meiji, 321; New Buddhist Fellowship, 321–22; Sinification in, 21–22; Zen literature in, 196
Japan Socialist Party, 326
Jewel Forest Biographies (Baolin zhuan), 15
Jiashan temple, 125n23
Jianzhong jingguo xudenglu, 162n77
Jichan, 291
Jifei Ruyi, 77, 78, 86
jikaku, 330, 331
Jikji, 245
jin, 324
Jin dynasty, 91n19
Jingde Chuandeng lu, 51, 219, 304
Jingde Era Record of the Transmission of the Lamp (Jingde chuandeng lu), 219
Jingde Monastery, 53
Jing Miaocheng, 16
Jingqing Daofu, 230n17
Jingshan si, 54
Jingyinchansi monastery, 5, 221, 233n37
Jingyin Daozhen, 19
Jinzong, 246
Jiuming Monastery, 47
Jiyin, 309–10
Jogye Order, 248, 270, 345; identity quest, 346; and Korean Buddhism, 257n3; legitimate descendent of, 252; legitimate founder of, 251, 256; Pojo Chinul and, 6, 7, 345; struggle of, 345–77
Jōjin, 131, 134–36, 160n45
Jōrakuji, 56, 189n26

Jordan, David Starr, 324
Juefan Huihong, 193, 194, 195, 206
Juehai, 74
Juelang Daosheng, 72, 198–99, 200, 296
Jūfukuji, 53, 171, 172, 173
Juhn Ahn, 5
Jurchen, 15–16, 20
Jushō, 195; tradition, 73

kaedang, 226
Kaibao Buddhist canon, 134
Kainoshō Masanobu, 69, 84
kairos, 184
Kaksu Posal, 351
Kakumon Kantetsu, 193, 194, 206
Kalton, Michael, 280
Kamakura, 42, 53–56, 128, 130, 169, 171, 174, 334; Engakuji in, 178; Jufukuji in, 171, 173; Kenchōji in, 147; sanctioned Zen compound in, 172; Yishan travel to, 183
Kameyama (Emperor), 173
kami, 205
Kamju, 227n2
kangdang, 218
Kang Hosŏn, 227
Kang Munsŏn, 251
Kanhua Chan, 356, 359, 360, 365; and Daruma-shū, 23; in Korea, 20–21; in Vietnam, 18
kanhwa, 244
Kanhwa kyŏrŭi ron, 354
Kanhwa Sŏn, 272, 273, 347, 348, 359–61; Chinul's, 242; Chinul's Buddhism, core of, 241; doctrine, inadequacy of, 362; four allusions to, 357–59; Hyesim's approach to, 240; Korean Sŏn Buddhist tradition, 253; Pou's practice to, 252; practice of, 355–56, 358, 360, 361, 366, 369; spread of, 240; and *Treatise on*

Resolving Doubts about Observing the Key Phrase, 355–57
Kani Uhyŏe, 78
Kansei period, 201
kanshi, 133
Kantō, 171, 172
Kanzan Egen, 185
Kapsin Coup, 249–50
Kaske, Elisabeth, 88n1
Katayama Sen, 327
Katō Tokijirō, 326
Katsura river, 204
Keizan Jōkin, 113–14
Kenchōji, 121, 147–48, 175, 177, 182; features of, 172; initial architecture of, 172; Mujō Ichien statement on, 150; translingual culture, 147; Yishan Yining's appointment to, 151; Zen monastery of, 147
Kenchōji ship, 131
Kenninji, 53, 144, 145, 147, 172
kenshō, 331
kenshū-style Zen, 174
Kenzeiki, **118,** 118–19
Keonjoo, Park, 346, 355–57; and four allusions to *Kanhwa Sŏn*, 357–59; and *Treatise on Resolving Doubts about Observing the Key Phrase*, 356
Keqin, 300
Ketelaar, James Edward, 332, 337
keyword meditation (KWM), 377n1
Keyworth, George, 4, 295
Khitan: canon, 222; and Koryo, 19; rebels against Mongols, 20–21; in Vietnam, 14–15
Khitan Liao, 220
ki (material force), 280
Kihwa, 57, 273, 362
Kikkawa Hiroyoshi, 82
Kilsangsa, 354
Kim Hyoungchan, 281

Kim Iryŏp, 251
Kim Kunsu, 240, 348, 352, 353, 356
Kim Suhwan, 377
Kim Youngmi, 242, 258n16
King U, 362
Kintaien (medical shop), 82
Kintaishi, 82
Kinugawa Kenji, 153
Kita Chōbei, 87
Kita Genki, 87
Kiyomizu Temple, 78
Kiyozawa Manshi: as Buddhist modernist, 320, 328; and D. T. Suzuki, 325
kōan-investigation, 99
Kobe People's Club, 323
Kŏboesa, 377
Kobong, 249
Kodalwŏn monastery, 217, 229n11
Kōfukuji, 74, *74,* 198
Kōhō Kennichi, 155, 165n112; brush-dialogue with Wuxue Zuyuan, 152–54, *153*; disciple of, 152; disciple of Wuxue, 178; recognition from Zuyuan, 153; *Recorded Sayings of Zen Master Bukkoku,* 152
koji, 334
Koji shinron, 334
Kōjosa, 269, 353, 354
Kokan Shiren, 142; and *Genkō shakusho*, 160n53; *Shūbun inryaku*, 142
Kōkoku Dōren, 83
kōkyō gishiki, 219
kongans, 272, 283, 375, 379n39; "brief critiques," 359; "dead words," 356
Kongmin, King, 361–62
Konoe Motohiro, 85, 93n30
Korea, 18–21; abbot system in, 217; Buddhist monasteries in, 216; Chan influence in, 56–58; Chan mythology, influence of, 219;

Korea *(continued)*
contemporary, 375; emergence of Sŏn in, 268–69; liberation of, 367; nuns' dharma lineage, 5–6; public monasteries in, 217–27; public Sŏn monasteries in, 216, 227; Song-style public monasteries, lacked, 225
Korean Approaches to Zen: Collected Works of Chinul (Buswell), 354
Korean Buddhism, 7, 345, 346, 369, 372, 373, 375, 376, 377; bhikṣuṇī Sŏn dharma lineage in, 249; Chinul's position in, 251–52; identity of, 363; Jogye Order, 6, 7, 248, 251, 252, 256, 257n3; nuns in, 251. *See* nuns in Korean Sŏn Buddhism; reformation of, 367; Susŏnsa within, 359, 361
Korean Sŏn, 1, 5, 195; Chinul's approach and, 57; connection to Hangzhou, 57–58; in Koryŏ period, 56; and Suzuki's interpretation of Zen, 42–43
Korean War, 367, 368
Koryŏ, 19–20, 26, 217, 223, 235n52, 247, 252, 265, 276, 279, 346, 376; carving, 235n47; international relations, 361; Paeg'un returned to (1353), 246; Pou returned to, 252; relationship with Southern Song, 20; relations with Song, 220; Sŏn in, 270; second "wave," 254; Yi Kyubo during, 242
Kōtaiji, 201
Kōtoku Shūsui, 321, 326, 327, 341n33, 342n40
Kubilai Khan (Emperor), 181
Kukch'ŏngsa, 268
kuksa, 347
Kulsanha, 236n53
Kumarajiva, 44
kŭmdang, 218

Kŭmgang Sŏnwŏn, 366
kundoku, 141
Kurokawa Masana, 69, 84
Kusanmun, 361
Kwangjong, King, 217
Kwangmyŏngsa monastery, 58, 222, 223, 234n43
Kwŏn Kŭn, 279
Kye ch'osim hagin mun, 216
Kyo (*kyo*), 269, 283, 351, 347
kyoga, 347
Kyo monasteries, 215
Kyŏnghŏ Sŏngu, 250
Kyŏnsŏngam, 248, 250, 253, 260n41, 261n58
Kyōto: print culture in, 132; Tōfukuji in, 172; Yishan travel to, 183

Lady Sa, 256n2
Laiguo, 291, 308
lamp traditions, 298–99
Lam-Te school, 72
Langdarma, 298
Laṅkāvatāra sūtra, 302
Lanxi Daolong, 4, 112, 155, 169, 171–75, 185; arrived at Hakata, 147; biographical sketches of, 168; disciple of Wuzhun Shifan, 54; "pure" Zen, 173, 174; Rinzai-style Zen, 173; Song style of Chan, 128; traveled to Jufukuji, 171; visited Sennyū-ji, 56, 171
Laozi, 266
Laozi Daode jing, 204
Lee, Seung-yeon, 218
Legends and History of the Three Kingdoms (Samguk yusa), 273
Leggett, Trevor, 164n99
Letan Kewen, 359
Levering, Miriam, 242
Liang Su, 273
Li Ao, 273, 312

Liao. *See* Khitan
Library of Old Mirrors of the Groove of Meditation, 370
The Light of Asia (Arnold), 37, 38
Lin Daorong, 79
lineage: Caodong, 72–73; Huqiu-based, 111–12; Imje's, 375; Korea nuns' dharma, 5–6, 253–56; Nine Mountain Sŏn, 223; Pŏmil's Mount Sagul, 223; Sagulsan, 223; Sanfeng, 309; Sŏkch'o, 230n17; Trúc Lâm, 17; Yuanwu Keqin, 98, 100
Lin Fenggao, 77
Lin Gongyan, 76, 78–79
Linguan Temple, **106**
Lingyin Chan monastery, 50
Lingyin [Hongli], 309
Lingyin si (monastery), 53
Linji Chan, 18
Linji School, 266–67, 346, 347, 375; Sanfeng lineage, 309; Yangqi branch, 363, 365, 369, 375
Linji-style exclusivism, 364
Linji Yixuan, 167
Lin Shoudian, 77
Lin Taiqing, 76, 78
Linzi Chan, 261n53
Li Tao, 232n33
Literary Chinese, 11–12; and Bai, 16; and Gozan, 25; in Japan, 23; and Korea, 18; and Tangut, 14; and Ŭichŏn, 19
Literary Sŏn, 360
Li Tongxuan, 20, 144, 240, 241, 296, 351, 371; and Bai, 16; and Chinul, 20; *Exposition of the Avataṃsaka sūtra*, 349, 350, 352
Liu Ban, 139
Liu Huayang, 311
Liuzu Huineng, 357, 365
Locke, John, 331
Lokasema, 44

Longcesi, 230n17
Lopez, Donald, 40, 319, 320
Lotus Sūtra, 144, 240, 249, 341n31; used by Uchiyama Gudō, 326, 329, 338
Lu Cheng, 46
Lü Chunyang, 311
Lü Dongbin, 311
Lu Guimeng, 139
Luo Yin, 47
Lushan Huiyuan, 302
Lu Zuqian, 275

Madhyamaka, 295
Madhyamaka Thought and Its Developments, 370
Mādhyamika/Sanlun (Three Treatise) school, 44
Mahāyāna, 307; bodhisattva, 334; Indian, 13; Japanese, 335; sutras, 332; teaching of Buddha Nature, 332; texts, 329; themes, 338
Makino Chikanari, 84
Manchu invasions, 362
Man'gong, 249, 250, 251, 261n58
Man'gong Wŏlmyŏn, 366–67
Manichaeism, 14
Mañjuśrī, 350
Manpukuji, 70, 79, 82, 87, 198
Mansŏng, 251
mantuo luo (mandala), 200, 201
Manu, 249
Manuscripts from Cold Pine (Kanshōkō), 148
Manzan Dōhaku, 194, 199
Marx, Karl, 330
Marxism, 325, 329, 331. *See also* socialism
Master Chaun, 369
matched rhyme poetry, 136–41
maximalism, 325, 327, 337, 338
Mazu, 243, 244, 297, 298

Mazu Daoyi, 56
McRae, John, 188n16, 313; "First Rule of Zen," 100–101
Meiji, 198, 311, 326, 328, 329; Buddhist modernism, 334; discourse of practical wisdom, 335; discourse on Buddhist degeneration, 334; government policy, 323; Meiji Zen, 333–37
Mencius, 324
Mencius, 280, 283
Menzan Zuihō, 119
Middle Path, 370
Min, 242, 258n16
Minatogawa Shrine, 338
mindfulness, 281–82
mind-to-mind transmission, 53, 57
Ming dynasty, 130, 227; Chan monasteries during, 308; *huatou* during, 301
Mingji Chujun, 132
Ming-Qing transition, 80
Min Hyŏn'gu, 242
Mit'aam, 248
Mito, 73, 195, 198, 202, 204
Mitsukuni, 203
Miyamoto Shoson, 370
Miyashita Takichi, 328
Miyun Yuanwu, 72, 309–10
modern Buddhism, 319–21
Mogam Ch'anyŏng, 362
Moguja, 347
Moheyan, 13
Mongols, 15, 21, 25, 130, 227, 276; alliance with Song dynasty, 170; authorities, 175; conquest of Bai, 16–17; failed invasion of Japan, 25; invasion of Koryŏ, 20–21; invasion of Vietnam, 18; soldiers, 176
Mongyŏ, 225, 226
moral cultivation, 334, 336
Mōri Saian, 322

Mount Ayuwang, 49, 50, 170, 223
Mount Chiri, 349, 365
Mount Chogye, 270
Mount Dongming, 200
Mount Haga, 349
Mount Hakusan, 113
Mount Hŏiyang, 229n11
Mount Huangbo, 72, 76
Mount Hyemok, 229n11
Mount Jiashan temple, 97, 100, 102, 104, 120, 125n23
Mount Jing, 172
Mount Kyejok, 224
Mount Ōbaku, 198
Mount P'algong, 366
Mount Putuoluo, 180, 182
Mount Sagul lineage, 223; Pŏmil's, 226
Mount Siming, 179
Mount Sumi, 234n46
Mount Tiantai, 47, 49, 50, 52, 53, 136, 138, 170, 180; Mushō Jōshō climbed, 136–37; stone bridge in, 136
Mount Tiantong, 53, 175
Mount Wutai, 134, 135
Mozi Ruding, 74, 81, 82
Mu'an Xingtao, 77, 78, 86
Muchen Daomin, 72, 309, 310
Muhak Chach'o, 348
mu hwadu, 360
Mujaku Dōchū, 194
Mujinjang, 368
Mujō Ichien, 150, 154
Mukyū Tokusen, 130, 135, 155
Müller, Max, 37
Munjong, King, 220, 268
Murai Shōsuke, 133
Murakami Senshō, 321, 338
Muromachi, 130, 174
Musang, 13; and Bai, 16; and Tibet, 13
Mushō Jōshō, 136–41, 160n53, 161n61

Musō Soseki, 9, 99, 152, 155, 178, 205
Muŭija sijip, 360
Muyeo, 273
Muyun Tongmen, 309
Myōan Eisai, 170
Myŏngjong, King, 278
Myōrakuji, 140
Myori Pŏphŭi, 248–49, 250
Myōshinji, 185, 194, 229
mysticism, 335

Nabeshima Katsushige, 84
naewŏndang, 228n2
Nagamatsu Nissen, 334
Nāgārjuna 375
Nagasaki, 134, 198, 199, 201; Buddhism in, 80–88; bugyō, 69, 79, 84; Chinatown, 198; Chinese Buddhist monasteries in, 73–76; Fuqing merchants in, 76; Fuqing native in, 78; interpreters, Chinese, 69; Meganebashi in, 81; merchants, Chinese, 69, 71, 76–79, 80, 83, 85; monk arriving at, Chinese, 69; temples, Chinese, 71, 86; trade, 70–71, 72, 73, 79. See also Japan
Nakae Chōmin, 341n35
Nakaseko Shōdō, 125n22
Nanjing, 135
Nankinji, 74
Nanquan, 297
Nanyang Huizhong, 14, 122; and Daruma-shū, 23; and Tangut, 14
Nanzenji, 183
Naoko, Iioka, 88n1
Naong Hyegŭn, 57, 246, 247, 252, 254, 348, 362
National Preceptor. See Pojo Chinul
NBF. See New Buddhist Fellowship
Neo-Confucianism, 6, 21, 46; adopted, 276; emergence of, 273–77; mindful practices in, 264; Mongol kingdom and, 276; ontologico-cosmological substructure of, 278; orthodox, 275; during Song dynasty, 275; spiritualism of, 263. See also Confucianism
New Buddhist Fellowship (NBF), 320, 321–22, 327, 328, 333, 335, 338; and anticlericalism, 334; Inoue Shūten and, 322–25; and secularity, 336; Uchiyama Gudō and, 328, 333
Newell, Catherine, 40, 41
Nguyen Phuc Chu, 72
Nguyen-Thieu tradition, 72
nianfo, 302, 310
nianfo chan, 295
Nichiren school, 329
Nie Xian, 304
Nine Mountain schools, 56; of Sŏn, 267, 268
Nine Mountain Sŏn lineages, 223
Nine Schools of Sŏn, 361, 362
Ningbo (port city), 134, 203
Ningbo-Nagasaki trade, 198
Ningen Zen Kyodan, 343n51
nirvāna, 331
Nishi Honganji, 321
Niutou school, 354
nôm, Vietnamese script, 17
Nōnin, 128
nonviolence. See ahimsa
Northern Chan: and Dunhuang, 13; in Japan, 22; and Tangut, 14, 15
Northern Wei, 217
North Kyŏngsang, 349, 368
nuns in Korean Sŏn Buddhism: gender and dharma lineage, 253–56; modern Korean Sŏn Buddhism, 248–51; overview, 239–40; practice of hwadu meditation under Hyesim, 240–45

450 | Index

Ōbaku: Buddhism, 88; business, 82; calligraphy, 86; monasteries, 83; monks, 82, 83, 84, 135, 200; portrait painting, 86–87; school, 72, 87; temple, 199; tradition, 3
Ōbaku bunka, 82
Ōbakushū monks, 199
Obeyesekere, Gananath, 37, 61n10
Ogyū Sorai, 82, 83
Olcott, Henry Steel, 38
Oldenberg, Hermann, 39, 61n8
ondoku, 141–42
One Hundred Odes, 97, 100, **115**, 116
Ŏnhŭm, 218
Ōsaka, 204
osoroshii, 148
ōtōkan, 185
Ō-Tō-Kan school, 196
Ouyang Xiu, 131, 221
Ouyi Zhixu, 310
Oxherder, 347, 356
oya-kata, 329

pacifism, 322, 324, 338; extreme, 325
paddy-rice agriculture, 16, 18, 21. *See also* farming
Paegil pŏmmun, 370, 372
Paeg'un Kyŏnghan, 245, 252, 254, 347–48; in China, 246; *Essentials*, 246, 247, 248; *Recorded Sayings of Master Paeg'un*, 246, 248
Paekp'a Kŭngsŏn, 363, 364
Paengnyŏnam, 369, 377
Paengnyŏn Pulgyo munhwa chedan, 377
P'agyesa, 368
Paine, Thomas, 331
Pak Chung-hee, 368, 369
pangjang, 218, 366
Pang Minho, 262n65
Park, Jin Y., 5
partial awakening, 371

pastoralism, and Chan, 13
Pearl String Collection of Verses on Old Cases, 300
Personal Admonitions to Neophytes Who Have First Aroused the Mind, 270
Philosophic Taoism, 283
pidgin Chinese, and North Chinese dynasties, 15
Pi Rixiu, 139
The Platform Sūtra of the Sixth Patriarch, 46, 63n38, 64n39, 151, 219, 265, 297, 304, 352, 353, 373; burning of, 15; and Chinul, 20; and Tangut, 14
Pŏbwŏn, 230n17
poetry, 130, 131, 136; Chinese, 86; Chinese, "ten scenic spots" in, 132; envoy, 133, 134; exchange poems, 133–34; matched rhyme, 136–41; rhymed Sinitic, 141–46; Sinitic, 127, 136, 137, 141–46; writing, 86; Xinyue's, 5
Pojesa monastery, 58, 220, 222, 234n43
Pojo Chinul, 6, 7, 19, 20, 56–57, 224, 225, 253, 346, 361, 363, 367, 376; *Admonitions to Beginning Students*, 5, 216, 226, 227, 270; awakening experiences, 355; Buddhism, 240, 241; *Encouragement to Practice: The Compact of the Concentration and Wisdom Society*, 269; *Essentials of the Exposition on the Huayan Sūtra*, 240; excerpts and posthumous works, 354; Kanhwa Sŏn, 242; Korean Buddhism, position in, 251–52; life of, impact of three awakenings on, 353; living on Mount Chiri, 349; mind-to-mind transmission of Chan Buddhism, 252; own account of

second "awakening," 350–51; and pathway to mindful Sŏn, 270–73; posthumous title, 269; *Pure Rules for Chan Monasteries,* inspired from, 227; *On the Resolution of Doubts in Kanhwa,* 272; retreat societies, 283; *Secrets of Cultivating the Mind,* 270–71; Sŏngch'ŏl's radical criticism of, 373; Sŏn tradition, ideas about, 284; stayed at Sangmuju hermitage, 352; sudden awakening, 371; sudden/gradual doctrine, 351, 364, 370, 372, 374, 377; three awakenings, *Funerary Inscription* account of, 348–49; *tono,* 371; triggered awakenings, 352, 378n9
Policy of Repression of Buddhism and Promotion of Confucianism, 362
Polo, Marco, 36
Pŏmnang, 265
Pomunsa, 349
Pongamsa *kyŏlsa,* 367
Pongamsa religious community, 367
Pon'gong Kyemyŏng, 251
pŏptang, 217
Poshan Haiming, 310
Pou's Buddhism, 261n53
practice-oriented meditation monk, 364
prajñā, 358
precepts: and Daruma-shū, 22; and Yōsai, 23
Precious Lessons of the Chan Forest, 105
Prince Gautama, 37
print culture, 132
Protass, Jason, 4
Protestant Buddhism, 37–38, 61n10
pseudo-Śūraṃgama-sūtra, 199
public monasteries in Korea, 217–27; Ch'ŏnhwasa, 223; during fourteenth century, 226–27; Jingyinchansi, 221; and Ming dynasty, 227; Susŏnsa and, 224–26; Tamjin and, 220–24; Xiangguosi, 221
Pulp'il, 366
Pure Land, 303, 310, 332; Buddhism, 269; dual practice of, 301–2; Maitreya tradition, 291–92, 301; practice of, 292; school's *nianfo,* 111
Pure Rules (*shingi*), 195, 196, 216–17, 221
Pure Rules for Chan Monasteries, 5, 227
Putuo island, 203
Pyŏngja Invasion, 346, 362

Qian Chu (King Zhongyi), 48, 49–50, 64n46
Qian Liu (King Wusu), 47
Qian Qianyi, 199, 303
Qiantang, 50
Qibai, 133
Qing dynasty: Chan monasteries during, 308; *huatou* during, 301; Yongzheng, 308; Yongzheng of, 303
qinggui, 2, 216; Rules for Purification, 52; for śila, 52
Qingliang Taiqin, 360
Qingzhuo Zhengcheng, 131, 132
quiet sitting, 263–64
Qu Ruji, 304

radical Chan, 11, 15; and Daruma-shū, 23; and Dōgen, 24; and Korea, 19; rejection by Tibetans, 13; and Son, 21
Ranzan Dōchō, 194
Ray, Reginald, 40
realization (*zong*), 302
recorded sayings, 303–7
Recorded Sayings of Master Paeg'un (Paeg'un hwasang ŏrok), 246

Recorded Sayings of National Master Chin'gak of Jogye (Chogye Chin'gak kuksa ŏrok), 242
Recorded Sayings of Zen Master Bukkoku (Bukkoku zenji goroku), 152
Record of Anecdotes from Lake Luo (Luohu yelu), 201
Record of Pilgrimage to Mount Tiantai and Wutai (San Tendai-Godaisan ki), 135
Record of the Source Mirror (Yongming Yanshou), 22
Record of the Transmission of the Lamp (Chuandeng lu), 222
Records of Chan Master Dahui Zonggao, 366
Red Flag Incident, 327
Reflections on Things at Hand (Jinsilu), 275
rejuvenated traditionalism, 274
Renzong (Emperor), 221
Rhee, Syngman, 368
Rinka, 120
Rinsenji, 326, 327
Rinzai sect, 98, 111–12; travelers, 99
Rinzaishū, 196
Rinzai Zen, 128, 175, 196; Buddhism, authentic transmission of, 200; Imakita Kōsen, 333; Japanese tradition, 272; priest, 334, 337; Shaku Sōen, 334
Ritual Text for the Rite of Water and Land (Shuilu yiwen), 220
Rōnen Myōzen, 53
Rujing, 53, 119, 145–46
Rulai chuxian pin, 350
Rules of Purity for the Chan Monastery (C. *Chanyuan qinggui*), 270
Russo-Japanese War, 322, 323, 326
Ruzhi, 180

Ryōkan Taigu, 141
Ryōkei Shōsen, 92n28
Ryōmō Kyōkai, 333–34, 343n51
Ryōō Dōkaku, 82
Ryūha Zenshu, 148

sabetsu byōdō, 332
Sacred Books of the East (Muller), 37
Sagulsan lineage, 223
sagyo ipsŏn, 347
sahwa, 278
Sakai Tadakatsu, 84
Sakai Tadakiyo, 84
Sakai Toshihiko, 321, 326, 327, 342n40
Sakoku policy, 85
"Sakoku" policy, 73
Sakura Sōgorō, 326
Śākyamuni, 35, 38–40, 59n1, 110, 300, 363, 370, 375; life and teachings of, 38, 40; reappearance of, 247; relics of, 49, 53; stūpa on Mt. Ayuwang, 50
samādhi, 162n75, 183, 358
Samādhi and Prajnā Society, 353
samgha, 363
samghārāma, 172
Samye debate, 13
Sanfeng: lineage, 309, 318n61; tradition, oppression of, 310
Sangch'ong, 215–16, 226–27; monastic rules, 216; recommendations, 228n6
sangdang, 218, 235n50
sangdang ŏgu, 223
sangha, 330
Sangmujuam, 349, 354
Sanjiao Laoren, 109–10
Sanmei, 162n75
Sanping Yizhong, 12
Sasaki Shigetsu, 343n51
satori, 331
Satyasiddhi, 295

Sawada, Janine, 342n49
Schafer, Edward, 133
Schlütter, Morten, 285n18
Schopen, Gregory, 38
Schopenhauer, Arthur, 37
script: Japanese, 21–22; Jurchen, 15; Khitan, 14; Tangut, 14; Tibetan, 13; Vietnamese, 17
Secrets of Cultivating the Mind, 270–71
self-awakening, 331
Senécal, Bernard, 7, 378n6
Seng shilüe, 51
Sengzhao, 296
Sennyūji, 56, 171
Seno'o Girō, 330, 342n42
Senseiden, 206
sentimentalism, 335
Seoru, 273
separate transmission: and Dōgen, 24; in Japan, 22
sermons, **106,** 144; Chan/Zen, 101, 151; Chinese-language, 145, 147, 148, 150–51; in *Extensive Record,* 121, 122; Gesshin's, 144–45; Pou's, 21; *sangdang,* 235n50; by Xingxiu, 15; Zhuxian's, 149
Sesson Yūbai, 170
Shaku Sōen, 41, 333–37; and Buddhist metaphysics, 335–36; and Buddhist unity, 335; as mentor of D. T. Suzuki, 323, 333; nationalism, issue of, 337; as Zen modernist, 321, 333, 338
Shaku Sōkatsu, 343n51
Shao Yong, 275
Shasekishū, 154
Shenhui, 11, 13, 296, 313; of Gao clan and Bai, 16; recorded sayings, 307
Shenzong (Emperor), 220, 221
She people, 12
Shidi lun, 228n5

Shields, James Mark, 6
shifangcha, 5, 216
Shigao, 44
Shilian Dashan, 72
Shimaji Mokurai, 332
Shingon, 172
Shinkei, Prince, 84, 93n29
Shin sect, 321
Shirayanagi Shūko, 321
Shiren, Kokan, 160n53
Shiwu Qinggong, 246, 252
Shiwu Qinhong, 57
Shōfuku-ji, 53
Shogun Tokugawa Ietsuna, 70
Shōnan kattoroku, 164n99
Shōshūji, 74
Shouchang [Hui]jing, 309
Shouzun Yuanzhao, 72, 89n6
Shūbun inryaku, 142
Shūhō Myōchō, 185
Shuilu yiwen, 220
Shuzenji, 182
Siddhārtha Gautama, 367
silent illumination, 310
silent illumination *(mozhao),* 303–4
Silla monks, 18
Silla period, 56
Simhak, 284n3
Simhŭi, 219
Sindŏk, Queen, 215, 228n3
Sinhaeng, 18
Sinification, 11–12; and Bai, 16; of Japan, 21–22; resistance to, 12; Tanguts and, 14
Sinitic poems/poetry, 127, 136, 137, 141–46, 151
Sino-Japanese trade, 3, 71, 72, 73, 78, 88
Sino-Japanese War, 321
Sino-Korean Connection, 346; Linji-style, 348; sociopolitical background of, 361–64

Sino-Korean connection, 362, 363
Sinophilism, 86
Sinophobe Motoori Norinaga, 198
Sino-Tibetan Doctrinal Institute, 292, 299
Smash the Old Mirrors and Come, 374
Snellgrove, David L., 38, 39, 41
social capital: Buddhism as source of, 83–86; definition, 83
socialism, 323, 324, 325, 326–27, 329–30, 332, 333, 337, 338; and NBF, 321; Uchiyama Gudō commitment to, 331. *See also* anarchism
Society for Cultivating Sŏn, 270
Sōfukuji monastery, 74, 76, 77, *77*, 78, 85, 86, 140
Sŏkch'o, 218; lineage, 230n17
Sōkei-an, 343n51
Sŏllim kogyŏng ch'ongsŏ, 370
Sŏmun yŏmsongjip, 346
Sŏn, 7, 347; emergence in Korea, 268–69; Korean, 42–43, 56, 57, 195, 245; and Kyo, 56; Linji, 57; monasteries, 215, 216; and Mongol empire, 21; revival of, 20, 21
Sŏn Buddhism, 7, 167, 283; center and margin in, 251–53; examination of nuns in, 255; and Hwaŏm, 267; Korean, 5, 6, 240–56; Korean, nuns practice, 240–45; modern Korean, nuns in, 248–51; revival of, 249, 250
sŏndang, 219
Sŏndŏk, Queen, 265
Sŏn'ga, 347
Song Buddhism, 1
Song Chan, 220; Beichan Zhixian (master), 143; and *Blue Cliff Record,* 98; masters, 53; *Pure Rules for Chan Monasteries,* 5; *Rules of Purity for Chan Monasteries,* 128; and schools of music criticism, 101; and Sinitic poem, 145; sources of, **117**
Song China, 5, 20, 22–23, 57, 147, 154, 220, 360; Chōnen traveled, 134; Cho's on traveling to, 360–61; developments in, 221; Dōgen awakening in, 145–46; Dōgen returned from (1227), 24; Enni Ben'en traveled, 128; and Five Mountains, 54; Japanese Tendai pilgrim to, 135; Mukyū Tokusen studied in, 130; Myōan Eisai visited, 52; and Tamjin, 221; Ŭich'ŏn returned to, 19
Song dynasty, 49, 58, 184; Buddhism in, 51; Buddhist region in, 52; Chan Buddhism during, 98, 101, 121, 263; Chan School Five Mountains monasteries in, **54**; Chan School Ten Temples in, **55**; matched-rhyme poetry during, 140; Mongols alliance with, 170; Neo-Confucianism in, 46, 275; Northern, 359; rhyme book, 142; Southern, 59, 206, 359; temple architecture, imitation of, 131; woodblock printed texts, 132
Song Gaoseng zhuan, 51
Songgwangsa, 216, 242, 367
Sŏng Hon, 280
Sŏngjŏnam, 368
Sŏngjusa, 231n21
Song of Enlightenment (Zhengdaojia), 365
Songtsän Gampo, King, 63n33
Sŏn'gyo ilch'i, 347
Sŏnhakwŏn, 250
Sŏnjo, King, 278
Sŏnjong, King, 220
Sŏn meditation, 242, 248; Huayan teachings and, 241; Korean

Buddhist nuns' participation in, 240; and Kyo teachings, 56; in Seoul, 250
Sŏn monks, 58, 225, 366, 368, 372; Ch'anyu, 219; in Korea, 216; Muyŏm, 19; T'aego Pou, 21; travel to Yuan China, 21
Sŏnmun chŏngno, 374
Sŏnmun chŏngno p'yŏngsŏk, 374
Sŏnmun Sugyŏng, 363
Sŏnmun yŏmsong chip, 228n5
Sŏnsa, 347
Sŏn school, 351
sŏnsil, 219
Sŏnwŏnsa, 224, 226, 227
Sŏong, 369
Sŏsan Taesa, 362, 363
Sōtō school, 375
Sōtō sect, 98, 113, 327
Sōtōshū, 196
Sōtōshū Daigakurin, 322
Sōtō Zen, 128, 327; in Japan, 198; Jushō, 195; monks, 199, 200, 326; temple, 322; traditions, 146
Sōtō Zen in Medieval Japan (Bodiford), 121
Sŏ Ŭihyŏn, 367
Southern Song, 15, 52, 54, 130, 275, 276; armies, 170; Chan School Five Mountains monasteries in, 54; Chan School Ten Temples, 55; Chinese Chan in, 51; Enni Ben'en studied in, 24; Hangzhou. *See* Hangzhou; Koryŏ relationship with, 20
South Korea, 242
South Kyŏngsang province, 349, 365, 368
Souza, George, 88n1
sŏwŏn, 279
State Preceptor, 347

State Preceptor Pojo Chinul, 367, 372
Stone Bridge, 53
Straight Talk on the True Mind, 354
Strict Transmission of Five Chan Lamps (Wudeng yantong), 200
sudden awakening, 49, 271, 297, 353, 364, 367; Chinul's, 371; cultivation of, 354; in *Huayan jing*, 240; and Jogye Order, 375; in Korean Buddhism, 57; Linji Sŏn tradition of, 57; memory of, 365; Sŏngch'ŏl's, 7, 371, 373, 376; and teaching of Sŏn Buddhism, 252
sudden cultivation, 271, 353–54
sudden enlightenment, 265, 266, 267, 271
Sudŏksa, 367
Sugimura Sojinkan, 322
Sugiura Kinzen, 201
Sui-Tang centrism, 43
Sŭkch'o, 218, 230n17
Sumi-san, 56
Suryuktang, 220
Su Shi, 132, 139, 140, 232n29
Susŏnsa, 224–27, 236n62, 243, 354, 359, 360, 361
Susŏnsa lineage monks, 5
Sūtra in Forty-Two Chapters, 294
Sūtra of Sturdy Lady (Fushuo Jiangunu jing), 243–44, 245
Suwang, 201
Su Wu, 184, 192n62
Su Zhe, 139
Suzuki, D.T. (Daisetsu), 7, 41, 100, 113, 120; contrasted with Inoue Shūten, 323, 325, 327; criticized by Inoue, 323; and NBF, 321, 322; realization, 302; as Sōen's interpreter, 336; *Yuanwu's Keeping the Beat to Smash the Barriers*

Suzuki, D.T. (Daisetsu) *(continued)*
  at the *Blue Cliff*, 114; as Zen
  modernist, 321, 333, 335, 336, 338
  syncretical Zen, 173

Tachi Ryūshi, 147
taedŏk, 235n52
Taedŏkhwa Posal, 369
T'aego Pou, 21, 57, 227, 227, 246,
  251, 252, 254, 348, 375; appointed
  by Kongmin, 362; sixth-generation
  disciple of, 363
Taehŭngsa, 222
T'aejo, King, 276, 362
T'aejong, 228n3
Taewŏnsa, 365
Taiping Cloister, 47
Taishō, 99; government policy, 323
Taishō period, 329
Taixu, 6, 291–314, 323; assessment
  of Baizhang and Mazu, 298; Chan
  school's traditional method, 296;
  Chinese Buddhist Learning, 292,
  305, 313; commentary on *gongans*,
  299–300; compiling and studying
  recorded sayings, 303–7; Gelugpa
  system of Tsongkhapa, 303; and
  Humanistic Buddhism, 292;
  Maitreya Pure Land tradition, 291–
  92; quoted several figures, 297–98;
  remarks on Chan's methodology,
  297; silent illumination, 303–4; and
  state of affairs in *sangha*, 308–10;
  and tantric Buddhism, 299; and
  tathāgata Chan, 298; yoga tantras
  in Tibet, 298; and Yongzheng's text,
  317n55
Taizu, 47, 303, 310
Takada Dōken, 334
Takasaki Jikidō, 146
Takashima Beihō, 322
Takeuchi Michiō, 113, 125n22

Tamamura Takeji, 129
Tamjin, 5–58, 220–24, 225, 226,
  232n33, 233n37, 233n39, 234n43,
  235n47, 235n48, 236n53, 236n55
tamsŏn pŏphoe, 222
Tang China, 13, 18, 133, 266; during
  Heian period, 169
Tang dynasty, 169, 267; Buddhism,
  267–68; Chan Buddhism during,
  263; diplomatic embassies to, 170;
  masters, 1; Trouble Free Chan of,
  359
Tanguts, 14
Tansoksa monastery, 222, 224,
  235n48, 236n56
Tantric Buddhism, 291
T'anyŏn, 223–24, 235n48; funerary
  epitaph, 223, 236n53; *sangdang*
  sermons, 235n50
Taoism: coattail, 310–11; and dual
  cultivation, 311; Philosophic, 283.
  See also Daoism
Tao Yuanming, 140, 294
tatchŭ, 229
tathāgata Chan, 298, 299
Tendai: monks, 22, 23, 130, 132; rites,
  172; school, 52, 329; and Zen, 22
*Ten Diagrams on Sage Learning
  (Sŏnghak sipdo)*, 272, 277, 278,
  283
Tengan Ekō, 152, 153, 165n112
Tenkei Denson, 102
Ten Ox-Herding Pictures, 140
Ten Temples, 54, **55**
Tentokuji, 195
Tetsugakkan, 322
Tetsugen Dōkō, 199
Theosophical Society, 38
Theravāda Buddhism, 61n10, 322,
  323, 342n2
Thiên, 18–19
Thien Uyen Tap Anh, 17

three awakenings: Funerary Inscription account of Chinul, 348–49; life of Chinul, impact on, 353; sequence of, 353–54
Three pillars of the Eightfold Path, 51
Three Teachings, 50–51
Tianhui Shiche, 308
Tianqi Benrui, 301
Tianran Hanshi, 310
Tianru Weize, 302
Tiantai Deshao, 48, 49
Tiantai school, 44, 47, 329, 365, 371
Tiantong, 310
Tianyin Yuanxiu, 309
Tianzhu monasteries, 57
Tibetan Buddhism, 63n33, 299, 313
Tibetans, 25, 26; and Chan, 13
Tieshan Shaoqiong, 21
Tobongwŏn monastery, 217
T'oegye, 265, 271, 284; Four-Seven Debate, evaluation of, 280; gradual guide to become sage, 277–82; and humanism, 280–81; learning of Confucian sages, 278; *Record of Self-Reflection*, 279; *The Ten Diagrams on Sage Learning*, 272, 277, 278, 283; view of "humanity," 279
T'oeong Sŏngchŏl, 6, 7, 251–53, 345, 346, 369; *Correct Path of Sŏn*, 374, 375; *Dharma Lineage of Korean Buddhism*, 375; dissatisfaction, 367; first part of works by, 370–72; influence of, critical evaluation of, 364–77; life as layman, 365–66; *Magnificence of the Origin*, 375; monastic life, 366; mountain monk, 364; *Old Mirrors of the Groove of Meditation's Library*, 375; radical criticism of Chinul, 373; retired old man, 369; second part of works by, 373–76; *Sermon of One Hundred Days*, 370, 371, 373; *Sŏngchŏl's Dharma Talk Collection*, 369; Sŏn monk, life as, 366–69; "theory ruins Sŏn," 372; thought of, critical approach to, 376–77; Tiger of Mount Kaya, 368; works and thought, 369–70
Tōfukuji, 54, 128, 172
Tohŏn, 219
tōji, 162n75
Tōjiji, 162n75
Tōkō kinpu, 201
Tōkō zenshū, 195
Tokugawa Ieyasu, 84
Tokugawa Mitsukuni, 195, 197, 199, 201
Tomoe, Moriya, 323, 325
Tonghwa monastery, 366
Tongli, 14–15
Tongsan Hyeil, 366, 369
t'ong Sŏn hoegyo, 347
tono chŏmsu sasang, 347
totalism, 325
Toŭi, 19, 257n3, 267
Touzi Yiqing, 300
Tower of Babel, 377
Toyotomi Hideyoshi, 73
tradition(s), 264
Trainor, Kevin, 40
Tran Nhan Tong, King
Treatise on Resolving Doubts about Observing the Key Phrase, 346, 354, 355–57
Treatise on the Complete and Sudden Attainment of Buddhahood, 354
Treatises, 174
Tripitaka Koreana, 269
Trisong Detsen, King, 63n33
Trouble Free Chan, 359
Trouble Free Sŏn, 360
Trúc Lâm lineage, 17
Truth (Caputo), 272

Truth and Method (Gadamer), 263
Tuiweng Hongchu, 309

Uchiyama Gudō, 7, 323, 325–32, 333, 337–38, 341n32, 341n33, 342n40; *In Commemoration of Imprisonment: Anarcho-communist Revolution*, 327–28; commitment to socialism, 331; *heibon*, 331; and High Treason Incident, 327; introduced to socialists, 326; and Kōtoku faction, 327; and land reform, 329; Meiji Restoration during, 328; *Ordinary Self-awakening*, 327–28, 330; priestly status, 327; and Red Flag Incident, 327; semifeudal system, destruction of, 331; as Sōtō Zen monk, 326; vision for better world, 330; Zen significance to, 329
Udakka Ramaputta, 367
Ŭich'ŏn, 20, 57, 220, 232n31, 232n33, 267, 283; Buddhist scriptures, collecting, 268–69; and Literary Chinese, 19; returned to China, 222
Uighurs, 14
Uijeong, 273
Ŭisang, 266, 285n15
Unitarianism, 324; modern Japanese Buddhism, influence on, 336
universalism, 333; pan-Mahayana, 49
Upper Tianzhusi, 220, 221

Vajrayāna, 298
van der Burgh, Adraen, 85
van Gulik, Robert H., 195, 201
verbal explanation *(yanshuo)*, 302
Vermeersch, Sem, 217
Verses on One Hundred Old Cases, 300
Victoria, Brian, 325, 341n27
Vietnam, 17–18; Chan Buddhism in, 73; Chinese emigration, 72; Shilian Dashan, 72; silk trade, 78; Tonkin, 78; Yuan Empire, 182
Vogel, Hans, 88n1
von Ruysbroeck, Willem, 36
Vulture Peak, 52–53

waka, 154–55
"Wakō" invasion, 73
Wan'an Daoyan, 109
Wanfu monastery, 69
Wang Anshi, 221
Wang Xiweng, 180
Wang Yin, 76, 78
Wanhesong, 201
Wanji Xingmi, 179
Wanshan tonggui ji, 49, 302
Wansong Xingxiu, 100, 309; *Congrong lu*, 300
Watanabe Kaikyoku, 322
Wei Gao, 86
Wei Gui, 86
Weiyan, 298
Wei Zhiyan, 76, 86, 91n18, 93n34; Fuqing native, 78; patronizing monasteries, 93n34; plaque donated by, 79; took over brother's business, 85
Wei Zhiyuan, 78
Welch, Holmes, 291, 310
Welter, Albert, 3, 267
White Deer Grotto Confucian Academ, 270
White Lotus Buddhist Cultural Foundation, 377
Wills, John E., Jr., 90n9
witness *(zheng)*, 302–3
Wŏllamsa temple, 224, 242
Wŏndon sŏngbullon, 354
Wŏnhyo, 266, 268; *Awaken Your Mind and Practice*, 270
Wŏnt'aek, 365, 370, 371, 372, 373, 374, 381n88

Wŏnyungbu, 362
World Parliament of Religions, 41
Wu'an Puning, 54, 147–48, 150, 151, 176
Wuben, 135
wu gongan, 243
wu hwadu, 243, 244, 252
Wu, Jiang, 3, 135, 195, 200
Wumen's Barrier, 102
Wuming Huijing, 200
Wuming Huixing, 171
Wunian Shenyou, 309
Wu of Liang (Emperor), 296
wushan, 170, 171, 185
Wushi Jiechen, 223
Wuxue Zuyuan, 54, 121, 129, 148, 155, 175–78, 185; biographical sketches of, 168; brush-dialogue with Kōhō Kennichi, 152–54, *153*; emigre monk, 147; invasion of Mongolian troops, 175–76
Wuyue (kingdom), 47–51
Wuyue Buddhism, 48, 51
Wuyue Chan, 48
Wuzhun Shifan, 54, 171
Wuzong (Emperor), 116, 268, 298
Wuzu Fayan, 105, 111, 302

Xiangfu Jiyin, 318n61
Xiangguosi monastery, 221
Xiangyansi, 221, 298
Xiangyan Zhixian, 300, 301
Xiaorong, 230n17
Xiao Ziliang, 139
Xingfusi, 200
Xingsi, 297
Xin Huayan jing lun, 349
Xinwen Tanben, 105, 107, 108, 110
Xinyue Xingchou. *See* Donggao Xinyue
Xiqian, 297
Xitang Zhizang, 18

Xi Xia, 52
Xixia. *See* Tangut
Xu'an Huaichang, 53
Xuanzhu, 48
Xuanzong, 116
Xu chuandeng lu, 233n34
Xuedou Chongxian, 97, 105, 113, 222, 300; *One Hundred Odes*, 97, 100, **115**, 116
Xueting Fuyu, 309
Xutang Zhiyu, 100
Xuyun, 291
Xu zhiyue lu, 304, 305
Xu zizhi tongjian changbian, 232n33

Yamanaka Kiyotaka, 340n22
Yamasaki Ansai, 277
Yampolsky, Phillip, 46, 196
Yanagisawa Kien, 82
Yanagisawa Yoshiyasu, 82
Yang Chŏngsŏk, 230n21
Yang Daozhen, 86–87
Yang E, 232n30
Yang Wenhui, 291
Yangzi Basin, and Korean monks, 18
Yankou, 310
Yaun Kagu, 270
Yejong, King, 222
Yelan Xinggui, 76
Yellow Sea interaction sphere, 45
Yelu Chücai, 100
Yet kŏul rŭl pusu'go onŏra, 374
Yi Chahyon, 19
Yifeng Fangtuan, 309
Yi Hwang, 265
Yi I, 277
Yijing, 164n101
Yi Kyubo, 242
Yingzong, 221
Yi Nŭnghwa, 249
Yinyuan Longqi, 3, 69–71, 78, 80, 83, 86, 195, 196; arrival in Sōfukuji,

460 | Index

Yinyuan Longqi *(continued)* 93n33; arrived in Nagasaki, 198; Chinese merchant community, relationship with, 73; disciples of, 77; Feiyin Tongrong, disciple of, 69–70; Fuqing merchants and, 76; invited to Fumonji, 70; in Japan, 70–71; Japanese disciple, 82, 92n28; Japanese royal family, relation to, 84–85; Lin met, 91n17; Miyun Yuanwu, disciple of, 72; Ōbaku, 70, 72; as poet, 70–71; relationship with political groups, 84; settled in Nagasaki, 70
Yiran Xingrong, 74, 90n11
Yi Saek, 246
Yishan Yining, 56, 99, 140, 155, 169, 175, 179–85; appointment to Kenchōji, 151; arrived in Dazaifu, 182; arrived in Japan, 24–25; awarded grand master title, 181; biographical sketches of, 168; brush-dialogue, 151–52; death of, 4; Guangli chansi, 179; singularity, 184
Yi Sŏnggye, 215, 276
Yi Tŏgmyŏng, 365
Yi Tongjun, 243
Yi Yŏngju, 365, 366
Yodo river, 204
Yogācāra, 291, 295, 313
Yogācāra-Mādhyamika school, 63n33
Yogācāra/Vijñānavāda/Faxiang/Weishi school, 44
Yŏhŭng Sŏnwŏn, 230n17
Yokoyama Toshio, 340n22
Yŏmbul yomun, 354
yŏmsong, 215
Yongansi, 198
Yŏngbo, 222, 234n46
Yongch'ŏnsa monastery, 227
Yongjia Xuanjue, 365
Yongming monastery, 50

Yongming Yanshou, 22, 48, 49, 50, 51, 302, 303
Yongmunsa, 222, 234n45
Yŏngwŏnsa, 223
Yongzheng (Qing emperor), 303, 308; criticisms, 310; *Yuxuan yulu*, 305, 306–7, 311
Yōsai *(see also* Eisai), 22, 23
Yoshida Kyū'ichi, 341n27, 341n32
Young Mi Kim, 243, 258n17
Youth League for Revitalizing Buddhism, 320, 330
Yoyŏn, 243, 244
Yuan. *See* Mongol empire
Yuan China, 21, 150, 154, 175, 246, 253; Gesshin Kei'en traveled to, 144; intellectual influence of, 273; Jinzong, 246; Korean monks traveled to, 252; Koryŏ Buddhists and, 255; sea trade with Japan, 25
Yuan dynasty, 170, 182; fall of, 150; *huatou* during, 301; Mongol, 347
Yuantong Ju'ne, 221
Yuanwu Keqin, 4, 97, 102, **103**, 107–13, 120–21, 300, 359, 365; *Blue Cliff Record. See Blue Cliff Record*; capping phrase expressions used by, 97; disciple of, 98, 100; *Essentials of Mind*, 100, 117; lineage, 98, 100; Lingyuan, cryptic warning from, 108–9; pedagogical efforts, 111; rhetoric, 104; teacher of, 105
Yuan Zhen, 139
Yu Dayou, 76
Yuefeng Daozhang, 82
Yuexi, 291
Yu Honggi, 249
Yuk Yŏngsu Yŏsa, 369
Yulgok, 277, 280
Yulin Tongxiu, 308
Yumen Zhengchuan, 309

Yunmen, 300
Yunmen Yuancheng, 309
Yunnan, 16–17
Yunp'ilam, 250
Yunqian Jiewan, 74
Yunqi Zhuhong, 72, 309
Yunyan, 298
Yushun, 201
Yusin declaration, 369
Yu Taech'i, 250
Yuxi Ruzhi, 179–81
Yuxuan yulu, 306–7

Zanning, 47, 48, 51
Zekkai Chūshin, 162n68
Zen and the Ways (Leggett), 164n99
Zen at War (Victoria), 325
Zen boom, 291
Zen Buddhism, 4, 7, 41–43, 167, 170–71, 174, 186, 329; Buddhist studies, 58–59; East Asian, 168; esoteric understandings of body, 129; institutional culture, 5; Japanese, 1, 3, 168, 198; and literary arts, 195–97; *Manuscripts from Cold Pine (Kanshōkō)*, 148; monastic institutions, 131; pilgrims, 131, 134, 135, 136; realization, 98; *satori*, 41–42; sermons, 101; and Suzuki Daisetsu, 41; texts, 132; and Tokimune, 178; translingual writing, 130; and Yishan Yining, 179
Zeng Fengyi, 303
Zenkōji, 148
Zen modernism, 321, 336, 338; in Japan, 333; progressive, 322. *See also* Buddhist modernism
Zen monasteries, 24, 172, 338; built environments of, 131; émigré teachers in, 155; Gozan, 147; growing, 54; Jōrakuji, 66n59; Kantō area, 172; Kenchōji. *See* Kenchōji; linguistic situation in, 25
Zen monks, 25, 99, 113, 127; communication with Chan monks, 129, 130, 136–54; Gidō Shūshin, 142, 155; Mukyō Tokusen, 130; Mushō Jōshō in China, 136–41; rhymed Sinitic poetry by, 141–46; Sōtō, 199, 200, 326
Zenrin bokuseki, 164n109
Zenrinji, 85
Zen sect, 323
Zen society Association for the Abandonment of Concepts of Objectivity and Subjectivity, 333
Zen temples, 131, 142; Five Mountain, 206; Japanese, 150; Kenninji, 53, 144, 145, 147, 172; Sōtō, 322
Zhang Mingyuan, 99
Zhang Zai, 275, 278, 280
Zhangzhou, 74, 135
Zhang Ziyang, 311
Zhanran, 47
Zhaojue temple, 105, **106**
Zhaojue Zhangxue, 310
Zhaozhou, 297
Zhaozhou gouzi, 357
Zhejiang, 179; Chan temples in, 102; Eastern, Chan monastery in, 170
Zhen Dexiu, 281; *Classic of the Heart and Mind*, 282
Zhengdaojia, 365
Zhenji [Guang]yin, 309
Zhenjing Kewen, 303–4
Zhenping, Wang, 159n36
Zhenyuan, 74
Zhiguang, 74
Zhihai, 221
Zhikong, 246–47; Certificates of Ordination, 247; ordinance, 247
Zhixian, 298
Zhiyi, 47, 48

Zhiyuan, 16
Zhiyue lu, 304, 305, 307, 314
Zhongfeng Mingben, 17, 111, 301, 309
Zhou Dunyi, 275, 278
Zhuangzi, 266
Zhuge Liang, 294
Zhuhong, 301
Zhuoan Deguang, 23
Zhu Shanshui, 203
Zhu Shunshui, 81, 197
Zhu Xi, 270, 275, 276, 279, 283; *Reflections on Things at Hand,* 278
Zhuxian Fanxian, 149, 150, 151
Zhu Xi's Family Rites, 277

Zibo Zhenke, 72, 303, 309
zong, 49
Zonggao. *See* Dahui Zonggao
Zongjinglu, 49, 50, 51, 174; in Japan, 22, 23; and Yōsai, 24
Zongmi, 56, 269, 297, 303; and Bai, 16; and Dunhuang, 13; in Japan, 21; and Khitan, 15; and Tangut, 14
Zongtong biannian, 308–9
Zuiryūji, 199
Zuisenji, 205
zuomosheng, 25
Zürcher, Erik, 292
Zuyinsi, 179

www.ingramcontent.com/pod-product-compliance
Lightning Source LLC
Chambersburg PA
CBHW021239240426
43673CB00057B/622